DICTIONARY
OF ART AND ARTISTS

PETER AND LINDA MURRAY

DICTIONARY OF ART AND ARTISTS

1250 illustrations
in color and black-and-white

FREDERICK A. PRAEGER, Publishers

New York · Washington

FOR OUR PARENTS

BOOKS THAT MATTER

PUBLISHED IN THE UNITED STATES OF AMERICA IN 1965
BY FREDERICK A. PRAEGER, INC., PUBLISHERS
111 FOURTH AVENUE, NEW YORK 3, N.Y.
ALL RIGHTS RESERVED
LIBRARY OF CONGRESS CATALOG CARD NUMBER 65-20073

PUBLISHED BY THAMES AND HUDSON LTD 1965
PART OF THE DICTIONARY WAS FIRST PUBLISHED
BY PENGUIN BOOKS LTD 1959
© PETER AND LINDA MURRAY 1959
PRINTED IN GREAT BRITAIN BY JARROLD AND SONS LTD, NORWICH

PREFACE

THIS DICTIONARY has grown from one originally published as a Penguin Reference Book. In this greatly extended form we have included the biographies of over a thousand artists and dealt with as many technical terms, including processes and movements, as we could discover. The provision of over twelve hundred illustrations has enabled us to demonstrate in colour the major techniques of painting, to supplement the summary of facts about every artist and movement by one or more illustrations of authentic works, arranged so that it should be possible to gain some idea of the life and style of any major artist and at the same time to see him in relation to his contemporaries and to the history of art as a whole. The opportunity has also been taken to add, as a distinct unit, both a classified bibliography of general books and a list of specialized monographs on individual artists or movements.

We have restricted ourselves to the arts of painting, sculpture, drawing, and the other graphic processes, chiefly in Western Europe, but also in those countries overseas in which the cultural forms and ideas of Europe have taken root, and we have limited ourselves, with occasional exceptions, to the period from about the year 1300 to the present day, which means that the special problems relating to the vast anonymous mass of medieval sculpture and illumination are not within the scope of this book. Where a term is already defined adequately, even in the technical sense, in a normal English dictionary, we have omitted it; examples of this are Vignette and Diorama. Where a dictionary definition seems to us not to cover a special usage in the arts we have given it here. These technical terms have, in fact, been given priority over the biographies, since we were necessarily limited to a restricted number of artists chosen from the many thousands in the thirty-seven volumes of Thieme and Becker's *Allgemeines Künstlerlexicon*, plus selections from among the best-known modern painters. Clearly, since so small a number had to be selected from so great a field, the system of a largely personal choice was the only one possible. An impartial historical judgement is against the present distinct overweighting in favour of contemporary artists, since a large contemporary following does not necessarily guarantee to an artist a long-term survival of his reputation, nor does this constitute automatically a valid reason for believing him to be more significant than a minor artist from an earlier period. But the considerable excitement provoked by, and the extravagant claims made for, certain current movements have prompted us to accede to an enlargement of this period, at the dual risk of abandoning the principle of proper proportion in representation, and a necessity for more frequent revision in this field.

In the biographies our aim has been threefold. We have tried, first to give the dates of birth and death, or known activity, and such other dates as seemed useful or important for an understanding of an artist's career. Next, we have tried to give the reader some idea of what his works look like, either in a descriptive phrase, or by relating him to other and perhaps better-known artists or movements through frequent cross-references. This task has now been greatly simplified by the provision of an illustration for every artist, usually juxtaposed to similar works by his contemporaries. Lastly, we have in most cases appended to the biography a list of museums which contain works by the artist, but these lists are only a rough guide and are not intended to be exhaustive or critical.

SPELLING

The spelling of names may present some difficulties as all prefixes have been disregarded though special Italian usages have been respected, so that, for instance, while de Witte or van Dyck will be found under W and D, Giovanni di Paolo will be found under G, not P. Though the cross-references will often be of great assistance here, the best rule will be to look under every variant before deciding that the artist has been omitted.

DATES

Dates are given with as much precision as possible, and the distinction between, say, 1520/5 and 1520–5 must be noted. The first means 'at some point in the period, but the exact point is unknown'; the second means 'beginning in 1520 and ending in 1525'.

CROSS-REFERENCES

Capital letters are used to indicate cross-references, and this has been made systematic, so that by following up the cross-references the reader can not only expand the information in the original entry, but should also be able to gain a better idea of an artist's relationship to his contemporaries. In any entry other names may occur in normal type; these may well have separate entries of their own, but we do not believe that following them up will, in such instances, add greatly to the reader's knowledge of the particular artist.

MUSEUMS

Obviously, we have tended to list museums in Great Britain or the United States, and to omit those in less accessible countries. For equally obvious reasons (but with one exception), we have not mentioned pictures in private collections unless they are crucial to the artist's development; this is very rare indeed. As far as we know, the pictures said to belong to a given museum are in that museum, but this is less simple than it sounds. Many museums have still not fully recovered from the last war; many have no modern catalogue, or even any at all; many seem to play a constant game of musical chairs with their possessions, lending them to Government offices, embassies, other museums, and the like; and some of the largest and most celebrated are like icebergs: only a small part of the mass can be seen. Possession unfortunately does not mean that the work is always exhibited, though most museums will arrange for a work kept in the depot or reserve to be seen if adequate notice is given. 'Royal Collection' denotes a picture in Hampton Court, Windsor Castle, Buckingham Palace (The Queen's Gallery), or any other Royal residence of the British Crown. In most cases, it will be permanently on view (Hampton Court), or for most of the time (Windsor and Holyroodhouse), but it is not always possible to distinguish, and pictures in the private apartments of any of the Royal residences are never available to the public except when on loan to exhibitions, or transiently included in the selection shown in the Queen's Gallery. The Royal Collection, because it is so large, so rich, and inalienable, and because so much of it is accessible, is the only exception to the rule by which we disregard private collections. It is a matter for much regret and concern that so many of the great American museums are inadequately catalogued or even have no catalogue at all. For this reason it is quite likely that we have omitted several masterpieces, despite efforts to keep track of major American acquisitions.

MONOCHROME ILLUSTRATIONS

The arrangement of the monochrome plates requires a brief note. Every artist or movement with an entry in the text has at least one illustration, but the choice has been governed by several considerations. Firstly, the work had to be both characteristic and authentic: either signed, and preferably dated as well, or documented, or at least as well documented as possible. In a few cases we have had to say 'Attributed to . . .', or 'Traditionally attributed to . . .', but where we say, in the caption, that a picture is documented we mean that the evidence for its authorship is sufficiently strong for it to be acceptable to the great majority of historians. Obviously, there is always room for argument here, and we can only ask our readers to believe that we have been rigorous in our selection. The captions state whether a work is signed (fully, or in monogram or initials), dated, or documented. If the date is on the picture or known with precision from documents it is given; in a few cases, where the date is fixed with less precision, we have used a form such as '*c.* 1637', '1637–8', or even '1637/8'.

Only in the rarest instances have we broken our rule that all the illustrations must be chosen from works in public collections, so that they shall be relatively accessible. Occasionally, however, no authentic example existed in a public collection, but here we have been able to choose works in country houses which are open to the public at certain times, and, of course, churches have been treated as public collections. A word is perhaps desirable to justify the choice of museums from which works have been chosen for illustration. It would have been easy to choose works consistently from the National Gallery in London, the Louvre, the Metropolitan Museum in New York, and similar capital collections, and in a good many cases we have done so, often because the best examples tend to be in such museums. On the other hand, we have often found very beautiful and characteristic works in smaller British, French, or American museums, and we have used these to avoid too hackneyed a choice. For the same reason we have sometimes reproduced a famous picture quite small, with a less famous work on a larger scale beside it. It was obviously impossible to reproduce all the works to the same scale, and therefore no attempt at any consistency of scale has been made, and because accurate sizes are so often impossible to discover, particularly with sculpture, no dimensions have been given either. Each pair of pages is, as far as it could be done, made up of similar works, usually from the same national school at a given time – e.g. Dürer and his contemporaries, Dutch portrait groups of the seventeenth century, and so on – but some other groupings based on wider relationships have been made, particularly with modern art, and occasionally we have deliberately gone outside a national grouping, as when an early Gainsborough landscape is put with Hobbema and Ruisdael. Sometimes these juxtapositions seemed more instructive and helpful than a more conventional arrangement; the references to plate numbers at the end of each entry will in any case always serve as a guide.

COLOUR PLATES

Fifty-two colour plates, mostly specially made, supplement the black and white plates with details, many of which are nearly full-size, designed to illustrate variety of technique. All the major techniques have been illustrated in this way, and on a scale which makes it possible to study the handling; there are twenty-four colour plates for oil-painting alone, so as to show variety of treatment from the smoothest application to the roughest impasto. A small black and white reproduction of every work has been included, to give an idea of scale, except when the colour plate reproduces all, or nearly all, of the original. The arrangement is very roughly chronological in each subdivision, but juxtapositions seemed more important than exact chronology. We feel that this is the most useful way to use colour plates, far better than to treat them merely as an embellishment, and we are very grateful to our publishers for having so many new photographs specially made for this book.

BIBLIOGRAPHIES

The bibliographies are in two parts, and are intended to help students who use this book as a guide to further study. The first is a classified list of books on particular schools or styles, and can be used as a reading list by anyone anxious to study, say, Italian painting in more detail. The second corresponds to the entries in the Dictionary, and lists one or more monographs, and occasionally a general book as well. The monographs chosen are those which seem to be the most useful and up-to-date, regardless of the language in which they are written, though an English translation of a foreign work is mentioned if one exists, and as some monographs are now rather old we have, where we thought necessary, given a reference to a more modern general book. All articles in periodicals have been excluded; we have given enough to enable the serious student to find these for himself.

ACKNOWLEDGEMENTS

Many people have helped us to remove errors and to sharpen definitions, and we are grateful for the help we have received in this way. Among friends and colleagues we particularly wish to thank Dr Anita Brookner, Professor L. D. Ettlinger, Mr Michael Kitson, Mr Michael Levey, and Dr M. D. Whinney, as well as Miss Nicolette Coates, Mr John Gage, and Mr Leslie Parris. Miss Ruth Rosenberg and Mr Alan Hockley of Thames and Hudson have helped enormously with the editorial work.

London

CONTENTS

x

BIBLIOGRAPHIES
The two bibliographies are intended to form a
short guide to art historical literature. The first is
classified by subject, so that anyone wishing to study,
say, Italian Renaissance art can find a list of useful
textbooks. The second bibliography is monographic
and will lead the reader to the principal books on individual artists or movements.

xii

LIST OF GENERAL ARTICLES

Absorbent Ground
Abstract Art
Abstract Expressionism
Academy
Academy Figure
Action Painting
Alla Prima
Altorilievo, *see* Relief
Amorino
Ancona
Anonimo
Anti-cerne
Antwerp Mannerists
Aquatint, *see* Engraving
Arabesque
Architectonic
Armory Show
Arricciato, *see* Fresco
Ars Moriendi
Art Nouveau
Ascription, *see* Attribution
Ashcan School
Atelier
Attribution
Au Premier Coup
Automatism

Bambino
Bambocciata
Barbizon School
Baroque
Bas-Relief, *see* Relief
Bauhaus, The
'Before all letters' *see* Proof
Bentname
Biedermeierstil
Biomorphic Art
Bistre
Bitumen
Blaue Reiter, Der
Blauen Vier, Die, *see* Jawlensky
Block-book
Blot Drawing
Blue Four, The, *see* Jawlensky
Bodegón
Body Colour
Bolus Ground
Bottega

Boucharde, *see* Stone Carving
Bozzetto
Broad Manner, *see* Fine Manner
Bronze
Brücke, Die
Brushwork
Burin

Cabinet Picture
Calligraphic
Camaïeu, *see* Grisaille *and* Chiaroscuro
Camden Town Group
Camera Obscura, Lucida
Capriccio
Cartellino
Cartoon
Cassone
Casting, *see* Plaster *and* Bronze
Cavo-Rilievo, *see* Relief
Charcoal
Chiaroscuro
Christus Patiens, Triumphans
Cinquecento
Cire Perdue, *see* Bronze
Classic, Classical, Romantic
Claw Chisel, *see* Stone Carving
Cloisonnisme, *see* Bernard
Cobra, *see* Appel
Cold Colour, Tone
Collage
Complementary Colour
Composition
Constructivism
Conté
Continuous Representation
Contour
Contrapposto
Conversation Piece
Cool Colour, Tone, *see* Cold Colour, Tone
Cosmati
Costruzione Legittima
Coulisse
Counterproof

Craquelure
Cross-hatching
Cubism

Dada
Dance of Death
Danube School
Deësis
Del., Delin.
Desco da Parto
Design
Diptych
Disegno
Distemper
Divisionism, *see* Optical Mixtures
Doelenstuk, Schutterstuk
Dotted Print
Drill, *see* Stone Carving
Drypoint, *see* Engraving
Dugento

Eclectic, *see* Carracci
Encaustic Wax
Engraving
Etching, *see* Engraving
Euston Road
Exc., Excudit
Expressionism

F., Fec., Fecit
Facture, Fattura
Fauve
Fine Manner
Fixative
Fontainebleau, Schools of
Foreshortening
Found Object
Fraglia
Fresco
Frottage
Futurism

Garzone
Genre
Gesso
Giotteschi, Giottesques
Glazing

Glyptic, *see* Sculpture
Golden Section
Gothic
Gouache
Graffito, *see* Sgraffito
Graphic Arts
Graver, *see* Burin
Grisaille
Grotesque
Ground
Guild

Handling
Hatching
History Painting
Hortus Conclusus
Hot Colour, Tone
Hours of Turin
Hudson River School

Icon
Ideal Art
Illusionism
Imago Pietatis
Impasto
Impressionism
Imprimitura
Inc.
Intaglio
International Gothic
Intimisme
Intonaco, *see* Fresco
Inv., Invenit
Italianizers

Journeyman
Jugendstil, *see* Art Nouveau

Keeping, *see* Values
Key
Kit Cat
Kortegaardjes

Laocoön
Lay Figure
Liber Studiorum, *see* Liber Veritatis
Liber Veritatis

Limning
Linear Composition
Linocut, *see* Engraving
Lithography, *see* Engraving
Local Colour
London Group
Lukasbrüder, *see* Nazarener

Macchiaioli
Madonnieri
Maestà
Mahlstick
'Mai'
Malerisch
Mandorla
Manière Criblée, *see* Dotted Print
Manner
Mannerism
Maquette
Masses
Matière
Mattoir, *see* Engraving
Medici e Speziali
Medium
Merz, *see* Schwitters
Mezzo-Rilievo, *see* Relief
Mezzotint, *see* Engraving
Miniature
Misericordia, Madonna della
Mixed Method
Mobile
Modelling
Modello, Modelletto
Monochrome
Monotype
Montage
Monumental
Morbidezza
Mosaic
Mural, *see* Wall-Painting

Nabis, Les
Nature Morte, *see* Still-Life
Nazarener
NEAC
Neoclassicism
Neo-Impressionism
Neue Sachlichkeit
New English Art Club, *see* NEAC
Niello
Nocturne
Norwich School
Novecento

Objet Trouvé, *see* Found Object
Oeuvre

Offset, *see* Counterproof
Oil Painting
Optical Mixtures
Orphic Cubism, Orphisme
Ottocento

P., Pinx., Pinxit
Painterly, *see* Malerisch
Painting Techniques, *see* Encaustic Wax, Fresco, Gouache, Oil Painting, Pastel, Size Colour, Tempera, Watercolour
Pala
Paliotto
Papier Collé
Paris, the School of
Pastel
Pastiche, Pasticcio
Patina
Pedigree, *see* Provenance
Peinture à l'Essence, *see* Degas
Pencil
Pentimento
Perspective
Picture Plane
Picturesque
Pietà
Plaster Casting
Plasticity
Plein Air
Pochade
Pointillism, *see* Optical Mixtures
Pointing Machine
Polychromatic Sculpture
Polyptych
Post-Impressionism
Poussinisme, *see* Rubénisme
P R B, Pre-Raphaelite Brotherhood
Predella
Primary Colours
Priming
Primitive
Profil Perdu
Proof
Proportion
Provenance
Punch, *see* Stone Carving
Putto

Quadraturista
Quadro Riportato
Quattrocento

Rayonism
Realism
Recession

Refusés, *see* Salon
Relief
Remarque Proofs
Renaissance
Replica
Repoussoir
Reredos
Retroussage
Rilievo, *see* Relief
Rococo
Romanists
Romantic, *see* Classic
Royal Academy, *see* Academy
Rubénisme

Sachlichkeit, Die Neue, *see* Neue Sachlichkeit
Sacra Conversazione
Salon
Sanguine
School
Schutterstuk, *see* Doelenstuk
Scorzo, Iscorzo
Sculp.
Sculpture
Scumbling
Section d'Or, *see* Golden Section
Seicento
Sepia
Serigraphy
Settecento
Sezession
Sfumato
Sgraffito
Shop Work, *see* Workshop Production
Significant Form
Silk-Screen, *see* Serigraphy
Silver Point
Sinopia
Size Colour
Sketch
Social Realism
Soft Ground Etching, *see* Engraving
Soft Style
Sopra Porte
Sotto in Sù
Spolvero
Squared
Stabile
Staffage
Stained Glass
Stanze
State
Steel Engraving, Steel-faced
Stiacciato, *see* Relief
Stijl, De

Still-Life
Stippled Drawing
Stone Carving
Stopping Out, *see* Engraving
Study
Stump
Style Criticism
Super-Realism, *see* Surrealism
Suprematism
Surrealism
Synthetism

Tachisme
Tactile Values
Taille-Douce, *see* Engraving
Tectonic, *see* Architectonic
Tempera
Tenebrism
Terracotta, *see* Plaster
Terribilità
Tesserae
Tondo
Tone Values, *see* Values
Torso
Totentanz, *see* Dance of Death
Trecento
Triptych
Trompe-l'œil, *see* Illusionism

Underpainting
Utrecht School

Values
Vanishing Point, *see* Perspective
Vanitas, *see* Still-Life
Variant
Veduta
Vehicle
Vesperbild, *see* Pietà
Vingt, Les
Vorticism

Wall-Painting
Wanderjahre
Warm Colour, Tone
Watercolour
Weepers
Weicher Stil, *see* Soft Style
Woodcut, *see* Engraving
Workshop Production

XX, Les, *see* Vingt, Les
Xylography, *see* Engraving

ABBREVIATIONS USED IN THE DICTIONARY

Acad.	Academy, Academia
Accad.	Accademia
Akad.	Akademie
ARA	Associate of the Royal Academy
b.	born
B.C.	Before Christ
Berks.	Berkshire
Bib.	Bibliothèque
BM	British Museum
c.	*circa*, about
Cal.	California
Cath.	Cathedral
cf.	*confer*, compare
Col.	Colorado
Coll.	Collection, College
Conn.	Connecticut
d.	died
DCL	Doctor of Civil Law
ed.	edition
e.g.	*exempli gratia*
Fdn	Foundation
ff	following
Fitzwm	Fitzwilliam
Fla	Florida
Fr.	French
Gall.	Gallery, Galleria
Ger.	German
Gk	Greek
Hist.	Historical
Hosp.	Hospital
i.e.	*id est*
ill.	illustration
Inst.	Institute
Ital.	Italian
KdK	Klassiker der Kunst series
K-H	Kunsthistorisches
Lat.	Latin
M of MA	Museum of Modern Art
Md	Maryland
Mass.	Massachusetts
Met. Mus.	Metropolitan Museum

Mich.	Michigan
Middx	Middlesex
MS, MSS	Manuscript, manuscripts
Mus.	Museum
Nat. Marit. Mus.	National Maritime Museum
Naz.	Nazionale
NEAC	New English Art Club
NG	National Gallery
NG of S	National Gallery of Scotland
NJ	New Jersey
NPG	National Portrait Gallery
nr	near
NSW	New South Wales
NY	New York
NZ	New Zealand
OED	*Oxford English Dictionary*
OM	Order of Merit
Pa	Philadelphia
Pal.	Palais, Palace, Palazzo
PRA	President of the Royal Academy
PRB	Pre-Raphaelite Brotherhood
RA	Royal Academy, Royal Academician
RAMC	Royal Army Medical Corps
RI	Rhode Island
Rijksmus.	Rijksmuseum
RSA	Royal Scottish Academy
S.	Saint, San, South
SC	South Carolina
SM	Santa Maria
SNPG	Scottish National Portrait Gallery
Soc.	Society
Span.	Spanish
SS.	Saints
St	Saint
Sta	Santa
Staffs.	Staffordshire
Sto	Santo
Univ.	University
US	United States
USSR	Union of Soviet Socialist Republics
V & A	Victoria and Albert Museum
Va	Virginia
Wilts.	Wiltshire

SOURCES OF ILLUSTRATIONS

The following plates are reproduced by gracious permission of Her Majesty the Queen: 54, 206, 229, 276, 280, 287, 306, 308, 309, 313, 315, 367, 368, 373, 394, 414, 415, 417, 521, 523, 577, 670, 678, 806, 813, 833, 849, 892, 929, 947, col. pl. 10.

The authors and publishers also wish to thank all authorities, museums, and galleries whose works are reproduced in this book, and the Syndics of the Fitzwilliam Museum, Cambridge; the Trustees of the British Museum, the Courtauld Institute, Trustees of the National Gallery, Trustees of the National Maritime Museum, Trustees of the Tate Gallery, Trustees of the Wallace Collection, London; the Governors of the John Rylands Library, Manchester; the Trustees of the Lady Lever Art Gallery, Port Sunlight.

They would also like to thank the following: A.C.L. Brussels 268, 335, 336, 342, 343, 348, 350, 362, 363, 370, 372, 378, 381, 389, 391, 403, 413, 418, 997, 1027, 1028, 1055; Cliché Agraci 991; Archives Photographiques 22, 102, 175, 178, 220, 228, 283, 289, 351, 412, 572, 665, 666, 667, 668, 672, 674, 675, 690, 695, 698, 701, 708, 711, 712, 713, 714, 719, 725, 727, 731, 733, 736, 737, 743, 745, 747, 748, 755, 756, 757, 773, 774, 775, 779, 786, 792, 793, 795, 796, 982, 989, 1008, 1048; Arts Council of Great Britain 1053, 1060, 1126, 1141; Osvaldo Böhm 297; F. Bruckmann AG 312, 426; Photo Bulloz 547, 676, 686, 689, 739, 742, 749, 755, 770, 787; Deutsche Fotothek Dresden 173, 216, 286, 293, 392, 533, 564, 569, 593, 598, 1013; Soprintendenza alle Gallerie, Florence 10, 70, 172, 319, 460; Photographie Giraudon 73, 195, 326, 330, 331, 349, 420, 568, 673, 677, 709, 723, 724, 741, 744, 771, 772, 782, 788, 791, 800, 981, 1004, 1007, 1036, 1052, 1101; Hirmer Verlag 299, 630, col. pl. 9; Gottfried Keller Foundation, Berne (on loan to the Kunstmuseum, Basle) 607; London County Council Architect's Department 430, 433, 498, 865, 925; Mansell Collection 5, 7, 8, 11, 12, 16, 17, 18, 19, 20, 23, 24, 26, 27, 28, 29, 30, 34, 35, 39, 40, 41, 45, 46, 47, 50, 51, 52, 55, 61, 65, 66, 68, 71, 72, 75, 83, 84, 86, 88, 90, 92, 93, 94, 95, 99, 101, 104, 106, 109, 116, 117, 121, 122, 129, 133, 144, 147, 148, 153, 155, 159, 160, 161, 162, 164, 165, 166, 167, 168, 174, 176, 184, 186, 187, 194, 197, 198, 204, 205, 209, 210, 211, 212, 215, 221, 223, 231, 232, 235, 237, 241, 245, 247, 249, 251, 256, 257, 270, 271, 274, 282, 285, 291, 303, 354, 405, 409, 592, 594, 638; Bildarchiv Foto Marburg 1, 541, 543, 550, 551, 611, 629, 631; Foto A. Yr. Mas 214, 217, 339, 377, 388, 556, 633, 634, 636, 640, 651, 653, 654, 659, 660, 661, 663; Georgina Masson 300; Ministry of Public Building and Works (Crown Copyright) 276, 703, 893; Jack Nisberg col. pl. 37; U. Pfistermeister 625; Soprintendenza alle Gallerie del Piemonte 213, 253, 279; Rheinisches Bildarchiv Cologne 584, 608, 1011, 1012, 1017, 1019, 1020, 1022, 1082; G.F.N. Rome 15, 49, 200, 201, 244, 255, 258, 262, 263, 283, 290, 332, 360, 463, 657, 887, 1123; Royal Commission on Historical Monuments (England) (Crown Copyright) 868, 877, 880; Royal Society of Arts, London 894; Scala col. pls. 1, 5; Skira col. pl. 8; Society for Cultural Relations with the USSR 384, 754; *The Times* 891; Cliché des Musées Nationaux, Versailles 735, 746, 1003, 1037, 1050, 1090; Warburg Institute, London 157, 868, 878, 879; Galerie Welz, Salzburg 1146; Dr M. D. Whinney 875; Professor G. Zarnecki 332.

DICTIONARY OF ART AND ARTISTS

Abbate, Niccolò dell' (*c.* 1512–71), was a Modenese painter whose style was founded on Mantegna's illusionism and especially on Correggio's softness. He painted frescoes in Modena (1546) and Bologna (1547: now in the University), and was in France by 1552, helping PRIMATICCIO with the decoration of the Royal château at Fontainebleau. Most of his work there has disappeared. He spent the rest of his life in France, where, with Primaticcio, he represents the end of the First School of FONTAINEBLEAU. He introduced the Mannerist landscape into France: there is a fine example in the NG, London, and other works are in Florence (Uffizi), Paris (Louvre), Rome (Borghese), Vienna, and elsewhere. [ill. 196, p. 302]

Abbott, Lemuel Francis (*c.* 1760–1803), was an English portrait painter, famous for his *Nelson,* of which many replicas and variants exist. These and other portraits are in London (NPG, Nat. Marit. Mus.). [ill. 853, p. 397]

Absorbent Ground. A chalk ground, on canvas or panel, prepared without oil so that it will absorb the oil from the paint, leaving it matt and very quick-drying.

Abstract Art depends upon the assumption that specifically artistic values reside in forms and colours and are entirely independent of the subject of the painting or sculpture. This view is of great antiquity and has resulted in much art of a semi-magical character as well as pure decoration. It also prevails in Moslem countries, where representation of the human figure is prohibited. The 'liberating' influence of the camera allowed the painter to neglect his social duty as a recorder of things and events, and, at the same time, late in the 19th century, Impressionism came to be regarded as a dead-end of naturalism, thus leading to an increased emphasis on formal values and ultimately to CUBISM, CONSTRUCTIVISM, TACHISME, and the rest. The philosophical justification of abstract art may be found in Plato: 'I do not now intend by beauty of shapes what most people would expect, such as that of living creatures or pictures, but . . . straight lines and curves and the surfaces or solid forms produced out of these by lathes and rulers and squares . . . These things are not beautiful relatively, like other things, but always and naturally and absolutely' ('Philebus').

Abstract Expressionism. A combination of ABSTRACT ART and EXPRESSIONISM which amounts to little more than automatic painting – i.e. allowing the subconscious to express itself (a SURREALIST idea) by the creation of involuntary shapes and dribbles of paint. Abstract Impres-

sionism – which appears to be another name for the same thing – is supposed to derive from the intricate mesh of paint which forms the surface of MONET's last pictures, as, half-blind, he struggled to find pictorial equivalents for his optical sensations. Abstract Impressionism has been defined (by E. De Kooning, 1956) thus: 'Retaining the quiet uniform pattern of strokes that spread over the canvas without climax or emphasis, these followers keep the Impressionist manner of looking at a scene but leave out the scene. . . .' *See also* ACTION PAINTING, TACHISME. [ills. 1096–8, pp. 428–9. Col. pls. 34–5]

Academy. The name, derived from Plato's Academy, was used in Italy in the 15th century by groups of humanists meeting together for discussion. During the 16th century these groups acquired more formal aims and character, and the term was, by extension, applied to groups of artists meeting privately for study. Baccio BANDINELLI founded one in 1531, in the quarters granted him by Leo X in the Vatican, and another in Florence *c.* 1550. The first Academy of Fine Arts, properly speaking, was founded in 1563 in Florence by VASARI, with at its head the Grand Duke Cosimo and the absent and eighty-eight-year-old MICHELANGELO, who, by his personal prestige, had done more than anyone to raise the fine arts from the level of the mechanical to the equal of the liberal arts. Vasari's Accademia di DISEGNO was intended to be a teaching as well as an honorific body, for the main purpose of an academy was always to raise the social status of the artist, but though almost every artist of repute in Italy became a member, its teaching programme was soon abandoned. The Accademia di S. Luca, founded in Rome in 1593, with Federico ZUCCARI as its president, also had a similarly ambitious programme which came to nothing. Other such bodies were founded in Italy – notably in Bologna in 1598, where it became intimately associated with the CARRACCI – and the custom of artists meeting under the patronage of an enlightened nobleman or connoisseur, to draw from the nude, thus forming private teaching academies, was widespread by the middle of the 17th century.
The French Academy, first founded in 1648, was closely modelled on the Italian ones, but did not reach its all-powerful position until 1661, when it came under the control of Colbert, who saw in it a golden opportunity to make the arts play a part in the aggrandizement of the monarchy. By 1664 he had obtained a new constitution for it, which made it primarily a teaching body, responsible for the training of artists who could then carry out the artistic programmes which he planned. He also founded the French Academy in Rome in 1666, as a school to which the most successful students could be sent for further training, and

intended to make POUSSIN its head, but the latter's death prevented this. The French Academy reached perhaps its greatest power under LEBRUN, who became Director in 1683. This dual character of learned body, with a strict hierarchy of members graded according to the form of art they practised (history painters at the top, portraitists next, and so on down to landscape and genre) and with the privilege of public exhibition exclusively reserved to it, combined with a state school, became the pattern for most of the Academies founded during the 17th and 18th centuries. The majority were not, however, successful until after the middle of the 18th century, when academies of all kinds were an established part of the pattern of intellectual life.

The Royal Academy in London, founded in 1768 with provision for forty Academicians and (in 1769) twenty Associates, later increased to thirty, was one of these latecomers. But it is an exception to the generality in that it was the outcome of private enterprise among artists, and though it enjoyed Royal patronage from the start (in fact, it owed its initial success to the keen interest of George III), has never had any state control, subsidies, or monopoly of exhibitions. The efforts of its first President, REYNOLDS, established it as a school and his personal prestige and intellectual attainments were reflected in the social status which membership conferred, while the open character of its yearly exhibitions ensured a flow of new talent. The first American Academy, founded in Philadelphia in 1805, grew out of a private institution, and the National Academy of Design was founded in 1826, under MORSE.

It was mainly during the reign of late-19th-century conservatism that the Academy, here as abroad, became the centre of opposition to all new ideas in art, with results that have brought nothing but discredit on itself, so that the term 'academic' has become the synonym of dullness, conventionalism, and prejudice. This cleavage between official bodies and the mass of artists outside the academic fold has bedevilled the relations between artists and public, has fostered unfortunate extremes of taste, has rendered the fair appreciation of academic art difficult and the criticism of art particularly unfruitful. There are, however, signs that it is now realized, inside and outside the Academies, that this cleavage is to the detriment of all. [ills. 202, 694–707, pp. 303, 376–7]

Academy Figure. A painting or drawing, generally about half life-size, of a nude figure executed solely for purposes of instruction or practice and not as a work of art.

Action Painting. Splashing and dribbling paint on canvas. The basic assumption is that the Unconscious will take over and produce a work of art. The technique is claimed to go back to Leonardo, who suggested using stains on walls as a starting-point for designing (cf. BLOT): the essential difference is that Leonardo used the method solely as a means of stimulating the creative imagination and not as an end in itself. Action Painting should not be confused with the intellectual type of Abstract art in which some thought is necessary, but its advocates claim that the beauty of the 'calligraphy' – i.e. the movements of the artist's wrist – constitute its justification, as well as distinguishing it from TACHISME. *See* POLLOCK. [ill. 1096, p. 429. Col. pl. 35]

Adam, Lambert-Sigisbert (1700–59), a French sculptor, went to Rome in 1723 and there won the competition for the Trevi Fountain (1731), which he did not execute. He returned to Paris in 1733 and was received into the Academy on his *Neptune calming the Waves* (1737: Louvre), which is derived directly from Bernini, while his *Neptune* at Versailles is also markedly Baroque; yet he also published a collection of Greek and Roman sculpture ('Recueil de sculptures antiques . . .', Paris, 1754). [ill. 711, p. 378]

Aertsen, Pieter (1508/9–75), was a painter, born in Amsterdam, who continued the tradition of peasant genre established by BRUEGEL, and was unaffected by the ROMANISTS. He settled in Antwerp c. 1535, where he married and entered the Guild, but he returned to Amsterdam in 1556, possibly on account of religion. Many of his pictures were destroyed in the religious troubles of 1566, but there are many survivors, mostly with kitchen or genre scenes in the foreground and a religious scene (such as Christ in the House of Martha and Mary) in the background. His still-life painting was very important in the development of the genre in the Netherlands and even in Italy: it has been argued that he influenced both Caravaggio and Velazquez. His surviving religious pictures, while less influential, show the straightforward, realistic tradition of Netherlandish art. His wife's nephew, Joachim BUECKELAER, was his pupil. There are works by him in Amsterdam (Mus. and Mus. Mayer van den Bergh), Berlin, Birmingham, Brussels, Copenhagen, Cracow, Genoa, Leningrad, Pisa, Rotterdam, Stockholm, Uppsala (University) and Vienna. [ill. 379, p. 326]

Afro (*b.* 1912), is an Italian abstract painter whose real name is Afro Basaldella. He lives in Rome, but his style derives from Picasso and Braque; he has worked a good deal in the US, where several museums own pictures by him. There are murals by him in the Banco Nazionale del Lavoro, Rome. Berlin has a painting and London (Tate) a drawing. [ill. 1103, p. 429]

Agostino di Duccio (1418–81), sculptor, was born in Florence. He became a mercenary soldier in 1433, and did not return to Florence until 1442, by which date he had executed the altar in Modena Cathedral, accepted as his earliest independent work. Its figures in deep relief against a plain background suggest that he was probably a pupil of Jacopo della QUERCIA, who worked at S. Petronio, Bologna, from 1425 to 1438. From about 1450 until 1457 he worked on his masterpiece – the tombs and the extensive series of low reliefs forming the sculptural decoration of the interior of the Tempio Malatestiano in Rimini, reconstructed by Sigismondo Malatesta who employed Alberti as architect and PIERO della Francesca as painter. Agostino worked on the façade of the Oratory of S. Bernardino, Perugia, until 1462, and in 1463 returned to Florence, where he entered the Guild, but in 1473 he went back to Perugia, remaining there until his death.

Agostino's marble reliefs are usually of an even lowness, and his flat, decorative, and intensely linear style has none of the illusionistic effects used by DONATELLO or the ROSSELLINO brothers. There are further examples in Florence (Bargello), London (V & A), Paris (Louvre), and Washington (NG). [ill. 65, p. 279]

Aikman, William (1682–1731), was a Scottish portrait painter, pupil of MEDINA, who succeeded to his business in Edinburgh, but after KNELLER's death in 1723 migrated to London, where he had many literary friends, including Swift and Pope. Allan Ramsay, the poet and father of the painter, was portrayed by him; the picture is inscribed: 'Here painted on this canvas clout By Aikman's hand is Ramsay's snout'. He is chiefly remarkable as having studied in Rome (1707–10) before this became common; after this he went on to Constantinople and Syria. There are self-portraits in Edinburgh (NG of S) and Florence (Uffizi). [ill. 821, p. 393]

Albani, Francesco (1578–1660), a Bolognese painter contemporary with Guido RENI whose fellow-pupil he was, first under CALVAERT and then at the CARRACCI Academy. There are many works by him in Rome, Bologna, Paris, and in most of the older galleries. [ill. 258, p. 309]

Albertinelli, Mariotto (1474–1515), was a Florentine painter who collaborated with Fra BARTOLOMMEO from before 1500, and whom the Frate took into partnership in 1508 in the S. Marco workshop. After three years he abandoned painting for inn-keeping which he said was less exacting and less open to criticism, declaring, so the tale goes, that he was 'sick of this everlasting talk of perspective'. His best work is the *Visitation* (1503) in the Uffizi, Florence. [ill. 169, p. 296]

Algardi, Alessandro (1595, not 1602–54), was a Bolognese sculptor who worked in Rome and represented the classicism of the Bolognese Academy in opposition to BERNINI. He was a pupil of Lodovico CARRACCI and worked in the Carracci Academy in Bologna before going to Rome *c.* 1625, where he became a friend of DOMENICHINO, also a Bolognese Carracci pupil. His early works – the Tomb of Cardinal Millini (*d.* 1629) in Sta Maria del Popolo, and the Frangipane portrait busts in S. Marcello – show his marked dependence on antique portrait types. His *S. Philip Neri* (Sta Maria in Vallicella), an imaginary portrait of the saint (canonized 1622), is another example of his skill in portraying people he never set eyes on; but his *Cardinal Zacchia* (1626: Berlin) and his *Bracciolini* (London, V & A) show what he could do when working from life. This latter was once attributed to Bernini and there are still several busts which are disputed between them, but on the whole Algardi's are more grave in deportment and have greater inward characterization than Bernini's highly extrovert portraits. There can be no doubt, though, that Algardi borrowed from Bernini, whose portrait statue of Urban VIII underlies Algardi's *Innocent X*, begun in 1645 for the Conservatori Palace in Rome as a companion to Bernini's *Urban*; while the Tomb of Leo XI (St Peter's, 1634–52) is a chastened and plain white marble version of Bernini's polychrome Tomb of Urban VIII. Algardi's position as leader of the classical opposition to Bernini was recognized in 1640 by his election as Principe of the Academy of S. Luke, but his real success came under Innocent X (1644–55), when Bernini was in disgrace. His only important relief also dates from this period: the *Attila* in St Peter's of 1646–53, which is a piece of technical virtuosity, but is less a relief than a Carracci altarpiece in marble. There are other

works elsewhere in Rome and in S. Paolo, Bologna, Cleveland Ohio, Minneapolis, New York (Met. Mus.), Paris (Louvre), and Ravenna. [ills. 264, 265, p. 310]

Allan, David (1744–96), sometimes called the 'Scottish Hogarth', was, more accurately, a painter of genre and portraits anticipating WILKIE. He lived in Rome 1764–*c.* 1777 and won a medal for a history picture in 1773. There are works in Edinburgh and Glasgow. [ill. 883, p. 400]

Alla Prima (Ital. at first) describes the technique, general since the 19th century but considered freakish and slapdash before then, of completing the picture surface in one session in full colour and with such opacity that neither previous drawing nor underpainting – if these exist – modifies the final effect. [Col. pls. 19, 29, 30]

Allston, Washington (1779–1843), was the first important American landscape painter. He was trained in London and elected ARA in 1818, the year in which he returned to America. His early works were Italianate landscapes in the Claude manner, but his intensely Romantic outlook caused him to admire FUSELI and TURNER, and ultimately to imitate the hyper-romanticism of MARTIN. Most of his works are in America, but his portrait of his lifelong friend, S. T. Coleridge, is in London (NPG) and Birmingham has an extravagant landscape attributed to him. *See* HUDSON RIVER SCHOOL. [ill. 944, p. 407]

Altdorfer, Albrecht (*c.* 1480–1538), a Bavarian painter, worked in Regensburg (Ratisbon), becoming City architect and a councillor. In 1511 certainly, and probably earlier, he travelled along the Danube and visited the Austrian Alps where the scenery moved him to become the first landscape painter in the modern sense. His earliest dated works (1507: Berlin and Bremen) show the influence of CRANACH and DÜRER, but the landscape is already very important, and by 1510 the figure is quite unimportant – only the rustle of the trees beside the mountain lake matters. The figures in his pictures are the complement of his romantic use of landscape (*S. George in the Forest*, Munich), and their gestures and facial expressions, as well as their colour, show his use of subjective distortion for dramatic and emotional ends. He also made many drawings and etchings of pure landscape, the importance of which makes him the head of the DANUBE School. His major works are the *S. Florian Altar* (1518: mostly still in S. Florian's Monastery, near Linz) and *Alexander's Victory* (1529: Munich): other works are in Regensburg and in Basle, Cologne, Florence (Uffizi), London (NG), Luton Hoo Beds. (Wernher Coll.), Nuremberg, and Vienna. [ills. 573–4, p. 357]

Altichiero was a Veronese painter of the late 14th century, whose style was formed on Giotto's frescoes in Padua. With his helper Avanzo he painted frescoes in Padua (Il Santo and, after 1377, Oratorio di S. Giorgio), and, at the end of the century, he founded the School of Verona with his frescoes in Sant' Anastasia. [ill. 34, p. 273]

Altorilievo *see* RELIEF.

'Alunno di Domenico', i.e. 'Pupil of Domenico' (GHIRLANDAIO): a name invented by Berenson for the Florentine painter to whom he ascribed most of the designs for Florentine woodcut book-illustrations of the late 15th century. This wholesale attribution has not won general acceptance, but the actual pupil and assistant of Ghirlandaio postulated by Berenson has been identified as Bartolommeo di Giovanni, who was commissioned to paint the predella of Ghirlandaio's *Adoration* in the Foundling Hospital, Florence, in 1488. [ill. 83, p. 281]

Amberger, Christoph (*c.* 1500–61/2), was an Augsburg portrait painter whose works resemble those of Holbein, but with a strong Venetian influence, perhaps due to Paris BORDONE, who may have visited Augsburg in 1540. There is a signed altarpiece, of 1560, in S. Anna, Augsburg, but the only signed portrait by him seems to be *The Emperor Charles V* (Berlin). There are works in Augsburg, Birmingham (Barber Inst.), Glasgow, Munich, Philadelphia (Johnson), Toledo Ohio, Vienna, and York. [ill. 587, p. 357]

'Amico di Sandro' (Friend of Sandro, i.e. Botticelli) was the name given by Berenson to the artist he invented as the painter of several pictures which seemed between the styles of BOTTICELLI and Filippino LIPPI, e.g. two Filippinos in the NG, London, and a Botticelli in the V & A, London. His creator later repudiated him and the pictures have been redistributed. [ill. 103, p. 285]

Amigoni (Amiconi), Jacopo (1682?–1752), was a Venetian history and portrait painter who worked all over Europe in a more or less international style, the Venetian Rococo, with elements compounded from Sebastiano RICCI and French Rococo and, later, TIEPOLO. He worked for some years for the Elector of Bavaria and then came to London in 1730, where he painted several decorative cycles and portraits; though these, according to Vertue, were 'not his inclination – nor Talent'. In 1739 he returned to Venice with a small fortune, and it was he who persuaded Canaletto to visit London (1746). In 1747 he went to Madrid as Court Painter: Vertue records that news of his death there reached London just as his finest works – in St James's Square – were destroyed. The altarpiece of Emmanuel College, Cambridge is his: other works are in Darmstadt, Madrid, Schleissheim, Sheffield, and Venice. [ill. 295, p. 315]

Ammanati, Bartolommeo (1511–92), was a Florentine sculptor influenced by Michelangelo and Sansovino. His best-known work is the *Neptune* fountain (1563–75) in the Piazza della Signoria at Florence, of which a contemporary said: 'Ammanato, Ammanato, che bel marmo hai rovinato!' (what fine marble you have ruined!). In his old age, affected by Counter-Reformation austerity, he is said to have destroyed some of his secular works. He also wrote an important letter (published in 1582) setting out his ideas on decency and on the sculptor's responsibility for his work, which is a document of Mannerist art after the Council of Trent. [ill. 162, p. 295]

Amorino (Ital. little love). A small Cupid or PUTTO.

Ancona (Ital.). A large altarpiece composed of several compartments made in one piece with the frame. *See* POLYPTYCH.

Andrea del Castagno *see* CASTAGNO.

Andrea del Sarto (1486–1531), was, with Fra BARTOLOMMEO, the most important painter working in Florence at the time when Raphael and Michelangelo were active in Rome. He was the best painter, as opposed to draughtsman, in 16th-century Florence and had more feeling for tone and colour than any of his contemporaries south of Venice. He was the first Florentine to depart from the coloured drawing approach in favour of composition by patches of coloured light and shade, although his actual draughtsmanship is derived from Michelangelo. He also borrowed from the newly arrived engravings of Dürer. As a fresco painter he made his name with a series of grisailles in the Church of the Scalzi (1511–26) and the *Miracles of S. Filippo Benizzi* (1509–10) in SS. Annunziata. These were followed by his most famous frescoes, epitomizing the High Renaissance style in Florence, the *Birth of the Virgin* (1514) and the *Madonna del Sacco* (1525), both also in the Annunziata. Andrea went to France in 1518/19 at the invitation of François I and was well received there, but he broke his contract in order to return to his wife, who, in the opinion of contemporaries, ruined him. Browning's poem is probably the best explanation of his failure to live up to his great promise, but his works are of great importance in the evolution of Florentine painting, especially the *Holy Families*, often in half-length. The *Madonna delle Arpie* (1517) in the Uffizi, Florence, is a purely classical work comparable with Raphael's Madonnas: it is also a starting-point for MANNERISM, since his pupils included PONTORMO, ROSSO, and VASARI. Outside Florence there are works by him in the Royal Collection and in Berlin, Dresden, London (NG and Wallace Coll.), Madrid, New York (Met. Mus.), Paris (Louvre: including some painted in France), Philadelphia, Vienna, and elsewhere. [ill. 184, p. 298]

Angelico, Fra (*c.* 1387 or perhaps *c.* 1400–55). Fra Giovanni da Fiesole, known as the Blessed Angelico, was a Dominican friar who was a friend of S. Antoninus and knew Popes Eugenius IV and Nicholas V. As a member of the Order of Preachers he used his art for didactic rather than mystic purposes and the style he evolved was correspondingly simple and direct; conservative, and yet based on the largeness of form of Giotto and Masaccio, so that the general development of his style begins with a Gothic quality akin to LORENZO Monaco and runs counter to the trend of Florentine painting in the 1440s as shown e.g. by Fra Filippo LIPPI. He entered the convent at Fiesole in or after 1407 and shared in its vicissitudes at Cortona and Foligno, but he does not seem to have painted much before 1428. The new theory that he was born *c.* 1400 goes a long way towards explaining this. The first certainly datable work by him is the *Linaiuoli Madonna* (Florence, S. Marco), commissioned in 1433. The convent of S. Marco was taken over by his Order in 1436 and he decorated it with a series of about fifty frescoes, most of them in the cells of the friars and intended as aids to contemplation. At the same time (*c.* 1440) he painted the altarpiece for S. Marco and two other convents: these show the Madonna surrounded by Saints and are important in the development of the type of altarpiece known as the SACRA CONVERSAZIONE. He was called to Rome, probably by Eugenius IV, to decorate a chapel in the Vatican (*c.* 1446–9), which still exists. In 1447 he also painted two frescoes in Orvieto Cathedral as part of a *Last Judgement*, a scheme which was later finished by SIGNORELLI. He was elected Prior of Fiesole in 1449 and probably returned to Rome after his three-year term expired to paint the Chapel of the Sacrament in the Vatican, now destroyed. He died in Rome in 1455. The biggest collection of his works is in the Museo di S. Marco, Florence, his own convent. Others are in Cortona, Fiesole, Florence (Uffizi), Perugia, and the Vatican, as well as Berlin, Cambridge Mass., London (NG), Madrid, Paris (Louvre), Munich, and elsewhere. His most important pupil was Benozzo GOZZOLI. [ill. 72, p. 278]

Anonimo (Ital. anonymous) often applied to any unknown Italian painter, but specifically it refers either to the Anonimo Morelliano (i.e. Marcanton Michiel), a writer on the art of Venice and N. Italy in the first half of the 16th century, or to the Anonimo Magliabechiano (or Gaddiano), a Florentine writer of the same period.

Antelami, Benedetto, was the chief Italian sculptor before the PISANI. In 1178 he signed and dated a relief of the *Deposition* in Parma Cathedral; the Baptistry at Parma, begun in 1196, and some of the sculpture at Borgo San Donnino (now called Fidenza) are attributed to him. [ill. 4, p. 269]

Anti-cerne (Fr. *cerne*, outline). A contour managed by leaving a white line of bare canvas between two or more areas of colour. It is, in fact, the opposite of a black outline, and is a favourite device of FAUVE painters.

Antonello da Messina (*c.* 1430–79) was the only major S. Italian painter of the 15th century and the only Italian decisively influenced by the minute oil-technique associated with the EYCKS. He may have been a pupil of the half-legendary Colantonio in Naples (where he could have seen Flemish paintings) and there is no reason to suppose he actually visited Flanders. His mature style combines Flemish detail with Italian breadth of form. In 1475/6 he was in Venice, where he painted the S. Cassiano altarpiece (now known only from copies and fragments in Vienna): this was contemporary with the altarpiece of PIERO della Francesca (Milan, Brera) and the one (now destroyed) by Giovanni BELLINI for SS. Giovanni e Paolo. One of these three was the first great SACRA CONVERSAZIONE to treat the picture space as a continuation of the real space – like a chapel opening out of the church – so that the spectator is drawn into the scene in active participation. Antonello's virtuoso technique also influenced the Venetians, especially Giovanni Bellini's portraits, which show traces of the Flemish type of design favoured by Antonello. Apart from the Vienna fragments there are works in London (NG), (*Salvator Mundi*, 1465, the first dated work, and others); Paris (Louvre), and Antwerp which both have works dated 1475, presumably painted in Venice; Berlin, Bucharest, Messina, Munich, New York, Philadelphia,

Rome (Borghese), Washington, and elsewhere. [ill. 137, p. 292]

Antwerp Mannerists, a term used to describe a group of Antwerp painters, mostly unknown, working in the early 16th century (*c.* 1510–30), and who, strictly speaking, have nothing to do with MANNERISM. Their style is characterized by its use of affected poses and florid ornament, some of which is Italianate in type. ISENBRANDT is related to this group. [ill. 373, p. 325]

Appel, Karel (*b.* 1921), is a Dutch painter, born in Amsterdam, who works in Paris. He exhibited with the group known as Cobra (i.e. Copenhagen, Brussels, Amsterdam) from 1949. In 1951 he painted a mural for the Stedelijk Museum, Amsterdam, and he has also produced some book-illustrations, but most of his works are in immensely thick layers of frenziedly moulded oil paint, Abstract Expressionist in type and similar to the work of the American KOONING. There are examples in Antwerp, Auckland NZ, Brussels, Buffalo, Copenhagen, The Hague, Liège, London (Tate), Manchester (Whitworth), New York (Guggenheim), Ottawa, Pittsburgh (Carnegie), and Utrecht. [ill. 1104, p. 428]

Apt, Ulrich the Elder (*d.* 1532), was active in Augsburg in 1481. He painted many portraits, mostly in the style of Hans Holbein I, and several have been confused with Holbein the Younger's. There are pictures by him in Augsburg, Florence (Uffizi), Munich, Vienna; and there are two replicas of a *Man and his Wife*, 1512, in the Royal Coll. and New York (Met. Mus.). [ill. 583, p. 356]

Aquatint *see* ENGRAVING.

Arabesque, a flowing linear decoration. *See* GROTESQUE.

Archipenko, Alexander (1887–1964), was a Russian-American abstract sculptor. He was one of the first Cubist sculptors. There are works by him in New York (M of MA), Detroit, and London (Tate). [ill. 1129, p. 430]

Architectonic in the technical sense means 'having the massive stability and calm grandeur of noble architecture'. A handy synonym for MONUMENTAL.

Arcimboldi, Giuseppe (1527–93), a Milanese painter of fantastic heads composed of fragments of landscape, vegetables, flowers, etc., much overrated in his own day (and now) and claimed as an ancestor by the Surrealists. He worked in a normal style for Milan Cathedral (1549–58) and designed tapestries for Como (1558). Court painter at Prague (1562–87), his bizarreries appealed to the Hapsburgs, especially Rudolf II, who made him a Count Palatine. Vienna has several pictures painted for Rudolf II; other works are in Brescia, Cremona, Graz, Hartford Conn. (Wadsworth Atheneum), and Innsbruck. [ill. 157, p. 294]

Aretino *see* SPINELLO.

Armitage, Kenneth (*b.* 1916), is a British sculptor who now works almost exclusively in modelled plaster, subsequently cast in bronze. His figures are exceedingly thin and sail-like, with much attention given to the effect of movement. In 1956 he won a competition for a war memorial at Krefeld, and in 1958 he was the British representative at the Biennale in Venice. There are works by him in Antwerp (Middelheim Park), Brussels, Buffalo, Leeds, London (Tate, V & A), New York (Brooklyn and M of MA), Paris, Rome, and elsewhere. [ill. 1151, p. 434]

Armory Show. Held in 1913 in a regimental armoury in New York this exhibition was the principal means of introducing 'modern' – i.e. Post-Impressionist – art to the United States. [ill. 1060, p. 422]

Arnolfo di Cambio (*d.* probably 1302), Italian architect and sculptor, designer of Florence Cathedral (1300). A pupil of Nicola PISANO, Arnolfo worked on his master's Shrine of S. Dominic, Bologna (1264–7), and Pulpit at Siena (1265–8), before going to Rome in 1277 where he made a portrait of Charles of Anjou (Rome, Conservatori Gall.), which is one of the first modern portrait statues. His tomb of Cardinal de Braye (*d.* 1282) in S. Domenico at Orvieto, now much altered, set the type of wall-tomb for more than a century, with its arrangement of the dead man lying on a bier below the Madonna and Child in glory, set in a vertical architectural frame. He also made a tomb and a bust of Boniface VIII, as part of the Pope's campaign of artistic propaganda, and built ciboria in S. Paolo fuori (1285) and Sta Cecilia (1293), both in Rome. The remains of his sculptural decoration for Florence Cathedral are in the Cathedral Museum, and other works are in the Bargello, Florence; Boston, and the V & A, London. [ill. 9, p. 270]

Arp, Hans (*b.* 1887), a French painter and sculptor. In 1916 he was one of the co-founders of DADA. There are works by him in New York (M of MA) and London (Tate). [ill. 1139, p. 433]

Arpino, Giuseppe Cesari, called Cavaliere d'Arpino (1568–1640), was 'the last melancholy champion' of conservative and anaemic MANNERISM in opposition to CARAVAGGIO's naturalist revolution (he employed Caravaggio and outlived him by 30 years), and was patronized by the Vatican and the Roman Princes. He designed the mosaics of the dome of St Peter's, painted the frescoes of S. Martino, Naples (1589–91), and painted huge and dull histories in the Conservatori Palace, Rome, the earliest of 1591 and the last of 1636. Most old galleries have examples, including London (Wellington Mus.), the Vatican, and Vienna. [ill. 278, p. 312]

Arricciato *see* FRESCO.

Ars Moriendi (Lat. The Art of Dying). One of the most famous BLOCK-BOOKS, printed in Germany *c.* 1465. It is a devotional work, like the *Biblia Pauperum*, and is based either on a Netherlandish block-book of *c.* 1450 (in London, BM) or on a set of engravings (Oxford) by the anonymous Master E.S. [ill. 561, p. 354]

Art Nouveau was a 'new art' which spread across Europe and America in the 1890s. It was mainly a style of architecture and interior decoration (Horta, van de Velde) and flourished in Belgium and Britain especially, using flat patterns of writhing vegetable forms based on a naturalistic conception of plants rather than a formalized type of decoration. Cast-iron lilies and copper tendrils are still with us, as is furniture with heart-shaped holes in it. ENSOR was associated with the creators of the movement in Belgium, but he is much less typical than MORRIS, whose Arts and Crafts movement may be the progenitor of *Art nouveau*, or, better still, BEARDSLEY, whose drawings appeared in the first issue of 'The Studio' (1893), a periodical which helped to spread the style. In Germany the movement was called *Jugendstil*, after a magazine 'Jugend' (Youth), which was first published in 1896. [ills. 997, 998, p. 415]

Ascription *see* ATTRIBUTION.

Ashcan School. A group of 19th/20th-century American 'realist' painters and illustrators – the best known was BELLOWS, although he was not one of the original eight – whose interest in the sordid side of city life (especially in New York) justifies the nickname.

Asselyn, Jan (1610–52). A Dutch Italianate painter, probably a pupil of E. van de Velde but who formed his style on the imitation of the Arcadian landscapes of CLAUDE. His best-known work is a political allegory of Dutch independence, *The Angry Swan*, in Amsterdam (Rijksmus.) but *Beggars at a Monastery* (1647) in Dresden is more typical. [ills. 425, 426, p. 333]

Atelier (Fr. studio). The *atelier libre* is a common feature of the Continental art world. It is a studio, open freely but not free, which provides a nude model in fixed sessions, but no tuition or control. The most famous was opened *c.* 1825–30 in Paris by a model called Suisse, and was used by Delacroix, Courbet, Manet, Monet, Pissarro, Cézanne, and other Impressionists. The Atelier Julian, opened in Paris in 1860, was not an *atelier libre* since it provided a teacher, though it was more liberal than the official École des Beaux-Arts for which it often served as forcing-ground or alternative. Most of the NABIS worked at the Julian, as did Matisse, Derain, and Léger. Sometimes these *ateliers libres* are called *Académies*.

Attribution. When a picture is signed or recorded in a document there can be little doubt that it is by the painter to whom it is attributed: 'attribution', however, usually means assigning a picture to its painter on the grounds of its likeness to works known to be his. This, which involves STYLE CRITICISM, can range from moral certainty to mere guess-work, depending on such factors as the number of certain works known to the person making the attribution, as well as the degree of his intimacy with them. For this reason, a conscientious cataloguer gives at least the main reasons for his decisions, and it is desirable to use phrases like 'Attributed to . . .', 'Ascribed to . . .', 'Circle of . . .', or 'Studio of . . .' with some precision. In normal English usage there is no distinction between Attributed and Ascribed, but it may be suggested that a useful terminology would be to keep 'Ascribed to . . .' to imply a slightly greater degree of dubiety than 'Attributed to . . .'. The distinction between 'Studio of . . .' and

'Follower of . . .', maintained in the catalogues of the National Gallery, is similar – Follower not implying any direct contact with the artist. A Follower may well be considerably later, whereas an Imitator is self-explanatory.

Au Premier Coup (Fr. at the first shot) *see* ALLA PRIMA.

Automatism. Doodling. Shut your eyes and draw – the subconscious will do the rest; hence it was a favourite SURREALIST technique.

Avanzo, Jacopo. A 14th-century Paduan painter who was the pupil and apparently inseparable partner of ALTICHIERO. [ill. 34, p. 273]

Aved, Jacques (1702–66). A French portrait painter trained in Amsterdam, who became a friend and collaborator of CHARDIN, whose splendid portrait of Aved is now in the Louvre, Paris. There are portraits by Aved in the Louvre and Versailles and in Amsterdam (Rijksmus.) and The Hague. [ill. 732, p. 380]

Avercamp, Hendrik (1585–1634). A landscape painter born in Amsterdam but influenced by BRUEGEL the Elder and CONINXLOO and making the transition to the realistic Dutch landscape of the 17th century. He specialized in ice scenes and there are works in Amsterdam (Rijksmus.), Edinburgh (NG of S), London (NG), Rotterdam, St Louis, Toledo Ohio, and Vienna. Barent Avercamp (1612–79) was his nephew, pupil, and imitator. [ill. 496, p. 344]

B

Baburen, Dirck van (c. 1590–1624) was one of the three principal painters of the UTRECHT SCHOOL. He was in Rome 1617–20/2 and there painted the *Deposition* (S. Pietro in Montorio) which is derived from Caravaggio's (now in the Vatican). His career was very short and only a handful of pictures survive, others being in Utrecht, Boston, Oslo, and York. [ill. 458, p. 338]

Baciccia, Giovanni Battista Gaulli called (1639–1709), was a Genoese whose style was formed by the study of Rubens and van Dyck. He soon made a name as a portrait painter but went to Rome very young and made a greater reputation as one of the most daring of all the Baroque decorators. He was friendly with BERNINI and studied the Correggio frescoes in Parma: his most celebrated work, the ceiling of the Gesù in Rome (1668–85) is a staggering piece of illusionism, with the painted figures merging into stucco figures which break out of the apparent frame into the plane of the spectator. It goes beyond even the ceiling of the Barberini Palace, by PIETRO da Cortona, and has in addition a Rubensian warmth of colour. Many other Roman churches were decorated by him and his portraits are also to be found in Roman galleries. Some of his later portraits have a quieter, almost Marattesque, character. [ill. 272, p. 313]

Backer, Jacob Adriaensz. (1608–51), was a pupil of Rembrandt about 1632 and painted portraits in Amsterdam. Occasionally he crossed the influence of Rembrandt with that of Hals, particularly in his use of light colour. Amsterdam and The Hague have good examples. [ill. 436, p. 334]

Backhuysen, Ludolf (1631–1708), was a Dutch marine painter, a pupil of A. van Everdingen. He is well represented in the NG, London, and his *Boats in a Storm* (London, Dulwich) may well have been one of the sea-pieces that influenced Turner. [ill. 503, p. 345]

Bacon, Francis (b. 1909), is a self-taught painter who destroys a large part of his output, so much so that virtually nothing of his early work has survived. Through his highly personal subject-matter, which concentrates chiefly on dogs, carcasses, and evocations of men, including elderly tycoons, and Velazquez's *Innocent X*, caged in plate-glass and screaming in a silent world of horror, dissolution, and fear, he expresses with energy and singleness of aim all the gradations of emotion from pity and disgust to horror, traumatic revulsion, and the unbalance of panic. His work, which can be interpreted as an attempt to evoke an essentially partial, since incomplete, catharsis

in the spectator, raises in its most acute form the problem of the relationship between art and pleasure. There are pictures by him in Aberdeen, Batley, Belfast, Birmingham, Buffalo NY, Chicago, Detroit, London (Tate), New York (M of MA), and Yale. [ill. 1116, p. 429]

Bacon, John (1740–99), began by modelling china figures. He also worked in Coade's artificial stone, and for Wedgwood and the Derby porcelain factory. He became an RA in 1770. He was a fashionable sculptor who executed many tombs, including the huge Chatham monument in Westminster Abbey (1779) and the one to Dr Johnson in St Paul's Cathedral (1796). He was considered the best sculptor of his day for tombs, as BANKS was for history pieces and NOLLEKENS for busts, and prided himself on his Christian sentiment: he was 'pious and zealously attached to Methodism . . . yet knowing in the ways of the world . . . and eager among stockbrokers'. His son John (1777–1859) was his pupil and finished his equestrian *William III* in St James's Square, London, and also executed a large number of tombs. [ill. 868, p. 399]

Baldinucci, Filippo (c. 1624–96), succeeded VASARI as historiographer of Florentine Art, his 'Notizie de' Professori . . .' appearing in many volumes, 1681–1728. He made greater use of documents than his predecessor, and the vast collection of drawings in the Uffizi is due to his appreciation of their importance in the study of paintings.

Baldovinetti, Alesso (c. 1426–99), was a Florentine painter and worker in mosaic and stained glass who was influenced by DOMENICO Veneziano. His experiments with the technique of fresco painting were unfortunate, witness the frescoes in SS. Annunziata (1460/2) and S. Miniato (1466), in Florence. He painted three panels in the series on the doors of the Silver Cupboard of SS. Annunziata (now in the Museo di S. Marco, Florence) which had been begun by Fra Angelico. There are other works by him in Florence as well as in London, Paris, and elsewhere. [ill. 82, p. 281]

Baldung, Hans (1484/5–1545) called Grien, was a Strasbourg painter and designer of woodcuts and stained glass. His woodcuts in particular show the influence of DÜRER, in whose shop he may have worked before 1505. His principal picture is the altarpiece in Freiburg Cathedral (1512–16), but his favourite theme was the female nude, often in horrible allegories such as the *Death and the Woman* (1517: Basle). Outside Germany and Austria there are pictures in the Royal Collection and in The Hague, Liverpool, and London (NG). [ill. 563, p. 355]

Balla, Giacomo (*b.* 1874), signed the FUTURIST Manifesto of 1910 and painted Futurist pictures for a while, including the only amusing one produced by that dreary movement – the *Dog on a Leash*. He later returned to more traditional forms of expression. [ill. 1034, p. 419]

Bambino (Ital. baby), usually specifically the Christ Child.

Bambocciata (Ital.), the name given to low-life and peasant subjects, generally small, with small figures, of the type painted by several Dutch and Flemish artists in Italy in the 17th century. These were popular even in Italy, although frowned on by the theorists of the Grand Style, as well as in the North. The name perhaps derives from BAMBOCCIO, although it also means 'jest, triviality'.

Bamboccio (Ital. fat and lively baby), name given as BENTNAME to Pieter van Laer (1592 or 1595–1642), a Dutch painter who lived in Rome 1627–39, where he was a friend of Poussin, Claude, and Sandrart. His pictures of peasants, soldiers, brigands, and similar subjects became popular in Italy and were much imitated by other Northern artists. He returned to his native Haarlem in 1639 and died there. There are pictures by him in the Royal Collection and in Amsterdam, Cambridge (Fitzwm), Dresden, Florence (Uffizi), New York (Met. Mus.), Paris (Louvre), Rome (Gall. Naz.), and elsewhere. [ill. 428, p. 333]

Bandinelli, Baccio (1493–1560), was a Florentine sculptor, goldsmith, and painter whose constant efforts to out-do Michelangelo generally rebounded on his own head. He was the rival of Cellini, who hated him both on his own account and on behalf of Michelangelo, but he enjoyed the favour of the Medici and through them he got the commission for his *Hercules and Cacus* (1534: Florence, Piazza della Signoria), made in direct emulation of Michelangelo's *David*. It was not much liked and Cellini and Bandinelli had a highly public quarrel over it. His best works are the reliefs in the choir of Florence Cathedral, but his greatest importance lies in the part he played in the development of ACADEMIES. [ills. 160, 202, pp. 295, 303]

Banks, Thomas (1735–1805), was one of the first British sculptors to be influenced by Neoclassic ideals. He went to Rome in 1772 on a scholarship from the RA and remained there seven years: while there he carved the *Thetis* (London, V & A). He spent 1781–2 in St Petersburg but in 1786 was elected RA and worked for the rest of his life on busts and monuments, the most famous of which was the dead child, *Penelope Boothby* (Ashbourne, Derbyshire) which moved Queen Charlotte to tears. There are works in London (NPG, Soane Mus., Westminster Abbey, and St Paul's), and elsewhere. [ill. 881, p. 399]

Baptiste *see* MONNOYER.

Barbari, Jacopo de' (*c.* 1440/50–*c.* 1516), is said to have been a Venetian painter, but from 1500 he worked in Germany and the Netherlands; about 1501 he wrote a curious letter to the Elector of Saxony called 'De la eccelentia de la pictura'. He influenced DÜRER and was also influenced by him; certainly his engravings fit into the development of German graphic art. There is a portrait of Pacioli, the mathematician and pupil of Piero della Francesca, with another man, signed and dated 1495 (Naples), but this is sometimes held to be the work of a different painter: on the other hand he certainly painted the first still-life, the *Dead Bird*, of 1504, at Munich. Berlin, Dresden, Paris, Philadelphia (Johnson), Verona, and Weimar also have works of his. [ill. 224, p. 306]

Barbizon School. A mid-19th-century group of landscape painters, centred on the village of Barbizon in the Forest of Fontainebleau. Its chief members were MILLET, Théodore ROUSSEAU, and DIAZ, their aims being an exact and unprettified rendering of peasant life and scenery, painted on the spot; this last making them the precursors of IMPRESSIONISM. [ills. 755, 762, 763, pp. 384–5]

Barisanus of Trani was a bronze-founder and sculptor working in South Italy in the last quarter of the 12th century. There are three large pairs of bronze doors by him at the Cathedrals of Trani, Ravello, and Monreale. Those at Trani have a self-portrait and a signature and are thought to date from *c.* 1175. The doors at Ravello are dated 1179 but are not signed. Those at Monreale are signed and are thought to be contemporary with the other set of doors made for the same cathedral by the Pisan BONANUS in 1185. The difference in style is considerable and emphasizes the much greater dependence of Barisanus upon Byzantine models – in some cases he even retains Greek inscriptions – as well as his far greater interest in decorative forms. Many of Barisanus's figures are repeated, even on the same door, and were thus cast from a single mould. His doors are made of plates of bronze nailed on to an oak framework, since the technique of bronze-casting in the 12th century was still comparatively rudimentary. [ill. 3, p. 269]

Barlach, Ernst (1870–1938), was a German EXPRESSIONIST sculptor and illustrator of great tragic power. His pessimistic art was condemned by the Nazis and many of his works destroyed: survivors are now in many German museums and there is a small Barlach Museum near Lüneburg. His best works are perhaps the woodcarvings of single figures of peasants, beggars, and similar subjects, many of them inspired by a visit to Russia. His wood-carving technique was closely based on German Late Gothic work. [ill. 1143, p. 432]

Barna was a Sienese painter, active *c.* 1350/6, who was the greatest of Simone MARTINI's followers. In the Collegiata at S. Gimignano he painted the *Life of Christ* and he is said to have died as a result of a fall from the scaffolding, leaving the frescoes unfinished. The *Christ carrying the Cross* (New York, Frick Coll.) is attributed to him. [ill. 44, p. 274]

Barnaba da Modena (active 1362–83), was a N. Italian painter who combined an almost purely Byzantine tradition with some Giottesque elements. There are dated works in Berlin (1369) and London (1374) and elsewhere. [ill. 33, p. 273]

Barocci, Federico (*c.* 1535–1612) was, after Raphael, the most important painter of Urbino. His soft, colouristic, and emotional art is a perfect expression of one aspect of the Counter-Reformation, and it is not surprising that S. Philip Neri regarded him highly. He was in Rome in the mid-1550s, when Michelangelo is said to have encouraged him, and he returned in 1560, making his name with the decorations in the Casino of Pius IV (1561–3: Vatican). Most of the rest of his life was spent in Urbino, where he worked for only two hours a day, crippled by ill-health (yet he lived to extreme old age). He became a Tertiary of the Order of S. Francis in 1566 and his greatest patron was the austere and pious Duke of Urbino, although he is better known for his connection with S. Philip. Many drawings made as studies for his carefully-prepared paintings survive, and, apart from the numerous works in Urbino, there are others in Brussels, Copenhagen, Florence (Uffizi, including the big *Madonna del Popolo*, 1575–9), London (NG), Madrid, Milan (Brera), Munich, Paris (Louvre), Rome (Borghese and churches), the Vatican, Vienna and Weimar. [ill. 212, p. 303]

Baronzio, Giovanni, was a Riminese painter, working in 1345 and earlier, who was much influenced by CAVALLINI and GIOTTO. He was dead by 1362. He is the best evidence for Giotto's activity in Rimini, recorded in old sources. There are two dated pictures (1345) in Urbino and Mercatello, near Urbino (but the attribution of this is open to doubt), and frescoes in Ravenna and Tolentino. Others are in Rimini, Birmingham (Barber Inst.), Baltimore, Berlin, Munich, New York (Met. Mus.), Paris (Jacquemart-André), Rome, Venice, and elsewhere. [ill. 31, p. 272]

Baroque. This is the style that succeeded MANNERISM and lasted, though with profound modifications, until well into the 18th century. The style is seen at its purest in the so-called 'High Baroque', which is virtually confined to Italy (to Rome even) and to the period covered by the years *c.* 1630–80, that is, roughly the maturity of its greatest exponent, BERNINI. The High Baroque, at its best and fullest, is a union of the arts of architecture, painting, and sculpture, acting in concert on the emotions of the spectator; inviting him, for example, to participate in the agonies and ecstasies of the Saints. Its blend of illusionism, light and colour, and movement is calculated to overwhelm the spectator by a direct emotional appeal. Owing to its essential links with Counter-Reformation Catholicism, pagan antiquity, and the Mediterranean generally, many Northerners are – or were until recently – queasy about it. At the beginning of the 17th century there was an upsurge of spiritual confidence and a new direction in religious art which combined with a new approach to classical art to create a new style. The confused and flaccid forms of Late Mannerism gave place to the simple subject-matter, the unidealized naturalism, the uncomplicated iconography, and strong chiaroscuro of CARAVAGGIO; the clarity of composition, the revival of the balance and harmony of Raphael and the tenderness of handling of Correggio, the nobility of form, the directness of meaning and imagery of Annibale CARRACCI, DOMENICHINO, Guido RENI, and GUERCINO. Of the painters of the High Baroque, LANFRANCO, PIETRO da Cortona, BACICCIA, and, at the end of the century, Padre POZZO, specialized in the florid and exuberant illusionism which is

one of the characteristics of the style, while Bernini pushed to their furthest limits the use of painterly effects in sculpture, the dissolved contour, the rendering of movement by means of flickering light, the expression of the most profound and passionately felt religious emotion. Some Roman artists, such as SACCHI, MARATTA, and ALGARDI were always more restrained: POUSSIN, who lived and worked in Rome for most of his life, developed the classical and intellectual aspects of the Baroque style almost to the exclusion of its emotional side. Outside Italy, astute politicians like Colbert, Louis XIV's great Minister, were quick to see that the religious style could easily be made to subserve autocratic régimes, by the glorification of the monarch, but in this process a good deal of pompous inflation was superimposed on the original religious fervour; and the French exponents of the Baroque, in LEBRUN and his team, replaced its emotional qualities with a conscious and frigid use of the antique. Even RUBENS, the greatest Northern Baroque artist, sometimes allowed himself to be used in this way. The style lasted longest in Catholic Germany and Austria, and had the least influence in Protestant countries – Britain, Scandinavia, and Holland, although there are aspects of Rembrandt which place him among the greatest artists of the Baroque, and there is certainly such a thing as English Baroque. In the North it is still possible to use the term as one of simple abuse (i.e. non-Gothic, unRuskinian), but this is now confined to the very old or the very unsophisticated. A more dangerous misuse is as a synonym for 'Seventeenth Century'. Late Baroque merges almost imperceptibly into the ROCOCO and the Age of Reason finally rejected both and produced NEOCLASSICISM. [ills. 259–84, pp. 310–13]

Barry, James (1741–1806), was an Irish painter who was brought to London by Edmund Burke in 1764. He was encouraged by Reynolds to persist in grand manner historical painting, and Burke paid his expenses to Italy, 1766–71, where he studied Raphael and Michelangelo with more enthusiasm than discretion. He was made an RA in 1773, and from 1777 to 1783 worked on a huge decoration in the Great Room of the Society of Arts of six pictures (two are 42 feet long) representing *The Progress of Human Culture*. When they were exhibited in 1783 Dr Johnson said of them: 'Whatever the hand may have done, the mind has done its part. There is a grasp of mind there which you find nowhere else.' He became Professor of Painting at the RA in 1782, but in 1799 was expelled for his bitter attacks on his fellow-members and on the memory of Reynolds. BLAKE's projected poem 'Barry' exists only as a fragment, which is a diatribe against Reynolds. He died in great poverty and squalor. There are works in Dublin (NG), Cork, London (Tate), and Manchester. He represents, with FUSELI and HAYDON, another instance of the failure of the English patron to appreciate history painting on a gigantic scale and on heroic themes, based on a studious adaptation of the Italian Grand Style. His portraits are very fine, but he could only rarely be persuaded to demean himself to paint one. [ill. 894, p. 401]

Bartolo di Fredi was a Sienese who died in 1410 but who worked in the style of the LORENZETTI and of BARNA. [ill. 45, p. 274]

Bartolommeo di Giovanni *see* 'ALUNNO di DOMENICO'.

Bartolommeo della Porta, Fra (*c.* 1474 – probably 1517), was born in Florence and apprenticed to Cosimo ROSSELLI in 1484. He was in the convent of S. Marco in 1498 when it was stormed and its Prior, Savonarola, dragged to prison, and he is said to have vowed then to become a monk, which he did in 1500. His earliest remaining work (a *Last Judgement*, 1499, Mus. di S. Marco) is now in very bad condition but enough remains to show its profound influence on the young RAPHAEL. In 1504 he became head of the monastery workshop, a position once held by Fra Angelico. He visited Venice in 1508 and after his return took Mariotto ALBERTINELLI into partnership, and he was in Rome in 1514 or 1515, both these visits being important for the development of his ideals of simplicity and balance in composition, decorum of presentation, the use of telling gestures and rapt expressions, the exclusion of picturesque detail, and the adoption of sober and rather generalized settings. He introduced figures in strong *contrapposto* for its own sake, and was among the first to replace contemporary costume with nondescript drapery in his religious figures, using this to stress the gulf between the divine and the earthly. All these ideas mark the change from the style of the 15th century to that of the 16th century, and he was one of its most important initiators, his influence being spread by his huge output of drawings. After his death the S. Marco workshop petered out. There are works in Berlin, Besançon (Cath.), Cambridge Mass. (Fogg Mus.), Florence (Accad., Pitti, Uffizi, Mus. di S. Marco), London (NG), Lucca (Mus. and Cath.), Paris (Louvre), Philadelphia (Johnson Coll.), Rome (Gall. Naz.), Stuttgart, the Vatican, Vienna, and Washington (NG). [ills. 167, 168, p. 296]

Barye, Antoine-Louis (1796–1875), the son of a Paris goldsmith, served in the Napoleonic Armies 1812–14 and began to study sculpture only in 1816. He worked for a goldsmith from 1823 to 1831 in the Jardin des Plantes, making models of the animals, and from then on devoted himself almost exclusively to animal sculpture. In 1848 he went bankrupt but was appointed Keeper of Casts at the Louvre (1848–50) and was later teacher of zoological drawing at the Musée d'Histoire Naturelle, Paris. His first major work of a non-animal subject was the *Napoleon dominating History and the Arts* (1855–7), a pediment on the Pavillon de l'Horloge of the Louvre, and in 1860 he made the equestrian *Napoleon* for Ajaccio, Napoleon's birthplace. He was one of the major Romantic artists of the 19th century and his choice of violent subjects – tigers, jaguars, and other carnivores, often shown devouring other animals and even human beings – gives him a certain affinity with DELACROIX, although Barye was never able to invest the human figure with Romantic overtones. One or two small statues of women are almost Greek in feeling. There is a large collection of his works in the Louvre and over 100 in Washington (Corcoran). [ill. 722, p. 379]

Basaiti, Marco (*c.* 1470–1530), was a Venetian painter much influenced by Giovanni BELLINI (*c.* 1500–10) and then by GIORGIONE. There is a signed *Madonna* in London (NG) which shows him using Bellini's types.

Pseudo-Basaiti is probably only a name for one aspect of Bellini. [ill. 142, p. 293]

Bas-Relief *see* RELIEF.

Bassano. This was the name of a family of Venetian painters of which there were four main members. Francesco da Ponte the Elder (*c.* 1475–1539) worked in Bassano and was a modest provincial follower of the Bellini. His son Jacopo (*c.* 1510/18–92) was the most considerable artist of the family. He was a pupil in Venice of BONIFAZIO de' Pitati, and was independent by the early 1530s. Although he worked almost entirely in Bassano he was by no means a provincial painter, and his works show successive waves of influence, proving him to have been in constant and sensitive touch with Venice. His was a highly personal style, robust and energetic, with stocky figures in strong chiaroscuro and heavy impasto, and he pioneered the large, rustic genre scene depicting the seasons, or the trades, with many figures and animals, often set in a mountainous and stormy landscape, and favoured religious subjects that allowed him to introduce peasants and animals (in which he was one of the first to be interested) and heaped-up still-lifes of fruit, game, vegetables, and utensils (cf. AERTSEN, BUECKELAER). Jacopo had three painter sons. Francesco the Younger (1549–92) ran the Venetian branch of the workshop. His paintings are often based on his father's drawings and closely, but more weakly, follow his style. He committed suicide a few months after his father's death. Leandro (1557–1622) worked in the Venetian studio under Francesco, and after the latter's death took over the workshop. He was the chief portrait painter of the family, and his portraits are closely allied to those of TINTORETTO. Gerolamo (1566–1621) entered the workshop under Leandro.
There are works by the family in the museums and churches of Bassano and Venice, and in the Royal Collection, Bergamo, Berlin, Cambridge (Fitzwm), Cambridge Mass. (Fogg Mus.), Cleveland Ohio, Copenhagen, Detroit, Dresden, Edinburgh (NG), Florence (Uffizi, Pitti), Greenville S. Carolina, Grenoble, London (NG, V & A), Madrid (Acad., Prado), Manchester, Mantua, Milan (Brera, Ambrosiana, Castello), Munich, Naples, New York (Met. Mus., Frick), Paris (Louvre), Philadelphia (Johnson), Rome (Gall. Naz., Borghese, Capitoline), Stockholm, Toronto, Turin, Vienna, and elsewhere. [ills. 227, 229, 232, p. 306]

Batoni (Battoni), Pompeo (1708–87), was the principal rival of MENGS in Rome, but, although he was an enthusiast for Raphael and the Antique, he was less wholeheartedly Neoclassic. The minute delicacy of his handling won him many foreign patrons and the greater part of his output must consist of portraits of Princes and Grand Tourists painted while they were in Rome. He painted three Popes and most Princes of Europe, but the idea of a portrait of an educated man, standing against a background of classical antiquity (e.g. the Colosseum), seems to be Batoni's speciality and was well suited to the travelling Englishman. Many of these still exist in private collections, and there is even one of *General Gordon* (1766) which shows the sitter in full Highland dress with a claymore, set against the Colosseum. Reynolds was more influenced by these than he would admit, and, in the 14th Discourse, he goes out of his way to praise Gainsborough at the expense of Mengs and Batoni. From 1735 Batoni had a great many commissions for altarpieces and also for historical and mythological pictures: in 1760–1 he painted an altarpiece for St Peter's but this was not very successful and is now in S M degli Angeli, Rome. There are works in Roman churches and galleries and in Berlin, Birmingham, Cardiff, Dresden, Dublin (NG), Edinburgh (NPG), Florence (Uffizi and Pitti), Frankfurt (Städel), Greenville SC, and London (NG, NPG), Madrid (Acad., Prado), Milan (Brera), Minneapolis, Munich, Oxford, Paris (Louvre), and Vienna. [ill. 296, p. 315]

Bauhaus, The. This was the most famous school of architecture, design, and craftsmanship of modern times and has had an inestimable influence on art school training all over the world. It was founded in 1919 at Weimar, in Germany, by W. Gropius, the architect. It moved to Dessau in 1925 and then to Berlin, where, in 1933, it was closed by the Nazis. Its great importance lay in the fact that its teachers included FEININGER, KLEE, and KANDINSKY, and it attempted to face the problem of machine production, which MORRIS had evaded. The New Bauhaus was at Chicago.

Baumeister, Willi (1889–1955), was a German abstract painter who began as a Constructivist. He was in Paris in 1912 and 1914 and was influenced at first by Lautrec, Gauguin, and Cézanne, but was later decisively influenced by the mechanical forms of LÉGER. He was dismissed from his teaching post for 'degeneracy' in 1933, but, unlike most others, he remained in Germany and was, in due course, reinstated. From *c.* 1936 his works were entirely abstract: examples are in Cologne and Frankfurt (Städel). [ill. 1082, p. 426]

Bayeu, Francisco (1734–95), was a Spanish painter who worked under MENGS on the decoration of the Royal Palace, but is better known as GOYA's master 1766–*c.* 71 and brother-in-law. There is a portrait of him by Goya in the Prado, Madrid, which also has some of his own works. His brother Ramón (1746–93) was also a painter and worked with Goya. [ill. 663, p. 370]

Bazaine, Jean (*b.* 1904), denies that he is an abstract painter, but since 1945 he has produced non-figurative pictures as well as stained glass and mosaics (churches at Assy (1950), Audincourt (1951), and for the UNESCO building in Paris). In 1948 he published 'Notes sur la peinture d'aujourd'hui', which went into a second edition in 1953. In 1953–4 he was in Spain. There is a painting by him in Paris (Mus. d'Art Mod.). [ill. 1105, p. 428]

Bazille, Frédéric (1841–71), was a pupil of the academician Gleyre at the same time as Renoir, and through him came into close contact with most of the IMPRESSIONISTS and with Manet. His chief aim was the study of figures painted out-of-doors, so as to relate the tones of the flesh with those of the landscape. He was killed in the Franco-Prussian War when still on the threshold of his career. Most of his pictures are in Paris (Mus. de

l'Impressionnisme) and his native Montpellier. [ill. 792, p. 389]

Beardsley, Aubrey (1872–98), was an illustrator whose highly wrought, stylized black and white drawings exude a typically *fin-de-siècle* atmosphere and express perfectly the ART NOUVEAU of which they were an ingredient. He is best known for his work on the 'Yellow Book' in 1894, and for his illustrations to Wilde's 'Salome', and to the 'Rape of the Lock'. There are drawings by him in the Tate, London. [ill. 998, p. 415]

Beccafumi, Domenico (1485/6–1551) was the most important MANNERIST painter in Siena, and the last of the great Sienese. The influence of Michelangelo is apparent in his developed style, but he has an intensity of emotion and a subtle use of shot colour that mark his style as highly personal. Most of his best works are in Siena, but there are others in Baltimore, Berlin, Birmingham (Barber Inst.), Cambridge (Fitzwm), Detroit, Dresden, Dublin, Florence (Uffizi, Pitti, and Horne Mus.), London (NG, V & A), Munich, Naples, Pisa (Cath.), Rome (Gall. Naz., Borghese, S M Maggiore), Sarasota Fla, Washington (NG), York, and elsewhere. [ill. 188, p. 299]

Beckmann, Max (1884–1950), was one of the leading German EXPRESSIONIST painters who taught at Frankfurt until his dismissal as a 'decadent' artist in 1933. He went to Amsterdam from 1938 to 1947 and then to America where he died. His nine Triptychs, painted from 1932 onwards, are his best works and show that the main influences on his style were BOSCH and German primitive paintings. He is represented in many American museums and now in German museums as well. [ill. 1066, p. 424]

Beechey, Sir William (1753–1839), was a portrait painter of far less skill than Sir Thomas Lawrence, but he may have had a more truthful eye and he was certainly more sober in approach. He was elected ARA in 1793 and made Portrait Painter to the Queen; in 1798 he exhibited the huge *George III and the Prince of Wales reviewing Troops* (Royal Coll.) for which he was knighted and elected RA. He was a very careful craftsman and most anxious to ensure the durability of his pictures, examples of which are in London (Tate, NPG, Courtauld Inst.), Ottawa, and many American museums. [ill. 846, p. 396]

'Before all letters' *see* PROOF.

Bellechose, Henri, *see* MALOUEL.

Bellini. There were three painters in this Venetian family: Jacopo, and his sons Gentile and Giovanni.
Jacopo (*c.* 1400–70/1) was a pupil of GENTILE da Fabriano, with whom he was in Florence where, in 1423, he was involved in a prosecution as a result of an affray with a youth who threw stones into the workshop yard. Only four certain pictures are known, all rather stiff and hieratic in pose and treatment. In 1441 he defeated PISANELLO in a competition portrait of Lionello d'Este of Ferrara, but this portrait cannot be identified with certainty. His major surviving works are his two sketchbooks (British Museum and Louvre) which were the source of many of

the ideas and designs used by his sons and by Mantegna. Four signed works are in Lovere, Milan (Brera), Venice (Accad.), and Verona; other, attributed, pictures are in Florence (Uffizi), Milan (Poldi-Pezzoli), Padua, Verona, and elsewhere.

Gentile (c. 1429/30–1507) probably worked in the family shop until his father died (an altarpiece said to have been signed by all three and dated 1460 is recorded), but he had achieved sufficient fame to be ennobled by the Emperor in 1469, though nothing is known of the work that procured him his honours. In 1479–81 he was in Constantinople, painting portraits for Sultan Mahomet II. He worked on the cycle of history pictures in the Doge's Palace in 1474 and again on his return from Turkey, but all were burnt in 1577. His series depicting the processions and ceremonies of two major charitable foundations in Venice became the popular type for this kind of picture, full of portraits and views of the city. His large *S. Mark preaching at Alexandria* (Milan, Brera) was unfinished at his death, and he bequeathed one of his father's sketchbooks to his brother on condition that he finished it. He also bequeathed to two of his pupils his sketchbook of Roman drawings (now lost), which may be evidence for his having visited Rome. There are works in Berlin, Boston (Gardner), Budapest, Chicago, Istanbul (University Library), London (NG), Milan (Brera), New York (Frick Coll.), San Francisco, Venice (Accad., Correr, S. Marco Mus.), and elsewhere.

Giovanni (c. 1430–1516) is usually accepted as the younger son, but his birth date is pure conjecture. There is some evidence that he was independent by 1459, but he can be presumed to have been connected with the family work-shop until Jacopo's death. His early work derives much from his father, but, like Gentile, he was strongly in-fluenced by MANTEGNA, who married their sister Nicolosia in 1454. The chronology of his works is difficult because he became the main teacher of his generation, the main source of new ideas and forms, with a large work-shop of pupils and assistants, so that 'OP. IOH. BELL.' is not only a signature, but a trade-mark, the sign of the workshop rather than the artist. His pupils included Giorgione, Titian, Palma Vecchio, and Sebastiano del Piombo, and he influenced directly or indirectly all the painters of his own and the next generation, even when they were the pupils of his brother or the Vivarini; Cima, Catena, Basaiti, Montagna, and Carpaccio are examples of this. Dürer wrote home from Venice in 1506 that he was 'very old, but still the best in painting'. He became the greatest of the Venetian *Madonnieri*, or Madonna painters, evolving a succession of designs and types of unparalleled imaginativeness and versatility for official commissions, such as the votive offerings of the Doges, large altarpieces, and small devotional works. He was influenced by ANTONELLO, and from the latter's S. Cassiano altarpiece and one of his own, painted for SS. Giovanni e Paolo (and burnt in 1867), stem the great SACRE CONVERSAZIONI painted for S. Giobbe (c. 1483/5; now in the Accad.) and S. Zaccaria (1505; in the church) and the later develop-ments of the form, notably those by Giorgione and Titian. His compositions of the Pietà, particularly those with the dead Christ supported in the tomb either by angels or by the Virgin and S. John, derive ultimately from Donatello and Jacopo Bellini, and were intended more as private devotional works than for churches. He frequently in-cluded landscapes as a background, and in the *Agony in the Garden*, painted in emulation of Mantegna's similar work (both in London, NG), he combines observation of nature with rare poetic feeling, but naturalistic details are never allowed to overwhelm the figures. In 1479, when Gentile went to Turkey, he took over the work in the Doge's Palace and eventually became chief painter to the State, a position he held until his death, despite Titian's attempts to displace him. The loss of these history paintings (together with those by Pisanello and Gentile da Fabriano) in the fire of 1577 means that the early style of Venetian history painting can only be surmised. His official work included painting portraits of the Doges – the *Doge Loredano* (c. 1501; London, NG) is the finest of these – and his portraits, many of which adapt the Flemish type of the three-quarter view against a landscape background, are simple, sensitive, and compelling. His last works break new ground. His *S. Jerome* (1513; Venice, S. Giovanni Crisostomo) with its spatial device of the saint seated in a landscape and seen through the arch before which the other life-size figures stand, is an entirely new invention. He had painted Christian and classical allegories before, but never a mythology on such a scale as the *Feast of the Gods*, painted in 1514 for the Duke of Ferrara (now in Washington), which depicts a rustic Olympian picnic in a mildly erotic pastoral vein. Titian later repainted the land-scape background to make it suit his own mythologies painted for the same room. The *Lady at her toilet* (1515; Vienna), a semi-mythological subject which possibly started as a portrait, combines the composition used for late Madonna pictures with genre detail and a nude figure. These three works show the old Bellini coming to terms with the new century. Technically, he learned from Antonello; stylistically, he digested Mantegna, yet sur-vived as an independent personality; iconographically, he was the most inventive painter Northern Italy produced. There are works in the Royal Collection, Baltimore (Walters), Bergamo, Berlin, Boston (Gardner), Bristol, Cambridge Mass. (Fogg), Detroit, Dresden, Florence (Uffizi), Glasgow, Houston Texas, Kansas City, London (NG, Courtauld Inst.), Milan (Brera, Poldi-Pezzoli), Naples, New Orleans, New York (Brooklyn, Frick Coll., Met. Mus., Morgan Library), Ottawa, Oxford (Ashmo-lean), Padua, Paris (Louvre, Mus. Jacquemart-André), Pesaro, Philadelphia (Johnson), Rimini, Rome (Borghese, Capitoline Mus.), San Diego Cal., San Marino Cal. (Huntington), Stuttgart, Toledo Ohio, the Vatican, Venice (Accad., Correr, Cà d'Oro, Doge's Palace, Querini-Stampalia, and churches), Verona, Vienna, Washington (NG), and elsewhere. [ills. 136, 139, 147, 150–2, pp. 292–3]

Bellotto, Bernardo (1720–80), was the nephew and pupil of CANALETTO, and is sometimes confusingly so called: he himself started the habit, doubtless because it paid. They appear to have separated by 1746, perhaps after a quarrel, for Canaletto came to London and Bellotto began travels in N. Italy before leaving for Dresden, in 1747. He became Painter to Frederick Augustus II in 1748 and painted many views of Dresden, Pirna, and Königstein for him. He also visited Vienna and Munich before going to Poland in 1767. Although nominally on his way to Russia, he settled in Warsaw and worked for King Stanislas Poniatowski until his death. His *vedute* of Warsaw are of great topographical exactness (and were used in the reconstruction of the city after the Second World War), and in general his style is very similar to that of his uncle; his colour is colder and he has a feeling for landscape and a certain humour in his figure groups lacking in Canaletto's work. Almost all his best works are in Dresden and Warsaw but there are examples in Boston, Cambridge (Fitzwm), Dublin, Glasgow, London (NG), New York (Met. Mus.), Vienna, and elsewhere. [ill. 305, p. 316]

Bellows, George (1882–1925), was an American illustrator and painter of city life, who was influenced by the ASHCAN School and was one of the organizers of the ARMORY Show. He also painted a number of fine portraits in a bold style – e.g. *Mrs T., No.* 2 (Minneapolis). [ill. 963, p. 411]

Benedetto da Maiano (1442–97), was a Florentine sculptor of the post-Donatello generation. His major work is the pulpit in Sta Croce, Florence (*c.* 1475), three sketches for which are in London (V & A). He also made several fine portrait busts, examples being those in Florence (Bargello), London (V & A), Paris (Louvre), and Washington (NG). [ill. 94, p. 282]

Bentname (Dutch), the nickname given to Dutch and Flemish members of the *Schildersbent*, or group of painters in Rome. They were also called *Bentvueghels* (birds of a flock) because they formed a group in 1623, partly in solidarity against the Italians and against the law, but ostensibly to defy the dues levied by the Roman Academy of S. Luke. The founders included BABUREN and BOR, but most of the members painted BAMBOCCIATE (Bamboccio was the Bentname of Pieter van Laer). As more Northerners flocked to Rome the Bentvueghels got more rowdy and held huge drinking parties ending in Sta Costanza, where scores of their names are still scratched on the walls. Their riotousness and mock baptisms caused the Pope to suppress them in 1720. [ill. 425, p. 333]

Berchem, Nicolaes (Claesz.) (1620–83), was born in Haarlem and studied under an assortment of masters, but his style was really formed in Italy, where he went with J.B. WEENIX 1642–5. He painted a few religious (e.g. *The Angel appearing to the shepherds*, 1656: Bristol) and allegorical subjects and some portraits, as well as some realistic Dutch landscapes (e.g. *Winter Scene, Haarlem* of 1647: Amsterdam, Rijksmus.); but most of his works are Italianate landscapes, seen through a golden haze and peopled with travellers and their mules or Arcadian shepherds and their flocks. The ruins and taverns blend to a nicety the classic past and the spirt of BAMBOCCIO, and it is not surprising that he and his rival, BOTH, were the principals among the popular ITALIANIZERS, the landscape painters influenced by Claude and, above all, by a nostalgic longing for the South. He may have returned to Italy 1653/6. Not only did he paint many pictures of his own but he also added the figures for others, including Hobbema and Ruisdael: he also made a number of etchings. There are representative works in London (NG, Wallace Coll., Dulwich). [ill. 427, p. 333]

Berckheyde, Gerrit (1638–98), was a Haarlem painter of town views. He was the pupil of Hals and of his own brother Job (1630–93) and was influenced by his Haarlem contemporary, the great architectural painter SAENREDAM. After 1660 he went to Germany and painted views of Cologne, Heidelberg, and Bonn; on his return he painted Amsterdam and The Hague, but in all cases he often rearranged the buildings to improve the composition – i.e. he painted VEDUTE long before the Italians. [ill. 481, p. 341]

Bergognone *see* BORGOGNONE.

Berlinghiero was active in Lucca from *c.* 1215 and died in 1242 or earlier. His signed crucifix in Lucca is of the more old-fashioned CHRISTUS TRIUMPHANS type which was to be superseded by GIUNTA Pisano. Berlinghiero's three sons were all painters and one, Bonaventura, painted the *S. Francis* (1235: Pescia) which is one of the earliest altarpieces dedicated to the saint. The Berlinghiero family exerted considerable influence on Florentine painting before CIMABUE. [ill. 13, p. 270]

Bermejo, Bartolomé (active 1474–95 or later), was a Spanish painter who was much influenced by the Flemings and was one of the first to practise oil painting in Spain. In 1474 he painted the *S. Dominic of Silos* (Madrid, Prado), which is very close to Jan van EYCK. From 1475 his contracts stipulate the use of oil, but the *Pietà* of 1490 in Barcelona Cathedral is less Eyckian and reflects a certain influence from MASSYS, and possibly even from French painting. There are other works by him in Berlin, Boston (Gardner Mus.), and Luton Hoo Beds. (Wernher Coll.). [ill. 633, p. 363]

Bernard, Émile (1868–1941), was the friend of van Gogh, GAUGUIN, and Cézanne. He experimented with Signac's POINTILLISM, *c.* 1886, but subsequently quarrelled with Signac and destroyed all the works of this type. He then went to Brittany, where he met Gauguin in 1886, and he evolved a style known as *Cloisonnisme* from its resemblance to *cloisonné* enamels; this was a method of painting strong, flat forms in strong, flat colours with blue or black contours separating the colour-patches. It was to lead eventually to a quarrel with Gauguin, who got all the credit. Bernard subsequently travelled in Egypt, Spain, and Italy (1893–1900); his later works are reactionary in style and often vitiated by a sentimental religiosity. Paris (Mus. d'Art Mod.) has a good early picture. [ill. 991, p. 415]

Bernini, Gianlorenzo (1598–1680), was born in Naples, the son of Pietro Bernini, a Tuscan sculptor in the Late Mannerist style, who moved to Rome *c.* 1605 to work for Pope Paul V. The young Bernini early attracted the patronage of the Pope's nephew, Cardinal Scipione Borghese. His first known work, the *Goat Amalthea* (*c.* 1615: Rome, Borghese) for long passed as an antique, and the *Aeneas and Anchises* (1618–19: Borghese) shows him working, perhaps with his father's help, within the Mannerist tradition; the group has no fixed viewpoint and the spectator is encouraged to walk round it, thus obtaining a varying silhouette which, coupled with the slipping movement and the strongly emphasized details of muscles, veins, and joints, creates an impression of uncertainty and strain. The *Neptune and Triton* (1620: London, V & A) shows this uncertainty resolved into energy and movement, though still within the tradition of the multiple viewpoint, but in the group of works executed for the Cardinal (*Rape of Proserpina* 1621–2; *David* 1623; *Apollo and Daphne* 1622–4: all Borghese) Bernini adopts a single frontal viewpoint and the indecisions are resolved into a clearcut expression of supreme energy, coupled with a psychological insight and a delicacy of finish that established him as the greatest sculptor since Michelangelo.

The roots of his style are not only in Michelangelo and the Antique, but also in contemporary painting, for his attitude to the Antique is conditioned by his admiration for Annibale Carracci, his naturalism is stimulated by Caravaggio, and his gestures and facial expressions are influenced by Guido Reni. He rejected Michelangelo's concept of the figure adhering closely to the block, just as he rejected the Mannerist multiple silhouette, and evolved the new concept of the figure with a single action and viewpoint freed from the limitations of the block and infringing the limits of its own space by breaking into that of the spectator, who is thus drawn into the action. This new concept lay at the root of the BAROQUE, of which Bernini was the virtual creator and greatest exponent. His search for a means of expressing different realms of the divine, the mystical, and the earthly, led him to imaginative mixtures of white and coloured marbles, bronze, stucco, stone, painting, and even coloured light through stained glass, and the combination of these varying materials has often been condemned, by uncomprehending critics, as tasteless overdecoration. The finest examples of this use of mixed materials are in the Cornaro Chapel (1645–52: Rome, S. Maria della Vittoria) with the *Ecstasy of S. Theresa*, and the tombs of Urban VIII and Alexander VII in St Peter's, the latter a dramatic conception, in white and coloured marbles, with a bronze figure of Death writing the Pope's name in his book. His busts prove his insight into character, and his religious statues and groups show his passionate concern with the expression of states of mind and soul, while his feeling for the unity of sculpture and its setting led him to become the architect who has most fully expressed the upsurge of religious confidence and militant faith that characterize the Counter-Reformation. He was a man of difficult and stormy character – his son, Domenico, described him as '*terribile nell'ira*' – but of deep piety who regularly practised the Jesuit Spiritual Exercises.

Papal patronage provided him with enormous architectural commissions (in and around St Peter's and the Vatican: tombs, fountains, churches) which demanded the participation of numerous assistants, and of these MOCHI, BOLGI, and Raggi were the best of his frequent helpers, while DUQUESNOY was a friendly, and ALGARDI a bitter, rival. Louis XIV invited him to Paris to redesign the Louvre in 1665; nothing came of the visit but the magnificent bust of the King (Versailles), and a later equestrian statue of Louis (1669–77) was, when it arrived in Versailles in 1685, so disliked by him that Girardon was employed to convert it into a garden ornament. This only too truly fulfils Bernini's prediction that after his death his reputation would suffer a decline. It is impossible to see his work properly outside Rome, and on no city has one man left a stronger imprint of his vision and personality. There are

also works in Bologna (Mus. Civico), Bordeaux (S. Bruno), Cambridge Mass. (Fogg), Copenhagen, Detroit, Florence (Bargello), London (V & A), Modena, New York (Met. Mus.), Paris (Louvre, Mus. Jacquemart-André), Washington (NG). [ills. 259–63, pp. 310–11]

Berrettini *see* PIETRO da Cortona.

Berruguete, Alonso (? *c.* 1489–1561), was the son of Pedro Berruguete and became the major Spanish sculptor of the 16th century. He was trained in Italy and brought back Italian Mannerist ideas both in sculpture and in painting. He went to Florence about 1504 where he saw and copied Michelangelo's lost *Battle* cartoon (he is even mentioned in Michelangelo's letters). He may have been in Rome before returning to Florence for about five years before his final return to Spain in 1517. He was, therefore, acquainted with the early work of PONTORMO and ROSSO at the very beginning of the Mannerist style. His own work as a painter is close to Rosso and he probably finished the *Coronation of the Virgin* (Paris, Louvre) which was left incomplete by Filippino LIPPI.

He was active in Spain principally as a sculptor on such works as the altar of the Irish College in Salamanca (1529–32) and especially the choir stalls in Toledo Cathedral (on the Epistle side) executed 1539–43. These works, like his paintings, show a combination of the influences of LEONARDO da Vinci, ANDREA del Sarto and RAPHAEL. He had an extremely successful career, being made Painter to the King on his return from Italy and ennobled in 1559. Other pictures attributed to him are in Arezzo, Budapest, Florence (Uffizi), Munich and Rome (Borghese). [ill. 636, p. 364]

Berruguete, Pedro (*c.* 1450–1503/4), was Court Painter to Ferdinand and Isabella. He was a Castillian who worked at Avila and in Toledo Cathedral from 1483. At some date before this he may have been in Italy since it is often held that he painted some of the pictures in the Palace at Urbino which are usually given to the Fleming JOOS van Gent. This problem is much confused by a document, purporting to be of 1477, which says that 'Pietro Spagnuolo' – Peter the Spaniard – was working in Urbino. Unfortunately nobody has set eyes on the document since 1822. On the other hand, a 16th-century Spanish writer says that the *Famous Men* at Urbino were by an unspecified Spanish painter. Some further evidence in favour of the attribution may be found in works by Berruguete at Avila and in his native village, Paredes de Nava, and also in the fact that his son Alonso studied in Italy. Other works by Pedro are in Madrid (Prado) and Paris (Louvre), these latter being part of the series from the Palace at Urbino. [ill. 634, p. 363]

Bertoldo di Giovanni (*c.* 1420–91) was the pupil and assistant of Donatello and the master of Michelangelo, since he was employed by Lorenzo de' Medici as Keeper of his Sculpture Garden. There are works by him in Florence (Bargello), Modena, and Paris (Louvre). [ill. 96, p. 283]

Bertram of Minden, Master. A German painter working in Hamburg from 1367 to *c.* 1415. The most important work attributed to him is the *Grabow Altar* (*c.* 1379/83:

Hamburg, Kunsthalle). Others are in Hanover, Paris (Mus. des Arts Décoratifs), and London (V & A). He was a precursor of the realistic Flemish approach of the 15th century but also of the SOFT STYLE, and may have had some contact with THEODORIC of Prague and with France. [ill. 536, p. 351]

Beuckelaer *see* BUECKELAER.

Bewick, Thomas (1753–1828), was the father of modern wood-engraving. His numerous book-illustrations, beautifully observed from nature, are expressed in terms of white-line engraving, which he revived. There are drawings by him in London (BM and Courtauld Inst.) and Newcastle (his home town). [ill. 902, p. 402]

Bibiena, a family of Bolognese stage-designers and architects active from the 1670s to the 1780s in most European countries. They were the most famous exponents of the elaborate perspectives and settings provided for theatrical productions and state occasions. The Opera House at Bayreuth was their work and about 200 engravings also exist. [ill. 302, p. 315]

Biedermeierstil is the name given to the style, roughly corresponding to Early Victorian, of furniture and decoration in Germany in the period 1815–48. It is an unaristocratic style, clear and simple, and is sometimes extended to cover painting and sculpture of the same period (cf. SPITZWEG). The name derives from two fictitious characters, Biedermann and Bummelmeier, who were supposed to represent genuine German Philistines.

Bill, Max (*b.* 1908), is a Swiss abstract sculptor who is also active as a painter, architect, and writer. He was trained in Zürich and at the BAUHAUS in Dessau (1927–9). In 1951 he went to Ulm to teach for six years, exerting considerable influence on young German artists. His writings include essays on the mathematical element in modern art and on Kandinsky. [ill. 1155, p. 434]

Bingham, George Caleb (1811–79), was an American painter of the great settlements in the Far West in the 19th century. Bingham was the most important of the so-called Frontier painters, but he had no real training, apart from a few months in Philadelphia in 1837–8. He worked for a time in Washington, but returned to Missouri *c.* 1844 and painted scenes from everyday life which were widely engraved. In 1856 he went to Düsseldorf and was much influenced by the sentimental German art of the period, but in 1859 he returned to America and wasted most of the rest of his life in politics. [ill. 960, p. 410]

Biomorphic Art is a form of Abstract art which purports to take its abstract forms from living organisms rather than from the geometrical basis of such abstract movements as CONSTRUCTIVISM.

Bird, Francis (1667–1731), was born in London, but studied in Flanders and Rome, and after his return about 1689 under Grinling Gibbons and Cibber. He executed most of the statuary on the outside of St Paul's Cathedral from before 1706 to 1721, and made the *Queen Anne* of

which a poor replica now stands before the Cathedral. He also made many tombs in Westminster Abbey. [ill. 877, p. 398]

Bistre (Fr.), a brown pigment, made from charred wood, used as ink, or chalk, or – principally in the 17th century – as a wash. Rembrandt's drawings are mostly in bistre.

Bitumen, a rich brown pigment made from asphaltum. Its use, though pleasant, is very dangerous, since it never dries completely. It was popular during the 18th and 19th centuries and has been the cause of severe damage in many paintings of those periods.

Blake, William (1757–1827), earned a meagre living by working for publishers as an engraver, usually of other men's designs, but between his bread-and-butter work he produced his own poems in books which he made and published himself, engraving the text and surrounding it with an illustration which he coloured by hand. In this manner he issued the 'Songs of Innocence' (1789) and 'Songs of Experience' (1794), and his various 'Prophetic Books' (1783–1804). His greatest works are his twenty-one large watercolours illustrating the Book of Job, produced from 1820 and engraved in 1826, 102 illustrations to Dante, of which seven were published in 1827, and his colour-printed drawings, which include the *Nebuchadnezzar*, the *Hecate*, and the *Elijah in the Chariot of Fire*. These were made by printing off a design prepared in distemper on millboard, and then finishing each individually. Most of his designs were carried out in normal watercolour technique, but his so-called 'frescoes' are in a highly unorthodox form of tempera which has deteriorated badly. His early work is within the current Neoclassical style, but as his verse and philosophy acquired a more visionary quality, so he turned to forms and ideas evolved from medieval and Mannerist examples, abandoned logical arrangement in space, and developed a purely subjective use of colour, light, and form to give substance to his visions. Whatever his sources, he always transmuted everything by the power of his imagination; this is his salient quality and marks the sharpest reaction against the Age of Reason and the dawn of Romanticism.
In 1800 he moved to Felpham, near Bognor, where he lived uneasily for three years in the circle of the poet Hayley, which included FLAXMAN and Romney. His difficulties with the engraver Cromek, over his illustrations to Blair's 'Grave' (1808) and his picture and engraving of the *Canterbury Pilgrims* (1810), are reflected in one of his typically pungent epigrams: 'A petty sneaking knave I knew – Ah! Mr Cromek, how d'ye do?'. His detestation of Reynolds's theory was expressed in his annotation to the 'Discourses': 'This Man was Hired to Depress Art'. He was also of the opinion that all the parts of Reynolds's 'Discourses' with which he found himself agreeing were due to BARRY or FUSELI. In his last years he was helped by LINNELL, and his circle of friends included Varley, Richmond, CALVERT, PALMER, and Fuseli, who admitted that he found Blake 'damned good to steal from'. The Tate Gallery, London, has a fine collection of his work, and there are also examples in Boston (Mus.), Cambridge (Fitzwm), Cambridge Mass. (Fogg), London (BM, V & A), Manchester (City Art Gall. and Whitworth), Melbourne,

New York (Met. Mus., Morgan Library, Brooklyn), San Marino Cal. (Huntington), and elsewhere. [ill. 906, p. 403. Col. pl. 45]

Blanchard, Jacques (1600–38), was in Rome in 1624. In 1625 he moved to Venice and then Turin, where he worked for the Dukes of Savoy, before returning to France in 1628. The principal influence on him was from Veronese, whose blond and silvery colour and limpid light he used most effectively in his small religious and mythological subjects. The several versions of *Charity*, depicted as a young woman with two or three children, are excellent examples of his tenderness of colour handling, and of a softness of sentiment more reminiscent of the 18th than the 17th century. He was also a sensitive portrait painter. There are examples in London (Courtauld Inst.), New York (Met. Mus.), Paris (Louvre and Notre Dame), Toledo Ohio, and in French provincial museums. [ill. 685, p. 374]

Blaue Reiter, Der (The Blue Rider), was the name given to a group of Munich artists in 1911 by the two most important members, KANDINSKY and MARC. They invented this name, according to Kandinsky, because they both liked blue, Marc liked horses and Kandinsky liked riders. The group was later joined by KLEE and, with Die BRÜCKE, was the most important manifestation of modern art in Germany before 1914. [ills. 1021, 1023, p. 418]

Blauen Vier, Die (The Blue Four), *see* JAWLENSKY.

Blechen, Karl (1798–1840), was a German Romantic painter influenced by FRIEDRICH, whom he probably met in Berlin in 1823. Blechen worked for the Berlin Theatre and went to Italy in 1828–9. On his return he became Professor of landscape painting at the Berlin Academy (1831). He visited Paris in 1835. His later works are more realist and show him moving away from his early romanticism. Most of his pictures are in Berlin, but there are others in Hanover, Karlsruhe, and Vienna. [ill. 605, p. 359]

Block-book. An early form of illustrated book, of a popular devotional character, in which the text and illustrations were cut together, from the same block. Oddly enough, the earliest block-books seem to date from *c.* 1460, after the invention of movable type, and are contemporary with books printed from movable type and illustrated with separately cut blocks. [ill. 561, p. 354]

Bloemaert, Abraham (1564–1651), was an Utrecht Mannerist. He was in Paris 1580–3 and returned to Utrecht to paint elaborate history and genre subjects, bright in colour and with an exaggerated figure style reminiscent of WTEWAEL. He is important in the formation of the UTRECHT School because he was the master of so many other painters, including Both, J.G. Cuyp, Gerard HONTHORST, Terbrugghen, Weenix, and others. He himself came strongly under the influence of Caravaggio in the early 1620s, just when his pupil Honthorst returned from Italy with the new ideas. His son Hendrick (*c.* 1601–72) was also a painter and his pupil. There are works by Abraham in the Royal Collection and in Amsterdam, Berlin, Brunswick, Brussels, Cape Town, Copenhagen,

Dublin, Frankfurt, Grenoble, Haarlem, The Hague, Hamburg, Leamington Spa, Leyden, London (V & A (Ham House)), Ottawa, Paris (Louvre), Stockholm, Toledo Ohio, Utrecht, and Vienna (K-H Mus.). [ill. 401, p. 328]

Blot Drawing was the name given by Alexander COZENS to the practice of evolving a composition from the forms suggested by allowing a few blobs of ink or colour to fall at random on a sheet of paper, if necessary folding the paper to create further blots. The method seems to have been known to Leonardo, who advocated the study of stains on a wall or the shapes in the fire as a stimulus to the creative imagination. Cozens's advocacy of the method as a means of teaching his numerous pupils led to his being dubbed 'Blotmaster to the Town': at the end of his life he published his system as 'A New Method of assisting the Invention in Drawing Original Compositions of Landscape' (1785/6). [ill. 918, p. 404]

Blue Four, The, *see* JAWLENSKY.

Boccioni, Umberto (1882–1916), was one of the original FUTURISTS, signing the Manifesto of 1910 and issuing the 'Manifesto of Futurist Sculpture' in 1912. He also wrote a book about it (1914). He volunteered for the War in 1915 and died as a result of an accident after being wounded. [ill. 1134, p. 431]

Böcklin, Arnold (1827–1901), was, with HODLER, the major Swiss painter of the 19th century, and he exerted a tremendous influence on the German-speaking countries through the expression of a heightened Romanticism and poeticism. He was trained in Germany, Flanders, and Paris, and spent seven years in Rome (1850–7), where he began to evolve a kind of heroic landscape. He was in Munich 1871–4, where he met THOMA, but, like many other German artists of the period (e.g. FEUERBACH), he spent much of the rest of his life in Italy, where he died. His most famous work was, and is, the *Island of the Dead*, which exists in several versions from 1880 onwards: it has a curious haunted quality which can be felt even in the elementary German grammars, where many people first saw it in reproduction. The same quality can be found in his *Pan* and some other landscapes. Most of his works are in Basle (the Museum also has a frescoed staircase), Munich, and other German museums. [ill. 607, p. 359]

Bodegón (Span. tavern), kitchen scenes in which the interest in still-life predominates. [ill. 658, p. 369. Col. pl. 17]

Body Colour is watercolour mixed with white to make it opaque: it is therefore identical with GOUACHE. Body colour is often used in drawings done on tinted paper, or on watercolours, to heighten the effect of highlights or give accent to strong passages of local colour. [Col. pl. 49].

Bol, Ferdinand (1616–80), was a pupil of Rembrandt before 1640, and for many years imitated his master so closely that many of his works have passed as Rembrandt's (e.g. *Lady*: London, Kenwood). By about 1660, when Rembrandtesque portraits were less in demand, Bol adapted his style to a more French manner, lighter and more courtly.

He painted several big group portraits, such as the *Governors of the Leper Hospital* (1649: Amsterdam, Rijksmus.). [ill. 437, p. 334]

Boldini, Giovanni (1845–1931), was a fashionable portrait painter, the Italian equivalent of SARGENT, whom he knew. He was born in Ferrara, but in 1867 went to Paris and was swept off his feet by MANET, whose dazzling skill he imitated, but without Manet's impeccable taste. He visited London before settling in Paris *c.* 1872, where he spent the rest of his life. Whistler and the Impressionists also influenced him, but he is best remembered as a virtuoso who recorded the Paris of La Belle Époque. There is a Boldini Museum in his native town, and other works are in Paris as well as Florence, London, and New York (Brooklyn Mus.: *Whistler*). [ill. 325, p. 318]

Bolgi, Andrea (1605–56), an Italian sculptor, was a pupil of BERNINI. His best-known work is the *S. Helena*, one of four huge statues in the crossing of St Peter's in Rome. The others are by Bernini, MOCHI, and DUQUESNOY. A bust of Laura Frangipane is signed and dated 1637 (Rome, S. Francesco a Ripa). [ill. 267, p. 311]

Bologna, Giovanni (da), (Giambologna, Jean de Boulogne) (1529–1608), the most famous sculptor in Florence after the death of Michelangelo, was born in Douai and trained in Flanders before arriving in Italy *c.* 1555. After a period in Rome he settled in Florence, where he competed with AMMANATI and CELLINI for the commission for the Fountain in the Piazza della Signoria. Ammanati won, but Giambologna assisted him and later made his own *Neptune Fountain* in Bologna (1563–7). His *Rape of the Sabines* (1579–83: Loggia dei Lanzi, Florence) shows the fully developed Mannerist principle of sculpture to be seen from all points of view equally by walking round it instead of regarding it from one main viewpoint. All his marbles are in Florence except the *Samson slaying a Philistine* (London, V & A, begun *c.* 1565). The best known of his bronzes are the *Mercury* (Florence, Bargello, 1564; Vienna, and other versions) and the equestrian statues of the Grand Dukes Cosimo I (1594: Florence, Piazza della Signoria) and Ferdinando (Piazza dell' Annunziata). Small bronze replicas of his works were produced in his shop in huge quantities. [ill. 163, p. 295]

Boltraffio, Giovanni Antonio (1467–1516), was one of LEONARDO's Milanese followers. Most of his works are in Milan, but others are in Berlin, Cambridge Mass. (Fogg), Florence (Uffizi), London (NG), New York (Met. Mus.), Paris (Louvre, Musée Jacquemart-André), and Philadelphia (Johnson). An interesting portrait by him is at Chatsworth, Derbyshire. [ill. 203, p. 302]

Bolus Ground. The canvas or panel is prepared with a dark brown or reddish earth, and the colour of the ground eventually shows through and affects the painting.

Bonanus made the bronze doors of Pisa Cathedral in 1179, but they were destroyed in 1595. The side door (Porta di S. Ranieri) is attributed to him as it is identical in style with the bronze doors of Monreale Cathedral, signed by him and dated 1185 (modern style). The other bronze doors at Monreale are by BARISANUS. [ill. 1, p. 269]

Bone, Sir Muirhead (1876–1953), was an architectural draughtsman and etcher, whose *Demolition of S. James's Hall* (1905) was the first major work in a field he made his own. There are many drawings and etchings by him of the First World War in the Imperial War Museum, London, while the Second World War produced the huge *Ruins of London from S. Bride's*. [ill. 968, p. 410]

Bonifazio de' Pitati (Bonifazio Veronese) (1487–1553), was born in Verona but trained under PALMA Vecchio and ran a large workshop in Venice. His style was much influenced by Giorgione and Titian, and to some extent his name is used to cover works which the owner dare not quite attribute to either of them. [ill. 226, p. 306]

Bonington, Richard Parkes (1801/2–28), was an English landscape painter who went to France as a boy and was trained there. He was a friend of DELACROIX as well as a pupil of GROS and began exhibiting in 1822. He returned to England in 1825 and 1827 and went to Italy in 1826. His historical pictures are much influenced by the Venetians, but Delacroix's remark that Bonington was carried away by his own skill is truer of them than of his landscapes. There are works by him in his native Nottingham, Paris (Louvre), and London (Tate, Wallace Coll., V & A, and BM). [ill. 937, p. 406]

Bonnard, Pierre (1867–1947), was the friend of Vuillard, and with him was one of the NABIS until, about 1905, they both adopted a more Impressionist technique and outlook, known later as *Intimisme*. There are works by him in Birmingham (Barber), Chicago, Glasgow, London (Tate), New York (M of MA), Paris (Mus. d'Art Mod.), Toledo Ohio, and elsewhere. [ill. 995, p. 415]

Bor, Paulus (*c.* 1600–69), was born in Amersfoort, Holland, and went to Rome in the 1620s, where he was one of the founders of the BENT. He returned to Amersfoort about 1628 and painted at first in a manner deriving from the young Rembrandt, but the influence of Caravaggio – whose works he must have seen in Rome – seems to have grown on him and he became a member of the UTRECHT School. There are works in Amersfoort, Amsterdam (Rijksmus.), Liverpool, and Utrecht. [ill. 461, p. 339]

Borch, Gerard ter, *see* TER BORCH.

Bordone, Paris (1500–71), was a Trevisan painter who spent most of his life in Venice, but probably visited France (in 1538?) and Augsburg; a portrait in the Louvre is signed and dated 1540 and inscribed 'Augusta', so he was probably in Augsburg in that year, and the Venetian influence on AMBERGER may well come from this visit. Vasari says that he was apprenticed to Titian but set himself to imitate GIORGIONE. There are works by him in the Royal Collection and in Augsburg, Baltimore, Bergamo, Boston (Mus. and Gardner Mus.), Cologne, Dublin, Edinburgh, Florence (Uffizi, Pitti), Genoa, Glasgow, London (NG), Milan (Brera), Munich, Paris, Philadelphia

(Johnson), Rome (Borghese), Toronto, Treviso, the Vatican, Venice, Vienna and Washington. [ill. 228, p. 306]

Borgognone, Ambrogio (*c.* 1450/60–1523), was a Milanese painter, influenced by FOPPA and not by Leonardo, whose best works are in the Certosa at Pavia, including some *trompe-l'œil* frescoes of monks looking through windows. Other works are in Bergamo, Birmingham, London (NG), and Milan (Brera). [ill. 117, p. 288]

Bosch, Hieronymus (*c.* 1450–1516), perhaps the greatest master of fantasy who ever lived, is first recorded in 's Hertogenbosch in 1480/1. He may have been born there and his name probably derives from it; certainly he spent his life there and died there. His obsessive and haunted world is that of Gothic twilight and is the best surviving expression of some aspects of the waning of the Middle Ages, but it is now largely incomprehensible. The Surrealists have claimed him as a sort of Freudian *avant la lettre*, but it is certain that his pictures had a very definite significance and were not free expressions of the unconscious mind. For example, the *Hay Wain* (Madrid, Prado) once belonged to Philip II of Spain and is obviously an allegory on the general theme 'All flesh is grass'; just as the *Ship of Fools* (Paris, Louvre) is a well-known late medieval allegory. About 1600 a Spanish writer apparently thought it necessary to defend Bosch's memory against imputations of heresy, which would seem to show that by then the real meaning of the pictures had largely been lost. In recent years there has been an elaborate attempt to 'explain' many of the pictures – in particular the *Earthly Paradise* (Madrid, Prado) – as altarpieces painted for a heretical cult which was addicted to orgiastic rites. Not only is there no evidence for this but it also fails to explain why so many of Bosch's pictures belonged to people of unimpeachable orthodoxy, such as Philip II. The problem of Bosch's patrons resembles that of BRUEGEL's, and there is much in common between the two although Bosch's fantasy is always far more inventive and seems to have deeper levels of symbolism, even in what appear to be purely erotic scenes. It is also worth noting that, according to a mid-16th-century Spanish writer, there were already forgeries in circulation apparently signed by Bosch: he cites the *Seven Deadly Sins* (Madrid, Prado) as an example, but it is now universally accepted as authentic. The chronology of Bosch's pictures is not clear, but it may be safe to assume that the *Crucifixion* (Brussels) is his earliest known work, on the grounds that the style is closer to that of BOUTS or Roger van der WEYDEN – the dominant styles in the Netherlands *c.* 1480 – than at any other time in Bosch's career. His master is unknown, and the origins of his style are very obscure but are probably to be sought in popular woodcuts and devotional prints. Other early works are probably the *Christ Mocked* (London, NG), the *Cure for Madness* (Madrid, Prado), and the *Seven Deadly Sins*: the later works seem to be those with great numbers of small-scale figures, painted in pale bright, transparent colours on a very white ground. There are examples in Antwerp, Berlin, Boston (Mus.), Chicago, Cologne (Wallraf-Richartz Mus.), Denver Col., the Escorial, Frankfurt (Städel), Ghent, Lisbon, Munich, New York (Met. Mus.), Philadelphia (Johnson), Princeton NJ, Rotterdam (Boymans Mus.), San Diego Cal.,

Valenciennes, Venice (Doge's Pal.), Vienna (Akad. and K-H), and elsewhere. [ill. 347, p. 322]

Both, Andries (*c.* 1608–41/9) and Jan (*c.* 1618–52), were Utrecht painters who were supposed to have worked together, Andries painting the figures and Jan the landscapes, until one day Andries fell into a canal in Venice on his way home from a SCHILDERSBENT party. Andries was probably in Rome *c.* 1636–41 and Jan *c.* 1638–41; Jan returned to Utrecht after his brother's death. Such a picture as the *Boors carousing* (Utrecht), signed and dated 1634, shows Andries as a painter of BAMBOCCIATE in a style closer to Brouwer than to his brother's idyllic landscapes. Jan was profoundly influenced by the works of CLAUDE in the period 1638–41. He became one of the leading ITALIANIZERS, and, like his chief rival, BERCHEM, painted Claudian landscapes with a golden light falling on the picturesque peasantry. The treatment of light in Cuyp's work owes much to him. Both brothers were pupils of the Utrecht Mannerist Bloemaert, and in their several ways they show the new directions taken by Dutch painting in the 17th century. Jan is represented in most older galleries, and there are typical works in London (NG, Wallace Coll., Dulwich), Detroit, Indianapolis, Toledo Ohio, and Worcester Mass. [ills. 421, 429, 505, pp. 332–3, 346]

Bottega (Ital. shop), the workshop or studio of an artist; specifically, that part in which pupils and assistants worked on productions commissioned from, and usually signed by, the master.

Botticelli, Sandro (*c.* 1445–1510), was the most individual, if not the most influential, painter in Florence at the end of the 15th century. He was probably a pupil of Fra Filippo Lippi but was influenced by the POLLAIUOLI for a short time around 1470, when he painted a *Fortitude* to go with a set of six other *Virtues* by Piero Pollaiuolo (all now in the Uffizi). The chronology of his work is difficult to establish since it ranges between the vigorous realism of the 1470 *Fortitude* and the languorous and anti-naturalistic ecstasy of his last dated (and only signed) work, the *Mystic Nativity* (1500: London, NG). It seems certain that the Victorian interpretation of his style as progressively more naturalistic (and more Pre-Raphaelite) is topsy-turvy: we know that he was neurotic, much troubled by the religious crisis of the Late Quattrocento and yet ambiguous in his attitude to Savonarola, and that he was at any rate accused of pederasty (this charge seems to have been made as freely in 15th-century Florence as that of Communism in modern America, and on about the same evidence). His extreme dependence on outline as a means of emotional expression is a summary of Florentine tendencies in the 15th century, but his style nevertheless to have been deliberately archaic; just as his most celebrated mythological pictures – the *Primavera* and the *Birth of Venus* (both in the Uffizi) – have very involved allegorical and Christianizing meanings. These were probably painted for a member of the Medici family, then still ruling Florence, but we know almost nothing about the commissioning or his relationship with the Medici and their humanist circle. In 1481/2 Botticelli was in Rome, painting frescoes in the Sistine Chapel along with Ghirlandaio, Rosselli, Signorelli, and Perugino, but this does not seem to have been particularly successful.

During the last twenty years of the 15th century he ran a large shop for the production of *Madonnas* of a gently devout kind well suited to the piety of the age: these made him prosperous and many of them are repetitions by different hands from a cartoon by him. They were also extensively forged in the 19th century, but these are now beginning to look strangely Victorian.

By about 1500 his style was so obviously opposed to the new ideas of Leonardo da Vinci and Michelangelo that he suffered a decline in popularity and the last ten years of his life are mysterious. It is probable that the clumsy and almost hysterical style of pictures like the *Pietàs* in Munich and Milan (Poldi-Pezzoli) or the S. Zenobius series in London (NG), Dresden, and New York (Met. Mus.) is that of his last period, i.e. after the 1500 *Mystic Nativity*, rather than works of his youth. Probably in the 1490s he made a series of splendid outline drawings illustrating Dante (Berlin and the Vatican), which show his sensitive feeling for contour at its most subtle. There are pictures by him in Bergamo, Berlin, Boston (Mus. and Gardner Mus.), Cambridge Mass. (Fogg Mus.), Chicago, Detroit, Dresden, Edinburgh (NG), Florence (Accad., Uffizi, Pitti, and Ognissanti and other churches), Frankfurt, Glasgow, London (NG, V & A, Courtauld Inst.), Milan (Ambrosiana, Poldi-Pezzoli), Munich, New York (Met. Mus.), Ottawa, Paris (Louvre, Mus. Jacquemart-André), Philadelphia, Rome (Borghese), the Vatican, Washington (NG), and elsewhere. Filippino LIPPI was his pupil. [ills. 99, 100, p. 285]

Botticini, Francesco (*c.* 1446–97), was a Florentine painter who imitated many others, including Botticelli. The most interesting picture ascribed to him is the *Assumption* (*c.* 1474/6: London, NG) which is the only Quattrocento picture known to have been painted to illustrate a heresy: Matteo Palmieri, the donor, held that human souls are the angels who remained neutral when Lucifer rebelled. [ill. 101, p. 284]

Boucharde *see* STONE CARVING.

Bouchardon, Edmé (1698–1762), was a French sculptor who worked under G. COUSTOU I and then went to Rome (1723) where he remained for nine years and enjoyed considerable fame. He worked at Versailles, but is best remembered for his Fontaine de Grenelle, Paris (1739–45); his *Cupid* (1750: Louvre); and his equestrian *Louis XV*, designed as the centrepiece of the Place de la Concorde, Paris, but destroyed in the Revolution: it had *Virtues* by PIGALLE which evoked the epigram:

> Oh! la belle statue! Oh! le beau piédestal!
> Les vertus sont à pied et le vice à cheval!

[ill. 712, p. 378]

Boucher, François (1703–70), was the most typical ROCOCO decorator and the friend and protégé of Mme de Pompadour. He began as an engraver of Watteau, won the Prix de Rome of the Academy in 1723, but did not go to Italy until 1727: there he admired little but Tiepolo, the greatest decorator of the age. He returned to France in 1731, became an Academician in 1734, and Director in 1765. He made many tapestry designs and painted charmingly indelicate mythological scenes, ultimately inspired by Veronese, Rubens, and Watteau. Reynolds, who visited his studio, was scandalized by his working without a model: 'he said, when he was young, studying his art, he found it necessary to use models; but he had left them off for many years'. The best collection of his works is in the Wallace Coll., London, but there are others in London (NG, Kenwood), New York, Paris, and Washington. [ill. 729, p. 381]

Boudin, Eugène (1824–98), was a direct precursor of Impressionism. He was born at Honfleur, son of a pilot, and he painted seascapes and harbour scenes with luminous skies taking up most of the picture space. These skies are the link between his friend Corot and his younger friends the Impressionists, especially MONET. He exhibited at the First Impressionist Exhibition, 1874. [ill. 760, p. 385]

Bourdelle, Émile-Antoine (1861–1929), was a pupil of RODIN, but soon reacted against his loose and impressionistic modelling and began to study Greek and Gothic sculpture for its more stylized forms. He did the sculpture and decorative paintings in the Théâtre des Champs-Élysées, Paris, but his major work is *The Virgin of Alsace*, an enormous statue on a mountain in the Vosges, the sketch for which is in Edinburgh. [ill. 1122, p. 431]

Bourdon, Sébastien (1616–71), was born in Montpellier, and spent his early years in Paris and Bordeaux. In 1634 he went to Rome; there he imitated current styles – the landscapes of CLAUDE, the genre subjects of CASTIGLIONE, and BAMBOCCIATE, the speciality of Dutch and Flemish painters in Italy. In 1637 he returned to Paris, visiting Venice on the way, and continued along the same lines, before turning to large religious and classical subjects in a more Baroque manner, with a Venetian richness of handling, though the influence of POUSSIN eventually subdued their exuberance. In 1652 he went to Sweden as Court portraitist to Queen Christina, and after her abdication and his return to Paris in 1654 he continued to paint portraits with great success. The years 1659–63 were spent in Montpellier, but he was finally compelled to leave through the jealousy of local artists, and he passed his remaining years in Paris. His late works show the strong influence of Poussin, with tenderness, charm, and cool colour.

There are works in Amsterdam (Rijksmus.), Cambridge (Fitzwm), Greenville SC (Bob Jones Univ.), The Hague, Hartford Conn. (Wadsworth), London (NG, Dulwich), Madrid (Prado), Montpellier, Montreal, Munich, Paris (Louvre), Providence RI, Sarasota Fla (Ringling), Stockholm, and elsewhere. [ill. 686, p. 374]

Bouts, Dieric (*c.* 1415–75), an early Netherlandish painter, was born in Haarlem but was working in Louvain (where he died) before 1448. His figures are stiff and unemotional, but his treatment of light and his landscape backgrounds are of great beauty, perception, and delicacy, especially in their colour. With Roger van der WEYDEN, who influenced him strongly, he was a powerful influence on German 15th-century painting. His only certain works are the *Five Mystic Meals* (1464–8: S. Pierre, Louvain) and the two large scenes of the *Justice of the Emperor Otho* (Brussels), one of which was unfinished at his death. There are other works in Lille, London (NG), Madrid, New York (Met. Mus.), Philadelphia, and elsewhere.

His two sons, Dieric II (*c.* 1448–90/1) and Aelbrecht (*d.* 1549), were also painters: of Dieric nothing certain is known; Aelbrecht's chief work is an *Assumption* in Brussels. [ills. 342, 343, p. 322]

Bozzetto (Ital. sketch), or MAQUETTE, usually applied to models for sculpture, but can also be used for painted sketches, usually called MODELLI. [ill. 262, p. 311]

Brancusi, Constantin (1876–1957), was a Rumanian sculptor whose most successful works are often simple, highly-polished shapes. He settled in Paris in 1904 and was influenced by RODIN, but by 1907 was more concerned with abstract shape: he was the friend of MODIGLIANI and induced him to turn to sculpture. He exhibited at the ARMORY Show (1913) in New York, and was involved in a notorious case in 1926–8, when the US Customs refused to admit a work of his as sculpture, claiming that it was turned metal and thus dutiable. In 1937 he began a column some 90 feet high at Targu Jiu, in Rumania. There are works in London (Tate), and the Museums of Modern Art in New York and Paris, but the biggest collection is in Philadelphia. [ill. 1135, p. 432]

Brangwyn, Sir Frank (1867–1956), was a Welsh painter of huge mural decorations, usually with many figures executed in a brilliantly colourful handling. He became an RA in 1919, and was knighted in 1941. There are examples of his decorations in the Skinners' Hall, the Royal Exchange, and Lloyd's Register, all in London; the Court House, Cleveland Ohio; Missouri State Capitol, and the Rockefeller Center in New York (where it replaced one by RIVERA). After many troubles his projected decorations for the House of Lords were erected in the Guildhall, Swansea. Most English provincial museums have an example of his paintings or his large and important etchings, and there are many scattered throughout the world. Bruges (his birthplace) and Orange in Southern France have museums devoted to his works. [ill. 967, p. 410]

Braque, Georges (1882–1963), learned to paint as an apprentice in a decorator's business, hence his superb technique. He was at the École des Beaux-Arts in Le Havre and, later, in Paris, but preferred to work on his own. He was friendly with Dufy and Friesz (both were from Le Havre) and by 1906 was in the FAUVE circle, but by 1909 he knew PICASSO well, and with him had started to work out the basis of a new approach to painting which developed into CUBISM. By the outbreak of war in 1914 this close collaboration was at an end: when Braque resumed painting in 1917 he tried to pick up Synthetic Cubism where he had left off, but by 1920–1 a less arbitrary spatial composition and not so much a return to reality as an acknowledgement of its existence, led to the ample, vigorous, splendid still-life and figure compositions, with a perfection of balance and harmony between the colour and the design, which he continued to develop for the rest of his life.

He also executed a certain amount of sculpture, incised plaster plaques, and plaster reliefs. There is a small body of graphic work – between forty and fifty lithographs, some woodcuts for book illustration, and some etchings for which the drawings were originally produced in 1931 as illustrations for Hesiod's 'Theogony'. There are works in Basle, Buffalo, Copenhagen, Detroit, Frankfurt (Städel), Glasgow, Le Havre, London (Tate), New York (M of MA, Guggenheim Fdn.), Ottawa, Oxford, Paris (Mus. d'Art Moderne, Petit Pal.), Philadelphia, San Francisco, Toledo Ohio, Washington (Phillips), and elsewhere, including many French museums. [ill. 1045, p. 420. Col. pl. 36]

Bray, Jan de (*c.* 1626/7–1697), was the son and pupil of Salomon. He worked in Haarlem and was much influenced by HELST, as well as by HALS. His best works are portraits and portrait groups such as the *Regents of the Children's Hospital* (1663: Haarlem), which clearly shows the influence of similar group portraits by REMBRANDT (e.g. the *Staal Meesters* of 1662), and Hals, but is much less free in handling. He also painted some more consciously poetical works such as the *Antony and Cleopatra* of 1669 (replicas in the Royal Collection and at Nuremberg). These works show him, like LIEVENS and MAES, aping the grand manner of contemporary French historical painting. Other works are in Amsterdam (Rijksmus.), Edinburgh (NG), London (NG), and Worcester Mass. [ill. 530, p. 349]

Bray, Salomon de (1597–1664), was an Amsterdam painter, poet, and architect who settled in Haarlem *c.* 1625. He was the pupil of GOLTZIUS, whose manner he occasionally imitated, but his portraits, like those of his son Jan, are often close to HALS. There are works by him in Bristol, Dresden, The Hague (1651: *Decorations for the House in the Wood*), and London (V & A). [ill. 533, p. 350]

Breu, Jörg (*c.* 1475–1537), was a painter and designer of woodcuts who worked in Austria 1496–1502, but settled in Augsburg in 1502 and came under the influence of HOLBEIN the Elder and BURGKMAIR. There are works by him in Augsburg, Basle, Berlin, Herzogenburg, London (Courtauld Inst.), Melk, Munich, San Diego Cal., and Vienna. [ill. 581, p. 356]

Breughel *see* BRUEGEL.

Bril (Brill), Mattheus (1550–83) and Paul (1554–1626), were brothers, born in Antwerp, but who both worked in Rome and painted landscapes which form the link between the panoramic views of Patenier or Bruegel and the ideal landscape evolved by Poussin and Claude. Mattheus was in Rome by about 1570 and painted several large frescoes, including the *Seasons* in the Vatican, but he died young and much of his work was completed by Paul, who also succeeded him in the Papal favour. Paul seems to have followed his brother to Italy *c.* 1574, and was certainly in Rome in 1582. He also painted frescoes, including the landscapes in the Casino Rospigliosi, Rome, accompanying Guido RENI's *Aurora*; but he is best known for his small easel pictures on copper, many of which are much influenced by ELSHEIMER. Among his pupils was Agostino Tassi, later to become Claude's master. His influence was also spread by his engravings. Among his pictures (some signed with a pair of spectacles – *Brille*) are examples in Amsterdam, Antwerp, Basle, Berlin, Brussels, Dresden, Dunedin NZ, Edinburgh, Florence (Uffizi, Pitti), Glasgow, London (NG, Wellington Mus.), Milan, Munich, Paris (Louvre), Rome (Gall. Naz. and Borghese), Stockholm, the Vatican, and Vienna. [ills. 399, 400, p. 328]

Broad Manner *see* FINE MANNER.

Broederlam, Melchior (active 1381 – *d.* 1409 or later), was a painter in Ypres who became Painter to Philip the Bold, Duke of Burgundy, in 1385 and was in Paris 1390/3. In 1392 he was commissioned to paint two wings for an altar, which he completed in 1399 (Dijon, Musée): this is probably the earliest example of INTERNATIONAL GOTHIC. [ill. 328, p. 319]

Bronze was used as a material for sculpture in ancient Greece and Rome as well as in Africa and China, but the art seems to have become almost lost in the Middle Ages, when bronze effigies were made by hammering thin plates of bronze on to a wooden core. The *S. Peter* attributed to Arnolfo di Cambio is one of the earliest modern cast bronzes on a big scale, but by the early 15th century the craft was well established in the hands of masters like Ghiberti. Modern bronzes are made either in sand moulds or by the *cire perdue* method, both these techniques being very ancient. Sand casting is done by simply making a mould of damp sand from the original PLASTER model, inserting a core, and pouring in the molten bronze. *Cire perdue* (Fr. lost wax) is economical of bronze because it consists of a model which is a few millimetres smaller in all directions than the enclosing mould, the space between being filled with wax and vent pipes inserted at top and bottom. The outer side of the wax is exactly what the desired bronze should look like; and molten bronze is poured through the top vent, taking the place of the wax which has previously been melted out. The amount of wax run out serves as a guide to the quantity of bronze needed. Any number of such casts can be taken. In Renaissance times it was usual to work on the casts with files and chasers, polishing and engraving the surface, but it is now the fashion to prefer a rough surface, showing the thumb-marks of the original clay model. Patina is the lovely greenish tint and matt surface which age and chemical reaction have imparted to Greek bronzes, but which is now artificially imitated by chemical means. A peculiarly vivid green bronze is characteristic of Epstein's work.

Bronzino, Agnolo (1503–72), was a Florentine painter who was the pupil of PONTORMO and was also influenced by Michelangelo. He was Court Painter to Cosimo I de' Medici, the first Grand Duke of Tuscany, and one of the most important Mannerist portrait painters, concentrating on expressing an inhuman elegance and restraint in his sitters, totally unlike the nervous sensibility of Pontormo. From Michelangelo he learned little but tricks of foreshortening. His few religious works are highly wrought and devoid of any kind of feeling, while his *Venus, Cupid, Time, and Folly* (London, NG) has a kind of icy obscenity. Most of his works are in Florence; others are in Antwerp (Mayer van den Bergh), Berlin, Boston (Gardner), Chicago,

Cincinnati, Detroit, London, Madrid, Milan, New York (Met. Mus. and Frick Coll.), Ottawa, Oxford, Paris, Pisa (S. Stefano), Rome (Barberini, Borghese), Vienna, Washington (NG), and Worcester Mass. [ill. 183, p. 298]

Brouwer (Brauwer), Adriaen (1605/6–38), was the link between Flemish and Dutch genre painting. He was born in Flanders but spent some time in Holland and may have been a pupil of Frans Hals. His pictures, apart from a few landscapes, represent sordid tavern scenes, usually with boors carousing. He himself lived like that and has been compared to Villon in consequence. His earliest works may start from the village scenes of BRUEGEL, and he may have known one of Bruegel's sons before going to Amsterdam in 1625 and on to Haarlem where he met Hals. In 1631/2 he was in the Guild in Antwerp and came under the influence of Rubens, who in turn admired him. His political activities led to imprisonment in 1633: the prison baker was Joos van Craesbeck, who became his pupil and imitator. His best works are comparable with those of STEEN and David TENIERS II (both of whom were influenced by him) and have a delicacy of colour combined with a breadth of handling that compensate for his subjects, in which his most fervent admirers see an almost Rembrandtesque pathos. The best collection of his works is in Munich: others are in Amsterdam, Antwerp, Berlin, Brussels, Dresden, Frankfurt (Städel), Haarlem, The Hague, Leipzig, London (NG, V & A, and Wellington Mus., Wallace Coll., and Dulwich), Madrid (Prado), New York (Met. Mus.), Paris (Louvre, Petit Pal.), Philadelphia (Johnson), Rotterdam, Vienna (Akad.), York. [ill. 504, p. 346]

Brown, Ford Madox (1821–93), was born in Calais and studied in Belgium, Paris, and Rome (where he met and was influenced by OVERBECK) before returning to England in 1845. In 1848 ROSSETTI asked him for lessons and in this way Brown was brought into contact with the PRB. He never actually became a member but his work was profoundly influenced by them for many years, as may be seen in his best-known works *The Last of England* (1855: Birmingham) and *Work* (1852–65: Manchester). He carried out decorations for the Town Hall at Manchester, and there are other pictures in the Tate Gallery, London. [ill. 954, p. 408]

Brücke, Die (The Bridge), was the name taken by a group founded in 1905 in Dresden by E. L. KIRCHNER, K. SCHMIDT-ROTTLUFF, Erich HECKEL, and F. Bleyl. There was no particular programme, but the name was chosen to indicate their desire to link like-minded artists. The group style, however, was that of EXPRESSIONISM and was manifested in forms very close to those of FAUVISM, since they admired the works of Gauguin, van Gogh, and Munch. The group broke up in 1913, but it had exerted considerable influence on public taste, and it was particularly important in the revival of woodcut and other graphic arts. *See also* BLAUE REITER, Der. [ills. 1016, 1018, 1020, p. 417]

Bruegel, Jan I (1568–1625), called 'Velvet Bruegel', was the younger son of Pieter I and brother of Pieter II. He was a successful painter of still-life and landscape in a highly detailed style which elicited much admiration from contemporaries. His chief claim to fame is the fact that Rubens collaborated with him. There are pictures in London (NG), Oxford, and many other museums. His son Jan II (1601–78) was also a painter. [ill. 393, p. 327]

Bruegel (Brueghel, Breughel), Pieter I (*c.* 1525/30–69), sometimes also called 'Peasant Bruegel', was the most important satirist in the Netherlands after BOSCH and one of the greatest landscape painters. The date of his birth is unknown but may be guessed at from the fact that he became a Master in the Antwerp Guild in 1551: immediately after this he went to France and Italy (*c.* 1552), travelling as far south as Sicily. He was in Rome in 1553 and returned over the Alps, probably in 1554. The Alps, and to a lesser extent the scenery of Italy, made a tremendous impact on him, as may be seen from the drawings he made on the journey and also from the whole development of his landscape style. The art of Italy seems to have made almost no impression on him. On his return he began to make drawings for engravers, very much in the manner of Bosch and dealing with the same subjects. His earliest painting to be dated is of 1553 and in the last ten or twelve years of his life he produced the genre scenes and the religious subjects set in vast landscapes which are his finest works. The old nickname 'Peasant Bruegel' is misleading if it is held to mean that he was himself a peasant: on the contrary, he was highly cultivated and is known to have enjoyed the friendship of humanists and the patronage of the Emperor's representative, Cardinal Granvella. Later many of his pictures belonged to Rudolf II. His attitude, and that of his patrons, is hard to define since it is not merely condescending but seems to show a real interest in village customs coupled with a satirical approach to drunkenness, gluttony, and other sins. Some pictures – for example the *Massacre of the Innocents* – have been held to be veiled allusions to the Spanish Fury and the subjection of the Netherlands in general, and it has also been held that Bruegel's move from Antwerp to Brussels *c.* 1563 was due to his membership of a heretical sect and fear of persecution: yet he was certainly patronized by Cardinal Granvella and Brussels was the centre of orthodoxy and of government. The great series of the *Months* consists of five pictures (now in Vienna, Prague, and New York), all but one dated 1565. They have no moral message comparable with his earlier works, such as the *Fall of the Rebel Angels* or the *Dulle Griet*, but they are among the great landscape paintings of the age, influenced by PATENIER and even Titian but surpassing both in their feeling for nature and the unity of man and his surroundings. The best collection of his works is in Vienna (K-H Mus.) but there are others in the Royal Collection and in Antwerp (Mus. Mayer van den Bergh), Berlin, Boston (Mus.), Brussels, Budapest, Darmstadt, Detroit, London (NG), Madrid (Prado), Munich, Naples, Paris (Louvre), Philadelphia, Rome (Doria), Rotterdam, Upton House (National Trust) Banbury, Washington (NG). [ills. 389, 390, p. 327]

Bruegel, Pieter II (*c.* 1564–1638), called 'Hell Bruegel', was the son of Pieter I and frequently copied his father's works. He was the master of Snyders and presumably of his own son, Pieter III. [ill. 391, p. 327]

Brushwork. With the development of the technique of oil painting it soon became clear that the use of stiff bristle brushes charged with oil paint and applied to a grainy surface such as canvas could give a special texture and quality of handling which is aesthetically pleasing in itself, independently of its function in representing form. A painter's brushwork is as personal as his handwriting (and is occasionally so referred to) and it is even harder to imitate. The encrustations of Rembrandt, the frenzied drama of the actual strokes of van Gogh's brush, the thin film of Gainsborough, the gem-like luminosity of Vermeer's small dabs of paint; all these are possible in one and the same medium, so that brushwork is one of the painter's most powerful tools in the creation of his own world. In some cases it becomes the end rather than the means, as in certain forms of Abstract Expressionism, where the word can perhaps hardly be legitimately applied to paint trickled, rather than brushed, on to the ground. [Col. pls. 18, 20, 21, 23, 29, 35]

Bruyn, Barthel (1492/3–1555), was a Cologne painter, chiefly of portraits. His religious works are much influenced by Netherlandish painters of the late 15th century and his portraits, which are grimly realistic representations of unaristocratic sitters, are very close to those of JOOS van Cleve. There are works in Cologne (Mus. and churches), churches in Essen and Xanten, and in Antwerp, Basle, Berlin, Brussels, Copenhagen, Dresden, Frankfurt (Städel), Göteborg, Gotha, The Hague, Hanover, Leipzig, London (NG, Courtauld Inst.), Munich, Oberlin Ohio, Ottawa, Paris (Louvre), Prague, Siena, Toronto, Vienna, York, and several other German museums. [ill. 584, p. 356]

Brzeska *see* GAUDIER.

Bueckelaer (Beuckelaer), Joachim (*c.* 1530/35–1573/4), was the nephew by marriage and pupil of AERTSEN, and painted very similar still-life pictures with ostensibly religious subjects. He often worked as a journeyman for other artists, but became a master in the Antwerp Guild in 1560. His first dated work is of 1561. There are pictures by him in Amsterdam (Rijksmus.), Antwerp (Mus. and Mayer van den Bergh), Brussels, Florence (Uffizi), Genoa, Hull, Paris (Louvre), Stockholm, Vienna, and York (The Treasurer's House). [ill. 378, p. 326]

Buffet, Bernard (*b.* 1928), is a French painter of extreme precocity who made his name as early as 1948. He is the principal figurative painter in Paris and was much influenced in the 1940s by the movement known as *Misérabilisme*; sad greys, thin spiky forms, and an obtrusively angular signature, characterize his style. In later years he has painted views of London, Paris, and New York, as well as series of Toreadors and S. Joan of Arc. There are works in Cincinnati, New York (Brooklyn), and Toronto, as well as London (Tate) and Paris (Musée d'Art Moderne) [ill. 1029, p. 418]

Buon, Bartolommeo (*c.* 1374–1464/7), was the leading Venetian sculptor of the first half of the 15th century. His work is strongly influenced by South German sculpture and most of it is in Venice (e.g. Porta della Carta, Doge's

Palace) but there is a *Madonna della Misericordia* (1441–5) by him in London (V & A). [ill. 90, p. 283]

Burgkmair, Hans (1473–1531), was an Augsburg painter who was not influenced by Dürer but, like him, formed his style by contact with Venetian art. He soon outdistanced the elder Holbein and also had a good connection with publishers, designing woodcuts. He was patronized by the Emperor Maximilian. There are works in Augsburg, Cologne, Munich, Nuremberg, Vienna, and elsewhere. [ill. 582, p. 356]

Burin or Graver, the principal tool used in ENGRAVING on wood or metal to plough the lines out of the surface of the plate or block.

Burne-Jones, Sir Edward (1833–98), was one of the painters in the circle round William MORRIS and ROSSETTI, by whom he was greatly influenced. He travelled in Italy in 1859, and was in Milan and Venice in 1862 with Ruskin, for whom he copied works by Tintoretto. He produced many tapestry and stained-glass designs for William Morris's firm, and these and his paintings evoke a dreamy, romantic, literary never-never land of Botticelli and Mantegna, executed in a flat technique and a colour aptly described by the phrase 'greenery-yallery, Grosvenor Gallery'. He was made a baronet in 1894.
The largest collection of his works is in Birmingham City Art Gallery (his native town), and there are many in the Tate, London; Cardiff, and in provincial museums in England. [ill. 952, p. 409]

Burri, Alberto (b. 1915), an Italian abstract painter, began by practising medicine, but started painting in a prisoner-of-war camp in Texas in 1944. He settled in Rome in 1945 and exhibited in New York in 1954. He was awarded a prize at the 1960 Biennale. His works are not so much paintings as compositions in patched sacking with an occasional blob of colour. New York (Guggenheim) has a painting. [ill. 1113, p. 428]

Bushnell, John (d. 1701), fled from England owing to matrimonial difficulties and went to Rome. He worked in Italy, France, and Flanders before settling in Venice, where he made the huge Alvise Mocenigo monument in S. Lazzaro dei Mendicanti. He returned to England after 22 years, but his impossible pride and conceit suggest that he was mentally unbalanced. He executed a number of tombs, including two in Westminster Abbey, but his work is very uneven in quality. A terracotta bust of Charles II at Cambridge (Fitzwm) is attributed to him. [ill. 867, p. 398]

Butler, Reg (b. 1913), one of the leading British sculptors, was originally an architect and has also worked as a blacksmith: most of his work is in metal, either forged or cast. He won the 1953 competition for a monument to The Unknown Political Prisoner, and he produced another version in 1957. His first one-man show was in 1949 and the works of this period were all Constructivist, but in the later 1950s he has returned to figurative work and his most recent works are superbly sensual figures of girls. He has also written a book on the processes of artistic creation. There are works by him in Cologne, London (Tate), New York (M of MA), and Ottawa. [ill. 1152, p. 434]

Bylert (Bijlert), Jan van (1603–71), was an UTRECHT painter who was the pupil of BLOEMAERT and then went to France and Italy, returning to Utrecht by 1625. His work between 1620 and 1630 is based directly on Caravaggio's in subject and handling; after c. 1630 he used much lighter and brighter colours and chose subjects which have a certain pastoral prettiness, as well as painting some portraits. There are works in Amsterdam (Rijksmus.), Berlin, Brunswick, Budapest, Cassel, London (NG), Lyons, Rotterdam, Utrecht (Mus. and elsewhere). [ill. 462, p. 339]

C

Cabinet Picture. A small easel picture, usually not more than about 3 or 4 feet across, and often much less. The minor Dutch masters were the principal painters of this type of furniture picture at its best.

Calder, Alexander (*b.* 1898), is an American sculptor, abstract painter, and illustrator of children's books. He was originally an engineer and his main inventions – STABILES (so named by ARP) and MOBILES (so named by DUCHAMP), both dating from *c.* 1931 – can be regarded as a marriage between engineering and sculpture. His paintings are influenced by MIRÒ. Most of his works are in America, but there is a Mobile (of 1959) in Leeds. [ill. 1141, p. 432]

Calligraphic is an adjective applied to an artist's handling. In drawing it means 'freely and rhythmically treated, with pen squiggles like handwriting': in painting it means 'free and loose BRUSHWORK'.

Callot, Jacques (1592/3–1635), was one of the greatest of etchers and produced some 1,500 plates. He was born in Lorraine, at Nancy, and went to Rome at some time between 1608 and 1611, when he went to Florence. There he made many etchings of fairs and festivals as well as of courtiers, beggars, and hunchbacks, many of them based on *Commedia dell'arte* types. In 1621 he returned to Nancy, where his work took a more serious turn, culminating in his masterpiece the *Grandes Misères de la Guerre* (1633), which was at least partly inspired by Richelieu's invasion of Lorraine. It is the most terrifying record of the savageries of the Thirty Years War, comparable with Goya's later *Desastres*. [ill. 682, p. 373]

Calraet, Abraham van (1642–1722), was a Dordrecht painter who may have been a pupil of CUYP. The similarity between some of Calraet's small pictures and those by Cuyp has led to a great deal of misattribution, some of it deliberate. The initials AC apply equally to both artists, but the still-life pictures so signed are certainly Calraet's and many of the stable scenes probably are his. There are three pictures signed AC in the National Gallery, London, all of which were previously attributed to Cuyp. [ill. 422, p. 332]

Calvaert, Dionisio (Denis) (*c.* 1545–1619), was an Antwerp painter who went to Italy *c.* 1562. He eventually set up an Academy in Bologna and became the first master of Reni, Albani, and Domenichino; his Academy seems to have inspired the CARRACCI one. There are

works by him in Bologna and other Italian museums and in Hull, Vienna, and Worcester Mass. [ill. 405, p. 329]

Calvert, Edward (1799–1883), joined the Navy as a young man and first exhibited at the RA in 1825. He met PALMER there in 1826, who described him as 'a prosperous, stalwart country gentleman . . . redolent of the sea, and in white trousers': between 1827 and 1831 he was deeply influenced by BLAKE and Palmer, but he lost his innocent eye and spent the rest of his long life absorbed in anti-Christian mythological musings. There are works by him in the Tate Gallery, London. [ill. 939, p. 406]

Camaïeu (Fr.). For paintings *en camaïeu see* GRISAILLE, and for engravings *see* CHIAROSCURO.

Cambio, Arnolfo di, *see* ARNOLFO.

Camden Town Group. A small secession from the NEAC which later developed into the LONDON GROUP. GILMAN and GORE were the major figures in it, but SICKERT was the principal inspiration. The group is usually said to have introduced Post-Impressionism into English art. [ills. 969, 972, p. 411]

Camera Obscura, Lucida. A mechanical means of securing accuracy in drawing, particularly of topographical detail. The *camera obscura* was invented in the 16th century and consists of an arrangement of lenses and mirrors in a darkened tent or box. The view seen by the lens is reflected through the mirrors on to a sheet of paper, so that all the draughtsman has to do is to trace round the edges. CANALETTO is known to have used the machine in making studies for his *Vedute*, and its use was undoubtedly widespread; CARLEVARIS also used it. Drawings made in this way are sometimes identifiable by distortions at the edges due to primitive lenses. A *camera lucida* is a more sophisticated optical instrument, incorporating a prism.

Campendonk, Heinrich (1889–1957), was the youngest member of the BLAUE REITER, which MARC and KANDINSKY invited him to join in 1911. He emigrated to Holland in 1933 and taught at Amsterdam. Most of his works are woodcuts, but his paintings are rich in colour with small, puppet-like figures reminiscent of Chagall and the Russians. [ill. 1025, p. 418]

Campin, Robert (1378/9–1444), is known to have been a painter active in Tournai from 1406. No pictures are certainly known to be his, but he had two pupils, Jacques DARET and (probably) Roger van der WEYDEN: he may therefore have been identical with the MASTER of FLÉMALLE. [ills. 337, 338, p. 320]

Canaletto, (Giovanni) Antonio (1697–1768), Venetian *vedutista*, went to Rome *c.* 1719 and was influenced in some not clearly definable way by PANINI. He had already worked as a scene painter with his father and was back in Venice by 1720, where he is recorded in the Guild 1720–67. His earliest datable works are four views of Venice painted in 1725–6 for Stefano Conti of Lucca (now in a private collection in Montreal): these show the strong contrasts of light and shade which made him famous at the expense of CARLEVARIS (who may have been his master, although this is not likely). It is clear that these *vedute* were extremely unusual in that they were painted on the spot instead of from drawings, although he later abandoned this practice and returned to the traditional method of working from drawings, some of which were made with the help of the CAMERA OBSCURA; occasionally he even worked from etchings by Carlevaris. By 1726 he was already working for the English market and by about 1730 he had come to an agreement with Joseph Smith, later British Consul in Venice, who had the pick of his output, arranged other sales, and probably forwarded his visit to England, which, with short intervals in Venice, lasted from 1746 until *c.* 1756. During this time he painted several English views and Capricci, although on his arrival he had some difficulty in establishing himself as Vertue observed that 'on the whole of him something is obscure or strange. he dos not produce work so well done as those of Venice or other parts of Italy . . . especially his figures in his works done here, are apparently much inferior to those done abroad. which are surprizeingly well done and with great freedom and variety – his water and his skys at no time excellent or with natural freedom. and what he has done here his prospects of Trees woods or handling or pencilling of that part not various nor so skillfull as might be expected . . . which has much strengthend a conjecture that he is not the veritable Cannalleti of Venice.' This was perhaps partly due to BELLOTTO's use of his uncle's name. During and after his English period Canaletto's style, as Vertue observed, became much harder and tighter, losing all the breadth and freedom of his earliest works. These later works were much imitated by English painters such as SCOTT and Marlow.
The Royal Collection has the largest and best collection of Canaletto's works, with more than 50 paintings and over 140 drawings from the Smith Collection. Most other galleries have an example. About 1741/4 he issued his etched *Vedute . . .* with a dedication to Smith. [ills. 306, 308, 309, p. 316]

Cano, Alonso (1601–67), was one of the leading painters and sculptors of Seville. He was the son of a sculptor who specialized in the construction of elaborate altars and he himself continued the business, but became a master painter in 1626. His early works were influenced by ZURBARÁN, but his style later became softer in handling. In 1636 he was imprisoned for debt; in the following year he was in trouble for duelling, and in 1638 he left Seville for the Court where he may have been invited by VELAZQUEZ, who had been his fellow-apprentice under PACHECO. In 1644 his young wife was found stabbed to

death; he was arrested but subsequently freed. He returned to Madrid in 1645, but obtained the salary of a Prebendary at Granada Cathedral, although he does not seem to have been very satisfactory to his ecclesiastical superiors. He designed the façade of Granada Cathedral *c.* 1664. A contemporary records his systematic use of prints, even the crudest street ballads, as a means of stimulating his imagination. Most of his sculpture is in Granada, but there are paintings and some carved wooden figures in Berlin, Budapest, Dresden, Kansas City, London (Wallace Coll.), Los Angeles, Madrid (Prado and Acad.), Munich, New York (Hispanic Soc.), Paris (Louvre), Seville, Stockholm, Worcester Mass., and York. [ill. 646, p. 365]

Canova, Antonio (1757–1822), was brought up as a mason and already had his own studio, in Venice, by 1774: he became the most famous NEOCLASSIC sculptor whose international reputation surpassed even those of FLAXMAN, THORWALDSEN, and GIBSON. His early work is still very much in the 18th-century tradition and reminiscent of French portrait sculpture in its liveliness, but by 1779 he had been converted to Neoclassic theory and this was confirmed by his visit to Rome and Naples in 1780 and his residence in Rome from 1781. He is said to have been influenced by Gavin HAMILTON. In 1782 he received his first major commission, the Monument to Pope Clement XIV (1782–7: Rome, SS. Apostoli), followed by that to Clement XIII (1787–92: St Peter's). The French invasion caused him to go to Vienna in 1797, and there he got the commission for the Monument to Maria Christina (in the Augustinerkirche). In 1802, pressed by the Vatican, he accepted Napoleon's invitation to Paris; although he did not approve of the French lootings of Italian works of art he became an admirer of Napoleon and made a bust of him from life. This was followed by many others and in the years 1806–8 he began several, including an equestrian bronze for Naples and two gigantic standing figures of the Emperor, stark naked. One of these, in bronze, is in Milan (Brera): another, in marble, was captured by Wellington and is now in the Wellington Mus., London. In 1807 he also began (but abandoned) a Nelson Monument. His best-known work is the portrait of Napoleon's sister, *Pauline Bonaparte Borghese as Venus* (1808: Rome, Borghese Gall.), one of several statues of members of Napoleon's family. In 1815, after the fall of Napoleon, Canova was sent by the Pope to Paris to try to secure the return of the works looted by the French. He succeeded in large measure, with English help, and he visited London on his way back, where he studied the Elgin Marbles (bought, after much controversy, for the British Museum in 1816). For his part in securing the return of the Italian treasures the Pope made him Marchese d'Ischia. In 1817 he transformed his equestrian *Napoleon*, destined for Naples, into *Charles III Bourbon* and in the same year he adapted his colossal *Religion* into a smaller figure for a Brownlow Monument in Belton, Lincs, where it is said to represent *Protestant Faith*. Two years later, at the expense of George III, he made the Monument to the Stuarts now in St Peter's, and in 1820 he made a *Washington* for N. Carolina (now destroyed). He seems to have been an extremely kind and generous man, spending his large fortune freely in helping young students and sending patrons to struggling sculptors. There is a large collection of casts of his works in his native village,

Possagno near Treviso: other works are in Bassano, Bergamo, Berlin, Florence (Pitti and Sta Croce), Forlì, Genoa (Pal. Bianco), London (V & A), Milan (Ambrosiana), Munich, Naples (Mus. Nazionale and Filangeri), Padua, Paris (Louvre), Parma, Rome (Mus. Capitoline and Napoleonico, S. Antonio dei Portoghesi, SS. Luca e Martina, S. Marco), Treviso, Turin, the Vatican, Venice (Accad., Correr, Mus. dell'Arsenale, Querini-Stampalia, Seminario Arcivescovile), and Vienna (K-H Mus.). [ill. 318, p. 318]

Cappelle, Jan van de (c. 1624/5–79), was an Amsterdam painter of calm seas with fleecy white clouds. He also painted a few winter landscapes. His style was based on that of Simon de VLIEGER, by whom he owned 9 paintings and 1,300 drawings: Cappelle seems to have been wealthy, since his collection also included 500 Rembrandt drawings and portraits of him were painted by Rembrandt, Hals, and Eeckhout. Examples of his work are in many Dutch museums and in Antwerp, Berlin, Birmingham (Barber Inst.), Brussels, Chicago, Detroit, Dublin, Glasgow, London (NG and Kenwood), Munich, New York (Met. Mus., Frick Coll.), Ottawa, Vienna, Washington (NG), and elsewhere. [ill. 500, p. 345]

Capriccio (Ital. caprice). A fantasy; but usually applied to quasi-topographical subjects and VEDUTE, e.g. Marlow's *St Paul's, London, with the Grand Canal, Venice* (London, Tate). *Los Caprichos* is the title of a set of highly phantasmagoric etchings by Goya. [ills. 308, 662, pp. 316, 370]

Caracciolo, Giovanni Battista called 'Battistello' (d. 1637), was one of the first Neapolitan painters to be influenced by CARAVAGGIO, whose works he may have seen in Rome before Caravaggio went to Naples in 1606–7. He thus exerted a decisive influence on Neapolitan painting of the 17th century. [ill. 242, p. 309]

Caravaggio, Michelangelo Merisi da (1573–1610), so called from his birthplace near Milan. In 1584 he was apprenticed for four years to Simone Peterzano, a Bergamasque who claimed to have been a pupil of Titian. After his apprenticeship ended he went to Rome, but his early years are so obscure that it is uncertain when he arrived there, and when he worked for the Cavaliere d'ARPINO. His earliest works were still-life subjects and small dramatized self-portraits of a distinctly Northern and vaguely Venetian character, with strong chiaroscuro and detailed execution. From the 1590s he worked for Cardinal del Monte, who commissioned several genre subjects, and through him he obtained in 1597 the commission to decorate a chapel in S. Luigi dei Francesi, the French church in Rome, with 3 scenes from the life of S. Matthew. This – his first public work – was finished only after many difficulties, including the rejection of the original altarpiece of *S. Matthew and the Angel* on the grounds of indecorum, and radical repaintings of the *Calling* and the *Martyrdom* of the Saint on the side walls, probably due to difficulties with the scale of the figures occasioned by unfamiliarity with working on such large canvases and on related works on opposing walls. The present altarpiece was substituted for the original one, and with the extensive repaintings the work may have lasted until 1603, although the chapel was opened in 1601.

During these years he also painted the *Martyrdom of S. Peter* and the *Conversion of S. Paul* for Sta Maria del Popolo (1600–1), and these too were rejected by the clergy and replaced by more acceptable renderings. These are smaller than the works in S. Luigi, with fewer figures much larger in scale, but with an even more dramatic chiaroscuro. Three further large altarpieces were bitterly criticized: the *Madonna di Loreto*, the *Virgin and Child with S. Anne*, and the *Death of the Virgin*. Basically, the objections were on the grounds of indecorum – the sweaty headcloth and dirty feet of the pilgrims in the *Madonna di Loreto*, the naked Child and peasant air of the Virgin and S. Anne, the coarse peasant types used for the Apostles, and the bloated figure of the dead Virgin, reputed to have been painted from a drowned strumpet fished out of the Tiber. These accusations, and opposition to his works among the Academic Late Mannerists such as ZUCCARI, were founded on his vivid realism, his use of contemporary costumes and settings, his rejection of idealization, the immediacy and simplicity of his approach, and the novelty of his use of strong chiaroscuro with a wealth of detail which, though appearing to conform to the new ideas favoured by Counter-Reformation artistic theory, were radically opposed to the forms and ideas expressed by the CARRACCI. But all his rejected works found ready buyers among Cardinals and noblemen against whom no accusations of insincerity and sensationalism can be made. His reputation as a stormy petrel was probably added to by the libel action brought against him in 1603 by Baglioni (later his biographer) because of scurrilous verses circulated by Caravaggio, and by the numerous fracas with the police due to his violent temper. His career in Rome was brought to an inglorious end in 1606 by just such an outburst, for during a game of tennis he quarrelled with his opponent and stabbed him. He fled to Naples where he painted several works before going on to Malta in 1607.

Here he was well received by the Grand Master of the Order of S. John, of whom he painted a full-length portrait (now in the Louvre), was made a Knight and commissioned to paint two works still in Malta. After assaulting a Justiciary, he was imprisoned but escaped and fled to Sicily in 1608. He was expelled from the Order, and pursued by its agents from Syracuse to Messina, then to Palermo, and finally back to Naples in 1609, where at a low tavern, haunt of German mercenaries and cut-throats, he was seriously wounded in a brawl and his death was generally reported. Meanwhile, in Rome, efforts were being made to obtain a pardon, but not daring to return to Rome until he was sure of it, he left Naples by sea for Porto d'Ercole, a Spanish enclave on the Tuscan coast. Here he was imprisoned by mistake and was released in time to see the felucca sail, as he thought, with all his goods. His rage brought on an attack of fever, and a few days later he died in a tavern. After his death, the Spanish Viceroy sent to Porto d'Ercole for his effects which were awaiting him in the customs house.

His last works in Malta and Sicily are very dark and somewhat damaged, but their direct iconography, their inspired simplicity and poignancy embody a new intensity of dramatic feeling. His technical methods were revolutionary and brought him into endless controversy: he is recorded as painting directly on to the canvas from a model, instead of working from sketches and squared-up preparatory drawings. Apart from Naples his methods and ideas had little lasting effect in Italy, where his principal followers were Orazio GENTILESCHI and his daughter Artemisia, MANFREDI, Borgianni, Serodine, and a number of lesser men who imitated his manner without catching more than his realism and light effects. He had some influence on Guido RENI and GUERCINO, and a decisive one on the UTRECHT School and in Naples. The realism of RIBERA and Maino links him with the early work of VELAZQUEZ and MURILLO, and in France LA TOUR and the LE NAIN brothers show the spread of his ideas. RUBENS also was a profound admirer of Caravaggio, and much of REMBRANDT's work stems from him.

There are works in Berlin, the Escorial, Florence (Uffizi, Pitti), Hartford Conn., Kansas City, Leningrad, London (NG), Madrid (Prado), Messina, Milan (Ambrosiana, Brera), Naples (S. Domenico Maggiore, Misericordia), New York (Met. Mus.), Palermo (S. Lorenzo), Paris (Louvre), Rome (Gall. Naz., Borghese, Capitoline, Corsini, Doria Galls. and churches), Valletta Malta, the Vatican, Vienna. [ills. 236, 237, 238, p. 308. Col. pl. 16]

Carlevaris, Luca (1665–1731), was the precursor of CANALETTO as the painter of Venice, and his *Vedute*, 103 etchings, were published in 1703. A sketch-book with preparatory drawings for these is in the British Museum; a volume of 53 oil-sketches is in the V & A Museum, and there are paintings in the Royal Collection, Birmingham, Detroit, Venice, and elsewhere. [ill. 303, p. 316]

Carpaccio, Vittore (active 1490–d. 1523/6), was probably a pupil, and certainly a follower, of Gentile BELLINI and was influenced by Giovanni Bellini and perhaps Giorgione. His best work is the cycle of large pictures of the *Legend of S. Ursula*, now in Venice (Accad.), the earliest dated one being of 1490. There are many other pictures of this pageant type in Venice (Accad. and churches) and other examples in Berlin, London (NG), Milan (Brera), New York (Met. Mus.), Paris (Louvre, Mus. Jacquemart-André), Philadelphia (Johnson), Rome (Borghese), Washington (NG), and elsewhere. His *Knight in a Landscape*, dated 1510?/26? (Lugano, Thyssen Coll.) may be the first full-length portrait, preceding CRANACH and MORETTO: if so, it is clearly derived from pictures of Saints, such as Giorgione's S. Liberale in the Castelfranco Altar. [ill. 149, p. 292]

Carpeaux, Jean-Baptiste (1827–75), was the principal French sculptor of his day and is, in some ways, parallel to Delacroix. He was a pupil of RUDE, whose influence he combined with the Romanticism of BARYE; he was also a precursor of Rodin and Rosso in the importance he attached to *chiaroscuro* in sculpture. He went to Italy in 1854 and made his name with a dramatic statue of *Ugolino*, before returning to Paris in 1862. His most famous works were a pediment for the Pavillon de Flore of the Louvre (begun 1863) and *The Dance*, begun in 1865 for the new Opera House in Paris. This caused a great sensation and was attacked on grounds of morality. It was even suggested that the group should be removed, but the outbreak of the Franco-Prussian War in 1870 prevented any action. He worked in England in 1871, to avoid the Commune. His last years were clouded by persecution mania and he died, at 48, of cancer. He worked as a painter as well as a

sculptor and his native Valenciennes has a museum of his works: others are in Paris (Louvre and Petit Pal.), and in Birmingham, Copenhagen, London (Tate), New York, Providence RI, and Washington. [ill. 724, p. 379]

Carrà, Carlo (b. 1881), was one of the original FUTURISTS until, in 1915, he was deeply impressed by Giotto and, after meeting CHIRICO, joined his *Pittura metafisica*, thus belonging to both the major modern Italian movements. Like many others he has since reverted to a more naturalistic mode. [ill. 1063, p. 424]

Carracci. There were three Carracci, all Bolognese: Ludovico, and his cousins Agostino and Annibale, who were brothers.

Ludovico (1555–1619) probably entered the Bologna Guild in 1578. With his cousins, he founded a teaching Academy in Bologna in 1585/6, which became the most celebrated of its kind and was responsible for the training of most major Bolognese painters of the next generation, including Domenichino, Reni, and Guercino. He ran the Academy alone after his cousins left Bologna, but after this there was a notable falling off in his work, and he dwindled into a painter of large, rather sentimental and didactic, Counter-Reformation altarpieces, with none of the originality that his cousins, particularly Annibale, had stimulated in him.

Agostino (1557–1602) was principally an engraver who executed many plates after works by High Renaissance, and particularly Venetian, artists. He visited Venice and North Italy in 1580–1 and was in Parma with Annibale c. 1585. His wide knowledge of North Italian painting reinforced the trend away from the dying forms of Roman Mannerism towards a fresh evaluation of the part to be played by the High Renaissance and classical tradition in the creation of the new and revitalized painting which culminated in the Baroque. He was in Rome in 1597–9, working with Annibale on the Farnese Gallery, but by 1600 had moved to Parma and was working there for the Farnese family when he died. His major altarpiece, the *Last Communion of S. Jerome* (Bologna), greatly influenced Domenichino.

Annibale (1560–1609) was a pupil of Ludovico, and was by far the greatest artist of the three. He may have travelled in Tuscany c. 1583–4, was in Parma with Agostino and almost certainly visited Venice c. 1585/6. He participated with Ludovico and Agostino in the Academy, and they all shared in the decoration of the Fava (1584) and Magnani (1588–91) palaces in Bologna. In 1595 he went to Rome to work for Cardinal Farnese on the decoration of the Farnese Palace, and for this he first executed the Camerino, with an elaborate ceiling with subjects from classical mythology in fresco surrounding an oil-painting of *Hercules at the Crossroads* (now in Naples). The Gallery, which he next undertook, is a room some 66 feet long by 22 feet wide, and he designed for the barrel-vault of the ceiling an elaborate illusionistic arrangement of mythological pictures supported by herms against an open colonnade, with, seated above the cornice, nude male figures reminiscent of those in Michelangelo's Sistine ceiling. The Farnese Gallery ranks with Raphael's decorations in the Stanze and the Farnesina and Michelangelo's Sistine ceiling as one of the great schemes of decoration. In its illusionism and imaginative scope, it has a lightness of touch, a sense of humour, and a freshness of vision and fancy transcending his other works, where the conscious re-creation of the grander aspects of the style of High Renaissance painters, particularly Raphael, Correggio, Andrea del Sarto, and the Venetians, is more readily perceptible. He was helped in the Gallery by Agostino until 1599, and by Domenichino (particularly in the landscapes) and Albani. It was finished by 1604, and in 1605 Annibale was first attacked by the illness which virtually prevented him from working and which eventually killed him.

There are works by one or more of the Carracci in the Royal Collection, Amsterdam (Rijksmus.), Berlin, Birmingham (City Mus.), Bologna (Mus., and churches), Boston (Mus.), Brussels, Dresden, Florence (Uffizi), London (NG), Milan (Brera), Modena, Munich, Naples, Oxford (Christ Church), Paris (Louvre), Parma, Rome (Borghese, Capitoline; Colonna, Doria, and Spada Colls.), Sheffield, the Vatican, Venice (Accad.), Vienna, and elsewhere.

Antonio (c. 1583–1618), an illegitimate son of Agostino, and Francesco, an illegitimate brother of Agostino and Annibale, were also painters and worked as assistants.

The term Eclectic, now discredited, was formerly applied to the Carracci as an imputation that their use of the High Renaissance and classical tradition involved a deliberate policy of selection and combination of the forms and concepts, often mutually incompatible, characterizing the style of their predecessors. There is no evidence of any such specific programme underlying either the teaching in their Academy or their own works, which illustrate the truism that all art is nourished by tradition. [ills. 245–7, 254, 255, pp. 308–9]

Carriera, Rosalba (1675–1757), was a Venetian woman pastellist who had a great vogue in Venice, Paris (1720–1), Vienna, and among English tourists. She painted numerous portraits in pastel, but she also had great success with her nearly pornographic girls, which are considerably earlier than those of GREUZE. There are 157 of her pastels in Dresden. [ill. 293, p. 314]

Carstens, Asmus (Erasmus) Jakob (1754–98), was Danish-born, but was the most *ernst* of the German Neoclassic artists; his difficult temperament prevented him from obtaining due recognition. He made his first Italian journey in 1783, but money soon gave out and he had to return. With OVERBECK's help he settled in Berlin in 1787 and became Professor at the Academy (1790), but in 1792 he was able to return to Rome, where he died. He made almost no paintings and his work consists of large cartoons in black and white chalk, very much influenced by Michelangelo, so that the combination of Neoclassical rectitude with Mannerist form is curiously reminiscent of BLAKE. There are examples in Berlin and Copenhagen and, especially, Weimar. His works became better known through the publication of engravings, 1864–84. [ill. 593, p. 359]

Cartellino (Ital. a little paper), a small scroll or piece of paper painted on a picture to appear like a real scroll affixed to the background or the small foreground parapet which is often supplied to limit the front of the foreground plane and provide something for the *cartellino* to be stuck

to. The commonest use for a *cartellino* is to take the painter's signature, as in the works of Giovanni Bellini and Antonello da Messina, but it sometimes carries a religious invocation or the motto of the sitter in a portrait.

Cartoon. Nowadays this normally means a drawing with a humorous or satirical intention, but the original meaning (from Ital. *cartone*, a big sheet of paper) is quite different. A cartoon in this sense is a full-size drawing for a painting, usually worked out in complete detail, ready for transfer to the wall, canvas, or panel. The cartoon was rubbed on the back with chalk and the main lines were then gone over with a stylus thus transferring them to the canvas or panel; sometimes the main lines had their contours pricked through and fine charcoal dust was then 'pounced' through or a SPOLVERO was used to preserve the cartoon itself. The procedure for FRESCO was more complex but essentially the same. Several cartoons still survive and it is possible to tell which were used for transfer, from the presence of prickings or the indentation of the lines. The most famous of all, by Raphael, were for tapestries and therefore were not transferred in this way. [ills. 176, 179, pp. 296, 298. Col. pl. 10]

Cassatt, Mary (1845–1926), was born in Pittsburg, the daughter of a banker who offered little encouragement to her desire to be a painter. In 1868, after travelling widely in Europe, she settled in Paris to study under Chaplin, a typical Academic painter, but was far more interested in Courbet, Manet, and the Impressionists. In 1877 she met Degas, who invited her to exhibit with the Impressionists, which she did in 1879, 1880, 1881, and 1886. She bought Impressionist paintings for herself and her family, tried to get other Americans to do so, and helped their dealer Durand-Ruel in some of his more difficult moments. She was partly blind by 1912, and totally so at her death. She is well represented in American museums. [ill. 959, p. 409]

Cassone is an Italian word for a special kind of coffer used as a marriage-chest and containing the bride's household linen. They were often very richly decorated, with carved and gilt mouldings and painted panels at the front and sides and sometimes also inside and outside the lid. The great age of *cassoni* was from the 14th to the 16th century, and the subjects were usually mythological, of the *Rape of Helen* type, or from classical antiquity. The exact significance of some of the paintings inside the lids is still not clear and may have been quasi-magical. Many panels from the fronts of *cassoni* are now framed and hung as Old Masters, although most of the original painters were not regarded as more than craftsmen by their contemporaries: Uccello is an exception. A panel from a *cassone* is nearly always recognizable on account of its shape – some four to six feet wide by about a foot or eighteen inches in height. [ill. 115, p. 288]

Castagno, Andrea del (perhaps 1421–57), was one of the most influential Florentine painters of the generation after Masaccio. The date of his birth is now thought to be as late as 1421/3, although it was formerly put at 1412 or even in the 14th century. He seems to have been precocious: traditionally he painted some effigies of rebels hanged by the heels, c. 1440, from which he derived the nickname Andreino degli Impiccati (of the hanged men). He was certainly in Venice in 1442, when he signed and dated some frescoes in S. Zaccaria; but these do not give an unequivocal picture of his style in his youth, since they were painted in collaboration with the unknown Francesco da Faenza. He was back in Florence in 1444, designing a stained-glass window for the Cathedral (still there), and soon after this he must have painted his frescoes of *Passion Scenes* and the *Last Supper* (Florence, S. Apollonia, now the Castagno Mus.). These were his first famous works and show the influence of Masaccio's scientific realism. In 1449–50 he painted an *Assumption* for S. Miniato fra le Torri (now in Berlin), which is far closer to the International Gothic style; and, for the last seven years of his short career, Castagno broke with the style of Masaccio (whom he could not have known) in favour of one based on the emotional and linear style of DONATELLO (who was alive and very famous): in fact Castagno translated Donatello's sculpture into terms of painting and thus influenced all 15th-century Florentine painters. The major examples of this Donatellesque style are the *Famous Men and Women*, painted for a villa at Legnaia, near Florence (now in the Castagno Museum). His last dated work was the equestrian fresco portrait of *Niccolò da Tolentino* in the Cathedral, a pendant to Uccello's *Hawkwood*. This is of 1456 and shows a more dynamic style than Uccello's, based partly on Donatello's *Gattamelata*. In recent years a number of Andrea's *sinopie* have been recovered, justifying the praise lavished on him by contemporaries as a draughtsman. There are other works by him in Florence (SS. Annunziata) and in Edinburgh (NG), London (NG), New York (Met. Mus. and Frick Coll.), Venice (S. Marco), and Washington (NG). [ill. 70, 71, p. 279]

Castiglione, Giovanni Benedetto (*c.* 1600?–65?), was a Genoese and a pupil of van DYCK, in whose studio in Genoa he worked from 1621. He was – for an Italian – much influenced by foreigners, for his style was formed by Flemish painters and Rembrandt's etchings, and later he was much influenced by POUSSIN and Rubens. Like Bassano, he was a great animal painter. He was in Rome by 1634, when he was in the Academy of S. Luke, and he remained until 1650 at least: it was at this time that he was influenced by Poussin. About 1648/50 he began to work for the Mantuan Court, which perhaps explains the influence of Rubens. His latest works have a deep mystical fervour, but he is principally remembered as the inventor of a kind of drawing in thin washes of oil paint, and, more important, of the MONOTYPE. Excellent examples of both are in the Royal Collection (Windsor) and other works are in Bergamo, Birmingham, Dresden, Dublin, Genoa, Hartford Conn., Munich, Madrid, Montpellier, Ottawa, Paris (Louvre), Rome (Doria), Rouen, Turin. [ill. 277, p. 312]

Casting *see* PLASTER *and* BRONZE.

Catena, Vincenzo (*c.* 1480–1531), was a Venetian painter who began as an imitator of Giovanni BELLINI and CIMA, but who entered into some kind of partnership with GIORGIONE in 1506 (according to an inscription on the back of Giorgione's *Laura* in Vienna); nevertheless, the influence of Giorgione did not make itself felt until after

1510 when Giorgione died. In the last twenty years of Catena's life he was also influenced by Palma Vecchio, Titian, and others. There are works by him in Berlin, Boston (Gardner), Budapest, Dresden, Edinburgh (NG), Frankfurt (Städel), Glasgow, Liverpool, London (NG), Madrid (Prado), Milan (Brera), New York (Met. Mus.), Ottawa, Paris (Louvre), Venice (Accad., Correr, Querini-Stampalia, SM Mater Domini), Vienna (K-H Mus.), Washington (NG), and elsewhere. [ill. 140, p. 293]

Cavallini, Pietro (active 1273–1308), was the great representative of the Roman School slightly before GIOTTO. He painted fresco cycles and designed mosaics in a purely classical style which forms the link between the painting of antiquity and the revived forms introduced principally by Giotto. The mosaics in Sta Maria in Trastevere in Rome are recorded as having been signed and dated 1291 and the fragmentary *Last Judgement* fresco in Sta Cecilia, also in Rome, is probably of 1293. He was in Naples in 1308 and the frescoes in S M Donna Regina are probably his. [ill. 15, p. 270]

Cavallino, Bernardo (1616–56), was a short-lived Neapolitan painter of small-scale figures set in a murky background. He was the major Neapolitan painter of the 1640s and early 50s until his death in the great plague of 1656. His only signed and dated work is the *S. Cecilia* of 1645, acquired by Hitler in 1941 and now the property of the Italian Government: the sketch for it is in Naples along with other works. Boston, Detroit, Hartford Conn. (Wadsworth Atheneum), London (NG), Munich, New York (Met. Mus.), Sarasota Fla, Stockholm, Verona, Vienna (K-H Mus.), Washington (NG), and York also have examples. [ill. 243, p. 309]

Cavo-Rilievo *see* RELIEF.

Cellini, Benvenuto (1500–71), Florentine sculptor, goldsmith, and amorist, is best known for his 'Autobiography' (1558–62: several English editions exist). This is one of the great autobiographies and gives us a glimpse into the processes of artistic creation as well as an insight into the troubled Italy of the years following the Sack of Rome in 1527; Cellini's love-life also features in considerable detail, not all of it quite credible. In 1519 he refused an invitation to go to England with TORRIGIANO, on the grounds that he could not do anything with the man who had broken the divine Michelangelo's nose. Instead he went to Rome, and, according to his own account, played a heroic part in the defence of the city during the siege. He also claims to have killed Charles de Bourbon, one of the Imperial commanders in the siege. As an artist Cellini was first influenced by the pupils of Raphael but later came very much under the shadow of Michelangelo, and his *Perseus* (1545–54: Florence, Loggia dei Lanzi) stood fittingly near Michelangelo's *David* and Donatello's *Judith*, its other main prototype. In 1537 and again in 1540–5 Cellini went to France to work for François I, for whom he made a salt-cellar (1540–3: now in Vienna) and the *Nymph of Fontainebleau* (1543–4: Paris, Louvre), whose sophisticated elegance and elongatedly Mannerist forms sum up the whole of the Second School of FONTAINEBLEAU. Imprisoned in 1556, apparently for immorality, in 1558

Cellini took the first steps towards becoming a priest but in 1560 he obtained his release from his vows. He also designed coins and medals and there are other works by him in Boston (Gardner Mus.), the Escorial, Florence (Bargello), and Oxford. [ill. 161, p. 295]

Cennini, Cennino, wrote, *c.* 1390 or a little later, the earliest Italian treatise on painting, 'Il Libro dell'Arte', which is the source of most of our knowledge of early TEMPERA technique. He says in it that he was a pupil of Agnolo GADDI – and could therefore trace his artistic descent back to Giotto – but no works of his are known.

Cerano *see* CRESPI, G.B.

César (*b.* 1921), was born César Baldacchini in Marseilles, but has lived in Paris since 1943. He is a sculptor who works with characteristic 20th-century materials – mostly crushed motor-cars and similar industrial debris. He has three workshops, one in a foundry, so that material is handy, and he can then weld the crushed scrap into assemblages that often take their titles from the location of the workshop, e.g. *Man of Saint-Denis* (London, Tate). [ill. 1153, p. 434]

Cézanne, Paul (1839–1906), was probably the greatest painter of the last 100 years. He was born in Aix-en-Provence, the son of a wealthy banker and tradesman, and was educated at the Collège Bourbon where he became friendly with Zola. The friendship, which meant a great deal to Cézanne, lasted until the publication of Zola's 'L'Œuvre' in 1886: the character of Claude Lantier seemed a travesty of Cézanne, and not only to Cézanne. In 1861, after abandoning the study of law, Cézanne went to Paris, where he met PISSARRO and from 1862 he devoted himself to painting, living in Paris until 1870. The Franco-Prussian War drove him to L'Estaque and in 1872 he joined Pissarro at Pontoise. In the 1860s his ardent Southern temperament expressed itself in a series of more or less erotic and melodramatic pictures – in particular the *Rape* of 1867 – which were not unnaturally received with no enthusiasm. While closely associated with Pissarro Cézanne began to paint landscapes in an Impressionist technique and he exhibited at the First IMPRESSIONIST Exhibition of 1874. One of his pictures was among those which incurred the greatest public displeasure. This was the most extraordinary of all his erotic fantasies, the *Modern Olympia*, so called as a rather dubious compliment to MANET: it represents a fat squatting female being disrobed by a negress while a man (probably Cézanne himself) watches with interest. In the midst of the chaste Impressionist landscapes the effect must have been startling, particularly as these early pictures are painted with great violence and the colour is often piled on with a palette-knife. During the 1870s Cézanne digested the theories of colour and light which the Impressionists were then developing: in the Third Impressionist Exhibition (1877) he showed 16 pictures and one critic praised them highly. Gradually he calmed down the exuberant Romanticism of his temperament and abandoned a Delacroix-like technique, to which he was not really suited. His great achievements lay in the direction of an ever more subtle analysis of colour and tone, totally different from the Impressionists' analysis in that they sought to capture the surface, the impression, and therefore painted quickly. Cézanne's analysis was infinitely prolonged and laborious because he sought to use colour as a means of modelling and as the ultimate expression of the underlying forms of visible objects. In this he was, of course, following classical prototypes and some of his recorded sayings are of great importance. He said that he 'wanted to do Poussin again, from Nature' and that he wanted 'to make of Impressionism something solid and durable, like the art of the Museums'. This was clearly because Impressionism was lacking in formal qualities, but 'when colour has its greatest richness then form has its plenitude': in particular, the basic ideas of CUBISM have been claimed to be implicit in his teaching that the painter ought to look for the cone, the sphere, and the cylinder in nature. Cézanne himself was no theorist and constant insults from public and critics made him very chary of exposing himself. When his father died in 1886 he found himself rich and able to live in seclusion in Provence, mainly at the Jas de Bouffan, near Aix, a house his father had bought and which once contained some very early Cézanne decorations. In 1890 he was invited to exhibit in Brussels by Les XX, in 1895 he had his first big show, and from about 1900 his genius was fairly widely recognized. In the last years of his life he returned to some of his favourite early themes – in particular, the big compositions of *Bathers*, with nude figures in a landscape setting. His great contribution was to show that colour and tone values must be considered as one thing and not two; in doing this he made Impressionism into something solid, like Poussin. Because his analysis was pursued with agonizing care many of his pictures were never finished – he is said to have abandoned a portrait of Vollard the dealer, after more than a hundred sittings, with the remark that he was not displeased with the shirt-front! Naturally, still-life and landscape offered the greatest freedom in this respect and most of his flowerpieces were probably painted from artificial flowers; his few portraits were of himself or of people whose sittings could be protracted almost indefinitely.

There are pictures by him in Amsterdam (Stedelijk Mus.), Basle, Berlin, Berne, Boston, Budapest, Cardiff, Chicago, Cleveland Ohio, Columbus Ohio, Essen (Folkwang Mus.), Glasgow, The Hague (Gemeente Mus.), Hamburg, Helsinki, Leningrad, London (NG, Tate, and Courtauld Institute), Los Angeles, Mannheim, Merion Pa (Barnes Foundation), Minneapolis, Munich, New York (Met. Mus., Brooklyn Mus., and Guggenheim), Northampton Mass. (Smith College), Oslo, Ottawa, Paris (Louvre), Philadelphia, Prague, Providence RI, St Louis, São Paulo, Stockholm, Washington (NG and Phillips), and Zürich. [ills. 981–3, p. 413. Col. pls. 31, 50]

Chadwick, Lynn (*b.* 1914), is a British abstract sculptor who works in welded iron and steel, copper, bronze, metal compositions, plaster, and glass. Like his contemporary BUTLER he was trained as an architect. After war service he turned to sculpture and produced mobiles under the influence of CALDER (he made three big mobiles for the 1951 Festival of Britain), but has now evolved 'balanced Sculptures' which do not attempt to exploit the quality of movement. He was awarded a prize at the 1956 Venice Biennale and is now represented in museums in Adelaide,

Brighton, Bristol, Brussels, Buffalo, Chicago, London (Tate and V & A), Manchester (Whitworth), Montreal, New York (M of MA), Ottawa, Paris (Musée d'Art Moderne), Pittsburgh, Rome, Rotterdam, and Turin. [ill. 1150, p. 434]

Chagall, Marc (*b.* 1887). Born in Vitebsk, Chagall was trained in St Petersburg and came under the influence of Bakst and the Ballet. He was in Paris 1910–14 and was influenced by Cubism; in 1917 he was made Commissar of Fine Arts in the Vitebsk area and founded an Academy. After disagreements with MALEVICH he resigned and worked for theatres in Moscow, returning to Paris in 1923. By now his highly imaginative style was fully formed, and he was painting more or less recognizable objects in unusual juxtapositions and floating rather insecurely in space, his colour was very rich and most of his subjects were poetic evocations of Russian village life, but he came increasingly to paint religious pictures. His fantasies have greatly influenced the SURREALISTS. In 1941 the Museum of Modern Art, New York, invited him to America, where he remained until 1946. In 1961 he completed a series of stained-glass windows of the Twelve Tribes of Israel for a synagogue near Jerusalem. [ill. 1079, p. 426. Col. pl. 37]

Champaigne, Philippe de (1602–74), was born in Brussels and received his first training there as a landscape painter. He went to Paris in 1621, and worked with POUSSIN on the decoration of the gallery in the Luxembourg Palace which was to house Rubens's series of the Life of Marie de' Medici. In 1628 he became Painter to the Queen Mother, Marie de' Medici, and also worked for Louis XIII and Richelieu, painting for the Cardinal the dome of the Sorbonne church, the fine full-length portrait, and the triple portrait similar to van Dyck's one of Charles I, made for the same purpose – to be sent to Bernini as a model for a portrait bust. About 1643 he began to work for the Jansenists of Port-Royal. This austere Catholic sect deeply influenced him and accentuated his tendency, observable as early as the middle 1630s, towards a form of classicism parallel to that then being developed independently in Rome by Poussin. His early portraits show his links with Rubens and van Dyck, but there is no strong Baroque feeling in his later works – no ecstasies, radiances, visions. All is kept clear and lucid, to appeal to reason rather than to the emotions, with severe composition, frequently of the frieze type used by Poussin, cool, strong colour, and an unexaggerated though strict naturalism. His portraits of lawyers, merchants, and the group portraits of the Sheriffs of Paris, show his human and sensitive grasp of character, and are as grave and sober as his sitters. His finest portraits are those in the votive picture made on the recovery of his daughter, a nun at Port-Royal, who was stricken with paralysis and cured in 1661 by the prayers of the community. There are works in the Royal Collection and in Amsterdam, Barnard Castle (Bowes Mus.), Berlin, Boston, Brussels, Detroit, Florence (Pitti, Uffizi), The Hague, Hull, Le Mans, London (NG, Wallace Coll.), Lyons, New York (Met. Mus.), Paris (Louvre), Rome (Gall. Naz.), São Paulo, Toledo Ohio, Toulouse, Versailles, Vienna, and Washington. [ill. 420, p. 331]

Chantrey, Sir Francis (1781–1841), was a celebrated

sculptor of portrait statues and busts, whose large fortune was bequeathed to the RA for the purchase of 'works of Fine Art of the highest merit . . . executed in Great Britain'. The choice of many works has been criticized. There are works by Chantrey in the Royal Collection, in Edinburgh (NPG), London (NPG, V & A, Soane Mus., RA, Westminster Abbey, St Paul's), Oxford, and elsewhere. [ill. 866, p. 399]

Charcoal is made from twigs of willow or vine which have been charred away from the air. Each twig will then make a blackish mark that is easily rubbed off if necessary. Charcoal is sometimes used for drawing on paper, but its principal use is for making the preliminary drawings on walls or canvases as the first stage in a painting.

Chardin, Jean-Baptiste-Siméon (1699–1779), the finest 18th-century French painter of still-life and genre, became a member of the Academy in 1728 and was its treasurer and hung its exhibitions for over 20 years. His early works are not so much inspired by similar Dutch paintings as extensions of the Netherlandish cabinet pictures so popular in France in the 18th century: they take up the modest size and restricted range of subjects, adapting them to French tastes and feeling. His still-lifes, composed of the simplest elements – kitchen utensils, vegetables, game, baskets of fruit, fish, and similar materials – are exceptional in their impasted technique and solid colour, with tremendous depth of tone achieved by extreme delicacy of touch and the subtle use of dragged and scumbled colour. They have a straightforward honesty of vision and truth of representation untainted by mere verisimilitude. His genre scenes are small in format, with small figures in homely interiors, redolent of the simple domesticity of everyday bourgeois life, unsentimentalized and unidealized, but not rendered picturesque by any concessions to low life, or titillating by excursions into modish society. In the Salons of 1771 and 1775 he exhibited pastel portraits of himself [Col. pl. 42] and his wife (all now in the Louvre) which are masterpieces of acute analysis and breadth of vision and technique, far excelling LATOUR's more fashionable pastel portraits. Fragonard was his pupil for a short time.
There are works in Amiens, Angers, Berlin, Boston, Cambridge Mass. (Fogg Mus.), Chicago, Detroit, Dublin, Edinburgh, Glasgow (Hunterian Mus. and Burrell Coll.), The Hague, Hartford Conn., Indianapolis, Kansas City, Leningrad, London, Merion Pa (Barnes Foundation), Minneapolis, New York (Frick Coll. and Met. Mus.), Oberlin, Ottawa, Paris (Louvre and Jacquemart-André), Potsdam, Princeton, Rotterdam, St Louis, Springfield Mass., Stockholm, Vaduz (Liechtenstein Coll.), Washington (NG and Phillips Gall.). [ill. 707, p. 377. Col. pl. 42]

Charonton *see* QUARTON.

Chassériau, Théodore (1819–56), was a pupil of Ingres who was deeply influenced by Delacroix – the only artist of his time to make this difficult synthesis with any success. He used subject-matter from the repertory of both: Biblical and Shakespearean illustration, scenes from North African life, reconstructions of classical life, religious and allegorical decorations, and portraits, often – like Ingres's –

in lead pencil. He is well represented in the Louvre in Paris, and in French provincial museums. [ill. 748, p. 382]

Chavannes, Puvis de, *see* PUVIS.

Chiaroscuro (Ital. light-dark). As generally used, chiaroscuro (or the French *clair-obscur*) means the balance of light and shadow in a picture, and the skill shown by the painter in the management of shadows. The word tends to be used mainly of painters like Rembrandt or Caravaggio whose works are predominantly dark in tone. A *chiaroscuro woodcut* is a woodcut, linocut, or other similar engraving which is printed from several blocks, in exactly the same way as a colour print, in imitation of a drawing in several shades of monochrome wash, each shade being cut on a separate block. Intermediate tones may be obtained by careful overprinting of two or more blocks. The first artist to specialize in this technique was Ugo da Carpi, and many designs for such woodcuts go back to PARMIGIANINO.

Chirico, Giorgio de' (*b.* 1888), an Italian painter who founded the quasi-Surrealist *Pittura Metafisica* movement. In the 1930s he abandoned his 'modern' ideals and returned to a form of imitation of the Old Masters. There are works by him (mostly unregenerate) in Rome (Gall. d'Arte Mod.) and in Chicago, Detroit, London (Tate), New York (M of MA), and elsewhere. [ill. 1062, p. 424]

Christus Patiens and **Christus Triumphans** are the names given to the two main types of the very large painted crucifixes which normally stood on the rood-screens of medieval churches. Very few still exist in their original positions, most of the surviving examples having been cut down in size and transferred to side chapels or sacristies. The Christus Patiens (Suffering Christ) represents Christ as dead on the Cross whereas the Triumphans type represents Him with open eyes and outstretched arms standing on, rather than hanging from, the Cross. The dramatic emphasis of the Patiens type is certainly to be connected with the influence of S. Francis. An early example is provided by the work of GIUNTA Pisano.

Christus (Cristus), Petrus (*d.* 1472/3), was the major Bruges master after the death of Jan van EYCK (1441). Christus settled there in 1444, but he is nevertheless sometimes said to have been Jan's pupil: two pictures – a *S. Jerome* (1442: Detroit) and a *Madonna* (probably finished 1443: New York, Frick Coll.) – have been claimed as works by Jan finished by Christus. His own dated works range from 1446 to 1452 (or 1457), the latter being a *Madonna* in Frankfurt (Städel) which has some of the characteristics of a *Sacra Conversazione* in the Italian manner. This is signed, but the date is not clear: there is also a portrait in Los Angeles which is very similar in style to ANTONELLO da Messina, but it is not signed and may not be his. These two pictures are often read with a Milanese document of 1457 referring to 'Piero di Burges' to endow Christus with an Italian period and an influence on Antonello. In fact, Christus's style is a simplification of Jan van Eyck's, with very smooth, rounded forms; but he also painted two versions of the *Lamentation* (Brussels and New York, Met. Mus.) which both derive more or less from Roger van der Weyden's Escorial *Deposition*. The New York picture is simpler and the two are put at opposite ends of Christus's career; whether early or late depending on individual choice of the moment of maximum Eyckian influence. There are other pictures by him in Berlin, Copenhagen, Dessau, Kansas City, London (NG), Madrid (Prado), and Washington (NG). [ill. 340, p. 321]

Cibber, Caius Gabriel (1630–1700), sculptor to William III, carved the bas-relief at the base of the Monument, London, in 1673–5 while imprisoned for debt. He worked at Hampton Court (1692–4) and at St Paul's Cathedral (1698–1700), but his best-known works are *Melancholy* and *Raving Madness* (inspired by Michelangelo's Medici tombs) formerly over the gate of Bedlam and now in the Guildhall Museum, London. [ill. 873, p. 398]

Cima da Conegliano, Giovanni Battista (1459/60–1517/18) was a Venetian painter much influenced by Giovanni BELLINI and also by Antonello. There are pictures by him in Amsterdam, Baltimore (Walters), Berlin, Birmingham, Bologna, Boston (Mus. and Gardner), Cambridge (Fitzwm), Conegliano near Treviso (Cath. and S. Fiore), Detroit, Dresden, Edinburgh (NG), Florence (Uffizi), Frankfurt (Städel), London (NG, Wallace Coll., Courtauld Inst.), Milan (Brera, Poldi-Pezzoli, Ambrosiana), New York (Met. Mus.), Paris (Louvre), Parma, Philadelphia (Johnson), Vicenza, Washington (NG), York, besides a large number in Venice. [ill. 141, p. 293. Col. pl. 41]

Cimabue (*c.* 1240–1302 ?) is generally put at the beginning of modern art, as the teacher of GIOTTO (which he may, in fact, have been). The basis of his fame is due to the choice of his name by Dante as an example of the transitory nature of earthly glory: 'Cimabue thought that he held the field in painting, but now Giotto is acclaimed and his fame obscured' ('Purg.' XI, 94–6). The early commentators drove home the moral by insisting that Giotto was Cimabue's pupil and he is consequently credited with the introduction of a more naturalistic style into the Byzantine formulae current in Tuscan Dugento painting. In fact, he is known to have been in Rome in 1272 and may well have been influenced by the classical current which is represented by CAVALLINI; but the sole securely documented work by Cimabue is a *S. John*, part of a large mosaic in the apse of Pisa Cathedral, on which he was working in 1302. This affords only the most tenuous grounds for stylistic generalizations, but there are several works attributed to him on what seem good traditions. These include the very damaged frescoes in the choir of the Upper Church at Assisi and the repainted *Madonna of S. Francis* in the Lower Church as well as the very large and impressive *Sta Trinita Madonna* (Florence, Uffizi) which can reasonably be compared with the *Ognissanti Madonna* by Giotto or the *Rucellai Madonna* attributed to DUCCIO (both in Florence: the latter was formerly attributed to Cimabue). Other works attributed to him are in Arezzo (S. Domenico), Bologna (SM dei Servi), Florence (Baptistry, Sta Croce, SM Novella), Paris (Louvre), and Washington (NG). [ills. 16, 18, p. 271]

Cinquecento (Ital. five hundred). The 16th century, i.e. the fifteen hundreds.

Cione, Nardo and Jacopo di, *see* ORCAGNA.

Cire Perdue *see* BRONZE.

Classic, Classical, Romantic. In addition to the meanings given in any standard English Dictionary there are some extra ones in common use in writings on art. *Classic* is usually used to mean an established excellence and *classicism* a form of art derived (or thought to be derived) from the study of Antique exemplars, which are by definition *classic*: this became a fixed dogma in the mid 18th century, though prevalent enough from the 16th century or even earlier. The 18th-century form is better referred to as NEOCLASSICISM, and, with its passion for rules and Academies, it soon led to a marked reaction. It is a curiosity of history that the French Revolution fostered both ideals simultaneously, but the Romantic movement, with its unbridled expression of the passions, its love of the exotic, and its occasional absurdities reached its apogee about 1830 in France, Britain, and Germany. In France the situation was clarified by the presence of INGRES and DELACROIX as the living embodiments of the two approaches to life and art, and indeed the dichotomy is still apparent in CUBISM and SURREALISM, the antithesis between form and content (or subject). The culmination of 19th-century art can be seen to some extent in CÉZANNE, who began as a positively orgiastic Delacroix follower and ended as one of the great classic French artists, like Poussin.

Claude Gellée (Claude Lorraine) (1600–82) was born near Nancy, and, according to Sandrart, was first trained as a pastry-cook. By *c.* 1613 he was in Italy, working as *garzone* for the Cavaliere d'ARPINO and the landscape painter Agostino Tassi. From 1618 until 1620 he was probably in Naples, then he settled in Rome as Tassi's pupil and assistant. In 1625 he returned to Nancy, but by 1627 was back in Rome; by the end of the 1630s he had a big reputation as a landscape painter and his popularity has remained undimmed ever since. The 195 drawings in the LIBER VERITATIS (now in London, BM) were his own record of his paintings, made to guard against copies and forgeries.

The obvious comparison is with POUSSIN, but while the latter derived his heroic landscapes from Titian and Annibale Carracci, Claude's sources lie chiefly in the romanticized poetic landscapes of the later Mannerists such as Tassi, and the northerners, ELSHEIMER and the BRILLS. Like them, Claude used the later Mannerist traditions of the division of the picture into areas of dark greenish-brown foreground, light green middle distance, and blue far distance, with the composition set out in COULISSES to create a sense of infinite distance, and tree forms treated as feathery fronds in silhouette. He also developed Elsheimer's landscape of mood created by poetic lighting effects, though not so much with strong chiaroscuro as by looking into the sun in a blaze of golden light. His composition remains virtually constant: a large mass of trees on one side counter-balanced by a smaller mass on the other, a middle distance with some small feature such as a bridge or a farm, and a far distance of mountains, rivers, or the Campagna in the most delicately atmospheric handling. In his seascapes and port scenes, the additive details of shipping, masonry, rigging, merchandise lying on quays, does not really alter this

arrangement of the parts, and allows him to concentrate on the magical effects of sunlight shimmering on water. He also uses small figures (possibly sometimes by other artists) not for themselves but as a part of nature, the drama of their action absorbed into immensities of light and space. His working drawings, loose and free in their handling, exemplify his way of looking at landscape by gradations of tone rather than colouristically, and his poetic rather than formal vision. Most older galleries have examples. [ill. 692, p. 375]

Claw Chisel *see* STONE CARVING.

Cleve, Joos van, *see* JOOS.

Clodion. Claude Michel, called Clodion (1738–1814), was a French sculptor who won the Rome Prize in 1759 and went there in 1762. In 1767 he left the French Academy in Rome but stayed on in the city working for Catherine II of Russia and other patrons until he was sharply reminded that he had been sent to Rome at the King's expense for the glory of France. He went home in 1771, but did not become an Associate of the Academy until 1793; never became a full Academician; and never received official commissions, other than the *Montesquieu* for the King (1779–83; the marble now in the Institut, Paris). His works were almost entirely small figures of nymphs, satyresses, and similar subjects treated in a frankly sensual way and he was nearly ruined by the Revolution and Republican Virtue. He rallied, however, and adopted the Greek taste so successfully that he was able to get work on the Colonne de la Grande Armée (1806–10) and the Arc de Triomphe du Carrousel (1806–9). There are works by him in the Louvre, Paris; London, Wallace Collection and V & A; Versailles and other French museums. [ill. 713, p. 378]

Cloisonnisme *see* BERNARD.

Clouet, François (*d.* 1572), was the son of Jean Clouet, whom he succeeded as Court Painter in 1541. He was sometimes called Janet. His earliest signed painting is the *Pierre Quthe* (1562: Paris, Louvre), which seems to indicate that he had been to Italy as it closely resembles the work of BRONZINO and other Florentines. He specialized in portrait drawings, most of which are now in Chantilly (Musée Condé): there are paintings in the Royal Collection and in Edinburgh (NG), Florence (Uffizi and Pitti), London (Wallace Coll.), New York (Met. Mus.), Versailles, Vienna, and Worcester Mass. [ill. 672, p. 372]

Clouet, Jean II ('Janet') (*d.* 1540/1), was probably the son of the Flemish painter Jean Clouet, painter to the Duke of Burgundy. Jean II is first recorded in a poem of 1509 – where he is referred to along with Leonardo and others – and he later became Court Painter, his son François succeeding him in 1541. He made a number of portrait drawings (mostly in the Musée Condé, Chantilly) which are comparable to those of Holbein as records of a Court though quite different in style. Paintings ascribed to him are in the Royal Collection and at Antwerp, Edinburgh (NG), New York (Met. Mus.), and elsewhere. [ill. 673, p. 372]

Cobra see APPEL.

Coello, Claudio (1642–93), was of Portuguese descent but became the last great painter of the School of Madrid. The principal influences on his work seem to have been RUBENS, van DYCK, and TITIAN – that is, he used his opportunities to study in the Spanish Royal Collection. He became Painter to the King in 1684, and was promoted Pintor de Cámara in 1686. His pictures tend to be over-crowded and rather complicated, and are reminiscent of Neapolitan Rococo. His masterpiece is *Charles II adoring the Blessed Sacrament* (1685–90: Sacristy of the Escorial), the space of the actual sacristy being continued in the picture, which contains the portraits of many courtiers and priests. There are other works by him in Frankfurt, London (Wellington Mus.), Madrid (Prado, Acad., and churches), and Munich. [ill. 641, p. 365]

Coello, Sánchez, see SÁNCHEZ.

Cold Colour, Tone: Cool Colour, Tone. Those colours and tones which are blue, blue-green, or blue-violet in general effect. The opposite of HOT or WARM.

Cole, Thomas (1801–48), was the principal painter of the HUDSON RIVER School of American landscape painting. He was born in England and worked as an engraver before emigrating to the US in 1818. In 1819 he went to the W. Indies and was deeply impressed by the beauties of the scenery. His efforts as a landscape painter met with little success until he settled in New York in 1825, when he began to be recognized, and in 1826 he was one of the founders of the National Academy of Design. He returned to England in 1829 and went on to Italy in 1832, living in a studio that traditionally had been Claude's: Cole admired Claude (and therefore Turner) more than any other painter, but his works are far more dramatically Romantic than theirs. He returned to America in 1832, but made another trip to Europe in 1841. He is represented in Cleveland, Hartford Conn., Minneapolis, New York (Met. Mus.), Toledo Ohio (an extraordinary fantasy, *The Architect's Dream*, 1840), and other US museums. [ill. 945, p. 407]

Collage (from Fr. *coller* to stick). A picture built up wholly or partly from pieces of paper, cloth, or other material stuck on to the canvas or other ground. The device was much used by the early Cubists, who would stick pieces of newspaper on to pictures painted in an otherwise normal way, and by the Dadaists. In his last years Matisse used pieces of coloured paper as a complete substitute for painting. *See* FROTTAGE. [ill. 1061, p. 426]

Complementary Colour. Each primary colour – red, blue, yellow – has a complementary formed by a mixture of the other two, and it is part of Impressionist theory that every primary has its complementary colour in the shadow cast by it. Thus, a yellow object will have violet in the shadows.

Composition. The art of combining the elements of a picture or other work of art into a satisfactory visual whole: in art the whole is very much more than the sum of the parts. A picture is well composed if its constituents – whether figures or apples or just shapes – form a harmony which pleases the eye when regarded as two-dimensional shapes on a flat ground. This is the sole aim of most abstract painting but in more traditional forms the task is made much more difficult by the need to project the forms in an ordered sequence into an imaginary depth or picture space without losing their effectiveness as a pattern. The word is often also used loosely to mean a work of art, a group etc.

Conca, Sebastiano (1680–1764), was a belated Baroque decorator. He was born near Naples and trained under SOLIMENA before moving to Rome in 1706. He was much employed in churches and also had a great reputation as a teacher. In 1751 he was commissioned to decorate the church of Sta Chiara in Naples (totally destroyed 1939/45) and he spent the rest of his life there. There are works by him in Augsburg, Dresden, London (NG), Parma, Rome (Accad., Borghese, Gall. Naz., and churches), Sarasota Fla, and elsewhere. [ill. 285, p. 314]

Conegliano see CIMA.

Coninxloo, Gillis van (1544–1607), was an important link in the chain of landscape painters between Bruegel and the early-17th-century Dutch realist painters such as E. van de Velde, van Goyen, or S. van Ruysdael. Coninxloo travelled in France and Germany as well as his native Flanders before settling in Amsterdam, where he died. His type of landscape has much realist detail, especially in the trees and foliage, but is combined with fantasy of shape and of viewpoint, as well as adhering closely to the 'three tone' scheme – warm brownish foreground, green middle distance, and blue distance. There are works in Brussels, Dresden, Graz, and Vienna. [ill. 392, p. 327]

Constable, John (1776–1837), was, with TURNER, the major English landscape painter of the 19th century. He first exhibited in 1802, but achieved only limited recognition, becoming an ARA in 1819 and an RA in 1829. His comment on the Suffolk countryside, 'These scenes made me a painter', takes little account of his skill in composition and his brilliant use of chiaroscuro as a unifying factor. In 1806 he travelled in the Lake District, but he was happiest with the vivid, dewy greens of water-meadows and mills, under fresh, windy skies, his deep knowledge of which he owed to the sky studies made under the influence of Luke Howard's 'The Climate of London' (1818–20). In 1824 his *Hay Wain* (shown at the Academy in 1821: now London, NG) and a *View on the Stour* were awarded a Gold Medal at the Paris Salon, and the great success of these and other works imported into France had an appreciable effect on the development of the BARBIZON School, and on the painting of the Romantic movement – Delacroix, for instance, was enormously impressed by them.
He left few successors. His art lay in the representation of nature modified by the tradition inherited from the Dutch landscape painters of the 17th century, and he was the last great painter in this tradition. After him, Turner's 'airy visions, painted with tinted steam' – the phrase is Constable's – and the meticulous descriptive attitude of the Pre-Raphaelites exploited different, and contradictory, aspects of nature.

A large collection of his work was bequeathed to the Victoria & Albert Museum, London, by his daughter. There are also examples in Boston (Mus.), Cambridge Mass. (Fogg), Chicago, Cincinnati, Detroit, Dublin (NG), Dunedin NZ, Edinburgh (NG), Hartford Conn., Leeds, Le Mans, London (NG, BM, RA Diploma Gall., Tate, Guildhall), Manchester, Montreal, New York (Met. Mus., Frick), Ottawa, Oxford (Ashmolean), Philadelphia (Mus.), San Marino Cal., Toledo Ohio, Toronto, Washington (NG, Corcoran, Phillips), Worcester Mass., Yale University. [ills. 933, 934, p. 406]

Constructivism was principally a Russian movement which grew out of COLLAGE. Vladimir TATLIN in Moscow developed this into hanging and relief constructions, abstract in concept, and made of a variety of materials, including wire, glass, and sheet-metal. He later turned to architectural and engineering schemes such as the projected monument to the Third International – a leaning spiral about 1,300 feet high with counter-rotating central sections. PEVSNER and his brother GABO evolved from Cubism, but only after returning to Moscow in 1917 did they become abstract Constructivists, publishing in 1920 – the year of the big Constructivist exhibition – their 'Realistic Manifesto', in which they restated the ideas of Archipenko and Boccioni that only movement in space and not volume was important in art.
By 1921 the movement was dead in Russia for political reasons and its practitioners turned to furniture design, the stage, typography – in fact, anything but painting and sculpture. Pevsner went to Paris in 1923, and Gabo worked in Germany until 1932. Constructivist ideas have had considerable influence on architecture and decoration, and their manifestations include abstract sculpture employing non-traditional materials such as perspex, or industrial methods such as welding. [ills. 1136–8, pp. 432–3]

Conté. A proprietary name for synthetic black, red, or brown chalk.

Continuous Representation. In many medieval – and some Mannerist – pictures there are representations of several successive incidents in the story, shown as taking place in different parts of the same picture. For example, a picture of the martyrdom of a saint may show all his miracles dotted about in the background. This is conveniently known as Continuous Representation.

Contour (Ital. *contorno*). The outline which, in drawing or painting, forms the boundary of one shape defining it in relation to another, so that the outline of a head against a wall is at once the pattern made by the head at that particular position against the wall, and also the shape as it were cut out of the wall by the impingement of the head. Contour means slightly more than outline, because an attentive study of any good drawing – and more especially one by INGRES – will reveal that the modulation of the contour traced by the point of the pencil can express the fullness and recession of forms and even the variety of texture and surface between bony structure and fatter tissue; whereas outline is no more than a boundary of forms or silhouette.

Contrapposto. An Italian word used to mean a pose in which one part of the body is twisted in the opposite direction from that of the other – usually with the hips and legs in one way and the chest and shoulders twisted on the opposite axis. Michelangelo's fantastic virtuosity in this led to a sort of mania in the 16th century to see who could invent the most elaborate and improbable *contrapposto* for a figure supposedly performing some simple action. *See* Tibaldi. [ills. 191, 201, pp. 300, 303]

Conversation Piece. A special kind of genre picture consisting of two or more small portraits of people represented in appropriate surroundings, usually domestic. It is an informal group portrait and usually represents members of the same family. HOGARTH, DEVIS, and ZOFFANY are among the best-known exponents of the genre.

Cooper, Samuel (1609–72), was an English miniaturist who enjoyed a European reputation: Aubrey called him 'the prince of limners' and his prices were not far short of LELY's. Unlike Hilliard, he regarded the miniature as a painting, not a drawing or piece of goldsmith's work, and he modelled his heads in light and shade. Walpole said: 'If a glass could expand Cooper's pictures to the size of Vandyck's they would appear to have been painted for that proportion. If his portrait of Cromwell could be so enlarged, I do not know but Vandyck would appear less great by the comparison. . . .' The *Cromwell* is the best-known image of the Protector (Coll. of the Duke of Buccleuch, replica in the Royal Coll.). Evelyn's 'Diary' (10 January 1662) records 'Being call'd into his Majesties Closet, when Mr Cooper (the rare limner) was crayoning of his face and head, to make the stamps by, for the new *mill'd* mony, now contriving, I had the honour to hold the Candle whilst it was doing; choosing to do this at night & by candle light, for the better finding out the shadows. . . .' A few days earlier, Pepys had been disappointed in his hopes of meeting Cooper; later, however (30 March 1668), he visited his house and saw his work 'which is all in little, but so excellent as, though I must confess I do think the colouring of the flesh to be a little forced, yet the painting is so extraordinary, as I do never expect to see the like again. . . . Being infinitely satisfied with this sight, and resolving that my wife shall be drawn by him. . . .' In fact, this miniature of Mrs Pepys cost him £30, and another £8. 3. 4. for its crystal and gold case, a large sum of money. Samuel's elder brother, Alexander (*d.* 1660), was also a miniaturist who worked in Holland, Sweden, and Denmark. Both were the pupils of their uncle John HOSKINS, who probably anticipated them in treating a miniature like an oil-painting. Both Coopers are represented in the V & A Museum, London. [ills. 808, 809, p. 392]

Copley, John Singleton (1738–1815), was a Boston painter, almost self-taught, who evolved a distinguished and direct portrait style for his New England clientele. In 1774 he left America for good, visited Italy and much of Europe before settling in London, where competition with Reynolds and West profoundly altered his style, although his children retain an engaging vivacity. His *Brook Watson and the Shark* (1778: Christ's Hospital and Boston), *Death of Chatham* (1780: London, Tate), and *Death of Major Pierson* (1783: Tate), are notable for being among the first large pictures of modern history and grand scale genre subjects, of a type common in France during the Napoleonic period and the Romantic movement. There are examples in the Royal Collection, Cambridge Mass. (Fogg, Harvard), Cleveland Ohio, Dundee, New York (Met. Mus., Brooklyn), N. Carolina, Philadelphia (Hist. Soc.), Providence RI, and Washington (NG, Corcoran), and Yale. The American museums contain most of his early portraits, of which there are many in Boston (Mus., and public buildings). [ills. 842, 915, pp. 394, 403]

Corinth, Lovis (1858–1925), was, like LIEBERMANN, one of the leading German Impressionists. He worked in Paris 1884–7 and painted in an Impressionist style until 1911, when he had a stroke. He was crippled by this, but forced his hand to work and from then on painted in a more violent and pessimistic way: some of his later works are crude and harshly Expressionist. There is a museum at Tapiau, in East Prussia (his birthplace), and he is well represented in German museums: other works are in Basle, Belgrade, London (Tate), New York (M of MA), Pittsburg, Vienna, and Zürich. [ill. 608, p. 359]

Corneille de Lyon (active 1533/4–74) was a painter of small-scale portraits who was born in The Hague but worked in Lyons and was Painter to Henri II and Charles IX of France. There is no known work by him, but a group of small portraits, similar to the work of François CLOUET but faintly Northern in style, is associated with him. They usually show half-length figures in black against a green or blue background: examples are in Boston, London (NG and Wallace Coll.), New York (Met. Mus.). [ill. 671, p. 372]

Cornelius, Peter von (1783–1867), went to Rome in 1811 and there worked with OVERBECK and the NAZARENER until 1819. He then returned to Munich and became head of the so-called Munich School, which sought to revive monumental fresco painting. Most of his works are in Munich, but he was also important as a teacher and administrator. [ill. 612, p. 360]

Corot, Jean-Baptiste-Camille (1796–1875), was born in Paris. His early training, from 1822 onwards, was with the classicizing landscape painters Michallon and Bertin, and in 1825 he went to Italy, via Switzerland, for two years. He spent most of his time in and around Rome, where he developed, through painting actually on the site, his sensitive treatment of light, form, and distance in terms of tonal values rather than by colour and drawing. In this he resembled MICHEL (whom he knew), but never to the point of abandoning, for works to be exhibited, the traditional classical or religious subject; this he used as a disguise for his unconventional vision, although these carefully composed landscapes have little of the spontaneity of his sketches from nature. He travelled widely in France between 1827 and 1834, and returned to Italy for several months in 1834 and 1843, his journeys being recorded in his drawings or his *pochades*, which are small and very freely handled, and remarkable for the justness of their tonal values and the freshness of their colour. By the early 1850s the tide of official and public favour had turned, possibly because by then he had developed for his

Salon exhibits a fuzzy, woolly, poeticizing manner entirely different from the directness and keenness of observation found in his sketches. This muzzy treatment of the landscape and trees in soft, grey-green tones became immensely popular, and has assured to Corot the most notoriously prolific of all posthumous productions. His very late portraits and figure studies are entirely free from the blurred and formless approach of his public manner, and show that in his seventies he was able to absorb the ideas of younger men, such as Courbet and Manet. His personal prestige with the younger generation was very great, and he did all in his admittedly limited power to soften the rigours of the Salon jury towards the works of unacademic artists. He was a man of great simplicity and generosity and extremely charitable, as witness his support of Daumier in his blindness, Millet's widow, and his benefactions during the Franco-Prussian War. There are examples of his art – autograph or attributed – in almost every museum of any size all over the world; the works of Caruelle d'Aligny and Édouard Bertin, who were his companions in Rome in 1825–7 on many of his painting expeditions, are all too frequently confused with his. [ills. 750, 757, 764, pp. 383, 385]

Correggio, Antonio (1494, or 1489–1534), worked mostly in Parma, in a style that looks forward to the Baroque and even, in its softness, to the French 18th century. His earliest works show the combined influences, oddly disparate, of MANTEGNA, whose pupil he traditionally was, and LEONARDO (who influenced all early-16th-century painters in North Italy). From Leonardo he developed a very soft painterly style, extolled by 18th-century critics as MORBIDEZZA, or the 'Correggiosity of Correggio'. This softness, which in works like the SS. *Placid and Flavia* (Parma) is allied to a virtually Baroque movement and emotion, is characteristic of all his oil-paintings and achieves, in his mythologies, a tender and voluptuous quality. His frescoes show so much of the influence of Michelangelo and Raphael as to make a visit to Rome before 1520 fairly certain. He is first documented as a painter in 1514, and his first set of frescoes was painted about 1518: these are the decorations in the Camera di S. Paolo, Parma, which derive partly from the SOTTO IN SÙ perspective of Mantegna's Mantuan frescoes and from his *Madonna della Vittoria*, and partly from Leonardo. Other frescoes in Parma are the cupolas of S. Giovanni Evangelista (1520–3) and the Cathedral (documented from 1522, but probably executed 1526–30). Both these have extremely illusionistic effects as seen from below, and anticipate the ceilings and domes of the 17th century, particularly those of LANFRANCO. The Cathedral dome, representing the Assumption, is composed of ascending concentric circles of flying figures and is said to have been described unkindly (but not altogether unreasonably) by one of the canons as 'a hash of frogs' legs'. Apart from Parma there are no other frescoes by Correggio, but oil-paintings are in the Royal Collection and Berlin, Budapest, Detroit, Dresden, Florence (Uffizi), Frankfurt (Städel), London (NG, Wellington Mus.), Madrid (Prado, Acad.), Milan (Brera, Mus. Civico), Modena, Munich, Naples, New York (Met. Mus.), Paris (Louvre), Philadelphia (Johnson Coll.), Pavia, Rome (Borghese), Vienna, and Washington. [ills. 209, 210, p. 302. Col. pl. 5]

Cortona, Pietro da, *see* PIETRO.

Cosmati. A name given to the marble and mosaic workers in Rome from the 12th to the 14th centuries, many of whom were of the same family. They made many pavements, pulpits, tombs, and other ecclesiastical furnishings in marble with inlays of coloured stones and glass, mosaic and gilding. Towards the end of the period they also produced sculpture. 'Cosmati work' is thus a generic term for work in coloured stone. [ill. 5, p. 269]

Cossa, Francesco del (1435/6–probably 77), worked in Ferrara from 1456 as a follower, to some extent, of Cosmè TURA; but his style was probably first formed in Florence and his *Crucifixion* (Washington, NG) although probably a late work shows clear traces of the style of Castagno. Like all the other Ferrarese of the 15th century he was basically influenced by MANTEGNA and also by Piero della Francesca, whose lost frescoes in Ferrara may well have influenced Cossa's best-known works, the frescoes of the *Months* in the Palazzo di Schifanoia at Ferrara. These were completed in 1470 and Cossa – who did not paint all of the cycle – was so ill-satisfied with his pay that he left the city and spent the rest of his life in Bologna. The Schifanoia frescoes are charming and mildly lascivious, but they can hardly rank with the Camera degli Sposi at Mantua, in which Mantegna also depicted the daily life of a Court, nor (presumably) would they have compared with the lost Pieros. Parts of the Schifanoia frescoes are lost, parts are by pupils, and one Month, *September*, is possibly the earliest work of Ercole ROBERTI. There are works by Cossa in Berlin (Schloss Mus.), Bologna (Pinacoteca and churches), Dresden, Forlì, London (NG), Milan (Brera), Paris (Musée Jacquemart-André), and Washington (NG). [ill. 131, p. 290]

Costa, Lorenzo (*c.* 1460–1535), was trained in Ferrara and brought up on the style of TURA, COSSA, and ROBERTI. He moved to Bologna by 1483 and worked there for the Bentivoglio Court, becoming the partner of Francesco FRANCIA and tempering the ferocity of his Ferrarese style with Francia's Umbrian softness. In 1506 he was appointed Court Painter at Mantua in succession to Mantegna and painted two *Allegories* for Isabella d'Este (now in the Louvre, Paris); later in life, however, ill-health led to his eclipse by GIULIO Romano. There are works by him in the Royal Collection and in Amsterdam, Berlin, Bologna (Pinacoteca, S. Giacomo Maggiore, and other churches), Boston, Dresden, Dublin, Florence (Uffizi), London (NG), Lyons, Mantua (S. Andrea), Milan (Brera), New York (Met. Mus.), Paris (Louvre, Mus. Jacquemart-André), Vaduz (Liechtenstein), and Washington (NG). [ill. 134, p. 291]

Costruzione Legittima. An early PERSPECTIVE system, described in the Treatise on Painting written in 1435 by the architect, humanist, and aesthetic theorist Leon Baptista Alberti (*c.* 1404–72). It is based on geometrically constructed picture space, in which the height of the figures to be represented in the finished picture is taken as the norm by which the base-line of the picture and also the height of the horizon are to be fixed and proportioned. A point approximately in the centre of the horizon then becomes the central Vanishing Point, on which all lines that recede into the picture are made to converge: lines which are parallel to the Picture Plane can have no point on which to converge and an element of distortion is thus introduced, since a house in the picture will seem to have one side subject to the effects of perspective while the other side remains unaffected, as a quadrilateral parallel to the picture plane. Examples of this construction can be found in e.g. the works of UCCELLO. [ill. 67, p. 278]

Cosway, Richard (1742–1821), was a fashionable miniaturist of great charm and ability. He became an RA in 1771, was a collector of Old Master drawings, dealt in pictures as a side-line, was a famous fop and a friend of the Prince of Wales (later George IV). In 1781 he married Maria Hadfield, who had been born and brought up in Florence, and was also a miniaturist, though not in her husband's rare class. They entertained lavishly, and perhaps imprudently in view of the odd rumours which circulated about their house. After her husband's death Maria Cosway returned to Italy, where she ran a girls' school at Lodi until her death in 1838. [ill. 810, p. 392. Col. pl. 52]

Cotes, Francis (1726–70), first made his mark in 1748 as a pastellist. He was a pupil of Knapton, but used brighter colour than his master, and shows the influence of Rosalba Carriera and Liotard. During the 1760s he worked more in oils, and adopted Reynolds's portrait style, in contrast to the more conservative patterns of Knapton. He was Reynolds's most serious competitor before Gainsborough arrived in London, but his portraits have neither Reynolds's inventiveness nor Gainsborough's charm, though at his best – in e.g. his portrait of Sandby (London, Tate) – he is fine indeed. He occupied the house and studio in Cavendish Square later used by Romney. There are examples in the Royal Collection, Leicester, London (Tate), and elsewhere. [ill. 827, p. 393]

Cotman, John Sell (1782–1842), was a painter in watercolour and oil, whose austere sense of design produced some of the finest English landscape paintings of the early 19th century. He was born in Norwich but worked in London, partly with Dr MONRO, and exhibited at the RA 1800–6. He then returned to Norwich and became the leading member of the NORWICH SCHOOL. While living in East Anglia he visited Normandy in 1817–18 and 1820, making drawings for Dawson Turner's 'Architectural Antiquities of Normandy' (1820–2), and in 1834 he returned to London. From 1831 he used watercolour mixed with rice-paste, producing an impasted and richly wrought surface which (to modern taste) is rather vulgar and totally different from his earlier work, which depends solely on simple flat washes of colour and clearly defined, almost geometric, planes. There are works by him in Norwich, London (BM, NG, Tate, V & A, and Royal Inst. of British Architects), and in Birmingham, Hull, Leeds, and Port Sunlight (Lady Lever Gall.). His sons Miles Edmund (1810–58) and John Joseph (1814–78) were also painters. [ill. 928, p. 404. Col. pl. 48]

Coulisse (Fr.). The side-pieces at either side of the stage, so arranged as to give room for exits and entrances. The idea has been taken over to describe the type of composition in which the effect of recession into space is obtained by leading the eye back into depth by the overlaps, usually alternately left and right, of hills, bushes, winding rivers, and similar devices.

Counterproof. A mirror-image reproduction made by damping an original drawing or engraving, laying a damp sheet of clean paper on it, and then running both through a press. It is sometimes done by the artist himself in order to bring a fresh eye to his work by seeing it in reverse, but is also the commonest and simplest method of faking 'original' drawings. Such fakes are easily detected because reversal turns right hands into left, makes the normal diagonal direction of shading appear left-handed and so on. An offset is the same as a counterproof, but has a wider meaning, e.g. in printing.

Courbet, Gustave (1819–77), was born at Ornans, near the Swiss border of France. After he went to Paris in 1840 he taught himself partly by copying in the Louvre, partly by working in the Atelier Suisse. He evolved a vigorous naturalism, tinged with Venetian and Caravaggesque influence, which he used in scenes from everyday life, portraits, nudes, still-life, flowers, seascapes, and land-scapes; these last are often of the mountain scenery near Ornans and sometimes include nudes, hunting scenes, or deer amid snow, and his scenes from daily life extend from the depiction of abject poverty in the *Stonebreakers* (1849: formerly Dresden, destroyed in 1945), to the representation of a peasant funeral in the *Burial at Ornans* (1850: Louvre) which contains over forty lifesize figures, and to a quasi-philosophical manifesto in the huge *Painter in his studio* (1855: Louvre). He was rabidly anti-clerical – his *Return from the Conference*, depicting drunken priests, was rejected both by the official Salon and the Salon des Refusés in 1863, and was finally bought by a strict Catholic who destroyed it – and he further injured himself by meddling in politics and involving himself in the aftermath of the 1848 Revolution and the Commune in 1871. The first added to his reputation of being a dangerous firebrand, as violent as his painting; the second caused him to be imprisoned and heavily fined for his part in the destruction of the column commemorating Napoleon in the Place Vendôme and eventually brought about his flight to Switzerland, where he died.

Courbet was strongly anti-intellectual, despite his friend-ship with Baudelaire and with the socialist writer and theorist Proudhon. He rejected all idealization in art, rebelled against both classicism and romanticism for their literary and exotic subjects, proclaimed that only realism was truly democratic, and that the noblest subject for the artist was the worker and the peasant. He also rejected selection and composition in landscapes, though his own prove this to have been more theory than practice. He exhibited regularly at the Salon, which awarded him a gold medal in 1849, but his works generally incurred bitter criticism. In 1855 and 1867, on the occasion of Inter-national Exhibitions in Paris, he held large private exhibitions of his works in an attempt to offset official neglect. Both attracted more unfavourable than helpful notice, but they established the precedent of privately organized exhibitions, also followed by Manet and the

Impressionists. His flight from France in 1873 prevented him from knowing much of the Impressionists, though he knew Monet personally; he was particularly valuable to them as an example of fairly successful intransigence towards academism. Courbet was a convivial Bohemian, of inordinate vanity, and with an unendearingly caustic tongue. His technique was imperfect; reworkings and bitumen have played havoc with many works, and his brushwork and use of the trowel-shaped palette-knife are often as insensitive as his colour, though in his best works this can be extraordinarily rich, his chiaroscuro deeply satisfying and his vivid, unconventional approach dramati-cally exciting. Many of his nudes range from the mildly to the highly erotic. In his last years, he employed un-worthy assistants in what was virtually a production-line system for painting Swiss landscapes, though at this time he was crippled by the payment of the indemnity exacted by the French State for the Vendôme Column. His ideas and works were more favourably received in Belgium, Holland, and Germany than in France; although he had a certain influence on Whistler, this was indignantly repudiated by the American. There are works in Baltimore, Basle, Berne, Birmingham (Mus.), Boston (Mus., Gardner), Bristol, Cambridge (Fitzwm), Cambridge Mass. (Fogg), Chicago, Cincinatti, Cologne (Mus.), Columbus Ohio, Detroit, Dublin (NG), Glasgow (Mus., Burrell Coll.), Hartford Conn., Kansas City, Leeds, Liverpool, London (NG, Tate, V & A), Manchester, Mannheim, Minneapolis, Montpellier, Montreal, New York (Met. Mus., Brooklyn), Northampton Mass. (Smith College), Ornans, Ottawa, Paris (Louvre, Petit Palais), Philadelphia (Mus., Acad.), Portland Oregon, Providence RI, Rochester NY, St Louis, Toledo Ohio, Toronto, Wash-ington (NG, Corcoran, Phillips), Yale University, and many French provincial museums. [ill. 756, p. 384]

Coustou, Guillaume I (1677–1746), was one of a family of French sculptors. He was a pupil of his uncle COYSE-VOX and went to Rome. He became Director of the Academy and worked for the Crown from 1707; his masterpieces, the *Chevaux de Marly*, were made for the Royal park at Marly 1740/5 and are based on Antique prototypes. They are now at the entrance to the Champs-Élysées in Paris. His son, Guillaume II (1716–77), became an Academician in 1742 and produced much sculpture for churches and public buildings. There is a bust by him in London (V & A) and his *Vulcan*, made for the Academy, is in Paris (Louvre). [ills. 718, 719, pp. 378–9]

Couture, Thomas (1815–79), was a French history and portrait painter whose best-known work is the *Romans of the Decadence* (1847: Louvre), which united the soft colour of the 18th century to the contemporary classic strictness, but is in fact a 19th-century orgy picture of a recognizable type. He was a pupil of GROS and was a good portrait painter, with a bold attack, and is now remembered as MANET's master. His *Etex* (Birmingham) shows his influence: much of the so-called Spanish influence on Manet's early work is in fact derived from Couture's free-dom of handling and sharp tonal contrasts. Outside France there are pictures in Boston, Bristol, Cambridge (Fitzwilliam Mus.) and Cambridge Mass. (Fogg Mus., a sketch for the *Decadence*), Cleveland, Edinburgh, Glasgow, London (Wallace Coll., including the first idea of the *Decadence*, dated 1843), Philadelphia, Providence RI, and Toledo Ohio. [ill. 777, p. 386]

Cox, David (1783–1859), was a watercolour painter who studied for a while under Varley (1804) and first exhibited at the RA in 1805. He lived by teaching and published several books, of which the best known is the 'Treatise on Landscape Painting and Effect in Water-colours', 1813–14 (reprinted 1922). His favourite painting ground was North Wales, but he visited Holland and Belgium in 1826 and France in 1829 and 1832. His effects are extremely broad, with a vigour of handling that sometimes appears forced, as if for exhibition. In 1836 he discovered accidentally a kind of cheap wrapping paper made in Dundee, which exactly suited his style, since the rough, slightly tinted paper absorbed the washes quickly. A similar kind of paper is now marketed as 'Cox Paper'. In 1840 he took lessons in oil-painting from MÜLLER, but his water-colours have always been more prized. The best collection of his work is in his native Birmingham, but other works are in Cardiff, London (BM, Tate, and V & A), Manchester (City Gall. and Whitworth), and other provincial museums. His son David (1809–85) was also a painter. [ill. 942, p. 407]

Coypel, a dynasty of French painters active in the 17th and 18th centuries. The founder was Noël (1628–1707) whose career began in 1646 and who painted in a style derived from POUSSIN. He decorated the Invalides in Paris (*c.* 1700–7), worked for the Gobelins tapestry factory from 1674, and had a distinguished career in the Academy. He became a Member in 1663, Professor 1664, and Director in 1695. The influence of LEBRUN got him the appointment as Director of the French Academy in Rome 1672–4. Some of his writings were published posthumously. There are pictures by him in Paris (Louvre), Madrid, and many French provincial museums.

His son Antoine (1661–1722) was the most famous of the family. He began his training in Rome in 1672 with his father and was made a Member of the Academy in Paris in 1681, becoming Director in 1714, and Rector in 1716. In 1717 he was ennobled. His works are evidence of the triumph of RUBÉNISME by the 1690s, but the vast ceiling of the Chapel at Versailles (1708) is much more reminiscent of Roman High Baroque illusionism as practised by BACICCIA at the Gesù. There are works by him in Berlin, Florence, Madrid, Paris (Louvre), and many French provincial museums.

Antoine's half-brother Noël-Nicolas (1690–1734), was also a painter and pastellist, and became a Member of the Academy in 1720. Antoine's son Charles-Antoine (1694–1752), also had a distinguished academic career, becoming First Painter to the King in 1743 and Director of the Academy in 1747. He was widely read and himself wrote forty pieces for the stage; Voltaire remarked that there was no other example in his day, 'De rimeur peignant de sa force, Ni de peintre rimant comme lui.' His huge output included book-illustrations and tapestry designs as well as religious pictures, portraits and writings on art. He was the originator of the idea of the École royale des Élèves protégés which was a special school for promising Academy students

who received a State pension and an education fitting them for further training at the French Academy in Rome and subsequent membership of the Academy itself. The programme of the school consisted of professional studies in painting and sculpture and courses in ancient and modern literature and history, mythology, and all the learning thought proper to the painter of history in the 18th century. There are works by him in Paris (Louvre, Mus. Jacquemart-André, and Gobelins Mus.) and in other French museums, and in Berlin, Cleveland Ohio, Hartford Conn., Minneapolis, New York (Met. Mus.), Philadelphia, and Sarasota Fla. [ills. 698, 701, pp. 376–7]

Coysevox, Antoine (1640–1720), was the chief sculptor to Louis XIV of France and worked much at Versailles, in a vigorous Baroque style derived ultimately from Bernini. This may also be seen in his portraits, such as the *Charles Lebrun* (London, Wallace Coll., the original terracotta) or the *Matthew Prior* (Westminster Abbey). He is well represented in the Louvre, Paris. [ill. 696, p. 367]

Cozens, Alexander (*c.* 1717–86), was born in Russia (though the picturesque story that Peter the Great was his father is not now credited). He was in Rome in 1746 and appears to have gone to the Continent again in 1764, but most of his time was spent as a drawing master. He is best known for his system of 'BLOT drawings' – in 1781 Beckford described him as 'almost as full of systems as the Universe' – which developed an idea adumbrated by Leonardo da Vinci. A blot or dots made haphazard on the drawing paper would suggest a landscape or other composition, which could then be worked out in full. This system was set out in his 'New Method of assisting the Invention in Drawing Original Compositions of Landscape' (1785/6). He also wrote several other books. There are drawings and blottings by him in London (BM, V & A, and Tate Gall.), and in Birmingham and Manchester (Whitworth). [ill. 918, p. 404]

Cozens, John Robert (1752–97), was the son of Alexander Cozens and was, according to Constable, the 'greatest genius that ever touched landscape' . . . 'Cozens is all poetry'. His entire work consists of landscape painting in watercolours and only one oil-painting, of 1791, is known (in a private collection). He went to Switzerland and Italy with the famous connoisseur Payne Knight in 1776–9 and was in Rome in 1778–9, when his style seems to have been modified by contact with Swiss watercolourists, notably Ducros, who was said to be an innovator in technique. He returned to Switzerland and Italy, going as far south as Naples, in 1782–3, this time in the train of William Beckford, the eccentric author of 'Vathek'. On these journeys Cozens discovered the grandeur of the Swiss Alps as well as the better-known classical beauties of the Italian landscape; his gentle and poetic landscapes are muted in colour and soft in lighting, being predominantly blue-green or blue-grey in tonality. Some time in 1793 his mind gave way, and early in 1794 he was under the care of Dr MONRO, who regarded him as incurable. He died in 1797 without recovering. He exercised an enormous influence on the next generation since both Turner and Girtin worked for Dr Monro and copied drawings by Cozens. There are watercolours by him in the Royal Collection and in Aberdeen, Birmingham, Cambridge (Fitzwm), Leeds, London (BM, V & A, Tate, Soane Mus.), Manchester (Whitworth), Oxford (Ashmolean), and elsewhere. [ill. 919, p. 404]

Cranach, Lucas I (1472–1553), painter, etcher, and designer of woodcuts, was in Vienna in 1503 and had probably been there since 1500. In 1505 he went to Wittenberg to become Court Painter to the Electors of Saxony and there he met Luther, became his friend and designed propaganda woodcuts for him. His earliest works are religious subjects in which the landscape plays a great part; they are therefore linked with the ideas of the DANUBE School. In Wittenberg his style changed considerably, partly on account of the large shop he set up. He seems to have invented the full-length portrait as an independent work of art, for the splendid pair of *Henry the Pious of Saxony* and his *Duchess* (1514: both in Dresden and probably originally on one panel) certainly ante-dates the Italian examples by MORETTO and others, and probably ante-dates other German examples; only CARPACCIO's *Knight* has a claim to be earlier. All his life Cranach continued to paint splendid portraits, including a large number of versions of *Luther*, but at the same time he developed a new kind of highly erotic female nude, usually full-length, painted with a glossy enamel-like finish and purporting to represent Lucretia, Venus, or some other character. From about 1505 to 1509 he made a number of woodcuts, much influenced by Dürer, and from about 1520 he designed many more, often rather crudely executed, to illustrate the Bible or the writings of the Reformers. Most of his pictures are signed with a winged snake and the monogram LC, but it is very difficult to distinguish his own works from those produced in his shop or by his sons Hans (d. 1537) and Lucas II (1515–86). There are pictures in the Royal Collection and in Augsburg, Basle, Berlin, Boston, Breslau (Mus. and Cath.), Bristol, Brunswick, Brussels, Budapest, Cincinnati, Cologne (Wallraf-Richartz), Darmstadt, Detroit, Dresden, Florence (Uffizi), Frankfurt (Städel), Glasgow (Burrell), Kansas City, Leipzig, Leningrad, Lisbon, Liverpool, London (NG, Courtauld Inst.), Milwaukee, Munich, New York (Met. Mus.), Nuremberg, Oslo, Ottawa, Paris (Louvre), Philadelphia, Sarasota Fla, Stockholm, Vaduz (Liechtenstein), Vienna (K-H Mus., Akad., and Albertina), Weimar, and many other German museums. [ills. 569–72, p. 356]

Craquelure. The network of fine cracks which covers the surface of any old painting, caused by shrinkages and the movement of the ground and the paint film and varnish. There are characteristic crack-formations for each type of ground and paint film and they also vary with age and with the skill of the original painter. *Craquelure* remains one of the principal means of proving forgery, even though really high-class forgers use elaborate electrical and chemical means of counterfeiting the effects of time.

Credi, Lorenzo di (c. 1458–1537), was a Florentine painter who was the fellow-pupil of LEONARDO under VERROCCHIO, whose principal assistant on the painting side of the business he seems to have become. He was in Verrocchio's shop in 1480/1 and was still there in 1488, when

Verrocchio died. His style is technically admirable but is otherwise an insensitive and highly-coloured version of Leonardo's earlier works. There are several works by him in Florence and others in Berlin, Boston (Gardner), Cambridge Mass. (Fogg), Cleveland, Dresden, Liverpool, London (NG), Naples, New York (Met. Mus.), Oxford (Ashmolean), Paris (Louvre), Philadelphia (Johnson), Princeton NJ, San Marino Cal., the Vatican, Yale, York, and elsewhere. [ill. 102, p. 284]

Crespi, Daniele (c. 1598–1630), was probably related to G.B. Crespi and was much influenced by him. His career was cut short by the plague of 1630, but like Cerano he expressed Counter-Reformation piety, and his best-known work is the *S. Charles Borromeo's Lenten Meal* (c. 1628) in S. Maria della Passione, Milan, which has many other paintings by him. His *S. Bruno* cycle in the Certosa at Garegnano, Milan, of 1629, shows the influence of Rubens and van Dyck and was followed by a similar, less good, cycle in the Certosa at Pavia. There are works in Milanese museums and churches and also in Berlin, Budapest, Florence (Uffizi), Madrid (Prado), Munich, Piacenza (S M di Campagna), Vienna (K-H Mus.), and Wellesley College, Mass. [ill. 214, p. 303]

Crespi, Giovanni Battista 'Il Cerano' (c. 1575–1632), was the major Lombard Mannerist of the early 17th century. He was born at Cerano, near Novara, and visited Rome and Venice; as a result, the main influence on his early style, Gaudenzio FERRARI, was overlaid by the influences of BAROCCI, Tintoretto, and Veronese. He settled in Milan c. 1598 and worked for Cardinal Federigo Borromeo, contributing to the scenes from the life of S. Charles Borromeo, painted for Milan Cathedral between 1602 and S. Charles's canonization in 1610. In 1620 he was appointed first Director of the painting section of the Cardinal's newly-founded Accademia Ambrosiana, and in 1629 he became head of the sculpture workshop of the Cathedral (his designs for sculpture are in the Cath. Mus.). His paintings reflect the piety of the age of S. Charles (d. 1584) and are Mannerist principally on account of their emotional quality and their pale, clear tonality with a favourite lemon, grey, and pink colour scheme. There are works in many Milanese churches and in the Ambrosiana, Brera and Castello Museums and also in Bristol, Detroit, Florence (Uffizi), Pavia (Certosa), Princeton NJ, Turin, Varese (S. Vittore), and Vienna. [ill. 213, p. 303]

Crespi, Giuseppe Maria (1665–1747), was a Bolognese painter, trained in the academic tradition, which he came to loathe. In his youth, Bologna was still the Mecca of foreigners studying in Italy, but he predicted its end as a School and lived long enough to see it replaced by Rome. He developed a vivid genre style: dark shadows and very strong lights – time has accentuated the contrasts – and a passion for effects of light, which often involved a surrender to anecdote and gives the details of his settings an almost Dutch character, although they are, in fact, derived from the Caravaggesque tradition. He influenced PIAZZETTA, who used his low tones, rich greys, and his light effects. He died blind. There are works in Birmingham, Bologna, Boston (Mus.), Cambridge Mass. (Fogg), Dresden (the *Sacraments*, his best-known works), Florence

(Uffizi, Pitti), Munich, Paris (Louvre), St Louis, the Vatican, Vienna, Washington (NG), and elsewhere. [ill. 279, p. 312]

Cristus, Petrus, *see* CHRISTUS.

Critz *see* GHEERAERTS.

Crivelli, Carlo (*d.* 1495/1500), was a Venetian, recorded there in 1457, and probably trained under the VIVARINI. He was deeply influenced by the Paduans, including MANTEGNA, to whom he probably owes the wiry outline which bounds his figures. There is a strong element of Late Gothic fantasy in his work, which was mostly done in the Marches and not in Venice at all. The Brera at Milan and the NG, London, have the best collections of his pictures. Vittorio Crivelli, perhaps Carlo's brother, worked in the same style. [ill. 135, p. 291]

Crome, John (1768–1821), was, with COTMAN, the major artist of the NORWICH School. He began life as an errand boy but apprenticed himself to a sign painter and is said to have taught himself by being allowed to copy Gainsborough and Hobbema: certainly the Dutch 17th century is the principal influence on his style, together with that of Wilson. His observation of Norfolk scenery has the same freshness as Hobbema and Ruisdael, while Cuyp and Wilson influenced his sense of design and of light. He founded the Norwich Society of Artists in 1803 and exhibited regularly there. In 1814, along with many other British artists, he went to Paris to see the pictures looted by Napoleon, and on the way he visited Belgium. He was a notable etcher and is well represented in the BM. There are paintings by him in Norwich and in Boston, Edinburgh, London (NG, Tate, Kenwood), New York (Met. Mus.), Ottawa, and elsewhere. He is often called 'Old Crome' to distinguish him from his son John Bernay Crome (1793–1842), who imitated him. The *Water Frolic* (London, Kenwood) is probably a joint work: others by the son are in Norwich. [ills. 925, 926, p. 405]

Cross-hatching *see* HATCHING.

Cubism is the parent of all abstract art forms. It grew out of the efforts of PICASSO and BRAQUE to replace the purely visual effects of Impressionist preoccupation with the surface of objects with a more intellectual conception of form and colour. Their starting-point was Cézanne, who had striven to the same ends, but Cubism carried much further the ideas of the unity of the two-dimensional picture surface, and the analysis of forms and their interrelation, since they deliberately gave up the representation of things as they appear in order to give an account of the whole structure of any given object and its position in space. This meant, in practice, combining several views of the object all more or less superimposed, expressing the idea of the object rather than any one view of it. The first exhibition of such pictures was in 1907 in Paris. The name Cubism was derisive, for it excited as much opposition as Impressionism itself, or the then recent FAUVISM: it was much influenced by Negro art, by Picasso's interest in Iberian sculpture, and by reaction from the pattern-

making of Fauvism. Gris, Léger, Delaunay, and Derain were among the early adherents and the new aesthetic was soon preached by two practising Cubist painters, Gleizes and Metzinger, whose book, 'Du Cubisme', was published in 1912 and later translated into English, while the poet Apollinaire followed in 1913 with 'Les Peintres Cubistes'. The first phase, under the influence of Cézanne, lasted from 1906 to 1909; the second, sometimes called High or Analytical Cubism, lasted from 1909 to 1912 and excluded interest in colour or handling while concentrating on the breaking down of forms; finally, Late or Synthetic Cubism (1912–14) allowed a re-emergence of tactile qualities, colour, and handling. ORPHIC CUBISM is a derivative. [ills. 1041, 1045–8, 1051, 1132, 1133, pp. 421, 422, 431. Col. pl. 36]

Currier, Nathaniel, published in 1840, three days after the disaster, a highly-coloured print of the burning of the steam-boat 'Lexington' in Long Island Sound. The edition went like wildfire, and established him as the most important publisher of 'Colored engravings to the People'. James Ives joined the firm in 1852, and it became Currier and Ives in 1857. The prints were lithographs, hand-coloured on a mass-production system of one girl to each colour, and for some 50-odd years they published about three new prints each week on every aspect of American life – views, portraits of notabilities, Wild West, Indian, sporting and pioneering scenes, fires and other disasters, the Civil War, temperance and political tracts – which reached into the farthest confines of the land, and also had a considerable sale abroad. [ill. 917, p. 403]

Cuyp, Aelbert (1620–91), was a Dordrecht painter, principally of landscape and animals, but also of seapieces, portraits, and still-life, such versatility being rare in the Dutch School. He was the son and pupil of Jacob Gerritsz. Cuyp (1594–after 1651), a painter of portraits and landscapes. In his earlier works Aelbert was influenced by van GOYEN and S. van RUYSDAEL and painted landscape with the same fidelity to nature; later, however, he became more and more interested in the play of light, and especially of those effects of golden glow which the Italianate Dutch landscape painters had learned from Claude. In his later works Cuyp resembles Jan BOTH in his light effects and his use of semi-Italian scenery and *staffage*. His light is, however, always poetic in feeling and exerted an incalculable influence on the development of English painting, since nearly all his best works are still in Britain; in the Royal Collection, in Glasgow (a rare religious work), London (NG, Wallace Coll., Dulwich, Kenwood), Oxford, and in other galleries and many private collections. Others are in Amsterdam (Rijksmus.), Antwerp, Berlin, Brussels, Cape Town, Dordrecht, Dublin, Frankfurt (Städel), The Hague, Munich, New York (Met. Mus.), Paris (Louvre), Philadelphia, Rotterdam, Toledo Ohio, Toronto, Vienna (K-H Mus.), and Washington (NG). Many pictures signed AC are by his imitator Abraham CALRAET.
Benjamin Gerritsz. Cuyp (1612–52), was Aelbert's father's half-brother and painted genre scenes in the manner of OSTADE, with some influence from the early Rembrandt. [ills. 430, 506, 527, 532, pp. 333, 346, 349–50]

Dada (Fr. hobby-horse) was a nihilistic precursor of SURREALISM, invented in Zürich during World War I, a product of hysteria and shock lasting from about 1915 to 1922. It was deliberately anti-art and anti-sense, intended to outrage and scandalize, and its most characteristic production was the reproduction of the *Mona Lisa* decorated with a moustache and the obscene caption LHOOQ (read: *elle a chaud au cul*) 'by' DUCHAMP. Other manifestations included ARP'S COLLAGES of coloured paper cut out at random and shuffled, ready-made objects such as the bottle drier and the bicycle wheel 'signed' by Duchamp, Picabia's drawings of bits of machinery with incongruous titles, incoherent poetry, a lecture given by 38 lecturers in unison, and an exhibition in Cologne in 1920, held in an annexe to a café lavatory, at which a chopper was provided for spectators to smash the exhibits – which they did.

Daddi, Bernardo (*c.* 1290–1349/51), was a pupil of Giotto but was influenced by the Lorenzetti: that is to say, he attempted to fuse the plastic qualities of Giotto with some aspects of Sienese art and in this he represents the trend of the generation after Giotto, both in Florence and Siena. His triptych of 1328 in Florence, Uffizi, is a typical work; other works are in Florence and in the Royal Coll. and Baltimore, Berlin, Boston (Mus. and Gardner), Cambridge Mass. (Fogg), Edinburgh, London (Wallace Coll.), New York (Met. Mus., Historical Soc.), Paris (Louvre, Musée des Arts Décoratifs), Philadelphia (Johnson), the Vatican, Washington (NG), and York. [ill. 25, p. 272]

Dahl, Michael (1656/9–1743), was a Swedish painter who was KNELLER'S only serious rival. He probably came to London about 1682, made a Grand Tour in 1685, travelling through Paris, staying long in Rome, and visiting Venice and Naples before returning via Frankfurt to London, where he decided to settle in 1689. He had a long and successful career. His style is softer than Kneller's, warmer and less forced. There are works in London (NPG, Nat. Marit. Mus., Dulwich), English provincial museums, and Stockholm. [ill. 820, p. 393]

Dali, Salvador (*b.* 1904), was originally a Cubist but became one of the leading Surrealists until he abandoned its implied Marxism and returned to the Catholic Church. Glasgow, New Brunswick, New York, and other US museums have pictures. [ill. 1054, p. 423]

Dance of Death (Ger. *Totentanz*). A typically macabre late medieval subject, in which Popes, Emperors, Lords, and so on down to Artisans are shown as being whirled off in a dance with skeleton Popes, Emperors, and so on

and not enjoying the experience. The most celebrated of these is the woodcut series by HOLBEIN the Younger. [ill 579, p. 357]

Danti, Vincenzo (1530–76), was a Perugian sculptor much influenced by Michelangelo. His first work was the bronze *Julius III* (1555: Perugia) but he later worked mainly in Florence, where he is best known for his completion of Sansovino's *Baptism of Christ*, on the Baptistry, and for his own bronze group of the *Decollation of S. John Baptist*, also on the Baptistry. There are other works in Florence, in the Bargello and elsewhere. [ill. 165, p. 295]

Danube School (Ger. *Donauschule, Donaustil*). This is really only a name for the pre-eminence of the Danube region in the formation of modern landscape painting: the romantic effects and the emotional sympathy between landscape and human action found in ALTDORFER'S pictures are the principal examples but other major painters of the 'School' are the young CRANACH and Wolf HUBER.

Daret, Jacques (*d.* after 1468), was a painter in Tournai who, in 1427, became the apprentice of CAMPIN. He painted an altarpiece for S. Vaast, Arras, 1434–5 (now in Berlin, Lugano (Thyssen Coll.) and Paris (Petit Pal.)), which is documented as his, and which shows very strongly the influence of the MASTER of FLÉMALLE: hence the identification of Flémalle with Campin receives strong support. Some light is also cast on the origins of Roger van der WEYDEN. [ill. 333, p. 320)

Daubigny, Charles-François (1817–78), was a French landscape painter much influenced by the BARBIZON School, who worked mostly near Paris but who went to Italy in 1836 and also visited England, Spain, and Holland. He was a friend of Corot and was admired by Monet; he thus forms a link between the Impressionists and their predecessors of the Barbizon School. There are pictures by him in Aberdeen, Boston, Edinburgh (NG), Glasgow, London (NG, Tate), Montreal, New York (Met. Mus.), and Washington, as well as many French museums. [ill. 758, p. 385]

Daumier, Honoré (1808–79), worked as a cartoonist on 'La Caricature', founded in 1830, and was imprisoned in 1832 for representing King Louis-Philippe as Gargantua. After the suppression of 'La Caricature' in 1835, he joined 'Charivari', and made, for this and other similar journals, some 4,000-odd lithographs, mostly of the aptest and bitterest political and social satire. His watercolours and wash drawings of scenes in the Courts of Justice, and every-day life, are untouched by any romantic feeling for picturesque poverty and his large oil-paintings, many on the theme of Don Quixote, are loosely handled, with calligraphic brushwork and intense light and shadow. He became blind in his old age, and was rescued from desperate povery by Corot.

There are works in Baltimore (Mus., Walters), Boston (Mus.), Cambridge Mass. (Fogg), Cardiff, Glasgow, London (NG, BM, V & A, Tate, Courtauld Inst.), Montreal, New York (Met. Mus., Brooklyn), Ottawa, Paris (Louvre, Petit Pal.), Philadelphia (Mus.), Washington (NG, Corcoran, Phillips), and elsewhere. [ills. 782, 783, p. 388]

David, Gerard (*d.* 1523), was born in Oudewater in Holland but was in Bruges by 1484. He was the last master of the Bruges School, painting gently pious pictures in a 15th-century style which was superseded in his own lifetime by the new, Italianate, Antwerp style, just as the commercial prosperity of Bruges faded before the rise of Antwerp. David seems to have gone to Antwerp and joined the Guild there in 1515, but he was certainly back in Bruges by 1521 and he died there. His only documented picture is a *Sacra Conversazione* (1509: Rouen), but two *Justice Scenes* of 1498 are certainly his (Bruges). Many pictures are ascribed to him, in Amsterdam (Rijksmus.), Antwerp, Berlin, Brussels, Chicago, Cleveland, Denver, Detroit, Dublin, Edinburgh, the Escorial, Florence (Uffizi), Frankfurt (Städel), Granada, Greenville SC, London (NG), Madrid (Prado), Munich, New York (Met. Mus., Frick Coll.), Paris (Louvre), Philadelphia (Johnson), St Louis, Stockholm, Toledo Ohio, Vienna, and Washington (NG), and elsewhere. [ill. 349, p. 323]

David, Jacques-Louis (1748–1825), was distantly related to Boucher, who recommended his being placed under VIEN in 1765. He won the Prix de Rome in 1774, and went there with Vien in 1775, remaining until 1781. He abruptly forsook Boucher's Rococo in favour of the new NEO-CLASSICISM and at the same time adopted the strong chiaroscuro of the Caravaggesques. In 1782 he became an Academician and in 1784 he returned to Rome to paint *The Oath of the Horatii* (1785: Paris, Louvre), which was acclaimed in Rome and again in Paris at the Salon of 1785. It was perhaps the most important French Neoclassic picture, simple, severe, and uncompromising in its subordination of colour to drawing; it was also highly topical in its Republican implications. It was followed by other large pictures extolling classical and republican virtues. During the Revolution David became a Deputy and voted for the death of Louis XVI. He became dictator of the arts, designed huge propaganda processions – such as the Feast of Reason – abolished the Academy, and helped to found the Institut which replaced it; he also painted memorial portraits of the martyrs of the Revolution, Lepelletier de Saint-Fargeau and Marat. After the fall of Robespierre he was imprisoned, and his release was due to the intercession of his pupils and his wife, who had divorced him because of his Revolutionary activities but who now remarried him and lived happily with him for another 31 years. The *Sabine Women* was begun in 1798, partly in recognition of her devotion, partly as a manifesto of his passion for the

Antique. In the same year he met Napoleon and became an ardent Bonapartist. Napoleon fully appreciated the uses of a great painter as a propagandist, and as part of the Napoleon Saga David painted *Napoleon crossing the Alps* and worked 1805–7 on the huge *Coronation*, containing over a hundred portraits, and followed this with *The Emperor distributing the Eagles*. After Waterloo he fled to Switzerland and eventually retired to Brussels, where he died.

Several contradictory strains combine in David's art – from the stern Neoclassicism of his youth he moved, in the Napoleonic pictures, towards a Venetian use of colour and light, and yet contemporary and later pictures of classical subjects show a concentration on drawing and a rigid antiquarianism at variance with all that Venetian influence implies. His portraits are always supremely well designed and full of realism, yet his later classical subjects betray a progressive sweetening of style, perhaps due to the stultifying influence of his self-imposed exile, cut off from the stimulating conflict of ideas resulting from the rise of Romanticism. He was a great teacher, whose many pupils included GÉRARD, GIRODET, GROS, and INGRES. Most of his large pictures are in Paris (Louvre, Petit Pal., Jacquemart-André, and École des Beaux-Arts; others in Aix-en-Provence, Algiers, Angers, Avignon, Berlin (Charlottenburg), Besançon, Boulogne, Buffalo NY, Cambridge Mass. (Fogg Mus.), Cherbourg, Cincinnati, Cleveland Ohio, Detroit, Hartford Conn., Kansas City, Le Mans, Lille, Lyons, Montauban, Montpellier, New York (Met. Mus. and Rockefeller Inst. for Medical Research), Northampton Mass. (Smith Coll.), Rome (Mus. Napoleonico), Rouen, Springfield Mass., Troyes, Versailles, Vienna (Belvedere), and Washington (NG). [ills. 742, 744, p. 382]

Deësis (Gk.). A group of Christ enthroned in Majesty, with the Virgin and S. John on either side. The idea is Byzantine, but the best-known representation is in the Ghent Altar. It is often used as the central group in a Last Judgement. [ill. 336, p. 321]

Degas, Edgar (1834–1917), was born in Paris of a wealthy family. He studied at the École des Beaux-Arts under a pupil of Ingres, whom he knew and deeply admired. His early works – family portraits and some history pictures – suggest that he was to develop into an academic painter in the Ingres tradition. By the late 1860s, however, he had begun to develop a deceptively casual composition, probably influenced by Manet and possibly also by Whistler. He knew Manet well, as he did Bazille, Berthe Morisot, and Tissot, and was a frequent member of the circle which gathered round Manet, where he also met Fantin-Latour, Renoir, Constantin Guys, Cézanne, Monet, Sisley, and Pissarro. During the Franco-Prussian War he remained in Paris and in 1872–3 he visited relations in New Orleans. Here he painted only a few works, but these – and those executed after his return to Paris – show him using unusual viewpoints and purely contemporary subject-matter. He ceased exhibiting at the Salon in 1870, and in 1874 he took part in the First Impressionist Exhibition, as he did in six of the subsequent seven. His works could only be seen in public at these group exhibitions (always received with hostility and ridicule) and at the dealer, Durand-Ruel, whose patient and persevering faith in IMPRESSIONISM nearly ruined him. Unlike Monet, and some others in the group, Degas had a private income which made him independent of sales of his work, and he was less than understanding over their defections from the group exhibitions (which he largely organized) in order to send works to the Salon in an endeavour to attract purchasers.

His first pictures of dancers were painted about 1873, and from then on ballet girls, working girls, models dressing and bathing, and cabaret artists became his principal subject-matter. He recorded the manners and movements of a society which he observed almost as if it were another world, and these figures were treated as the material of his investigations into light, colour, and form as much as the pastel or paint he used. Technically, he was one of the greatest experimenters and innovators. His sound knowledge of the traditional technique of oil painting enabled him to make endless trials of various media and mixtures such as oil-paint thinned with turpentine after the oil has been partly extracted with blotting-paper (*peinture à l'essence*), pastel used in superimposed layers, or with watercolour or turps-thinned oil-paint, or thinned with water, gouache, egg tempera, etching, drypoint, monotype, lithography, aquatint, and drawing in every material [Col. pl. 43]. In later life, he used pastel more than any other medium, and as his eyesight weakened so that handling became broader and freer. There are also 74 pieces of sculpture – late works – including ballet dancers and figures in movement, originally executed in wax, but now generally cast in bronze. The most unusual is the large figure of the little ballet girl wearing a real net *tutu* (London, Tate).

There are works in Baltimore (Walters), Berlin, Birmingham, Boston (Mus., Gardner), Cambridge Mass. (Fogg), Chicago, Cleveland Ohio, Columbus Ohio, Copenhagen, Detroit, Dumbarton Oaks, Frankfurt (Städel), Glasgow (Burrell Coll.), Hartford Conn., London (NG, Tate, V & A, Courtauld Inst.), Los Angeles, Lyons, Minneapolis, Moscow, New York (Met. Mus., M of MA, Brooklyn, Frick Coll.), Ottawa, Paris (Louvre, Mus. de l'Impressionnisme, Mus. Gustave Moreau), Pau, Philadelphia (Mus.), Rochester NY, São Paulo, St Louis, Stockholm, Toledo Ohio, Toronto, Vienna, Washington, and elsewhere. London (Tate) and New York (Met. Mus.) have good collections of the sculptures. [ills. 751, 779, 795, 798, pp. 383, 386, 389. Col. pls. 25, 43]

Del., Delin. (Lat. *Delineavit*, he drew it) after a name on an engraving or drawing is an assertion of authorship.

Delacroix, Eugéne (1798–1863), was the major painter of the Romantic movement in France. He was a pupil of Baron Guérin (teacher also of GÉRICAULT) whose lack of artistic authority made his studio tolerant of new ideas. Delacroix was the ardent admirer rather than an intimate friend of Géricault, but in the grim year which preceded his death was a frequent visitor to his studio. To Géricault's influence is probably due Delacroix's interest in English art and in animal painting, and his revolt from the classicizing forms. and classical literary subject which still dominated French painting in the early 19th century. He admired GROS, studied Rubens and Veronese, and was a friend of Bonington and an admirer of Constable. He was

in England in 1825 and was much impressed by the charm of English colour and freshness of handling, particularly in landscape, and the predominance of medieval and anecdotic subject pictures.

His first Salon exhibit (*Dante and Virgil crossing the Styx*, 1822: Paris, Louvre) was well received, but subsequent ones (*The Massacre at Chios*, 1824; *Sardanapalus*, 1829: both Louvre) were bitterly attacked for his use of brilliant colour, contemporary and exotic literary subjects, and free handling, in which was seen the influence of Géricault and English art and a rejection of traditional French classicism. In 1832 he visited North Africa and this opened to him a whole new field of subjects: scenes from Arab and Jewish life, animal subjects, innumerable combinations of illustrations to Byron and allusions to the Greek wars against the Turks abound in his gigantic *œuvre* after this, and share the honours with Scott and Shakespeare as constant sources of inspiration. From the mid-1830s he was in official favour, receiving commissions for large-scale decorations in which INGRES, his greatest rival and inveterate opponent, was unsuccessful. His principal decorations were the *Justice of Trajan* for Rouen Town Hall (1840), the ceiling of the Salon d'Apollon in the Louvre (1849), and works in the Libraries of the Chamber of Deputies and the Senate (1838–47), S. Sulpice (1857–60), and the Hôtel de Ville (destroyed in 1870). But the works he is happiest with are small, freely handled, colourful subjects – battles, hunts, animals in combat, and portraits of intimate friends such as Chopin (1838: Louvre). His Diary, kept from 1822 to 1824 and again from 1847 to 1863 is a precious source for his life and work and as a commentary on the social, intellectual, and artistic world of Paris. Delacroix only occasionally had pupils, and never taught in the sense that Ingres did, though he had assistants for his large decorations. He left no artistic succession, for the essence of Romanticism is its personal quality. His contribution to the struggle of the non-conforming artist against entrenched classicism is reflected in his long wait for election to the Institut (1857), the frequent battles over the admission of his works to the Salon and the veneration in which he was held by younger artists.

There are works in Baltimore (Mus., Walters), Bordeaux, Boston (Mus., Gardner), Bristol, Buffalo, Cambridge Mass. (Fogg), Chantilly, Chicago, Cincinnati, Cleveland Ohio, Dublin, Edinburgh (NG), Glasgow, Hartford Conn. (Wadsworth), Lille, London (NG, Wallace Coll.), Los Angeles, Metz, Minneapolis, Montpellier, Montreal, New York (Met. Mus., Brooklyn), Northampton Mass. (Smith), North Carolina (Univ.), Paris (Carnavalet), Philadelphia, Princeton Univ., Rheims, São Paulo, St Louis, Toledo Ohio, Toronto, Toulouse, Versailles, Victoria NSW, Washington (NG, Corcoran, Phillips), and elsewhere. [ills. 772–4, p. 387. Col. pl. 27]

Delaunay, Robert (1885–1941), was the inventor of ORPHIC CUBISM. He was mainly concerned with the emotional effects of pure colour, which may have grown out of his early preoccupation with Impressionism. In 1911 he exhibited with the Independents in the Cubist Room and was also invited by KANDINSKY to exhibit with the BLAUE REITER group. Delaunay began to paint a series of the city of Paris and the Eiffel Tower in 1910–12 and he returned to these themes in 1924, after a seven-year stay

(1914–21) in Spain and Portugal. In 1937 he was commissioned to paint vast murals – one was 9,000 square feet – for the Universal Exhibition in Paris. There are works by him in Amsterdam (Stedelijkmus.), Minneapolis, New York (Guggenheim), and Paris (Musée d'Art Moderne). Delaunay's wife Sonia Terk (*b.* 1885) was a Russian who went to Paris in 1905, where she was influenced by Gauguin. She married Delaunay in 1910. In 1937 she also painted a huge mural for the Paris Exhibition. [ill. 1048, p. 421]

Delvaux, Laurent (1698–1778), was a Flemish sculptor who came to London in 1717 to work with SCHEEMAKERS. In 1728 they went to Italy together, but soon afterwards Delvaux returned to Brussels where in 1733 he received a Court appointment. In Brussels he made a large number of statues for churches, several important pulpits, and a number of tombs; he worked on two tombs in Westminster Abbey with Scheemakers, and there are works (including terracotta models) by him in the V & A and the RA in London, and in Brussels (Mus. d'Art Moderne). [ill. 875, p. 399]

Denis, Maurice (1870–1943), was a co-founder and principal theorist of the NABIS. In Paris in 1888 he met BONNARD, VUILLARD, and SÉRUSIER, who knew Gauguin. Denis's early style, in reaction against Impressionism, was strongly decorative and much influenced by PUVIS de Chavannes, as well as Gauguin: in 1900 he painted his celebrated group portrait, *Homage to Cézanne* (Paris, Mus. d'Art Mod.). He made several trips to Italy and particularly studied the decorative style of Giotto, Fra Angelico, and Piero della Francesca; in 1903 he accompanied Sérusier to Beuron, the German Benedictine monastery which was a centre of religious art, and from 1910 he painted many religious works, including the decoration of St Paul, Geneva (1914). In 1919 he founded the Ateliers d'art sacré. His interest in subject-matter seems to run counter to his famous dictum that a picture is essentially a flat surface covered with colours assembled in a certain order, but the contradiction is more apparent than real. Denis was a prolific writer on art, his best-known works being 'Théories' and 'Nouvelles Théories'. There are paintings by him in Paris (Mus. des Arts Décoratifs, and Mus. d'Art Mod.). [ill. 992, p. 415]

Derain, André (1880–1954), was one of the original FAUVES. He was much influenced by Vlaminck, Matisse, and Cézanne and, before 1914, painted in very bright colours and a Pointillist handling: after 1919 he became more traditionalist and used principally browns and olive-green. There are works in Paris (Mus. d'Art Mod.) and in Chicago, Cleveland, Detroit, Glasgow, Leeds, Liverpool, London (Tate), Manchester (Rutherston), New York (M of MA), Oxford, Washington (NG), and elsewhere. [ill. 1006, p. 416]

Desco da Parto (Ital. birth plate). In medieval Italy there was a charming custom of visiting a woman who had just given birth to a child and carrying her sweets or small gifts on a special small tray: these *deschi da parto* were frequently painted with appropriate subjects, e.g. a visit to a lady in childbed by ladies carrying *deschi,* as in the famous *desco* in Berlin, attributed to Masaccio. [ill. 59, p. 277]

Desiderio da Settignano (1428/30–64) was probably the most promising sculptor of the followers of Donatello. He adopted the technique of very low relief (*rilievo schiacciato*) which had been invented by Donatello, but Desiderio used it for purposes of extreme delicacy of effect quite different from the heroic style of Donatello. Desiderio's sensitive treatment of women and children is best seen in his busts: examples are in Berlin, Florence (Bargello), London (V & A), Paris (Louvre), Philadelphia, Toledo Ohio, Washington (NG). His major monumental work is the tomb of Carlo Marsuppini (*d.* 1453) in Sta Croce, Florence, which derives from Donatello and the ROSSELLINI. [ill. 85, p. 283]

Design. Roughly the same, in normal usage, as COMPOSITION. It may mean a part of a composition considered in isolation, as 'The design of the lower left-hand group of Mr Blank's composition . . .' The arts of design are the visual arts. For the distinction between Design and Disegno *see* DISEGNO.

De Smet *see* SMET.

Despiau, Charles (1874–1946), was a French sculptor who was influenced by RODIN from 1903 and worked for him 1907–14. Despiau's *Paulette* of 1907 (Paris, Musée d'Art Moderne), his earliest major work, attracted Rodin's attention, but later Despiau rejected the softness and vagueness of Rodin's forms and, like MAILLOL, returned to the simplicity and formal severity of Antique sculpture, particularly of the archaic period. His only large-scale work was the war memorial for his native Mont-de-Marsan (Landes), of 1920–2, but he was a sensitive and famous portraitist. There are works by him in Buffalo, Detroit, London (Tate), New York (M of MA), Philadelphia, and Rotterdam, and several in the Musée d'Art Moderne, Paris. [ill. 1125, p. 430]

De Stijl *see* STIJL.

Devis, Arthur (1711–87), was a successful painter of small portraits and conversation pieces of great charm, cool delicate colour, and high finish. His solidly middle-class patrons are usually portrayed in their gardens or parks, or in sparse interiors detailed with as much care as the personages, who are assembled rather than grouped before the painter. His brother Antony (1729–1816) was a minor landscape painter, and his son Arthur William (1763–1822) was a topographical draughtsman.
There are works in Liverpool, London (Tate, V & A), Manchester, Preston (his native town), and elsewhere. [ill. 836, p. 394]

De Wint, Peter (1784–1849), was born at Stone, Staffs., of Dutch-American descent. He was trained in London and, through Dr MONRO, was influenced by Girtin. He was also helped by Varley. Apart from a visit to France in 1828 and to North Wales in 1829 he painted only the English landscape, and especially the flat country round Lincoln which lends itself to his favourite format, very wide in comparison to its height. In breadth of handling he sometimes approaches Cox, but his washes are simpler and more liquid, and the whole atmosphere calmer. There are examples in Cambridge (Fitzwm), Edinburgh, Leeds, Lincoln, London (BM, Tate, V & A), Manchester, and elsewhere. [ill. 923, p. 404]

Diaz de la Peña, Narcisse-Virgile (1807/8–76), was a French landscape painter of the BARBIZON School, but his earlier works were Romantic compositions in the manner of Delacroix. There are pictures by him in Boston, Glasgow, London (NG, Tate), New York (Met. Mus.), and French museums. [ill. 763, p. 385]

Diderot, Denis (1713–84), was the most important 18th-century French writer on art and a precursor of the modern critic. He wrote informative and penetrating accounts of the SALONS in 1759–71, 1775, and 1781, which circulated in Grimm's privately subscribed 'Correspondance Littéraire'. His plays, the earliest examples of the *comédie larmoyante*, by their emphasis on tableaux and on incident rather than character, explain his admiration for GREUZE's development of narrative bourgeois genre. [ill. 736, p. 381]

Diptych. A picture consisting of two parts, usually hinged together like the pages of a book: a POLYPTYCH in two parts. A *Consular Diptych* is a pair of ivory reliefs commemorating a Consulship. There are several extant examples of Flemish 15th-century diptychs which consist of a portrait of the owner, represented in prayer, gazing on the Madonna and Child on the other panel: these were intended as objects of private devotion and as memorials.

Disegno. An Italian word, capable of a variety of meanings, the simplest of which is Drawing, and the next simplest DESIGN. The *arti del disegno* are the visual arts in general, not just drawing alone, and the 16th-century usage became more and more complicated as the MANNERISTS evolved theories about design which perhaps found their climax in the anagram *Disegno, segno di Dio* – i.e. Design is the sign-manual of God. This may be an over-statement. In this involved theory the idea of *disegno interno* plays an important part; the artist is thought of as having a Platonic Idea of an object in his mind, implanted by God, so that the perfect idea of a human figure which exists in the painter's mind is what he has to realize, not contenting himself with the mere copying of any figure which he happens to have in front of his eyes. This theory, explicit in Mannerists like Federico ZUCCARI, is implicit in all theories of IDEAL ART and is at the back of most anti-naturalistic modern movements. In its purest 16th-century form it has much in common with the Counter-Reformation, a fact which might well surprise some of its more recent exponents.

Distemper. A painting technique in which the powdered colours are mixed with size. As anyone who has ever done home decorating will know, it is easy and cheap but very impermanent; for this reason alone it should not be confused with TEMPERA. [Col. pl. 10]

Divisionism *see* OPTICAL MIXTURES.

Dix, Otto (*b.* 1891), learned to paint in Dresden. His experiences in 1914–18 and in the Inflation after the War

led him to paint with a pitiless realism, even in his portraits, though never in quite so caricatural a manner as Georg GROSZ. He was naturally attracted to the NEUE SACHLICHKEIT group and in 1933 his big triptych 'disappeared' from Dresden Gallery and Dix himself was later arrested by the Gestapo. Since 1946 he has painted mainly religious subjects, and in his later works the influence of early German masters such as Altdorfer and Baldung has been evident. [ill. 1067, p. 424]

Dobson, William (1610–46), was born in London. He was described by his contemporary Aubrey as the 'most excellent painter England hath yet bred', and as such he succeeded to the office of van DYCK as Court Painter and to the position of van Dyck, whose assistant he may have been. Nevertheless, his impasted and robust style is more Italianate than van Dyck's and may have been partly formed by a study of the superb Venetian pictures in the collection of Charles I. He appears first in 1642, at Oxford where the Civil War had driven Charles I and his Court; between then and his early death he painted many of the Royalists and also the Royal children, but never the King himself. There are works in the Royal Collection, Birmingham, Dunedin NZ, Edinburgh (NPG), Hull, Liverpool, London (Tate, NPG, Nat. Marit. Mus, Courtauld Inst.), and elsewhere. [ill. 811, p. 392]

Doelenstuk, Schutterstuk. Dutch words meaning group portraits of the Civic Guards formed in Dutch towns during the Wars of Independence. HALS and REMBRANDT painted the most celebrated examples, but most of the late-16th- and early-17th-century portrait painters received commissions. [ill. 524, p. 348]

Doesburg, Theo van (1883–1931), was born in Utrecht and began his career as a painter (there are pictures by him in Amsterdam and The Hague), but in 1917, with MONDRIAN, he founded the magazine De STIJL and most of the rest of his life was spent as a publicist. He had some influence on BAUHAUS ideas. [ill. 1089, p. 427]

Dolci, Carlo (1616–86), was the leading painter in Florence in the mid 17th century, and an exponent of the restrained style of Late Baroque comparable with SACCHI's Roman works. Dolci was extremely precocious and one of his finest pictures is the portrait, painted when he was 16, of Fra Ainolfo dei Bardi (1632: Florence, Pitti). Nevertheless, he became very neurotic and felt himself to be professionally inadequate. Most of his later works are small devotional pictures, often painted on copper in an extremely finicky and detailed style: when GIORDANO was in Florence in 1682 he said jokingly that his own virtuoso style had brought him a fortune of 150,000 scudi, but if Dolci spent so much time in finishing his works he would starve, an idea which preyed upon Dolci's mind. One of his best works is *The Martyrdom of S. Andrew* of 1646 (Florence, Pitti) for which there is a sketch of 1643 in Birmingham. [ill. 251, p. 308]

Domenichino (1581–1641), one of the chief pupils of the CARRACCI, was an assistant to Ludovico in Bologna before he joined Annibale in Rome in 1602 to work in the

Farnese Palace. He exemplified the Carracci doctrines of a return to the Antique and Raphael and was also, with Annibale Carracci and the Northerners Elsheimer and the Brills, one of the pioneers of landscape painting.

In 1621 he returned to Rome from Bologna – where he had been since 1619 – to work as Papal Architect for the newly elected Pope Gregory XV, but his main work of this period was the decoration of the choir and pendentives of S. Andrea della Valle (1624–8), the dome being by LANFRANCO. The bitter enmity between them was exacerbated by Domenichino's neurotic temperament and his jealousy at having to share the commission. In 1631 he went to Naples to decorate the Chapel of S. Gennaro in the Cathedral, a commission that had been hawked around due to the difficulty of getting any major Roman artist to brave the hostility of the Neapolitan artists, before whom the Cavaliere d'Arpino prudently retired, and Guido Reni fled after the murder of one of his assistants. Domenichino's acceptance of this ungrateful task was prompted by the increasing unpopularity of his style in Rome, where the day was being carried by the more exuberant Baroque of Lanfranco and Pietro da Cortona. Domenichino also had trouble with the Neapolitan faction and worked reluctantly and not very successfully, with several flights, and again in bitter competition with Lanfranco, until his death there. Outside Rome and Naples (where there are too many to list) examples may be found in the Royal Collection, and in Berlin, Béziers, Bologna, Bristol, Cambridge (Fitzwm), Chatsworth, Florence (Pitti, Uffizi), Genoa (Pal. Rosso), Glasgow (University), Grottaferrata, Hartford Conn., Indiana, Leeds, Leningrad, London (NG, Dulwich), Madrid (Prado), Milan (Brera), Montpellier, Munich, Newcastle (King's College), Oxford (Christ Church), Paris (Louvre), Vicenza, York. [ill. 248, p. 308]

Domenico Veneziano (d. 1461), was probably a Florentine painter, although his name may be held to imply that he came from Venice. The date of his birth is unknown, but he is first recorded in 1438, in Perugia, when he wrote to the Medici in Florence asking for a job. He may have been successful in this, for he was working in Sant' Egidio (SM Nuova) in Florence 1439–45, on frescoes which are now lost. One of his assistants was PIERO della Francesca, and Domenico's greatest influence on the future was probably exerted through Piero rather than in Florence proper. His main concern was with the mutation of colour by light, a subject that hardly interested the Florentines, obsessed as they were by drawing. In recent years there have been attempts to represent Domenico as the most important influence after Masaccio, but there are only two signed pictures by him and barely half a dozen plausibly attributed. What is probably his earliest surviving work is the *Carnesecchi Madonna* and two *Saints* from the same street tabernacle (London, NG): these fresco fragments are in bad condition, but the *Madonna* is signed. The other signed picture is his masterpiece, the *S. Lucy Altarpiece*, painted for a church in Florence and now dispersed. The main panel is in Florence (Uffizi) and represents the Madonna and Saints in one of the earliest SACRE CONVERSAZIONI; the *predelle* are now in Berlin, Cambridge (Fitzwm), Washington (NG), and a private collection. It has been suggested that, before this, he painted the lower half of Angelico's *Coronation of the Virgin* (Paris, Louvre) and

after the *S. Lucy Altarpiece* he was sufficiently influenced by Castagno to paint the fresco of *SS. John and Francis* (Florence, Sta Croce): there is no compulsion to believe either of these theories. One of the few things known with certainty about him is that he died in 1461, and therefore could not have been murdered by Castagno (d. 1457). Nevertheless, this story was current in the late 15th century. Other works attributed to him are in Berlin, Boston (Gardner Mus.), New York (Met. Mus.), and Washington (NG). [ill. 73, p. 279]

Donatello (c. 1386–1466), was not only the greatest Florentine sculptor before Michelangelo; he was the most influential individual artist of the 15th century. Much of the later 15th-century painting in Florence stems from him, as does the whole Paduan School, while, through MANTEGNA and the BELLINI, his influence was felt even in Venice. Practically every later sculptor, including Michelangelo, was deeply indebted to him; while the heroic types he invented have coloured our whole conception of 15th-century Florence. He was apprenticed to GHIBERTI and worked on the First Doors in 1403 but had left by 1406, when he was working with NANNI di Banco on the Cathedral: he continued to work for the Cathedral on and off for the next 30 years. In 1408/9 he carved his marble *David* (reworked 1416: Florence, Bargello): this shows him as still very influenced by Gothic formal ideas, but his own heroic style is first seen in the *S. Mark* (1411–12: Florence, Orsanmichele) and the *S. John Evangelist* (1413–15: Cathedral) which made his reputation. In both these he created a new kind of humanity, slightly larger than life and exemplifying those qualities of will that were so highly prized in the Early Renaissance. In 1415 he began his series of statues for the Campanile and from 1416 to c. 1420 he worked on his *S. George* for Orsanmichele (now in the Bargello). The Saint is a portrayal of the Christian hero, but perhaps even more significant was the relief below (still on Orsanmichele) of *S. George killing the Dragon*. This is the earliest datable example (c. 1417) of the new science of perspective being used to create a definite, measurable space for the figures to inhabit: it was probably contemporary with the theoretical studies of Brunelleschi, Donatello's friend, but precedes the work of MASACCIO by many years. About 1425 Donatello entered into partnership with the sculptor and architect MICHELOZZO, with whom he produced a series of works, including the Tomb of the Antipope John XXIII (Florence, Baptistry) and the Tomb of Cardinal Brancacci (S. Angelo a Nilo, Naples), both of which were being worked on in 1427, in which year he also finished the *Salome* for the Baptistry Font, Siena. The Tomb of John XXIII established a type of wall-tomb, with the dead man lying on a bier, which derived from earlier examples (e.g. by ARNOLFO di Cambio) but which was decisive for the later Florentine examples (e.g. those by the ROSSELLINI or DESIDERIO). Both the marble relief from the Brancacci Tomb and the bronze one of *Salome* show Donatello exploiting the dramatic possibilities of a combination of very low relief (*rilievo schiacciato*) with the new perspective effects, and these mark his full maturity as a tragic artist. (The *Ascension* in London (V & A) is another example of about the same date.) In 1431–3 he was in Rome, probably with Brunelleschi, and there he seems to have produced little, presumably as he was absorbed in studying the classical remains. Certainly his later work is saturated in the spirit of antiquity, which he understood more fully than any other 15th-century artist, with the possible exception of Mantegna. It was probably after his return to Florence that he made the very classic bronze *David* (Bargello), one of the earliest of Renaissance independent nudes. He was also commissioned to carve the *Cantoria* ('Singing Gallery') for the Cathedral (1433–9: Cath. Mus.) to match the one already begun by Luca della ROBBIA. During these years he also made the Pulpit for Prato Cathedral and carried out the elaborate decorations of the Old Sacristy in S. Lorenzo, Florence, including the bronze doors, which, much less ambitious than Ghiberti's, far surpass his in the interpretation of human character. From 1443 to 1453 Donatello was in Padua, where he made the High Altar of the Santo (now altered) and the equestrian monument to Gattamelata, the first reworking in modern times of the ancient Roman type and clearly owing much to the most famous antique example, the *Marcus Aurelius* in Rome. His works in Padua were the models for all North Italy.

On his return to Florence Donatello explored new possibilities of romantic distortion and religious emotion in his carved wood *Magdalen* (c. 1455: Baptistry), which shows the dramatic impact of extreme ugliness. This statue was of great importance in the development of Florentine painting, for it has the qualities of expressive contour and tense drama that painters like Castagno or, later, Botticelli, sought. At his death he left two unfinished pulpits in S. Lorenzo which show the extreme distortion he was prepared to practise in his old age. They were completed by his pupil BERTOLDO. Apart from those mentioned, there are works by or attributed to Donatello in Berlin, Boston, Faenza, Florence (Sta Croce Mus. and Piazza della Signoria), Lille, Pisa, Rome (St Peter's, Aracoeli), Siena (Cath.), Venice (SM de' Frari), and Washington (NG). [ills. 61–3, pp. 277–8]

Dongen, Kees van (*b.* 1877), is a Dutch painter who has lived in Paris since 1897. From 1905 he was influenced by the FAUVES (especially MATISSE and DUFY), and from their formal simplifications he evolved a style which, coupled with the experience of making satirical drawings for newspapers, has allowed him to become a successful painter of 'cruel' portraits of the rich and fashionable. There are examples in Chicago, New York, and Paris (Mus. d'Art Mod.). [ill. 1003, p. 416]

Donner, Georg Raphael (1693–1741), was the leading Austrian Baroque sculptor. He probably went to Italy before 1715, although the evidence for such a journey is purely stylistic. The influence of Michelangelo is very marked in his works, as well as that of contemporaries. He worked in Salzburg 1725–8, in Pressburg 1728–38, and then in Vienna. Most of his best works are in lead (e.g. the *S. Martin* of 1735 in Pressburg Cath.), but the lead figures for the Fountain in the Mehlmarkt, Vienna (now in the Barockmus.), of 1737–9, had to be replaced by bronze copies. This was his masterpiece, and in the opinion of some critics it shows him moving away from Baroque exuberance. [ill. 628, p. 362]

Dossi, Dosso (*c.* 1479/90–1542), was the last of the Ferrarese painters, much influenced by Giorgione and Titian and also by Raphael. He is first recorded in Mantua in 1512, but had presumably already been in Venice. His most famous work, the *Circe* (Rome, Borghese) shows the unearthly light which plays about his fantastic landscapes inhabited by gorgeously dressed actors. There are works in the Royal Collection and in Baltimore, Detroit, Dresden, Ferrara, Florence (Uffizi, Pitti), Glasgow, London (NG), Modena, Naples, New York (Met. Mus.), Parma, Philadelphia (Johnson), Rome, (Borghese, Capitoline), Trent, Vienna (K-H Mus.), Washington (NG), Worcester Mass., and elsewhere.

His brother, Battista Dosso (*d.* 1548) was his helper, but pictures in Modena and Dresden may be by Battista alone. [ill. 230, p. 306]

Dotted Print. Among the earliest forms of ENGRAVING were prints made from metal plates treated as relief blocks, the white lines being cut out of the metal. The surface was extensively ornamented with dots made by using punches to produce a decorative effect, often regardless of the design as a whole. [ill. 562, p. 354]

Dou, Gerard (1613–75), a portrait and genre painter of Leyden was a pupil of the young REMBRANDT 1628–31, although it is difficult to see any trace of Rembrandt's handling (or intellectual powers) in the elaborately wrought small scenes of everyday life that brought Dou great prosperity and are now in every major gallery. The extreme minuteness of his handling may be connected with his horror of dust – he would sit immobile in his studio, waiting for it to settle, before beginning work. METSU was his pupil. [ills. 441, 515, pp. 334, 346]

Downman, John (*c.* 1750–1824), travelled in Italy with Wright of Derby in 1773–5, and made a number of landscape drawings, but on his return to London he turned to small portraits (often on copper), being particularly successful with pencil and charcoal drawings delicately tinted with watercolour. He became an ARA in 1795. There are examples in London (Tate and Wallace Coll.). [ill. 835, p. 395]

Drill *see* STONE CARVING.

Drouais, François-Hubert (1727–75), wa sa French portrait painter who studied under his father, BOUCHER, and others. His father painted actresses and so did he: his *Mme Favart* (1757: New York, Met. Mus.) is a good example. He became a serious rival to NATTIER and worked for Mme du Barry and the Royal family, being particularly successful with children. There are works in Paris (Louvre), London (NG), and New York (Met. Mus.). [ill. 734, p. 380]

Drypoint *see* ENGRAVING.

Dubuffet, Jean (*b.* 1901), is inspired by *graffiti* on walls ('the art of the ordinary man') and produces works, called *pâtes*, which are not painted but made of junk – tar, sand, glass and so on – which has been scratched, coloured, and manipulated into shapes resembling human beings – e.g. aggressively female women. He prefers amateur spontaneity to professional skill, and has a large collection of what he calls *art brut* (raw art), much of it produced by psychotics. He has travelled a good deal and worked for a while in America, producing *Bowery Bums*. There are examples in London (Tate) and New York (M of MA). [ill. 1108, p. 429]

Duccio di Buoninsegna (*c.* 1255/60–in or before 1318, probably 1315/18), was the first great Sienese painter, and he stands in relation to the Sienese School as GIOTTO does to the Florentine; yet without the powerful naturalism which makes the art of Giotto so revolutionary, for Duccio rather sums up the grave and austere beauty of centuries of Byzantine tradition and infuses it with a breath of the new humanity which was spreading from the new Orders of S. Francis and S. Dominic. He is first recorded in 1278 and 1279, working for the Comune, and then in 1280 he was heavily fined for an unspecified offence, probably a political one. It was the first of many fines to be inflicted on him, but the others were all very much smaller. In 1285 a large *Madonna* was ordered from him for the Florentine church of Sta Maria Novella: this was very probably the *Rucellai Madonna* (now temporarily in the Uffizi, Florence), but the picture is sometimes called a work of the Master of the Rucellai Madonna, and Vasari, in one of his patriotic moods, ascribed it to the Florentine Cimabue. The picture was probably painted in Siena, where Duccio is recorded at intervals (1285–99), when he was again fined for refusing to swear fealty to the *Capitano del Popolo*, a civil official. In 1302 he was fined again – probably one of several for debts incurred – and was also commissioned to paint a *Maestà* for Siena Town Hall, but the picture is now lost. He was also fined again, this time for refusing military service, and yet again for some activity apparently connected with sorcery. This last accusation cannot have been very serious since in 1308 Duccio achieved the consummation of his career with the contract for the huge *Maestà* for the High Altar of the Cathedral. The work was finished in 1311 and carried in solemn procession from the workshop to the Cathedral. Most of the *Maestà* is now in the Cathedral Museum at Siena, a few small pieces are missing, and the other panels (all small ones from the *predelle*) are in London (NG), New York (Frick Coll. and a private (Rockefeller) coll.), and Washington (NG). Wellesley College, Mass., has an *Angel* which may have come from the *Maestà*. In its original form the *Maestà* proper – that is, the Enthroned Madonna and Child surrounded by Saints and Angels – occupied the whole of the main panel facing the congregation. Above and below were scenes from the Life of Christ and the Virgin, with small figures of Saints. Most of these smaller scenes would have been visible only to the officiating priest. The whole of the back of the main panel was taken up by 26 scenes from the Passion, while above and below, as on the front, were smaller panels with scenes from the Life of Christ. The whole of this narrative cycle, being in the Sanctuary, was normally easily visible only to the clergy, and it is perhaps for this reason that the narrative is more important, as a kind of commentary on the Scriptures; while the front is principally an image for the contemplation of the devout. From the artistic point of view both sides show Duccio as a profound innovator, for the front has figures with greater weight and solidity, and more characterization, than had

been seen previously in Siena; while the back shows him as a master of narrative, equal to Giotto in his power of story-telling though less fresh in iconographical invention, for Duccio was content to use the old Byzantine models for most (though not all) of his scenes from the New Testament. The superb craftsmanship, the use of gold as a decoration and a compositional feature at the same time, the rich and subtle colour which is made into an aesthetic feature in its own right rather than treated (as in Giotto's works) as explaining the forms, and above all the use of varied and elegant outlines as a surface pattern as well as a description of form; all these features characterize the Sienese School for nearly two centuries. In the next generation artists as profoundly different as Simone MARTINI and the LORENZETTI started from aspects of Duccio's work, although the influence which Giovanni PISANO's sculpture had had on Duccio himself was also a potent factor in the development of the Lorenzetti.
Other works ascribed to Duccio are in the Royal Collection, in Badia a Isola near Siena (a *Madonna* often ascribed to the Badia a Isola Master rather than to Duccio himself), Berne, Boston, Budapest, Cambridge Mass. (Fogg), London (NG), New York (Met. Mus., Frick Coll.), Perugia, Philadelphia (Johnson), Siena (Pinacoteca, Opera del Duomo, and Cathedral itself (stained glass)), and Utrecht (Archiepiscopal Mus.). [ill. 37, p. 274. Col. pl. 40]

Duchamp, Marcel (*b.* 1887), was one of the original Dadaists. Before the invention of DADA he had shocked New York with his *Nude descending a Staircase* in the ARMORY SHOW of 1913. Most of his works are in Philadelphia. [ill. 1060, p. 422]
His brothers were Raymond DUCHAMP-VILLON and Jacques VILLON.

Duchamp-Villon, Raymond (1876–1918), was the brother of Marcel DUCHAMP and Jacques VILLON. From 1898 his sculpture was under the influence of RODIN, but he later came to sympathize with Cubist ideals, and, from 1912 to 1914, there is a series of *Horses* which have something of the quality of a Cubist manifesto, combined with BOCCIONI's interest in movement. He was gassed in 1916 and died in 1918. Paris, Musée d'Art Moderne has one of the *Horse* series (1914). [ill. 1130, p. 430]

Dufy, Raoul (1877–1953), worked in a sub-Impressionist manner until 1905, when the impact of the FAUVE movement (particularly of Matisse's *Luxe, Calme et Volupté*) impelled him to adopt simplified form and bright colour. He designed textiles and ceramics and developed a gay, light-hearted, decorative style, eminently suited to his range of subjects – esplanades, racecourses, regattas, etc. – and used odd tricks of technique, such as white patches ('neutrals') for shadows, and a rapid, modish, calligraphic draughtsmanship. There are examples in London (Tate and Courtauld Inst.), New York (M of MA), Paris (Mus. d'Art Mod.), and large collections at Le Havre and Nice. [ill. 1008, p. 416]

Dugento (*Duecento*: Ital. two hundred). The 13th century i.e., the twelve hundreds.

Dughet, Gaspard, *see* POUSSIN.

Dujardin, Karel (1622–78), was born in Amsterdam. He was a pupil of BERCHEM, and twice went to Italy. He painted chiefly Italianate landscapes with figures, occasional religious subjects, and an exceptionally fine group portrait of the *Regents of the Women's Prison in Amsterdam* (1669: Rijksmus.). He died in Venice. There are examples in the Royal Collection, Berlin, Brussels, Dresden, Edinburgh (NG), The Hague, Hartford Conn., Leningrad, London (NG, Dulwich, Wallace Coll.), Munich, Paris (Louvre), Vienna, York, and elsewhere. [ills. 431, 440, pp. 333, 335]

Dunlap, William (1766–1839), was an American painter of portraits – e.g. the picture of himself, on his return from London in 1788, showing his *Hamlet* to his parents (New York, Hist. Soc.). He was also a playwright and kept 30 volumes of Diary (1786–1834) of which 11 survive and have been published; above all, he wrote 'A History of the Rise and Progress of the Arts of Design in the United States', 1834, which is the best source-book on early American painting. [ill. 843, p. 395]

Duquesnoy, François (1594–1643), known as Il Fiammingo, was a sculptor, born in Brussels, who worked in Rome from 1618 to 1643. He died on his way to Paris to become Court Sculptor. He was the most famous non-Italian sculptor of his day, and, like ALGARDI, he represented a more classical tendency than the full Baroque of BERNINI, by whom he was nevertheless influenced, especially in portraiture. Poussin, the most classical artist of the age, was his close friend. His major works are the *S. Andrew* (1628–40: St Peter's. *See* BOLGI) and the *S. Susanna* (1629–33: Sta Maria di Loreto, Rome). Numerous smaller works spread his fame outside Italy: there are examples in Berlin, London (V & A), Paris, and elsewhere. His *putti* were especially praised by contemporaries: good examples are those in Sta Maria dell' Anima, Rome. [ill. 269, p. 311]

Durand, Asher B. (1796–1886), began as an engraver whose reputation was established in 1820 with the engraving, after TRUMBULL's painting, of the *Declaration of Independence*. As early as 1830 he projected a serial publication of engravings devoted to the American landscape, but it was not successful and had to be suspended after the first number. By this time he had turned to painting portraits and landscapes, and he eventually became one of the leading landscape painters of the HUDSON RIVER School. In 1840 he made a trip to Europe and copied the Old Masters, and in 1846 he was elected President of the National Academy of Design, one of the first landscape painters in any country to receive such recognition. Unlike his friend COLE, he worked out-of-doors and the artless realism of his landscapes is their principal attraction, but he began by working in a tradition close to that of the Dutch 17th-century painters (e.g. Hobbema). There are pictures by him in many American museums, but there do not seem to be any outside the United States. [ill. 946, p. 407]

Dürer, Albrecht (1471–1528), was the son of a goldsmith who settled in Nuremberg in 1455, and in 1467 married his master's daughter. The young Albrecht was first apprenticed to his father, and was then bound for three years to the painter Michael WOLGEMUT, whose large workshop also produced woodcut book-illustrations for the printer Anton Koberger, Dürer's godfather. He travelled for eighteen months, from Easter 1490, and then visited Colmar (intending to work under Martin Schongauer), Basle, and Strasbourg, and in May 1494 he returned to Nuremberg and married. In the autumn of 1494 he went to Venice (his great friend, the humanist Wilibald Pirckheimer, was then a student at Padua) and returned home by spring 1495. Late in 1505 he again went to Venice, travelling via Augsburg, and stayed until February 1507. During this visit he met Giovanni Bellini, whom he greatly admired, and painted several works including the *Madonna of the Rose Garlands* (Prague; now very damaged) for the German merchants in Venice, and the *Christ among the Doctors*, which shows some knowledge of Leonardo. On his return he intensified the learned side of his art and personality; he studied mathematics, geometry, Latin, and humanist literature, and sought the company of scholars rather than that of his fellow-artisans. This departure in mode of life and thought was directly traceable to the influence of Leonardo and Mantegna and the example of Bellini, and though it was common enough in Italy, it was unprecedented in Germany. In 1512, he became Court Painter to the Emperor Maximilian, and in July 1520 he journeyed to the Netherlands to obtain from his successor, Charles V, the ratification of his post and pension. He saw the coronation of the new Emperor at Aix-la-Chapelle and was confirmed in his office, visited Antwerp, Brussels, Malines, Cologne, Middelburg, Bruges, and Ghent, and was honoured and fêted all along the route. He returned home in July 1521, and despite ill-health resulting from fever, probably contracted in the swamps of Zeeland, where he had ventured in the hope of seeing a dead whale, he worked unremittingly until his death.

Dürer's enormous *œuvre* consists of woodcuts and engravings, paintings, preparatory and independent drawings, and he also wrote treatises on measurement (1525), fortification (1527), proportion and artistic theory (1528), besides his detailed diary of his Netherlands journey. He was the main channel through which Italian Renaissance forms and ideas were introduced into the North, and he combined these with the individualism general in German art and inherited from the Gothic tradition. His greatest influence was through his graphic work. He is one of the supreme masters of woodcut and copper engraving, and these easily transportable models carried his technique, subjects, designs, and style all over Europe, and even had a considerable influence in Italy. He extended the range of woodcut and engraving by perfecting the technique of both, and raised the standard of graphic art by the training he gave to the workmen who executed his designs.

His main works in woodcut were series such as the *Apocalypse* (1498), the *Great Passion* (1498–1510) and the *Little Passion* (1509–11), the *Life of the Virgin* (1501–11), and single prints such as the *Men's Bathhouse* (1497), and in engraving the *Engraved Passion* (1507–12) and the many single plates such as the *Sea Monster* and the *Prodigal Son* (1497), the *S. Eustace* (c. 1501), the *Great Fortune* (1501/2), the *Adam and Eve* (1504), the *Knight, Death and the Devil* (1513), *S. Jerome* and the *Melencolia* (1514). The *Apocalypse* was the first book to be entirely the work of an artist; Dürer here was his own artist, printer, and publisher. All his works combine vivid imagery, technical refinement, expressiveness, and masterly draughtmanship with deeply thought out, and often involved, iconography which must be read, layer upon layer, before the meaning of the design becomes clear, although its visual impact is immediate. He shared in the Emperor Maximilian's commissions for the huge woodcut *Triumphs*, and executed some blocks for them, but they added little to his fame.

Compared with his graphic work, his paintings are few in number; they are more traditional in type and usually less packed with significance. One of his greatest contributions is his watercolour and gouache landscapes, some made during his Italian journeys, for they are among the most evocative expressions of mood and atmosphere in landscape painting. In October 1526, he presented to his native city, as a memorial of himself, the *Apostles* (Munich), probably designed as a part of a *Sacra Conversazione* which was not executed because of the Reformation. In form, the Saints owe much to Bellini's Saints in the Frari Altarpiece (Venice), and their significance is bound up with the spiritual conflicts of the Reformation, which affected him deeply. Melancthon was a close friend, and he knew and admired both Luther and Erasmus. Despite his large workshop he left no succession; his art was too universal and yet too personal to breed imitators.

There are works in Augsburg, Berlin, Boston (Gardner), Budapest, Cassel, Cologne (Wallraf-Richartz), Dresden, Florence (Uffizi), Frankfurt (Mus. and Städel), Lisbon, London (NG), Madrid (Prado), Munich, New York (Met. Mus.), Nuremberg, Ober St Veit (near Vienna), Paris (Louvre, Bib. Nat.), Toledo Ohio, Vienna, Weimar, and elsewhere. [ills. 556–9, p. 354. Col. pl. 46]

Dyce, William (1806–64), painter, scientist, and administrator, was born in Aberdeen and studied in London and Rome. He was much influenced by the NAZARENER and introduced their ideas to England with a *Madonna* in 1828: he thus transmitted the new German ideas to the Pre-Raphaelite Brotherhood (founded in 1848). There are works in the Royal Collection and in Aberdeen, Edinburgh (NG), Liverpool, and London (Tate). [ill. 947, p. 408]

Dyck, Sir Anthony van (1599–1641), was born in Antwerp. He became RUBENS's chief assistant while still in his teens, his forte being for subjects requiring pathos rather than movement. He visited England in 1620 (James I desired to employ him as Court Painter), but after four months returned to Flanders and in 1621 he went to Italy, where, except for a visit to Flanders in 1622 when his father died, he remained for four years. He was in Rome, Florence, Venice, Palermo, and particularly in Genoa, where he laid the foundation of his great career as a portrait painter, and evolved the repertory of patterns of which he made such

constant use during his years in England. He was not at his best in Rome, which was then full of brilliant artists – Domenichino, Guercino, Bernini, Pietro da Cortona – and the Baroque that Rubens saw coming to birth was fully developed.

Between his return to Flanders in 1625/6, when he tried to obtain the patronage of the Regent Isabella, and worked for the House of Orange, and his departure for England, he produced most of his finest portraits for, less forceful as a personality than Rubens, he was more sensitive to his sitter's individuality which he expressed with an unfailing sense of style that reflects something of his own introspective melancholy. In religious works, he leaned heavily on Rubens, and on Titian and Correggio, though he digested these influences less successfully than Rubens did. Technically, his paint is thinner than Rubens's, drier, more dragged, and with greyer underpainting, less limpid and free in handling. His years in England – from 1632 until his death – were outwardly successful, with immense prestige at the Court of Charles I, a knighthood, and an enormous practice as a portrait painter, for he supplanted MYTENS and overshadowed JOHNSON. But his efforts to re-establish himself on the Continent in 1640, first to succeed Rubens (cf. JORDAENS), and then to obtain the commission for the decoration of the gallery in the Louvre which, when he arrived in Paris, had already been given to Poussin, suggest that he realized how precarious Charles I's position had become, and how limiting was the patronage of the English Court. But by now he was very ill, and he returned to England to die.

His nine years in England were prolific, but involved the constant repetition of his Genoese types, with varying success according to whether he himself or a studio hand executed the work. None of his helpers was of any significance, and he lacked Rubens's ability to control a large workshop. Among the most famous of his English portraits are the equestrian ones of Charles I, the triple portrait of the King sent to Bernini to serve as a model for a bust, the groups of the Royal children, and the great family group at Wilton. These show him creating a model that lasted until the end of the great tradition of English portrait painting, through DOBSON, Lely, Reynolds, and Gainsborough to Lawrence.

Most of the older galleries have one or more examples, Antwerp, Brussels, London (NG, Wallace Coll.), and the Royal Collection being exceptionally rich. The following American and Canadian museums also have examples: Baltimore, Boston (Mus., Gardner), Chicago, Cincinnati, Cleveland Ohio, Columbus Ohio, Denver, Detroit, Hartford Conn. (Wadsworth), Kansas City, Los Angeles (Mus., Univ. of S. Cal.), New York (Met. Mus., Frick), Ottawa, Raleigh N. Carolina, St Louis, San Diego, Toronto, Washington (NG, Corcoran, Nat. Coll.), and others. [ills. 415–17, p. 330]

E

Eakins, Thomas (1844–1916), was an American painter, principally of portraits. He went from Philadelphia to Paris in 1866, where he came under the influence of MANET's realism. After a visit to Spain in 1870 he returned to Philadelphia and became a sucessful teacher whose quest for realism led him to attend medical classes to improve his knowledge of anatomy and led indirectly to his *Gross Clinic* (1875), with its representation of a surgeon operating, which caused an uproar, as did his *Agnew Clinic*. These Rembrandtesque subjects were treated in the 'Spanish' style of Manet, which also caused uproar rather earlier in Paris. His works are well represented in US museums. [ill. 962, p. 410]

Earl, Ralph (1751–1801), was an American portrait painter who is first recorded in 1775, making sketches for engravings of the Revolution. He worked in England 1778–85, exhibiting at the RA 1783–5 and probably coming into contact with the Loyalist WEST. In 1785 he returned to New England and painted portraits there until his death: he was twice married and deserted both wives, and from 1799 his work deteriorated under the influence of the alcoholism which killed him. His *Roger Sherman* (c. 1775/7: Yale Univ. Gall.) has a gaunt Yankee quality which seems preferable to the pastiche of fashionable English painting apparent in his later works. Many American museums have a picture by him: the only one outside the US appears to be the *Admiral Kempenfelt* (1783) in the NPG, London. [ill. 844, p. 395]

Eclectic *see* CARRACCI.

Eeckhout, Gerbrand van den (1621–74), was an Amsterdam painter who was the pupil, friend, and close imitator of Rembrandt. About 1655 he painted a number of scenes in the totally different manner of TER BORCH. [ill. 439, p. 335]

Elias, Nicolaes, called Pickenoy (1590/1–1654/6), was an Amsterdam portrait painter of the generation before Rembrandt. His *Company of Captain Jan van Vlooswijck* (Amsterdam, Rijksmus.) was painted in 1642, the year of Rembrandt's *Night Watch*. [ill. 438, p. 334]

Elsheimer, Adam (1578–1610), was a German landscape painter whose most important work was done in Italy. He was in Venice c. 1598 and in Rome by 1600, where he spent the rest of his life. His landscapes are among the first ideal ones, in which the figures have a considerable but not overwhelming part to play, and in which the effects of light are studied with great care. He probably learned the effectiveness of a variety of points of light from Tintoretto and Caravaggio and many of his small landscapes have several sources of light – e.g. a warm sunset with the cold light of the moon in another part of the picture, together with the light of a torch elsewhere. His works are small, always on copper, and executed with great precision: they had great influence on his friend Rubens and on younger men such as Rembrandt and Claude. Rubens, in a letter of 14 January 1611, refers to Elsheimer's death as causing him great grief and goes on: 'I pray that God has forgiven Signor Adam his sin of sloth by which he has deprived the world of the most beautiful things, caused himself much misery and finally, I believe, reduced himself to despair; whereas with his own hands he could have built up a great fortune and made himself respected by all the world.' He then goes on to offer to sell any of Elsheimer's pictures on behalf of the widow for considerable sums of money – 'and if the painting should not be sold immediately, we shall in the meantime find a way to advance her a good sum of money on it without prejudice to the sale'. There are examples in Cassel, Cambridge (Fitzwm), Dresden, Florence (Uffizi), Frankfurt (Städel), The Hague, London (NG, Dulwich), Munich, Paris (Louvre), Venice (Accad.), Vienna (K-H Mus.), and elsewhere. [ill. 402, p. 328]

Encaustic Wax was a painting technique apparently practised in antiquity with success but since fallen into disuse. The principle seems to have been to work on a wall with colours mixed with wax, which, when heated with irons or similar means, were driven into the wall itself. Pliny gives an account, and this probably inspired LEONARDO's disastrous attempt at reviving the technique in 1503–5 as well as the late-19th-century attempts.

Engraving. A generic title often used to cover all the methods of multiplying prints, although strictly the word should apply only to the second of the processes described below. The first distinction to be drawn is between Reproductive and Original Engravings, a reproductive engraving being a means of divulgating an idea expressed in a painting, drawing, statue, or other medium, invented by an artist other than the engraver. An original engraving is an independent work of art invented by the engraver himself.
The three main types of engraving may be classified as (1) Relief or cameo, (2) Intaglio, and (3) Surface or planar. Each of these types corresponds to one or more of the main techniques, and each type has a special method of printing.
1) Relief. The main techniques are Woodcut and Wood-engraving, Linocut and its simpler forms, such as Potato-cuts. A plain block of wood, if covered with printing ink

and pressed on a sheet of paper, would print as a black rectangle: but if channels were cut into the surface with a gouge these would not catch the ink, and, therefore, would print as white patches. The principle of a woodcut is therefore to leave the black lines or patches as untouched wood and to cut away the parts intended to print as white. A single black line has to have the wood on each side of it cut away, and this is done with special knives and gouges. Woodcuts are done on blocks of soft wood, cut plank-fashion, and will give hundreds, or even thousands, of impressions before wearing out. Lino is often used nowadays, as it is easier to work, but its life is shorter. Colour prints are produced by cutting a special block for each colour as well as a key-block, usually printed black, which carries the linear structure (see CHIAROSCURO CUT), and these have to be printed 'in register', so that the forms do not overlap. The earliest woodcuts date from the end of the 14th century, but wood-engraving hardly occurs before the mid 18th century, and found one of its greatest exponents in Thomas BEWICK, who revived white-line engraving. Wood-engraving is very similar to engraving on copper, using the same kind of tool, called a graver or burin. The main difference between wood-engraving and woodcut is in the block itself, which is of boxwood, cut across the grain, for wood-engraving. On this smooth, grainless surface the sharply pointed graving tools can plough very fine furrows each of which will print as a fine white line. Obviously, it is far easier to think in terms of white lines on a predominantly black ground, and the great modern revival (since about 1920) of wood-engraving has been of the white-line or Xylographic type, which offers a means of stylized design.

2) Intaglio. The intaglio techniques are all forms of engraving on metal, usually copper, and they are distinguished from the other techniques by the method of printing. When the plate has been engraved by one or more of the processes to be described – and several processes are often used in combination – the plate is dabbed all over with a thin kind of printing ink, which is then rubbed off again with muslin or the palm of the hand, leaving the ink in the engraved furrows. A piece of paper is then damped and laid on the plate and both are rolled through a heavy press not unlike a mangle. The damp paper is forced into the engraved lines and so picks up the ink in them: when dry the engraved lines stand up in relief. This explains the great difference between a copper-engraving, or any other intaglio print, and a wood-engraving which has been cut in a very similar way – the ink lies on the surface of a wood-engraved block instead of being forced into the lines cut (*intagliate*) into the metal plate. A wood-engraving cannot be printed in the intaglio manner as it would break under the great pressure. The main intaglio processes are: (*a*) Line-(or copper-)engraving, (*b*) Dry-point, (*c*) Etching, including Soft-ground etching, (*d*) Stipple- and crayon-engraving, (*e*) Mezzotint, and (*f*) Aquatint and the related processes.

a) *Line-engraving*. The sharp graver is pushed into the copper, exactly like a plough into the earth, throwing up small shavings and leaving a line which has a V-section. This is the earliest of the intaglio techniques, as the earliest dated print is of 1446, but it is also the one demanding the greatest discipline and precision of hand since the sharp tool has to be pushed ahead of the hand – and polished

copper is very slippery. DÜRER is incomparably the greatest original artist in this medium, which was later used mainly for reproducing pictures and other works of art.

b) *Dry-point*. This is the simplest technique, since it consists of drawing on the metal plate with a 'pencil' made of hard steel. The great quality of dry-point lies in the burr, which is the shaving of metal turned up at the side of the furrow. When burr occurs in line-engraving it is scraped off, but it is left in a dry-point because it catches the ink and prints with a richness which adds to the directness of the artist's work. Unfortunately, it is soon crushed by the pressure of printing, so that less than fifty good impressions can be taken. Dry-point is often used to reinforce etching or even engraving; Rembrandt, in particular, often combined it with etching.

c) *Etching*. Here the plate is covered with a resinous ground, impervious to acid, and then the etcher draws on the ground with a needle, exposing the copper wherever he wants a line to print. The plate is put in an acid bath, which eats away the exposed parts, but subtlety is given by taking the plate out of the acid as soon as the faintest lines are bitten. These faint lines are then 'stopped-out' with varnish and the plate re-bitten until the medium-dark lines are stopped-out in their turn, and so on. The first dated etching is of 1513, but the great period came with the 17th century, culminating in Rembrandt, and the process has been popular ever since. *Soft-ground Etching* looks like a pencil or chalk drawing, because the ground is mixed with tallow, and has a sheet of thin paper laid on it, on to which the etcher draws directly with a pencil; part of the ground sticks to the paper giving a grainy effect when the plate is bitten.

d) *Stipple-, crayon-engraving*, and *colour printing* were popular 18th-century techniques. Stipple- and crayon-engraving were used particularly for the reproduction of portrait drawings, giving an effect remarkably similar to that of a chalk drawing. It is obtained by a combination of etching and engraving techniques, stippling dots over a grounded plate with the point of an etching needle or, more usually, by the use of special tools; a *Roulette* is a spur-like wheel which gives an effect similar to the grainy quality of chalk, and it can be combined with a *Mattoir*, which is an instrument like a tiny club with sharp points projecting from the head. These points produce a grained effect on the bare copper which prints as black, chalk-like dots. Occasionally the effect of two-colour chalks is obtained by printing from two plates, usually black and red. Colour engravings of the 18th century fall into two main categories, English and French. The finest English colour prints are usually based on the aquatint process (see (*f*) below) and are made by a single printing from a plate coloured in the appropriate areas. Some English colour prints are, in fact, monochrome aquatints hand-coloured in watercolour, and both GIRTIN and TURNER earned a living colouring engravings at the beginning of their careers.

The French technique, sometimes called *manière de lavis*, is an imitation of a wash drawing or a watercolour obtained by the use of a great number of *roulettes*, *mattoirs* and gravers. The use of these tools gave the tones, but the actual colours were printed from four separate plates – yellow, red, blue, and black, printed in that order, the black being the most important since it defined the contours. The most difficult part of this technique is to ensure that one plate is printed exactly on top of another – 'in register'.

e) *Mezzotint*. This was the great reproductive process of the 18th century (though invented in the 17th century), especially famous and successful in England, where the portraits of Reynolds and Gainsborough were normally reproduced by it. The plate is first covered with a mesh of small burred dots, made by a toothed chisel-like 'rocker'. In this state the plate would print as a solid, rich black. The half-tones and lights are obtained by scraping off the burr with a scraper, or polishing the plate smooth again with a burnisher so that the ink may be wiped off the highest lights. The technique is rarely practised now, as photographic methods have superseded it for reproduction.

f) *Aquatint*. Like mezzotint, aquatint is a tone process rather than a line method, but it is admirably adapted to the rendering of transparent effects, such as watercolour gives. It is basically a form of etching, using a porous ground which the acid can penetrate to form a network of fine lines. Any pure whites are stopped out in the usual way before the biting begins, then the palest tints are bitten and stopped out, and so on as in etching. Variations of texture can be obtained by pressing a piece of sand-paper on the grounded plate, mixing sugar with the ground, or attacking the plate with sulphur ('sulphur-tint'). Paul SANDBY was the first imaginative artist to use the process, followed by the greatest of all aquatinters, GOYA, but it has been revived by John Piper, and Picasso used the sugar process for his illustrations to Buffon. [ill. 1042, p. 420]

3) Surface Printing. The one major process which involves no cutting into the block or plate, and therefore no 'engraving' in the proper sense, is Lithography, usually executed on a thick slab of stone, although zinc is now more common as it is both lighter and less fragile. The whole technique, invented in 1798 by Alois Senefelder, is based on the fact that water runs off a greasy surface. The design is drawn or painted on the stone with a greasy chalk and then the stone is wetted. When the greasy ink is rolled on the stone it will not take on the wet parts but it sticks on the parts which are already greasy, off which the water ran. The new process was taken up by several 19th-century artists, including Delacroix, Goya, Géricault, Daumier, Manet, and others, and it is still a popular medium. It is used very widely for posters and other forms of commercial art. Its great advantage is that there is almost no limit to the number of prints it is possible to take. *See also* SERIGRAPHY. [ills. 81, 545, 557–8, 560–2, 662, 798–9, pp. 281, 352, 354, 370, 389. Col. pls. 44, 45]

Ensor, James (1860–1949), was a Belgian painter whose father was English. Apart from his training in Brussels Ensor spent his life in Ostend. He had a peculiarly macabre outlook, taking the subjects of Callot, Bosch, or Bruegel and treating them in the technique of Manet, Courbet, and Rubens. He frequently used masks and skeletons for Expressionist purposes before Expressionism was invented. In 1884 he exhibited with Les XX, who, in 1889, rejected his *Entry of Christ into Brussels in 1889* (1888: Knocke-le-Zoute, Casino) and voted for his expulsion. His best work was done by 1900: in 1929 he was made a Baron. There are pictures in Antwerp, Brussels, Detroit, London (Tate),

New York (M of MA), and Paris (Mus. d'Art Mod.). [ill. 997, p. 415]

Epstein, Sir Jacob (1880–1959), was born in New York and went to Paris in 1902; from 1905 he lived in England. In 1907 he was commissioned to carve 18 statues for the British Medical Association building. They were erected in 1908 and caused great scandal: after that, it became customary for any new imaginative work of his to be greeted with uproar – e.g. the *Rima* in Hyde Park (1925) or the carvings on the London Transport Building in Westminster (1928–9). His portraits in bronze have an over-lifesize quality, partly due to the rugosity of the handling, reminiscent of Rodin, and are generally admired: the last example was the official commission of *Smuts* outside the Houses of Parliament. Other works are in Aberdeen, Auckland NZ, Birmingham, Hull, Llandaff Cathedral, London (Westminster Abbey, St Paul's, Tate, Imperial War Mus., and outside the Convent of the Holy Child, Cavendish Square), Manchester, New York (M of MA), Oxford (New College), Paris (Cemetery of Père Lachaise, Tomb of Oscar Wilde), and elsewhere. [ill. 1126, p. 431]

Ercole de' Roberti *see* ROBERTI.

Erhart (Erhaert), Gregor (*d.* probably 1540), was a German sculptor, born in Ulm, who worked in Augsburg from 1494 until his death. There are no documented works by him, although he is known to have made a stone crucifix in 1498, and in 1509 he was working on an equestrian monument for the Emperor Maximilian. Nothing is known of his later work, but he seems to have been an important sculptor of the transitional period, whose work was influenced first by MULTSCHER, the leading Ulm artist, while his later works come close to those of RIEMENSCHNEIDER. The most important attributions to Erhart are the altarpiece at Blaubeuren (1493–4), and *Madonnas* in Berlin (1502–4) and Frauenstein, Austria (*c.* 1515). Other works attributed to him are in Cleveland, Ohio, Detroit, London (V & A), and Paris (Louvre). [ill. 622, p. 360]

Ernst, Max (*b.* 1891), introduced the DADA movement into Cologne in 1919. He also made *collages* and *frottages* and from 1924 was a Surrealist. He has published *collage* novels. There are examples in Hartford Conn., Manchester and New York (M of MA). [ill. 1057, p. 423]

Etching *see* ENGRAVING.

Etty, William (1787–1849), was one of the very few English artists to paint the nude almost exclusively. This he did in a manner derived from Titian and Rubens, and therefore glowing and sensual, but subject to the requirements of IDEAL ART. Many of his pictures consist of extremely faithful studies from the nude, done in the Academy Life School which he frequented all his life, presented as mythological characters. He made several journeys to the Continent and met Delacroix in 1825, so he must have been aware of the French Romantic movement. The best collection of his work is in his native York, but there are other pictures in Boston, Leeds, London

(Tate), Manchester, New York (Met. Mus.), Oxford, Port Sunlight (Lever Gall.), Preston, and elsewhere. [ill. 912, p. 403]

Euston Road was the name given to an English group, founded in the late 1930s, which takes its name from the Euston Road in London. They sought to return to a more realistic conception of painting, neither abstract nor Surrealist. The principal members were Coldstream, Gowing, Rogers, and PASMORE (who has since become an abstract painter).

Everdingen, Allart van (1621–75), was a Dutch landscape painter who visited Scandinavia (1640–4) and returned to Holland with a new type of romantic mountain landscape, with pine forests and waterfalls, which was strange and successful. His type of scenery influenced some of the later works of J. van RUISDAEL. There are pictures by him in many Dutch and German galleries, the NG and Wallace Coll., London, and elsewhere. He also produced over one hundred landscape etchings. [ill. 490, p. 342]
His elder brother, Caesar Boetius (1617–78), was a figure painter in Alkmaar and Haarlem who was much influenced by Caravaggio and therefore represents a sort of offshoot of the UTRECHT School. There are pictures by him in Alkmaar, Amsterdam, Dresden, The Hague, and Stockholm. [ill. 464, p. 339]

Eworth, Hans, who signed his works HE, was an Antwerp painter working in London from 1549 (or 1545) to 1574. He painted chiefly portraits, sometimes allegorical, such as the *Sir John Luttrell*, of 1550, or straightforwardly Holbeinesque, such as the *Mary Tudor* (1559: Soc. of Antiquaries). His style is sensitive and nervous, employing a great deal of delicately rendered detail, ultimately dependent on HOLBEIN – who preceded him as Henry VIII's Court Painter – yet without his robustness. Eworth's *Queen Elizabeth confounding Juno, Minerva and Venus* (1569: Royal Coll.) is an example of the unsubtle flattery expressed in highly sophisticated and involved Mannerist imagery which was typical of Elizabeth's Court. The *Lord Darnley and his Brother* (1563: also Royal Coll.) is a straightforward portrait but equally introspective and elegant in the painter's conception. There are several pictures signed HE in private collections and others attributed to him in the Royal Collection and in Antwerp, London (NPG, Tate, and Wallace Coll.), Ottawa, Oxford (Ashmolean), and Wellington NZ. [ill. 367, p. 325]

Exc., Excudit (Lat. he executed it) on an engraving usually refers to the publisher, who was often identical with the engraver.

Expressionism. The search for expressiveness of style by means of exaggerations and distortions of line and colour; a deliberate abandon of the naturalism implicit in Impressionism in favour of a simplified style which should carry far greater emotional impact. In this general sense of emotional force Expressionism is a feature of non-Mediterranean art in general, GRÜNEWALD being the standard example. In the more limited context of modern art, the Expressionist movement may be said to spring from van GOGH's use of drastically simplified outline and very strong colour. In France this has clear affinities with FAUVISM, but the principal exponents, apart from Toulouse-Lautrec, were mostly German (or at least 'Nordic', like the Norwegian MUNCH, whose hysterical art is one of the foundations of the movement). The tendency to a sentimental hysteria and the clear derivation from Negro art are two of the factors which explain Hitler's denunciation of 'Degenerate Art' and the esteem it now enjoys. The BRÜCKE and the BLAUE REITER are two of the principal sub-groups, while some of the major individual artists are BECKMANN, ENSOR, NOLDE, KOKOSCHKA, ROUAULT, and SOUTINE. The nature of their subject-matter and the emphasis placed on outline are two reasons for the important part played by Expressionist graphic art. [ills. 996, 997, 1012, 1015, 1026, 1031, 1066, pp. 415, 417, 418, 424]

Eyck, van. On the frame of the polyptych of the *Adoration of the Lamb* in S. Bavon, Ghent, is a Latin quatrain which may be roughly translated as 'The painter Hubert van Eyck, than whom none was greater, began it; Jan, second in art, having completed it at the charge of Jodocus Vyd, invites you by this verse on the 6th May to contemplate what has been done.' The last line is a chronostich containing the date 1432. On the problems raised by the meaning of this verse, more ink has been spilt than on any other subject in the history of art. The only facts assumed to relate to Hubert are these four: in 1424/5 a Master Luberecht was paid by the Ghent Magistrates for two designs for an altarpiece, and a Master Ubrechts was visited by the Magistrates in his workshop; in 1426, a 'Master Hubrechte the painter' had in his workshop a statue and other works connected with an altarpiece, and later in that year the heirs of Lubrecht van Heyke (not specified as a painter) paid inheritance tax on his property. Except for two copies said to have been made of the epitaph on his tomb before its destruction in 1578, and according to which he died on 18 September 1426, that is all that is known of Hubert.
Jan van Eyck is well documented. From 1422 to 1424 he was working for Count John of Holland at The Hague, and around, or before, this date was perhaps connected with the Turin HOURS. In 1425 he was appointed Court Painter and 'varlet de chambre' to Philip the Good, Duke of Burgundy, and from then until late in 1429 he lived in Lille. He removed to Bruges probably in 1430, bought a house there in 1431 or 1432, and lived there until he died. Between 1426 and 1436 he made several secret journeys on the Duke's business, two of which – concerned with marriage negotiations – took him to Spain in 1427 and to Portugal in 1428. Many records testify to his presence and activity in Bruges (payments of salary, a visit in 1432 to his workshop by the town councillors, and one by the Duke himself in 1433) until the final record of his burial in July 1441. In addition to the documented facts, there are a number of signed and dated pictures: the *Portrait of a man*, inscribed 'Tymotheos Leal Souvenir 1432', the *Man in a red turban*, 1433, bearing the painter's challenging motto 'Als ich kan' (As I can) on the frame, and the *Arnolfini marriage group*, 1434, with the declaration of his own participation as a witness – 'Johannes de Eyck fuit hic' (. . . was here) – all in London, NG; the *Madonna and Child* in Melbourne,

1433 (though the inscription here is not contemporary); the *Madonna of Canon van der Paele*, 1436, in Bruges; the *S. Barbara*, an elaborate drawing on a gesso ground, 1437, and the *Madonna of the Fountain*, 1439, in Antwerp; the *Portrait of his wife*, 1439, in Bruges. In all these works the stupendous Eyckian technique is a major factor. For long the brothers were credited with the invention of oil painting, and though this is no longer a tenable idea, it is clear that Jan perfected an oil medium and varnish which has enabled his brilliant colour to survive almost unchanged, and which was fluid enough to allow him to achieve the subtlest effects of light and the most detailed rendering of objects. [Col. pl. 22] It is through his astounding analysis of surfaces that he reaches the larger understanding of form and space; from his capacity to observe the minute he achieves a complete expression of the whole, and his technique is the perfect servant of his realistic, unidealizing, and unemotional attitude.

The Ghent Altar is a very large and complex polyptych. It consists of two superimposed rows of paintings: the upper row has, inside in the centre, *Christ as King* flanked by the *Virgin* and *S. John the Baptist*, and on the insides of the wings *Musician* and *Singing Angels*, and *Adam* and *Eve*; the lower row has, in the centre, the *Adoration of the Lamb*, and on the insides of the wings are continuations of the processions of the faithful coming to adore the Lamb, in the form of four groups of *Judges*, *Knights*, *Hermits*, and *Pilgrims* (the panel of *Judges* is a modern copy of the original, stolen in 1934). On the outside of the wings, in the upper row, is an *Annunciation*, and in the lower row portraits of the *Donor and his wife*, flanked by their patron Saints, *John the Baptist* and *John the Evangelist*. This huge and heterogeneous work is rendered more difficult to interpret by the extensive restorations and repaintings disclosed by recent scientific investigation. The quatrain would make it – with the *Leal Souvenir* portrait – the earliest of Jan's dated works, but it is impossible to decide how much or what parts are due to an earlier hand (that is, to Hubert). The theory has been advanced that the quatrain is a later forgery and Hubert a legendary figure to whom no works or participation in the Ghent Altar can be allowed. This is certainly going too far, for the verse appears to be genuine, and there exist certain works (the *Three Maries at the Sepulchre*, Rotterdam, and the so-called *Friedsam Annunciation*, New York, Met. Mus.) which are related to works by Jan, but not to the point of being attributable to him, and which possess characteristics from which his style could well have developed.

Other works attributed to Jan with reasonable certainty include the *Virgin in a Church*, Berlin; *Annunciation*, Washington, NG; *Madonna with Saints and Donor*, triptych, Dresden; *Madonna with Chancellor Rolin*, Paris, Louvre; *Madonna and Child*, Frankfurt, Städel; and the so-called *Cardinal Albergati*, Vienna, the preparatory drawing for which, in Dresden, is the only surviving silverpoint unanimously attributed to Jan.

Jan's ability and inventiveness make him easily the major artist of the Early Netherlandish School, and his position is challenged only by the MASTER of FLÉMALLE. In Jan, the opulent, politically opportunist, and aristocratic Burgundian Court found its most complete artistic expression. The Ghent Altar was extremely influential throughout the 15th century and the technique evolved by Jan became the accepted Flemish one. His formal influence, however, in the succeeding years was less than that of Roger van der WEYDEN, due to the greater appeal of Roger's warmer and more emotional approach. Jan's chief follower was Petrus CHRISTUS, who is believed to have completed the *Madonna and Child with Saints* (New York, Frick Coll.) commissioned in 1441 a few months before Jan died, and who probably took over his workshop and something of his position as the principal Bruges painter of his day.

Margaret van Eyck, said to have been a sister of Jan and a miniaturist, is pure fiction.

Besides the works already mentioned there are others in Berlin, New York (Met. Mus.), Philadelphia (Johnson), Turin, and Vienna. [ills. 334–6, pp. 320–1. Col. pl. 22]

F

F., Fec., Fecit (Lat. he made it) frequently follows a name on paintings, engravings, etc. as an assertion of authorship.

Fabriano *see* GENTILE da Fabriano.

Fabritius, Barent (1624–73), was the younger brother of Carel. Like his brother, he was probably a pupil of Rembrandt *c.* 1640, but unlike Carel he remained a Rembrandt imitator all his life. He painted portraits, Biblical and mythological subjects, good examples of which can be found in Amsterdam, The Hague, Hartford Conn., and London. [ill. 443, p. 334]

Fabritius, Carel (1622–54), was the finest of Rembrandt's pupils, whose brilliant promise was cut short by the great Delft explosion of 12 October 1654, which killed him as he was working on a portrait. He was in contact with Rembrandt about 1641–3 and was himself probably the master of Vermeer: the extraordinary gap between Rembrandt and Vermeer being bridged by Fabritius's reversal of Rembrandt's practice, in that he painted dark objects against a light background (e.g. the *Self-portrait*, Rotterdam). Several Rembrandtesque portraits have recently been attributed to him, but the few known works – only five are dated, and less than ten are signed – do not seem to confirm these attributions, and there is still considerable confusion with his brother's work. The *Goldfinch* (1654: The Hague) is almost unique in Dutch art, but it has much more in common with Vermeer than with Rembrandt. There are pictures in Amsterdam (Rijksmus.: one apparently dated 1640, but probably 1648/9), Groningen, The Hague, Innsbruck, London (NG: dated 1652 and 1654), Paris (Louvre), Rotterdam, Schwerin (dated 1654), and Warsaw. [ill. 444, p. 334]

Facture, Fattura are the French and Italian equivalents for HANDLING.

Falconet, Étienne-Maurice (1716–91), worked under J.-B. LEMOYNE and was accepted into the Academy in 1714. In 1757 he was appointed Director of Sculpture at the Sèvres Porcelain Manufactory, where he remained until 1766, supervising the production of many pieces from his own models. He also worked for Mme de Pompadour. Through Diderot the Empress Catherine II invited him to Russia in 1766 to make a bronze equestrian monument to Peter the Great at St Petersburg: this is his masterpiece and a great feat of technique as the horse rears up on its huge plinth of rough granite with both forelegs unsupported. He left Russia in 1779, before the statue was unveiled, returning to France in 1781. A stroke in 1783 forced him to stop working. He also wrote on sculpture and was notorious for his opinion that the warmth and softness of the human body were better rendered by his own contemporaries than by the Ancients ('Réflexions sur la sculpture', 1761); most of his own works are of Venus, nymphs, and similar subjects tending to warmth and softness. His more formal *Milo of Croton* (1754: made for the Academy) is in the Louvre, and the *maquette* for the *Peter the Great* is in the Hermitage, Leningrad: the Wallace Coll., and V & A, London, and the Frick Coll., New York, have more characteristic works. [ills. 714, 720, p. 378]

Fantin-Latour, Henri (1836–1904), was a French painter of Romantic figure subjects, portrait groups, and still-life. He exhibited at the Salon regularly from 1861, but found himself in the SALON des Refusés in 1863, and, for all that he seems a straightforward Salon painter, he was friendly with most of the advanced artists of the day, including Manet and Whistler, and also admired the Pre-Raphaelites. He painted several portrait groups, the best known being the *Hommage à Manet* (*L'Atelier aux Batignolles*) (1870: Louvre, Paris), but his Romantic imagination and, later, a passion for Wagner, led him to paint some extraordinary figure subjects. In England he has always been popular for his still-life and flower paintings, executed in a meticulous 'Dutch' manner totally unlike his sub-Delacroix fantasies. There are pictures in Birmingham, Boston, Cambridge (Fitzwm), Cleveland, Dublin, Glasgow (Burrell Coll. and University), Kansas City, London (NG, Tate, V & A), Manchester, Ottawa, Oxford, Port Sunlight (Lever Gall.), Toledo, St Louis, Washington (NG and Phillips), and elsewhere. [ill. 749, p. 382]

Farington, Joseph (1747–1821), was a topographical draughtsman of no great ability who became an RA in 1785 and whose talent for intrigue gave him an enormous influence in that institution. He kept a very full Diary which is one of the principal sources for the history of English art (and the RA) in the last years of the 18th and the early 19th century: extracts from it have been published. The original text is mostly at Windsor Castle, but some parts have been dispersed. Farington's drawings are in London (BM, V & A) and elsewhere. [ill. 921, p. 405]

Fattori, Giovanni (1825–1908), was one of the leading members of the MACCHIAOLI. He was trained in Florence and then fought in 1848–9: in 1861 he won a prize with his *Battle of Magenta* (1861–2: Florence, Gall. d'Arte Moderna). This was followed by other military subjects as well as landscapes and scenes of peasant life.

He visited Paris in 1875, the year after the First Impression-ist Exhibition, but was little influenced by them. There are works by him in Florence, Leghorn, Milan and Rome, as well as about 200 etchings (a technique unusual in 19th-century Italy). [ill. 319, p. 318]

Fauve. At the Paris Salon d'Automne of 1905, the works of a number of painters were hung together in one room: these were MATISSE, MARQUET, DERAIN, VLAMINCK, ROUAULT, Manguin, Camoin, Jean Puy, and Othon Friesz. Their works, full of distortions and flat patterns and painted in violent colour, created a furore, and a critic dubbed them collectively 'Les Fauves' (the wild beasts). They were not, until then – or even afterwards – a par-ticularly coherent group. Matisse came to be regarded as their leader, possibly because he was not unwilling, but the parts of the group had various origins. Matisse, Marquet, Rouault, and Camoin had all been pupils of Gustave MOREAU at the École des Beaux-Arts; Matisse and Mar-quet had often worked together; Rouault pursued a solitary course and found himself among the Fauves rather than sought their company; Derain and Vlaminck worked to-gether, strongly influenced by EXPRESSIONISM; the others adhered temporarily, mostly out of rebellion against the academic system and because their brightly coloured works could be hung in no other company. In 1906 DUFY, and in 1907 BRAQUE and METZINGER, exhibited with them, but by 1908 the Fauves had fallen apart as a group and a number of its members had seceded to CUBISM. [ills. 1001, 1002, 1004, 1006, 1007, p. 416]

Feininger, Lyonel (1871–1956), was born and died in New York, but is really a German Cubist. He went to Germany in 1887 and finally returned to America only in 1937: he was trained in Germany and went to Paris in 1892–3. From 1911 he was interested in Cubism, and DELAUNAY was the main influence on his painting. In 1912 he met the members of the BRÜCKE group and in the following year exhibited with the BLAUE REITER. He was particularly close to KLEE and KANDINSKY, but after his return to the US his works became more abstract. Many German and American museums have examples. [ill. 1049, p. 422]

Ferguson, William Gouw (1632–95), was a Scottish painter of still-life so much in the Dutch manner that he is often confused with painters like Jan WEENIX. He worked in Holland and England. There are four pictures by him in Edinburgh and others in Barnsley, Berlin, London (Tate, V & A at Ham House), and elsewhere. [ill. 473, p. 341]

Ferneley, John (1782–1860), was an English sporting painter whose works were made widely popular in reproduction. He worked in Ireland 1809–10. His *Bay Horse* (1826: London, Tate) is typical. [ill. 901, p. 402]

Ferrari, Gaudenzio (1471/81–1546), was a Lombard painter who combined the influence of Leonardo with that of both Perugino and Correggio and sometimes added a strong dash of German art. His principal fresco cycles are in Lombardy, in the Sacro Monte, Varallo (begun 1517), in S. Cristoforo, Vercelli (1529–32), and in Saronno

(1534–6). The Sacro Monte frescoes, which contain an element of overcrowding derived from German examples, are further complicated by the addition of terracotta figures in the round, also by Gaudenzio, to add to the illusion. There are pictures by him in Amsterdam, Bergamo, Berlin, London (NG), Milan (Brera, Poldi-Pezzoli, Castello, and churches), Paris (Louvre), Sarasota Fla, Turin, and elsewhere. [ill. 155, p. 294]

Ferri, Ciro (1628/34–89), was the closest follower of PIETRO da Cortona, some of whose frescoes he completed in the Pitti Palace, Florence, and elsewhere. He worked mainly in Rome, Florence, and Bergamo and he also made many designs for engravers. [ill. 274, p. 313]

Feti (Fetti), Domenico (1589–1623), was born in Rome and began as a follower of Caravaggio's followers and an admirer of ELSHEIMER. He was taken to Mantua in or before 1613 by Cardinal Ferdinando Gonzaga (who became Duke of Mantua) and worked there as Court Painter until he went to Venice in 1621. In 1622 he settled there and is recorded as gravely ill early in 1623. In Mantua he saw the Rubens portraits and was also influenced by Venetian painting, and these influences, together with his early admiration for Elsheimer, led him to produce smallish genre pictures, usually representing one of the Parables, which are very broadly treated and rich in colour. He painted some frescoes in Mantua, but they are less successful. There are examples in the Royal Coll. (a series at Hampton Court) and in Dresden, Florence (Uffizi, Pitti), Frankfurt (Städel), Manchester, Mantua (Palazzo and Cath.), Munich, New York (Met. Mus.), Paris (Louvre), Venice (Accad.), Vienna, Washington (NG), and York. [ill. 280, p. 312]

Feuerbach, Anselm (1829–80), was, like BÖCKLIN, a German Romantic painter who came under the spell of Italy and Italian art (in his case, Raphael). He was trained in Germany and Antwerp before going to Paris and work-ing in COUTURE's studio (1852–3); he was also simul-taneously influenced by Delacroix and Courbet. In 1855 he went to Italy and spent most of the rest of his life there except for three unsuccessful years (1873–6) teaching in Vienna. He painted some fine portraits, 16th-century Italian in feeling, especially those of Nanna, whose features obsessed him from 1860 to 1865. Karlsruhe has a whole room of his works and most German galleries possess examples. [ill. 616, p. 360]

Fiammingo see DUQUESNOY.

Fine Manner. Early Florentine engravings, of the mid and later 15th century, are divided into two classes – the Broad and Fine Manners. The Fine Manner is so called because it uses fine lines, often cross-hatched, to give a general effect not unlike a wash drawing. The Broad Manner uses bolder lines, parallel but farther apart, often with small hooks at the end, the general effect being similar to a bold pen drawing. MANTEGNA, although not a Florentine, was influenced by the Broad Manner.

Finson (Finsonius), Ludovicus (before 1580–1617), was a rather mysterious Caravaggesque who was born in Bruges, died in Amsterdam, formed his style in Naples, and seems to have worked principally in Aix-en-Provence. He was there in 1610, but his *Annunciation*, still there, is signed and inscribed '1612 in Naples', and another version is in Naples Mus. His style was closely modelled on Caravaggio's Neapolitan followers (cf. the UTRECHT School) and he actually owned a part-share of Caravaggio's *Madonna of the Rosary*. There are two pictures of 1613 in Marseilles, and the *Martyrdom of S. Stephen* (1614) is in Arles Cathedral; most of his works are in the South of France, especially Aix, but there are attributed pictures in Chicago and Oxford. [ill. 404, p. 329]

Fixative. A kind of thin varnish sprayed on to drawings and pastels to prevent their being rubbed.

Flaxman, John (1755–1826), was an English NEO-CLASSIC sculptor with an enormous European reputation in his own day. He first exhibited in 1767 and became friendly with ROMNEY early in his career. He went to the RA Schools in 1770 and met BLAKE at about this time: much of his sympathy for Gothic art is probably due to this friendship. In 1775 he began to work for Wedgwood, who was then popularizing Neoclassical designs in his new 'Etruscan' ware. With Wedgwood's help he went to Italy in 1787, where he remained until 1794, looking at a great variety of works of all periods. A sketchbook in the V & A, London, shows the catholicity of his tastes, for it includes drawings after Bernini although he loathed everything he stood for. His dislike of the Baroque was probably partly religious in origin, reflecting his Low Church sympathies; and it is interesting that BACON was a Methodist and BANKS an atheist, and all employed only generalized Christian symbolism – non-Catholic – in their funerary sculpture, although Flaxman prided himself on Christianizing monumental sculpture. After he returned from Italy Flaxman devoted himself almost exclusively to monuments, two of his most famous having been begun in Rome. These are the *Mansfield*, erected in Westminster Abbey in 1795, and the *Collins* of the same year in Chichester Cathedral. While still in Rome he had also begun the book-illustrations which brought him the greatest fame on the Continent and influenced later generations – INGRES and the NAZARENER among them. These are pure outline drawings of strictly Neoclassical simplicity, which give the impression of being sketches for relief sculpture: they include long series of plates for the 'Odyssey' and the 'Iliad', Aeschylus, Hesiod, Dante, as well as Milton and Bunyan drawings. He became an RA in 1800 and was made Professor of Sculpture in 1810, his lectures being published posthumously in 1829. Among his few statues in the round which are not monuments are the *Fury of Athamas* (1791–2: Nat. Trust, Ickworth House) and *S. Michael overcoming Satan* (1821) and the *Pastoral Apollo* (1824: both Nat. Trust, Petworth). University College, London, has a large collection of his drawings and models, and the Soane Mus., London, also has models. Other works are scattered as far as Madras and Quebec and include works in Bath, many in Chichester Cath., Copenhagen, Edinburgh (SNPG), Glasgow, Gloucester, London (NPG, V & A, RA, Westminster Abbey, and St Paul's), and many English churches and cathedrals. [ill. 880, p. 399]

Flinck, Govaert (1615–60), was a pupil of REMBRANDT, and imitated him until the mid 1650s, though always with a greater striving for elegance, which brought him a successful practice as a portrait painter. He had ambitions, however, as a historical painter, and was commissioned by the City Council of Amsterdam to decorate the interior of the new Town Hall with large historical works, but he died before executing the work, which was then divided among different artists – including Rembrandt. There are works in Amsterdam (Rijksmus.), Antwerp, Berlin, Boston (Mus.), Brunswick, Cape Town, Dresden, Dublin, London (NG, Wallace Coll.), Leningrad, Munich, New York (Met. Mus.), Paris (Louvre), Rotterdam, Vienna, and elsewhere. [ill. 445, p. 335]

Floris, Frans (Frans de Vriendt) (*c.* 1517–70), was a Flemish painter who went to Italy, where he studied Michelangelo, Raphael, and the Antique. He entered the Antwerp Guild in 1540, and was prominent among the Antwerp ITALIANIZERS.
There are works in Amsterdam (Rijksmus.), Antwerp, Berlin, Brussels, Dresden, Florence (Uffizi), The Hague, Madrid, Vienna, and elsewhere. His two sons, Jan Battista and Frans, were also painters; the second worked in Rome. [ill. 382, p. 326]

Fontainebleau, First and Second Schools of. The First School of Fontainebleau is the name given to the combination of Mannerist painting and stucco decoration introduced by the Italians ROSSO, PRIMATICCIO, and Niccolò dell'ABBATE into the Royal Palaces of France, particularly that of Fontainebleau, under the patronage of François I. The style begins in 1530, with Rosso's arrival in France, and continues to *c.* 1560 under Niccolò dell' Abbate. The extreme elegance of Parmigianino's art is characteristic of this First School. The Second School of Fontainebleau represents an attempt at a similar decorative tradition in the second half of the 16th century, mostly under Henri IV. The Palaces decorated by him have suffered greatly, but the Salle Ovale at Fontainebleau is an example of the revival. The names usually associated with the Second School are not illustrious: Ambroise Dubois (1542/3–1614), Toussaint Dubreuil (1561–1602), and Martin Fréminet (1567–1602). [ills. 195, 675, 676, pp. 302, 372]

Foppa, Vincenzo (1427/30–1515/16), was the leading painter of the Milanese School before it was transformed by the influence of Leonardo da Vinci. He was born near Brescia and may have been a pupil of the Paduan SQUARCIONE, who was Mantegna's master: in any case his first dated work, the *Crucifixion* (1456: Bergamo) shows the influence of Jacopo Bellini, and Foppa's later works amply prove that he knew the work of Jacopo's son Giovanni and son-in-law Mantegna. From 1456 to 1490 he worked in Pavia and was employed a good deal by the Dukes of Milan. There are works by him in Milan (Brera, Castello, Poldi-Pezzoli, S. Eustorgio) and in Baltimore (Walters), Bergamo, Berlin, Brescia (Accad. and Carmine), London (NG and Wallace Coll., all that is left of the frescoes in the Medici Bank), Milan, New York (Met. Mus.), Pavia, Philadelphia (Johnson), Washington (NG), and Worcester Mass. [ill. 116, p. 288]

Forain, Jean-Louis (1852–1931), was a draughtsman and illustrator working for satirical papers in Paris from 1876 onwards. He was greatly influenced by Rembrandt and Goya, by DAUMIER, who preceded him in his chosen field, and by Manet. He was a friend and follower of Degas, and exhibited four times with the Impressionists between 1879 and 1886. Until *c.* 1909 his subjects were chiefly scenes from Parisian life, with occasional cartoons on political scandals, e.g. the Panama Canal; after 1909 he turned to the depiction of social misery and the callousness and inhumanity of the processes of justice. He also illustrated the New Testament. Most of his drawings are in limpid watercolour washes of sepia on a loose and evocative outline, full of movement and luminosity, highly reminiscent of Daumier. There are works in Boston (Mus.), Chicago, Dresden, London (Courtauld Inst., Tate), Paris (Louvre), Washington, and elsewhere. [ill. 785, p. 388]

Foreshortening is perspective applied to a single object. An arm pointing directly at the spectator so that little more than the hand can be seen is said to be strongly foreshortened. Extreme foreshortening can have emotional overtones, as is best demonstrated by Mantegna's *Dead Christ* (Milan, Brera). The work of Uccello is sufficient proof that a mastery of foreshortening is not necessarily accompanied by the ability to construct coherent perspective systems.

Found Object (*Objet trouvé*). In SURREALIST theory an object of any kind, such as a shell found on a walk, can be a work of art; and such 'Found Objects' have been exhibited. If a little judicious touching-up has been indulged in, the object is known technically as a 'Found Object Composed'.

Fouquet, Jehan (*c.* 1420–in or before 81), was the major French painter of the 15th century. He went to Italy and was in Rome at some time between 1443 and February 1447, since he is said to have painted a portrait of Eugenius IV and two attendants: this, however, depends on the identification of Jehan the Frenchman with *Giachetto francoso*, which is not self-evident. He may have gone to Rome with a French embassy in 1446, or he may have gone to get a dispensation to enter the priesthood, since there is a letter of 1449 from Nicholas V to 'Johanni Fouquet Juniori clerico....' By 1448 he was back in his native Tours, where he soon began to work for Charles VII. He was appointed Painter to Louis XI in 1475. He is known to have designed sculpture and to have worked for the Order of S. Michel, but the only documented works extant are the miniatures in a copy of 'Les Antiquités Judaïques' (Paris, Bibliothèque Nationale). On grounds of style several other MSS and some easel pictures are attributed to him: they include works in Paris (Louvre (portraits of *Charles VII* and *Jouvenel des Ursins*) and Bib. Nat.), Antwerp and Berlin (the two halves of the Melun Diptych: *Étienne Chevalier* and *Madonna*), Chantilly (Musée Condé), London (BM), Munich (Staatsbibliothek), and Nouans Indre-et-Loire, Parish Church (*Deposition*).
A very fine portrait of a young man, dated 1456, in the Liechtenstein Coll., Vaduz, used to be attributed to Fouquet but is now generally given to the Master of 1456,

and another portrait, *Man with a Glass of Wine*, in the Louvre, has also been attributed to him. [ills. 668, 669, pp. 372–3]

Fraglia. The Venetian painters' GUILD.

Fragonard, Jean-Honoré (1732–1806), was the typical painter of gallant and sentimental subjects in the reign of Louis XV during the ascendancy of Mme du Barry, and during the reign of Louis XVI. He was a pupil of Chardin for a few months in 1750 and then went to BOUCHER until 1752, when he won the Rome Prize: he did not go directly to Rome, however, but worked under Carle van Loo 1753–6. From 1756 until 1761 he worked at the French Academy in Rome, where he studied the living TIEPOLO more than any of the Old Masters. He also went, with Hubert Robert, to the South under the patronage of the Abbé de Saint-Non, who later wrote a book about the trip. In 1761 Fragonard returned to Paris and made his name in 1765 with his *High Priest Coresus sacrificing himself to save Callirhoe* (Paris, Louvre), a piece in the very Grand Manner. He soon abandoned History (having been elected *Agréé* of the Academy) and turned to more congenial subjects, such as *The Swing* (*c.* 1766: London, Wallace Coll.). This was originally commissioned from a serious history painter by the Baron de St Julien: 'I desire', he said, 'that you should paint Madame [pointing to his mistress] on a swing which is being set in motion by a Bishop. You must place me where I can have a good view of the legs of this pretty little thing. . . .' The serious history painter could think of nothing else to say except to recommend M. Fragonard as a more suitable person. He continued in this light-hearted and sometimes frankly erotic vein with great success, being commissioned by Mme du Barry to paint a series of the *Progress of Love* for her new house; unaccountably, however, she rejected them and Fragonard took them back to his native Grasse when he fled there during the Terror. They are now in New York (Frick Coll.). In 1773 he went to Italy again, returning via Austria and Germany. The Revolution put an end to his patrons and to the demand for his kind of art, which was entirely superseded by the high-mindedness of DAVID and Republican Virtue. In desperate poverty, he returned to Paris from Grasse, and it was David who got him a job in the Museums Service. He died in Paris, almost totally forgotten. There are works by him in Besançon, Paris (Louvre and Banque de France), and other French museums: outside France the best collection is in London (Wallace Coll.), and there are others in Boston, Cincinnati, Cleveland, Detroit, St Louis, New York (Met. Mus.), Washington (NG), and elsewhere. [ill. 728, p. 380]

Francesca, Piero della (dei Franceschi), *see* PIERO.

Francesco di Giorgio (1439–1501/2), was a Sienese who worked principally as an architect and designer of fortifications, but who also executed sculptures, and a few paintings in a tender and linear style. There are examples in Amiens, London (NG), New York (Met. Mus.), and Siena. [ill. 112, p. 288]

Francia, Francesco (*c.* 1450–1517/18), was a Bolognese goldsmith who is first recorded as a painter in 1486. It used to be thought that a *Madonna* (London, NG) of

1492 was his earliest known dated work; this is now regarded as a forgery and the earliest picture would now seem to be the large *Felicini Madonna* (signed and dated 1494: Bologna, Pinacoteca), which shows a blend of the style of PERUGINO with that of COSTA and the Ferrarese and almost no personal character. Until 1506, when Costa went as Court Painter to Mantua, they worked in partnership, but after that date he was more and more influenced by Raphael and the soft style of Perugino and the Umbrians. There are works by him in the Royal Coll. and in Berlin, Bologna (Pinacoteca, Mus. Civico and several churches), Boston (Gardner), Budapest, Chantilly, Dresden, Dublin, Ferrara (Cath.), Florence (Uffizi), Glasgow, London (NG), Milan (Brera, Poldi-Pezzoli), Munich, New York (Met. Mus.), Paris (Louvre), Philadelphia (Mus. and Johnson), Rome (Gall. Naz., Capitoline, Borghese), San Marino Cal. (Huntington), Turin, Vienna (K-H Mus., Akad.), Washington (NG), Worcester Mass., and elsewhere. [ill. 121, p. 289]

Franciabigio (*c.* 1482/3–1525), was a Florentine painter who was the assistant of ANDREA del Sarto and a pupil of ALBERTINELLI. Franciabigio's best works are his rather introspective portraits, and he is a characteristic representative of the generation between Andrea del Sarto and Fra BARTOLOMMEO, as may be seen in his frescoes in the Chiostro dello Scalzo, Florence, of about 1518. There are works by him in Florence (Uffizi, Pitti, and churches) and in the Royal Collection, Barnard Castle (Bowes Mus.), Berlin, Brussels, Detroit, London (NG), Munich, New York (Met. Mus.), Oxford, Paris (Louvre), Rome (Borghese and Gall. Naz.), and Vienna. [ill. 173, p. 296]

Francis, Sam (*b.* 1923), is a Californian Tachiste painter. He served in the US Air Force 1943–5, and, after a long spell in hospital, became an abstract painter in 1947. In 1950 he went to Paris, joining the circle of American painters around RIOPELLE. He has painted murals for the Kunsthalle, Basle (1956–8) and, on a visit to Japan in 1957, for a School of Flower Arrangement there. His technique of dribbling paint differs from the more 'calligraphic' style used by many Americans. There are paintings by him in London (Tate) and New York (M of MA). [ill. 1110, p. 429]

Francke, Master (active *c.* 1405–after 24), was the most important Hamburg painter after Master BERTRAM, but was (like KONRAD von Soest) an exponent of the SOFT STYLE. He was probably in France about 1405, since his style owes much to French illuminated MSS. His major work was the *S. Thomas à Becket Altar*, painted for the merchants trading with England, of which only fragments are known (begun 1424: Hamburg). Other works are in Hamburg, Helsinki, and Leipzig. [ill. 539, p. 351]

Fresco (Ital. fresh). Wall-painting in a medium like watercolour on plaster. *Fresco secco*, painted on dry plaster, gives an effect not unlike an ordinary distempered wall and suffers from the same defect of the paint scaling off, but true fresco, or *buon fresco*, practised in Italy from the 14th century and perfected in the 16th century, is one of the most permanent forms of wall decoration known. The wall is first rough-plastered and then a coat, known as the

arricciato, is applied. On this the CARTOON is traced, so that the whole composition is transferred to the wall, and then an area sufficient for one day's work is covered with the final layer of plaster, called the *intonaco*. The cartoon is redrawn over this, joining up with the parts still uncovered, and the damp plaster is then painted with pigments mixed with plain water or lime-water, allowance being made for the fact that the colours dry much lighter. Because the plaster is still damp a chemical reaction takes place and the colours become integrated with the wall itself, so that scaling cannot occur. The use of a detailed, full-size cartoon means that several assistants can work simultaneously on different parts of the wall, provided that all work is done from the top downwards so that the splashes fall on the unpainted parts. At the end of the day all the unpainted *intonaco* is cut away, to be relaid next day, so that the working surface is always damp: careful examination of a fresco reveals the joins in the plaster and from these the number of days taken to paint the whole can be estimated approximately. *Fresco secco* may legitimately be employed to retouch or to add accents, but during the 16th century it was almost obligatory to work entirely in *buon fresco*, and some of the finest examples of the technique are Raphael's decorations in the Stanze of the Vatican. Climatic conditions outside Central Italy are not always favourable and the attempts to revive the technique for the decoration of the House of Lords, early in the 19th century, were not successful, although RIVERA has practised a form of fresco in Mexico in the present century. [ill. 1072, p. 425, Col. pls. 1–9]

Friedrich, Caspar David (1774–1840), was the most purely Romantic of German landscape painters, and in his vision of the great forests one of the purest of European Romantics. He was particularly interested in the expression of effects of light and of the seasons, but his feeling for the woods has perhaps no parallel outside Altdorfer. The best collection of his works is in Dresden, where he spent most of his life. [ill. 603, p. 358]

Frith, William Powell (1819–1909), was the son of an innkeeper in Harrogate, who virtually forced him to become an artist. He started as an itinerant portrait painter, and after 1840 specialized in costume history and genre subjects, becoming one of the most successful painters of contemporary life. *Ramsgate Sands* (1853: Royal Coll.), *Derby Day* (1858: London, Tate), *The Railway Station* (1862: Royal Holloway College, near Windsor) depict with minute detail an enormous variety of anecdotal incidents, which made his works so popular that barriers had to be erected at the Royal Academy to protect them from the crush of admirers. He travelled a good deal in Holland, and visited Italy; he published three volumes of memoirs, recounting in the most matter-of-fact way the sources of his subjects, and the details of his phenomenal success. [ill. 953, p. 408]

Froment, Nicolas (active 1450–90), worked in the South of France and was painter to René of Anjou. There are two documented works by him: the curious *Mary in the Burning Bush* (1476: Aix-en-Provence, Cath.) and the *Raising of Lazarus* (1461: Florence, Uffizi). A diptych of

René and his wife, attributed to Froment, is in Paris (Louvre). [ill. 667, p. 373]

Frottage (from Fr. *frotter*, to rub). Most people know the parlour game which consists of putting a piece of thin paper over a penny and rubbing a soft pencil over it, causing an image of the monarch's head to appear on the paper. This simple device, dignified by the name of *frottage*, has frequently been used to obtain effects of texture in abstract or semi-abstract painting. It is normally done by making a *frottage* on a piece of paper and then applying one or more of these to a canvas as COLLAGES. Max ERNST frequently used the method, employing the floorboards and other wooden surfaces.

Frueauf, Rueland I and II were Austrian painters from Passau. Rueland I (*c.* 1440/5–1507) worked in Passau and Salzburg from 1470 in a style derived from Flemish painters such as Jan van Eyck and the Master of Flémalle. There are four *Passion Scenes* of 1490–1 by him in Vienna (K-H Mus.).
His son Rueland II (*c.* 1470/5–1545 or later) was a citizen of Passau before 1497, a Councillor in 1533, and was still active as a painter in 1545. He painted a series of scenes from the life of S. Leopold, some of which are signed RF and dated 1507, for Klosterneuburg, near Vienna, as well as a *S. Anne with the Virgin and Child* (1508: Vienna K-H Mus.). Other works by father or son are in Boston, Budapest, Cambridge Mass. (Fogg), Detroit, Munich, Prague, and Venice (Correr). [ills. 554, 555, p. 353]

Fuller, Isaac (*d.* 1672), was probably trained in France and was working in Oxford in 1644, at the same time as DOBSON. He seems to have been a very Bohemian character, and his few surviving works are all painted with a fierce bravura and an impasto distantly reminiscent of Rembrandt. His altarpiece in All Souls College, Oxford, is now lost but was described by Evelyn as 'too full of nakeds for a chapell' ('Diary', 1664). He died in London. There are works in London (Tate, NPG, and Dulwich) and Oxford (*Self-portrait*, 1670, in the Bodleian Library and a version in Queen's College). [ill. 817, p. 393]

Fuseli, Henry (1741–1825), was Swiss by birth, his name, Füssli, being modified to suit the Italian tongue. His father, a painter, forced him to become a clergyman, and he was ordained in 1761, but his exposure of a dishonest magistrate ended his career as a parson. In 1763 he began studying art in Berlin and later came to England to work as a hack translator of French, German (WINCKELMANN, as early as 1765), and Italian books, and occasional illustrator. He was encouraged by Reynolds to become a painter, and in 1770 went to Rome for eight years, where he taught himself, mainly by copying Michelangelo in the Sistine Chapel. On his return to England he began ex-

hibiting works of imaginative power, executed in a deficient technique, his first success being *The Nightmare* (1782), a picture redolent of Romantic horror. He then worked for Boydell's Shakespeare Gallery, became an ARA in 1788 and an RA in 1790, and began a series of huge paintings illustrating Milton (46 in all) to which public and patrons remained indifferent. He was made Professor of Painting at the Academy in 1799 and Keeper in 1804, and he held the double office until his death. Among his pupils were Etty, Haydon, Mulready, Leslie, Constable, Landseer, and the artistic memoirs of the period are full of anecdotes of his eccentricities and sarcasms. Fuseli's art, with its extravagance of movement and gesture, its distortions and stylizations of form (particularly in his often erotic drawings of women), its exploitation of the murky layers of horror and fear in the imagination, is the antithesis of Reynolds's classicism and Gainsborough's charm, but is a less dedicated form of the visionary quality which inspired BLAKE whom he first met *c.* 1787. He also knew DAVID (in Rome 1775/8) and GÉRARD. In 1831 a 'Life' was published with an edition of his writings.
There are works in Auckland NZ, Birmingham, Cambridge (Fitzwm), Frankfurt (Goethe Mus.), London (Tate, Courtauld Inst.), Weimar, Zürich, and elsewhere. [ill. 909, p. 403]

Futurism. This word, used by 'Punch' and others to mean any art more recent than 1900, has in fact a precise meaning. It was the only important modern movement to be largely independent of Paris (for which reason it is not popular in France), and it can be dated from 20 February 1909, to its virtual demise in World War I (*c.* 1915). It was actually born in Paris, in an article in 'Le Figaro' by MARINETTI, poet, dramatist, mountebank, and future friend of Mussolini, in which he announced '. . . a new beauty . . . a roaring motor-car, which runs like a machine-gun, is more beautiful than the *Winged Victory of Samothrace* . . . We wish to glorify war. . . .' This general Manifesto was followed by a 'Manifesto of Futurist Painting' (1910) and a 'Technical Manifesto' (also 1910), which is the key to the aesthetics of Futurism. They wished to represent machines or figures actually in motion – 'We proclaim . . . that universal dynamism must be rendered as dynamic sensation; that movement and light destroy the substance of objects.' The 'Manifesto of Futurist Painting' was signed by BOCCIONI, CARRÀ, Russolo, BALLA, and SEVERINI; Boccioni also issued a Manifesto of his own, on sculpture, in 1912. In that year the Futurist Exhibition was held in Paris and caused great scandal; from Paris it went on to London and Berlin and eventually all over Europe, causing riots and general excitement. Nevertheless, Futurism as an aesthetic force died early in World War I and all the major Futurists who survived have since returned to a more traditional method of expressing their ideas. [ills. 1033, 1034, p. 419]

G

Gabo, Naum (*b.* 1890), was born in Russia and is the younger brother of PEVSNER. He abandoned a medical career and began to study in Munich under the great German art historian Wölfflin. In 1910 he met KANDINSKY and in 1913/14, while visiting his brother, then a Cubist painter in Paris, he met other artists and, on returning to Russia in 1917, he found himself involved in art and politics. He and his brother opposed TATLIN and in 1920 issued their 'Realistic Manifesto', beginning: 'We deny volume as an expression of space. . . .' Inevitably, he had to leave Russia and he spent the years 1922–32 in Berlin, leaving at the time of the Nazi rise to power. He spent many years in England, broadcasting for the BBC during the war, and in 1946 he settled in America. There are works by him in London (Tate) and New York (M of MA). [ill. 1137, p. 432]

Gaddi, Taddeo (*d.* 1366), was one of the most faithful of the followers of GIOTTO, for whom he is supposed to have worked for 24 years – thus transmitting, through his son Agnolo, the Giotto tradition to the very end of the Trecento, and even, through Agnolo's pupil Cennini, into the Quattrocento. Since Giotto died in 1337 Taddeo must have been apprenticed to him not later than 1313, but by 1332 he took an important independent commission to paint the fresco cycle of the *Life of the Virgin* in the Baroncelli Chapel in Sta Croce, Florence, where Giotto himself painted four chapels. These frescoes were completed in 1338 and form his most important work; they show a strong dependence on Giotto and also a certain desire to break away, which is confirmed by the signed and dated triptych (1334: Berlin) which shows affinity with the art of Bernardo DADDI. Several other dated works are known, and in 1347 his name heads the list of famous painters who might be employed to paint a polyptych for S. Giovanni Fuorcivitas, Pistoia. He was given the commission, and the altarpiece (dated 1353) is still in the church. He also painted a series of scenes from the Life of Christ and of S. Francis on the panels of a Sacristy cupboard door (now in Florence, Accad., Berlin, and Munich): these are often adapted from Giotto's frescoes in Sta Croce and Assisi. Other works are in Berne, Bristol, Florence (Uffizi, Accad., Horne Mus., Bargello, and churches), New York (Met. Mus.), Pisa (S. Francesco), Yale University, and elsewhere. [ill. 26, p. 272]

His son, Agnolo (*d.* 1396) was working in the Vatican as an assistant to his brother Giovanni in 1369 and seems to have had a very prosperous career, founding the fortunes of the Gaddi family. He painted a series of frescoes in Sta Croce, so that his style is easily comparable with that of both Giotto and his own father: the most important of

his frescoes is the cycle in the choir of the *True Cross* (perhaps of the early 1380s). There are documented frescoes in Prato Cathedral (1392–5) and panels in S. Miniato al Monte, Florence (1393–6). Other works are in Florence and in Berlin, London (NG), Montreal, Munich, Paris (Louvre), Perugia (Cath.), Washington (NG), Yale, and elsewhere. [ill. 27, p. 272]

Gainsborough, Thomas (1727–88), was born in Sudbury, Suffolk, but went to London in 1740, where he worked for the next few years under GRAVELOT and probably met HAYMAN, then working on his Vauxhall decorations. The connection with Hayman is not very clear, but it is certain that many of the small portrait groups, with the figures set in a realistic landscape, which Gainsborough painted at the beginning of his career are markedly dependent on Hayman. One of the principal influences on him at this stage, however, was Dutch 17th-century landscape painting. In London he seems to have copied and restored such pictures for the dealers, and it is certain that he thought of himself as a landscape painter in this style. His earliest landscapes, painted in Suffolk, are very close to the example of Wynants, Ruisdael, and Hobbema as may be seen from the most famous of them, the *Cornard Wood* (finished 1748: London, NG), of which Gainsborough himself wrote: '. . . as an early instance how strong my inclination stood for Landskip, this picture was actually painted at Sudbury in the year 1748; it was begun *before I left school*; – and was the means of my Father's sending me to London . . .' All his life he was to regard landscape as his real bent, but he painted portraits for a living and set up in Sudbury *c.* 1748. He moved to Ipswich *c.* 1750 and remained there until he moved to Bath at the end of 1759. In Suffolk he continued to paint landscapes as well as the little portrait groups, like conversation pieces in a park, which distantly echo Watteau – perhaps through the French influence of Gravelot as well as from Hayman. A pair of early landscapes at Woburn Abbey (1755) are also French in style. His move to Bath, then a highly fashionable town, was probably in order to find more sitters. This he did, and he remained the most sought-after painter there until his final removal to London in 1774. His Bath period is characterized by a loss of the ingenuous quality of his early work, which gives way to a sense of fashionable elegance, now often displayed in full-length portraits, life-size, set against an imaginary landscape background. The influence of van Dyck, whom he now had opportunities to study, is very apparent in such pictures as the *Blue Boy* (San Marino, Calif.) and some others in which he actually dresses the sitter in van Dyck costume. He continued to paint landscapes but they are now more Arcadian in quality, obviously composed rather than observed, although the finest of them, such as the *Harvest Wagon* (Birmingham, Barber Inst.), have a new richness of colour. He began to exhibit in London (at the Society of Artists) in 1761 and was sufficiently well known there to be among the original members of the Royal Academy when it was founded by George III in 1768. He was later elected to the Council of the Academy, but his relations with it were always uncertain: in 1773 he quarrelled with the hanging of his pictures and did not exhibit again until 1777; after another dispute in 1784 he ceased to exhibit there. His move to London in 1774 was in order to match himself against Reynolds, and most people relished the rivalry. Their styles are utterly different and Gainsborough, who was fortunate in seizing a likeness much better than Reynolds could, is often empty and mechanical in his later portraits; yet he has always, as Reynolds has not, a superb handling of paint. The rivalry was rendered the more piquant by the fact that Reynolds was knighted and the head of the King's own Academy – yet all the Royal Family preferred Gainsborough to paint them, although RAMSAY was Painter to the King until his death in 1784, when Reynolds succeeded to the title but not the favour. From about 1780 Gainsborough painted several 'fancy pictures', more or less in imitation of Murillo, of a poetic quality which was an extension of his interest in landscape. His later landscapes are much influenced by Rubens and were composed of 'broken stones, dried weeds and pieces of looking-glass . . . magnified and improved into rocks, trees and water'. The *Watering Place* (RA 1777: Tate) was described by Horace Walpole: 'the landscape in the style of Rubens is the most beautiful which has ever been painted in England and equal to the great masters'.

Contrary to normal 18th-century practice Gainsborough painted all his pictures himself and never employed a drapery man. His technique was, he realized, an essential part of the effect he sought and he made it a beauty in its own right: it is best described in the noble tribute paid by his rival Reynolds in an obituary 'Discourse' (the 14th) at the RA in which he says, 'all those odd scratches and marks which, on a close examination, are so observable . . . and which even to experienced painters appear rather the effect of accident than design; this chaos, this uncouth and shapeless appearance, by a kind of magic, at a certain distance assumes form . . .' He seems to have used very long brushes and to have diluted the paint with turpentine to the consistency of watercolour. As a result, his works have lasted much better than those of almost any other 18th-century British painter. His wife's nephew Gainsborough Dupont (c. 1755–97) was his pupil and imitator. There are pictures by him in almost every major museum. [ills. 485, 839, 845, 931, pp. 343, 395–6, 405. Col. pl. 21]

Galgario, Fra, *see* GHISLANDI.

Garzone is an Italian word for a boy apprentice, less skilled than an assistant or JOURNEYMAN. When a part of a picture is apparently ill-executed it is usual to blame the *garzone*.

Gaudier-Brzeska, Henri (1891–1915), was a French sculptor who lived in London (Brzeska was the name of a

Polish woman he lived with). He was associated with the Vorticist movement, but he joined the French Army in 1914 and was killed before he had time to develop as a sculptor: he is perhaps at his best in the calligraphic drawings made in the Zoo, where the taut pen line perfectly expresses the grace of a puma or a jaguar. He is well represented in the Tate Gallery, London, and also in Chicago, Liverpool, Manchester, New York (M of MA), Southampton, and elsewhere. [ill. 1124, p. 430]

Gauguin, Paul (1848–1903), was born in Paris. Part of his childhood was spent in Peru, whence his mother's family came, and from 1865 to 1871 he was at sea. He became a stockbroker in 1871, and a Sunday-painter who collected the works of the Impressionists and joined in their exhibitions (1881–6). He gave up his job in 1883, and after many vicissitudes separated from his family and went to live in Britanny at Pont-Aven and Le Pouldu, where he worked from 1886 to 1890, except for visits to Paris, a trip to Panama and Martinique in 1887, and a disastrous stay of two months with Van Gogh in Arles in 1888. In 1891 he went to Tahiti, returned to Paris in 1893 for lack of money, but went back to the South Sea Islands in 1895. His health was failing and he had been seriously hurt in a brawl with sailors in Britanny in 1894. His remaining years were spent in poverty, illness, and continual strife with the colonial authorities through his championing of native causes. He died at Atuana in the Marquesas.

His early works may be ranged with those of the Impressionists, particularly with Pissarro and Cézanne, but after 1886 when his works hung in the eighth and last Impressionist Exhibition with those of Seurat he endeavoured to introduce more colour and this tendency became more marked after his voyage to Martinique. In 1888 at Pont-Aven he met Émile BERNARD, the influence of whose knowledge of medieval art joined with Gauguin's interest in primitive sculpture, Japanese, Romanesque, and Far and Near Eastern art, to encourage him to abandon Impressionism and all attempts at the representation of nature in favour of SYNTHETISM. His rejection of Western civilization led to his departure for Tahiti, and to his efforts to express through an art free from the conventions of the naturalistic tradition the simplicity of life among primitive and unspoiled peoples. His influence has been enormous, since he is one of the main sources from which non-naturalistic 20th-century art has emanated.

There are works, including sculpture, in Baltimore, Basle, Birmingham (Barber Inst.), Boston (Mus.), Brussels, Buffalo, Chicago, Cleveland Ohio, Edinburgh (NG of S), Essen, Glasgow, Grenoble, Hartford Conn., Indianapolis, Kansas City, London (Tate, Courtauld Inst.), Los Angeles, Manchester (City Mus.), Minneapolis, Moscow, Newcastle, New York (Met. Mus., M of MA), Oslo, Ottawa, Paris (Louvre, Petit Palais), Prague, Rheims, Stockholm, Toledo Ohio, Washington (NG, Phillips), and elsewhere. [ills. 986, 987, p. 414]

Gaulli *see* BACICCIA.

Geddes, Andrew (1783–1844), studied from 1807 onwards in the RA Schools, where he met Wilkie, whose lifelong friend he became. He painted portraits in Edinburgh from 1810 to 1814, when he removed to London although he frequently visited Edinburgh. In 1828 he travelled in France, Germany, and Italy, and was elected an ARA in 1832. He died soon after a visit to Holland. His portraits, direct and in a solid technique with a skilful use of grey, have much charm; his subject paintings tend to be sentimental and vaguely Nazarene in type. He is well represented in Edinburgh (NG). [ill. 850, p. 397]

Geertgen tot Sint Jans (i.e. 'little Gerard of the Brethren of S. John') was a Dutch painter active in the late 15th century. He was born at Leyden and is said to have died at about 28, perhaps *c.* 1485/95. He was a pupil of Albert van OUWATER and the only works which can reasonably be connected with his name are two very large panels in Vienna, K-H Mus., originally back and front of a single panel from an altarpiece in the Monastery of S. John at Haarlem, for which Geertgen worked. They represent the *Lamentation over the Dead Christ* and *Julian the Apostate burning the bones of S. John Baptist, with members of the Order saving some relics.* The curious egg-shaped heads make it easy to group some other works around these two, but a picture of the Cathedral at Haarlem (in the Cathedral) which is traditionally his shows no characteristics in common. The principal pictures attributed are in Amsterdam (Rijksmus.), Berlin, Cleveland, Leipzig, Leningrad, London (NG), Milan (Ambrosiana), Paris (Louvre), Prague, Utrecht. [ill. 345, p. 323]

Gelder, Aert de (1645–1727), was a pupil of Rembrandt in the 1660s and continued his late style well into the 18th century. He painted principally Biblical subjects and portraits, and his Old Testament scenes are often markedly Rembrandtesque in their strong, warm colour as well as in their use of Oriental types and costume. There is a series of New Testament scenes, of *c.* 1715, in the galleries of Aschaffenburg and Munich and other pictures in Amsterdam, Berlin, Birmingham (Barber Inst.), Boston, Brighton, Chicago, Dordrecht, Dresden, Frankfurt, The Hague, London (Dulwich), Melbourne, Paris (Louvre), Providence RI, Rotterdam, Vaduz (Liechtenstein Coll.), and Vienna. [ill. 456, p. 336]

Genre (Fr. kind, variety). A type of picture, usually small in size, depicting not so much a subject as everyday life and surroundings, though the opportunity for narrative content leads easily into subdivisions such as moralities and the conversation piece, which is a form of genre portrait. The important thing is that it should not represent idealized life. Small touches of genre – interest in setting, in objects – can be found in 14th- and 15th-century Italian painting and in early Flemish painting, but not so strongly developed as to affect its status as religious art. Although genre appears in Italy in e.g. CARPACCIO and, later, in CARAVAGGIO, CRESPI, and Piazzetta, it plays a minor role until the 18th century when Pietro LONGHI devoted his whole life to it. It is in the North that it first gains a strong hold and appears as a distinct form, as in the engravings of the MASTER of the HOUSEBOOK and in the *Bankers* of Massys and Reymerswaele. In 17th-century Holland the absence of patronage for religious and decorative painting stimulated the development of genre, and OSTADE, STEEN, METSU, TER BORCH, VERMEER, and de HOOCH produced little else, each specializing in sub-varieties such as peasant and tavern scenes, musical or genteel drinking parties, with displays of glittering satin, or simple interiors with dazzling effects of light. In the 18th century, in France CHARDIN imbued his humble subjects with supreme dignity and beauty; in England the main forms were the moralities of HOGARTH, the 'fancy pictures' of GAINSBOROUGH, and the rustic scenes of MORLAND. In the 19th century the genre subject became the commonplace anecdotic painting of the Victorian narrative painters like Mulready, and the PRE-RAPHAELITES, with their mixture of costume-history and religious subjects and scenes from contemporary life, blurred further the line dividing genre from History Painting. MANET used the form occasionally and so did the IMPRESSIONISTS, RENOIR and DEGAS, and it survives into our own times with Sickert and the Camden Town Group, the Euston Road painters, and even the new Realists, for much the same reasons as caused its enormous development in Holland.

Gentile da Fabriano (*c.* 1370–1427), is first recorded in 1408, when he was in Venice. In 1409 he was working on historical frescoes in the Doge's Palace which were later finished by PISANELLO but were subsequently destroyed. From 1422 to 1425 he was in Florence where he completed, in May 1423, the resplendent altarpiece of the *Adoration of the Magi*, now in the Uffizi. This was one of the masterpieces of the INTERNATIONAL GOTHIC style and exerted enormous influence on Florentine art; it was followed by the *Quaratesi Altarpiece*, completed in May 1425, of which the *Madonna* is now in the Royal Coll. and the remainder divided between the Uffizi, the Vatican, and Washington. In 1425 he left Florence and worked in Siena and Orvieto, and by 1427 he was working on frescoes in the Lateran Basilica in Rome, which have also been destroyed. His art is the charming, elegant, and courtly art of the International Gothic style; he shows little or no interest in the intellectual problems of space and volume which exercised MASACCIO, who was working in Florence at precisely the same time (cf. the *Madonna* in the Royal Coll. with Masaccio's Pisa Polyptych *Madonna*, in the NG).
There are other pictures by him in Berlin, Harvard Univ. Gall., Milan (Brera and Poldi-Pezzoli), New York (Met. Mus.), Orvieto, Paris (Louvre: part of the Uffizi *Adoration*), Perugia, Pisa, Washington (NG), Yale Univ. Gall. [ills. 54, 55, p. 276]

Gentileschi, Orazio (1563–1639), was a follower of CARAVAGGIO who worked in Paris *c.* 1623/4 and arrived in London as Court Painter to Charles I in 1626. He remained in England until his death and was – with HONTHORST – one of the first practitioners of Caravaggism in England. There are works by him in the Royal Coll. and in Birmingham, Fabriano (Cath. and churches), Florence (Pitti), Madrid, Milan, Paris (Louvre), Rome (Corsini and churches), Vienna (K-H Mus.), and Washington (NG).
His daughter Artemisia (*c.* 1597–1651/3), worked in a similar style, mainly in Naples. She joined her father in London in 1638–9. [ill. 241, p. 309]

Gérard, Baron François (1770–1837), was born in Rome. While he was a pupil of DAVID – from 1786 onwards – he worked for engravers to earn a livelihood and during the

Revolution, to evade military service, he obtained through David's influence a position as judge on the Revolutionary tribunal, but contrived to be continuously ill so as to avoid its dreadful duties. His reputation as a portrait painter was made by 1795, and during the First Empire he rivalled David in Court favour. It was Gérard who suggested to David that in his huge *Coronation of Napoleon* the Emperor should crown Josephine rather than himself. Later, there was bitter animosity between them, and also between him and GROS, whom he defeated both in the speed with which he turned his political coat and in his efforts to secure the Court appointment to the restored Bourbons. He was ennobled by Louis XVIII, and kept a large studio of assistants to help with his glossy, showy, superficial portraits that compete with Lawrence for facility and charm, but lack the vision and solidity which make David's portraits outstanding. There are works in Paris (Louvre, Carnavalet), Versailles, London (Wellington Mus.), and elsewhere. [ill. 745, p. 382]

Gerhaert, Nicolaus (von Leyden or Leyen) (active 1462–73/8), was the last great German Gothic sculptor in the realist tradition – at least, if he was not Dutch, as the 'Leyden' often added to his name would imply. He is first recorded in Trier in 1462, when he signed and dated the Tomb of Archbishop von Sierck (Diocesan Mus.), but he was in Strasbourg from 1463 until 1467 in which year he carved the Baden-Baden Crucifix and went to Vienna to work on a Tomb for Friedrich III (Vienna, S. Stephan). He seems to have died in Vienna between 1473 and 1478. Other works by him are in Chicago, Downside Abbey Somerset, Frankfurt, New York (Met. Mus.), Passau Cath., and Ranshofen. A fine *Madonna* formerly in Berlin was destroyed 1939/45. [ill. 621, p. 360]

Géricault, Théodore (1791–1824), was born in Rouen of well-to-do parents. In 1808 he became the pupil of Carle VERNET, but left him after two years ('One of my horses would have devoured six of his', he said) for Guérin, in whose studio DELACROIX was also a pupil. He was strongly influenced by GROS, particularly in his painting of horses, and his choice of contemporary subjects. His technical innovations, too, are noteworthy: he abandoned the use of detailed preparatory drawings and squared-up studies, painting directly on to the final canvas from models posed according to a painted sketch. From being an ardent Bonapartist he eventually sided with the liberal opponents of the Restored Monarchy, an alignment reflected in many of his drawings (scenes from the Greek Wars of Independence, anti-slavery subjects, the ending of the Inquisition) and particularly in his most celebrated work, the *Raft of the 'Medusa'*, a shipwreck which was a political scandal of the day (1819: Louvre). In 1816 he visited Italy for a year, and in 1820–2 he was in England, where his *Raft* was shown in a travelling exhibition. During this long stay, he made many lithographs of horses and scenes of the poverty in the London streets, as well as small paintings of horses and racing subjects. His influence on the development of the Romantic movement exceeded what might have been expected from his total of no more than three exhibited works, a few portraits and horse pictures, and his lithographs and drawings. But his art, as

much as that of Gros and Rubens, was one of the starting-points for the young Delacroix, who admired him deeply. There are works in Baltimore (Walters), Bayonne, Buffalo, Cambridge Mass. (Fogg), Chicago, Detroit, Geneva, Ghent, Glasgow, Hartford Conn., London (NG), Montpellier, Munich (Bavarian State Mus.), Northampton Mass. (Smith College), Paris (Louvre), Providence RI, Rouen, Springfield Mass., and elsewhere. [ills. 770, 771, p. 387]

Gesso is the name given to the ground used in TEMPERA painting and in certain types of oil painting. It is a dense and brilliantly white ground with a rather high degree of absorbency (in Italy it was usually gypsum, but in N. Europe usually chalk). In Italian practice it was usual to prepare a panel with several coats of *Gesso Grosso*, which is simply gesso mixed with size, like white distemper. This is highly absorbent. The panel was then given ten or more coats of *Gesso Sottile*. This is plaster of Paris slaked in water for a month or more, so that all the setting power goes out of it. It is then made into a silky smooth mixture with size and painted on over the *gesso grosso*. The result is a smooth, brilliant white surface with a pleasant 'feel' and low absorbency. [Col. pl. 41]

Gheeraerts. The Gheeraerts, the de Critzes, and Isaac OLIVER were all Huguenot refugees in England who intermarried and were probably members of one workshop, to which most English portraits of the later Elizabethan period tend to be attributed. John de Critz (*c.* 1554–1642) was well established in England by 1598 and was Sergeant Painter to the Crown from 1605 until his death, at a very great age, in 1642. His sister, Susanna, married in 1571 Marcus Gheeraerts the Elder, a decorative painter from Bruges who fled from the Alvan persecution in 1568 and was in England 1568–77: he died before 1604. He made a signed engraving of the *Garter Procession* in 1576 and may have painted the *Queen Elizabeth* (Coll. the Duke of Portland), which is signed MGF (but this may also be his son's signature). Marcus Gheeraerts the Younger (*c.* 1561–1636) was a child of an earlier marriage and married, in 1590, Magdalen de Critz, his stepmother's younger sister. No works can be attributed to John de Critz, and there is not much evidence for Marcus Gheeraerts I as a portrait painter. Marcus the Younger is documented as a portrait painter and as working for the Crown: the *Duke of Württemberg* (Royal Coll.) is of *c.* 1608 and is signed 'Gerardi Brugiense'. There are other works, notably in Oxford (Bodleian), in the Duke of Bedford's Coll., and at Penshurst, which are certainly by him. The portraits (there was no other possible subject) which usually sail under the Gheeraerts colours are full- or half-length, life-sized effigies of noblemen and women in full dress with heavy curtains, a table, or chair or a Turkey carpet as accessories. They have a formal, heraldic air and, when clean, are bright in colour. The portraits of Queen Elizabeth in English country houses are always lumped together under the name Gheeraerts (when not called ZUCCARO).
Emmanuel de Critz (*d.* 1665) was a younger son of John. He is usually credited with the fine de Critz and Tradescant family portraits (one is dated 1645) in the Ashmolean Mus., Oxford, but no convincing reason can be adduced in support. [ills. 368, 812, pp. 325, 392]

Ghent Altar *see* EYCK.

Ghiberti, Lorenzo (1378–1455), was the Florentine
sculptor who made two of the three bronze doors of the
Baptistry in Florence. He was younger than Brunelleschi
but older than DONATELLO or Masaccio, and, in spite of
his collection of Antique sculpture and his desire to be
regarded as a humanist he was not really like the Masaccio-
Brunelleschi-Donatello triumvirate and had only a superficial feeling for classical art, at least in the earlier stages of
his career, although it deepened in his later years. In 1401
a Competition was announced for a bronze door for the
Baptistry, to match the one by Andrea PISANO, but to
consist of Old Testament scenes. The competition was
won by Ghiberti in 1402, against Brunelleschi (who subsequently devoted himself to architecture), Jacopo della
QUERCIA, and four others: according to his own account
'The palm of victory was conceded to me by all the experts
and by all my fellow-competitors. By universal consent
and without a single exception the glory was conceded to
me. . . .' Up to this time Ghiberti had been active as a
goldsmith and painter but the rest of his life was principally
devoted to his first Doors (1403–24) and to the second pair
commissioned immediately afterwards (1425–52). The
reliefs, of the *Sacrifice of Isaac*, submitted by Ghiberti and
by Brunelleschi survive (Florence, Bargello), but all the
others are lost. When the commission was given to
Ghiberti in 1403 (and renewed in 1407) the subjects were
changed from Old to New Testament but the doors remained very close to the type established by Andrea
Pisano, with high reliefs enclosed in Gothic frames, the
figures being gilt and set against a neutral ground.
Ghiberti established a large workshop to carry out this
great undertaking, and this shop was the principal training-
ground for the next generation of artists – including
Donatello as well as painters like MASOLINO and
UCCELLO.

In spite of a restrictive clause in his contract Ghiberti made
several other works during the period 1403–24. Two large
statues – the *S. John Baptist* (1414) and the *S. Matthew*
(1419–22, but dated 1420) – made for the church of
Orsanmichele, show the movement of his style away from
Gothic linear rhythms towards a graver and more Antique
treatment. Between 1417 and 1427 he made two reliefs
for the Font of the Baptistry in Siena, where the pictorial
treatment of the relief foreshadows his own second Doors
but is probably derived from Donatello's contribution to
the Font. Finally, in 1418 Ghiberti was paid for a model
of the dome of Florence Cathedral, thus proving that he
was also involved in the greatest architectural enterprise of
the day: his share in the dome as built by Brunelleschi is
still controversial.

After a trip to Venice in 1424 Ghiberti returned to Florence
and was commissioned in 1425 to make the remaining
(third) pair of doors. Such had been the success of his first
pair that he was left to exercise his own judgement. He
altered the whole layout and reduced the number of Old
Testament scenes to 10 (against 28 New Testament scenes
on the earlier doors), allowing each rectangular field to
appear like a picture in a frame, with the plane of the background representing the sky or the ground, and not simply
a neutral foil as in the earlier door. The perspective is
carefully calculated and depends on the recent researches

of Brunelleschi and Donatello: Ghiberti himself described
the doors thus 'There were ten scenes, each framed so that
the eye measures them from a distance and they appear in
relief. The relief is very low and the figures are so disposed
on the planes that those which are nearest are seen to be
larger than those farther off, just as happens in reality. The
whole work is based on these principles.' These doors were
very richly gilded, thus adding to the painterly effect, but
the gold was completely obscured by time and dirt until
the doors were taken down during the Second World War
and cleaned. This pair is often called the Door of Paradise
– the *Porta del Paradiso* – because Michelangelo is said to
have called them worthy to be the Gates of Paradise.

During this period 1425–52 Ghiberti also made the bronze
shrine of the Three Martyrs (1428: Florence, Bargello) and
the bronze Reliquary of S. Zenobius (1432–42: Florence,
Cath.) as well as another statue, the *S. Stephen*, for
Orsanmichele (1428). There are other works by him in
Florence (Sta Croce, S. Egidio, and Sta Maria Novella)
and he also designed a number of stained-glass windows
for the Cathedral.

In the last years of his life Ghiberti also wrote his 'Com-
mentarii' – already quoted from – the Second of which is the
principal source of our knowledge of Trecento art in
Florence and Siena and also includes Ghiberti's Autobiography, the earliest to survive by an artist. His interest
in the art of the Trecento links him firmly with his Gothic
predecessors: his consciousness of his own individuality in
his Autobiography shows him to have been also a man of
the Renaissance and perhaps the vital link between the
two worlds. [ills. 51, 52, p. 276]

Ghirlandaio, Domenico (1449–94), was the best fresco
executant of his generation in Florence, whose main claim
to fame is that he had Michelangelo as an apprentice. With
his brother Davide (1452–1525) and other relatives he ran
an extensive and well-organized studio, but he himself
preferred fresco to tempera, and he never attempted oil
painting. He worked in the Sistine Chapel in the Vatican
(1481–2), along with Botticelli and others, and his contribution is notable for the fact that it is nearest in spirit to
Masaccio – i.e. it was old-fashioned in the 1480s – and that
the nominal subject, the Calling of the First Apostles, is
half-swamped in the rows of life-like portraits of prominent
Florentines living in Rome. His essentially prosaic mind
and the naturalistic detail in all his works made him very
popular in his own day and in the late 19th century, but it
is significant that he received only one commission (now
lost) from the Medici family and none from any cultivated
patron. His frescoes are, of course, of great historical
interest. Most of them are in Florence: the *S. Jerome*
(1480: Ognissanti) shows strong Flemish influence in the
treatment of detail, and the two major cycles are those in
the Sassetti Chapel, Sta Trinita (completed 1485) and in
the choir of Sta Maria Novella (completed 1490). Outside
Florence, there are works of his in Berlin, Cambridge
(Fitzwm), Cambridge Mass. (Fogg), Detroit, London
(NG), Munich, New York (Met. Mus.), Paris (Louvre),
Philadelphia (Johnson), Washington, and elsewhere. His
son Ridolfo (1483–1561) was much influenced by his
friend Raphael and was a portrait painter of distinction.
He is well represented in Florence, and there are portraits
by him in Chicago, London (NG), Philadelphia (Johnson),

Washington (NG), and Worcester Mass. [ills. 78, 171, pp. 280, 296]

Ghislandi, Vittore, called Fra Galgario (1655–1743), was an Italian portrait painter, active mainly in Bergamo, who was trained in Venice and whose portraits reflect the best qualities of Late Baroque Venetian painting in their solid handling and strong but subdued colour. His sitters are usually simple people and he represents them in informal poses, often with a strength of light and shade indicating a knowledge of Rembrandt. He has lately been connected with the Realist tendency in Lombard painting of the early 18th century, but the closest parallels among his contemporaries seem to be Hogarth's portraits. His works are best represented in Bergamo, but there are others in Milan, Minneapolis, and Venice. [ill. 291, p. 314]

Giacometti, Alberto (*b.* 1901), is a Swiss sculptor, painter, and poet. He was trained in Italy 1920–2 and then spent three years in Paris under BOURDELLE, but he was also much influenced by BRANCUSI and became a Surrealist in the 1930s. The sculpture of this period has been called 'still-life sculpture' or 'magic objects', and the most famous is *The Palace at 4 a.m.* (1932–3: New York, M of MA). Later he returned to more realistic single figures, extremely emaciated in form, usually built up by working directly in plaster of Paris on a wire foundation. A characteristic example is the *Man Pointing* (1947: London, Tate). [ill. 1148, p. 433]

Giambologna *see* BOLOGNA, Giovanni.

Giambono, Michele, was a Venetian painter and mosaic worker. He is recorded in 1420 as a married man and is last recorded in 1462. He came of a family of painters but his Venetian workshop tradition was profoundly influenced by the International Gothic style imported into Venice by GENTILE da Fabriano and PISANELLO in their major works in the Doge's Palace (destroyed in the 16th century, and known to us mainly from reflections in the style of artists like Giambono). He worked on the mosaics in the Mascoli Chapel in S. Mark's from 1444 and his *Coronation of the Virgin*, ordered in 1447, is probably the painting now in Venice (Accad.) which was copied from an earlier picture of the same subject. There are other works by him in Rome (Gall. Naz.) and Venice. [ill. 49, p. 275]

Giaquinto, Corrado (1703–65), was a Neapolitan painter who was a pupil of SOLIMENA until 1723, when he went to Rome and began to work under CONCA who had also been a Solimena pupil. Giaquinto worked with Conca in Rome and Turin and was elected to the Academy of S. Luke in Rome in 1740 and became President in 1750. In 1752 he was invited to Madrid to succeed AMIGONI as Court Painter. He arrived in 1753 and became Director of the Academy, but in 1761 Charles III summoned MENGS to Madrid, and Giaquinto, whose Neapolitan Rococo style was the antithesis of Mengs's Neoclassicism, at once returned to Italy. One of his most important works is the vast *Birth of the Virgin* in Pisa Cathedral (1751/2) for which several sketches exist, one in Oxford. There are pictures in Madrid and a sketch in London (NG) for a proposed ceiling in the Royal Palace at Madrid. [ill. 290, p. 315]

Gibbons, Grinling (1648–1721), was born in Rotterdam of English parents but came to England by 1672. He was one of the most skilful wood-carvers who ever lived, as witness such virtuoso performances as the wooden cravat in the V & A Museum, London. With the help of Evelyn the diarist he was introduced to Charles II and became Master Carver in Wood to the Crown: as a sculptor proper his finest work is certainly the *James II* outside the National Gallery, but, as with all his work other than wood-carving, it is probable that most of it is by others. He worked with Arnold QUELLIN on the Chapel at Whitehall Palace (1685–6) and it is likely that Quellin actually modelled the *James II*, although Gibbons was paid for it. [ill. 874, p. 398]

Gibson, John (1790–1866), was apprenticed to a mason in Liverpool in 1804 but contrived to get to Rome in 1817 and spent the rest of his life there ('I thank God for every morning that opens my eyes in Rome'). He worked under CANOVA and THORWALDSEN and enjoyed a reputation little below theirs, revisiting England only in 1844 and 1850, on both occasions to work for the Queen. His principal innovation was to reintroduce the tinting of marble, which, although certainly practised by the Greeks, seemed to a contemporary 'a dangerous departure from true art'. Many stories are told of his simplicity: a woman pupil said of him that 'he is a god in his studio, but God help him out of it', and to a puzzled railway porter he is said to have replied 'No, I am not a foreigner, I am a sculptor.' Nevertheless, he left a large fortune and his bequest to the Royal Academy (to which he had been elected in 1838) paid for most of the building of the Diploma Gallery, which now contains work by him: there are others in the Royal Collection and in Cardiff, Durham Cath., Liverpool, and London (NG, NPG, Tate, V & A, Wellington Mus., and Westminster Abbey). [ill. 871, p. 399]

Gill, Eric (1882–1940), English engraver, letter-cutter, sculptor, typographer, and writer. The *Stations of the Cross* (Westminster Cath.) and *Prospero and Ariel* (Broadcasting House) are his best-known carvings: others are in the Tate Gallery. He will probably best be remembered as the designer of the lettering known as Gill Sans-serif, and for many other fine alphabets. [ill. 882, p. 399]

Gilman, Harold (1876–1919), was trained at the Slade School, met GORE and joined SICKERT's circle, against which he subsequently reacted violently, coming under the influence of van Gogh. He was a member of the CAMDEN TOWN GROUP and became the first President of the LONDON GROUP on its foundation in 1913. He is represented in Cardiff, Liverpool, London (Tate) and Ottawa. [ill. 972, p. 411]

Gilpin, Sawrey (1733–1807), was an English animal painter of Romantic ambitions. He was the younger brother of the Rev. William Gilpin, the celebrated writer on the PICTURESQUE. Sawrey studied in London from 1749 under SCOTT: his work is less sensitive than that of STUBBS and is somewhat marred by anthropomorphism.

This may be seen in his *Election of Darius* (York) –
according to legend the election was influenced by the
neighing of Darius's horse – but most of his works are
straightforward sporting pictures. He exhibited at the RA
from 1786, and was elected RA in 1797. [ill. 897, p. 402]

Giordano, Luca (1632–1705), was a Neapolitan painter
known as 'Luca fa presto' (Luke, paint quickly) from the
alleged habit of his father in urging ever greater speed and
facility. Certainly he was able to paint in an amazing
variety of styles, which has earned him praise and disdain
in about equal measure. He was probably a pupil of
RIBERA in Naples but went on to Rome, where he was
influenced by the lighter style of PIETRO da Cortona, and
to Florence and Venice, where the influence of Venetian
art was instrumental in getting away from the darkness of
Ribera's style. In Florence he painted a chapel, and, in
1682–3, the huge ceiling of the Ballroom of the Palazzo
Medici-Riccardi. His great renown led Charles II to
summon him in 1692 to Spain, where his ceilings in the
Escorial are probably his masterpieces. He returned to
Naples in 1702 and spent his last years there. He was the
most important Neapolitan painter of the second half of
the 17th century, and his lighter and more colouristic style
marks a great change from the Neapolitan painting of the
first half of the century. His output was huge and most older
galleries have examples of his easel-paintings. [ill. 284,
p. 313]

Giorgione (*c.* 1476/8–1510), was a Venetian painter, a
pupil of Giovanni BELLINI, who was ranked by Vasari
with Leonardo da Vinci as one of the founders of modern
painting. He was the first exponent in Venice of the small
picture in oils, intended for private collectors rather than
for churches, and frequently mysterious and evocative in
subject. Many of his contemporaries were unable to
interpret the subject of such a picture as the *Tempest*
(Venice, Accad.), of which we can say only that it appears
to be the first 'landscape of mood', expressing the heat and
tension of an approaching thunderstorm. His career is
almost entirely mysterious. In 1506 he shared a studio with,
of all people, CATENA; in 1507/8 he was working in the
Doge's Palace, but these works are lost; in 1508 he was
painting frescoes on the outside of the Fondaco dei
Tedeschi, the headquarters of the German merchants in
Venice, and TITIAN was also working there in a subordinate
capacity. Only faded fragments of these frescoes now exist,
but the link with Titian is important, for it seems to prove
that it was Giorgione, and not Titian, who was the great
innovator. This would be less controversial if we had more
knowledge of Giorgione's style, but no extant pictures can
be regarded as completely documented and there are only
about half a dozen which are generally agreed to be
attributable to him on adequate evidence. The problem is
much complicated by the fact that he died, of the plague,
in 1510 and several pictures seem to have been completed
by Titian and SEBASTIANO del Piombo, both of whom
were, at that date, profoundly influenced by him; nevertheless, optimistic attributions to him continue to be made.
The *Castelfranco Madonna* (Castelfranco Veneto – his
birthplace – S. Liberale) is derived from the large altarpieces of Giovanni Bellini, and is therefore probably an
early work: it is universally accepted as Giorgione's. Other

86

works, in Dresden, Leningrad, Venice, and Vienna (K-H
Mus.), including the *Laura* in Vienna which is dated 1506,
are almost beyond controversy, but the debate continues
over works in the Royal Collection and in Berlin, Boston
(Gardner), Budapest, Florence (Uffizi and Pitti), Glasgow,
London (NG, Courtauld Inst.), Madrid, Oxford, Paris
(Louvre), San Diego Cal., and Washington as well as
other less likely candidates. [ills. 215, 218, pp. 304–5.
Col. pl. 13]

Giotteschi, Giottesques. The name given to a number of
14th-century painters working in the shadow of GIOTTO.
Many of them are anonymous, others are known by names
like the MASTER of S. CECILIA, while others again are
distinct personalities such as DADDI, GIOTTINO,
Taddeo GADDI, or MASO di Banco.

Giottino, active in the mid 14th century, probably painted
the *S. Remigio Deposition* in Florence (Uffizi) which was
regarded as a work of MASO by Vasari and earlier writers.
The distinction of hand is evident, but it is by no means
certain that Giottino was identical with a Giotto di Maestro
Stefano who was painting in the Vatican in 1369, who in
turn cannot be reconciled with Vasari's Maso/Giottino
figure. No other work can reasonably be attributed to the
painter of the Uffizi *Deposition*, unless one accepts the
attribution of it to ORCAGNA's brother Nardo di Cione.
[ill. 24, p. 272]

Giotto (1266/7 or, less probably, 1276–1337), was a
Florentine, who, with CIMABUE, is generally regarded as
the founder of modern painting, since he broke away from
the stereotyped forms of Italo-Byzantine art and tried to
give his figures the maximum solidity and naturalism and
gave passion and imagination to his scenes, just as
Giovanni PISANO had done slightly earlier in sculpture.
His dramatic power can be felt in his frescoes of scenes
from the lives of SS. Joachim and Anne and the Virgin,
and of the Life and Passion of Christ, in the Arena Chapel,
Padua. These were completed by 1313, perhaps *c.* 1306.
Before then Giotto had probably painted the fresco cycle
of the Legend of S. Francis in the Upper Church at Assisi,
although his authorship is denied by some critics on stylistic
grounds. These frescoes are imbued with the humanity
which S. Francis himself had brought into the religious
life of the 13th century, and which was so potent an
influence on the arts.
Probably just after 1300 Giotto designed the *Navicella*, a
huge mosaic of the Ship of the Church, in St Peter's, but
this has been so reworked that his hand is no longer
discernible in it. Much later, perhaps in the 1320s, he
decorated four chapels in Sta Croce, Florence, of which
two chapels (Bardi and Peruzzi: *Life of S. Francis* and
Lives of SS. John Baptist and Evangelist), and an *Assumption* from a third chapel, survive. A slight influence from
Gothic sculpture is perceptible in them. Giotto also
worked in Naples (1329–33), but all his work there is lost.
There are several panel pictures – some of them signed –
attributed to him: in Bologna, Florence (Sta Croce),
London (NG), Munich, Paris (Louvre), Upton Park
(National Trust) near Banbury, Washington, and elsewhere, but all of these are held to be works of his school
or shop, and even the signed ones are, as it were, trade-

marked rather than signed in the modern sense. This is true even of the *Stefaneschi Altar* in the Vatican, which is mentioned as his in a document of 1342; on the other hand, the *Ognissanti Madonna* (Florence, Uffizi) is universally accepted as his although it is neither signed nor documented. Other works with some claim to be considered as his include the *Dormition of the Virgin* (Berlin) and a Crucifix in Sta Maria Novella, Florence.

On account of his great fame – he and Cimabue are both mentioned in Dante – Giotto was appointed Supervisor of Florence Cathedral in 1334, and he began work on the Campanile ('Giotto's Tower'), but his design was altered later. Nearly all Florentine and many Sienese painters of the mid 14th century were influenced by him (the Giotteschi), but his influence waned in the later 14th century, to be revived in MASACCIO and even in Michelangelo. [ills. 17, 20–23, pp. 271–3. Col. pls. 1, 39]

Giovanni d'Alemagna *see* VIVARINI.

Giovanni da Bologna *see* BOLOGNA.

Giovanni di Paolo (1403–82/3), was, with SASSETTA, the leading Sienese painter of the 15th century. There are documented works from 1426 down to about 1475 and it is likely that he ceased painting towards the end of his long life. His style is a rather more archaic and tortured version of Sassetta's, with a certain influence from GENTILE da Fabriano (who was in Siena 1424/6): his later works seem to show that he had visited Florence. Nevertheless, like Sassetta, he seems always to be looking back over his shoulder to the masters of the Trecento. There are works in Altenburg, Baltimore (Walters), Berlin, Boston (Mus. and Gardner), Cambridge (Fitzwm) and Cambridge Mass. (Fogg), Chicago, Cologne (Wallraf-Richartz, Rheinisches Mus.), Florence (Uffizi, Bargello), London (NG), Minneapolis, Modena, Münster, New York (Met. Mus. and Frick Coll.), Oxford (Ashmolean and Christ Church), Paris (Louvre), Philadelphia (Johnson), Siena (Pinac., Cath. Mus., and churches), Utrecht, the Vatican, Vienna (Akad.), Washington (NG), and Yale University. [ill. 111, p. 288]

Girardon, François (1628–1715), was the most classical of the sculptors working at Versailles for Louis XIV. His *Apollo and the Nymphs*, commissioned in 1666 for the Grotto of Thetis and now much altered by the regrouping of the figures, is severely classical in style and based on the *Apollo Belvedere* and on Poussin, whose type of composition it translates into sculpture. His *Rape of Proserpine*, in the gardens, though full of movement, consciously avoids both the Mannerism of Giovanni da Bologna's group, and the Baroque movement in depth of Bernini's group of the same subject. [ill. 709, p. 378]

Girodet de Roucy-Trioson, Anne-Louis (1767–1824). He became a pupil of DAVID in 1785 and won the Prix de Rome in 1789. He was in the Academy in Rome when in 1793 David's order to replace the Royal arms by the Republican ones touched off the riot in which the mob wrecked the Academy and murdered the French agent. Girodet escaped to Naples, but there found his republicanism dangerous and after a gruelling flight across Italy

arrived, very ill, in Genoa where he was succoured by GROS. His *Endymion*, sent from Rome in 1793, reflects not only his romantic temperament but also the drift from David's classicism towards more poetic and romantic themes. David disapproved of him, and of GÉRARD, declaring that they had debased the art by their pandering to poetry and portraiture. In 1812 Girodet inherited a large fortune and abandoned painting to compose unreadable poems on aesthetics, writing in a house shuttered against daylight. There are works in Montpellier, Malmaison, Orléans, Paris (Louvre), Versailles, and elsewhere. [ill. 746, p. 382]

Girtin, Thomas (1775–1802), was the friend and contemporary of TURNER, but all his important work was done in watercolour and in his short life he revolutionized landscape painting in that medium. With Turner he worked for Dr MONRO and also copied Canaletto drawings, from which he learned much about topographical drawing. In 1801–2 he went to Paris where he made a series of softground etchings of views of that city, published posthumously in 1803. On his return from Paris he resumed work on an enormous panorama of London (*The Eidometropolis*) which he exhibited in 1802. The panorama is lost, but half a dozen sketches for it are in the BM. In his watercolours Girtin bridged the gap between the 18th-century stained drawing and the 19th-century watercolour painting: the *White House at Chelsea* (1800: London, Tate), one of his finest works, shows this transition and the poetic spirit which informs his work. He made several technical innovations, including the use of rather absorbent offwhite cartridge paper, but his most radical change was the abandonment of the older monochrome underpainting in favour of a richer handling, with broad washes of strong colour often offset by dark blobs. There are works by him in Bedford (Higgins Mus.), Birkenhead, Birmingham, Brighton, Bristol, Cambridge (Fitzwm), Cardiff, Dublin, Edinburgh, Leeds, Lincoln, London (BM, Tate, V & A, Guildhall, Courtauld Institute), Manchester (Whitworth), Newcastle, New York (Met. Mus.), Ottawa, Oxford, Sheffield, Swansea, Victoria NSW, York, and other British museums. [ill. 927, p. 405]

Gislebertus was a French Romanesque sculptor who worked c. 1125–35 at Autun Cathedral in Burgundy, where he carved a tympanum *Last Judgement* (conspicuously signed), and also executed many capitals. His figures are characterized by vivid imagery, and by minutely pleated drapery in rhythmic folds and flutters. The fragments of the North transept door include the famous *Eve*. There affinities between the work at Autun and some of the sculpture at Vézelay, which suggest that he may have worked there before going to Autun, and his iconographic dependence on Cluny suggests close links with the Abbey there. Other places in Burgundy have works deriving from Autun, probably by his workshop. [ill. 664, p. 371]

Giulio Romano (1492 or 1499–1546), painter and architect and one of the creators of MANNERISM. From about 1515 until RAPHAEL's death in 1520 Giulio was his chief assistant and was working on the frescoes in the Sala dell' Incendio in the Vatican, a fact which makes it unlikely that he was born in 1499. Before going to Mantua in 1524

Giulio completed some of Raphael's unfinished works, including the *Transfiguration* and the Vatican frescoes (Sala di Costantino), and he also painted an altarpiece for Sta Maria dell'Anima, Rome, and the *Stoning of S. Stephen* for Sto Stefano, Genoa (1523). All these works show an exaggeration of Raphael's style and also a melodramatic invention coupled with the influence of MICHELANGELO and these qualities are carried further in the frescoes in the Palazzo del Tè, designed by him for the Gonzaga of Mantua. The *Fall of the Giants*, occupying the whole of one room, is a piece of brutal illusionism deliberately designed to overwhelm the spectator who finds himself involved in the crushing of the Giants by the thunderbolts of Jove in the sky above. The whole of the room is painted from floor to ceiling to increase the illusion, and Vasari – who admired it greatly – tells us that the flames in the fireplace were intended to add to the effect of general destruction. This series was painted 1532–4, and there are other frescoes by him in Mantua. Florence, London, Naples, Paris, Rome, and Vienna also have paintings of his. [ill. 182, p. 299]

Giunta Pisano was, with BERLINGHIERO, one of the earliest Italian painters known to us as individuals. Giunta was active in Pisa *c*. 1229–*c*. 1254 and is known from three surviving crucifixes in Assisi, Pisa, and Bologna. He is also known to have painted a crucifix in Assisi (dated 1236 but now lost) and he may have painted the dramatic *S. Francis* (Pisa). His style is more consciously realistic than that of Berlinghiero and he uses the modern CHRISTUS PATIENS type of crucifix. [ill. 14, p. 270]

Glazing is the process of applying a transparent layer of oil paint over a solid one so that the colour of the first is profoundly modified. Thus, a transparent glaze of crimson over a solid blue will give effects of purple to mulberry colour, depending on the thickness of the glaze or the intensity of pigment used. It is thus the opposite of SCUMBLING and is impossible in direct, or ALLA PRIMA, painting. The use of glazes is now very rare, as it implies a deliberation and a craftsmanly approach to painting which is often thought inconsistent with inspiration: by a paradox the principal exponents of glazing are now probably the TACHISTES. The exact use made of glazes by different Old Masters is a highly controversial subject, since every time a picture is cleaned someone will claim that the 'Master's final glazes have now irretrievably vanished': occasionally this may be true, but it usually means that the dirty varnish layer has been regarded as a glaze in its own right. There is an added complication in that some glazes were undoubtedly put on with fugitive colours and have therefore vanished of their own accord: this has affected many pictures by Reynolds.

Gleizes, Albert (1881–1953), was overwhelmed by CUBISM in 1910, and in 1912 published with METZINGER 'Du Cubisme', the first book on the subject (English translation 'Cubism', 1913). He was one of the flat-pattern Cubists, and also produced abstract works. In 1917, when in America, he turned to religion, and many of his later works are a marriage of traditional Catholic themes with Cubist ideas. He also wrote on religion and art. There are works in London (Tate), Paris (Mus. d'Art

Mod.), New York (M of MA), and Toronto. [ill. 1051, p. 422]

Glyptic *see* SCULPTURE.

Goes, Hugo van der (*d.* 1482), was the most important Ghent painter in the period after Jan van Eyck, and one of the most gifted of all the early Netherlandish painters. He was probably born at Ghent and was in the Guild there in 1467, becoming Dean in 1473/4 and 1475. About 1475 or a little later he completed the *Portinari Altarpiece* (Florence, Uffizi) for a Florentine resident in the Netherlands: the picture went direct to Florence and had little influence in the Netherlands, but it made a considerable impression on several Florentines, notably Ghirlandaio. It is unusual in Flemish work in that it is on a huge scale (over 8 ft high), and the great size is a positive gain to Hugo's composition, whereas to any other Flemish painter it would have been an embarrassment. The cool but rich colour and the virtuosity of the oil technique must also have been regarded with wonder in Florence. About 1475 (or perhaps later) Hugo joined his brother as a lay-brother in the Augustinian monastery at Roode Clooster, near Brussels; but he continued to paint, to receive noble visitors, and apparently to travel, since he went to Louvain to value the estate of Bouts in 1479/80 and, about 1481, went to Cologne. On this journey he was seized by madness (from a contemporary description, a form of religious melancholia) and he died, still insane, the following year. The *Portinari Altar* is rather exiguously documented as his, but all other attributions are based on it; his dramatic, almost *exalté* style is easily recognizable. There are two other very large pictures by him, both in Berlin, and other works in Baltimore, Bruges (Mus. and S. Sauveur), Brussels, Cassel, Edinburgh (NG, on loan from the Royal Coll.), Frankfurt (Städel), Leningrad, New York (Met. Mus.), Oxford (Christ Church), Philadelphia (Johnson), Vaduz (Liechtenstein), Venice (Correr), Vienna, and Wilton House, Wilts. [ills. 355, 356, p. 323]

Gogh, Vincent van (1853–90), was the son of a Dutch pastor. He was first employed in The Hague, London, and Paris by the picture dealers for whom his brother Theo worked. He then taught in two English schools, worked in a bookshop in Holland, began studying for the Church, and became a missionary in the coal-mining district of the Borinage in Belgium, where he shared the poverty and hardships of the miners. He did not begin to become an artist until he was living in great poverty after his dismissal from the mission in 1880, and from then until 1886 he lived variously at Brussels, Etten, The Hague, Drenthe, Nuenen, and Antwerp, teaching himself to draw and paint, with occasional lessons in Brussels, from Antoine Mauve in The Hague, and at the Academy in Antwerp, which appear to have contributed little to his development. In 1886 he joined Theo in Paris and came immediately into contact with the works of the Impressionists, which Theo endeavoured to sell in the gallery devoted to modern art that he directed. He met Toulouse-Lautrec, Pissarro, Degas, Seurat, and Gauguin, and in 1888 went to Arles where he was later joined by Gauguin. In December 1888 he became insane, and from then until his death suffered intermittent attacks of mental trouble. During the intervals between them he continued to paint, both in the asylums at Arles and S. Rémy and after his removal to Auvers, where, in July 1890, he shot himself. His brother Theo, to whom most of his long and revealing letters were addressed, and who was his constant support, moral and financial, died six months later.

Van Gogh's Dutch period is characterized by his use of dark colour, heavy forms, and subject-matter chiefly drawn from peasants and their work. He ignored Theo's advice to lighten his palette as the Impressionists were doing, but during his short stay in Antwerp he became more interested in Japanese prints and the work of Rubens. After his arrival in Paris a complete change took place in his palette and subject-matter; he adopted the Impressionist technique, leaning briefly towards the Pointillism of Seurat, and turned to flowers, views of Paris, and portraits and self-portraits which enabled him to experiment with these new ideas. After he went to Arles, he painted many landscapes and portraits in heightened colour and with a vivid, passionate expression of light and feeling, and after the arrival of Gauguin his work shows the influence of SYNTHETISM in the greater simplification of his forms and his use of less modulated colour. His paintings done at S. Rémy and Auvers are vivid in colour and with writhing, flame-like forms in the drawing, completely expressive of his tormented sensibility. His greatest influence was on MUNCH and the German Expressionists.

He left a vast volume of work, the largest amount of which is in the collection of Theo's son, Ir. V.W. van Gogh at Laren in Holland, and in the Kröller-Müller Museum at Otterlo in Holland. There are also works in Amsterdam (Stedelijk Mus.), Baltimore, Boston (Mus.), Cambridge Mass. (Fogg), Chicago, Copenhagen, Edinburgh (NG), Essen, Glasgow, London (Tate, Courtauld Inst.), Minneapolis, Moscow, New York (Met. Mus., M of MA, Brooklyn), Paris (Louvre, Mus. Rodin), São Paulo, Washington (NG, Phillips), and many other museums. [ills. 984, 985, p. 414. Col. pl. 30]

Golden Section (Golden Mean) is the name given to an irrational proportion, known at least since Euclid, which has often been thought to possess some aesthetic virtue in itself, some hidden harmonic proportion in tune with the universe. It is defined strictly as a line which is divided in such a way that the smaller part is to the larger as the larger is to the whole (AB cut at C, so that CB:AC = AC:AB). In practice it works out at about 8:13 and may easily be discovered in most works of art.

In 1912 an exhibition was held in Paris, called *Section d'Or*, which marks the break between Analytical and Synthetic CUBISM. The initiative came from J. VILLON and all the followers of Cubism were represented: only the inventors, Picasso and Braque, did not exhibit.

Goltzius, Hendrik (1558–1617), was a Haarlem engraver and painter, who, with SPRANGER, BLOEMAERT, and WTEWAEL, was a leading Mannerist. He founded a school of engraving in Haarlem in 1582, but did not begin to paint until 1600, under Italian influence – he had been in Italy in 1590–1. His portraits, both painted and engraved, have a sober realism and grasp of character quite different from his fancy subjects, and occasionally they seem to foreshadow Hals, his fellow-townsman. His engravings,

executed by himself or by others to his designs, are very numerous and of superb technique. There are paintings in Amsterdam, Arras, Baltimore (Walters), Basle, Haarlem, The Hague, Leningrad, Munich, Paris (Louvre), Philadelphia, Providence RI, and Rotterdam. [ill. 384, p. 326]

Gonçalves, Nuno (active 1450–72), was the most important Portuguese painter of the 15th century. His *S. Vincent Altar* for Lisbon Cathedral was destroyed in 1755, but another, of six panels dedicated to the same Saint (now in Lisbon Mus.), is reasonably attributed to him. It contains many portraits and may be dated *c.* 1465–7: the style is ultimately Flemish, based on BOUTS, but simpler and more austere. The influence of wood-carving is discernible in the treatment of the heads. [ill. 635, p. 363]

González, Julio (1876–1942), was, with LAURENS and LIPCHITZ, a Cubist sculptor. He was born in Barcelona, into a family of metal-workers. The family moved to Paris in 1900 and González soon came in contact with Picasso, whom he had already met in Barcelona: in 1930–2 he taught Picasso the technique of ironworking. For many years a painter, González worked in the Renault factories during the First World War and subsequently devoted himself to sculpture in iron. He was influenced by ARCHIPENKO and produced a form of Cubist sculpture: in turn, his work has had great influence on British and US sculptors (e.g. Butler). His masterpiece is the *Montserrat* (1936–7: Amsterdam, Stedelijk Mus.) made for the Spanish Pavilion at an International Exhibition, but it is more naturalistic than most of his works – e.g. the *Woman doing her Hair* (1936: New York, M of MA). Many of his works are in Paris, Mus. d'Art Moderne. [ill. 1131, p. 430]

Gore, Spencer Frederick (1878–1914), was strongly influenced by SICKERT and Late Impressionist painting, and from 1910 (when Roger Fry organized the First Post-Impressionist Exhibition in London) he was deeply influenced by Cézanne and Gauguin. In 1911 he was the first President of the newly founded CAMDEN TOWN GROUP. There are works by him in the Tate, London. [ill. 969, p. 411]

Gorky, Arshile (1904–48), was born Vosdanig Adoian in Turkish Armenia, fled before the Turks in 1915 and finally arrived in the US in 1920. His life began in tragedy – his mother starved to death – and ended in suicide, following a cancer operation in 1946 and a car crash in which he broke his neck. He worked in New York from *c.* 1925 and began to paint Cubist pictures in 1927: his earliest works are imitations of Cézanne, later of Picasso and finally of MIRÒ. His *Artist and his Mother* (*c.* 1926–36: New York, Whitney Mus.) is an able pastiche of Picasso's figure style of *c.* 1920. In 1935 and 1939 he painted two large murals on the theme of aviation, but both are lost. In 1940 he met MATTA, who inspired him with Surrealist ideas similar to those of Mirò. Other American museums with pictures by Gorky include Baltimore, Buffalo, Chicago, New York (M of MA), Oberlin Ohio, San Francisco, Tucson Ariz. University, and Utica NY (Munson-Williams-Proctor). [ill. 1084, p. 426]

Gossaert, or Gossart, Jan, *see* MABUSE.

Gothic is a term normally used to describe the architectural style of N. Europe from the early 12th century until the 16th, and, as such, has no place in this Dictionary. It is, however, often used to describe the other arts of the same period, particularly when emphasizing their transcendental qualities in contradistinction to Renaissance art. The phrase 'Late Gothic' is useful in this connection, since it means that artists such as NOTKE, HOLBEIN the Elder, and even GRÜNEWALD, continued to practise a style which was not affected by Renaissance ideas, as late as the end of the 15th century and into the 16th. The genuine Gothic art of France in the 14th century influenced some Italians, notably Simone MARTINI, and the result of this was the stylistic offshoot known as INTERNATIONAL GOTHIC.

Gouache is opaque watercolour paint (known to many people as Poster Paint). With gouache effects very similar to those obtainable in oil painting may be got with less trouble, so that it is a useful means of making studies for a large picture in oils; although, like its kin DISTEMPER and TEMPERA, it has the defect of drying much lighter in tone than it seems when wet. The medium lacks the peculiar charm of pure watercolour, but has always been popular on the Continent. Paul SANDBY was one of the few British artists to use it extensively. *See also* BODY COLOUR. [Col. pl. 49]

Goujon, Jean (active 1540–62), was a French sculptor who is also recorded as an architect. His elongated, elegant figures are derived from Parmigianino, Rosso, and Cellini, but these influences are so completely assimilated that he possesses a striking personal style, which also shows the influence of classical sculpture, known possibly through a visit to Italy before 1540. He worked in Paris on the roodscreen for S. Germain l'Auxerrois (from 1544: Louvre), on the *Fontaine des Innocents* (1547–9: most of the reliefs are now in the Louvre), and on decorations for the Louvre, much restored during the 19th century. These include figures and reliefs on the exterior, and the caryatides of the Gallery in what is now the Salle des Caryatides. He disappears from sight in 1562. Besides the works now in the Louvre, there are works in Rouen (Cath., S. Maclou) by or attributed to him. [ill. 674, p. 372]

Goya. Francisco de G. y Lucientes (1746–1828), was born near Saragossa and studied there until (apparently) his amours and knifings caused him to leave: in 1766 he was in Madrid working under BAYEU, whose sister he married. He was in Rome in 1771, but was back in Saragossa later in the year, working in the Cathedral. By 1775 he was in Madrid and from 1776 began producing tapestry cartoons for the Royal manufactory; this started his successful career and he became Deputy Director of the Academy in 1785, *pintor del rey* 1786, *pintor de cámara* 1789, and *primer pintor de cámara* (i.e. Principal Painter to the King) in 1799, so that his contemporaries certainly recognized his genius. In 1792, however, he was very ill and became deaf, which undoubtedly made him still more introspective, so that we find Goya the official portrait painter also producing works

which, he said, were 'to make observations for which commissioned works generally give no room, and in which fantasy and invention have no limit'. This fantasy was typified in the series of etchings called *Los Caprichos*, produced 1796–8 and announced for sale in 1799 (eight more were added in 1803). These are savagely satirical attacks on manners and customs and on abuses in the Church, yet in 1798 he painted the frescoes of the cupola of S. Antonio de la Florida in Madrid (technically fascinating, because apparently executed with sponges in dabs and wipings of colour). The dilemma in which Goya and other liberal Spaniards found themselves became acute in 1793 when Charles IV declared war on the new French Republic; for Charles was very reactionary and most liberals were then partly in sympathy with France. In 1808 the troops of Napoleon invaded Spain and drove out Ferdinand VII, replacing him with Joseph Bonaparte. Many Spaniards welcomed his liberalism, yet hated the foreigners – in particular the French troops, who behaved with almost 20th-century savagery. These atrocities were recorded by Goya in the series of etchings called *The Disasters of War* (1810–13: first published in full in 1863) and, above all, in the two paintings called *2 May* and *3 May 1808* (c. 1814: Madrid, Prado). The French were driven out with the aid of Wellington (whom Goya painted in 1812) and in 1814 Ferdinand VII was restored. Goya was pardoned for having worked for Joseph Bonaparte and continued to work for the Spanish Court until 1824 when there was a fresh wave of reaction and he went to Paris and then settled in voluntary exile in Bordeaux. What seems so difficult to understand is how the Bourbons could continue to employ him, for his portraits of Charles IV and his family have been described as making them look like prosperous grocers; but in fact these portraits, and those of Ferdinand VII, make them appear brutish, moronic, and arrogant.

From 1819 Goya began to practise the new art of lithography and he produced some bull-fighting scenes as well as single prints and several more etchings and aquatints. There are good examples of his prints in the BM, London, in Madrid, and New York (Hispanic Soc.).

As a painter Goya began his decorative works very much under the influence of Tiepolo's Spanish frescoes, while his portraits are influenced by Mengs and, oddly, by English 18th-century portraits (he is known to have owned engravings): an intensive study of Velazquez, his predecessor as Court Painter, led to a breadth of style which ends as a kind of Impressionism. He had great influence on 19th-century French painting, especially on Manet, and he has been called the last of the Old Masters and the first of the moderns (whatever that may mean). There are pictures in Agen, Baltimore, Barnard Castle, Bayonne, Berlin, Besançon, Boston (Mus.), Castres, Chicago, Cincinnati, Cleveland, Detroit, San Diego Cal., Edinburgh, Hartford Conn., Houston Texas, Kansas City, Lille, London (NG, Courtauld Inst., Wellington Mus.), St Louis, Madrid (Prado, Acad., and S. Antonio de la Florida), Minneapolis, Montreal, Munich, New York (Met. Mus., Frick Coll., Brooklyn Mus., and especially Hispanic Soc.), Northampton Mass. (Smith Coll.), Ottawa, São Paulo Brazil, Paris (Louvre), Seville, Toledo and Toledo Ohio, Valencia, Washington (NG and Phillips Coll.), and Worcester, Mass. [ills. 659–62, p. 370. Col. pl. 8]

Goyen, Jan van (1596–1656), was, with Salomon van RUYSDAEL, the most important Dutch landscape painter of the realist school before Jacob van RUISDAEL. He spent a year in France as a young man and then worked under E. van de VELDE in Haarlem *c.* 1617 before settling in The Hague in 1634. He travelled extensively in Holland and also went to the neighbourhood of Antwerp and Brussels (a sketchbook exists of his Belgian trip): many of his pictures represent identifiable places. He speculated all his earnings on tulips and houses and died insolvent, in spite of his huge production, but a portrait of the family by his son-in-law, Jan STEEN, shows a very prosperous-looking group, complete with Negro page. His earliest works, up to *c.* 1630, show the influence of Esaias van de Velde, with rather crowded compositions and strong local colours. About 1630 a marked change is observable in his style. His composition is simplified, with the horizon set very low in the picture, and a great breadth of handling and tonality is obtained by the use of near-monochrome, with the light green and yellow-brown which is typical of him (Houbraken, writing before 1718, said that the blues had faded out of his greens, leaving yellows – cf. PYNACKER). At this stage it is often difficult to distinguish his pictures from those of S. van Ruysdael (a Ruysdael of 1631 in London, NG, passed for years as by van Goyen, and reasonably so). Later on his colour becomes richer again, until, at his death, the poetic imagination of Jacob van Ruisdael carried Dutch landscape painting to fresh heights. Van Goyen made some etchings as well as very numerous drawings, some of which were certainly made for sale as independent works of art. He painted his own figures in his landscapes, the earliest of which dates from 1618: about 1,200 are recorded, so that he is well represented in Museums. [ill. 495, p. 344]

Gozzoli, Benozzo (*c.* 1421–97), was the assistant of Fra ANGELICO, but was entirely secular in outlook. His numerous frescoes give a picture of 15th-century life, the most famous being the *Medici family as the Magi* (*c.* 1459: Florence, Medici Palace). A typical panel is in London (NG). [ill. 76, p. 280]

Graf, Urs (*c.* 1485–1527/28), was a Swiss draughtsman, engraver, and goldsmith. He painted only one picture, *War* (*c.* 1515: Basle), and possibly one other, the *S. George*, which is also in Basle. He was a vile man who frequently went off as a mercenary soldier and his drawings of the life of these brutes have a morbid fascination, enhanced by the sweeping rhythms of the pen stroke. He disappeared from Basle in 1527 – perhaps to take part in the Sack of Rome – and his wife remarried in 1528. The great majority of his drawings and engravings are in Basle. [ill. 567, p. 355]

Graff, Anton (1736–1813), was born in Switzerland, but was the leading German portrait painter of the 18th century. He was a younger contemporary of Reynolds, with whom he is often compared, but Graff really belongs to a later generation, since most of his portraits lack the trappings of the Grand Style, and he worked almost into the BIEDERMEIER period. He was in Augsburg by 1756 and removed to Dresden in 1766 to teach at the newly founded Academy. He recorded himself as having painted some 1,240 portraits in his long career and his sitters included many of the most famous of his contemporaries – Lessing, Herder, Schiller (whom he records as having fidgeted the whole time). He also made some 322 portrait drawings in silver point, a very rare technique in the 18th century. Some fragments of an autobiography were posthumously published in Zürich in 1815. There are pictures in many German museums, including Berlin, Dresden, and Leipzig. [ill. 598, p. 359]

Graffito *see* SGRAFFITO.

Granacci, Francesco (1469/70–1543), was a Florentine painter of the generation immediately preceding MICHELANGELO whose friend he was from early youth. Like Michelangelo, Granacci was a pupil of Domenico GHIRLANDAIO, whose assistant he later became. Granacci was one of the assistants engaged by Michelangelo in 1508 for the beginning of the Sistine Ceiling but, like the others, was dismissed after about one month. On his return to Florence Granacci fell under the influence of Fra BARTOLOMMEO, and his later works have elongated figures in an attempt at monumentality. The Dublin *Holy Family*, which is usually attributed to him, has also been attributed to Michelangelo and shows the approximation of their styles. Basically, however, Granacci was a Quattrocento artist and is thus very similar to such transitional painters as Ridolfo Ghirlandaio and FRANCIABIGIO. There are works by him in Florence and in Baltimore (Walters), Berlin, London (V & A), Munich, Oxford, San Francisco, Sarasota Fla, and Washington. [ill. 172, p. 296]

Grandi, Ercole di Giulio Cesare, *see* ROBERTI.

Graphic Arts. The phrase is an importation into English from the German *Graphik* and is used to mean those arts which depend for their effect on drawing and not on colour: in other words the arts of drawing and engraving in all its forms.

Gravelot, Hubert (1699–1773), was a French book-illustrator and engraver. He came to London about 1732 and returned to Paris in 1745, after having been Gainsborough's master. He came back to London and remained till 1755 and then finally returned to Paris: he is the most important link between the French School – especially the Watteau followers – and the British in the mid 18th century. [ill. 860, p. 397]

Graver *see* BURIN.

Greco. Domenikos Theotocopoulos (1541–1614), called El Greco, was born in Crete and probably received his early training there. Crete then belonged to Venice, but it was a centre of the survival of Byzantine art in the 16th century, and it would be natural for a young artist who wished to receive further training to go to Venice for it, as Greco did. The references to his Italian years are very scanty, the most important being the letters of his friend, the illuminator Giulio Clovio. One, written in 1570, seeks the patronage of Cardinal Farnese for him: 'There has arrived in Rome a young Candiote, a pupil of Titian, who seems . . . to have a rare gift for painting.' Another letter was said to contain the strange reference: 'Yesterday I visited Greco, thinking to take a walk with him through the city. It was a most lovely day, with the spring sunshine at its best and would have given pleasure to anybody. The whole city was festive. When I went into his studio I was astonished: the shades were pulled so completely over the windows that you could hardly distinguish the objects in the room. Greco was seated in a chair – neither working nor asleep. He would not go out with me as he said the daylight blinded the light within him.' This, however, is now known to be a falsification, concocted in 1923 – i.e. at a time when MANNERISM was being discovered.

One early-17th-century source, not very reliable, records him as working during the Pontificate of Pius V (1566–72) and says that he had studied under Titian, coming to Rome at a propitious moment and with a great opinion of himself – saying, when Pius proposed to cover the nudities in Michelangelo's *Last Judgement* (eventually done by Daniele da Volterra), that if the whole thing were demolished he would paint another as good and decorous into the bargain. This caused such resentment that Greco was forced to go to Spain, where he had to compete for Court favour with established painters such as TIBALDI, ZUCCARO, and others, whose intrigues caused him to retire and die in obscurity. There is an element of truth in all this, including his lack of success at Court.

Greco's early works show his wide range of sources; Titian, Michelangelo, Bassano, Raphael, Dürer, the Mannerists of Central Italy, such as Pontormo and Parmigianino, and, underlying all these, his Byzantine heritage. It is not known why he went to Spain, but he is recorded in Toledo from 1577 until his death. Soon after his arrival he received his first major commission – the High Altar and two transept altars in San Domingo el Antiguo (1577–9). The High Altar has been dispersed but the transept altars remain. It astonishes by the completeness with which he has assimilated all the varied elements of his style and also by its great scale – *The Trinity* (now in the Prado) is nearly 10 feet high and the *Assumption* (now in Chicago) is over 16 feet. His next major commission was for the *Disrobing of Christ* (*El Espolio*), for Toledo Cathedral: it was refused and he had to bring a lawsuit, but the verdict of the assessors was enthusiastic and may explain the number of repetitions. Soon after this he made a bid for Court favour with his *Dream of Philip* (in the Escorial; sketch in London NG), a sort of counterpart to Titian's *Gloria, or Vision of Charles V*. It represents the adoration of the Name of Jesus, and is an allegory of the Holy League against the Turks. This was painted *c.* 1579, and in 1581 Philip commissioned the *Martyrdom of S. Maurice and the Theban Legion*, delivered in 1584, and immediately refused by the King, whose secretary wrote: 'The picture does not please His Majesty, and that is no wonder, for it pleases few, although it is said that there is much art in it and its author understands much for there are excellent things of his to be seen.' Philip was devoted to the balanced, serene art of Titian and this highly Mannerist work, asymmetrical, violent in scale changes, disturbing, and acid in colour, was bound to clash with the King's tastes. Philip tried hard to attract major artists into his service, but he got only feeble exponents of a style

one of whose greatest masters he rejected out of hand. Greco passed the remainder of his life in Toledo and his ecstatic and passionate style becomes heightened with time, often increasing with successive repetitions of a subject, and so personal that his pupils and assistants do not even attempt to follow his example except for occasional weak imitations by his son Jorge Manuel. The background of Mannerism in Italy lies partly in the Sack of Rome and the Counter-Reformation: in Spain the background to Greco is in the Wars with the Netherlands and in the long tragedy of the Expulsion of the Jews and the Moriscos from 1585 to 1609, which ruined Toledo and left whole districts desolate, with grass growing in the streets. It lies also in the 'Spiritual Exercises' of S. Ignatius, the founder of the Jesuits, which insist upon immediacy of experience, even of the events of the Passion, for the person practising the devotions. Greco's use of colour, often eerie and strident, with sharp contrasts of blue, yellow, shrill green, and a livid mulberry pink, the elongated limbs and nervous tension of his fingers, the feeling that the draperies swathing them have a life of their own – all these suggest the intensity of the painter's mystical experience and the catharsis he found in his art. The finest collections of El Greco's works are in Spain; in the Escorial, the Prado in Madrid, and in the museums and churches of Toledo. There are others in Barnard Castle (Bowes Mus.), Boston, Cadiz, Cambridge Mass. (Fogg Mus.), Chicago, Cincinnati, Cleveland Ohio, Copenhagen, Detroit, Dresden, Edinburgh (NG), Hartford Conn. (Wadsworth Atheneum), Kansas City, London (NG), Los Angeles, Milan, Minneapolis, Modena, Montreal, Munich, Naples, New York (Met. Mus., Frick Coll., Hispanic Soc.), Oslo, Ottawa, Palencia (Cath.), Paris (Louvre), Parma, Philadelphia, Princeton, Providence RI, Rochester NY, St Louis, San Diego Cal., San Francisco Cal., Saragossa, Sarasota Fla, Seville, Stockholm, Strasbourg, Toledo Ohio, Villanueva y Geltrú, Washington (Dumbarton Oaks, NG, and Phillips Coll.), and Worcester Mass. [ills. 648–52, pp. 366–7. Col pl. 11]

Greco, Emilio (*b.* 1913), is a Sicilian sculptor. As a boy he worked for a tombstone-maker, but while in the Army managed to attend art school in Palermo. His first one-man show in Rome in 1946 brought him immediate success. His principal works are bronze portrait busts, and life-size bronze female figures, tall, slender, posturing with great elegance, and often in sharp and witty parody of classical statues. His pen drawings express form through hatchings, with only an occasional fine contour. [ill. 1145, p. 432]

Greuze, Jean-Baptiste (1725–1805), made his name in the Salon of 1755 with *A Grandfather reading the Bible to his Family*, a piece of Dutch-inspired narrative genre painting, extolling the simple virtues of the poor. Enormously popular works such as *L'Accordée de Village* (1761: Louvre) and the *Paralytic tended by his Children* (1763: Leningrad, Hermitage) exploit this Rousseauish field with skill and determination, winning him extravagant praise from DIDEROT, who later came to a juster appreciation of Greuze's talent. His excessive vanity so antagonized his fellow-artists that his attempt in 1769 to secure election to the Academy as a History painter with the inadequate and ill-drawn *Septimius Severus reproaching Caracalla* met with a deservedly humiliating rebuff, and caused his withdrawal from all further Salons. He exhibited his works privately, enjoying a great vogue during the 1770s when much of his fame derived from the popularity of engravings after his works, fully exploited by a number of engravers, and, less profitably, by the artist, whose wife embezzled most of the proceeds. During these years a severe and Poussinesque composition and a more restrained use of accessory detail, were combined with turgid colour, strong chiaroscuro, and a heightened rendering of the gamut of the passions, displayed in vivid facial expressions and gestures and in a mountingly high moral tone. He also painted some excellent portraits and charmingly tender studies of children. During the late 1770s and in the 1780s, to offset his dwindling popularity, adversely affected by Neoclassicism, he produced increasing quantities of titillating semi-draped figures of young girls, grossly deficient in drawing and of mawkish sentimentality, and numerous 'Expression Studies' arbitrarily named 'Sorrow' or 'Innocence' and so on. His life was embittered by his disastrous marriage to the pretty model of his early pictures who later degenerated into a sleazy drab, whom he eventually divorced. After the Revolution, which ruined him, he endured poverty and neglect, occasionally relieved by a charitable commission from Napoleon and his circle. He died unnoticed, having – like Fragonard – outlived his time and his reputation. The largest collections of his pictures are in the Louvre and the Wallace Coll., London, Montpellier, and his native Tournus. There are others in most French provincial museums and in Baltimore, Berlin, Berne, Budapest, Dublin, Edinburgh, Glasgow, Leningrad, London (NG), Minneapolis, Moscow, Munich, New York (Met. Mus.), Rotterdam, Stockholm, Vienna, and York. There are also many drawings in Russia, where he was very popular. [ill. 731, p. 381]

Grien, Hans Baldung, *see* BALDUNG.

Gris, Juan (1887–1927), left Madrid in 1906 and settled in Paris, living near PICASSO. At first he broke up the objects in his pictures into many-facetted planes, but by 1911 he was using the analytical form of Cubism, and later used *collage* and synthetic forms, with an understanding and an originality that preserve him from inclusion among the more obvious Picasso followers. He did some work for Diaghileff in 1922–3, but found the world of ballet too hectic.
His 'Possibilités de la peinture' was given as a paper at the Sorbonne in 1924. There are works in New York (M of MA) and Paris (Mus. d'Art Mod. [ill. 1046, p. 421]

Grisaille is a painting executed entirely in monochrome, in a series of greys. Strictly speaking, a monochrome painting is one executed in any one colour, red, blue, or black; a *grisaille*, as its name implies, is in neutral greys only. A *grisaille* may be executed for its own sake as a decoration, or as a model for an engraver to work from, or it may be the first stage in building up an OIL PAINTING. [ill. 499, p. 345]

Gros, Baron Antoine-Jean (1771–1835). His parents were both minor artists, and he became a pupil of DAVID in 1785. In 1793 he was in Italy and was introduced by Josephine into the entourage of Napoleon (whom he painted) in Milan after the Italian campaign; he was one of the committee which selected the looted works of art taken from Italy to France. His strength lay in large pictures illustrating the Napoleonic Saga, such as *Napoleon visiting the plague-stricken at Jaffa* (1804: Louvre) and battlepieces full of movement and colour. He was David's closest friend and fervent admirer, and after his death in 1825 assumed the leadership of the classicist school. He was made a Baron by Charles X for his dome of the Panthéon which he had originally planned as an apotheosis of Napoleon and had to convert into an apotheosis of the Restoration Bourbons. His late classicist pictures were received with derision, and partly in despair at his failure, partly because of his miserable married life, he drowned himself. His influence on GÉRICAULT and DELACROIX was important for the development of the Romantic movement.
There are works in Algiers, Besançon, Bordeaux, Chartres, Grenoble, Malmaison, Moscow, Paris (Louvre, Carnavalet, Invalides), Toulouse, Valenciennes, Versailles, and elsewhere. [ill. 769, p. 387]

Grosz, Georg (1893–1959), was the leading German satirical draughtsman of this century. He was trained at the Dresden Academy from 1909 and served in the Army from 1914, but his dislike of authority resulted in a court martial for insubordination and he was nearly shot. In 1918 he was one of the founders of DADA in Berlin and in 1920 produced a book of satirical drawings – 'Gott mit Uns' – as a result of which he was fined for insulting the German Army. In 1923 he was again fined for an insult to morality, and in 1928 for blasphemy. Fortunately for him, he began to exhibit in America in 1931 and in 1933 he went to New York, remaining in America until he revisited Germany in 1951. He returned to Berlin, with the intention of staying there, in 1959, but died soon after his arrival. His autobiography has been published in German and English. There are examples of his work in Berlin, Cologne, and Stuttgart, as well as Boston, Cambridge Mass. (Fogg), Chicago, and New York (M of MA). [ill. 1068, p. 424]

Grotesque in its technical sense has nothing to do with its normal usage. It refers to the kind of ornament, sometimes also called Arabesque (though this is not really identical), which was used as a decoration in antiquity. This consists of medallions, sphinxes, foliage, and similar elements and the name Grotesque derives from the fact that these classical ornaments were rediscovered in places like the Golden House of Nero, in grottoes; and were thus named *Grotteschi*. Raphael was one of the first modern artists to use these motives.

Ground is the surface on which a painting is made. If on canvas, the ground is usually white oil paint, sometimes with a tinted layer on top; on panel the ground may be the same or GESSO. Some incompetent artists do not use a ground and paint direct on to the support – i.e. the bare canvas or wood. On canvas this practice is always, eventually, fatal. *See also* BOLUS GROUND.

Grünewald. Mathis Neithardt-Gothardt, called Grüne-wald (*c.* 1470/80–1528), was the contemporary of Dürer, and his exact opposite. Little is known of his life – he is first documented in 1501 in Seligenstadt – but he may have been in Aschaffenburg before then and was perhaps born in Würzburg. From 1508 to 1514 he was Court Painter to the Archbishop-Elector of Mainz and then to Cardinal Albrecht, Elector of Mainz; but he seems to have had Lutheran sympathies and in 1526 he was in Frankfurt and 1527 in Halle, where he died. Unlike most of his German contemporaries he seems never to have designed any woodcuts or made etchings or engravings, and relatively few drawings by him have survived. The first datable work is the *Mocking of Christ* (formerly dated 1503: Munich) but his masterpiece is the large folding altar for a church in Isenheim (finished *c.* 1515: Colmar, Musée), which shows how completely his outlook differed from that of Dürer. Dürer attempted to learn the Italian technical methods in order to penetrate into the serene world of the Italian and classical tradition: Grünewald seems to have been well acquainted with the Renaissance ideas in, for example, perspective and the definition of a given space, but he uses these Renaissance technical means simply to heighten the emotional impact made by his essentially Late Gothic religious imagery. The terrible figure of the Crucified Christ in the *Isenheim Altar* is anti-Renaissance in its intensity, but the altarpiece as a whole combines a passionate expression of the Visions of S. Bridget with an Italian (or rather Renaissance) feeling for drawing, light, and colour. The terrible afflictions of so many of the figures are probably due to the fact that the altarpiece was painted for a hospital for skin diseases. His few paintings are in Basle, Donaueschingen, Frankfurt (Städel), Freiburg i. B., Karlsruhe, Munich, Stuppach in Württemberg, Washington (NG). [ill. 568, p. 355]

Guardi, Francesco (1712–93), was a Venetian VEDUTA painter, whose free handling and atmospheric effects now appeal more than CANALETTO's meticulous views of Venetian architecture, which were the more highly valued until the Impressionists taught us to see transient effects of light. Most of Guardi's views of Venice – he painted little else – were produced as souvenirs for tourists, and a contemporary diarist records him as a disciple of Canaletto, working for an Englishman. He worked with his brother, Giovanni Antonio (1698–1760) and collaborated with him on some religious pictures, but Francesco's activity as a figure painter has only recently been clarified by the discovery of such works as the altarpiece at Roncegno in Valsugana, of *c.* 1777, and five large decorative panels (London, private coll.). His *vedute*, for which he got only about half Canaletto's prices, were produced in great numbers and have also been imitated ever since the 18th century. The vivacity and bravura of his little figures, and his pale, bright colour, may owe something to his brother-in-law, TIEPOLO. Most large galleries have works by him, but the following are dated sets of pictures: *Election of Doge Alvise IV Mocenigo*, 1763, based on engravings after drawings by Canaletto, in the Louvre (7), Brussels, Grenoble, Nantes (2), and Toulouse; *Pius VI's visit to Venice*, 1782, in Oxford and private collections; *Fêtes for the Archduke Paul of Russia and Maria Feodorowna* ('*I Conti del Nord*'), 1782, in Munich and private collections.

Other dated pictures include *Faith* and *Hope*, 1747, in the Ringling Mus., Sarasota Fla. [ills. 301, 307, 310, pp. 315–16]

Guercino (1591–1666), was born at Cento, near Bologna. His nickname means 'squint-eyed', his real name being Francesco Barbieri. He was first strongly influenced by Ludovico CARRACCI, but early overlaid his Carraccesque training with the strong chiaroscuro associated with the Caravaggesques, which he invested with a charm and softness unknown to its originator, though he later abandoned it for an even characterless illumination more suitable for the didactic, mechanical Counter-Reformation altarpieces of his late Bolognese period. In 1621 he was in Rome working for Pope Gregory XV, and his masterpiece is the *Aurora* on the ceiling of the Casino Ludovisi, one of the finest Baroque illusionistic decorations. In the landscape parts he was helped by Tassi and the BRILLS. He returned to Cento on the death of the Pope in 1623, and set up a studio, but on the death of RENI – who loathed him, and accused him of fishing in his ideas and copying his handling – he moved to Bologna in 1642 and took over the Reni religious picture factory.

There are examples in the Royal Collection (rich in fine drawings), Bologna (Mus. and churches), Berlin, Birmingham, Brussels, Budapest, Cento, Detroit, Dresden, Dublin, Florence (Uffizi, Pitti), Genoa, Greenville SC, Hartford Conn., Leningrad, London (NG, Dulwich, Lancaster House, Wellington Mus.), Madrid (Prado), Milan (Brera), Minneapolis, Modena, Munich, Naples, Parma, Paris (Louvre), Piacenza, Providence RI, Rome, Sarasota Fla, Toulouse, Vaduz (Liechtenstein Coll.), Vicenza, Vienna. [ills. 252, 253, 256, pp. 308–9]

Guido da Siena was the all but mythical founder of the Sienese School. He signed a picture in the Pal. Pubblico, Siena, and dated it 1221, but there are other pictures, also in Siena, associable with him which are datable 1262 and in the 1270s. There are therefore two schools of thought: (i) that 1221 is correct, in spite of the evidently repainted surface of much of the picture. In this case (*a*) Siena precedes Florence in the development of Dugento painting, and (*b*) the other pictures mentioned are by Guido's followers, not by Guido himself. (ii) The other school (which contains few Sienese) holds that 1221 is an old tampering with an original date *c.* 1261 – perhaps MCCXXI was altered from MCCLXI – and the other pictures are therefore his and contemporary. Recent X-rays give no grounds for believing this. Another theory, more reasonable, assumes that the picture was painted perhaps 1260/70, but was a copy and replacement of an older image, and the date 1221 was copied faithfully from this older image. [ill. 36, p. 274]

Guild. In the Middle Ages tradesmen formed themselves into Guilds for economic, religious, and social purposes, and often several different trades would unite in a single guild; at Florence, for example, painters belonged to the Doctors' and Apothecaries' Guild (*Medici e Speziali*). Much of our knowledge of early painting comes from Guild records, since all painters had to join unless they were in the personal service of the ruling prince. Only a Master could set up in business, take pupils, and employ JOURNEYMEN, and to become a Master it was necessary to submit a master-piece to the Guild as evidence of competence. The Guild officers also supervised the number of apprentices and the conditions of work and often also materials. Some Guilds bought in bulk for members, others allowed only panels stamped with their seal to be used for painting on. The tendency to uniformity of practice and to a 'Trade Union' mentality led to painters like Leonardo and Michelangelo insisting on the freedom and originality of the artist and his status as a professional man and a scholar (and gentleman). This new conception of the inspired being, instead of the honest tradesman, led to the decline of the Guilds and the rise of the ACADEMIES, which took over the all-important function of teaching. As one might expect, the power of the Guilds lasted longer in N. Europe than in Italy. As late as 1655 the Guild at Malines made itself ridiculous by trying to prevent Jan Cossiers from completing a commission, painted in his Antwerp studio, *in situ* in Malines – on the grounds that he was not a resident and was therefore forbidden to work in their town. A similar situation arose in Toronto in 1960.

Günther, Ignaz (1725–75), was the great Bavarian sculptor of the Rococo period, who used its light and gay forms to create deeply religious images. Most of his work is in painted wood and is in Munich and its neighbourhood. [ill. 630, p. 362]

Guttoso, Renato (*b.* 1912), was born in Sicily and is the leading Italian (or European) exponent of SOCIAL REALISM. He studied Law and began to paint only in 1931. His works attacked Fascism and the Nazis (especially in his bitter drawings 'Gott mit uns'), and his style is necessarily realistic, but the influence of Picasso is evident. There are works in London (Tate), New York (M of MA), Prague and Sydney NSW. [ill. 1074, p. 425]

Guys, Constantin (1802–92), was a draughtsman who chronicled the wars and the fashions of Europe in the 19th century. He travelled enormously and took part in the Greek War of Independence and the Crimean War (which he reported as correspondent of the 'Illustrated London News'), but he is best known for his witty drawings of soldiers, horses, and courtesans. Baudelaire wrote a long essay on him as *le peintre de la vie moderne*. [ill. 784, p. 388]

H

Hals, Frans (1580/5–1666), was born in Antwerp of Flemish parents but spent most of his life in Haarlem. He was a pupil of Karel van MANDER (1600–3), and entered the Haarlem Guild in 1610. His earliest dated work (*Jacobus Zaffius*, 1611: Haarlem) was painted in Haarlem, but by 1616 he was probably in Antwerp and may have been in contact with Rubens, who may later have visited him. His great gift was for portraiture, and especially for catching the fleeting expression, and he is best known for the huge but lively groups of the companies of Archers and Musketeers raised during the Wars against Spain, the earliest of which was painted in 1616. These groups solve the very difficult problem of composing a picture out of a number of figures all of whom demand the same prominence (since all the sitters subscribed), thus precluding the classical solution of subordinating the minor figures. Hals used a very virtuoso technique to enliven the whole picture surface and each portrait is caught in a fleeting gesture or expression. The whole is perhaps a little like a school photograph, but that is what the sitters wanted, and the very informality caused his work to be a great influence on Manet and the Impressionists. In his single figures his dazzling skill sometimes runs away with him – as in the *Laughing Cavalier* (1624: London, Wallace Coll.) – and he never quite achieved the sympathy and insight of his greater contemporary Rembrandt. During the years 1624–8 he was strongly influenced by the UTRECHT School and adopted the type of genre portrait common to Terbrugghen and Honthorst. He used these largely for technical experiments, making his drawing even more simplified and his handling appear almost monochromatic and *alla prima*: he did in fact employ a very limited colour-range and used greys a great deal, but all the bravura of the handling is a deal less spontaneous than it appears at first sight. After the Peace of 1648 the Military Companies were disbanded, but their place was taken, for artists, by the great group portraits commissioned by Regents and Governors of Charities. Hals painted several of these, particularly in his last years when he was destitute and dependent on charity for himself and his wife: these have greater feeling for character and greater humanity than many of his earlier groups, and they are also strangely closer to the late Rembrandt in handling.

Both his brothers were painters, but only Dirk (1591–1656) achieved any independence, though his subjects and style were similar to Frans's. All seven of his sons were also painters, though of little significance. His pupils probably included BROUWER, Jan MOLENAER and his wife Judith LEYSTER, A. van OSTADE, and WOUWERMAN, while Jan de BRAY owed much to Hals's development of the Regent groups. Hals had a large workshop, and as many as twenty versions of some works are known. The most important collection, including five Officer groups and three of Governors, is in the Hals Museum at Haarlem. Other works, by him or from his studio, include those in the Royal Coll. and in Amsterdam (Rijksmus.), Antwerp, Baltimore, Berlin, Birmingham (Barber Inst.), Boston (Mus.), Brussels, Cape Town, Cassel, Chicago, Cincinnati, Cleveland Ohio, Cologne (Wallraf-Richartz Mus.), Denver, Detroit, Dresden, Edinburgh (NG), Frankfurt (Städel), The Hague, Hartford Conn., Houston Texas, Hull, Kansas City, London (NG and Kenwood), Munich, New York (Met. Mus. and Frick Coll.), Paris (Louvre), Richmond Va, San Diego Cal., St Louis, Sarasota Fla (Ringling), Stockholm, Toledo Ohio, Toronto, Vienna, Washington (NG), and elsewhere. [ills. 509, 524, 525, 535, pp. 346, 348–50. Col. pl. 19]

Hamilton, Gavin (1723–98), was a Scots laird who graduated at Glasgow and then went to Rome and trained as a painter in the 1740s. After practising as a portrait painter in Britain in 1753/4 he returned to Rome for good and became well known as a dealer and antiquary and as a member of the NEOCLASSIC school centred round Mengs and Winckelmann. He was painting Poussinesque historical compositions by 1758 and is thus one of the original exponents of the doctrine preached by DAVID some 15 years later. There is a picture ascribed to him in Edinburgh (NG), but his most influential works are in the Villa Borghese in Rome. [ill. 887, p. 400]

Handling (Fr. *facture*; Ital. *fattura*) is the name given to the most personal part of a work of art, the actual execution. The general features of composition, of subject, of drawing or colour, can be used to assign a picture or other work to a given School or period; the handling of the paint, pencil, clay, or other medium is personal to the artist and is what the forger tries hardest to imitate. Just as a man's signature is highly personal and executed without thinking about it, so a painter will handle shapes and planes and even come to see in terms of his own BRUSHWORK.

Harpignies, Henri (1819–1916), was a French landscape painter who was principally influenced by Corot. In his old age his failing eyesight forced him to generalize in a manner not unlike the late Corot. He was popular in England and there are four pictures by him in the NG, London. [ill. 766, p. 385]

Hartung, Hans (b. 1904), was born in Leipzig and began as an Expressionist, but became an abstract painter about

1922: in 1925 he saw works by KANDINSKY, which confirmed him in this trend. He has lived in Paris since 1935, fought in the Foreign Legion and lost a leg at Belfort (1944), and is now a French citizen. His works are a mesh of calligraphic brushstrokes, usually dark on a light ground, which an admirer has described as 'a blend of the exacting discipline that governs French art with what is best and most distinguished in Germanic poetry'. The effect is often similar to the works of KLINE, the American, for whom no such background has been claimed. His paintings have no titles, but are distinguished by numbers, thus: T54-16 means Toile (i.e. canvas), 1954, number 16. There are examples in Basle, Grenoble, New York (Guggenheim), Paris (Musée d'Art Moderne), and Philadelphia. [ill. 1094, p. 428]

Hatching is shading carried out in parallel lines; cross-hatching is shading in two layers of parallel lines, one layer crossing the other at an angle.

Haydon, Benjamin Robert (1786–1846), British historical painter. Like BARRY, Haydon attempted to be a pure history painter in the Grand Style adumbrated by Reynolds in his 'Discourses'. His life was a tragi-comedy of high endeavour and High Art which ended in imprisonment for debt, and suicide. His tireless propaganda forced the Government and nobility to accept the novel idea that the patronage of the arts was socially desirable, and he was partly responsible for the Government's purchase of the Elgin Marbles in 1816. There are pictures in London (NPG and Tate), but his best memorial is his 'Auto-biography and Memoirs'. [ill. 910, p. 403]

Hayman, Francis (1708–76), was a scene-painter and illustrator who became one of the Founder-Members of the RA in 1768 and was later its first Librarian. He painted several small portrait groups which influenced Gainsborough (who may have worked under him), but his most famous pictures were the decorations for the fashionable Vauxhall Gardens, begun in the mid 1740s. Two of these survive in the V & A, London, and show the strong French element in his style, perhaps derived from his friend GRAVELOT. His *Sir Robert Walpole in the Painter's Studio* (London, NPG) and his *Finding of Moses* (1746: London, Coram Foundation, formerly Foundling Hospital) are other aspects of his work. [ill. 856, p. 396]

Heckel, Erich (b. 1883), studied architecture in Dresden in 1904, where he met KIRCHNER and SCHMIDT-ROTTLUFF, with whom he founded the BRÜCKE in 1905. A trip to Italy in 1909 was a great influence on him, and so were FEININGER, MACKE, and MARC, whom he met in 1912 and who introduced him to the DELAUNAY form of Cubism. He served in the Army Medical Corps, 1915–18, and met Ensor and Beckmann in Belgium. From 1918 he lived in Berlin until he fled to Switzerland in 1944, after no fewer than 729 of his works had been removed from German museums. From 1949 to 1956 he taught at Karlsruhe, but has since returned to Switzerland. There are pictures by him in Berlin, Cologne, Detroit, Hagen, Harvard University, and New York (M of MA). [ill. 1016, p. 417]

Heda, Willem Claesz. (1594–1682), was a Dutch painter of still-life subjects, usually in cool greyish colour against a plain background, with elaborate goblets of wine and pewter vessels. There are examples in Amsterdam (Rijksmus.) and other Dutch museums, Dresden, Karlsruhe, Munich, and elsewhere. [ill. 470, p. 339]
His son Gerrit (c. 1620–before 1702) was also a still-life painter in a similar vein. There are works in Amsterdam (Rijksmus.), London (NG), Munich, Oxford (Ashmolean), Rotterdam and Worcester Mass. [ill. 467, p. 339]

Heem, Jan Davidsz. de (1606–84), worked at Utrecht and Leyden before the religious troubles drove him to settle in Antwerp. Usually his pictures contain a profusion of flowers, or fruit, oysters, etc., with elaborate goblets, but occasionally he painted a 'Melancholia' type of still-life, with a figure surrounded by books, papers, and pictures. He was the most brilliant still-life painter in a family of them; his father David (1570–1632) worked in Utrecht, and his son Cornelis (1631–95) worked in Leyden and Antwerp. There are works in Amsterdam (Rijksmus.), Berlin, Brussels, Darmstadt, Dresden, Edinburgh (NG), The Hague, London (NG, Wallace Coll.), Munich, Oxford, Toledo Ohio, Vienna, and elsewhere, by one or other member of the family. [ills. 465, 469, 471, pp. 338–9]

Heemskerck, Maerten van (1498–1574) worked with SCOREL in Haarlem 1527–9 and learned most of the Italianate manner from him before going to Italy in 1532 himself. Before he left he gave his *S. Luke painting the Virgin* to the Haarlem Guild (now in Haarlem, Hals Mus.): this is almost a parody of the Italian manner, as conceived by a Northerner at second hand. In Rome he made a large number of drawings (1532–5) of the antiquities and works of art, and two of his sketchbooks (Berlin) are invaluable evidence for the monuments of antiquity as they existed in the 16th century as well as for such things as the building of New St Peter's. He settled in Haarlem in 1537 and worked there for the rest of his life except for a flight to Amsterdam (1572–3) while the Spaniards were besieging Haarlem. He painted a number of fine portraits, like those of Scorel, as well as Italianate religious pictures. There are works by him in Amsterdam (Rijksmus.), Barnard Castle (Bowes Mus.), Berlin, Brussels, Cambridge (Fitzwm, *Self-portrait with the Colosseum in the background*), Cassel, Ghent, The Hague, Lille, Linköping Cath. (Sweden), New York (Met. Mus.), as well as in Haarlem and elsewhere. [ill. 361, p. 325]

Helst, Bartholomeus van der (1613–70), was a fashionable Amsterdam portrait painter and one of the founders of the Guild there (1653). He was probably a pupil of ELIAS and was influenced by both Hals and Rembrandt. There are works by him in Amsterdam, Berlin, Brussels, Cambridge (Fitzwilliam Mus.), Detroit, Dublin, The Hague, London (NG and Wallace Coll.), New York, Paris, Philadelphia (Johnson Coll.), Vienna, and elsewhere. [ill. 442, p. 334]

Hepworth, Barbara (b. 1903), is a British abstract sculptor. She is a direct carver in wood and stone and has only recently turned to modelled forms, mostly partly cut in plaster before being cast in bronze. In 1931 she began piercing holes in her sculpture and has since exploited hollowed-out forms. She was trained in Leeds, where she met Henry MOORE, and was later also influenced by BRANCUSI. From 1938 she has carved abstract forms in which the large masses are set off by string or wire, giving an effect like a musical instrument. Her works can be seen in the open at Harlow New Town, Essex; Hatfield, or the Royal Festival Hall, London, where she has also made large-scale decorative works for several new buildings, e.g. State House, Holborn (1963). There are works in Aberdeen, Birmingham, Bristol, Leeds, London (V & A and Tate), Manchester, Wakefield, as well as several American and European museums. [ill. 1140, p. 433]

Herring, John F. (1795–1865), was a stage-coachman who turned animal painter. After driving local coaches for four years he drove the 'High Flyer' between London and York until he devoted himself entirely to painting racehorses. He worked for many years in the Doncaster district and painted thirty-three successive winners of the St Leger before settling in Newmarket, and, in 1833, in London. He exhibited at the RA from 1818 to 1846 and worked for George IV and Queen Victoria. His works were very popular in the United States through engravings. His son John Frederick Herring the Younger worked in the same style and died as recently as 1907. [ill. 904, p. 402]

Heyden, Jan van der (1637–1712), was the first painter in Amsterdam to paint townscapes, although this was being done in Haarlem by the BERCKHEYDES. Van der Heyden began as a still-life painter and at the end of his life he took it up again, but his architectural subjects date mostly from the 1660s. He painted walls and masonry with minute skill, but his topography is often wilful. From c. 1670 he designed fire-engines and street lighting, both of which activities made him very rich: his 'Fire-engine Book', with etchings by him, was published in 1690. There are works by him in the Royal Coll., in Amsterdam, Berlin, Dresden, Edinburgh, Florence (Uffizi: *Amsterdam Town Hall*, 1667, which has been in Florence at least since 1672), Glasgow, The Hague, Hamburg, London (NG, Wallace Coll., Wellington Mus., and Dulwich), Paris (Louvre), Philadelphia, Rotterdam, Vaduz (Liechtenstein Coll.), Vienna, Washington (NG), and elsewhere. [ill. 482, p. 341]

Hicks *see* PRIMITIVE.

Highmore, Joseph (1692–1780), was an English portrait painter, contemporary with HOGARTH, who retired in 1761, when Reynolds had established himself. Apart from portraits Highmore also painted some illustrations to literature, the most famous being a Hogarth-like series from 'Pamela', by his friend Samuel Richardson (there are twelve in all, completed by 1745 and now divided between Cambridge (Fitzwm), London (Tate Gall., V & A), and Melbourne). In 1746, inspired by Hogarth, he presented a history picture to the Foundling Hospital, where it still hangs. He was originally bred to the law, and in his later years published various writings on art. Other pictures are in the Royal Coll., Cambridge, Cardiff, Liverpool, London (NPG, Tate, Dulwich), and Oxford. [ill. 859, p. 397]

Hildebrand, Adolf von (1847–1921), was the leading German sculptor of the classic tradition in the late 19th century. He went to Rome in 1867 and met the writer Konrad Fiedler, as well as the painter MARÉES, who had a decisive effect upon him. In 1872 he returned to Italy for five years, and in 1873 helped Marées on his frescoes in Naples. His most famous work is the Wittelsbach Fountain in Munich, begun in 1891; but he is probably better known as a writer, whose book on aesthetics, 'Problem der Form', first published in 1893, had reached its 9th edition by 1914. This was written under the influence of Fiedler, but became one of the most famous books on aesthetics ever published in Germany. Hildebrand's realist strain is seen in his portrait busts and monuments, which include one to Brahms. There are works in Berlin, Dresden, Frankfurt, Munich, and other German galleries. [ill. 632, p. 362]

Hilliard (Hillyarde), Nicholas (c. 1547–1619), is the first great British artist about whom we know a few details. He was the son of a goldsmith and was himself trained in, and practised, that art although he was painting miniature portraits by 1560. He is recorded in the Goldsmiths Company in 1570 and in the same year he painted his first dated portrait of Queen Elizabeth, to whom he had probably already been appointed Limner and Goldsmith: in the latter capacity he designed a Great Seal for her. He was certainly in France between 1576 and 1578 and was probably the Nicholas Belliart who was attached to the Duc d'Alençon, the Queen's suitor. About 1600 he composed a treatise 'The Arte of Limning' (first published in 1912), in the course of which he records conversations with the Queen and, in particular, their agreement that portrait painting should be done without shadows '. . . . best in plaine lines without shadowing, for the lyne without shadowe showeth all to a good jugment, but the shadowe without lyne showeth nothing'. About this time he was in financial difficulties, perhaps partly caused by his old-fashioned insistence on line without modelling, for his pupil Isaac OLIVER was by now a serious rival to him. In 1617 he was actually imprisoned, although it seems to have been as a surety for someone else. His miniatures are always intended to be thought of as jewels, to be held in the hand and in this his goldsmith's training was no doubt decisive. There are no known oil-paintings which can be attributed to him with any confidence, but a small group of portraits shows his style: the so-called 'Pelican' portrait of Queen Elizabeth (Liverpool) is the best known. There are works by him in the Royal Coll., and in London (V & A) and in Cambridge (Fitzwm), Cleveland, London (NPG, Nat. Marit. Mus.), New York (Met. Mus.), and Oxford (Bodleian Library). His son, Laurence Hilliard (1582–after 1640), was also a limner. [ill. 805, p. 391. Col. pl. 51]

History Painting, in fully developed academic theory, is the noblest form of art and consists of generalized representations of the passions and intellect as symbolized in classical history or mythology or in subjects taken from Christian iconography. The word 'history' was usually meant to refer to ancient history and mythology, but the Christian story was admitted as conformable to the highest flights of imaginative art. Modern history, and particularly subjects which involved modern dress instead of nondescript drapery, was admitted only in the late 18th century in England (WEST's *Death of Wolfe* is one of the classic examples) and even later elsewhere. The theory of history painting was pushed to extremes by men like HAYDON, who died of it, but it was also truly responsible for some of the greatest works of such masters as Raphael and Poussin.

Hitchens, Ivon (*b.* 1893), is the son of a painter, and studied at the Royal Academy Schools. In 1940 he went to live in Sussex, and his main subject-matter is the richly wooded landscapes around his home, expressed in non-naturalistic, almost abstract and Tachiste terms, usually in long rectangular format. He has also painted flowers and figures; these culminated in his enormous (69 × 20 ft) mural for the English Folk Song and Dance Society (1954), and for the University of Sussex (1963). There are characteristic works in many British museums, including Aberdeen, Birmingham, Cambridge (Fitzwm), London (Tate, V & A), Nottingham, and in Adelaide, Buffalo, Gothenburg, Melbourne, Montreal, Oslo, Ottawa, Paris (Mus. d'Art Mod.), Seattle, Toledo Ohio, Toronto, and Wellington NZ. [ill. 977, p. 412]

Hobbema, Meindert (1638–1709), was the friend and pupil of Jacob van RUISDAEL, whom he met in Amsterdam before 1659. His earliest pictures are dated 1658 (Detroit) and 1659 (Frankfurt and Grenoble) and not only are some of his works virtually indistinguishable from Ruisdael's, but they also occasionally painted the same views, e.g. the pair in Amsterdam and Washington. In 1668 he married the maid of the Burgomaster of Amsterdam, and through the influence of one of his wife's fellow-servants he obtained a minor post in the Excise, and from then onwards he seems to have painted much less. It used to be thought that his most famous work, the *Avenue at Middelharnis* (London NG), was dated 1669 and was his swan-song, but the date is now read as 1689, and there are pictures of 1671 (also in the NG) and 1689 (Bridgewater Coll.), so he presumably continued to paint but omitted to date his pictures. In any case it is difficult to understand how a man of such gifts could bring himself to stop painting and spend 40 years gauging wine in casks. Unlike Ruisdael he painted quiet landscapes, usually with watermills, with none of the romantic quality or the splendid clouds and skies of Ruisdael's pictures. Although his work was little prized in his own time it was very much sought after by English collectors of the 18th and 19th centuries and exerted great influence on English landscape painting: for this reason the best collection of his works is in the NG, London. There are others in the Royal Collection and Amsterdam, Antwerp, Berlin, Brussels, Cambridge (Fitzwm), Cape Town, Chicago, Cincinnati, Detroit, Frankfurt (Städel), Glasgow, The Hague, Indianapolis, London (Wallace Coll. and Dulwich), Minneapolis, Munich, New York (Frick Coll., Historical Soc., and Met. Mus.), Ottawa, Paris, Philadelphia, Rotterdam, Vienna, and Washington. [ill. 483, p. 342]

Hodler, Ferdinand (1853–1918), was, with BÖCKLIN, the leading Swiss painter of the 19th century. He visited Madrid (1878–9) and Paris (1891), where he was influenced by Corot and Courbet, but he ultimately developed a very linear, flat style, much closer to PUVIS de Chavannes.

About 1891 he was much influenced by Symbolist ideas, by ART NOUVEAU, and, like many others, by the Rosicrucians. From the mid 1890s he concentrated on large-scale historical and mythological works, such as those for Jena University (1907) and Hanover Town Hall (1910). There are works by him in Zürich and other Swiss and German museums. [ill. 1000, p. 415]

Hofer, Carl (1878–1955), is usually classed as an Expressionist, but his art is profoundly French in its adherence to classical ideals. He first went to Paris in 1900, after which he worked for two years under THOMA in Karlsruhe and then spent five years in Rome (1903–8). He returned to Paris, 1908–13, except for two trips to India, and was interned in France 1914–17. He became a Professor in Berlin in 1918, was dismissed in 1933, and reinstated in 1945. An air-raid in 1943 destroyed many of his works, and he set himself to paint some again from memory. His sober classicism, influenced by MARÉES, and above all by CÉZANNE, is very similar to that of DERAIN. He wrote an autobiography and also a book, published posthumously, on discipline in art. There are works in Cologne, Detroit, and Harvard University. [ill. 1069, p. 424]

Hogarth, William (1697–1764), was apprenticed to a goldsmith but began engraving *c.* 1720. He studied at the St Martin's Lane Academy, but never really achieved any proficiency as a draughtsman: he was, however, well aware of the need for academic training and later promoted another Academy in St Martin's Lane which was the principal forerunner of the Royal Academy. He began painting small groups and conversation pieces and by 1729, when he married THORNHILL's daughter, he had begun to make a name. The *Beggar's Opera* (several versions exist, one in the Tate Gall.) was perhaps the most successful of these, and it was probably the transition from portraiture to his best-known works, the moralities. Hogarth himself said 'I then married, and commenced painter of small conversation pieces, from twelve to fifteen inches high. This having novelty, succeeded for a few years . . . I therefore turned my thoughts to a still more novel mode, *viz.* painting and engraving modern moral subjects, a field not broken up in any country or any age. . . I therefore wished to compose pictures on canvas, similar to representations on the stage; and farther hope, that they will be tried by the same test, and criticised by the same criterion . . . I have endeavoured to treat my subjects as a dramatic writer; my picture is my stage, and men and women my players, who by means of certain actions and gestures, are to exhibit *a dumb show*.' The first of these moral subjects was the *Harlot's Progress*, showing the downfall of a country girl at the hands of the wicked Londoners (several of whom were recognizable). The original paintings were probably executed in 1731/2 (they are now lost) but the popularity of the series depended on the engravings made from them in 1732; this was so great that they were frequently pirated and Hogarth ultimately got a Copyright Act passed in 1735 which was of great benefit to artists and engravers alike. The next series was the *Rake's Progress* (1735: paintings in the Soane Mus., London) and it was followed by the *Marriage à la Mode* (1743–5: London, NG) and the *Election* (1754: Soane

Mus.). He visited Paris in 1743 and again in 1748 and was strongly influenced by French Rococo, but the influence was perhaps strongest at the beginning of his career – e.g. in *Before* and *After* and other pictures of the 1730s. He was in fact rabidly anti-French (his chief characteristics seem to have been pugnacity and self-assertion) and his xenophobia was not helped by the fact that, in 1748, in company with HAYMAN, he was arrested as a spy for drawing the fortifications at Calais, an event that he celebrated in his picture *O the Roast Beef of Old England!* ('*Calais Gate*') (1748: London, NG). His efforts in the Italian Grand Manner had little success, although the *Pool of Bethesda* and *Good Samaritan* (1735–6: London, S. Bartholomew's Hospital) were certainly better received than the *Sigismunda* (1759: Tate Gall.) which he painted to show that he could treat a tragic subject in as grand a manner as a Bolognese picture of the same subject which was sold at auction for a price higher than Hogarth thought right. This was painted at the end of his life and was savagely attacked by John Wilkes who had recently been roughly handled by Hogarth in an engraving.

His fame was, and is, most firmly based on the engravings of his moral subjects, which have to be read, detail by telling detail, rather than contemplated as works of art; nevertheless, all through his life he was capable of pieces of superb painting. He continued to paint portraits, the most successful being those of sitters of his own type, e.g. the *Captain Coram* (1740: the Foundling Hospital, London). This was painted for the great charitable institution which Coram founded and of which Hogarth himself became a Governor. Not only is the portrait itself important as an adaptation of the Baroque State portrait to a middle-class sitter, but Hogarth managed to persuade a number of other artists, including HAYMAN and HIGHMORE, to join with him in presenting a history picture each to the Foundling Hospital. These were shown to the public for the benefit of the Hospital, but the Exhibition was so popular that it led ultimately to the establishment of public exhibitions in London and thus to the Royal Academy. Hogarth also wrote a treatise on aesthetics, 'The Analysis of Beauty' (1753), and an Autobiography, the MS. of which is in the BM, printed in J. Burke's edition of the 'Analysis' (Oxford, 1955).

There are pictures in the Royal Collection and in Birmingham, Bristol, Buffalo, Detroit, Edinburgh (NG), Liverpool, London (NG, NPG, Tate, Nat. Marit. Mus., Dulwich Coll., Soane Mus., and Coram Fdn., i.e. Foundling Hospital), Manchester, Minneapolis, Montreal, New York (Met. Mus. and Frick Coll.), Northampton Mass., Oberlin Coll. Ohio, Ottawa, Philadelphia, St Louis, Toledo Ohio, Vancouver, Washington (Corcoran and Nat. Coll.), and in many English provincial galleries. [ills. 830, 857, 858, pp. 394, 396–7]

Holbein, Hans the Elder (*c.* 1465–1524) was a Late Gothic painter with a large workshop in Augsburg in which his sons Hans the Younger and Ambrosius worked. By 1514 the shop had broken up, and Holbein senior moved to Isenheim probably by 1517. His major work was the *S. Sebastian Altar* (1515/17: Munich) but there is also a sketchbook, mostly of portrait drawings, in Berlin, which includes a double portrait of his two sons. [ill. 576, p. 356]

Holbein, Hans the Younger (1497/8–1543), was probably the most accomplished and penetratingly realist portrait painter the North has produced. He began in his father's shop, but by 1515 he and his brother were in Basle working for a local painter. He was soon working for publishers, notably for Froben, probably through whom he met Erasmus about 1515/16. His early portraits (*Burgomaster Meyer* and his *Wife*, 1516, and *Bonifacius Amerbach*, 1519: Basle) show his gift for characterization, and his religious works (*Dead Christ*, 1521, Basle; *Solothurn Madonna*, 1522, Solothurn) shown him either grimly realist or decorative rather than devotional. In 1517 he left Basle, visited Lucerne, and probably went to Italy; he returned to Basle after the death of his brother in 1519, became a citizen in 1520, and married. He was commissioned to paint the Council Chamber with frescoes of justice scenes, civic virtues, and law-givers in 1521, but the work was interrupted by the disturbances connected with the Reformation and by his absences and was not finished until 1530. He illustrated the Luther Bible and published the 'Dance of Death', 1523/4, and the 'Alphabet of Death', 1524. Both these add the bitterness of the Peasants' War to the medieval theme, and the Dance is dropped in favour of Death depicted as the harvester of every class of man. The 'Dance of Death' was published in Lyons, and ran to ten editions in twelve years. His international reputation as a portraitist was established by three portraits of Erasmus in 1523 which were strongly influenced by MASSYS. In 1526, possibly because the continued religious troubles were affecting his business, he left Basle and travelled via Antwerp (where he met Massys) to London, bringing introductions from Erasmus to Sir Thomas More and Archbishop Warham. He stayed for eighteen months, during which time he painted the large group of the More family (now only known from copies and sketches) and may have been temporarily employed by the Crown on decorations. He returned to Basle until 1532, but the religious strife was now more acute, and even an offer by the Town Council of a pension could not retain him. When he arrived back in London in 1532 More was in disfavour, and from 1532 to 1536 he worked mainly for the Merchants of the Steelyard (the wool staple and the Hanseatic League) on half-length portraits of amazing virtuosity. He probably entered the Royal service after painting *The Ambassadors* (1533: London, NG) – a *tour de force* of representation and iconographical allusion. One of his chief works for Henry VIII was the dynastic group of Henry with his Queen, Jane Seymour, and Henry VII and Elizabeth of York (burnt in 1698; part of the cartoon is in London, NPG). The figure of Henry served as a model for the many versions of the King, who also employed Holbein as a goldsmith's designer and on painted and architectural decorations, and sent him abroad to paint prospective brides (the *Duchess of Milan*, 1538, London, NG; *Anne of Cleves*, 1539/40, Paris, Louvre). His late practice of painting from drawings instead of from the sitter was strengthened by the requirements of extensive Court portraiture. His portraits – life-sized and in miniature – became more linear in style and more hieratic in treatment than his early works, partly through their emphasis on detail, partly because working only from drawings led him to be less sensitive in handling and perception. None of his decorations or goldsmith's work in England has survived, though drawings and miniature versions exist. A pair of organ shutters in Basle, and many drawings for the now destroyed Council Chamber decorations and house façades in Basle and Lucerne, are the only records of his large decorative works, which were strongly influenced by Italian – particularly Milanese – style.

The largest collections of Holbein's works are in Basle and the Royal Coll. (there are 85 of the drawings for portraits at Windsor). Other works, by him or his studio, include those in Berlin, Boston (Mus. and Gardner), Brunswick, Darmstadt, Detroit, Dresden, Florence (Uffizi), Frankfurt (Städel), Freiburg im Breisgau (Cath.), The Hague, Karlsruhe, Liverpool, London (NG, NPG, V & A, Wallace Coll., Guildhall), Los Angeles, Munich, New York (Met. Mus., Frick Coll.), Ottawa, Paris (Louvre), Parma, Philadelphia (Johnson), Rome (Gall. Naz.), St Louis, Stuttgart, Toledo Ohio, Vienna, Washington (NG), and Zürich. [ills. 577–80, pp. 356–7]

Hollar, Wenceslaus (1607–77), was born in Prague but was the most important illustrator and topographer working in England in the 17th century. He travelled in Germany after leaving Bohemia in 1627 and was taken into the service of the Earl of Arundel in Cologne in 1636. He was captured by the Parliamentarians at the siege of Basing House in 1645 and left England for Antwerp in the same year but returned in 1652 and, after the Restoration, was appointed 'H.M. Scenographer and Designer of Prospects'. His work consists of etchings and watercolour drawings dealing with almost everything that could interest the 17th-century Englishman: they are principally illustrations to books but include maps, portraits, plates of contemporary events, and, above all, the series of views of London before the Great Fire of 1666 and the plates of buildings like St Paul's, as well as reproductions of works of art, all of which are now invaluable historical material. [ill. 394, p. 327]

Hölzel, Adolf (1853–1934), was a German painter who went to Paris in 1882. He began to experiment with what he called 'coloured sounds' in 1917–18, and from 1923 produced many pastels of abstract compositions. His school at Dachau, opened in 1893, numbered NOLDE, SCHLEMMER, and BAUMEISTER among its pupils. There are works by him, including stained-glass windows, in Cologne, Hanover, and Stuttgart. [ill. 1058, p. 422]

Homer, Winslow (1836–1910), was, with EAKINS, one of the most influential of late-19th-century American painters. After two years in England and Paris (1866) he earned a living as an illustrator – he recorded the Civil War – and this sense of actuality remained in all his works even after 1875, when he devoted himself to painting. In the 1880s and 1890s he revolutionized American painting by his quasi-Impressionist style allied to Courbet-like studies of the sea and shooting and fishing subjects appealing to the American male. He was also affected by the Japanese craze which arrived in Europe in the 1860s and is visible in his work in the 1870s. He is represented in the NG, Washington, and many other US museums. [ill. 961, p. 410]

Hondecoeter, Melchior (1636–95), was the last and best of a family of Dutch painters. He specialized in still-life and scenes of birds, many of them exotic, and his speciality was the representation of a farmyard, or a courtyard, with a great number of different birds. He was the pupil of his father Gysbert (1604–53) and of his uncle J. B. WEENIX. He worked at The Hague and Amsterdam and his numerous pictures include examples in the Royal Collection, Amsterdam (Rijksmus.), Boston, Brussels, Cologne, Derby, Glasgow, The Hague, London (NG and Wallace Coll.), Lyons, Munich, New York (Met. Mus.), Nottingham, Paris (Louvre), and Vienna (Akad.). [ill. 472, p. 340]

Hone, Nathaniel (1718–84), was a Dubliner who painted portraits in the English provinces (often in miniature or in enamel), until a fortunate marriage allowed him to spend two years (1750–2) in Italy. After this he settled in London and became a Founder-Member of the RA, exhibiting regularly from 1769 until his death. In 1775, however, he submitted *The Conjuror*, which represented a conjuror, remarkably like Sir Joshua Reynolds, who points with a wand to prints after Michelangelo, Maratta, Pietro da Cortona, and others, clearly implying plagiary; there was also a young woman, and Angelica KAUFFMANN (whose exact relationship with Reynolds was a matter of interested debate) felt herself impugned. She petitioned the Council and the picture was rejected: it was subsequently exhibited elsewhere. The picture (now in a private coll.) was rediscovered in 1944, and it is clear that the imputations were not without foundation. Other pictures by Hone are in London (NPG *Henry Fielding*, 1762; RA, V & A), Birmingham (Barber), Cardiff, Dublin, Leeds, Manchester, and Oxford. [ill. 823, p. 393]

Honthorst, Gerard van (1590–1656), was one of the leading masters of the UTRECHT School. He was trained under BLOEMAERT and was in Rome *c.* 1610/12–1620, where he was much influenced by Caravaggio (who died in 1610), and, according to Sandrart, who was his pupil, by Caravaggio's follower MANFREDI. He worked for the Marchese Giustiniani, who had been Caravaggio's patron, and for him he painted the *Christ before the High Priest* (London NG). This has the characteristic Northern Caravaggesque device of using one candle as the sole source of light, the direct rays being shielded by the figures. His night scenes were very popular and earned him the nickname in Italy of 'Gherardo delle Notti': he had 'much of ye manor of Caravaggioes colouringe; wch is nowe soe much esteemed in Rome' (letter from Lord Arundel, 1621). He settled in Utrecht until 1628, when he visited England and painted the huge *Charles I and Henrietta Maria with the Liberal Arts* (Hampton Court), which marks the transition from his early Caravaggesque style and genre or mythological subjects to his second, Court, style based on realistic portraiture in a version of the elegant van Dyck manner. He succeeded MIEREVELD as Court Painter at The Hague (1637), and his later works are in a style very like Miereveld's. His brother Willem (1594–1666) worked with him. There are pictures in the Royal Coll. and in Alkmaar, Amsterdam, Berlin, Cologne, Dresden, Florence (Uffizi), Glasgow, Greenville SC, The Hague (a series of Court portraits), Haarlem, London (NG), Munich, Ottawa, Paris (Louvre), Rome (Borghese and churches), Utrecht, Vienna, and elsewhere. [ills. 459, 523, pp. 338, 348]

Hooch (Hoogh), Pieter de (1629–after 84), was the Dutch genre painter who came nearest to VERMEER in his feeling for the play of light. His first datable work is *Delft after the Explosion* (1654) and for the next decade or more he worked mainly in Delft, so that he must have known Vermeer. He chooses the same kind of subject – an interior with two or three figures engaged in some household task – and he occupies himself with rendering the fall of sunlight on surfaces, his favourite effect being that of a dark foreground with an open door leading through into a second room which is brightly lit. As in the case of Vermeer this interest in light is an ultimate legacy, via the UTRECHT School, of Caravaggio. De Hooch moved to Amsterdam in 1667. The works of the Amsterdam period are poorer in quality and also different in subject: unlike his simple interiors of the Delft period they are now rather bogus scenes of High Life, such as hardly existed in Holland, based on adaptations of the grand new Town Hall of Amsterdam or of Italian architecture. There are pictures in the Royal Collection and in Amsterdam, Berlin, Boston, Cape Town, Cincinnati, Cleveland, Copenhagen, Detroit, Dublin, London (NG, Wallace Coll., and Wellington Mus.), Los Angeles, Minneapolis, New York (Met. Mus.), Paris (Louvre), Philadelphia, Rome (Borghese and Gall. Naz.), St Louis, Stockholm, Toledo, Ohio, Vienna (K-H Mus. and Akad.), and Washington (NG and Corcoran). [ill. 517, p. 346]

Hoppner, John (*c.* 1758–1810), was one of the principal followers of Reynolds and a rival to LAWRENCE. He was a student at the RA in 1775, became Portrait Painter to the Prince of Wales in 1793 and RA in 1795. There are works by him in the Royal Coll. and in London (NG, NPG, Tate, V & A, and RA), New York (Met. Mus.), Ottawa, Washington (NG), and many other museums. [ill. 833, p. 395]

Hortus Conclusus (Lat. enclosed garden). The phrase is taken from the Song of Songs (iv. 12: *Hortus conclusus soror mea, sponsa* . . . A garden enclosed is my sister, my spouse . . .) and is used to describe paintings of the Madonna and Child in a garden with a fence round it, and often with a fountain inside it (*Hortus conclusus, fons signatus*. . . . A spring shut up, a fountain sealed). Occasionally there are also several female Saints present, as in one of the finest examples, the *Paradise Garden* by an unknown German master of about 1415 (Frankfurt, Städel). The *Virgo inter Virgines* type has the female Saints, but need not have the fenced garden. (*See* MASTER OF THE VIRGO INTER VIRGINES.) [ill. 542, p. 352]

Hoskins, John (*d.* 1665), was, according to his earliest biographer, 'bred a Face-painter in Oil but afterwards taking to *miniature,* he far exceeded what he did before'. His earliest miniatures date from *c.* 1620, so he was probably born at the end of the 16th century and some of his early works show some influence from HILLIARD and OLIVER. Nevertheless, he was probably the first 'who gave the strength and freedom of oil to miniature', although this was actually said of his nephews and pupils, Alexander and Samuel COOPER. Hoskins was Limner to Charles I and naturally came under the influence of van DYCK whose style he adapted to miniature. There are examples in the Royal Collection, Amsterdam (Rijksmus.), Cambridge (Fitzwm), London (V & A, Ham House and Wallace Coll.), and Oxford. [ill. 807, p. 392]

Hot Colour, Tone. Colours which tend to be reddish in hue. The phrase has generally a pejorative sense, implying that the balance of colour or tone is unduly inclined to the red end of the spectrum. It is sometimes due to BOLUS grounds.

Houdon, Jean-Antoine (1741–1828), was the most celebrated French sculptor of the 18th century. He was a pupil of LEMOYNE and PIGALLE before going to the École royale des Éléves protégés (where his father was for many years the concierge) with a Rome Prize in 1761. He went on to Rome in 1764 and made his name with his simple and classical *S. Bruno* in Sta Maria degli Angeli. In 1769 he was back in Paris and an associate of the Academy; he became a full Academician in 1777 with his *Morpheus* (now in the Louvre). He narrowly escaped imprisonment during the Revolution and continued to work under the Empire. He retired in 1814 but continued to teach at the École des Beaux-Arts until 1823, when he became senile. Among his better-known works are the *Girl Shivering* (1783: Montpellier), the *Diana* (1780: Gulbenkian Coll., and 1790: Louvre), and the *Minerva* in the Institut, Paris, which is reproduced on all the Institut's publications. His portraits are, however, his most numerous as well as his finest works and they include many of the greatest men of his time, among them the seated *Voltaire* of 1781 in the Comédie-Française (there are several other *Voltaires,* including one in London, V & A, and another in the Comédie, where there is also a *Molière*); his *Franklin* led to a commission from the State Parliament of Virginia for a statue of Washington. Houdon went to the US in 1785 to execute it and spent 14 days at Mount Vernon. The marble was completed by 1791 (although it is signed and dated 1788) and is in Richmond, Va; perhaps ironically, there is a bronze copy in London, outside the NG. There is a *Franklin* in New York (Met. Mus.) – the original plaster is in St Louis – and a *Diderot* in the Louvre, two busts in the Wallace Coll., London, and many others in France and elsewhere. [ills. 715, 721, p. 378]

Hours of Turin. A manuscript (the 'Très Belles Heures') begun by JACQUEMART de Hesdin *c.* 1385/90 but left unfinished at his death and divided *c.* 1412/13, so that the unfinished parts went to Count William of Holland (*d.* 1417), elder brother of Jan van EYCK's patron. This part, finished by various artists by the middle of the 15th century, was later subdivided between the Prince Trivulzio (Milan) and the Royal Library, Turin: the Turin parts were burnt in 1904 and the Trivulzio portion has now passed to the Mus. Civico, Turin. Hulin de Loo was the only scholar to study both portions and he declared that some 25 of the miniatures were by the van Eycks; controversy now rages – and presumably always will – over the exact attributions, since some of those destroyed had close links with the mature style of Jan van Eyck. [ill. 327, p. 319]

Huber, Wolf (*c.* 1490–1553), was a painter and designer of woodcuts, who, after ALTDORFER, was the most important member of the DANUBE School. He was in contact with Altdorfer by *c.* 1510 and may have been his assistant; certainly he shares Altdorfer's feeling for the poetry of landscape, as may be seen in his drawings of pure landscape as well as his pictures. From 1515 he worked in Passau, where he was much disliked by the local painters.

There are pictures by him in Dublin, Munich, and Vienna, and drawings in London (BM and University College). [ill. 575, p. 357]

Hudson River School. A school of American landscape painting, highly Romantic in feeling and glorifying the wonders of Nature as visible in the American landscape. The type begins soon after 1800 with the landscapes of Washington ALLSTON, but the name is properly applied to the period from 1825, when COLE settled in New York, until the 1870s. DURAND was a typical painter of the school. [ills. 945, 946, p. 407]

Hudson, Thomas (1701–79), was the son-in-law of Jonathan RICHARDSON I and inherited the same kind of stereotyped face-painting practice. He is best known as Reynolds's master (1740–3) but he painted a considerable number of portraits 1745–60, after which he virtually retired, probably because Reynolds was getting the business. He is well represented in London (Tate, Nat. Marit. Mus., Dulwich, NPG, Foundling Hospital), in Bristol, Edinburgh (NG), Manchester, New York (Met. Mus.), and elsewhere. [ill. 825, p. 393]

Hunt, William Holman (1827–1910), was in the RA Schools in 1844, and there met MILLAIS and ROSSETTI with whom he founded the PRB in 1848. He went to Egypt and the Holy Land in 1854, 1869, and 1873 to paint Biblical scenes with accurate local settings and types, and was the only member of the group to remain in any way faithful to PRB principles. In 1905 he published 'Pre-Raphaelitism and the Pre-Raphaelite Brotherhood', the best documented memoir of the movement. He was given the OM in the same year. There are works in Birmingham, Liverpool, London (Tate, St Paul's Cath.), Manchester, Oxford (Ashmolean, Keble College, Jesus College), and Port Sunlight. [ill. 949, p. 408]

Huysum, Jan van (1682–1749), was a Dutch flower-painter, son of the flower-painter Justus van Huysum (1659–1716), many of whose works are confused with his more famous son's. His flower pictures are very highly detailed, rich and crowded in composition and sometimes set against a light background (an innovation made by him). There are examples in many museums. He also painted a few landscapes and there is a *Self-portrait*, probably unique in his work, in Oxford.
His younger brother, Jacob (1687–1740), who often imitated him, worked in England and died in London. [ills. 477, 478, p. 341]

I

Icon (*Ikon*, Gk. image) originally meant a picture of Christ or a Saint on a panel, as distinct from a wall-painting. These icons were extremely limited in subject-matter and the actual forms and shapes were prescribed and maintained unchanged for centuries in the Greek Orthodox world: thus, the earliest surviving examples may date from the 6th to 7th century but are virtually indistinguishable from those painted as late as the 17th century or even later. An *Iconostasis* is a screen dividing the Sanctuary of a Greek Orthodox church from the lay part and covered with rows of icons. *Iconoclasm* is the breaking of images, the most famous outbreak being the Iconoclastic Controversy of the 8th century. The *Iconoclasm* of the Dutch provinces, under Calvinist influence in the mid 16th century, led to the destruction of most early Dutch religious painting. *Iconography* and *Iconology* are the knowledge of the meanings to be attached to pictorial representations: thus, a lamb with a flag is a simple problem in Christian iconography but many of the more complicated Baroque allegories, in which Christian and pagan mythological figures are used side by side, may now be almost beyond interpretation. There is also an older meaning of Iconography, namely a collection of portraits, as in van Dyck's *Iconography*.

Ideal Art. 'Any work of Art which represents not a material object, but the mental conception of a material object, is in the primary sense of the word, ideal; that is to say, it represents an idea, and not a thing. Any work of Art which represents or realizes a material object is, in the primary sense of the term, un-ideal' (Ruskin). According to Plato the only realities are ideas, and everything perceptible to the senses is merely an imperfect realization of the primary idea: thus, the idea of a dog is the true dog and all dogs in the visible gutter merely approximate to the idea of dogness. From this arises a perennial theory that the true function of art is to mirror those Ideal forms that are the sole realities, approaching them by way of the physical phenomena which are their distorted images. The story, told by Pliny, which served for centuries as the basis of this Ideal Art, tells how Zeuxis had to paint a *Venus* and, after inspecting all the most beautiful girls in Crotona, he selected five and painted the mouth of one, the legs of another, and so on: the theory being that a sum of perfect parts must add up to a perfect whole. Later, a similar story was told of Raphael; the point of it is the same but he is made to add, significantly, that not only must he see many beautiful women, but that he must also have a *certain idea* in his mind. This theory is obviously not impregnable, but such is the hold of PROPORTION, classic harmony, and geometry on the human mind that for centuries, but most vocally in the NEOCLASSIC period, artists have

sought to select, to refine, and to ennoble various details of the human figure into a whole which should express all these ideals and symbolize the highest aspirations of the mind. Naturally, this has meant an exclusive concern with the nude ('The human figure concealed under a frock-coat and trowsers is not a fit subject for sculpture. I would rather avoid contemplating such objects.' John GIBSON). Nevertheless, fallacious or not, the theory has produced many of the greatest works of art in existence and its perennial quality is perhaps best illustrated by the fact that it is still, under a new guise, one of the most fertile theories of aesthetics; for many forms of abstract art depend upon it and the works of BRANCUSI, MALEVICH, or MONDRIAN ultimately spring from Platonic Idealism.

Illusionism is the virtuoso use of pictorial techniques such as perspective and foreshortening to deceive the eye into taking that which is painted for that which is real. The principal moments when this was practised were the Late Antique period (at Pompeii and elsewhere) and the Italian Baroque, when it was common to use sculptural and architectural means to heighten the impression of actuality, e.g. by using plaster figures in three dimensions attached to a frame so that the painted and carved figures are indistinguishable. One of the first pieces of illusionism is, however, the Camera degli Sposi at Mantua by MANTEGNA, completed in 1474. When such technical skill is lavished on things like a fly painted on a frame or a view through a non-existent window the French term *trompe-l'œil* is often used, while the Italian word *quadraturista* is sometimes used for the professional painter of illusionist decorations (*quadrature*). [ill. 126, p. 290]

Imago Pietatis (Lat. Image of Pity). A representation, most popular in the late Middle Ages, of the Dead Christ standing upright in the Tomb. He is sometimes surrounded by symbols of the Passion and sometimes supported by the Virgin, Saints, or Angels, but in any case the stress is laid on the suffering involved in the Redemption. The PIETÀ expresses the same basic idea in less symbolical terms. [ill. 145, p. 293]

Impasto is a word, Italian by origin, used to describe the thickness of the paint applied to a canvas or panel. When the paint is so heavily applied that it stands up in lumps with the tracks of the brush clearly evident it is said to be 'heavily impasted'. [Col. pl. 30]

Impressionism was the derisive name given to the most important artistic phenomenon of the 19th century and the first of the Modern Movements. The name was derived from a picture by MONET, *Impression, Sunrise* (1872:? Paris, Musée Marmottan) which represents the play of light on water, with the spectator looking straight into the rising sun. The occasion of the derision was the First Impressionist Exhibition, held in 1874, when Monet, RENOIR, SISLEY, PISSARRO, CÉZANNE, DEGAS, Guillaumin, BOUDIN, Berthe MORISOT, and others held an independent exhibition. In fact, the true aim of Impressionism was to achieve ever greater naturalism, by exact analysis of tone and colour and by trying to render the play of light on the surface of objects. This is a form of sensualism in which traditional ideas of composition and drawing – that is, putting a line round a concept – were bound to suffer. Impressionist interest in colour and light was at least partly due to the researches into the physics of colour carried out by scientists like Chevreul; and the idea that an object of any given colour casts a shadow tinged with its complementary was (though known already to Delacroix) one of the principal ways in which they animated the surface of their canvases. The flickering touch, with the paint applied in small, brightly-coloured dabs, and the lack of firm outline, combined with the brightness of the colour, even in the shadows, and the generally high key undoubtedly alienated the public. In the course of time these technical devices became petrified into a quasi-scientific method of applying paint (NEO-IMPRESSIONISM) which was supposed to give the maximum of truth – optical truth – to Nature: it also led naturally to POST-IMPRESSIONISM; that is, to a purely artistic and anti-naturalistic movement. The great decade of Impressionism was 1870–80, but most of the major figures, such as Monet, Pissarro, and Sisley continued to produce masterpieces in a more or less Impressionist style for many more years. Degas, Renoir, and Cézanne are only dubiously Impressionists even in the 1870s (many of the original group felt that Cézanne was more than they could swallow) and they very soon moved away from it. Cézanne said that he wanted 'to make of Impressionism something solid and durable, like the art of the Museums', thus clearly defining the main weakness of the movement, its lack of intellectual rigour. Nevertheless, most painting of the last 90 years has been profoundly affected by it, and even the RA and the Salon would nowadays be lost without it. There is a special Musée de l'Impressionnisme in Paris; but the very nature of the movement, with its emphasis on painting landscapes out of doors and catching the fleeting impression, meant an enormous output of pictures so that they are not difficult to find. The eight Impressionist Exhibitions were held in 1874, 1876, 1877, 1879, 1880, 1881, 1882, and 1886. [ills. 760, 793–5, 800–4, pp. 381, 389–90. Col. pl. 34]

Imprimitura (Ital.). The priming or ground, often tinted, laid on canvas or panel.

Inc. (Lat. *incidit*, he cut it) on an engraving refers to the engraver, or more commonly etcher: *see also* SCULP.

Ingres, Jean-Auguste-Dominique (1780–1867), was born at Montauban. His father, a mediocre artist, recognized his son's abilities and sent him to Toulouse Academy (1791) and on to DAVID in Paris in 1797. He won the Prix de Rome in 1801 with the *Ambassadors of Agamemnon* which was praised by FLAXMAN, who had a great influence

on him. He earned a living by portraits until 1806, when he finally went to Italy intending to stay three or four years and remaining eighteen. His Rivière family portraits (1805: Louvre), with their stress on sinuous line forming a silhouette that both contains and explains the form, established a type that he developed and perfected, but hardly modified. Works sent back from Rome were bitterly criticized, and the fall of Napoleon forced him to seek a precarious livelihood making pencil drawings of visitors to Rome. In 1820 he settled in Florence and completed the *Vow of Louis XIII*, commissioned for Montauban Cathedral and exhibited in the 1824 Salon with enormous success. This work placed him in the front rank and established him as the official opponent of the ideas expressed by DELACROIX, and the main prop of a rigid classicism in opposition to the Romantic movement. While his main works were portraits – which he professed to dislike, and in which he both influenced and was influenced by the earliest photographs – he also painted subject pictures and poeticized Oriental scenes providing an excuse for voluptuous nudes. His wall-paintings were not happy; the *Golden Age* (1842–9) was abandoned and has deteriorated, leaving only the superb nude studies made for it. In 1834 he returned to Rome as Director of the French Academy, having applied for the position in a fit of pique over the reception accorded his *Martyrdom of S. Symphorian*. After his return to Paris in 1841, his intransigent opposition to any ideas but his own, backed by his academic standing, gave him an influence which he used blindly, not only against Delacroix, but also against younger rebels against what had become in the hands of his imitators, entrenched in mediocrity, a stereotyped and official style. His own style hardly changed and to the end he pursued his piercingly exact vision, his sinuous line, and his worship of Raphael; while his charmless handling stresses his supreme draughtsmanship. He said 'Drawing is the probity of art' and 'Drawing includes everything except the tint': opposed views were those of Théophile Sylvestre '. . . he is a Chinese painter lost . . . amid the ruins of Athens' and Delacroix's 'His art is the complete expression of an incomplete intelligence.' He became a Member of the Institut in 1825, a Grand Officer of the Legion of Honour in 1855, and a Senator in 1862. None of his many pupils except CHASSÉRIAU achieved lasting reputation: his real continuator was DEGAS.

There is a large Musée Ingres at Montauban and other works are in Aix-en-Provence, Algiers, Antwerp, Baltimore, Bayonne, Brussels, Cambridge Mass. (Fogg Mus.), Chantilly, Cincinnati, Florence (Uffizi), Hartford Conn., Kansas City, Leningrad, Liège, London (NG, V & A), Lyons, Montpellier, Northampton Mass., New York (Met. Mus., Frick Coll.), Paris (Louvre, Carnavalet, Invalides), Philadelphia, Stockholm, Toulouse, Versailles, Washington, and elsewhere. [ills. 747, 775–6, pp. 382, 386. Col. pl. 26]

Innes, James Dickson (1887–1914), was a Welsh landscape painter with a powerful sense of design and a feeling for strong colour. He first worked in the Wilson Steer brand of Impressionism, and was then strongly influenced by Augustus JOHN. His premature death invites speculation whether he might not have developed into an English *Fauve*.

There are works in Aberdeen, Cardiff, Leeds, London (Tate), and Manchester. [ill. 976, p. 411]

Intaglio (*Cavo-rilievo*) consists of cutting forms out of a surface so as to form a kind of relief in reverse. The commonest example is an engraved seal-ring, hence the opposite term is often Cameo. It is also used to describe a form of ENGRAVING, and there has recently grown up a new usage in this connection: many modern prints are a mixture of processes – line-engraving, etching, mezzotint, aquatint, etc. – and such prints are now often described as Intaglio Prints.

International Gothic. Towards the end of the 14th century there arose a new approach to Nature which first found expression in the Court art of France and Burgundy (*see* BROEDERLAM, LIMBOURG), but which rapidly spread to Italy, Germany, and Bohemia. As a style it remained fundamentally Gothic, for the new realism was confined to details, particularly to details of landscape, of animals, and of costume. This form of realism has almost nothing in common with the slightly later realism, classical and naturalistic in inspiration, practised by MASACCIO and DONATELLO. Aspects of both may, however, be detected in the work of GHIBERTI. In Italy the principal exponents of International Gothic were GENTILE da Fabriano and PISANELLO: a comparison between the *Madonna* by Gentile in the Royal Coll. and the Masaccio *Madonna* in the NG, London; or the Gentile *Adoration* in the Uffizi, Florence, and the Brancacci Chapel will make clear the difference of intention as well as of style. The influence of International Gothic remained active for many years, and was even revived towards the end of the 15th century. [ills. 51–8, 326, 328, 542, pp. 276–7, 319, 352]

Intimisme. A form of Impressionist technique applied to the depiction of everyday life in domestic interiors rather than to landscape. The work of BONNARD and VUILLARD is usually meant.

Intonaco *see* FRESCO.

Inv., Invenit (Lat. he invented it) often appears on an engraving as the credit title of the original author of the design, which may have been drawn (DEL.), engraved (INC. or SCULP.), and published (EXCUDIT) by other people.

Isenbrandt (Ysenbrandt), Adriaen (*d.* 1551), was a painter active in Bruges from 1510. He is said to have been a pupil of Gerard DAVID and for this reason a diptych of the *Madonna of the Seven Sorrows* (Bruges, Notre Dame, and Brussels Mus.) has been ascribed to him: around this not very certain attribution a large accretion of early-16th-century Bruges School work has accumulated under his name. To make it worse, some of these were once attributed to MOSTAERT by Waagen; hence *Der Waagen'sche Mostaert* or *The Pseudo-Mostaert* = 'Isenbrandt'. [ill. 350, p. 323]

Italianizers are Northern artists, generally Dutch or Flemish, who adopt as far as possible a style based on Italian models or who import Italian motives into their repertory. The word is often used of 17th-century Dutch landscape painters like ASSELYN, BOTH, and BERCHEM, but it is also used of 16th-century Flemings like MABUSE or van ORLEY, although these are usually called ROMANISTS.

Ives, James, *see* CURRIER.

Jacobello del Fiore (*d.* 1439) was a Venetian painter who was active from 1394. He broke away from the Byzantine tradition typified by PAOLO Veneziano which dominated Venetian art until the end of the 14th century, but was in turn influenced by the International Gothic style of the early 15th century. Most of his works are in Venice but the earliest signed and dated work by him is of 1407 (formerly US private coll.). [ill. 48, p. 275]

Jacquemart de Hesdin (*d. c.* 1411) was the Painter to the Duke of Berri from 1384 until 1411, when he was succeeded by the LIMBOURG brothers. He made the 'Grandes Heures du Duc de Berri' (Paris, Bibliothèque Nationale), as well as the 'Très Belles Heures' (Brussels, Bibliothèque Royale), but is principally remembered as having started what became the HOURS of Turin. [ill. 329, p. 319]

Jamesone, George (*d.* 1644), was an Aberdeen painter who was trained in Edinburgh, and not, as a highly improbable tradition would have it, by Rubens. He painted portraits in a style not unlike that of Cornelius JOHNSON – i.e. basically a Flemish manner. He was painting in Aberdeen in 1619/20; in 1633 he painted Charles I in Edinburgh and also visited Italy; and from 1634 he worked mainly in Edinburgh. There are pictures by him in Edinburgh (NG) and a number in Aberdeen (Gall. and especially the University Collection). [ill. 526, p. 349]

Janet *see* CLOUET.

Jansens (Janssen), Cornelius, *see* JOHNSON.

Jawlensky, Alexej (1864–1941), was a Russian painter, originally an officer in the Imperial Guard, who spent most of his life in Germany, although the major Western influence on his style was MATISSE. He studied in Munich from 1896, meeting KANDINSKY there, although he did not join the BLAUE REITER group. Later, with Kandinsky, KLEE, and FEININGER he formed a group known as the Blue Four. He settled in Wiesbaden in 1921 and his later works became more abstract, more Byzantine, and more expressive: he himself said that 'art is nostalgia for God'. There are many works in Wiesbaden and in Pasadena Cal. [ill. 1024, p. 418]

Jean de Boulogne *see* BOLOGNA.

John, Augustus Edwin, OM (1878–1961), was born at Tenby in Wales. He was trained at the Slade, taught at Liverpool (1901–2), and joined the NEAC in 1903, gaining early recognition through his superb draughtsmanship. He was strongly influenced by Puvis de Chavannes and Post-Impressionism, 1910–14, and made many cartoons for large decorations, only one of which (Johannesburg) was executed. His brilliant portraits derive from the Grand Manner tradition enlivened by a semi-Impressionist handling, colour high in tone, and a very un-Impressionist solidity of drawing. He travelled much in England and France, often gipsy-fashion, and was always a passionate opponent of academism, in art and life. He became an RA in 1928, later resigned with *éclat*, but was re-elected in 1940. There are works in Aberdeen, Birmingham, Brighton, Buffalo, Cambridge (Fitzwm), Cardiff, Detroit, Dublin, Glasgow, Leeds, Leicester, London (Tate), Manchester, Melbourne, Ottawa, Oxford, Sheffield, Stockholm, Swansea, Sydney, Toronto, Washington (NG), and elsewhere. [ill. 974, p. 411]
His sister Gwen (1876–1939) was also a painter, studied at the Slade and in Paris, and lived mostly in France – much with the Dominican sisters at Meudon. In feeling her pictures are the antithesis of her brother's: retiring, delicate, grey in colour, and of an almost neurotic sensibility. There are examples in Cardiff, London (Tate), Manchester, and elsewhere. [ill. 971, p. 411]

Johnson (Jonson), Cornelius (also called Jansens, Janssen van Ceulen) (1593–1661), was born in London of Netherlandish parents and became one of the most notable portrait painters in England before the arrival of van Dyck in 1632. He painted in a straightforward but sensitive Dutch manner sometimes indistinguishable from that of MYTENS, but he tended to confine himself to bust portraits set in an oval. After 1632 he came under van Dyck's influence until, in 1643, the Civil War caused him to retire to Holland, where he adopted a more Dutch manner, closer to that of MIEREVELD. There are works by him in Amsterdam (Rijksmus.), Bath (Holburne Mus.), Boston, Dublin, The Hague, Liverpool, London (NG, NPG, Tate, BM, V & A (Ham House), and Dulwich), and New York (Met. Mus.). [ill. 534, p. 350]

Jongkind, Johan Barthold (1819–91), was a Dutch landscape and marine painter, who, along with BOUDIN, was a precursor of Impressionism and a formative influence on MONET (who wrote to Boudin in 1860 that Jongkind 'is quite crazy'). He met Boudin in 1862 and exhibited at the SALON des Refusés in 1863. He spent most of his later life in France, living in squalor near Grenoble and ending in madness like van Gogh. He never painted in oils out of doors, working from drawings and watercolours made on the spot, but the results are very like those of the early Impressionists. [ill. 761, p. 385]

Joos van Cleve (Cleef) (*c.* 1485–1540/1), became a Master in Antwerp in 1511. He is usually identified with the MASTER of the DEATH OF THE VIRGIN, but there are wide discrepancies between the portraits and the religious pictures attributed to him (or them). Joos was a contemporary of MASSYS, and many of the portraits attributed to him are in a cool, realistic style not unlike that of Massys or even Holbein and Mabuse; they are perhaps closest to Barthel BRUYN. Joos seems to have been to Genoa and is reasonably supposed to have worked at the Court of François I of France *c.* 1530: certainly many portraits of François and his Queen exist and are attributed to him, but there are no portraits ascribed to him which are signed or satisfactorily documented; the *Self-portrait*(?) in the Royal Coll. is recorded in the 1639 Inventory of Charles I's Collection 'Sotto Cleve done by himself . . .' (see below), but the features are those of Joos as known from 16th- or 17th-century engravings. Other pictures attributed to Joos van Cleve are in the Royal Coll. and in Antwerp, Berlin, Boston, Brussels, Cambridge (Fitzwm), Cologne (Wallraf-Richartz), Detroit, Dresden, Florence (Uffizi), London (NG, Courtauld Inst.), Madrid, Manchester New Hampshire, Michigan (University), Munich, New York (Met. Mus.), Paris (Louvre), Philadelphia (Johnson), Vienna, Washington (NG, Corcoran), and Worcester Mass. [ills. 359, 369, p. 324]
His son Cornelis (1520–67), known as 'Sotte Cleve', was also a painter and visited London *c.* 1554, hoping for Royal patronage. He was, however, anticipated by MOR and he went mad in 1556.

Joos van Gent (van Wassenhove), called Justus of Ghent, (active 1460–after 1475), became a Master in Antwerp in 1460 and in Ghent in 1464. There he met Hugo van der Goes and is recorded up to 1469, but by 1475 he had gone to Rome. In 1473–4 he was in Urbino, painting *The Institution of the Eucharist* (Urbino), the commission for which was originally given to PIERO della Francesca, while the predella is by UCCELLO, who was paid for it 1465–9. Among the works attributed to him are a *Crucifixion*

(Ghent, Cath.) and a series of 28 *Famous Men* (*c.* 1476: half in Paris, Louvre, and half in Urbino), the hands (at least) of the Duke of Urbino in Piero della Francesca's *Brera Madonna*, and other works in the Royal Coll., London (NG), New York (Met. Mus.), and Urbino. Two formerly in Berlin were destroyed in 1945. The *Famous Men* and the Duke's hands (and some of the other pictures) have been ascribed to P. BERRUGUETE, in spite of a specific mention in a 15th-century Italian writer of the *Famous Men* as by 'a Netherlander'. Joos is the only Netherlandish painter known to have worked in Urbino. [ill. 354, p. 323]

Jordaens, Jacob (1593–1678), was born and died in Antwerp where he worked as an assistant to RUBENS. After Rubens's death he finished the incomplete works ordered for Spain, van DYCK's pretensions making it impossible to negotiate with him. He is an example of the pervasive effect of Rubens's style, for he uses a boisterous, restless type of Baroque derived from Rubens, but without his taste and control, or his imagination and versatility in design and colour. He worked for the House of Orange on portraits and decorations during the 1630s, and his late works include large genre scenes of drinking bouts – *Le roi boit* in Brussels is an example – full of overtones of BROUWER and STEEN. There are works in Antwerp, Brunswick, Brussels, Budapest, Cassel, Dresden, Karlsruhe, Lille, London (NG, Wallace Coll.), Madrid, New York (Met. Mus.), Paris (Louvre), Stockholm. [ill. 410, p. 329]

Journeyman (from Fr. *journée*, a day). An artist who had completed his apprenticeship but was not yet a Master in a GUILD. He earned his living as a day-labourer in the shops of various Masters (often making it difficult to distinguish between the products of shop A and shop B when he crossed the road to work in the other shop for a change). Some painters spent their WANDERJAHRE in this fashion; others never set up for themselves.

Jugendstil *see* ART NOUVEAU.

Justus of Ghent *see* JOOS van Gent.

K

Kalf, Willem (1619–93), was a Dutch still-life painter who worked in Rotterdam, Paris, and Amsterdam. The depth and brilliance of his colour and the sureness of his touch suggest the influence of Vermeer. Usually his pictures contain elaborate gold, silver, and glass vessels, fruit, a Turkey carpet, against a dark ground with, often, a watch in the front of the group. There are works in Amsterdam (Rijksmus.), Berlin, Cleveland Ohio, Dresden, Frankfurt (Städel), Munich, Oxford, Paris (Louvre), Vienna, and elsewhere. [ill. 468, p. 338]

Kalraet, Abraham, *see* CALRAET.

Kandinsky, Wassily (1866–1944), was born in Moscow but trained in Munich, after abandoning a legal career. He painted his first purely abstract work in 1910 (one such is in the Tate Gallery, London), and was therefore one of the founders of 'pure' abstract painting. In 1911 he was one of the founders of the BLAUE REITER group and in 1912 he published a book which was translated into English in 1914 as 'The Art of Spiritual Harmony'. He returned to Russia 1914–21 and then went back to Germany and taught at the Bauhaus from 1922, again coming into contact with KLEE. In 1933 he went to France. New York (Guggenheim Mus.) has many works, and so have Munich and Russian museums. [ills. 1021, 1085, pp. 418, 427]

Kauffmann, Angelica (1741–1807), was a Swiss decorative painter. She seems to have been an accomplished musician and painted an allegory of herself hesitating between the Arts of Music and Painting (1760: later versions exist). Having chosen painting she went to Rome in 1763, where she painted a portrait of WINCKELMANN (1764: Zürich, Kunsthaus) which helped to make her name. In 1765 she went to Venice and was in London the following year, where she remained until 1781. She became friendly with Reynolds (there were rumours of a romantic attachment) and imitated his style in her portraits. She was a Founder-Member of the RA in 1768. Her rather anaemic little decorative history pieces were widely engraved and the engravings used in the manufacture of *objets d'art*: from this has grown the habit of associating all decorative painting in all houses of the Adam period with her, although in fact only four such panels are known (two in the RA). Later, when she lived in Rome, her portraits became more Neoclassic in feeling. There are pictures in Brighton, Edinburgh (NG), London (NPG, Kenwood), Manchester, New York (Met. Mus.), Plymouth, and elsewhere. [ill. 595, p. 358]

Keeping *see* VALUES.

Kent, William (1685–1748), is celebrated as an architect, interior decorator, and furniture designer. He studied painting in Rome in 1714/15, and there met Lord Burlington, his most constant and influential patron. He completed, in 1719, the paintings which RICCI had left unfinished in Burlington House (now the Royal Academy) and the commission to decorate Kensington Palace was given to him in 1723 instead of to THORNHILL. This was virtually his last work in painting. In Rome he decorated the vault of S. Giuliano dei Fiamminghi. [ill. 892. p. 401]

Kettle, Tilly (1735–86), was an English portrait painter who was the first to seek his fortune in India. He was born in London and was influenced at the beginning of his career by Reynolds, as may be seen in the portraits he painted in Oxford in 1762 and 1763. In 1769 he went to India, where he had a great success, and remained there until 1776. On his return to London he found competition greater than he expected and his extravagant living forced him to return to India in 1786, but he died in the desert near Basra. There are pictures by him in London (Tate, NPG, V & A, Nat. Marit. Mus., Dulwich, and Courtauld Inst. which has an important double portrait painted in India), Oxford, and Versailles. There are also works said to be still in India. [ill. 837, p. 394]

Key. A painting is said to be high or low in key according to the average of the tone and colour values: thus an Impressionist picture is high in key, all the tones being kept nearer white than black and all the colours being pale and bright. Very low-keyed pictures, such as those by the followers of Caravaggio, are TENEBRIST.

Keyser, Thomas de (1596/7–1667), an Amsterdam portrait painter of the ELIAS generation, he first influenced REMBRANDT (e.g. Keyser's *Constantine Huyghens*, 1627; London NG) and was then influenced by him. Later works include small equestrian portraits with landscape backgrounds often by other painters. Other works are in Amsterdam, Haarlem, The Hague, New York, Paris, Philadelphia, Raleigh NC, Toledo Ohio, and elsewhere. [ill. 450, p. 336]

Kirchner, Ernest Ludwig (1880–1938), was a German Expressionist painter who was an original member of the BRÜCKE. From 1917 Kirchner lived in Switzerland suffering from tuberculosis until his eventual suicide in 1938. Many of his pictures were confiscated by the Nazis, but the best collection is now in Stuttgart. He also made a large number of woodcuts and some sculpture. Kirchner formulated the programme for the Brücke in 1906 and wrote its obituary in 1913, although his close friend Heckel was the most enterprising member. It is said that Kirchner occasionally deliberately dated some of his pictures too early in order to claim priority. There are works by him in New York and other American museums as well as those in Germany. [ill. 1020, p. 417]

Kit Cat (Kitkat). A canvas, size 36 × 28 inches, which is adapted to a portrait showing the head and one hand. *See* KNELLER.

Klee, Paul (1879–1940), was a Swiss painter and etcher, whose art of free fantasy, perhaps the most poetic of modern times, is best defined in his own words as 'taking a line for a walk'. He was trained in Munich and went to Italy (1901–2), after which he returned to Switzerland and began etching. His early graphic work was influenced by Blake and Beardsley as well as Goya, and later ENSOR. He worked in Germany from 1906 until 1933, teaching for many years at the celebrated Bauhaus in Weimar and Dessau, and later at Düsseldorf Academy. He was an impassioned teacher and many of his 'Pedagogical Sketchbooks' and theoretical writings have been published. From 1911 he was associated with the BLAUE REITER artists, and was especially close to KANDINSKY, FEININGER, and JAWLENSKY (they were known, from 1924, as the 'Blue Four'). In 1914 he went to Tunisia with MACKE, an experience which revealed a new world of colour to him. From the 1920s he was famous, and no fewer than 102 works of his were confiscated from German galleries by the Nazis. There are works in most galleries of modern art now, and there is a Klee Foundation in Berne. [ill. 1081, p. 426]

Klimt, Gustav (1862–1918), was the principal Austrian Jugendstil (ART NOUVEAU) painter, and one of the founders of the Vienna Sezession (1898), although he resigned in 1903. He was essentially a decorator and, from 1883 to 1892, he shared a studio for decorative painting with his brother and another artist: they did decorations in the Kunsthistorisches Museum, Vienna, in 1891. From c. 1898, after a barren period of about six years, he was influenced by Japanese art and by contemporary English painters like BURNE-JONES and Alma-Tadema. A more realist style characterized his ceilings for Vienna University (1900–3), which were very unpopular. He was perhaps most successful as a designer for the applied arts (e.g. mosaic), but he was also a great influence on SCHIELE and KOKOSCHKA. There are works in Vienna (Oesterreichische Galerie). [ill. 999, p. 415]

Kline, Franz (1910–62), was one of the leading representatives of the post-war American movement which has had so great an influence in the 1950s and 1960s. He was an exponent of ABSTRACT EXPRESSIONISM who was deeply influenced by Oriental calligraphy and whose colour schemes were normally limited to black, white, and grey. He is well represented in American museums and there is a picture in the Tate Gallery, London. [ill. 1099, p. 428]

Knapton, George (1698–1778), was a pupil of Richardson and went to Italy for seven years in 1725. He was a Founder-Member of the Society of Dilettanti in 1736, and painted between 1741 and 1749 twenty-three portraits of fellow-members (all but one in fancy dress) which brought him into contact with the principal patrons of his day. From about 1737 he used pastel a good deal, which provoked Vertue to remark 'Small pains and great gains in this darling modish study.' He was the master of Cotes.
There are examples in the Royal Collection, Birmingham (City Art Gall.), London (Dulwich), and Sheffield. [ill. 831, p. 394]

Kneller, Sir Godfrey (1646 or 1649–1723). Born in Lübeck, Kneller was trained in Amsterdam under Rembrandt's pupil Bol, and he may even have come into contact with the aged Rembrandt himself. He then went to Italy and finally arrived in England in 1674/5, rapidly becoming the leading portrait painter. He was made Principal Painter jointly with RILEY in 1688 and succeeded to the whole office when Riley died in 1691; in 1692 he was knighted and in 1715 he became the first painter in England to be made a baronet. There is a gap in his career between 1678 and 1682 and it has been conjectured that he was then abroad again. His first works in England are entirely in the style of Bol but they later take on some of the softness of MARATTA: by 1683 Kneller had established his mature style and from then on there are hundreds of documented portraits by him, many signed and dated. Of these a great many are careless and mechanical in handling, and some are simply based on LELY's style and poses; yet his best works show a great grasp of character and are painted *alla prima* in a free and vigorous technique which became the normal English style for many years to come – in fact, until the more French manner of Allan Ramsay superseded it. Part of his influence is due to his large employment of assistants, part due to Kneller's Academy, founded in 1711, which was the first attempt at an ACADEMY in England. His best works are the 42 portraits, now in the NPG, London, known as the Kit Cat series. These all date from 1702 to 1717 and are a standard size (36 × 28 inches, known later as Kit Cat), showing the head and one hand. They represent the members of a Whig club and were painted for the Secretary. A direct comparison with Lely may be made in the two series of *Beauties*, at Hampton Court, and the *Admirals*, in the National Maritime Mus. There is a picture at Lübeck dated 1668 and one in the Tate Gall. of 1672: others are in the Royal Coll. and London (NG, NPG, and Tate) and elsewhere.
Kneller's conceit was vast. He is said to have swallowed the suggestion that things might have been better managed had the Deity consulted him at the Creation. [ill. 819, p. 393]

Koch, Joseph Anton (1768–1839), was an Austrian landscape painter, born in the Tyrol, who was fundamentally a Romantic artist, but, like many others, was influenced by Neoclassic principles. In 1791 an English patron financed a trip to Italy, and in Rome he met CARSTENS and THORWALDSEN (1795). He worked in Vienna 1812–15 before returning to Rome, where he took part in the decoration of the Casa Massimo (1824–9) by the NAZARENER. He died in Rome. His landscapes are of the Italianate type deriving from Poussin which were popular in the early 19th century, and he said himself that he wanted to give landscape 'an elemental character such as one may imagine when reading the Bible or Homer'. There are works by him in Berlin, Cologne, Copenhagen, Düsseldorf, Karlsruhe, Munich, Vienna, and other Austrian and German galleries. [ill. 604, p. 358]

Kokoschka, Oskar (*b.* 1886), is an Austrian painter who developed, between 1908 and 1914, a highly imaginative Expressionist style. He taught at the Dresden Academy from 1919, was influenced by painters who had worked in the BRÜCKE group, and from 1924 to 1931 travelled widely in Europe, North Africa, and the Near East. He lived in Vienna from 1931 to 1934, and in England from 1935 to 1953. His portraits, landscapes, and, chiefly, town views, often seen almost in bird's-eye view, are vivid in colour and of a restless energy of drawing; he has also painted many allegories, inspired by legends or, more commonly, by ideological themes; one of these, in London, is a large ceiling decoration. There are works in Edinburgh (NG), London (Tate), New York (M of MA), and many other museums of modern art. [ill. 1015, p. 417]

Kollwitz, Käthe (1867–1945), was one of the most powerfully emotional German artists of this century. She married a doctor in 1891 and settled in Berlin where she soon began to make etchings, woodcuts, and lithographs mainly of the Mother and Child theme and often with Left-wing intentions. Most of her best works are tragic and many of them are specifically pacifist – her son was killed in 1914 and her grandson in 1942. In 1927 she made a journey to Russia, but was subsequently disillusioned. In 1933 she was expelled from the Academy and in the following years made eight large lithographs called *Death*. In her later years she also made some bronzes of which the most important is a war memorial at Eessen in Flanders. [ill. 1010, p. 417]

Koninck, Philips de (1619–88), may have been a pupil of Rembrandt before learning landscape painting from his brother Jacob de Koninck. He painted several rather unpleasing genre scenes in the manner of Brouwer, some not very distinguished portraits, and some superb panoramic views of the flat landscape and luminous skies of Holland. The figures in these are sometimes his own and sometimes by Lingelbach or Adriaen van de Velde. His very numerous drawings are in most big museums and have frequently been confused with Rembrandt's – a further possible confusion is between Philips and Salomon Koninck. There are pictures in the Royal Coll. and in Amsterdam (Rijksmus.), Berlin, Cape Town, Frankfurt (Städel), Glasgow (Univ.), The Hague, London (NG, V & A), Munich, New York (Met. Mus.), Oxford, Philadelphia (Mus.), Rotterdam, and elsewhere. [ill. 491, p. 342]

Koninck, Salomon (1609–56), was an Amsterdam painter who, from the early 1630s, imitated Rembrandt, especially in his small figures and groups of bearded old men. Like Philips de Koninck – to whom he may have been distantly

related – many of his drawings have passed as Rembrandt's. There are works in Amsterdam (Rijksmus.), Berlin, The Hague, Liverpool, Vaduz (Liechtenstein Coll.), and elsewhere. [ill. 452, p. 336]

Konrad (Conrad) von Soest was the principal Westphalian painter of the early 15th century. His only certain work is the signed polyptych in Niederwildungen Parish Church, obscurely dated, but probably 1404. This shows the influence of the SOFT STYLE, and, more precisely, contemporary Franco-Burgundian work. Other works attributed to him are in churches in Soest and Dortmund. [ill. 541, p. 352]

Kooning, Willem De (*b.* 1904), was born in Rotterdam, but has lived in the US since 1926. He was trained under the influence of De STIJL, but has since become a leading Action painter. His works have a brutal quasi-realism similar to that of the Dutchman APPEL. He painted a mural for the New York World's Fair of 1939 and there are pictures by him in Buffalo and New York (M of MA). [ill. 1098, p. 428]

Kortegaardjes, a Dutch word, from Fr. *corps de garde*, used to describe the guard-room scenes popular in the 17th century, which show soldiers drinking, gambling, quarrelling, and similar military occupations.

Kricke, Norbert (*b.* 1922), is a German sculptor who is fascinated by the movement of water. His *Water Forest*, 9 feet high, in the grounds of the Gelsenkirchen Opera House (1957), is made of plexiglass, through which water circulates. He has also made compositions in wire, e.g. at Münster Theatre (1959). [ill. 1156, p. 434]

Krüger, Franz (1797–1857), was the leading painter of the BIEDERMEIER style in Berlin, where he was Professor at the Academy and Court Painter. He specialized in horses, portraits, and ceremonial pictures very similar to those of his contemporary C. VERNET, whom he met on a visit to Paris in 1846. He also met DELACROIX and was influenced by him. Many of his portrait drawings were published as lithographs after his death. Most of his works are in Berlin. [ill. 602, p. 358]

Kulmbach, Hans Süss von (*c.* 1480–1522), was a Nuremberg painter who, with SCHÄUFFELEIN, was the best and closest of DÜRER's followers. He formed his style on Dürer's with a leaning towards the Venetians who had so profoundly influenced Dürer himself, as transmitted to him by Jacopo de' BARBARI. He probably went to Cracow in 1510/11 and was certainly there 1514–16. There are works by him in Berlin, Cracow, Dublin, Florence (Uffizi), Hanover, Leipzig, Munich, New York (Met. Mus.), Nuremberg, Turin, Vaduz (Liechtenstein Coll.), and Vienna. [ill. 565, p. 355]

Kupka, Frantisek (Frank, Franz) (1871–1957), one of the founders of abstract art, was trained in Prague and Vienna before going to Paris in 1894/5. He practised as a spiritualist medium, as well as a Fauve painter, but, *c.* 1911, he began to evolve an abstract style under the influences of KLIMT, ORPHISME, and the Section d'Or Cubists led by Jacques VILLON: his *Planes by Colours* (1911: Paris, Mus. d'Art Mod.) is comparable with KANDINSKY's abstract watercolours and antedates the work of MALE-VICH and MONDRIAN. Kupka also wrote a book on artistic creation. There is a Kupka Mus. in Prague (some 50 pictures) and other works are in London (Tate), New York (M of MA), and Paris (Mus. d'Art Mod.). [ill. 1090, p. 427]

Laer, Pieter van, *see* BAMBOCCIO.

Laguerre, Louis (1663–1721), was a French painter who, after working for some time under Lebrun, came to England in 1683/4. He worked for VERRIO at Christ's Hospital in 1684, and, with a French architectural painter called Ricard, decorated the Chapel, the Painted Hall, and several State Rooms at Chatsworth, 1689–94. He worked in many country houses, including Burghley and Blenheim (his best work) and also at Marlborough House in London. In his last decade, he suffered from the competition of THORNHILL, who learned much from him. [ill. 703, p. 377]

Lam, Wifredo (or Wilfredo) (*b.* 1902), was born in Cuba of Negro and Chinese parents, and studied in Havana, Madrid, and Paris. He lived in Spain, 1923–38, and afterwards in Paris, where he became a Surrealist. He returned to Cuba in 1942, and then went to the US. His pictures make use of folk-lore and include totems and jungle scenes. There are examples in London (Tate) and New York (M of MA). [ill. 1056, p. 423]

Lancret, Nicolas (1690–1743), was, with PATER, the principal imitator of WATTEAU. After failing as a history painter he was influenced by Gillot's theatrical scenes, as Watteau had been, and he spent the rest of his life painting *fêtes galantes*. He is well represented in the Wallace Coll., London. [ill. 730, p. 381]

Landseer, Sir Edwin (1802–73), the celebrated painter of sentimental animal subjects, was an infant prodigy who first exhibited at the RA at the age of twelve. He was the son of an engraver and his eldest brother devoted his life to making engravings of his pictures, examples of which were once to be found in practically every public house in England. At the beginning of his career he was an excellent painter of animals who owned STUBBS's drawings for the 'Anatomy of the Horse', but he very soon discovered that by giving animals, and especially dogs, quasi-human expressions he was able to touch the hearts of a large public. He was entranced by his first visit to Scotland in 1824 and very soon began to move in the highest society, particularly on deer-stalking expeditions; he was Queen Victoria's favourite painter and the life-long friend of the Duchess of Bedford. Landseer was elected ARA at the earliest possible age (24), RA in 1831; he refused the Presidency in 1865, as he had already refused a knighthood in 1842 (though he accepted in 1850). His best-known work is the group of lions at the foot of the Nelson Monument in Trafalgar Square, London, made in 1858. It has been observed that many of his pictures of animals have an unpleasant substratum of cruelty; in 1869 his mind gave way and he died four years later hopelessly insane. There are many pictures by him in the Royal Collection and others in Birmingham, Liverpool, London (Tate, NPG, RA, V & A, Kenwood), and elsewhere. The *Stag at Bay*, one of his numerous Highland subjects, is now in a private collection in Dublin. [ill. 903, p. 402]

Lanfranco, Giovanni (1582–1647), was born in Parma, where he was a pupil of Agostino CARRACCI, and was also much influenced by the domes by Correggio. He was in Rome in 1612, and about 1616 decorated the ceiling of the Casino Borghese in a manner derived entirely from the Farnese Gallery. He developed Correggio's SOTTO IN SÙ type of illusionism to an extravagant point, and painted several domes and apses in Roman and Neapolitan churches in this manner. To him DOMENICHINO lost part of the commission for the decoration of S. Andrea della Valle, a slight he resented so bitterly that – so the story goes – he weakened part of the scaffolding, hoping that Lanfranco would break his neck. From 1633/4 to 1646 he was in Naples, and in 1641–3 painted the dome of the S. Gennaro Chapel in the Cathedral, which, by its more up-to-date illusionism and greater showiness appealed far more to local tastes than Domenichino's works there. His dome is based on Correggio's type of illusionism and replaces one actually begun by Domenichino. He died in Rome, where his last work was the apse of S. Carlo ai Catinari.
Apart from Rome and Naples, there are works in Berlin, Dresden, Florence (Pitti), London (Foundling Hospital), Oxford (Ashmolean), Paris (Louvre), Parma, and Vienna. [ill. 271, p. 312]

Laocoön. The famous Antique statue, now in the Vatican, was discovered in 1506. It represents the death agonies of Laocoön and his two sons, crushed by the serpents. The horrible naturalism of this Late Hellenistic work led to erroneous ideas about the nature of Greek art and to a long controversy over whether Laocoön was really suffering in noble silence (WINCKELMANN, 1755) or (as he obviously is) howling with pain; part of this controversy was Lessing's 'Laocoön' published in 1766, and dealing with the relationship between painting and poetry.

Largillierre (Largillière), Nicolas de (1656–1746), was born in Paris but passed his youth in Antwerp and, from *c.* 1674, spent some years in England as LELY's assistant. He was thus almost a Flemish painter when he returned to Paris in 1682. He became a member of the Academy in 1686 and ultimately its Director. His principal rival was

RIGAUD, but he specialized in portraits of the wealthy middle classes, leaving the aristocrats to Rigaud. There are typical examples in London (NG, Wallace Coll.), New York (Met. Mus.), and Paris (Louvre). The *S. Geneviève* (Paris, S. Étienne) is the only survivor of the large ex-voto type of picture that he painted for the Corporations. He also painted a few pictures of still-life. [ill. 695, p. 376]

Lastman, Pieter (1583–1633), was an Amsterdam history painter who went to Italy *c.* 1604 and was influenced by Caravaggio – which makes him akin to the UTRECHT School – and by ELSHEIMER. He was back in Amsterdam by 1607. His real importance lies in the fact that LIEVENS was his pupil in 1617 and REMBRANDT in 1624/5. There are good examples in Amsterdam, Dublin, and London (NG). [ill. 453, p. 336]

La Tour, Georges de (1593–1652), worked all his life in Lorraine. He painted religious and genre subjects in a style that stems ultimately from Caravaggio although it seems more likely that he derived from the UTRECHT School than directly from Caravaggio or his Italian followers. In his later works he adopts a form of indirect lighting from a candle or other concealed source of light, which is close to Dutch Caravaggisti like HONTHORST. In his last works he evolves a figure style in which all masses are reduced to the simplest, almost geometrical, shapes, arranged in static calm which is itself an expression of French classicism. His religious subjects seem to be connected with a contemporary religious revival in Lorraine which was particularly associated with the Franciscans. There are works by him in Berlin, Cleveland, Detroit, Épinal, Grenoble, Hartford Conn., Kansas City, Le Mans, Nancy, Nantes, New York (Met. Mus. and Frick Coll.), Paris (Louvre), Rennes, Rouen, Stockholm. [ill. 679, p. 373].

Latour, Maurice-Quentin de (1704–88), was, with PERRONNEAU, the most celebrated French pastellist of the 18th century. He was born in Saint-Quentin and went to Paris as a young man; after visits to London and other places he settled in Paris 1724–84. He soon found that the vogue for pastel portraits started by Rosalba CARRIERA in 1719/20 was still capable of exploitation and he devoted the rest of his life to it. His portraits are characterized by an extreme vivacity of handling – sometimes rather vulgar – and a firm grasp of character. As a very old man the study of politics drove him crazy, and he retired to Saint-Quentin, where the largest and best collection of his works is to be found: it includes many studies and sketches which are sometimes superior to the finished portraits. [ill. 739, p. 381]

Laurana, Francesco (*c.* 1430–1502?), was Dalmatian by birth (at La Vrana, now Zadar) but Venetian by nationality although he worked much in Sicily and France. He was in France 1461–6 and in Sicily in 1467 – two *Madonnas* still there are dated 1471 – returning to France in 1477 for six years. He must have gone back to France once more (*c.* 1498?), since he died there before 12 March 1502. He is best known as the sculptor of a series of busts of enigmatic-looking women, now in several French provincial museums as well as in Berlin, Florence (Bargello), Paris (Louvre),

Vienna, and Washington (NG). He worked on the Triumphal Arch at Naples in 1453, and may have been there 1483/98. [ill. 88, p. 282]

Laurens, Henri (1885–1954), was a Cubist sculptor whose works are often of still-life subjects and are coloured, thus approaching COLLAGE: from 1911 he associated with Picasso, Braque, Léger, Gris, and other Cubist painters and thus, like LIPCHITZ, evolved a Cubist sculpture. From the late 1920s his work became more realistic, particularly when he treated Greek mythological themes. He also illustrated several books. There are works in London (Tate) and Paris (Mus. d'Art Mod.). [ill. 1128, p. 430]

Lautrec, *see* TOULOUSE-LAUTREC.

Lawrence, Sir Thomas (1769–1830), was born in Bristol but was so precocious that, at the age of 10, he was in practice as a portrait draughtsman in crayons in Oxford: at 17 he wrote to his mother '. . . excepting Sir Joshua, for the painting of a head I would risk my reputation with any painter in London'. In 1787, however, he was a student at the RA Schools for a short time and exhibited at the Academy of that year. From then on he was enormously successful, being made ARA in 1791, appointed Painter to the King on the death of Reynolds in 1792, and elected RA in 1794; he became President of the RA in 1820, having been knighted five years earlier. He had a European reputation as a portrait painter, partly because of the very real glitter and force of his best works, partly because he was commissioned by the Regent (later George IV) to paint all the great personalities of the struggle against Napoleon, making a kind of triumphal progress through Vienna and Rome to do so. His income was huge but he was always heavily in debt, which probably explains the empty flashiness of his worst work. He formed a superb collection of Old Master drawings – probably one of the best ever made – and his will offered it to the nation on very easy terms: by a piece of quite exceptional Governmental imbecility it was refused, and many of the finest drawings dispersed. Fortunately, a part was later bought for Oxford (Ashmolean). The best collection of his works is in the Waterloo Chamber at Windsor Castle, which houses the set of European sovereigns and statesmen painted for George IV. Other works are in museums all over the world, including London (NG, NPG, BM, Tate, V & A, Wallace Coll., RA, Dulwich, Guildhall, Soane, Kenwood, and Wellington Mus.), Ottawa, Paris (Louvre), San Marino Cal., the Vatican, Vienna, and Washington (NG, Corcoran, and Phillips). [ill. 849, p. 397]

Lay Figure. A jointed wooden figure, often life-size, which can be used either to arrange drapery on or as a guide to a complicated pose. It is said to have been invented by Fra Bartolommeo, but no doubt small clay figures or manikins were in use much earlier.

Leal, Valdés, *see* VALDÉS.

Lebrun, Charles (1619–90), was the virtual dictator of the arts in France under Louis XIV, until the death of his protector Colbert. He was the type of the artist-politician and as early as 1641 he gained Richelieu's patronage by an allegorical portrait of the King *en riche lieu*. He was a pupil of VOUET and went to Rome, probably with Poussin, in 1642; he studied partly under Poussin and partly from the works of the Roman Baroque decorators, such as PIETRO da Cortona. He returned, without permission, in 1645, as he was bored with Rome. In 1647 he exhibited an altarpiece for Notre Dame (a MAI), which began his success, and in 1648 he had so far taken over Vouet's position that he was one of the leaders in the foundation of the ACADEMY in 1648. He was to be Rector, Chancellor, and Director of it. He began the decorations for Vaux-le-Vicomte, for the minister Fouquet, in 1658. After Fouquet's fall Colbert realized Lebrun's talent as well as the advantages of a centralized institution as an instrument of policy, and advanced Lebrun, who became Director of the huge undertakings at the Gobelins Factory as well as *premier peintre* in 1664 (though he may have held the post since 1658). In 1665 Bernini arrived in Paris, where he seems to have been critical of Lebrun's gifts. This may have some connection with the sabotaging of Bernini's plans for the Louvre and the general failure of his visit: on the other hand, Lebrun was elected to the Academy of S. Luke in Rome in 1675 and made Director in the same year (and in 1676). For the French Academy he laid down a strict system of rules and even wrote a treatise on the expression of the passions. His most important paintings are at Versailles, where he decorated the Galerie des Glaces (1679–84) and the Salons de la Guerre et de la Paix (completed 1686). After the death of Colbert in 1683 Lebrun, though promoted Director of the Academy in that year, was gradually superseded by MIGNARD. There are paintings by him in Bristol, London (Dulwich), Montreal, Munich, Nottingham, Ottawa, Paris (Louvre), Venice, and many French provincial museums. [ill. 694, p. 376]

Le Brun, Mme Vigée, *see* VIGÉE.

Lega, Silvestro (1826–95), like FATTORI, fought in 1848–9 and was a leading member of the MACCHIAIOLI *c.* 1860. Unlike Fattori, however, Lega carried his political opposition to the French to the length of disliking French art: nevertheless, his masterpiece *The Pergola* (1868) is unthinkable without the example of COROT and the beginnings of Impressionism. He suffered from eye trouble from 1880 and was blind for some years before his death, in great poverty, in Florence. There are works in Florence, Milan, and Rome. [ill. 321, p. 318]

Léger, Fernand (1881–1955), met BRAQUE and PICASSO in 1910 and eventually from his early block-like figures evolved, by *c.* 1917, a form of curvilinear CUBISM, dependent on the dynamic shapes of machinery and their geometrical bases: cones, cylinders, cogged wheels, pistons, and brilliant metallic surfaces. These forms also influenced his massive, robot-like figures, and increased the effect of his clear greys and his strong, unbroken colours. He designed for the Swedish Ballet in 1921–2, and in 1924 made the first abstract film, 'Le Ballet Mécanique', from actual objects, not animated abstract drawings as had been used by Eggeling and Richter some seven years earlier. Among his last works were the huge murals for the UN building in New York.

There are works in London (Tate), New York (M of MA), Paris (Mus. d'Art Mod.), and there is a Musée Léger at Biot, Côte d'Azur. [ill. 1044, p. 420]

Lehmbruck, Wilhelm (1881–1919), was a German sculptor trained in Düsseldorf, where he was a contemporary of MACKE. He went to Italy in 1905 and lived in Paris 1910–14. He was influenced by both RODIN and MAILLOL, but his own forms are more elongated, and his masterpiece, the *Kneeling Woman*, of 1911, has a Gothic expressiveness. He committed suicide in 1919. There are many works in his native Duisburg and others in Buffalo, London (Tate), New York (M of MA), Otterlo, and several German museums. [ill. 1127, p. 431]

Leibl, Wilhelm (1844–1900), was a Cologne painter who was the leader of German Realism in the late 19th century. He met Courbet in Munich at the time of Courbet's exhibition in 1869, and later spent six months in Paris before the outbreak of the Franco-Prussian War (1870). His technical experiments included the use of tempera to obtain an enamel-like surface, and the minuteness of his handling can be seen in his masterpiece *Three Women in a Village Church* (1881: Hamburg). He lived in Bavarian villages and used peasant models, thus exerting a great influence on THOMA and the School of Munich. Many German museums possess examples, including Berlin, Cologne, Hamburg, and Munich. [ill. 617, p. 360]

Lely, Sir Peter (1618–80), was born in Germany of Dutch parents – his real name was van der Faes – and studied in Haarlem under Pieter de Grebber, becoming a Master in the Haarlem Guild in 1637. No works of this Dutch period are known, but he was certainly in London ten years later, and the earliest works produced in this country are still more or less in the style of de Grebber: they are history and subject pieces, even religious pictures, which he continued to paint throughout the Commonwealth. By 1647, however, he had painted the King as well as the Royal children and the double portrait of Charles I and the Duke of York (1647: Syon House, Middx.) inspired Lovelace's poem 'See what a clouded majesty. . . .' With the Restoration Lely at once began the production of that huge flood of portraits which made him the most influential of English 17th-century painters; more important even than van Dyck, to whose position he succeeded when he became Principal Painter to Charles II in 1661. From then until his death he maintained a large studio turning out hundreds of portraits painted in an International Baroque style and exactly catching that atmosphere of sensual languor which most of Charles's Court saw themselves as possessing. The two poles of his art are represented by the sleepily voluptuous *Beauties* of Charles II's Court (Royal Coll., Hampton Court) and the splendidly masculine *Admirals* (Nat. Marit. Mus.). These represent the twelve Admirals under the command of the Duke of York (later James II), for whom the set was painted to commemorate the victories in the Second Dutch War. Pepys records (18 April 1666): 'To Mr Lilly's, the painter's; and there saw the heads, some finished, and all begun, of the Flaggmen in the late great fight. . . .' There are other pictures by him in the Royal Coll. and in Birmingham, London (NG, NPG, Tate, Courtauld Inst., Dulwich, Guildhall, and

Ham House), New York (Met. Mus.), Ottawa, York, and elsewhere. [ill. 816, p. 393]

Le Moyne (Le Moine), François (1688–1737) continued, in the age of WATTEAU, the Grand Manner of LEBRUN. He did many decorations at Versailles, and his *Time revealing Truth* in the Wallace Coll., London, painted just before he committed suicide, shows the pure 17th-century style unaffected by Watteau, although it does show the triumph of RUBÉNISME. Boucher was his pupil. [ill. 702, p. 377]

Lemoyne, Jean-Baptiste (1704–78), was the son of a sculptor. He won the Rome Prize in 1725 but never made the journey. His *Baptism of Christ* (1731: Paris, S. Roch) is his most famous religious work, but he is best known for his splendid portrait busts and as a teacher – his pupils included Falconet, Pigalle, Pajou, and Houdon. There are works in Paris (Louvre, Musée Jacquemart-André, and Comédie-Française), Versailles, Stockholm, Vienna, and many French provincial museums. [ill. 716, p. 379]

Le Nain. There were three painter brothers of this name, all born in Laon. Antoine (c. 1588–1648) was in Paris from 1629 and his two brothers Louis (c. 1593–1648) and Mathieu (c. 1607–77) from 1630. All three were elected members of the Academy on its foundation in 1648. The snag is that there are about 15 signed and dated pictures – but no signature has any initial and all the dates are in or before 1648; i.e. there is no certain means of telling one from another. However, there is a group of small pictures, mostly on copper, with small figures painted in strong colours: these are usually associated with Antoine. Another group is much larger in scale, painted in cool greyish tones, sometimes (like Antoine's) of peasant families but also sometimes of religious subjects: these are called 'Louis' and are perhaps the most valuable artistically. Louis is supposed to have been to Rome. Any remaining tend to get ascribed to Mathieu. Pictures by one or other are in Boston, Bristol, Glasgow, Hagerstown Md, Hartford Conn., London (NG, V & A), New York (Met. Mus.), Paris (Louvre), San Francisco (Legion of Honor), and several French provincial museums. [ills. 680–1, 683–4, pp. 373–4]

Lenbach, Franz von (1836–1904), studied at Munich before going to Rome in 1858–9. In 1863 he returned to Rome with BÖCKLIN. He visited Spain in 1867 before settling in Munich in 1868, where he became a successful portrait painter working in a style derived from Rembrandt and Reynolds. He painted some 80 versions of Bismarck. There is a Lenbach Gallery in Munich, and other German galleries have examples. [ill. 600, p. 359]

Leonardo da Vinci (1452–1519), was one of the greatest of the Universal Men produced by the Renaissance. His intellectual powers were such that he anticipated many later discoveries in anatomy, aeronautics, and several other fields, as well as being one of the greatest of Italian artists. He has always been counted as one of the three great creators of the High Renaissance of the 16th century, yet he was born in 1452 and was thus a contemporary of Perugino or Signorelli and much older than either Michel-

angelo (b. 1475) or Raphael (b. 1483). The intellectual powers which allowed him to overcome the 'dry and hard manner' (as Vasari called it) of the Quattrocento were, however, so diffused over an enormous range of interests that he brought hardly any major enterprise to a conclusion: he almost discovered the circulation of the blood, he invented the first armoured fighting vehicle, projected several aircraft and helicopters, and anticipated the submarine, but not one of these discoveries was completed; and in the same way he left thousands of notes and drawings but only a handful of paintings, and fewer still completed ones.

He was born at Vinci, the illegitimate son of a Florentine notary, but was brought up in his father's house and trained as a painter, traditionally under VERROCCHIO. He is said to have painted the left-hand Angel in Verrocchio's *Baptism* (Florence, Uffizi), as a result of which Verrocchio gave up painting. On stylistic grounds there is every reason to accept the truth of the story, and Verrocchio may well have felt that he could stick to sculpture if he could have so good a painter in the firm; for it is certainly true that Leonardo was living in Verrocchio's house in 1476, presumably as his assistant, for in that year an anonymous accusation of homosexuality which was made against him says so. He had already become a Master in the Guild in 1472, and his earliest datable work is a drawing of an Arno landscape (1473) which already shows his interest in rock-formation and the structure of the earth. There are also some drapery studies, made in the 1470s, which show him breaking new ground, for earlier painters had been content to invent a formula for the folds in drapery and stick to it all their lives, but it is typical of Leonardo that he should have made a special study of fold-structure. In the 1470s he was also experimenting with the technique of oil painting, as may be seen in the *Madonna* in Munich, in which the detail of the dewdrops on the crystal vase astounded his contemporaries, and in the *Ginevra de' Benci* (probably 1474: Vaduz, Liechtenstein Coll.), which may originally have had hands, like the Verrocchio bust of a lady with flowers. This half-length with the hands shown would thus be a new type of portrait, looking forward to the *Mona Lisa*. In 1481 his reputation must have been considerable, for he was commissioned to paint a large *Adoration of the Kings* for the monks of S. Donato a Scopeto, near Florence. The composition of this work is of great importance as summing up all the aims of the later 15th century in creating a surface pattern which should also be a pyramidal form in depth, compact yet dynamic. Many drawings of this period exist, but the picture (now in the Uffizi) was never finished and the payments to Leonardo ceased in 1481. Nothing is known of his activities until he is documented in Milan in 1483, where he may have gone in the previous year. A draft letter exists, in which Leonardo offered his services to Lodovico Sforza, Il Moro, Duke of Milan, and in which he claimed at great length to be a highly skilled military engineer, ending with the words: 'In peace I believe that I can give you as complete satisfaction as anyone in the construction of buildings, both public and private. . . . I can further execute sculpture in marble, bronze or clay, and in painting I can do as much as anyone, whoever he may be. Moreover, I would undertake the commission of the bronze horse, which will endow with immortal glory and eternal honour the auspicious memory of your father and of the illustrious house of Sforza. . . .'

Soon after his arrival he probably painted the *Lady with an Ermine* (now in Cracow) which almost certainly represents Cecilia Gallerani, the mistress of Lodovico Il Moro (Gallerani is almost Greek for 'ermine'): this picture shows the same stylistic characteristics as those attributable to his earlier Florentine period, a point which it is important to bear in mind when considering the problems raised by the two versions of the *Virgin of the Rocks* in Paris (Louvre) and London (NG). Briefly, the problem may be stated thus: Leonardo rarely finished one work, so that it is not likely he would have painted two versions, almost, but not quite, identical of a picture for which only one set of documents seems to exist. These documents run from 1483 to 1506 and they seem to refer to a picture which must be identified with the NG one, the history of which is known in detail. Nevertheless, the Louvre version is indubitably the earlier – i.e. more Florentine – in style, which corresponds with a date *c.* 1483 for the commission. Leonardo remained in Milan until 1499, working on a few artistic projects and several scientific ones but principally acting as resident genius at the Court. Originally he had intended to carry out the elaborate bronze equestrian monument to Francesco Sforza, father of Lodovico Il Moro, but the project got no further than a huge clay model of the horse without its rider. It was never cast, and perished early in the 16th century, but there are some superb drawings of horses connected with it. Leonardo was a famous horseman and he seems to have projected a book on the anatomy of the horse while he was working on the Sforza Monument. One other major work was carried out at this time – the *Last Supper* in Sta Maria delle Grazie, Milan, on which he was working in 1497. Owing to his slow methods and his desire for experiment he worked on the plaster in oil instead of fresco, with the result that the painting was already a wreck in his own lifetime. Nevertheless, this is the first work of the High Renaissance, with its stress on the psychology of the Disciples and the tension of the moment when Christ announces that one of them is about to betray Him, a subtlety of interpretation quite foreign to the 15th century. The stories of Leonardo's slowness in working on this wall-painting and his search for psychological expressiveness justify the claims made by a later generation which regarded Leonardo as the originator of the idea of the artist as a contemplative and creative thinker, the equal of the philosopher, and not a mere artisan who was paid to cover so many square yards of wall a day. Certainly all the 16th-century ideas on the dignity of the artist can be traced back to the example set by him.

In 1499 the French invaded Milan, the dynasty fell, and Leonardo left the city, returning to Florence in 1500 and working in 1502–3, with what seems a cynical detachment, as a military engineer for Cesare Borgia. During his second Florentine period he did a great deal of dissection and made himself into incomparably the finest anatomist of his day, but he also worked on three major artistic projects. The most important was the commission given by the city to its two greatest artists, Leonardo and Michelangelo (who disliked each other intensely). This was for two gigantic wall-paintings, to commemorate Florentine victories, in the Council Chamber of the new Republic. Neither was ever finished. Leonardo's was to represent the Battle of Anghiari, but no more than the central group was ever painted; and this was apparently in some wax medium, in imitation of an antique technique, which failed miserably. Work was begun in 1503 and stopped in 1505. During these years he was also working on a number of versions of the Madonna and Child with S. Anne, seeking a solution to the problem of creating a single compositional form from two adult figures and one or more children. The two survivors are probably the first and last of the series, the one in London (NG) being probably begun in Milan and taken to Florence, and the one in the Louvre dating from *c.* 1506. One of his few finished works is the celebrated portrait of the wife of a Florentine official, known as *Mona Lisa* or 'La Gioconda'. This was painted between *c.* 1500 and *c.* 1504, and, apart from its accretions of fame as a *femme fatale*, is important as a type of portrait and as a feat of oil-technique, particularly in its SFUMATO effects.

In 1506 Leonardo returned to Milan and was made *Peintre et Ingénieur* to Louis XII of France in 1507: he died in France, at Cloux near Amboise, in a château given him by François I. His last years were spent mainly in scientific pursuits but he also projected another equestrian monument, this time to Trivulzio, the commander of the French troops, but the idea got no further than drawings. His last painting, probably done before he moved to France in 1517, was the *S. John* (*c.* 1514/15: Paris, Louvre). In this androgynous object the defects of Leonardo's qualities are painfully apparent: the search for solidity of modelling has led to inky shadows and the total suppression of colour in favour of chiaroscuro; and the search for subtlety of facial expression has led to the smirk with which Leonardo's Milanese followers have made us all too familiar.

A treatise on painting, for which many notes were made, was never written by Leonardo, but it was published from the notes for the first time in 1651 (and recently in full). Incomparably the finest collection of his drawings is in the Royal Library, Windsor Castle. There are other paintings by him in Leningrad, Milan (Ambrosiana), and the Vatican. [ills. 106–9, pp. 286–7. Col. pl. 12]

Lépine, Stanislas (1835–92), was a pupil of Corot and the friend of Boudin, Jongkind, and the Impressionists. He spent his life painting views of Paris in a style derived from Corot and Impressionism. There are good examples in Glasgow and London (NG). [ill. 765, p. 385]

Le Sueur, Eustache (1616/17–55), was, from 1632, a pupil of Vouet, whom he closely followed. He worked at the Hôtel Lambert, first on a *History of Cupid* for the Cabinet d'Amour, 1646–7, then in the Cabinet des Muses, 1647–9, where he turns more consciously towards Raphael and Poussin, the great influences on the later part of his career. Poussin, whom he may have known in 1640–2, dominates the *Life of S. Bruno* series painted for the Charterhouse of Paris (*c.* 1648: Louvre), and in his last works his imitation of Raphael (though he never went to Rome) turns him into a dully derivative artist. There are works in Paris (Louvre) and French provincial museums, and in London (NG). [ill. 687, p. 375]

Le Sueur, Hubert (active 1610–43), worked first in France, where he was Sculptor to the King by 1610, and mentioned as working in 1624. He was in England by 1629, when he made figures for the catafalque of James I, and soon after was employed to make the monstrous tombs of the Duke of Lennox and Richmond, and the Duke of Buckingham, in Westminster Abbey. His equestrian statue of Charles I at Charing Cross, begun in 1630, is an effective pastiche of the *Henri IV* on the Pont-Neuf in Paris, but like all his works, suffers from his pedestrian style and his emptiness of form. Charles I seems to have been aware that his sculptor was far below his painter, van Dyck, in quality. There are works in the Royal Collection, and in London (V & A), and Oxford (St John's College, Schools Quadrangle, Bodleian Library). [ill. 861, p. 398]

Lewis, Wyndham (1884–1957), was an English painter and writer who flourished on controversy. He was the founder of VORTICISM, which derived from Cubism and Futurism, and edited its paper 'Blast'. He is supposed to have painted the first English picture to be influenced by Cubism, in 1912. The Vorticist group amalgamated itself with the LONDON GROUP – but Lewis soon resigned. He wrote a number of novels and satires, and is represented as a painter in London (Tate), Manchester, and elsewhere. [ill. 973, p. 411]

Leyden, Lucas van, *see* LUCAS.

Leyden, Nicolaus Gerhaert von, *see* GERHAERT.

Leyster, Judith (1609–60), and her husband, Jan MOLENAER, whom she married in 1636, were Haarlem painters and were probably pupils of Frans HALS. They painted groups of people laughing and drinking which are strongly influenced by, if not entirely derived from, Hals, against whom Judith brought a lawsuit for the enticement of an apprentice from her workshop into his. Her *Lute Playing Fool* (Amsterdam, Rijksmus.) – a very UTRECHT SCHOOL subject – for many years passed as a Hals. There are works by her in Amsterdam (Rijksmus.), Dublin, The Hague, London (NG), Philadelphia, Stockholm, and elsewhere. [ill. 511, p. 347]

Liber Studiorum *see below.*

Liber Veritatis (Lat. book of truth) was the name given by CLAUDE to the collection of 195 drawings after his own paintings which he assembled as a record of authentic works. The number was later made up to 200 by the addition of five drawings not related to paintings: the entire collection, for centuries the property of the Dukes of Devonshire at Chatsworth, is now in the BM. They were engraved in mezzotint by R. Earlom in 1777, with a note based on Baldinucci's account of the origin of the drawings. This collection inspired TURNER to compile his own *Liber Studiorum: Illustrative of Landscape Compositions, viz., Historical, Mountainous, Pastoral, Marine, and Architectural . . .* (1807 onwards). These were compositions drawn, and partly engraved, by Turner, intended to form a corpus of landscape types, quite different in intention from Claude's index to his paintings. Turner was particularly stringent in his demands on the engravers' skill and the *Liber* may have raised standards in this respect.

Liebermann, Max (1847–1935), was the principal Impressionist painter in Germany. In 1874 he went to BARBIZON and was much influenced by MILLET. He returned to Germany in 1878 and painted rather sentimental genre scenes until the 1890s when he began to work more and more in the Impressionist manner. When the Berlin SEZESSION was founded in 1899 Liebermann became its President. He is well represented in German museums (though out of favour under the Nazis) and in London (Tate) and New York (Met. Mus.). [ill. 601, p. 359]

Lievens, Jan (1607–74), of Leyden was the friend and contemporary of REMBRANDT. He was a pupil of LASTMAN in Amsterdam and then shared a studio with Rembrandt in Leyden in the later 1620s: many works of this period show one influencing the other. Lievens went to England, probably in 1632 after Rembrandt moved to Amsterdam, but he was in Antwerp by 1635, where he was influenced by the Courtly style of van Dyck. He returned to Holland in 1639 and became a successful painter of portraits and allegories. There are works in Amsterdam, Berlin, Besançon, Brighton, Copenhagen, Dublin, Edinburgh (NG), The Hague (Mauritshuis and Huis ten Bosch), Leyden, Lille, London (NG), Nancy, Ottawa, Paris (Louvre), Rotterdam, and Vienna. [ills. 455, 529, pp. 336, 349]

Limbourg, Pol, Hennequin, and Herman de. Pol was the eldest of the brothers, but the first mention of any of them occurs in the accounts of the Duchy of Burgundy for 1400/1 (probably May 1400): there the story is told of Herman and Jacquemin (Hennequin), 'young children' who had been sent as apprentices to a Flemish goldsmith in Paris. The plague broke out and they were on their way home when they were caught up in a war and imprisoned in Brussels. The Duke of Burgundy paid the ransom, presumably because they were related to his painter Jehan MALOUEL. Immediately after this they began working for the Duke and from 1411 they were the Court Painters of the Duke of Berri, for whom they made the most splendid of all his fabulous collection of manuscripts, the 'Très Riches Heures du Duc de Berri' (Chantilly, Musée Condé), one of the greatest achievements of the INTERNATIONAL Gothic style. It is now known that all three were dead by 1416, when their heirs claimed property in Bourges. [ill. 326, p. 319]

Limning. An old-fashioned word, now coming back into use, for portrait painting 'in little' – i.e. miniatures.

Linear Composition. A composition which depends for its effect on the pattern made by the outlines of the forms represented (whether naturalistic or not) rather than on the masses of tone and colour, which tell as shapes rather than edges.

Lingelbach, Johannes (1622–74), was an Amsterdam painter of Italianate landscapes and BAMBOCCIATE. He often painted figures in landscapes by others, e.g. Hobbema and Wynants. [ill. 423, p. 332]

Linnell, John (1792–1882), painted miniatures, landscapes, and Bible illustrations. He was disliked by many fellow-artists and Constable is usually blamed for spreading the gossip about sharp practice in dealing which caused his constant rejection at RA elections. His son-in-law PALMER loathed him, and his one saving grace was the help he gave to Blake, whom he met in 1818. There are works by him in Brighton, and London (Tate, V & A). [ill. 943, p. 407]

Linocut see ENGRAVING.

Liotard, Jean-Étienne (1702–89), was a Swiss pastellist who worked in Paris from 1725, went to Italy in 1738 and there met two English noblemen who took him to Constantinople, where he adopted Turkish dress and a beard which he retained afterwards for the notoriety they brought him. He was in England from 1753 to 1755 painting portraits which Walpole described as 'too like to please', but their liveliness of colour and expression had great success and much influenced Cotes. He worked in Holland after his English visit, and returned to London from 1772 to 1774, but without his earlier success. There are works in Amsterdam (Rijksmus.), Dresden, Geneva (many of his best works), London (V & A), Vienna, and elsewhere. [ill. 594, p. 358]

Lipchitz, Jacques (b. 1891), was born in Lithuania but went to Paris in 1909. His sculpture shows the influence of CUBISM – he met Rivera and Picasso in 1913 – but by c. 1925 he had evolved a personal style of openwork sculpture (sculptures transparentes). In 1941 he went to America, where he has mostly lived since, but in 1946 he was commissioned to make a Madonna for one of the new French churches, at Plateau d'Assy. The Barnes Foundation, Merrion Pa, has many works bought in 1922 by Dr Barnes: others are in Amsterdam (Stedelijk), London (Tate), New York (M of MA), Paris, and elsewhere. [ill. 1133, p. 431]

Lippi, Fra Filippo (c. 1406–69), was probably the only direct pupil of Masaccio. He was an orphan and was put into the Carmine in Florence in 1421, presumably to get him out of the way although he was temperamentally unfitted to be a monk. In the 1420s Masaccio was painting the Brancacci Chapel there and in 1430 (after Masaccio's death) Fra Filippo is first recorded as a painter. The hypothesis that he was Masaccio's pupil is much strengthened by the fresco fragments, datable c. 1432, of the Relaxation of the Carmelite Rule which are his earliest works: they reflect the influence of Masaccio to the exclusion of almost everything else. In 1434 Fra Filippo had left the Carmine and was in Padua, but his work there has disappeared. The first picture by him which bears a date is the Tarquinia Madonna (1437: Rome, Gall. Naz.), and this shows that Masaccio's influence is being gradually superseded by that of Donatello and of Flemish painting. The Barbadori Altarpiece (Paris, Louvre) was also begun in 1437 and shows him using the new SACRA CONVERSAZIONE type of composition, with the old divisions of a triptych modified into a unified composition, the kneeling figures at the sides being used to form a pyramidal shape which stretches across the old divisions. His frescoes at Prato are perhaps his major achievement, and show him developing a progressively more dramatic style, with great

interest in the problem of rendering movement, with by now no trace of Masaccio. The Prato cycle was begun in 1452 and was still incomplete in 1464: these years include Lippi's trial for fraud and his abduction of the nun Lucrezia (and the consequent birth of Filippino). The Medici family, his constant patrons and friends, seem to have obtained him a dispensation to marry Lucrezia – but he does not seem to have been suitably grateful. In spite of his activities, his late works are infused with religious feeling and are far more lyrical than the early ones. The series of Nativities (Berlin and Florence) are examples. His last works were the frescoes in Spoleto Cathedral, but from the beginning in 1466 until his death there in 1469 he seems to have been in bad health and most of the work was done by pupils and assistants. The final receipts are signed by his son Filippino, who was then about 12. BOTTICELLI was probably also Fra Filippo's pupil in the 1460s. There are works by him in Baltimore, Berlin, Empoli, Florence (Uffizi, Pitti, Pal. Medici, and S. Lorenzo), London (NG, Courtauld Inst.), Milan (Castello), Munich, New York (Met. Mus.), Oxford, Prato (Mus.), Rome (Pal. Venezia), Washington (NG), and elsewhere. [ill. 74, 75, pp. 279–80]

Lippi, Filippino (1457/8–1504), was the son of Fra Filippo and completed his father's works (or at least cleared up his estate) in Spoleto, after which – at the age of about 12 – he set off alone for Florence on 1 January 1470. He was with BOTTICELLI in 1472 but the first certainly datable work by him is the Annunciation (1483/4: S. Gimignano) on two tondi. This long gap, coupled with the existence of a group of pictures which are close to both Filippino and Botticelli, led to the creation of AMICO di SANDRO, but the group has now been redivided between the two. His first major commission was to complete the fresco cycle in the Brancacci Chapel in the Carmine, Florence, which had either been left unfinished by Masaccio or had been partially destroyed. This he probably painted about 1484 and in 1486 he completed one of his best-known and most typical paintings, the Vision of S. Bernard (Florence, Badia) which shows his restless, fluttering line and bright colour. Between 1487 and 1502 he painted a fresco cycle in the Strozzi Chapel in Sta Maria Novella, and another one in Rome. This was the cycle in the Caraffa Chapel, S. Maria sopra Minerva (1488–93), and his years in Rome gave him the opportunity to study Antique remains: ever afterwards he introduced bits and pieces of antiquity into all his pictures, whether suitable or not. There are many panels datable in the 1490s and the last years of his life, but, like Botticelli, his style went out of date in his lifetime: it is sometimes called 'Quattrocento Mannerism'. There are pictures by him in Berlin, Chantilly, Cleveland, Copenhagen, Edinburgh (NG), Florence (Accad., Uffizi, Pitti, Horne Mus., S. Spirito), Genoa, London (NG), Munich, New York (Met. Mus.), Ottawa, Washington (NG), and elsewhere. [ill. 97, p. 284]

Liss (Lys), Johann (c. 1597–1629/30), was a German painter who seems to have trained in the Netherlands, perhaps under GOLTZIUS, before settling in Venice by 1621. He died there of the plague. His Roman BENTNAME 'Pan' sufficiently expresses his robustly Rubensian art, crossed with Venetian colouring, and his preferred subjects. There are examples in Berlin, Bremen (Kunsthalle, Roseliushaus), Budapest, Cassel, Dresden, Florence (Uffizi), The Hague (Bredius Mus.), London (NG), Nuremberg, Pommersfelden (Schloss Schönborn), Venice (Accad., S. Niccolò dei Tolentini), and Vienna (K-H Mus. and Akad.). [ill. 409, p. 329]

Lithography see ENGRAVING.

Local Colour is the actual colour of an object, uninfluenced by reflected light or colour: thus, the local colour of lips is pink although they may appear brown in certain lights.

Lochner, Stefan (d. 1451), was active in Cologne from at least 1442 and is the major master of the Cologne School, an important representative of the soft and pretty style associated with INTERNATIONAL GOTHIC. He seems to have been trained in the Netherlands, at least under the influence of the MASTER of FLÉMALLE (he was a contemporary of Roger van der Weyden) and perhaps also of the LIMBOURG brothers. His masterpiece is the *Patron Saints of Cologne* (*Das Dombild*) in Cologne Cath. Other works include the dated one (1447) in Darmstadt and others in Cologne (Wallraf-Richartz Mus. and Archiepiscopal Mus.), Frankfurt (Städel), London (NG), Munich, and Nuremberg. The Gulbenkian Coll. has one dated 1445. [ill. 540, p. 352]

Lombardo, Pietro (c. 1435–1515), and his sons Tullio (c. 1455–1532) and Antonio (c. 1458–1516?), were the major Venetian sculptors and architects of their time. Pietro, who came from Lombardy, was first recorded in Padua in 1464 (Roselli Tomb in the Santo, 1467), but his style suggests that he had already been in Florence. He settled in Venice probably c. 1467, and with his sons ran the principal sculpture workshop; they executed many tombs, the Mocenigo Tomb in SS. Giovanni e Paolo, finished by 1481, being the most important. He also worked at Treviso, and made Dante's tomb in Ravenna. His style is characterized by rather thick-set figures of markedly Antique derivation, soft modelling, and a certain hesitancy in form and movement. Tullio's career depends from his father's, but in style he is more emphatic, dramatic, and even more influenced by the Antique. Antonio was also strongly classical in inspiration, reflecting the tastes of his patrons, but he finally dwindled into decorative work for the Estes of Ferrara. Tullio and Antonio did most of the decorative sculpture and statues for S. Maria dei Miracoli, which their father built (1481–9), and they also did the odd perspective reliefs on the lower part of the façade of the Scuola di S. Marco. Besides numerous works in churches in Venice and in Treviso Cathedral, there are examples by Tullio in New York (Met. Mus.), Northampton Mass. (Smith Coll.) and Vienna (K-H Mus.). [ills. 87, 154, pp. 283, 294.]

London Group. Founded in 1913, the London Group arose from a fusion between the CAMDEN TOWN GROUP and the VORTICISTS, together with some other artists. The first President was GILMAN and the members included SICKERT and Wyndham LEWIS. The Group still exists.

Longhi, Alessandro (1733–1813), was the son of Pietro Longhi and a well-known portrait painter. His reputation was established as early as 1760 and two years later he published a book on Venetian painters of his own times ('Compendio delle Vite . . .' 1762) which is an important source-book. There are pictures in Venice and in London (NG), Boston, New York (Met. Mus.), and elsewhere. [ill. 292, p. 314]

Longhi, Pietro (1702–85), was a Venetian genre painter, whose scenes of everyday patrician life in Venice are of value to the historian. These pictures are very numerous and were often repeated by pupils or imitators and are therefore very common: the largest collection is in the Querini-Stampalia Gall., Venice. Others are in London, New York (Met. Mus.), Washington (NG). [ill. 294, p. 315]

Loo, van. A family of painters of Flemish descent working in France, of whom the most important were Jean-Baptiste, Carle, and Louis-Michel. Jean-Baptiste (1684–1745) was the eldest, but was the fourth generation of the family to be a painter. He was born in the South of France and worked there until he went to North Italy and on to Rome in 1714. From 1720 he was settled in Paris, becoming a Member of the Academy in 1731. He established himself as a portrait painter in the circle of the Regent, and also painted a version of the State portrait of Louis XV. In 1737 he moved to London, for reasons which are not clear; he had an immediate success, and was patronized by the Prime Minister, Sir Robert Walpole. He had great facility in catching a likeness, and by 1738 VERTUE wrote: 'The English painters have had great uneasines it has much blemishd their reputation – and business.' According to van Loo's own account, Walpole said he would have made him Painter to the King, but this was impossible since no foreigner could hold the post. In 1741 Vertue recorded his complaints about the English climate, and in 1742 he retired to his native Aix. His work had considerable influence on his English rivals such as HUDSON and HOGARTH. There are works by him in Aix, Brussels, Glasgow, Leningrad (Hermitage: a portrait of Walpole), London (NPG), New York (Hist. Soc.), Paris (Louvre and churches), Turin, Versailles, and Worcester (Town Hall). Carle (1705–1765) was Jean-Baptiste's brother and pupil and went with him to Rome in 1714, and back to Paris in 1720. After study in Paris he returned to Rome in 1727, and worked in Turin for two years before returning to Paris in 1734. He was elected to the Academy in 1735, and became the most famous member of the family in France, being appointed Principal Painter to the King in 1762, and Director of the Academy in 1763. There are works by him, principally decorations, in many French museums and also in Florence (Uffizi), Glasgow, Leningrad (Hermitage), London (Wallace Coll.), Madrid, New York (Met. Mus.), Paris (Louvre, Notre Dame and churches), Potsdam, Quebec, Stockholm, and Vienna.
Louis-Michel (1707–71), was the son of Jean-Baptiste and the brother of three further painters. Like his uncle Carle, who was only two years his elder, he was Jean-Baptiste's pupil in Turin and Rome, and he won a prize at the Academy in Paris in 1725. With his uncle he went to Rome 1727–32, but in 1736 he became Court Painter in Madrid

where he painted many portraits. He was a Founder-Member of the Academy in Madrid in 1752, but returned to Paris in 1753, and made many versions of the State portrait of Louis XV for presentation to the Courts of Europe. In 1765 he succeeded his uncle as Director of the special school of the French Academy known as the École royale des Élèves protégés (*see* COYPEL). There are works by him in Copenhagen, Leningrad, London (Wallace Coll.), Madrid (Prado and Acad.), Paris (Louvre), Versailles, and other French museums. [ills. 700, 705, 736, pp. 376–7, 381]

Lorenzetti, Pietro (active 1320–45), and Ambrogio (active 1319–47) were brothers, Pietro probably being the elder. They were Sienese painters who extended the side of Duccio's art that was concerned with rendering solidity of form and emotional depth: in this they were opposed to Simone MARTINI and were influenced by the sculpture of Giovanni PISANO (as Duccio himself was) and also by contemporary work in Florence by Giotto and his immediate followers. Like some of their Florentine contemporaries such as DADDI they form a stylistic link between Duccio and Giotto, between the Schools of Siena and Florence. Pietro was perhaps Duccio's pupil, but his earliest work, the polyptych in the Parish Church, Arezzo, which was commissioned in 1320, shows an independent style already, even though it has Ducciesque characteristics and is comparable with the polyptych by Simone Martini at Pisa, also of 1320. There are several frescoes and other panel pictures by Pietro, the most notable being the frescoes at Assisi (S. Francesco, Lower Church), the *Carmine Altar* (1329: Siena, Pinacoteca), and the *Birth of the Virgin* (1342: Siena, Opera del Duomo). The Assisi frescoes show the impact of the art of Giotto on him, and they are probably the most tragically grand and simple works produced by a Sienese in the 14th century. The *Birth of the Virgin* is probably later – the date of the Assisi frescoes is very controversial – and, by comparison with the more complex *Presentation* by his brother (also 1342: Florence, Uffizi), it seems very simple, yet it has great narrative power and it shows Pietro as a colourist. The setting is reminiscent of his brother's *Presentation*, but simpler and less accurate in its perspective, and it is thought that Ambrogio was the more inventive of the two. He may have been in Florence c. 1318 and the earliest work attributed to him, a *Madonna* of 1319, at Vico L'Abate (now in Florence, Mus. Diocesano), is much more influenced by Florentine ideas than by Sienese. He entered the Guild at Florence in 1327 and was in the city again in 1331–2, so that he was in constant touch with the art of Giotto and his followers. His most important works are the frescoes of *Good and Bad Government* in the Town Hall of Siena (1337–9). There is a large allegorical fresco, a sort of political manifesto, which shows the influence of Giotto in the bulky forms of the allegorical females, but the two most interesting are those representing Good Government in the Town and in the Country, where the streets of Siena are represented in perspective of astonishing mastery at that date, and the great panoramic landscape in the *Country* with its small figures riding through the peaceful countryside (the bandits have been hanged by the Good Government) is perhaps the first landscape in modern art to be used as an essential component of a composition, both reflecting and creating a mood. Ambrogio

is last recorded in 1347, and it is possible that both brothers died in the Black Death of 1348/9 which ravaged Siena with particular severity and killed off most of the artists – hence the rapid decline of the second half of the 14th century.
There are works by one or both in Baltimore (Walters), Berlin, Borgo San Sepolcro, Budapest, Cambridge Mass. (Fogg), Cleveland Ohio, Cortona, Dijon, Fiesole, Florence (Uffizi, Horne Mus., Sta Lucia), Frankfurt (Städel), Le Mans, London (NG), Massa Marittima, Milan (Poldi-Pezzoli), New York (Met. Mus.), Philadelphia (Johnson), the Vatican, Washington (NG), and elsewhere. The so-called 'UGOLINO-LORENZETTI' had no real existence and was not another member of the family. [ills. 40–2, p. 275]

Lorenzo Monaco (i.e. Lorenzo the Monk) (c. 1370/2–1422/5, probably 1425), was a Sienese who settled in Florence and took vows in the Camaldolensian monastery of S. Maria degli Angeli, which was famous as a school of manuscript illuminators: Don Lorenzo is also known to have painted illuminations. He was a follower of Agnolo GADDI and the Sienese strain in Late Trecento art, but he was also influenced by GHIBERTI, and, like him, by INTERNATIONAL GOTHIC. His principal works are the *Coronation of the Virgin* (1413 Florentine Style, i.e. 1414: Florence, Uffizi), painted for his own monastery, and a similar *Coronation* (London, NG), probably also for a Camaldolensian house. Both these are traditional Trecento altarpieces, with gold backgrounds and flat figures, bright in colour and occupying no space in the picture. What is probably his last picture is the *Adoration of the Magi* (Florence, Uffizi) and this shows a complete change to the International Gothic style – dark colour, realistic detail, and landscape background and an attempt at depth, though with very elongated figures. He is thus important as one of the introducers of the style into Florence at the time of GENTILE da Fabriano. There are other works in Florence (Accad., Uffizi, Bargello, Mus. di S. Marco, and churches) and in Amsterdam, Baltimore (Walters), Berlin, Cambridge (Fitzwm), London (NG), New York (Met. Mus.), Paris (Louvre), Philadelphia (Johnson), Siena, the Vatican, Washington (NG), Worcester Mass., Yale University, and elsewhere. [ill. 46, p. 274]

Lotto, Lorenzo (c. 1480–1556), was probably born in Venice. He worked in Treviso, Bergamo, Venice, and Ancona, and in 1509 was painting in the Vatican, though what he did there and how long he stayed is unknown. He settled in the monastery of the Santa Casa at Loreto in 1552, becoming a lay-brother in 1554.
His early works are strongly influenced by Giovanni Bellini, but after his removals to Bergamo and Venice he develops a chameleon-like quality, reflecting Botticelli, Fra Bartolommeo, Raphael, Correggio, Giorgione, Titian, and even something of Dürer and Holbein, though always with an intensely personal quality and with a steady development from the detailed, episodic vision of the 15th century to the broader handling of the 16th century. His account book (a rare survival), kept from 1538 onwards, suggests a troubled and difficult character and little material success.
His principal frescoes are in and near Bergamo, and there

are works by him in the Royal Coll., Ancona and the sur-rounding district, Bergamo (Accad. Carrara and churches), Berlin, Brescia, Cambridge Mass. (Fogg), Cleveland Ohio, Dresden, Edinburgh (NG), Florence (Uffizi), Jesi, Lenin-grad, London (NG), Loreto, Madrid (Prado), Milan (Brera, Castello, Poldi-Pezzoli), Munich, Naples, New Orleans, Oxford (Christ Church), Paris (Louvre), Phila-delphia (Johnson), Princeton, Recanati (Mus. and churches), Rome (Borghese, Barberini, Capitoline, Castel S. Angelo, Doria Gall.), Sarasota Fla, Treviso, Venice (Accad., Correr, and churches), Vienna, Washington (NG), and elsewhere. [ills. 205, 206, p. 303]

Lucas van Leyden (1494?–1533), is said to have been precociously capable by 1508. He was the pupil of his father, by whom no works are known, and Cornelius Engelbrechtsz., with whose paintings his are confused: almost nothing is known about the Leyden School. He married in Leyden in 1515, met Dürer in Antwerp in 1521, and may have entered the Guild there in 1522. He visited Mabuse in Middelburg, and travelled in Flanders with him in 1527, when Lucas gave banquets for local painters. His paintings are characterized by fluid, calligraphic brushwork and surprising colour. His numerous woodcuts and engravings lean heavily on Dürer; they display sensitive, brilliant draughtsmanship and the inventiveness in subject common in the North. The volume of his *œuvre* belies Van Mander's stories of his dilettante travelling, working in bed, and wining and dining in yellow silk clothes. There are works in Amsterdam, Boston (Mus.), Bremen, Brunswick, Brussels, Leningrad, Leyden, London (NG), Munich, Nuremberg, Paris (Louvre), Philadelphia (Johnson), and elsewhere. [ills. 374, 375, p. 324]

Luini, Bernardino (*c.* 1481/2–1532), was one of the most popular Milanese painters in the early 16th century, principally because he succeeded in vulgarizing the style of Leonardo (as indeed all his Milanese followers tried to do). He was certainly active by 1512, but there is a picture in the Musée Jacquemart-André, Paris, which is dated 1507 and is the work of a Bernardino: partisans for and against the attribution to Luini may be found. Before his domination by the style of Leonardo he seems to have been influenced by Bramantino and other Milanese and to have painted gay and enjoyable works like the fresco fragments in Milan (Brera), Pavia, Paris (Louvre), and London (Wallace Coll.), all from a villa at Monza. His very numerous works are mostly in Milan (Brera, Castello, Poldi-Pezzoli, Ambrosiana, and churches), but there are others in the Royal Coll. and in Berlin, Boston, Cambridge Mass. (Fogg), Chiaravalle nr Milan (the fresco *Madonna* dated 1512), Cleveland Ohio, Como (Cath.), Detroit, Florence (Uffizi), London (NG, Wallace Coll., Wellington Mus., Courtauld Inst.), Lugano (SM degli Angeli), Minneapolis, Ottawa, Paris (Louvre), Pavia (Mus., Certosa), Philadelphia (Johnson), Sarasota Fla, Saronno nr Milan (S. Maria dei Miracoli), Vienna, Washington (NG), and elsewhere. [ill. 204, p. 302]

Lukasbrüder *see* NAZARENER.

Lurçat, Jean (*b.* 1892), is the most important living tapestry designer. He began as a painter and was in-fluenced by Cézanne and by Cubist ideas, but, after being wounded in 1914, he began to work on tapestries in 1917. He lived for years in Spain and eventually abandoned Cubism. From 1937 he worked as designer at Aubusson, and from 1939 for the Gobelins; in the post-war period he has done much to revive this art, many of his tapestries being woven for the French Government to use in Em-bassies abroad. There are paintings by him in Paris (Musée d'Art Moderne), Melbourne, Toledo Ohio, and Washington (NG). [ill. 1078, p. 426]

Lyon, Corneille de, *see* CORNEILLE.

Mabuse, Jan Gossaert called (*d. c.* 1533), probably came from Maubeuge in Hainault, and is first documented in the Antwerp Guild in 1503. His early style derives from Gerard David, Hugo van der Goes, and Dürer, but he introduces flamboyant, over-abundant detail, amounting almost to a *horror vacui*. In 1508 he went to Italy, and after this his works display florid Italianized detail, particularly in the architectural settings, and borrowed poses, with no understanding of the essentials of the Italian Renaissance. He became an important ROMANIST, and was the first to introduce into Flanders classical subjects with nude figures. There are works in the Royal Collection, and in Antwerp, Brussels, Berlin, London (NG, Courtauld Inst.), Ottawa, Palermo, Paris (Louvre), Prague, Toledo Ohio, Vienna, and elsewhere. [ill. 376, p. 325]

Macchiaoli, I (Ital. *Macchia*, a stain or blot). A group of Italian painters working mainly in Florence *c.* 1855/65, who, in revolt against Academism, exploited the individual blob or touch of paint (cf. TACHISME). Influenced by COROT and by COURBET's Realism, some produced landscapes and genre subjects (the best among these were LEGA, FATTORI, and SIGNORINI), while others turned out pseudo-Romantic costume history pieces (Vito d'Ancona, Costa). The only ones influenced much by Impressionism were Degas's friends De NITTIS and ZANDOMENEGHI, and BOLDINI who became a glossily fashionable portraitist in Paris. Diego Martelli, who was painted by Degas (Edinburgh, NG) was their chief critic and apologist. [ills. 319–25, p. 318]

Macke, August (1887–1914), was a German painter deeply influenced by contemporary French painting, particularly by DELAUNAY's very bright colour used in conjunction with near-Cubist ideas. He was associated with MARC and KANDINSKY in the BLAUE REITER, and also influenced by Futurist ideas, but remained a more visual and representational artist than these associations would suggest. In 1914 he went to Tunisia with Klee. He was killed in France. [ill. 1022, p. 418]

Madonnieri. A Venetian word, applied to anonymous producers of devotional Madonna images, often of no artistic value.

Maelwel *see* MALOUEL.

Maes, Nicolaes (1634–93), was a Dordrecht painter who became a pupil of Rembrandt *c.* 1648. From then until about 1665 he painted genre and portraits in a Rembrandt-esque manner and some genre subjects rather like those of P. de Hooch. About 1665/6 he went to Antwerp and was much impressed by the modishness of Flemish portraiture in the French taste: this elegance he took back with him and applied to his Dutch sitters. There are examples in Amsterdam (Rijksmus.), Antwerp, Boston, Brussels, Dordrecht, The Hague, London (NG, Wallace Coll.), New York (Met. Mus.), Ottawa, Oxford (a *Still-life*), Washington (NG), and elsewhere. [ills. 451, 528, pp. 336, 349]

Maestà (Ital. majesty) is an abbreviation for the Madonna and Child enthroned in Majesty and surrounded by Saints and/or Angels. The subject is most common in the Dugento and Trecento and the best-known example is the *Maestà* by Duccio, painted for the High Altar of Siena Cathedral 1308–11. [ill. 37, p. 274]

Magnasco, Alessandro (1677–1749), painted extremely melodramatic landscapes, usually with storm-tossed trees and frenetic monks, in an 18th-century version of Salvator ROSA's 'savagery'. Some of Marco RICCI's works are almost indistinguishable from his. [ill. 312, p. 317]

Magnelli, Alberto (*b.* 1888), is an abstract painter of the type of LÉGER and MONDRIAN, practising what is sometimes called 'Concrete Art'. He was born in Florence, but went to Paris *c.* 1910, and came in contact with the Cubists and Futurists. Later, he met Picasso and Léger. He began painting abstract pictures in Florence in 1915, but reverted to figurative forms until he returned to France, settling in Paris in 1933. In 1958 he was awarded the Guggenheim Prize. There are works in Paris (Mus. d'Art Mod.) and several other museums in Europe and in the US. [ill. 1091, p. 427]

Magritte, René (*b.* 1898), is a Belgian Surrealist painter who was trained in Brussels and travelled in France, Britain, Germany, and Holland. He lived near Paris, 1927–30, and came into contact with the French Surrealist movement, although he painted some Impressionist-style pictures during the Second World War. He lives in Brussels and has painted murals for Belgian public buildings. His pale and dryly painted works have a dreamlike clarity. There are examples in Chicago and New York (M of MA). [ill. 1055, p. 423]

Mahlstick (Maulstick), a short stick with a padded knob used as a rest for the right hand when painting detailed passages.

'Mai'. A large altarpiece, commissioned by the Goldsmiths' Guild of Paris from one of the major painters of the day, and presented by them to the Cathedral of Notre Dame on 1 May. The custom seems to have died out at the beginning of the 18th century, and very few of these pictures have survived.

Maiano, Benedetto da, *see* BENEDETTO.

Maillol, Aristide (1861–1944), was a French sculptor whose works are devoted almost exclusively to the female nude. He returned to the ideals of Greek art of the 5th century B.C. in a reaction against RODIN's fluid forms, changing silhouettes, and dramatic content, although it was Rodin who helped to make his name. By contrast, Maillol stressed the static and monumental qualities of the human figure. He sometimes made use of the 'fragment' device, but never sought the dramatic contrasts of the partly unfinished figure. From 1889 he was friendly with BOURDELLE, although he did not begin sculpture until 1895; from 1900 he had links with the NABIS and became a life-long friend of Matisse. In 1908 he went to Greece. One of his most famous works, the Cézanne Monument, commissioned in 1912 for Aix, was formally rejected by the city in 1925 and was finally placed in the Tuileries in Paris. He is represented in the museums of modern art in London, Paris, and New York. [ill. 1121, p. 431]

Malerisch. This German word, meaning *painterly*, *pertaining to a painter*, was given a special sense by the great Swiss art historian Heinrich Wölfflin. In this technical sense it is used to denote the opposite of linear; that is, a feeling for form which does not see in terms of outline or drawing, but in patches of coloured light and shade, or painting in which the edges of the forms merge into one another or into the tone of the background. Titian and Rembrandt are among the most *malerisch* of painters, Botticelli or Michelangelo among the least.

Malevich, Kasimir (1878–1935), was a Russian artist who, not content with Cubism, invented SUPREMATISM and painted the picture which should have ended all abstract pictures – a white square on a white ground (*c*. 1918: New York, M of MA). From *c*. 1904 in Moscow he was aware of modern French painting, mainly from the splendid Shchukin Collection; about 1912 he went to Paris for a month and came back a Cubist. He claimed to have invented Suprematism as a purer form of Cubism in 1913, but it was more probably in 1915. After the Revolution he had a violent disagreement with CHAGALL over aesthetics: part of his 'Decree A in art. Vitebsk, 15 November 1920' reads '1. The fifth dimension is established . . . 18. To summon an economic council (of the fifth dimension) for the liquidation of all the arts of the old world. . . .' [ill. 1087, p. 427]

Malouel (Maelwel), Jean (*d.* 1419), was a Dutch painter working in Paris by 1396. He became Court Painter to the Dukes of Burgundy in 1397 and was succeeded by Bellechose in 1415. Malouel is known to have painted five works for Dijon in 1398 but no work certainly by him can now be identified. On the other hand, the large round *Pietà* (Paris: Louvre) which dates from 1400/10 is probably either by him or by Bellechose. Another picture in the Louvre, the *Martyrdom of S. Denis*, has been identified

with one of the five Dijon altarpieces of 1398, but it seems more likely that it is a picture completed in 1416 by Bellechose. It has been suggested that the *S. Denis* was begun by Malouel and completed by Bellechose but this is pure guesswork.
Henri Bellechose was born in Brabant but worked mostly in Dijon. He is known to have worked for the Dukes of Burgundy at Dijon from 1415 to 1425 and he died at Dijon 1440/4. [ills. 330, 331, p. 319]

Mander, Karel van (1548–1606), was a Flemish painter who was in Rome in 1575 and in Vienna in 1577. He settled in Haarlem where he opened an academy with GOLTZIUS and Cornelis van Haarlem which propagated Italianizing tendencies in the North. He is most celebrated for his 'Schilderboek', published in 1604 – a poor imitation of Vasari's 'Lives', which, despite its gossipy inaccuracies, is the best early source on Northern painters. [ill. 386, p. 326]

Mandorla (Ital. almond). An almond-shaped glory of light which is shown as enclosing the whole figure of the Resurrected Christ or of the Virgin at the Assumption.

Manessier, Alfred (*b.* 1911), is a French abstract painter who differs from many others in that some, at least, of his pictures have a specifically religious intent. He made a retreat at the Trappist monastery at Soligny and has designed stained-glass windows for churches in Bresseux (Jura), Arles, and Basle (1953). His picture of the Crown of Thorns (Paris, Musée d'Art Moderne) is clearly based on a meditation on the Passion, but the connection between his *Salve Regina* and the great 11th-century Latin antiphon is less evident (though probably susceptible of exegesis by the Dominicans of S. Germain-des-Prés). There are pictures by him in Basle, Brussels, London (Tate), New York (Guggenheim), Oslo, Paris, Pittsburgh, Stockholm, and Turin. [ill. 1106, p. 428]

Manet, Édouard (1832–83). His well-to-do bourgeois father reluctantly allowed him to study under COUTURE from 1850 to 1856. He then reacted very strongly against the academic history painting of his teacher and began his career as an artistic rebel with the *Absinthe Drinker* (1859: Ny Carlsberg Mus., Copenhagen), a scene from the seamier side of life. His brilliant technique, founded on the opposition of light and shadow with as little half-tone as possible, on painting directly from the model with intense immediacy, and on a restricted palette in which black was extremely important, helped him to create a new style; yet one founded on Velazquez, Goya, and Hals. His early works include many Spanish subjects inspired by troupes of dancers visiting Paris and he did not actually visit Spain until 1865. These Spanish pieces include numerous bull-fighting scenes, *Lola de Valence* (1862: Louvre) and the *Guitarist* (1860: private coll.), his only successful Salon exhibit before *Le bon Bock* (1873: Philadelphia). He had previously travelled in Italy, Holland, Flanders, and Germany.
His work was frequently rejected by the SALON jury (he played an important part in the 1863 Salon des Refusés) and, if hung, was ill-received by critics, his friend Zola being almost alone in defending him. After 1870, due partly to the influence of Berthe MORISOT, he adopted the

Impressionist technique and palette, abandoning the use of black and his genius for analysis and synthesis for a lighter, sweeter colour and a freer handling. He also tended more to sentimental subjects, such as *Washing Day* (1875: private coll.), *Chez le père Lathuile* (1879: Tournai), lacking the sober gravity of his earlier works – *Le Déjeuner sur l'herbe* (1863: Louvre, sketch in Courtauld Institute, London), *Olympia* and *The Fifer* (1865 and 1866: both Louvre). He always longed for official recognition and refused to take part in the Impressionist exhibitions organized by Degas. Although he was friendly with Monet, Renoir, Sisley, and Pissarro he bitterly resented being coupled with them in newspaper criticisms as the leader of 'Manet's gang'. At the end of his life he was given the Legion of Honour and the vilification of his works abated, chiefly because Impressionist handling and colour were beginning to affect academic painting. The tragedy of his life was that he was the perfect academic painter, unrecognized and rejected by the body whose dying traditions he alone could have revivified.

Apart from those mentioned already the following cities have works: Baltimore, Berlin, Berne, Boston, Bremen, Budapest, Buenos Aires, Cardiff, Chicago, Copenhagen, Dijon, Dresden, Essen, Frankfurt (Städel), Glasgow (Burrell Coll.), Hamburg, London (NG, Tate, Courtauld Inst.), Lyons, Mannheim, Melbourne, Merion Pa (Barnes Foundation), Moscow, Munich, Nancy, New York (Met. Mus. and Frick Coll.), Oslo, Philadelphia (Johnson Coll.), Providence RI, St Louis, São Paulo, Stockholm, Toledo Ohio, and Washington (NG and Phillips). [ills. 796, 797, p. 389. Col. pl. 29]

Manfredi, Bartolommeo (*c.* 1580–1620/1), was a Mantuan follower of Caravaggio, who seems not to have been above a little Caravaggio-faking immediately after the latter's death in 1610. His greater claim to fame lies in the fact that it seems to have been he – and not Caravaggio – who popularized subjects such as cardsharpers and soldiers in guard-rooms, with half-length figures on a largish scale. These were the works which influenced the Northerners in Rome (Honthorst and other UTRECHT painters, as well as French and Germans) and there are cases where the early writers mention such painters as being followers of Manfredi rather than of Caravaggio. It is also recorded that his works were exported to Holland. There are no signed or fully documented works by him, and most of what are now regarded as characteristic examples of his style were, at one time or another, called Caravaggios. There are examples in Brunswick, Brussels, Dresden, Florence (Uffizi, Pitti), Rome (Gall. Naz.), and Vienna. [ill. 244, p. 309]

Manière Criblée *see* DOTTED PRINT.

Manner. Usually now used as a pejorative alternative for 'style': my friends have style, yours merely manner (cf. MANNERISM). The original Italian term *maniera* meant personal style, 'handwriting', and the word manner is usually used in this sense in 18th-century criticism – 'a fine, free manner'.

Mannerism is a term developed in the present century to describe the artistic manifestations, principally Italian, of the period *c.* 1520–1600. During these years many major works were produced which cannot be called RENAISSANCE or BAROQUE without rendering these terms meaningless. The word *maniera*, from which Mannerism is derived, was used by Vasari (himself a notorious practitioner) to describe the schematic quality of much of the work produced, based on intellectual preconceptions rather than direct visual perceptions. Much of Mannerism consists of deliberately flouting the 'Rules' deduced from classical art and established during the Renaissance. This presupposes an educated spectator; otherwise there is no point in breaking the rules. The effect is more obvious in architecture, since the Rules there are both more simple and more rigid, and the works of GIULIO ROMANO show him to have been a major Mannerist architect although less important as a painter.

The principal characteristics of a Mannerist work of art are an insistence on the primacy of the human figure, which, however, is set in strained poses, wilfully distorted and elongated, while the muscles are sometimes also grossly over-emphasized. The composition is usually forced and unclear, with the principal subject set in a corner or in the background, with great discrepancies of scale between the figures and with the perspective treated more often as a piece of virtuosity than as a contribution to the lucidity of the narrative. The colour of a Mannerist picture is always vivid and often harsh, since it is intended to heighten the emotional effect rather than describe the forms; many Mannerists also have a preference for 'shot' colours, red blending into orange, yellow into green, and so on. It is essentially an unquiet style, subjective and emotional, and was therefore well fitted to be rediscovered and defined during the 1920s, but it is certainly wrong – as Marxist critics do – to equate it wholly with the disturbed political and social conditions prevailing in Central Italy after the Sack of Rome in 1527. These conditions, however influential, were more or less permanent; but it is fair to say that these disturbances, and particularly the unsettling effect of the Reformation (with its doctrine of private judgement) and the Counter-Reformation (with its repressive and didactic aspects) led to the abandon of the serenity and calm classicism of the High Renaissance, of the art of Bramante and Raphael, and much of Mannerism is a conscious artistic revolution against the qualities summarized in Raphael: it is even possible to see Michelangelo's *Last Judgement* as a renunciation of the ideas underlying his own Sistine Ceiling. By about 1520 it was clear that the very perfection of Raphael was an impasse for his successors, leading only to pointless emulation; and his most gifted pupil, Giulio Romano, therefore turned to an exaggeration of facial expression, gesture, and lighting, derived partly from Raphael himself (the *Transfiguration*) but even more from Michelangelo, in an attempt to conquer entirely new fields of emotional expressiveness. The overwhelming greatness of Michelangelo is another major factor. His single-minded and sculptural devotion to the male nude led to many minor painters eschewing the painting of landscapes and accessories in a desire to storm the artistic heights of DISEGNO, with all its difficulties of anatomy, composition, and *contrapposto*.

On the whole, Mannerism is a style best adapted to neurotic artists such as Pontormo, Rosso, and Parmigianino, all of whom produced major works, as well as such great masters as Michelangelo, Tintoretto, and El Greco. There were also many very dull painters who strained every nerve to be neurotically interesting, but produced only frenziedly gesticulating and twisted figures in insipidly repetitive *contrapposto* derived from Michelangelo. It should be observed, however, that Mannerism had relatively little effect in Venice, where the political conditions which favoured the style in Central Italy did not obtain. From Vasari and Pellegrino TIBALDI elegant petrification set in – as in the splendidly null Court portraits of Bronzino – and the style eventually died of inanition at the hands of the Cavaliere d' ARPINO. It was succeeded by a wave of returning confidence and vitality coupled with a return to Nature in the BAROQUE. (For Antwerp Mannerism *see* ANTWERP.) [ills. 182–3, 185–6, 195–202, pp. 298–9, 302–3. Col. pl. 11]

Mantegna, Andrea (*c.* 1431–1506), was a pupil and adopted son of the archaeologist-painter SQUARCIONE, and is first recorded in the contract for the decoration of the Ovetari Chapel in the Eremitani Church (destroyed 1944) in Padua, where he completed a fresco cycle in 1459 with four scenes from the Life of S. James, an *Assumption* and a *Martyrdom of S. Christopher* (which alone survives). In these, as in his *Madonna and Saints* (*c.* 1456/9: Verona, S. Zeno) and in all his other works, his forms appear to be made of tinted stone or bronze, a result of the powerful influence of DONATELLO. The *S. Zeno Madonna* is extremely important as an early example of a SACRA CONVERSAZIONE treated as a group of figures in a single, comprehensible space instead of as a triptych or other form of subdivided space. The *S. Sebastian* (*c.* 1460: Vienna) is referred to by Vasari as in his 'stony manner' and it also shows the painter's interest in the details of classical antiquity, an interest that made him a leading expert on archaeology and tended to swamp his paintings. In 1460 he left Padua and settled as Court Painter at Mantua. There he painted the frescoes of the Camera degli Sposi (finished in 1474) in the Castello as a memorial to the Gonzaga family, whose portraits on the walls appear to the spectator to be in an extension of the room-space; while on the ceiling is a view of a balcony with figures looking down, beneath an open sky, into the room. This is the first completely illusionistic SOTTO IN SÙ decoration of the Renaissance but the idea was not exploited again until CORREGGIO and not fully developed before the Baroque. Other works executed for the Gonzaga include the *Triumph of Caesar* (*c.* 1486–94: Hampton Court, The Royal Coll.) and the *Madonna della Vittoria* (1495–6: Louvre). He painted the *Parnassus* (Louvre) for Isabella d'Este. The BELLINI were his brothers-in-law. There are other works by him in Berlin, Copenhagen, Dresden, Dublin, Florence, London, Madrid, Milan (Brera, Museo del Castello, Poldi-Pezzoli), Naples, New York, Tours, Venice, Vienna, Washington, and elsewhere. [ills. 125–8, pp. 290–1]

Manzù, Giacomo (*b.* 1908), the leading Italian sculptor, was born of poor parents in Bergamo and apprenticed to a wood-carver in 1919: after military service he went to Paris, *c.* 1927, and settled in Milan in 1930, where the Archbishop gave him his first large commission, for the Catholic University chapel. Among modern sculptors he has been influenced by Medardo ROSSO, RODIN, and

MAILLOL, but it is probable that DONATELLO has been the greatest factor, both in his exploitation of very low relief and in the feeling for drama in religious imagery. In 1939 and during the war years he made many religious works, including eight reliefs of Christ, and these culminated in the great bronze doors for St Peter's, Rome, and for Salzburg Cathedral. The commission for St Peter's was the subject of an international competition in 1949 and was given to Manzù in 1950. They were consecrated in the summer of 1964. The subject of the panels is Death in various forms. The doors for Salzburg Cathedral were completed in 1958. Manzù is also a painter and has illustrated several books. There are works by him in Antwerp (Middelheim Park), Bristol, Cleveland, London (Tate), Milan (SM in Chiesa Rossa), New York (M of MA), Rome (Gall. Moderna and S. Eugenio), and Turin. [ill. 1144, p. 432]

Maquette (Fr. small model), used only of sketches in clay, wax, etc., for sculpture. A BOZZETTO. [ill. 1138, p. 433]

Maratta (Maratti), Carlo (1625–1713), was the last representative of one aspect of Baroque art and the first Neoclassic: his ideal was a return to the calm and noble style of Raphael and the Carracci and he was opposed to the more dramatic style of PIETRO da Cortona or BACICCIA. Not surprisingly, he was a pupil of Andrea SACCHI and, like him, a fine portrait painter although most of his works are altarpieces. His enormously long career began before 1645 and he made his name in 1650 with a *Nativity* for S. Giuseppe dei Falegnami, Rome; he was still painting in 1706 and continued to teach for some years after that. Much of his work looks forward to the 18th century, as for example the *Robert, 2nd Earl of Sunderland in antique costume* which was painted in 1661 (Althorp, Earl Spencer). There are pictures by him in many of the churches and galleries of Rome, in the Royal Coll., and in Ancona, Berlin, Brussels, Cambridge (Fitzwm), Cassel, Chatsworth, Dresden, Dublin, Florence (Pitti), Greenville SC (Bob Jones University), Hanover, Leningrad, Lille, London, Madrid, Munich, Naples, Paris, Stockholm, Vaduz (Liechtenstein Coll.), Versailles, Vienna, and elsewhere. [ill. 283, p. 313]

Marc, Franz (1880–1916), was a German Expressionist painter, associated with MACKE and KANDINSKY in the BLAUE REITER. His chief subjects were animals, and his variants on the theme of the Blue Horse are perhaps his best-known works. He met DELAUNAY in Paris in 1912 and his last works (1914) are more abstract. He was killed at Verdun. [ill. 1023, p. 418]

Marées, Hans von (1837–87), was a German landscape painter who went to Italy in 1864. In 1869 he visited Spain, France, and Holland with the writer on art, Konrad Fiedler, his future biographer (*see* HILDEBRAND). He served in the Franco-Prussian War of 1870–1, but was able to return to Italy in 1873 and began his most famous work, the frescoes in the Aquarium at Naples. He spent the rest of his life in Italy, and, like BÖCKLIN and FEUERBACH, he was essentially a German Romantic who longed for Italy: unlike LEIBL, he was untouched by the Realist movement and all that it implied. In spite of his interest in wall-painting and the success of his Naples frescoes he never succeeded in obtaining another monumental commission. The style of the frescoes is similar to that of his great French contemporary, PUVIS de Chavannes. There are oil paintings by Marées in Berlin, Hamburg, and Munich. [ill. 618, p. 361]

Margarito(ne) of Arezzo, active about 1260–90 (*d.* 1293?) was one of the few Italian painters of the mid 13th century who are known to us from signed works, such as those in Arezzo, Siena, London (NG), and Washington. The London example was acquired in 1857 'to show the barbarous state into which art had sunk even in Italy previously to its revival' (under CIMABUE and GIOTTO). [ill. 6, p. 269]

Marieschi, Michele (1710 not 1696–1743), was a Venetian painter whose works have often been confused with those by other members of the same family. He was working in Saxony before 1735 but on his return to Venice he was much influenced by CANALETTO; but the vivacious quality of his own handling probably made him an influence on GUARDI. His early works seem mostly to be architectural CAPRICCI, but after his return from Germany the VEDUTE are much more accurate representations of Venice. He made a series of twenty-one etchings of views of Venice, published in 1741 as *Magnificentiores . . . Urbis Venetiarum Prospectus. . . .* There are paintings by him in Bristol, Cambridge (Fitzwm), Dublin, London (NG and Guildhall), Philadelphia, Stockholm, Venice, and Vienna (Akad.). [ill. 304, p. 316]

Marin, John (1870–1953), was an American painter, best known for his semi-abstract watercolours, often of the sea. He began as an architect, but in 1905 he went to Paris, where he was influenced by WHISTLER. He returned to the US from Europe in 1911, and in 1913 he took part in the ARMORY Show. New York (Met. Mus.), Washington (Phillips) and many other American museums have works. [ill. 1030, p. 418]

Marinetti, Filippo (1876–1944), was an Italian poet and publicist closely associated with the FUTURIST movement, which he is said to have named. His career reached its apogee in friendship with Mussolini.

Marini, Marino (*b.* 1901), is one of the leading Italian sculptors, although he began as a painter and continues to produce paintings and graphic work. He was trained in Florence and Paris and travelled extensively before settling in Milan. His bronze and wood sculpture includes many versions of the horse-and-rider theme, all of which show his great interest in archaic Greek art. Most major European and American museums have examples. [ill. 1146, p. 432]

Marinus van Reymerswaele (active 1509?–after 1567?), was a painter of three themes, all more or less caricatural. He painted a number of straightforward *S. Jeromes*, all derived from Dürer's picture of 1521 (Lisbon) but stressing the crabbedness of scholarship. The other two themes are interdependent: two exceedingly ugly and covetous *Tax Gatherers* and a *Banker and his wife* (the

banker counting his profits). The *Banker* is closely related to MASSYS's picture of the same subject, and it may be that the *Tax Gatherers* derive from Massys's borrowings from the caricatures of Leonardo da Vinci. There are about 30 versions of the *Tax Gatherers* (the best is in London, NG; another has the date 1552) and what nobody has so far explained is why so many people should want to own a picture of tax-men (and excessively ugly ones at that) gloating over their imposts. There are also examples in the Royal Coll. and in Antwerp, Berlin, Ghent, Madrid, Munich, and Vienna. [ill. 377, p. 325]

Marmion, Simon (active 1449–*d.* 89), was a painter and illuminator who worked in Amiens and Valenciennes. The most important painting attributed to him is the *S. Bertin Altarpiece* (*c.* 1459: Berlin and London, NG); other paintings attributed to him are in London (NG), New York (Met. Mus.), Paris (Louvre), Philadelphia (Johnson), Rome (Gall. Naz.), and Strasbourg. [ill. 352, p. 322]

Marquet, Albert (1875–1947), exhibited at the original FAUVE show in 1905, but never shared either the ideas or the style of the other participants. He developed into a good latter-day Impressionist, specializing in simple landscapes and town views, executed with an undemanding technique, but with a nice perception of tonal values. He was a great friend of Matisse. [ill. 1004, p. 416]

Marshall, Benjamin (1767–1835), was a British sporting painter who travelled in Italy, but who was principally influenced by STUBBS, and, in his brushwork, Raeburn. In 1819 he was crippled in a coach smash. He also wrote on horse racing, which was almost exclusively the subject of his pictures. There are examples in the Royal Coll. and in London (Tate), San Marino Cal., and Toronto. [ill. 900, p. 402]

Martin, John ('Mad') (1789–1854), was the most spectacularly melodramatic history painter of the early 19th century. He exhibited at the RA from 1811 and soon attained fame with his *Joshua commanding the Sun to stand still* (1816) and others in the next few years. He developed a type of enormous canvas, crowded with tiny figures set in fantastic architecture and beneath lowering skies that now looks merely Hollywood, but which seems to have influenced the French Romantics. He chose subjects like the *Destruction of Herculaneum* (1822: Manchester) or *The Great Day of His Wrath* (*c.* 1853: London, Tate), and the public taste soon faded, to be revived by the *Coronation of Queen Victoria* (1839: Tate). He also illustrated Milton's 'Paradise Lost' in 1827. [ill. 907, p. 403]

Martini, Simone (*c.* 1284–1344), was a Sienese painter, the pupil of DUCCIO, who developed the use of outline for the sake of linear rhythm as well as the sophisticated colour harmonies implicit in Duccio. He was also deeply influenced by the sculpture of Giovanni PISANO, and even more by French Gothic art. His first work was a large fresco of the *Maestà* (1315, reworked 1321) painted for the Town Hall of Siena as a counterpart to the huge *pala* by Duccio in the Cathedral. This shows the formative influence of Duccio on him, but there is already a perceptible Gothic influence in it which is much strengthened in his next work, the *S. Louis of Toulouse* (1317: Naples). At this date Naples was a French kingdom, ruled by Robert of Anjou, who sent for Simone and commissioned him to paint a new kind of picture; Robert's claim to the throne of Naples was not impeccable, and he therefore caused Simone to paint a large votive image of the newly canonized S. Louis of Toulouse (a member of the French Royal House) shown in the act of resigning his crown to Robert. From this time on, Simone's is essentially a Court art, refined and elegant, and much influenced by France. The type of *Madonna* evolved by Simone was of great importance in Sienese painting and may be seen in his Pisa polyptych (1320) and in several others. In 1328 Simone painted another fresco for the Town Hall, Siena, this time a commemorative equestrian portrait of the mercenary soldier Guidoriccio da Fogliano. It is one of the earliest of such commemorative images, and contains a vast panoramic landscape with the tents of the soldiers in the background. At some date not yet established Simone went to Assisi and painted a fresco cycle in S. Francesco, of scenes from the life of S. Martin, which again show both the interest in French Gothic art and the sense of chivalric pomp that distinguish Simone. His best-known, and perhaps his finest, work is the *Annunciation* (1333: Florence, Uffizi) which was painted in collaboration with his brother-in-law Lippo Memmi (d. 1357). Lippo often worked with him, but in this case they both signed the picture. It is perhaps the most splendid example of pure craftsmanship produced in Siena in the 14th century, with its elaborate tooling of the burnished and matt gold, but it is also an almost abstract essay in pure line and two-dimensional pattern, at the furthest possible remove from either Giotto or even their Sienese contemporary Ambrogio LOREN-ZETTI. In 1340/1 Simone went to France. It seems that he went on official business, and not as a painter, to the Curia at Avignon, where the Papacy was then established, and in this Franco-Italian enclave he spent the rest of his life. There he painted the jewel-like *Christ returning to His Parents after disputing with the Doctors* (1342: Liverpool), a most unusual subject that probably once formed half of a diptych. In Avignon he met Petrarch and became friendly with him, illustrating a Virgil codex for him (Milan, Ambrosiana); he also painted frescoes in the Cathedral, of which a few fragments remain. His influence on French 14th-century painting is hard to assess, but a century later the Sienese (so Ghiberti informs us) regarded him as their greatest painter. There are works in Antwerp, Berlin, Birmingham (Gall. and Barber Inst.), Boston (Gardner Mus.), Cambridge (Fitzwm) and Cambridge Mass. (Fogg), Leningrad, London (Courtauld Inst.), Naples, New Haven Conn. (Jarves Coll.), New York (Met. Mus.), Orvieto (Cath.), Ottawa, Paris (Louvre), Siena (S. Agostino), the Vatican, Washington (NG), and elsewhere. [ill. 43, p. 275]

Masaccio (1401–probably 28), was born Tommaso di Ser Giovanni di Mone and nicknamed 'Masaccio' (Hulking Tom). He was the first and arguably the greatest of the succession of great masters in 15th-century Florence; certainly the greatest in that he achieved so much in a lifetime of 27 years. He is first recorded as a painter in 1422, when he entered the Guild in Florence, which disproves the tradition that he was MASOLINO's pupil,

since Masolino did not register with the Guild (and therefore could not take pupils) until 1423. The first major work by Masaccio for which documentary evidence exists is the Pisa Polyptych, painted for the Carmelite Church in Pisa in 1426, but now dismembered and largely lost. The central panel, of the *Madonna and Child*, is now in the NG, London, and shows that, at the age of 25, Masaccio had already developed his austere and heroic style in opposition to the INTERNATIONAL GOTHIC then being so successfully practised in Florence by GENTILE da Fabriano. This new style, in its realism, sobriety of gesture, narrative power, and the economy with which it creates its effects of space, light, and solidity of form, is akin to Giotto's, and is comparable among contemporaries only with the humanist and intellectual art then being developed by the much older DONATELLO in sculpture and Brunelleschi in architecture. For this reason Masaccio has always been regarded as one of the founders of modern painting. Between the end of 1425 and his death, probably at the end of 1428, Masaccio certainly painted a fresco of the *Trinity* in Sta Maria Novella, Florence, and his major surviving work, the frescoes in the Brancacci Chapel of the Carmelite Church in Florence (Sta Maria del Carmine). The Chapel was decorated with scenes from the Lives of the Apostles and may have been begun by Masolino in 1425, but a large part of the frescoes, including the earlier ones, perished in the 18th century. Those that survive are by three hands – a 15th-century source says that the Chapel was 'painted by three masters, all good but he [Masaccio] was marvellous' – and the puzzle is to sort out the shares. The parts by Filippino LIPPI are half a century later and easily distinguishable, and approximate agreement has now been reached over the remainder, it being generally accepted that the *Expulsion* on the entrance arch, the *Tribute Money*, parts of the *Raising of the Praetor's Son* and all of *S. Peter enthroned*, *S. Peter's shadow healing the sick*, *S. Peter giving alms*, are by Masaccio, while the *Baptism of the Neophytes* is probably by him, but is sometimes contested. The remainder of the original commission is by Masolino. Again, Masaccio's style is fully realistic and uncompromisingly grand, which probably explains why these frescoes long served as an art school without enjoying general popularity. Indeed, much of later 15th-century painting flatly contradicts the principles enunciated in the Brancacci Chapel. Parts of the frescoes may still have been incomplete when Masaccio went to Rome and died there. The remaining parts of the Pisa Polyptych are in Naples, Pisa, Vienna, and Berlin. Other works by or attributed to him are in Berlin, Boston (Isabella Gardner Mus.), Florence (Uffizi and Horne Mus.), London (NG), Montemarciano, and Washington (NG). [ills. 57, 58, 59, p. 277. Col. pl. 2]

Maso di Banco, active in the second quarter of the 14th century, was perhaps the greatest of Giotto's followers, and the only one to retain something of Giotto's amplitude of form; indeed, some of his figures are even more massive than Giotto's. The only work that can be attributed to him with certainty is the fresco cycle of *S. Sylvester and the Emperor Constantine* in Sta Croce, conveniently placed for comparison with Giotto. Other works are attributed to him – in Assisi, Berlin, Edinburgh, Florence, and elsewhere – but it is now agreed that he is not identical with

GIOTTINO, and a good many revisions will be necessary. [ill. 28, p. 273]

Masolino (*c.* 1383/4–1447?), was not the master of MASACCIO, as Vasari thought, but rather his pupil for a short time, in spite of the great difference of age. Masolino may have worked under Ghiberti on the First Baptistry Doors (1403/7), and this would explain his normal INTERNATIONAL GOTHIC style. He entered the Guild of Painters in Florence in 1423 – there is nothing to explain what he was doing 1407–23 – and in the same year painted a *Madonna* (Bremen) which shows the influence of Late Trecento art, and Lorenzo Monaco in particular. In 1427 he went to Hungary, but it is probable that he worked in the Brancacci Chapel in Sta Maria del Carmine in the interval; there he came under the influence of Masaccio to such an extent that it is not easy to distinguish them. He may also have worked in the Brancacci Chapel after Masaccio's death (1428) and before he went to Rome *c.* 1430 to decorate a chapel in S. Clemente for Cardinal Branda Castiglione, for whom he later worked in Castiglione d'Olona, near Como, one of the frescoes being dated 1435: the frescoes in the Collegiata and the Baptistry are very markedly less Masacciesque than those in the Brancacci Chapel and it would seem therefore that Masolino reverted in his last years to the style he had practised as a young man. There are other works in Detroit, Empoli, London (NG), Munich, Naples, New York (Met. Mus.), Philadelphia (Johnson), Todi, the Vatican, and Washington (NG). [ill. 56, p. 276]

Masses. In art criticism, the masses are the largest, simplest, and most fundamental shapes to which the component parts of a painting, a piece of sculpture, or a building can be reduced. To think (or see) in masses means the ability not to be distracted by unimportant detail and to concentrate on the forms which must be completely realized for a satisfactory aesthetic effect. Such an effect may be totally different from a naturalistic representation.

Massys (Matsys, Metsys), Quentin (1464/5–1530), was born at Louvain but became a Master in the Antwerp Guild in 1491. His earliest certain work is the *S. Anne Triptych* (1509: centre in Brussels, wings in the Liechtenstein Coll.), a large work painted in clear, pale, cool colour, with a subject – the Kinship of the Holy Family – traditional in the North. Many of his works introduce landscape backgrounds of fantastic wooded and rocky mountains some of which may have been painted by PATENIER, and the type became common among Antwerp painters. His use of *contrapposto* and of florid architectural detail of a debased classical type suggest some knowledge of Italian art, and he also knew a version of Leonardo's *Madonna and Child with S. Anne* (Louvre). He may have visited Italy between 1514 and 1519. In the latter year he built himself a house in Antwerp with a frescoed façade and a polychromed statue, which was visited by Dürer in 1520, although he failed to find Massys at home. He painted genre subjects such as the *Banker and his Wife* (1514: Louvre) which may have a recondite religious or moral significance, and is connected with other contemporary paintings of bankers, money-lenders, or tax-gatherers (cf.

MARINUS), and the *Ill-matched Pair*, with caricature types and an equivocal moral lesson. This is probably connected with Prodigal Son subjects and is the ancestor of the Flemish tavern scene picture. Besides his portraits of sitters seen against a landscape, Massys introduced a new type, derived from paintings of S. Jerome, of the scholar in his setting of desk, books, and papers, and used this form appropriately for his *Erasmus* (1517: Rome, Gall. Naz.) and his *Egidius* (Longford Castle Coll.), both of which look forward to portraits by van Orley and Holbein. There are works by him in Antwerp, Berlin, Brussels, Chicago, Detroit, Frankfurt (Städel), Lisbon, London (NG), Lyons, Madrid (Prado), Munich, New York (Met. Mus.), Ottawa, Paris (Louvre, Mus. Jacquemart-André), Philadelphia (Johnson), Poznan, Vaduz (Liechtenstein Coll.), Venice (Doge's Pal.), and Vienna. [ill. 370, p. 324]

Master of the Aix Annunciation. A triptych of the *Annunciation* and two *Prophets* was completed in 1445 and placed in the Église des Prêcheurs, Aix-en-Provence. The *Annunciation* is still there, but one of the wings is now in Brussels and the other is divided into two parts, one in Amsterdam (Rijksmus.) and the other in Rotterdam. The style of the altarpiece shows many points of contact with Flemish art, and others with the art of Naples; various identifications have been suggested, but it is likely that the painter was a Frenchman, and Jean Chapus, who lived in Aix and was working for King René of Anjou in 1437 and 1448, seems to fit the bill. [ill. 665, p. 372]

Master of S. Bartholomew (active in the late 15th and early 16th centuries). A German painter whose name derives from an altarpiece formerly in S. Columba, Cologne, and now in Munich. Two other altarpieces by him are still in Cologne and probably date from *c.* 1500, although the *S. Bartholomew Altar* itself is perhaps as late as 1510. The painter was probably a Cologne man, but his earliest works show the influence of the Netherlands, especially Roger van der WEYDEN and the School of Utrecht, so that it is sometimes suggested that he may have worked in Utrecht *c.* 1470. This influence is seen in a *Virgin and Child with S. Anne*, now in Munich. His work is characterized by bright enamel-like colour; there are examples in Berlin, Brussels, London (NG and Courtauld Inst.), and Paris (Petit Palais and Louvre: based on Roger van der Weyden's Escorial *Deposition*). [ill. 552, p. 353]

Master of S. Cecilia, an unknown Italian painter active before 1304, influenced by GIOTTO, who painted the *S. Cecilia Altarpiece* (Florence, Uffizi). The most important attribution to him is the beginning and end of the fresco cycle of S. Francis at Assisi. In recent years attempts have been made to attribute the whole cycle to him, an honour for which he seems unfitted. [ill. 19, p. 271]

Master of the Death of the Virgin. A painter, active 1507–37, who is named from two altarpieces of the *Death of the Virgin* in Cologne and Munich. He is often identified with JOOS van Cleve, and certainly he influenced BRUYN. [ill. 369, p. 324]

Master of Flémalle. A name given to the painter of some pictures in Frankfurt (Städel) which are (wrongly) supposed to have come from Flémalle. He is also supposed to have painted another fragment in Frankfurt, the *Merode Altar* now in New York (Met. Mus.), the *Werl Altar* dated 1438 in the Prado, Madrid, pictures in the NG, London, and some other works. His style is slightly earlier than that of Jan van Eyck, but almost as revolutionary in its naturalism. An *Entombment* (private coll., London), thought to be his earliest work, is probably earlier than any surviving painting by Jan. Various attempts have been made to identify him, the most satisfactory being that which equates him with CAMPIN and the least satisfactory that which identifies him with Roger van der WEYDEN, whose style is certainly similar but more subtle – and there is evidence that Roger was Campin's pupil. [ills. 337, 338, p. 320]

Master of S. Giles (active *c.* 1500) was a Flemish painter (or Flemish-trained painter) who worked in France. He is named after the two *Scenes from the Legend of S. Giles* in London (NG); two other panels, now in Washington (NG) have been connected with the *S. Giles* ones, but they seem to come from another altarpiece by the same hand. Other pictures attributed to him are in Berlin, Boston, Brussels, Chantilly (Musée Condé), and Paris (Louvre). [ill. 353, p. 322]

Master of the Housebook (Meister des Hausbuchs) was a Rhenish or Dutch painter, draughtsman, and engraver active in the last quarter of the 15th century. He is named from a series of drawings in the so-called *Hausbuch* in Schloss Wolfegg; many of the drawings show scenes of everyday life and so do the engravings (about 90 are known) attributed to him. By far the best collection of the engravings is in Amsterdam Print Room, and he was therefore once known as the *Master of the Amsterdam Cabinet*. Because of this, and because he seems to fit into the Bosch-Bruegel tradition, he is often thought to have been Dutch and various identifications have been suggested: the latest is Erhard Reuwich, who worked on the Middle Rhine *c.* 1480. A few paintings are also ascribed to him, including the *Pair of Lovers* (Gotha) and one in Frankfurt (Städel), but his work as an engraver was historically far more important. [ill. 545, p. 352]

Master of the Life of Mary (Master of the Life of the Virgin, Meister des Marienlebens) (active *c.* 1463/5–*c.* 1480/90) was a Cologne painter whose name derives from a series of 8 panels of *Scenes from the Life of the Virgin*, formerly in S. Ursula, Cologne, and now divided between Munich (7) and the NG, London (1). The altarpiece is known to have been the gift of a Councillor who was active *c.* 1460, while a *Crucifixion with Nicholas of Cusa as Donor* (Cues, Hospital church) seems to date from *c.* 1465. The Master may have been trained in the Netherlands, since his style is based on Roger van der WEYDEN and, especially, BOUTS, with skinny figures, rather small in scale and lost among their surroundings. The Master of the Lyversberg Passion may be identical with the Master of the Life of Mary, while the Master of Werden is probably only an aspect of his studio. [ill. 553, p. 353]

Master of the Life of the Virgin *see* MASTER of the LIFE of MARY.

Master of the Lyversberg Passion. A German painter responsible for a Passion series (now in Cologne), which

was at one time thought to be the work of the MASTER of the LIFE of MARY. The relationship between the two masters is very close indeed, but is not necessarily that of identity.

Master of Merode *see* MASTER OF FLÉMALLE.

Master of Moulins (active *c.* 1480–*c.* 99), has been identified with PERRÉAL and a number of other painters including, most recently, Jean Prévost (active 1470–*d.* 1504), a Lyons painter who collaborated with Perréal. He was one of the great French 15th-century painters, much influenced by Hugo van der Goes, and takes his name from a triptych of the *Madonna and Child with Angels and Donors* in Moulins Cathedral datable *c.* 1498/9. Other works attributed to him are in Autun (Mus.), Brussels, Chicago, Glasgow, London (NG, Wallace Coll.), Munich, Paris (Louvre). [ill. 351, p. 323]

Master of the Osservanza *see* SASSETTA.

Master of Oultremont *see* MOSTAERT.

Master of Třeboň *see* MASTER OF WITTINGAU.

Master of the Virgo inter Virgines. The Virgo Master was a Dutch painter active *c.* 1470–*c.* 1500 who was influenced by BOSCH and GEERTGEN and who ranks with them as an artist, although almost nothing is known about him. He was perhaps working in Delft 1490/95, where he seems to have influenced woodcut book-illustrations for which he may have made the designs. His name is derived from the *Madonna and Child with Four Female Saints* (*Virgo inter Virgines*) in Amsterdam (Rijksmus.). There are important pictures by him in Barnard Castle (Bowes Mus.), and Liverpool, and others in Berlin, Brussels, Chicago, Florence (Uffizi), Glasgow (Burrell Coll.), St Louis, Milan (Brera), New York (Met. Mus.), Philadelphia, Rotterdam, Vienna, and elsewhere. [ill. 346, p. 323]

Master of Werden. The painter of a series of panels, in the NG, London, which have now been reattributed to the Studio of the MASTER of the LIFE of MARY.

Master of Wittingau (Master of the Třeboň Altarpiece). In the NG of Prague there are three double-sided panels representing three Passion scenes and three sets of Saints, from an altarpiece in a church at Třeboň (Wittingau) in Czechoslovakia. They date from about 1390 and represent the next stage in Bohemian painting after Master THEODORIC, being related to the SOFT STYLE. The Master may have gone on working until *c.* 1420. [ill. 538, p. 351]

Master of 1456 *see* FOUQUET.

Matière (Fr. material). The *matière* of a picture is simply paint.

Matisse, Henri (1869–1954), was the principal artist of the FAUVE group. He was a pupil of the academician Bouguereau for a few months in 1892, and from 1892 to 1897 was a pupil of Gustave MOREAU, in whose studio he met Rouault, Marquet, Manguin, Camoin, and Piot. He copied in the Louvre, and was strongly influenced by Impressionism, and his *Dinner Table* (*La Desserte*) of 1897 shows him working close to Bonnard and Vuillard. In 1901 he first met Vlaminck in the company of Derain, whom he already knew. He tried the Divisionist technique about 1899, but turned to Cézanne by 1901–3, painting in strongly modelled form and dark tones to offset the rather superficial quality of Signac's bright colour. The influence of Signac was renewed in 1904 when Matisse stayed with him in the South of France, and this renewed contact probably started the train which led to the explosion of colour of the FAUVE movement. This came in 1905, but in the midst of the general abuse Matisse acquired patrons in the Stein family who encouraged him, bought pictures and encouraged other Americans to buy, and later the Russians Shchukin and Morosov became his chief patrons. Exhibitions in Germany followed and in 1908–10 Matisse ran a school which was thronged by American, German, and, above all, Scandinavian pupils. By this time Picasso had appeared on the scene, and after all the years of pre-paration for the leadership of modern painting, Matisse found that the artistic centre of gravity had shifted to CUBISM. In 1910 Matisse saw the exhibition of Near Eastern art at Munich, and it is clear that this highly decorative and brilliantly coloured art had a deep and lasting influence on him, particularly in his development of flat patterns with arabesques, flowered backgrounds, and in his use of brilliant and pure colours either juxtaposed or separated only by thin white lines or contours (*anti-cernes*). He travelled widely in Europe and North Africa (and also visited America and Oceania), and in 1914 went to Nice for the winter, to remain for most of the rest of his life on the Riviera, where he painted the long series of Odalisque and still-life subjects which are his main *œuvre*. He had done a certain amount of sculpture from the start of his career, but it never assumed an importance equal to that of his painting; he also made several illustrated books, notably editions of Ronsard and Baudelaire, done at the end of the Second World War. His last major work was the decoration of the interior of the Chapel of Dominican nuns at Vence, and in his last years he used a mixture of cut-outs in coloured paper with gouache and crayons to overcome the handicaps of age and illness.

Matisse's works are to be found in nearly every museum of Modern Art throughout the world. The two largest collections are the Moscow collection, made up of paintings bought by Shchukin and Morosov, and that at the Barnes Foundation at Merion Pa, which contains, among other important works, the huge murals of the *Dance* done in 1932–3. [ills. 1001, 1002, p. 416]

Matsys *see* MASSYS.

Matta (i.e. Roberto Sebastiano Matta Echaurren) (*b*. 1912) is a Chilean painter, now living in Paris, who began as an architect (1934) under Le Corbusier. From 1938 to 1947 he was a Surrealist, and is still a Freudian. He went to the US in 1939, where he met DUCHAMP. There are works by him in New York (M of MA). [ill. 1117, p. 429]

Matteo di Giovanni (*c*. 1435–95), a Sienese painter, was a pupil of VECCHIETTA. In Borgo San Sepolcro he com-pleted in 1465 the polyptych of which the central panel

(*Baptism of Christ*, London, NG) was by PIERO della Francesca. His linear and decorative style also shows the influence of POLLAIUOLO. There are works in Bir-mingham (Barber Inst.), London (NG), and Siena (Mus. and Cath.). [ill. 113, p. 288]

Mattoir *see* ENGRAVING (*d*).

Maulbertsch (Maulpertsch), Franz Anton (1724–96), was the major Viennese painter of the 18th century, becoming a member of the Academy in 1759 and Professor in 1770. There is no record of his having been to Italy, although it seems highly likely that he did so. Almost all his works are frescoes and altarpieces in Austrian, Hungarian, and Czech churches, which combine a certain Rembrandt influence with a very marked similarity to contemporary Venetian decorative painters such as PITTONI. There are sketches by him in Vienna (Barock-mus.) but most of his works are still in the churches for which they were painted. [ill. 590, p. 358]

Mazo, Juan Bautista del (*c*. 1612/16–67), was the pupil of VELAZQUEZ, whose daughter he married in 1634. He had an appointment in the Royal Household by 1646 and succeeded to his father-in-law's position as Court Painter in 1661. His close relationship to Velazquez has led to the attribution to him of several pictures not considered good enough for Velazquez: his own style is not sufficiently dis-tinguished to prevent this. There are very few certain works by him, but one is the *Queen Mariana* of 1666 (London, NG). The *Artist's Family* (Vienna) is almost certainly his, and there are other pictures in Madrid (Prado). A good example of the Velazquez-type portrait is the *Admiral Pulido Pareja* (London, NG) which is now attributed to Mazo. [ill. 643, p. 364]

Medici e Speziali. The Florentine GUILD of Doctors and Apothecaries to which the painters belonged. This seems to have been on account of their using rare minerals like lapis lazuli, which were part of the druggist's stock-in-trade.

Medina, Sir John Baptist (*c*. 1655/60–1710), was a portrait painter of Spanish descent, born in Brussels, who worked in London – in the style of KNELLER – from 1686 until 1693/4 when he went to Edinburgh and introduced the Kneller style there with a stock of ready-painted figures requiring only the faces. There are 31 portraits by him in the Royal College of Surgeons, Edinburgh, and others in Edinburgh (NPG), Glasgow, and Florence (Pitti), and Providence RI [ill. 818, p. 393]

Medium. The liquid used to bind powdered colour to make paint. By extension, the various techniques of painting: thus, the oil medium is oil painting; powdered colour mixed to a thick consistency with oil, usually linseed. Other media are size (for distemper), egg yolk (for tempera), and gum arabic for watercolour or pastel. In a more general sense it is possible to talk of pen-and-ink or pencil as media.

Melozzo da Forlì (1438–94), was famous in the 16th century as the inventor of extreme foreshortening –

SOTTO IN SÙ. Most of his works exist in such fragmentary condition that it is impossible to be sure if this is correct, but it is clear that he was connected with PIERO della Francesca. His *Platina appointed Vatican Librarian* (1477: Vatican) shows his knowledge of perspective and a certain link with Piero. Some fragments of an important fresco are in the Vatican, but his dome (1493/4) in S. Biagio, Forlì, was destroyed 1939/45. There are frescoes at Loreto. [ill. 119, p. 289]

Memlinc (Memling), Hans (*d.* 1494), was born at Seligenstadt, near Frankfurt-am-Main, but was traditionally – and very probably – a pupil of Roger van der WEYDEN. His art is purely Netherlandish and he seems to have spent his life in Bruges, where he became a citizen in 1465 and where, in 1480, he was one of the largest tax-payers. He painted calm and pious pictures, full of the restrained piety of the later Middle Ages, and some excellent portraits, but he added nothing to what he took from Roger van der Weyden and Dirk BOUTS. There are several dated works in Bruges (Mus. and Hôpital de S. Jean) and others range from 1472 (Ottawa) to the *Passion Altar* in Lübeck, commissioned in 1491 and finished by his shop. Other works are in the Royal Coll. and Antwerp, Berlin, Boston, Brussels, Chicago, Cincinnati, Cleveland, Cologne, Copenhagen, Danzig (Marienkirche), Florence (Uffizi), Frankfurt (Städel), Granada (Capilla Real), The Hague, Lisbon, London (NG, Wallace Coll.), Madrid (Prado), Melbourne, Montreal, Munich, New York (Met. Mus.), Paris (Louvre, Mus. Jacquemart-André), Philadelphia (Johnson), Toledo, Turin, Venice, Vicenza, Vienna (K-H and Akad.), and Washington (NG). [ill. 348, p. 322]

Mengs, Anton Raffael (1728–79), the most celebrated exponent of NEOCLASSICISM, was the son of the Dresden Court Painter who named him Anton (after Correggio) and Raffael (= Raphael) and brought him up with excessive severity to be a great painter. The boy was taken to Rome in 1741 and soon developed into something of a prodigy, specializing in pastel portraits. He was made Court Painter at Dresden in 1745, but his real career began in 1755, when he met WINCKELMANN, who praised him highly and whose theories Mengs adopted in return. He wrote a treatise on Beauty in Painting (published in 1762), which was apparently borrowed by an Englishman named Daniel Webb who published it as his own in 1760, when it had a considerable success. Mengs's first major work in Rome was the ceiling of S. Eusebio (1757–8), which cannot be called Neoclassical, but after this he went to see the antiquities then being excavated at Herculaneum, drew them, and returned to Rome to paint his best-known work, the *Parnassus* (1761: Rome, Villa Albani), which breaks completely with the Baroque tradition of illusionism and treats the ceiling like a relief, composed from drawings after the Antique, and seen orthogonally – i.e. as if it were at the spectator's eye-level, and not SOTTO IN SÙ. In 1761 he went to Spain as Court Painter and began decorating the Royal Palaces; when TIEPOLO arrived he found Mengs formidably entrenched, but Mengs's ceilings are markedly less Neoclassic in face of the competition from Tiepolo. In 1771 he returned to Italy and worked in the Vatican 1772–3. He went back to Spain 1773–7 and died in

Rome. He had met VIEN in Rome, and, like him, he was not really more than a precursor for the full Neoclassicism of DAVID, who arrived in Rome in 1775. Mengs was a fine portrait painter, and in this he was close in style to his principal rival, BATONI. There are works by him in Dresden and in Cardiff, Liverpool, London (NPG, Wellington Mus.), Madrid (Prado), Milan, Naples, Oxford (All Souls College), Paris (Louvre), and Vienna. [ill. 592, p. 359]

Menzel, Adolf (1815–1905), was one of the leading German painters of the 19th century. He was trained in Berlin and took over his father's business as a lithographer in 1832, thus beginning a long career as an illustrator. Perhaps his most important graphic works are the drawings for the Life of Frederick the Great (1840–2), which were admired by Degas. In 1839 he saw some pictures by Constable in Berlin and in the 1840s and 1850s he made a series of paintings which are very free in handling and seem to anticipate Impressionism, although later he rejected the theory. There are pictures by him in many German museums and in London (Tate). [ill. 619, p. 361]

Meryon, Charles (1821–68), ranks with Piranesi as the greatest of architectural etchers. He was the illegitimate son of an English doctor and a dancer at the Opéra and began his career in the French Navy, spending 1842–6 in the South Pacific. There are some drawings of exotic scenes and ships, but his reputation rests on the great series of views of Paris, described by Victor Hugo as 'visions', which he began *c.* 1850. The series ranges from straightforward *vedute* through Romantic horror (the *Gargoyle of Notre-Dame*, the *Morgue*) to uncomfortable fantasies like the *Ministry of Marine with flying Devils*. The series was not popular, and Meryon was very difficult in his personal character: he spent 1858–9 in an asylum and also the last two years of his life, believing himself to be Christ. All his etchings date from 1849 to 1866. He also drew Dr Gachet, later to befriend Van Gogh in his madness. [ills. 789–90, p. 388]

Merz *see* SCHWITTERS.

Meštrović, Ivan (1883–1962), was the greatest Yugoslav sculptor. He was the son of Dalmatian peasants and began as a wood-carver, later serving an apprenticeship to a mason. He studied in Vienna until 1904 and his early works, reflecting the Yugoslav patriotic movement, soon brought him fame. The freedom of his handling gave his work a certain kinship to that of RODIN. He went to America in 1947 and died there. There are examples of his religious works and also of his portraiture in London (Tate), and others in American museums, Belgrade, and in Zagreb. [ill. 1119, p. 430]

Metsu, Gabriel (1629–67), was a Dutch painter, born in Leyden but mainly active in Amsterdam, of interiors and genre subjects, representing nice, clean, and well-behaved people. He also painted a few portraits, religious subjects, and perhaps some still-life. He was probably a pupil of DOU and was slightly influenced by Rembrandt, but on the whole he closely resembles Ter Borch and De Hooch and his works can be confused with theirs. In his best works, such as the *Sick Child* (Amsterdam, Rijksmus.), he approaches Vermeer. There are works by him in the Royal Coll. and in Aix, Amsterdam, Berlin, Boston, Brussels, Cape Town, Cheltenham, Dresden, Florence (Uffizi), The Hague, Leningrad, London (NG, Wallace Coll.), Montpellier, Munich, New York (Met. Mus.), Oxford, Paris (Louvre), Rotterdam, Stockholm, Venice, Vienna (Akad., K-H Mus.), and Washington (NG). [ill. 512, p. 347]

Metzinger, Jean (1883–1956), became a Cubist painter and, with GLEIZES, published in 1912 'Du Cubisme', the first book on the movement (English edition, 1913). He used the flat-pattern type of Cubism in rather bright colour. [ill. 1047, p. 421]

Mezzo-Rilievo *see* RELIEF.

Mezzotint *see* ENGRAVING.

Michel, Georges (1763–1843), was employed by the Louvre on the cleaning and restoration of, principally, Dutch pictures, and the influence of Dutch 17th-century landscapes is clearly visible in his own works. He rarely moved away from his native Paris, and declared that no painter needs more than four square miles in which to find all the subjects he desires. Michel's simple pictures of muddy lanes, stormy skies, and unprettified fields and heaths are probably late works; they presage the landscape based on the observation of nature alone, exploited by the BARBIZON School, and his concentration on tone rather than colour links him with COROT. There are works in Besançon, Berwick-on-Tweed, Cambridge (Fitzwm), Edinburgh, Glasgow, Hanover, Leningrad, London (NG and V & A), Paris (Louvre), Strasbourg, and elsewhere. [ill. 759, p. 385]

Michelangelo Buonarroti (1475–1564), was born at Caprese, in Florentine territory, where his father was resident magistrate. A few weeks after Michelangelo's birth the family returned to Florence, and, in 1488, after overcoming parental opposition he was formally apprenticed to Domenico GHIRLANDAIO for a term of three years. Later in life Michelangelo tried to suppress this fact, probably to make it seem that he had never had an ordinary workshop training, for it was he more than anyone else who introduced the idea of the 'Fine' Arts having no connection with the craft which painting had always previously been. In fact his stay in the Ghirlandaio shop must have been very short, for it was probably later in the same year that he was transferred to the School set up in the Medici Garden under the direct patronage of Lorenzo de' Medici, 'Il Magnifico', and supervised by BERTOLDO; nevertheless, it must have been Ghirlandaio who taught him the elements of fresco technique, and it was probably also in that shop that he made his drawings after the great Florentine masters of the past (copies after Giotto and Masaccio; now in the Louvre, in Munich, and in Vienna). In 1492 his patron Lorenzo de' Medici died. The next few years were marked by the expulsion of the Medici and the gloomy Theocracy set up under Savonarola, but Michelangelo avoided the worst of the crises by going to Bologna, and, in 1496, to Rome. There he carved the first of his major works, the *Bacchus* (Florence, Bargello) and the St Peter's

Pietà, which was completed at the turn of the century. It is highly finished and shows that he had already mastered anatomy and the disposition of drapery, but above all it shows that he had solved the problem presented by the representation of a full-grown man stretched out nearly horizontally on the lap of a woman, the whole being contained in a pyramidal shape: in this it is the consummation of everything the sculptors of the 15th century had striven to attain. The *Pietà* made his name and he returned to Florence in 1501 as a famous sculptor, remaining there until 1505. During these years he was extremely active, carving the gigantic *David* (1501–4: now in the Accad.), the *Bruges Madonna* (Bruges, Notre Dame), and beginning the series of the *Twelve Apostles* for the Cathedral which was commissioned in 1503 but never completed (the *S. Matthew* now in the Accad. is the only one which was even sketched in). At about this time he also painted the *Doni Tondo* (Florence, Uffizi). After the completion of the *David* in 1504 he began work on the cartoon for a huge fresco in the Council Hall of the new Florentine Republic, as a pendant to the one already commissioned from Leonardo da Vinci. Both remained unfinished and the grandiose project of employing the two greatest living artists on the decoration of the Town Hall of their native city came to nothing. Of Michelangelo's fresco, which was to represent an incident in the Pisan War, we now have a few studies by him and copies of the only fragment of the whole which was actually begun as a full-scale cartoon (the best copy is the painting in Lord Leicester's Coll., Holkham, Norfolk). This cartoon, which is known as the *Bathers*, was for many years the resort of every young artist in Florence, and, by its exclusive stress on the nude human body as a sufficient vehicle for the expression of all emotions which the painter can depict, had an enormous influence on the subsequent development of Italian art – especially MANNERISM – and therefore on European art as a whole. This influence is more readily detectable in his next major work, the ceiling of the Sistine Chapel. In fact, however, the *Battle of Cascina* was left incomplete because the Signoria of Florence found it expedient to comply with a request from the masterful Pope Julius II, who was anxious to have a fitting tomb made in his lifetime. The Julius Monument was, in Michelangelo's own view, the Tragedy of the Tomb. This was partly because Michelangelo and Julius had the same ardent temperament – they admired each other deeply – and very soon quarrelled, and partly because, after the death of Julius in 1513, Michelangelo was under constant pressure from Popes and Princes to abandon his contractual obligations and work for them while equally under pressure from the heirs of Julius, who at one time went so far as to accuse him of embezzlement. The original project was for a vast freestanding Tomb with forty figures but this was substantially reduced in the second contract (1513), drawn up after Julius's death; under this contract the *Moses*, which is the major figure on the extant Tomb, was prepared as a subsidiary figure. Two others, the *Slaves* in the Louvre, were made under this contract but were subsequently abandoned. The third contract (1516) was followed by a fourth (1532) and a fifth and final one in 1542, under the terms of which the present miserably mutilated version of the original conception was carried out by assistants, under Michelangelo's supervision, in S. Pietro in Vincoli

(Julius II's titular church) in 1545. Michelangelo was then 70 and had spent nearly 40 years on the Tomb.

Meanwhile, the original quarrel of 1506 with Julius was made up and Michelangelo executed a colossal bronze statue of the Pope as an admonition to the recently conquered Bolognese (who destroyed it as soon as they could, in 1511). In 1508, back in Rome, he began his most important work, the Ceiling of the Sistine Chapel in the Vatican for Julius, who, as usual, was impatient to see it finished. Dissatisfied with the normal working methods and with the abilities of the assistants he had engaged, Michelangelo determined to execute the whole of this vast area virtually alone. Working under appalling difficulties (amusingly described in one of his own sonnets), most of the time lying down and never able to get far enough away from the ceiling to be able to see what he was doing, he completed the first half (the part nearer to the door) in 1510. There followed a longish break, while new scaffolding was prepared. The whole enormous undertaking was completed in 1512, Michelangelo being by then so practised that he was able to execute the second half much more rapidly and freely. It was at once recognized as a supreme work of art, even at the moment when Raphael was also at work in the Vatican Stanze. From then on Michelangelo was universally regarded as the greatest living artist, although he was then only 37 and this was in the lifetimes of Leonardo and Raphael (who was even younger). From this moment, too, dates the idea of the artist as in some sense a superhuman being, set apart from ordinary men, and for the first time it was possible to use the phrase il divino Michelangelo without seeming merely blasphemous.

The Sistine Ceiling is a shallow barrel-vault divided up by painted architecture into a series of alternating large and small panels which appear to be open to the sky. These are the Histories. Each of the smaller panels is surrounded by four figures of nude youths – the Slaves, or Ignudi – who are represented as seated on the architectural frame and who are not of the same order of reality as the figures in the Histories, since their system of perspective is different. Below them are the Prophets and Sibyls, and still lower, the figures of the Ancestors of Christ. The whole Ceiling completes the Chapel decoration by representing life on earth before the Law: on the walls are frescoes, painted in 1481–2, representing the Life of Moses (i.e. the Old Dispensation) and the Life of Christ (the New Dispensation). The Histories begin over the altar and work away from it (though they were painted in the reverse direction): the first scene represents God alone, in the Primal Act of Creation and the story continues through the rest of the Creation to the Fall, the Flood, and the Drunkenness of Noah, representing the human soul at its furthest from God. The whole conception owes much to the Neoplatonist philosophy current in Michelangelo's youth in Florence, perhaps most in the idea of the Ignudi, perfect human beauty, on the level immediately below the Divine story. Below them come the Old Testament Prophets and the Seers of the ancient world who foretold the coming of Christ; while the four corners have scenes from the Old Testament representing Salvation. The Prophet Jonah is above the altar, since his three days in the whale were held to prefigure the Resurrection. On the lowest and darkest parts – and very freely painted – are the human families who were the Ancestors of Christ. There can be no doubt that the splendour of this conception and the size of the task distracted Michelangelo from the Tomb, but he at once returned to it as soon as the Ceiling was finished, from 1513 to 1516, when he returned to Florence to work for the Medici.

His new master was Pope Leo X, the younger son of Lorenzo de' Medici, who had known Michelangelo from boyhood and who now commissioned him to complete the façade of S. Lorenzo, the family church in Florence. Michelangelo wasted four years on this and it came to nothing. In 1520 he began planning the Medici Chapel, a funerary chapel in honour of four of the Medici – two of them by no means the most glorious of their family. The chapel is attached to S. Lorenzo. Leo X died in 1521 and it was not until after the accession of another Medici Pope, Clement VII, in 1523 that this project was resumed. Work began in earnest in 1524 and at the same time he was commissioned to design the Laurenziana Library in the cloister of the same church. Both these buildings are turning-points in architectural history, but the sculptural decoration of the Chapel (an integral part of the architecture) was never completed, although the figures of Giuliano and Lorenzo de' Medici set over their tombs, above symbols of Time and Mortality – Day and Night, Dawn and Evening – eternally symbolize the Active and the Contemplative Life and are among his finest creations. The unfinished Madonna was meant as the focal point of the Chapel. In 1527 the Medici were again expelled from Florence, and Michelangelo, who was politically a Republican in spite of his close ties with the Medici, took an active part in the defence of Florence up to the capitulation in 1530, although in a moment of panic he had fled in 1529. After the reinstatement of the Medici he was pardoned and set to work once more on the Chapel which was to glorify them until, in 1534, he left Florence and settled in Rome for the 30 years remaining to him. He was at once commissioned to paint his next great work, the Last Judgement on the altar wall of the Sistine Chapel, which affords the strongest possible contrast with his own Ceiling. He began work on it in 1536. In the interval there had been the Sack of Rome and the Reformation, and the confident humanism and Christian Neoplatonism of the Ceiling has curdled into the personal pessimism and despondency of the Judgement. The very choice of subject is indicative of the new mood, as is the curious fact that the mouth of Hell gapes over the altar itself. It was unveiled in 1541 and caused a sensation equalled only by his own work of 30 years earlier. Most of the ideas of Mannerism are traceable implicitly or explicitly in the Judgement and, more than ever, it served to imprint the idea that the scope of painting is strictly limited to the exploitation of the nude, preferably in foreshortened – and therefore difficult – poses. Paul III, who had commissioned the Judgement, immediately commissioned two more frescoes for his own chapel, the Cappella Paolina; these were begun in 1542 and completed in 1550. They represent the Conversion of S. Paul and the Crucifixion of S. Peter. Michelangelo was now 75 years old, but since 1546 he had been increasingly active as an architect; in particular, he was Chief Architect to S. Peter's and was doing more there than had been done for 30 years. This was the greatest architectural undertaking in Christendom, and Michelangelo did it, as he did all his late works, solely for the glory of God. In his last years he made a number of drawings of the Crucifixion, wrote much of his finest poetry, and carved the *Pietà* (now in Florence Cathedral) which was originally intended for his own tomb, as well as the nearly abstract *Rondanini Pietà* (Milan, Castello) charged with emotional intensity which contemporaries recognized as Michelangelo's *terribilità*, and in which the very forms of the Dead Christ actually merge with those of His Mother. He was working on this *Pietà* within a few days of his death, in his 89th year, on 18 February 1564. Unlike any previous artist, Michelangelo was the subject of two biographies in his own lifetime. The first of these was by VASARI, who concluded the first (1550) edition of his 'Vite' with the Life of one living artist, Michelangelo. In 1553 there appeared a 'Life of Michelangelo' by his pupil Ascanio Condivi (there is an English translation by C. Holroyd, 1903): this is really almost an Autobiography, promoted by Michelangelo to correct some errors of Vasari and to shift the emphasis in what Michelangelo regarded as a more desirable direction. Vasari, however, became more and more friendly with Michelangelo and was also his most devoted and articulate admirer, so that the very long Life which appears in Vasari's second edition (1568), after Michelangelo's death, gives us the most complete biography of any artist up to that time and is a trustworthy guide to the feelings of contemporaries about the man who can lay claim to be the greatest sculptor, painter, and draughtsman that has ever lived, as well as one of the greatest of architects and poets. He is the archetype of genius.

Apart from the works mentioned above there are others in Florence (Accad., Bargello, Casa Buonarroti – the house of his family, which contains relics of him – and Pal. della Signoria) and in Bologna (S. Domenico), London (NG and RA), Rome (Sta Maria sopra Minerva), and Siena (Cathedral). There are also about 500 drawings by him the majority of which are in the Royal Coll., Florence (Uffizi and Casa Buonarroti), London (BM), Oxford, and Paris. [ills. 189–94, pp. 300–1. Col. pl. 6]

Michelozzo Michelozzi (1396–1472), though most famous as an architect, was the collaborator of Ghiberti and DONATELLO. He worked with Ghiberti from c. 1417 on his bronze Doors and was in partnership with Donatello 1423–38, during which time he was mainly responsible for the architecture and the decorative sculpture in their joint works. During 1427 the partners were engaged on three major commissions, the Monuments for Antipope John XXIII (Florence, Baptistry), Cardinal Brancacci (Naples, S. Angelo a Nilo), and Bartolommeo Aragazzi. Most of the sculpture on the Aragazzi Monument was Michelozzo's, and pieces of it survive in Montepulciano and in the V & A, London. He also made the *Baptist* for the Silver Altar (1452: Florence, Cath. Mus.). [ill. 66, p. 279]

Miereveld, Michiel Jansz. (1567–1641), was a prolific portrait painter, who was born and died in Delft, but was in The Hague in 1625 and became Painter to the Princes of Orange. His portraits are mostly small in size, often busts only, and always sober in handling. There are examples in Amsterdam (Rijksmus.), Boston, Delft, The Hague, London (NG, NPG, Wallace Coll.), Manchester,

New York (Met. Mus.), Rotterdam, and elsewhere. [ill. 531, p. 350]

Mignard, Pierre (1612–95), was the rival of LEBRUN but an exponent of the same Academic theories. Like Lebrun he was a pupil of VOUET but he went to Rome in 1636 and remained there until 1657, forming his style on the approved models of the Carracci, Domenichino, and Poussin. He returned to Paris on the orders of Louis XIV and decorated the dome of the Val-de-Grâce (1663), but his principal importance was as portrait painter to the Court. He revived the earlier Italian type of allegorical portrait, and a good example is *The Marquise de Seignelay as Thetis* (1691: London, NG). He was strongly opposed to the Académie royale and, in spite of his own stylistic origins, championed the Venetian or 'colourist' school (*see* RUBÉNISME); this, however, was probably only to oppose Lebrun. When Lebrun died in 1690 Mignard was at once made *premier peintre*, and, on the King's orders, the Academy had, in one sitting, to appoint Mignard Associate, Member, Rector, Director, and Chancellor of the body he had so long opposed. There are pictures by him in the Royal Coll., London (NPG), and most French museums. [ill. 697, p. 376]

Millais, Sir John Everett (1829–96), was in the RA Schools in 1840 – an infant prodigy. In 1848, he, HUNT, and ROSSETTI founded the PRB, and in 1853 he was elected an ARA. In 1854 he married Ruskin's former wife, and his friendship with Ruskin was broken off. Millais developed into a fashionable and technically brilliant academic painter of portraits, costume history, and genre pieces, forsaking his original PRB theories, and went on to become RA, President of the RA, and a baronet.

There are works in Cambridge (Fitzwm), Birmingham, Liverpool, London (Tate, NPG, Guildhall), Manchester, and Oxford. [ill. 948, p. 408. Col. pl. 28]

Milles, Carl (1875–1955). Probably the greatest of Swedish artists, Milles was one of the most famous sculptors since Rodin, by whom he was much influenced at the beginning of his career. Milles started to emigrate to Chile in 1897, but got no farther than Paris, where he stayed for eight years. His strong feeling for architecture distinguishes him from Rodin, and most of his best works are fountains, in which the figures must be seen against the water and sky as part of an architectural whole. Much of his best work is in the USA where he soon became famous. There is a fountain by him in Kansas City, his last work, and another forms part of the Metropolitan Mus., New York. [ill. 1120, p. 431]

Millet, Jean-François called Francisque (1642–79), worked in Paris from 1659, painting landscapes in the style of Gaspar POUSSIN. He had relatives of the same name, and it is not clear what is by him: a good example of what is usually associated with his name is in London (NG). [ill. 691, p. 375]

Millet, Jean-François (1814–75), was the son of a peasant. He was trained under a local painter at Cherbourg and then in Paris (1837) under Delaroche. His earliest works are pastiches of the pastorals of the 18th century and rather erotic nudes, but he also painted portraits for a time. The influence of DAUMIER seems to have been decisive, and in 1848 he exhibited at the Salon a peasant subject, *The Winnower* (destroyed: two versions are in Paris, Louvre). From *c.* 1850 his choice of subject-matter led to accusations of Socialism (e.g. *The Sower*, Salon of 1850). In 1849 he moved to BARBIZON and remained there for the rest of his life, painting scenes of peasants and their labours and also some ordinary landscapes and marines. The *Angelus* (1857–9: Louvre) shows him with an unusually sentimental approach. His works are particularly well represented in Boston, and in America generally. There are also works in several French museums and in Cardiff, Edinburgh, Glasgow, London (NG, V & A), and Vienna. [ill. 755, p. 384]

Miniature. A painting in little, usually a portrait, executed in gouache or watercolour. The 16th-century type of miniature, as exemplified in the work of HILLIARD or OLIVER, was normally executed in body colour on playing cards or on vellum, the material used by the medieval illuminator. This type of portrait, with its allegories and symbolism, is a direct descendant of manuscript illumination. In the hands of men like COOPER, in the 17th century the portrait miniature became more closely allied to contemporary oil painting (some miniatures were actually executed in oil, usually on metal). In the 18th century the whole character of miniature painting was changed by the introduction of ivory as a ground and support; this could be left as a white ground and was most effective in conjunction with transparent watercolour. COSWAY used this technique. [Col. pls. 51, 52]

Mino da Fiesole (1429–84) was a Florentine sculptor who was traditionally a pupil of his contemporary DESIDERIO da Settignano, but was in Rome by 1454, where he did several works for churches. His principal Tombs are those in Fiesole and Florence, particularly the Tomb of Count Ugo in the Badia, Florence, of 1469–81: this shows both the delicacy and virtuosity of his marble carving and also the influence of the Antique on him. He also made a number of strongly characterized portrait busts, the earliest (and one of the best) being that of Niccolò Strozzi (1454: Berlin). There are works by him in Florence (Bargello), London (V & A), Paris (Louvre), and Washington (NG). [ills. 86, 92, pp. 282–3]

Mirò, Joan (*b.* 1893), is a Surrealist painter of Spanish origin who lived for some time in the US. In 1925 he took part in the First Surrealist Exhibition, and, with DALI, was recognized as the leading Spanish Surrealist. His work has tended to become abstract, although he says: 'For me a form is never something abstract; it is always a sign of something. It is always a man, a bird, a something else. For me painting is never form for form's sake.' He designed the ballet 'Jeux d'Enfants' in 1932. There are works in several US museums, London (Tate), Paris (Mus. d'Art Mod.), and elsewhere. [ill. 1083, p. 426. Col. pl. 38]

Misericordia, Madonna della (Ital. Madonna of Pity). A representation of the Madonna standing erect and sheltering under her outspread mantle a number of people, usually members of a *Confraternità della Misericordia* or other charitable organization.

Mixed Method. Oil glazes over TEMPERA underpainting.

Mobile. A form of sculpture invented in 1932 by CALDER, and named by DUCHAMP. Essentially a mobile consists of a series of shapes cut from wood or sheet-metal and connected by wires or rods of metal so that a gentle touch will cause the whole to revolve like a planetarium, giving an ever-changing sequence of planes, solids, and colours in three-dimensional movement. The interior decoration of the 1950s and 1960s has been much affected by coloured shapes linked with wire. [ill. 1141, p. 432]

Mochi, Francesco (1580–1654), was an Italian sculptor whose *Annunciation* group in Orvieto Cathedral, finished in 1609, has been called the first piece of Baroque sculpture. He made two equestrian statues in Piacenza, but his best-known work is the *S. Veronica* in St Peter's (1629–40: *see* BOLGI). [ill. 266, p. 311]

Modelling. (i) The three-dimensional representation of forms, by means of some plastic material, usually modelling clay. The opposite of carving. (ii) The representation of three-dimensional forms on a two-dimensional surface, in such a way that they appear solid. Thus it is usual to speak of the modelling of a hand or figure, meaning the apparent solidity of it, or the painter's comprehension of the form.

Modello, Modelletto. Italian words used to describe a small version of a large picture, not strictly speaking a preliminary sketch, which was shown to the person or body commissioning the large work for approval before the final design was put in hand. Many such small versions, often quite highly finished, still exist, e.g. by TIEPOLO. *See also* BOZZETTO. [ill. 298, p. 314. Col. pl. 11]

Modersohn-Becker, Paula (1876–1907), was the most important German woman artist of her day and one of the main precursors of EXPRESSIONISM. She was born in Dresden and trained in Berlin (1896–8) before settling in the artists' colony of Worpswede, near Bremen. She went to Paris in 1900 and again in 1903, 1905, and 1906: these visits brought her under the influence of Gauguin and the Fauves (who exhibited in 1905). The simplification of form and colour and the stress on line were introduced by her into Germany, making her a link with the development of the BLAUE REITER and BRÜCKE groups. There are several works in Bremen and in other German museums. She was a friend of the poet Rainer Maria Rilke, who wrote a biography of her, and her portrait of him is in a private collection. [ill. 1011, p. 417]

Modigliani, Amedeo (1884–1920), was known as 'Modi' for short, from which by natural corruption the French referred to him as *un peintre maudit* – and those who were like him were equally accursed. He was born in Leghorn of a distinguished Italian-Jewish family and had his first training in Italy before going to Paris in 1906. He spent the rest of his life there, working at first in a manner influenced by Toulouse-Lautrec, but his *Cellist* of 1910 won him recognition and shows that his real style was based on African sculpture, Cézanne, and Picasso and, above all, his Italian heritage. He was a superb draughtsman, and all his work contains echoes of Botticelli, of Sienese Trecento painters, and of some of the Mannerists, so that he is truly the greatest Italian artist of the 20th century, and not a French painter at all. He was handsome, amorous, and addicted to drink and drugs. He said, 'I am going to drink myself dead', and he did. There are paintings or sculpture by him in Buffalo, Chicago, London (Tate, V & A, Courtauld Inst.), New York (M of MA), Paris (Mus. d'Art Moderne), Philadelphia, São Paulo, Washington (Phillips), and elsewhere. [ill. 1076, p. 425]

Moholy-Nagy, László (1895–1946), was a Hungarian law student who, after the First World War, studied art in Berlin and by 1923 was teaching at the BAUHAUS. In 1928 he went to Berlin. He emigrated to Amsterdam in 1934, lived in London 1935–7, and then settled in Chicago, where he was head of the New Bauhaus (later called the Institute of Design), 1937–9. His greatest importance was as a teacher, writer, and experimenter, especially with new materials, such as plexiglass, and he also used semi-industrial techniques. His constructions, called Space Modulators, have interchangeable elements. As early as 1919 he came under the influence of MALEVICH, and in the early 1920s he was associated with SUPREMATISM, CONSTRUCTIVISM, De STIJL, and DADA. At the Bauhaus he edited the Bauhausbücher and he also did much film and stage design, including the sets for H. G. Wells's 'Shape of Things to Come' in London; the last book he published in his lifetime was called 'The New Vision'. There are works by him in Cologne, Harvard University, and New York (Guggenheim). [ill. 1142, p. 432]

Molenaer, Jan Miensz. (c. 1609/10–68), was a Haarlem genre painter, active from 1629, who married Judith LEYSTER in 1636. He spent his life in Haarlem and Amsterdam and his earlier works, like those of his wife, are strongly influenced by HALS. The later pictures are more like the genre scenes of A. van OSTADE. There are works by him in Amsterdam, Berlin, Boston, Brussels, Frankfurt (Städel), Haarlem, The Hague, London (NG), Stockholm, and Vienna. [ill. 510, p. 346]

Monaco, Lorenzo, *see* LORENZO.

Mondrian, Piet (1872–1944), was a Dutch painter who went to Paris in 1911 and abandoned his realistic landscapes for Cubist ones. In 1914 he returned to Holland but he lived in Paris 1919–38, then in London, and he went to New York in 1940. His form of Abstraction was a peculiarly rigorous one known as Neo-Plasticism, which consists principally of restricting forms to purely geometrical shapes, set at right angles to the horizontal or vertical axes and coloured in the three primary colours, and white, black, or grey. The only enlivening touch he permitted himself was in his titles – *Boogie-Woogie*, for example. As might be expected, he was a prolific writer (often in De STIJL) and his 'Plastic Art and Pure Plastic Art' (1937) summarizes his theories. [ill. 1086, p. 427]

Monet, Claude (1840–1926), was the leading member of the IMPRESSIONIST group, and the one who longest practised the principles of absolute fidelity to the visual sensation and painting directly from the object, if necessary out of doors. Cézanne is said to have described him as 'only an eye, but my God what an eye!' and this description is certainly true in that his constant search for verisimilitude led at times to a neglect of form. He was born in Paris but went as a child to Le Havre. There he met BOUDIN – whose work he did not then like – and was persuaded by him to become a landscape painter (1856/8); at this time he also bought his first Japanese prints, then newly coming into Europe. In 1859 he went to Paris to study, meeting PISSARRO in the ATELIER Suisse. From 1860 to 1862 he was in Algeria as a conscript, but in 1862 he met JONGKIND – who influenced him considerably – and returned to Paris, where he met most of the major artists of his own time; in 1862 Bazille, Sisley, and Renoir, in 1864 Courbet, in 1865 Cézanne and Whistler, and in 1866 Manet, whose work he had earlier admired. Then and for many years to come he was extremely poor. In 1870 to escape the Franco-Prussian War he came to London, where he painted some views, and, in 1871, with Pissarro he visited the National Gallery and the V & A, where they studied Turner and Constable, but, according to Monet himself, were not tremendously impressed. He returned to Paris via Holland and in 1872 visited Le Havre, where he painted two views called *Impression*, one of which, when exhibited in 1874 at the First Impressionist Exhibition, was used derisively to name the whole movement IMPRESSIONISM. During the 1870s and 1880s he gradually became known and for the last thirty years of his very long life he was generally regarded as the greatest of the Impressionists. From about 1890 he began to paint series of pictures of one subject, the first being the *Poplars* and the *Haystacks*, representing them under various conditions and at different times of day; other series are those of *Rouen Cathedral* (1892–5), of the *Thames* (these were certainly finished in France, as he had by now given up the original practice of painting exclusively from nature) (1899–1904), the second *London* series (1905) and the *Venice* series (1908), and, most famous of all, the *Water-lilies* painted in the elaborate garden he had made for himself. He painted these over and over again, but the most important are the very large ones begun in 1916 and retained by him until his death. They were painted for the State and are now in a special museum (Paris, Orangerie), and it has recently been claimed that these shimmering pools of colour, almost totally devoid of form, are the true starting-point of abstract art, or at least certain forms of it, particularly that now called ABSTRACT IMPRESSIONISM. They were, however, painted after CUBISM had been invented and can be seen equally as the logical outcome of Monet's lifelong devotion to the ultimate form of naturalism, truth of retinal sensation. He was enormously prolific, and many museums possess works: two very rich collections are Paris (Musée de l'Impressionnisme) and Boston. [ills. 800–2, p. 390. Col. pl. 34]

Monnoyer, Jean-Baptiste (1636–99), called 'Baptiste', was a Franco-Flemish flower painter who was trained in Antwerp, but became a member of the Academy in Paris in 1665 and worked for Louis XIV. It is said that he was annoyed by his son Antoine, an inferior flower painter, who was allowed to alter some of his works, and in a fit of pique he went to London *c.* 1685. There he worked for the Duke of Montagu's new (and very French) town house (many of these pictures have passed by inheritance to the Duke of Buccleuch), and he remained in London until his death. His flowerpieces are rich and splendid, yet painted with the greatest regard for botanical accuracy: they frequently appear in English sale-rooms under his nickname 'Baptiste'. He also published books of engravings of flowers. Apart from those in English private collections and French provincial museums there are paintings by him in Munich and New York (Met. Mus.). [ill. 475, p. 340]

Monochrome. A painting or drawing executed in any one colour. *See* GRISAILLE.

Monotype. A single print, not strictly an engraving at all, made by painting, with oil paint or printer's ink, on an untouched copper plate, and printing on paper in the normal way. The only reason for doing this instead of painting direct on the paper is the quality of texture given by the pressure of printing. It is also possible to follow some of the indications left on the plate and repeat the process with slight variations. The technique was practised by CASTIGLIONE and DEGAS, among others. [ill. 798, p. 389]

Monro, Dr Thomas (1759–1833), was a London physician and amateur draughtsman who befriended or patronized many artists, including Turner and Girtin, De Wint, J.R. Cozens, and Cotman. According to FARINGTON '(Diary', 1794 and 1798) Turner and Girtin were employed by Dr Monro to draw at his house in the evenings, and in the winter evenings his house was like an Academy, being full of young painters whom he encouraged to use it as a studio. Some of his own drawings are in the V & A, London. [ill. 930, p. 404]

Montage is the sticking of one layer over another, especially as in photomontage when photographs of objects are applied to a photograph of an unusual or incongruous background. The technique was much used by the Cubists, who frequently stuck newspaper cuttings on to their canvases: it is now much exploited by advertising agents. *See* COLLAGE.

Montagna, Bartolommeo (*d.* 1523), was the principal painter of Vicenza in the late 15th century. He is first documented in 1459 and is recorded as living in Venice in 1469. He was then presumably training as a painter, since he is first mentioned as such in Vicenza in 1474. His works are markedly influenced by Giovanni BELLINI, the VIVARINI, and ANTONELLO. There are works by him in Vicenza, and in Amsterdam (Rijksmus.), Baltimore (Walters Gall.), Bergamo, Berlin, Columbus Ohio, Dublin, Glasgow, London (NG), Milan (Brera, Poldi-Pezzoli, and Castello), Naples, New York (Met. Mus.), Ottawa, Oxford, Paris (Louvre), Philadelphia (Johnson), Rome (Borghese), San Francisco, Springfield Mass., Venice, Verona, Washington (NG), Williamstown Mass., and Worcester Mass. [ill. 148, p. 293]

Monumental. The most overworked word in current art history and criticism. It is intended to convey the idea that a particular work of art, or part of such a work, is grand,

noble, elevated in idea, simple in conception and execution, without any excess of virtuosity, and having something of the enduring, stable, and timeless nature of great architecture. The word may properly be applied to the Pyramids, the paintings of Poussin or Piero della Francesca, and some few other works of art. It is not a synonym for 'large'.

Moore, Henry (*b.* 1898), is the most eminent living British sculptor. He was trained in Leeds – where he met Barbara HEPWORTH – and in London, winning a travelling scholarship to Paris and Italy in 1925. He was one of the advocates of direct carving and has always used his material to express natural forms in terms of stone or wood. His earliest major work was the *North Wind* (1928) for the London Underground building and it has been followed by several commissions for architectural sculpture, e.g. the Time-Life building in London (1952–3), and works in the open air in London, Paris, Rotterdam, and Arnhem. From 1940 he made many drawings of the underground air-raid shelters and of coal-miners, while his *Madonna* statue for S. Matthew, Northampton, was completed in 1944. His international reputation dates from 1948, when he was awarded the sculpture prize at the Venice Biennale, and he is now well represented in museums. [ill. 1149, p. 433]

Mor, Anthonis (Antonio Moro) (*c.* 1517/21–76/7), was an Utrecht portrait painter, the pupil of SCOREL, who became the Court Painter of the Spanish Netherlands and superimposed the grand air of Titian's portraits on to his own acute Dutch sense of character and polished technique. He was working for Cardinal Granvella in 1549 and visited Rome soon afterwards. In 1554 he painted Queen Mary Tudor (Madrid, Prado), presumably in London and to celebrate her marriage with Philip of Spain. His portraits had enormous influence on the development of a Court style of portraiture in both Spain and the Netherlands, but the presence of a Holbein tradition in England meant that he had no influence here, and in any case he could have had little opportunity in what must have been a very short visit. He was Court Painter to Philip II of Spain by 1560 and the Spaniard SÁNCHEZ COELLO was his pupil. There are pictures by him in Amsterdam (Rijksmus.), Berlin, Brussels, Cambridge (Fitzwm), Dresden, Florence (Uffizi), The Hague, London (NG, NPG), Madrid (Prado), Munich, New York (Met. Mus.), Ottawa, Paris (Louvre), Sheffield, Vaduz (Liechtenstein), Vienna (K-H), and Washington (NG). [ill. 365, p. 325]

Morales, Luis, 'El Divino' (active 1547–86). Morales is the most typical Spanish Mannerist, whose style was formed by a combination of the Flemish-Italianate painters such as MASSYS, and the Italian artists who influenced them, principally LEONARDO and his Milanese followers. Morales seems to have studied under a Dutch painter called Sturmio who worked in Spain, but the final result is a highly personal style. He is first documented in 1547, but there is a *Madonna* attributed to him which is dated 1546. He spent most of his life in Badajoz where there are still works by him, although he may have worked in Madrid for Philip II in 1564. He thus precedes EL GRECO as an exponent of extreme Mannerism in Spain. Outside Spain and Portugal there are works by him in Berlin, Cardiff, Catania, Dresden, Dublin, Florence (Uffizi),

Leeds, Leningrad (Hermitage), London (NG), Mexico City, Minneapolis, New York (Hispanic Soc.), Oxford, Paris (Louvre), and Rome (Gall. Naz.). [ill. 638, p. 364]

Morandi, Giorgio (1890–1964), was an Italian still-life painter. He never left his native country, but, apart from such Italian masters of the 15th century as Piero della Francesca, Cézanne and Chardin were the painters most akin to his withdrawn and meditative outlook. He lived in Bologna and painted some landscapes and flowerpieces, but most of his works are simple arrangements of bottles, treated with simple brownish tones approximating to monochrome. He was also a celebrated etcher – also mainly of bottles – and made some 90 plates, mostly dating from 1921 to 1924 and 1927 to 1933. There are pictures by him in Birmingham, Hamburg, London (Tate), and Toledo Ohio. [ill. 1064, p. 424]

Morbidezza (Ital. softness), a term much used in 18th-century criticism to indicate a softness of edges and a fusion of tones which is characteristic of CORREGGIO: hence the 18th-century mockery 'the Correggiosity of Correggio' as a cant phrase suitable for the would-be connoisseur. Its use is not now recommended.

Moreau, Gustave (1826–98), painted elaborate Biblical and mythological fantasies in a detailed, almost encrusted, technique. His importance – except for his slight influence on Surrealism – lies in his tolerant and intelligent teaching at the École des Beaux-Arts in Paris from 1892 to 1898, when ROUAULT, MATISSE, and MARQUET were his pupils. He left his collections to the State as a Museum, of which Rouault was to be the Curator. [ill. 786, p. 388]

Moretto of Brescia (c. 1498–1554) worked mainly in the Brescia and Bergamo districts until he visited Milan and Verona in the 1540s. His religious works are of a warm, late Bellini and Giorgionesque type; his portraits are outstanding, showing the influence of Lotto and Titian, and developing types that Titian did not use until much later. He was probably the first to introduce the full-length portrait into Italy as an independent subject, not part of a religious work (cf. the *Nobleman* dated 1526 in the NG, London) – an idea developed from German examples, notably from CRANACH, although CARPACCIO may have been one of the first to use it. MORONI was his pupil. There are works in Bergamo, Brescia (Mus., churches), Cambridge Mass. (Fogg Mus.), Detroit, Frankfurt (Städel), London (NG), Milan (Ambrosiana, Brera, Castello), New York (Met. Mus.), Paris (Louvre), Philadelphia (Johnson), the Vatican, Venice (Accad.), Verona, Vienna, and elsewhere. [ill. 207, p. 303]

Morisot, Berthe (1841–95), was the first woman to join the IMPRESSIONISTS – the other was Mary CASSATT. She met Fantin-Latour in 1859, and in 1860 was encouraged by Corot, who influenced her early work. In 1868 she met MANET and in 1874 married his younger brother Eugène. She exhibited in all but one (1879) of the Impressionist Exhibitions. Her great importance lies in her influence on Manet, for it was partly through her that he came to adopt the Impressionist palette and to abandon black of which he was so great a master. She could never persuade him

into joining the group, but their close family tie made it even more difficult for him to dissociate himself from them. After about 1885 she was very strongly influenced by Renoir.
There are works in Boston (Mus.), London (Tate), Paris (Musée de l'Impressionnisme), and Washington (NG). [ill. 793, p. 389]

Morland, George (1763–1804), was an exponent of picturesque rustic genre painting who based himself on Dutch and Flemish 17th-century models such as BROUWER. Like them, he refused to work for individual patrons and preferred to sell through an agent, thus altering the whole basis of patronage in 18th-century England. His very numerous works were popularized through engravings, many of which were executed by William Ward, brother of James WARD, Morland's own brother-in-law and imitator. The son of a painter, Henry Morland (c. 1730–97), he exhibited drawings at the RA at the age of ten (1773), and his first oil-painting was shown there in 1781. From then on he lived wildly, and in 1799 was arrested (as a French spy) while on the run from his creditors; after which he was in the King's Bench Prison until 1802. He died in prison after producing an enormous amount of scamped work to pay his debts. His reputation immediately declined and his place was taken by WILKIE. Among his most purely Dutch works are the *Industry* and *Idleness* (Edinburgh, NG), while the *Stable* (1791: London, NG) is one of his best rustic subjects. Other works are in London (Tate, V & A, Kenwood) and Birmingham, Glasgow, Leeds, Leicester, Manchester, New York (Met. Mus.), Nottingham, Ottawa, Port Sunlight (Lever Gall.), Wellington NZ, Wolverhampton, and York. [ill. 898, p. 402]

Moro *see* MOR.

Moroni, Giovanni Battista (c. 1525–78), was a pupil of MORETTO, and was also much influenced by Lotto. His religious works are dull and derivative, but he excels as a painter of quiet family portraits and, like his master, he blends the realism of Holbein with the feeling for style of the Venetians to produce the placid, intimate, human portrait style of the Lombards.
There are works in Baltimore, Bergamo (Mus. and churches), Berlin, Boston (Mus.), Brescia, Detroit, Florence (Pitti, Uffizi), London (NG), Milan (Ambrosiana, Brera, Castello), Minneapolis, New York (Met. Mus.), Ottawa, Paris (Louvre), Philadelphia (Johnson, Wilstach, Widener), Princeton, Sarasota Fla, Vienna, Worcester Mass., and elsewhere. [ill. 208, p. 303]

Morris, William (1834–96), met BURNE-JONES when at Exeter College, Oxford. He then studied architecture under Street, but abandoned it to become a painter under the influence of ROSSETTI. In 1861 he founded the firm of Morris and Co., to produce wallpapers, furniture, tapestries, and stained-glass windows (many designed by Burne-Jones), carpets and furnishing materials in a style entirely different from that of contemporary Victorian decoration, but one which, nevertheless, tended towards a different kind of *horror vacui* and the use of equally dark and heavy colours. He is particularly important for the development of the private press, and did much with his Kelmscott Press, founded in 1890, to raise the standards of book design and printing, although he favoured a revival of medieval black-letter where Lucien Pissarro's Eragny Press (1896) concentrated on modern type faces. His poems and other writings are anti-industrialist and support a Socialist theory for the regeneration of man by handicraft. There are drawings and a painting in the Tate and the V & A, London, the latter also having a room entirely decorated with Morris products. [ill. 951, p. 409]

Morse, Samuel (1791–1872), was an American painter and first President of the National Academy (1826), but is better known as the inventor of the electric telegraph (hence Morse code). After leaving Yale in 1810 he went to London and trained under ALLSTON and WEST: his ambitions as a history painter led him to exhibit a *Hercules* at the RA, but on his return to America in 1815 he had to live by portrait painting. He invented the telegraph in 1832 and painted relatively little after that. His best-known portraits are the *House of Representatives* (Washington, Corcoran) and *Lafayette* (1825: Brooklyn Mus.). [ill. 851, p. 397]

Mosaic. One of the oldest and most durable forms of mural decoration, mosaic was in constant use from the earliest times up to about the 13th century, when it was largely superseded by fresco and other forms of painting which are both much cheaper and much more adaptable to a realistic style. Recently, however, the very stylization inherent in mosaic has led to its revival as a decorative art. The technique is simple but laborious. A cartoon is drawn on the wall to be decorated and a small area covered with cement. Previously, small cubes (called *tesserae*) have been chipped from slabs of coloured stone, marble, and coloured or gilt glass; the *tesserae* are then stuck into the cement. Great care was taken in the best early mosaics to ensure that all the *tesserae* were not perfectly flat and level, since an uneven surface catches the light and reflects it in different ways according to the angle of incidence and the material used for the *tesserae*. Mosaic was much used for the decoration of Early Christian and Byzantine churches and there are splendid cycles in Rome, Ravenna, Venice, and Sicily as well as in Greece. [Col. pl. 39]

Moser, Lucas, is known only from the *Magdalen Altar* in the church at Tiefenbronn, near Pforzheim, which is signed and dated 1431 and has an inscription roughly translatable as: 'Cry, Art, cry and lament loudly, nobody nowadays wants you. So alas, 1431'. In fact, the style of the picture is markedly modern and forms a German counterpart to the realism of WITZ or van EYCK and CAMPIN. [ill. 543, p. 352]

Mostaert, Jan (c. 1475–1555/6), was a Haarlem painter who is recorded, on fair evidence, as having painted a *West Indian Landscape* as well as having worked for the Regent of the Netherlands. A picture at Haarlem (Hals Mus.) is presumably the landscape, and a group of pictures showing stylistic affinities with GEERTGEN – i.e. 'Dutch', rather than Flemish – can be considered as his. He must be distinguished from the 'Waagen'sche Mostaert', who is now identified with ISENBRANDT: on the other hand,

the Master of Oultremont is probably identical with Mostaert. There are pictures ascribed to him in Amsterdam (Rijksmus.), Brussels, Cologne, Liverpool, London (NG), Paris (Louvre, Petit Palais), Philadelphia (Johnson), St Louis, Sarasota Fla., Worcester Mass., and elsewhere. [ills. 364, 387, pp. 325, 327]

Motherwell, Robert (b. 1915), is an American Abstract Expressionist painter who began by studying philosophy at Harvard. He has said: 'Without ethical consciousness, a painter is only a decorator.' After a visit to Europe in 1938 he exhibited with the Surrealists in New York (1939) and later associated with POLLOCK, KOONING, and ROTHKO (with whom he founded an art school). He was editor (1944–57) of the important 'Documents of Modern Art' series. [ill. 1097, p. 428]

Müller, Otto (1874–1930), was a member of the BRÜCKE who experimented with techniques involving the use of distemper and beeswax rather than oil paint. The flatness inherent in this medium, and his passion for Egyptian art, led to striking simplifications of form which influenced the other members of the group. He studied lithography in Breslau from 1890 to 1895 and was trained at the Dresden Academy before going to Berlin in 1908, where he met HECKEL and subsequently joined the Brücke. He was much influenced by the sculptor LEHMBRUCK as well as by Gauguin, and his decorative paintings of gipsies and skinny nudes are less brutal than the works of most of his contemporaries. There are examples in Berlin, Cologne, and Harvard University. [ill. 1019, p. 417]

Müller, William James (1812–45), was a landscape painter, born at Bristol of German extraction, who was much influenced by Constable and Cox. He visited Egypt in 1838–9, and was one of the first English artists to paint Arabian subjects. In 1842–3 he was a member of an expedition to Asia Minor in search of Antique marbles. The largest collection of his work is in Bristol, but there are others in London (BM, Tate Gall., V & A). [ill. 941, p. 406]

Multscher, Hans (c. 1400–before 67), was active in Ulm for some 40 years, principally as a sculptor. His sharp sense of realism, noticeable in his sculpture, is even more marked in the first documented picture by him, the eight panels of the *Wurzach Altar*, of which the central part is lost (1437: Berlin). These panels belong to the same slightly crude realist school as MOSER's *Tiefenbronn Altar* or even the work of WITZ. A second altarpiece, including eight paintings, was commissioned in 1456 and completed in 1459: it was for Storzing (S. Tyrol) and is now in the Museum there. [ill. 544, p. 352]

Munch, Edvard (1863–1944), a Norwegian painter, was one of the forerunners of EXPRESSIONISM, whose most formative years were spent in Paris and Berlin, where a large Exhibition of his work, as early as 1892, was a formative influence on much German painting. Formally, he was much influenced by GAUGUIN but his subjects (especially his *Frieze of Life* project) deal with basic themes of love and death, for which he sought pictorial equivalents. He was friendly with Strindberg and his art, though sometimes powerful, is always neurotic and frequently hysterical. His graphic works were perhaps even more influential than his paintings. About 1,000 of his pictures are in the Munch Mus., Oslo, but there is also one in London (Tate). [ill. 996, p. 415]

Mural *see* WALL-PAINTING.

Murillo, Bartolomé Esteban (1617–82), was born in Seville where he passed the greater part of his life. He started as a painter of the kind of pictures that are sold at fairs (in Spain a bad painting is called a *pintura de feria*, and a good one, irrespective, a '*Murillo*'), but no certain example survives. He visited Madrid, probably in 1648, and stayed there for about three years, being apparently helped by Velazquez. His change of style from his earliest works in the Cloister of San Francisco in Seville, dated 1646, to his later style, could not have been effected without a knowledge of Rubens, van Dyck, Titian, and Velazquez. He also studied BAROCCI in the Royal Collection. In 1660 he was one of the founders, and the first President, of the Seville Academy. The Spaniards mark off his stylistic progression by his changes in the use of colour. First, the rather hard naturalism of the early beggar-boy pictures, with their hints of Ribera and Velazquez; then the *estilo frio* of the early religious subjects, cool, detached, with only a little idealization; then the *estilo cálido* of the type of the *Madonna del Rosario* (Madrid, Prado), above all a devotional image, with idealized forms, a certain Baroque flutter to the draperies, a certain artificiality, but with warmth, charm, and quiet religious feeling; then the *estilo vaporoso* of his late works, where all tends towards the softening and sweetening of style and colour, to the sentimental emotionalism of a pious image. His later beggar-boy scenes also exploit this sentimental attitude, and he found a ready market for these glamourized, picturesque urchins in fancy-dress rags, exuding the charms of Bohemianism and serving to exorcize poverty by robbing it of its power to inspire pity and horror. He had a large shop with many assistants, and his simple undemanding

pictures enjoyed huge popularity, so much so that 'Murillos' were painted until well into the 19th century, as a style in art, not primarily as forgeries. His best works are of moderate size, when he is versatile and inventive in composition, but his large decorations in the Hospital de la Cáridad in Seville (1671–4) are involved compositions without clear organization and with an uneasy blend of the naturalistic and the idealized.

There are works by him in Amsterdam, Baltimore, Berlin, Boston, Cadiz, Cambridge Mass. (Fogg Mus.), Chicago, Cincinnati, Detroit, Dresden, Genoa, Hartford Conn. (Wadsworth Atheneum), Indianapolis, Kansas City, Leningrad, Liverpool, London (NG, Dulwich, Wallace Coll., Wellington Mus.), Madrid, Minneapolis, Munich, New York (Met. Mus.), Notre Dame Univ. Indiana, Ottawa, Paris, Philadelphia (Widener), Raleigh N. Carolina, Rome (Corsini Gall.), St Louis, San Diego Cal., Seville (Mus. and churches), Sheffield, the Vatican, Vienna, and Washington. [ill 647, p. 365]

Mytens, Daniel (*c.* 1590–before 1648), was trained in The Hague, probably under MIEREVELD, but was in England by 1618 and was working for the Crown soon after that. He was appointed Painter to Charles I in 1625 and painted a number of portraits, including several full-lengths, which had a great success before the arrival of van DYCK in 1632. Some of his works are difficult to distinguish from JOHNSON's, but his masterpiece is the full-length *Duke of Hamilton* (on loan to Edinburgh, NG) which was painted in 1629 and therefore shows most of the elegance associated with van Dyck before his arrival in England. From *c.* 1635 Mytens seems to have lived in Holland. There are works by him in the Royal Coll. (including portraits of Charles I and his Queen that show why van Dyck's success was immediate) and in Leeds, London (NPG, Tate, Nat. Marit. Mus.), New York (Met. Mus.), Ottawa, and St Louis. [ill. 522, p. 348]

N

Nabis, Les (from Hebrew, Prophet), was the name taken by a small group of French artists, including BONNARD, VUILLARD, SÉRUSIER, and MAILLOL, between *c.* 1889 and 1899. They were attracted by GAUGUIN's advice to paint in flat, pure colours; and one of them, Maurice DENIS, 'uttered one of the great battle-cries of modern art' when he said: 'Remember that a picture, before being a horse, a nude, or some kind of anecdote, is essentially a flat surface covered with colours assembled in a certain order.' They reacted sharply away from the naturalism implicit in Impressionism, but their links with the Symbolist writers meant that they attached considerable importance to subject-matter. The best painters of the group, Bonnard and Vuillard, eventually reverted to a modified Impressionist style known as INTIMISME.

Nain, Le, *see* LE NAIN.

Nanni di Banco (*c.* 1384–1421) was a Florentine sculptor who was working with his father on the Cathedral in 1406/7 and received the commission for a *Prophet* on the Porta della Mandorla (1407/8), the companion figure being by Donatello. In 1408 he and Donatello again shared a commission for the Cathedral (Donatello: *David*; Nanni: *Isaiah*). His best-known works are the four *Saints* (*Quattro Santi Coronati*) in a niche on Orsanmichele, where there are others by him, and the *Assumption* over the Porta della Mandorla of the Cathedral. His early death cut short a career which promised to rival Donatello's and in some respects, such as the use of classical exemplars, Nanni may have been in advance. [ill. 60, p. 277]

Nash, Paul (1889–1946), was trained at the Slade School and served in the First World War at the front before being appointed an Official War Artist in 1917. He was again appointed in the Second World War. His poetic imagination was rather stimulated by Surrealism and he exhibited with the Surrealists in their Paris Exhibition, 1938. He did much work as a designer and book-illustrator. There are paintings by him in Belfast, Blackpool, Durban, Leeds, Leicester, Liverpool, London (Tate, Imperial War Mus.), Manchester, Ottawa, Sheffield, and Toronto. [ill. 979, p. 412]
His brother, John Nash RA, was born in 1893 and is also represented in the Tate Gallery.

Nattier, Jean-Marc (1685–1766), began his career as an engraver of the Rubens *Marie de' Medici* cycle in Paris but later became established as the painter of the ladies of Louis XV's Court. There are works in Versailles and Paris (Louvre and Mus. Jacquemart-André), French provincial museums and London (NG, Wallace Coll.), New York (Met. Mus., Frick Coll.), Stockholm, Toledo Ohio, and elsewhere. [ill. 733, p. 380]

Nature Morte (Fr. STILL-LIFE).

Nay, Ernst Wilhelm (*b.* 1902), was born in Berlin but now lives in Cologne. He was trained under HOFER at the Berlin Academy (1925–8), and then went to Paris, where he was influenced by Picasso. He was in Rome, 1930–1, and with MUNCH in Norway, 1936–7. He was fortunate in being able to continue painting when he was stationed at Le Mans in Northern France, 1942–4, and, beginning from Nolde and the Expressionists, he developed towards abstraction. There are works in Cologne. [ill. 1109, p. 429]

Nazarener. In 1809 two young painters, OVERBECK and Pforr, founded a quasi-religious order, the *Lukasbrüder*, in Vienna with the intention of regenerating German religious art in imitation of the works of Dürer, Perugino, and the young Raphael. Both went to Rome in 1810 and began working in the deserted Monastery of Sant' Isidoro, where they were soon joined by others, the most important of whom was CORNELIUS. Several, including Overbeck, became Catholics and the group became known mockingly as 'Nazarenes'. As an experiment in medieval workshop practice they painted jointly some frescoes (1816–17: now in Berlin) and decorated the Casa Massimo in Rome (1819). Their ideas were known and admired in England, e.g. by DYCE, and influenced the Pre-Raphaelites; they also influenced INGRES. [ills. 609–13, pp. 360–1]

NEAC (New English Art Club). The New English was founded in 1886 as a challenge to the complacent conventionalism of the Royal Academy (*see* SEZESSION), by a group of artists who were either French-trained or admirers of the French elective jury system. WHISTLER was admired by most of them, and he actually sat on the jury for a while before his inevitable resignation. STEER was an original member and SICKERT joined in 1886, and within a few years the Club tended to become an appanage of the Slade School, reflecting its tradition of draughtsmanship in the work of members like JOHN. The CAMDEN TOWN GROUP was founded in 1911, by GILMAN, GORE, and SICKERT, but in the winter of 1910/11 the Post-Impressionist Exhibition in London led to schism in both groups and the foundation of a new group, influenced by Cézanne, Gauguin, and van Gogh rather than the Impressionists. This was the LONDON GROUP, presided over by Gilman, and consisting of most of the Camden

Towners, the VORTICISTS, and a few others. The NEAC still exists.

Neer, Aert van der (1603/4–77), was a Dutch landscape painter who specialized in moonlight effects, usually showing the canals around Amsterdam, where he lived. He seems to have had difficulty in making a living and took to keeping a wineshop 1658–62, but he was no more successful at this and returned to painting. He also painted some winter scenes, rather in the manner of Hendrik Avercamp; but his moonlights are unique. There are typical examples in Amsterdam (Rijksmus.), London (NG, Wallace Coll.), and New York (Met. Mus.). [ill. 493, p. 343]
His son Eglon Hendrik (1634–1703) painted a few landscapes but is best known as a genre painter in the manner of Metsu. He is represented in Boston, London (NG, Wallace Coll.), New York (Met. Mus.), and elsewhere. [ill. 514, p. 347]

Neoclassicism is the name given to the movement which originated in Rome in the middle of the 18th century and spread rapidly over the civilized world. It arose partly in reaction against the 'excesses' of BAROQUE and ROCOCO – the former of which was also largely a Roman movement – and partly from a genuine desire to recreate the art of Greece and Rome, a desire much stimulated by the chief prophet of the movement, WINCKELMANN. From 1748 the discoveries at Herculaneum and Pompeii gave impetus to the movement – it has been argued that they created it – but, even more important, they provided some evidence of what ancient art actually looked like. This knowledge was disseminated by publications like 'Le Antichità di Ercolano' (1757 and later), plates from which were much used as models by MENGS, VIEN, and others. Even Winckelmann knew practically nothing of Greek originals; and one main reason for the tendency of the Neoclassic movement in the 18th century to equate the Antique with Roman art, where the 19th century equated it with the purer style of the Greeks (as they would have expressed it), lies in the great discoveries of the archaeologists in the late 18th century and early 19th century.
Neoclassicism differs from all the earlier Classic revivals in that for the first time, artists consciously imitated Antique art and knew what they were imitating, both in style and in subject-matter. This is particularly true of sculpture, which survives in much greater quantity and in better preservation than either painting or architecture. This is one reason for the adaptation of bas-reliefs as pictures, in sharp reaction against the composition in depth of Baroque artists. The imitation of ancient subject-matter was carried very far – as by DAVID, whose *Horaces* drew an ancient moral for modern circumstances – and is a different matter from the earlier type of history painting, where a subject such as the *Death of Caesar* was an excuse for dramatic grouping, not an incitement to tyrannicide. Some of the principal exponents of various forms of Neoclassicism were BARRY, CANOVA, FLAXMAN, HAMILTON, MENGS, PIRANESI, THORWALDSEN, VIEN, and WEST. [ills. 317–18, 592, 741–2, 744, 870, 880, 887, 889, 894, pp. 317–18, 359, 382, 399, 400–1]

Neo-Impressionism has, properly speaking, little to do with Impressionism. In its purest form, as it is found in SEURAT, it involves the use of Divisionism (*see* OPTICAL MIXTURES) and a strict, formal composition; both were too cerebral and too consciously applied by the artist to have much relation to the fleeting colour effects and the accidental, 'snapshot' composition of Impressionism. Neo-Impressionism was first seen in an exhibition held in 1884 in Paris by the Salon des Artistes Indépendants, where Seurat exhibited the *Bathers at Asnières* (London, NG), and in 1886 Seurat, SIGNAC, and PISSARRO all showed works based on Seurat's theories at the last Impressionist exhibition, hence the tendency to regard the movement as an offshoot of Impressionism. According to Signac it 'guaranteed all the benefits of luminosity, colour, and harmony by the optical mixture of pure pigments (all the colours of the prism and all their tones); by the separation of differing elements (local colour, the colour of the light, and their interactions); by the balancing of these elements and their proportions (according to the laws of contrast, of gradation, and irradiation); by the selection of a size of touch proportionate to the size of the picture'.
The theory had a strong but passing effect on van Gogh during his years in Paris (1886–8), on Gauguin *c.* 1886, on Toulouse-Lautrec *c.* 1887, and on Segantini *c.* 1891; other adherents include Maximilien Luce (1858–1941), Henri-Edmond Cross (1856–1910), Charles Angrand (1854–1926), Albert Dubois-Pillet (1846–90), and Théo van Rysselberghe (1862–1926). [ills. 988–90, p. 414. Col. pl. 33]

Neue Sachlichkeit (Ger. new objectivity). About 1920 a reaction against EXPRESSIONISM took place in Germany and the phrase *die neue Sachlichkeit* was coined in 1923 to distinguish a new attention to realistic representation of actual objects in a detailed way – thus also reacting against the muzziness of Impressionism. DIX was influenced by it. The movement petered out, but the new feeling for the subject is distantly related to SURREALISM.

New English Art Club *see* NEAC.

Nicholson, Ben and William. Sir William (1872–1949) was an English painter, especially of still-life, who is best known for his woodcuts of Victorian types and characters and for having contributed much, with his brother-in-law James Pryde (1866–1941), to the development of the poster. The two were known as the Beggarstaff Brothers. Nicholson is well represented in London (Tate) and in Cambridge (Fitzwm). [ill. 970, p. 411] His son, Ben (*b.* 1894) is the best-known British abstract painter and the first winner of the Guggenheim Award. His paintings and reliefs (plain and coloured) are geometrically inspired and derive from the austerer forms of Cubism and from Mondrian. Of his own *Au Chat Botté* (Manchester) he wrote: 'About space-construction: I can explain one aspect of this by an early painting I made of a shop window in Dieppe.... The name of the shop was "Au Chat Botté" ... the words themselves had also an abstract quality – but what was important was that this name was printed in very lovely red lettering on the glass window – *giving one plane* – and in this window were reflections of what was behind me as I looked in – *giving a second plane* – while through the window objects on a table were performing a kind of ballet and forming the "eye" or life-point of the painting – *giving a third plane*.' He is represented in Edinburgh (NG Modern Art), London (Tate), Manchester, New York (M of MA), Toronto, and elsewhere. [ill. 1088, p. 427]

Niello is a branch of goldsmiths' work which was of great importance in the early development of line ENGRAVING. A *niello* is a small plate of silver or gold which has a pattern engraved on it, the pattern being then filled with *niello*, a mixture of lead, silver, copper, and sulphur. This composition is fused into the lines of the pattern and the plate is then polished, so that the pattern is in black on a burnished ground. Sometimes the goldsmith would test his work by making a sulphur cast from the *niello* or by printing from it on to paper: from this it is a short step to making engravings for the sole purpose of being printed on paper. A few such impressions and sulphur casts still exist.

Nittis, Giuseppe de (1846–84), was trained in Naples, but was expelled in 1863 and went to Florence, where he came in contact with the MACCHIAOLI. From Florence he went to Paris, where he spent the rest of his life except for a visit to London in 1875. He was much influenced by the Impressionists, particularly by DEGAS, like his contemporary, ZANDOMENEGHI. His *vedute* are similar to those of SIGNORINI, who was his friend and companion on the trip to Britain. The largest collection of his works is in his native Barletta (190 pictures bequeathed by his widow), but there are others in Florence, Paris, Philadelphia (Wilstach), and Rome. [ill. 324, p. 318]

Nocturne. A night-piece. The term was first used by WHISTLER, who frequently gave his paintings musical titles, but the idea of painting landscapes as night scenes goes much further back, and most of A. van der NEER's works are of this kind.

Nolan, Sidney (*b.* 1917), is recognized as the leader of the modern Australian school. He was born in Melbourne and trained there. His grandfather was a policeman who told stories of the 'Kelly Era', and Nolan has painted a series of works on the theme of the semi-mythical outlaw in his home-made armour, which express the violence of his deeds and death and the hallucinatory quality of the Outback with a visionary intensity. Another Australian folk hero, Mrs Fraser, has also figured in his private mythology, as has the better-known Leda, more accessible in symbolism but equally the vehicle for his multi-layered exploration of the significance of form, colour, and emotional content. The series of the carcasses of sheep in the Outback has an almost Surrealist quality. Nolan first saw modern European painting in 1939, and in 1940 had his first one-man show, of abstract works. In 1951 he visited Europe, and in 1958–60 worked in the US. There are works in Australian museums and in Bedford, Liverpool, London (Tate), and New York (M of MA). [ill. 1115, p. 429]

Nolde, Emil (1867–1956), was a German Expressionist painter of landscapes, Biblical scenes, and figure subjects based on a private mythology. He shared in the BRÜCKE movement in 1906–7, and in 1913–14 travelled through Russia, China, Japan, and Polynesia, where he was impressed by the demoniac quality of primitive art and religion. He was persecuted by the Nazis. His pictures have a particularly ferocious quality, distorted drawing, violent colour, and a tormented technique. He also worked in etching, lithography, and woodcut. There is a Nolde Foundation at Seebüll, on the German-Danish border. [ill. 1012, p. 417]

Nollekens, Joseph (1737–1823), was an English sculptor who, from 1759 to 1770, worked in Rome where he also dealt in antiques and fragments which he restored and sold to English tourists. He became an ARA in 1771, an RA in 1772, and enjoyed a very considerable reputation. His able and lifelike busts ensured him a position in sculpture almost equal to that of Reynolds in painting; his character, mercilessly delineated by his pupil J.T. Smith in the first 'debunking' biography 'Nollekens and his Times' (1828), is that of a grasping man only outdone in miserliness by his wife. He made the bust of Dr Johnson in Westminster Abbey, where there are also several tombs by him, and there are works in the Royal Collection, Cambridge (Fitzwm), Edinburgh (NPG), and London (V & A, Wellington Mus., and Kenwood). There are said to be over 70 replicas of his bust of *Pitt*, which contributed handsomely to his fortune of £200,000. [ill. 865, p. 399]

Northcote, James (1746–1831), was pupil and assistant of Reynolds (1771–5), and he studied in Rome (1777–80). He was a tame follower of Reynolds's portrait style, and his history pictures – mostly for Boydell's Shakespeare Gallery – are full of figures from the Antique and the Italian Grand Manner, roughly transplanted into an alien land and made to toil humbly at unsuitable tasks. He wrote a biography of Reynolds and some gossipy reminiscences. [ill. 888, p. 400]

Norwich School. This is the only regional School of painting in England which had an internal cohesion comparable to the Italian local Schools. Its two great masters were COTMAN and CROME, and it began at a meeting at Crome's house in Norwich on 19 February 1803, when his friends, patrons, and pupils formed the Norwich Society 'for the purpose of an Enquiry into the Rise Progress and present state of Painting, Architecture, and Sculpture, with a view to point out the Best Methods of study to attain to Greater Perfection. . . .' From 1805 it became an Exhibiting Society and was joined by Cotman in 1807. Among the many minor artists the sons of Crome and Cotman, Joseph Stannard, Stark, and Vincent are the best known. All are well represented in Norwich Museum.

Notke, Bernt (*c.* 1440–1509), was the most important painter and wood-carver active in the late 15th century in the Baltic area. He was recorded at Lübeck in 1467 and was specifically exempted from the regulations of the Guild, so he may have been of higher social status than most German artists of his time. His main work, the High Altar for Aarhus Cathedral in Denmark, was being worked on in 1478/9 and was completed by 1482. The paintings are probably his, but the sculpture may be by his assistants. In 1477 he had carved the great cross for Lübeck Cathedral in polychromed wood with a combination of Late Gothic pathos and light-hearted elegance. The spiky elegance, coupled with an extreme realism of detail, is best seen in his most famous work, the huge statue of S. George killing the Dragon, completed in 1489 (Stockholm, S. Nicholas). This was an important commission given by a leading Swedish statesman and was intended as a national memorial to a victory over the Danes. Notke appears to have spent several years in Stockholm and he also made the High Altar for Reval Cathedral (1482/3). [ill. 550, p. 353]

Novecento (Ital. nine hundred). The 20th century, i.e. the nineteen hundreds. It was also the name given to a movement, founded in 1926, which became associated with Fascism on account of its 'back-to-the-great-Italian-past' character.

O

Objet Trouvé *see* FOUND OBJECT.

Ochtervelt, Jacob (*c.* 1635–1708/10), was a Dutch genre painter much influenced by Pieter de HOOCH, and, through him, by Vermeer. The NG, London, has typical examples of his work. [ill. 518, p. 346]

Œuvre (Fr. work). The *œuvre* of an artist is the total of his output, and an *Œuvre Catalogue* is, therefore, an attempt to record every single painting, or drawing, or statue, by a given artist.

Offset *see* COUNTERPROOF.

Oil Painting is the most usual technique for painting pictures of some size and importance. Basically, it consists of covering a slightly absorbent surface (usually primed canvas) with one or more layers of pigment ground in just enough oil to make the mixture pleasantly sticky. The oil used is normally linseed, but poppy or nut oils have also been used, since they remain workable for long periods. On the other hand, 'dryers' are sometimes mixed with linseed oil to speed up the drying processes. The use of oil mixtures for house and decorative painting probably goes back to antiquity, but the 'invention of oil painting' – i.e. the technique adapted to the painting of pictures – is traditionally credited to the EYCKS. This is not true, but it does seem certain that a much improved technique probably based on better-quality oil, was introduced into Flanders early in the 15th century. Italian painters were slow in catching up, and a picture like the *S. Sebastian* by the POLLAIUOLO brothers (1475: London, NG) shows that they were still far from proficient towards the end of the century.

There are two principal ways of painting pictures in oil. One, known as ALLA PRIMA or 'direct' painting, consists of just putting the paint on and hoping it comes out right. If this fails the proper cure is to take another canvas and start again. The second, more elaborate, technique is the one favoured by the Old Masters. This involves a good deal of planning ahead, since the canvas is first drawn on, then covered with one or more layers of monochrome so that the whole picture is virtually complete except for the colour; this is then applied in layers, so that the underlying layers show through to a predetermined extent, while the colours themselves are modified by their application as transparent films (GLAZES) or as opaque pastes (SCUMBLES), much extra effect being gained from IMPASTO and BRUSH-WORK. This technique, in the hands of a master craftsman such as Rembrandt, Rubens, or Titian, is capable of almost unlimited subtlety and variety; which is why oil painting has practically superseded all its rivals. [Col. pls. 11–36]

Oliver, Isaac (*d.* 1617), was brought to England as a child in 1568 to escape the persecution of the Huguenots. He learned the art of miniature painting from HILLIARD and became his chief rival by about 1595. He may have gone abroad in 1588, and he was certainly in Venice in 1596 – when he described himself as a Frenchman – and he must have seen a good deal of Italian art, principally that of Parmigianino, for he had ambitions, unlike Hilliard who painted only portraits, towards history painting in miniature. One of his three wives was a GHEERAERTS and he was popular at the Court of James I. He is well represented in the Royal Coll. and in the V & A, London. His son Peter (1594?–1647) completed some of his works. [ill. 806, p. 391]

Opie, John (1761–1807), was launched in London in 1781 as the 'Cornish Wonder', an untutored natural genius, by John Wolcot, doctor, sometime pupil of Wilson, satirist ('Peter Pindar') and skilful impresario. The young Opie's talent lay in painting peasant types in strong chiaroscuro, and he is best with old people and children, whom he treats with Rembrandtesque effects of light: 'Ah!' said Reynolds to Northcote, newly back from Italy, 'there is *such* a young man come out of Cornwall ... like Caravaggio, but finer!' His large compositions for Boydell's Shakespeare Gallery, popular in engravings, were influential in establishing the costume-history piece, but once his Tenebrist vision was smothered by elegant face-painting, he declined into insipidity. His second marriage, in 1798, to the novelist Amelia Alderson led to his painting more 'literary' subjects. From 1799 he had a studio in Norwich and knew CROME. He became an RA in 1787, was made a Professor at the RA in 1805, and gave a series of lectures, published posthumously in 1809. There are works in London (Guildhall, Tate, NPG), Aberdeen, Birmingham, Brighton, Bristol, Cardiff, Exeter, Glasgow (City Mus.), Leeds, Norwich, Plymouth, Southampton, Truro, and elsewhere. [ill. 886, p. 400]

Optical Mixtures. According to the colour-theory of NEO-IMPRESSIONISM, it is possible to obtain brighter secondary colours, such as green, by making a series of blobs of both primaries (which in the case of green would be blue and yellow) so that the blue and yellow blobs are very closely intermingled but not actually mixed. In this way, the colours mix in the spectator's eye at a certain distance from the picture, giving a much brighter and cleaner green than is obtainable by actual mixing of the pigments on the palette. For this reason, the Neo-Impressionists painted their pictures entirely in small dots or commas of colour, either the colours of the spectrum used pure, or blended only with white, and they varied the size of the blob according to the size of the picture and the distance at which it was to be seen, relying always on distance to make the mixture in the spectator's eye. The Neo-Impressionists disliked the term Pointillism, preferring Divisionism as a description of their technique: a full description is given in SIGNAC's book 'De Delacroix au Néo-Impressionnisme' (Chap. I). The Impressionists had already used a known variant of the technique, in their use of juxtapositions of different shades and tones of one or more colours, so as to enhance the brilliance and shimmering quality of their colour. Optical greys are also obtained in this way, and are claimed to be superior to mixtures with black pigment in them; they were essential to Impressionism, the theory of which does not recognize the existence of black in Nature. Many of Degas's pastels show the use of optical mixtures – not in the rigid manner of the Neo-Impressionist theory, but in a much more elaborate form than that used by the Impressionists, and he frequently used superposed scumbles to achieve depth of colour. [Col. pls. 32, 33, 43]

Orcagna, Andrea (c. 1308–68), was a painter, sculptor, and architect active in Florence in the mid 14th century, one of the first major figures to arise after Giotto, whose ideals he did not entirely share. The first document to mention him (1343) speaks of his 'many defects and faults'. He was admitted to the Guild of Painters in 1343/4 and Stonemasons in 1352. His only certain painting is the large altarpiece in the Strozzi Chapel of S. Maria Novella, Florence (1354–7). This shows a wiry sense of form and a rejection of the sense of spatial depth that had been one of Giotto's greatest achievements: in its place Orcagna creates a much more hieratic art, in which gold backgrounds play an important part, probably directly related to a change in religious feeling after the Black Death of 1348. His main work in sculpture is the Tabernacle, with a relief of the *Death and Assumption of the Virgin* (signed and dated 1359), in Orsanmichele, Florence. In 1368 an altarpiece of *S. Matthew* (Florence, Uffizi) was completed by his brother Jacopo di Cione on account of Orcagna's illness, and almost certainly he died in that year. His brothers Nardo (active 1343/6–d. 1365/6) and Jacopo (active 1365–98) di Cione were the most influential painters in Florence at the end of the 14th century. The fresco of the *Inferno* in the Strozzi Chapel does not seem to be by the same hand as the altarpiece (i.e. it is not by Orcagna) – and Ghiberti ascribes it to Nardo. There are many works which are vaguely Orcagnesque and seem to date from the end of the 14th century: these are usually attributed to Jacopo. Pictures by one or the other are in the Royal Collection and in Berlin, Florence (Accad., Uffizi, SM Novella, and other churches), Liverpool, London (NG, V & A), New York (Met. Mus., Hist. Soc.), Philadelphia (Johnson), St Louis, the Vatican, Washington (NG), and Yale University. [ills. 29, 30, 35, pp. 272–3]

Orley, Bernard (Barent) van (c. 1488–1541), was a Brussels painter, head of a large workshop. He was called in his own day the Raphael of the Netherlands, from his garbled imitation of Italian Renaissance ideas and forms, derived from his knowledge of the Raphael tapestry cartoons, which were woven in Brussels c. 1516/19, and from two conjectural visits to Italy. He was Court Painter to the Spanish Governors of the Netherlands; was one of the principal ROMANISTS; was a prolific designer of tapestries and stained glass, and executed occasional portraits in the Massys and Holbein style. There are examples in the Royal Collection (tapestries), Antwerp, Brussels, Detroit, Munich, Toronto, Turin, Vienna, and elsewhere. [ill. 372, p. 325]

Orozco, José (1883–1949), was a Mexican painter who used an Expressionist style for his frequently huge decorations (often in fresco or in imitations of fresco achieved with modern building materials). Most of his works have strong political overtones, and, like RIVERA, he executed many commissions for revolutionary governments. [ill. 1071, p. 425]

Orphic Cubism, Orphisme. A term invented in 1913 by Apollinaire to describe 'the art of painting new structures out of elements that have not been borrowed from the visual sphere but have been created entirely by the artist himself, and have been endowed by him with the fullness of reality'. This art was attributed to DELAUNAY, who was mainly concerned with the primacy of colour over form. He thus produced a fusion of CUBISM, Futurism, and the independent colour of Fauvism to produce a precursor of pure Abstract painting. Through KANDINSKY and KLEE his ideas exerted great influence in Germany. He also used the spectrum to produce what he called the Law of Simultaneous Contrasts.
Orphic Cubism is so called because it was regarded as more oracular and esoteric (and therefore 'purer') than ordinary Cubism. [ill. 1048, p. 421]

Ostade, Adriaen van (1610–84), was a Haarlem genre painter who was a pupil of Frans Hals, though it is difficult to see any influence of Hals in his interiors with drunken peasants or conversations between hags. In the 1640s he was influenced by Rembrandt (the *Slaughtered Pig*, 1643, Frankfurt, Städel, is a case in point), but the principal influence seems to be that of BROUWER, in the sense that both painted the same kind of peasant scenes. He painted about 1,000 pictures, so that he is well represented in museums. Jan Steen was his pupil. [ill. p. 507, 347]

Ostade, Isack van (1621–49), was the younger brother and pupil of Adriaen. In his short life he painted a large number of pictures, some of genre subjects like his brother's, but the best are of landscape: there are good winter scenes by him in London (NG, Wallace Coll., and Kenwood). [ill. 498, p. 344,]

Ottocento (Ital. eight hundred). The 19th century, i.e. the eighteen hundreds.

Oudry, Jean-Baptiste (1686–1755), was one of the greatest French painters of hunting, animal, and still-life subjects, particularly those with game and dead beasts in the open air. He was a pupil of his father and of Largillierre, and was influenced by Desportes, his only equal in his chosen genre. After painting portraits, still-life and flower subjects, he concentrated from *c.* 1720 on animals, hunts, and landscapes, with occasional portraits. He was appointed Court Painter to Louis XV, and painted the Royal hounds, and from 1726 onwards he worked for the Beauvais tapestry works. After he became manager (in 1734) he designed the illustrations to the 'Fables' of La Fontaine that brought the factory world fame. He also worked for the Gobelins from 1736, and designed for it the *Hunts of Louis XV*. His works show a careful attention to detail, but also have a largeness of handling in light and shade and feeling for colour.

There are works in Barnard Castle (Bowes Mus.), Caen, Cambridge Mass. (Fogg), Compiègne, Copenhagen, Fontainebleau, Leningrad (Hermitage), London (Wallace Coll.), Marseilles, Moscow, New York (Met. Mus.), Paris (Louvre, Carnavalet, Mus. des Arts Décoratifs, Petit Palais), Schwerin (the largest collection: 43), Stockholm, and elsewhere. [ill. 706, p. 377]

Ouwater, Albert van (mid 15th century). All that is known about this painter is that he was a Haarlemer who was the master of GEERTGEN tot Sint Jans, and that he made a painting of the *Raising of Lazarus* which is unmistakably the one in Berlin under his name (or perhaps the Berlin picture is a copy of a lost original). By deduction from Geertgen's activities it is possible to assume that Ouwater was contemporary with the other major 15th-century Haarlem painter, BOUTS the Elder. A tiny fragment in New York (Met. Mus.) is also attributed to him. [ill. 344, p. 322]

Overbeck, Johann Friedrich (1789–1869), was the most important of the NAZARENER group, which he founded with another painter, Pforr, in 1809. From 1810 he lived almost entirely in Rome and painted in a purely 'Quattrocento' style; like INGRES, he idolized Raphael. He became a Catholic in 1813. There are works in Assisi (SM degli Angeli), Basle, Berlin, Cologne (Cath.), Munich, and elsewhere. [ill. 609, p. 360]

Ovile Master, The, *see* 'UGOLINO-LORENZETTI'.

Ozenfant, Amédée (*b.* 1886), is a French painter who invented PURISM. In 1928 he published 'Art' (English edition in 1931 as 'Foundations of Modern Art'). He has lived in New York since 1938. There are works in London (Tate), New York (M of MA), and Paris (Mus. d'Art Mod.). [ill. 1052, p. 422]

P., Pinx., Pinxit (Lat. he painted) following a name on a painting or, more commonly, an engraving after a painting, refers to the authorship of the original picture.

Pacheco, Francisco (1564–1654), was a Spanish painter and writer on art. He was the master of CANO and VELAZQUEZ who was also his son-in-law. Pacheco worked mostly in Seville and is not known to have visited Italy, although he had a large collection of engravings including some after Michelangelo, Veronese, Dürer, and Lucas van Leyden. In 1611 Velazquez became his pupil, and in the same year he made a trip to Madrid and Toledo where he visited GRECO. In 1618 he was appointed Censor of Paintings to the Inquisition and in 1619 was made a Painter to the King. His book 'El Arte de la Pintura' took thirty years to write and was completed in 1637/8. It was published in 1649, but a new and fuller edition appeared in 1956. Pacheco claimed to have painted one hundred and fifty portraits by 1647. Most of his works are in Seville, but there is one in Williamstown Mass. [ill. 644, p. 364]

Pacher, Michael (c. 1435–98), was the principal Tyrolean painter and was almost certainly active also as a wood-carver. As his geographical position would imply, Pacher is a sort of half-way house between the Gothic qualities of German 15th-century painting and the more intellectual interests of the Italians – in his case, Mantegna seems to have been the principal influence. There is an altarpiece by him in Munich and other works in Cologne (Schnütgen Mus.), and Vienna (Belvedere) and a panel of his school in London (NG), but the majority of his works remain in the parish churches for which they were painted or carved, his masterpiece being the *S. Wolfgang Altarpiece* completed by 1481. [ill. 551, p. 353]

Painterly *see* MALERISCH.

Painting Techniques *see* ENCAUSTIC WAX, FRESCO, GOUACHE, OIL PAINTING, PASTEL, SIZE COLOUR, TEMPERA, WATERCOLOUR.

Pajou, Augustin (1730–1809), was a French sculptor who was a pupil of J.-B. LEMOYNE and studied in Rome 1752–6. He is best known for his decorative sculpture in the Opera House at Versailles (1768–70) and for his numerous portraits – *J.-B. Lemoyne* (1758) and *Buffon* in the Louvre, *Descartes* and *Bossuet* in the Institut. He worked much for Mme du Barry. In 1777 he was appointed Keeper of the King's Antiquities and in 1792 he served on a Revolutionary Committee on the Conservation

of Works of Art. His *Psyche abandoned* (1791: Louvre) is a piece of Neoclassic sentiment. [ill. 717, p. 379]

Pala. An Italian word for a large altarpiece: unlike an ANCONA a pala may consist of one picture only. A 'Pala of a unified type' is one in which all the action (if any), and all the figures, are represented as inhabiting one single space, which is treated as a consistent pictorial continuum. In most POLYPTYCHS each scene, or even each Saint, has its own space. [ill. 125, p. 290]

Paliotto is Italian for an *antependium* or altar frontal, i.e. the hanging which covers the front of an altar. These are normally of cloth, the colour agreeing with the liturgical colour of the day, but there are examples of carved, painted, or enamelled frontals. They are often very ancient, and the most famous is perhaps the golden one in St Mark's, Venice, which is 13th-century, or that in Sant' Ambrogio, Milan, of the 9th century.

Palma Giovane (1544–1628) was the grand-nephew of Palma Vecchio. He was much influenced by Tintoretto and Veronese. There are works by him in the Royal Coll. and in Florence (Uffizi), London (NG), Madrid, Milan (Brera), Munich, Naples, Vienna, as well as many in Venice. [ill. 234, p. 307]

Palma Vecchio (Jacopo Palma) (1480–1528) was a Venetian painter who was a pupil of Giovanni Bellini and was much influenced by Titian, as well as by Giorgione and Lotto. He is chiefly remembered as the painter of a particularly splendid type of blonde, said to be characteristically Venetian in her ample charms. For this reason, many of his works are *Sacre Conversazioni* with several female Saints. His masterpiece is perhaps the *S. Barbara and other Saints* in SM Formosa, Venice, but there are other works in Venice and in the Royal Coll. and Berlin, Cambridge (Fitzwm), Chicago, Detroit, Dresden, Florence (Uffizi), Glasgow, London (NG and RA), Milan (Brera), Paris (Louvre), Philadelphia, Rome (Gall. Naz., Borghese, Capitoline), San Marino Cal. (Huntington), Sarasota Fla, Vienna, Worcester Mass., York, and elsewhere. [ill. 216, p. 304]

Palmer, Samuel (1805–81), was a painter of pastoral landscape and the most important follower of BLAKE, whom he met in 1824. He was very precocious and exhibited at the RA from 1819. His 'Shoreham Period' (1826–35) was the moment of perfect balance between inner and outer vision – a landscape charged with fecundity and Christian symbolism, expressed in terms of observed detail. This 'primitive and infantine feeling' (his own words) for landscape began to fade *c.* 1832; in 1838 he married the daughter of John LINNELL and visited Italy, and his son later wrote of these events 'After the Shoreham and Italian periods, the whole of my father's life became a dreadful tragedy.' His early work has influenced modern Romantic painters, e.g. SUTHERLAND: examples are in London (BM, V & A, and Tate), Oxford (Ashmolean Mus.), and elsewhere. [ill. 940, p. 406]

Panini (or Pannini), Giovanni Paolo (*c.* 1692–1765/8), was the first painter to specialize in ruins, treating them as Roman VEDUTE of a special kind. He was working in Rome by *c.* 1717, but the earliest datable picture is of 1727 (London, Wellington Mus.); in 1729 he was concerned in a Fête given by Cardinal de Polignac in honour of the birth of the Dauphin and this began a long connection with France and the French Academy in Rome. Paintings of the Fête are in the Louvre (1729) and Dublin (1731). His views of modern Rome, as well as his *capricci* based on the better-known ruins, had an enormous vogue among tourists and examples are to be found in most galleries. PIRANESI, though more of an archaeologist, was influenced by him, and so was CANALETTO. [ill. 316, p. 317]

Paolo Veneziano (*d. c.* 1362), was the principal painter working in the Byzantine style in 14th-century Venice. In 1358 he and his son Giovanni jointly signed a *Coronation of the Virgin* (New York, Frick Coll.) which is the last known work by him, but another *Coronation* (Washington, NG) attributed to him is dated 1324. His son Luca was also a painter and the father and both sons jointly signed the cover which they made for the great altarpiece, the *Pala d'Oro*, in S. Mark's in 1345. [ill. 50, p. 275]

Papier Collé (Fr. stuck paper) is a form of COLLAGE built up from layers of paper stuck on a ground such as canvas.

Paris, The School of (L'École de Paris). Since about 1900 Paris has been the Mecca of young painters of every nationality, Picasso being perhaps the most obvious example. The term now means little more than contemporary painting, predominantly non-figurative, without regard to national schools: Eastern European and German refugees, Spanish and American painters can all be included in the term, and De STAËL, HARTUNG, and RIOPELLE equally with SOULAGES, MANESSIER, or DUBUFFET are covered by it. The phrase tends to mean different things to French writers, who would like to imply hegemony.

Parmigianino, Francesco (1503–40), was one of the most sensitive and elegant of the early Mannerists. He was born in Parma and was commissioned to decorate the S. transept of Parma Cathedral as early as 1522 and was painting frescoes in S. Giovanni Evangelista there in 1522/3: as this church contains frescoes by CORREGGIO the principal influence on his style was Correggio, soon followed by Pordenone and Raphael. He was in Rome by late 1523 and was captured in the Sack of Rome (1527) while working on the *S. Jerome* (now London, NG). He was able to escape to Bologna and travelled to Verona and Venice

before returning to Parma in 1530. The last ten years of his life were spent in painting frescoes in Sta Maria della Steccata, Parma, and quarrelling with the overseers of the works; although he was supposed to start in 1531 he did so little that, finally, in 1539 the authorities sacked him and had him imprisoned for breach of contract. The next year he died, and it is an adequate description of his neurotic temperament to quote Vasari: 'having his thoughts filled with alchemy . . . [he] changed from the delicate, amiable, and elegant person that he was, to a bearded, long-haired, neglected, and almost savage or wild man . . . he was there interred naked, as he had wished, and with a cross of cypress placed upright on his breast in the grave'. His work, both in painting and perhaps even more through his etchings, which had wide currency, was very influential in Italy and also in N. Europe. His figures have long necks and hands and seem almost swooning in their ecstasy, much of which is truly Counter-Reformation in taste. His portraits, when he had a congenial sitter, have deep spiritual insight (especially, perhaps, the early *Self-portrait* in Vienna, in which he saw himself distorted in a convex mirror). There are paintings by him in the Royal Coll. and in Berlin, Bologna (Pinac., S. Petronio), Copenhagen, Detroit, Dresden, Florence (Uffizi, Pitti), Frankfurt, Glasgow, Madrid (Prado), Milan (Ambrosiana), Naples, Parma (Gall., S. Giovanni Evang., Sta Maria della Steccata, Canonica di Bardi), Rocca di Fontanellato nr Parma, Rome (Borghese, Doria Pal.), Vienna, York. Parmigianino was, after Dürer, one of the earliest painter-etchers – i.e. to use the medium for making works of art of his own. His compositions were also very widely reproduced as engravings and as CHIAROSCURO WOODCUTS, for which he was probably among the first to make designs. [ill. 211, p. 302]

Pascin, Jules (1885–1930), was born Julius Pincas in Bulgaria, but settled in Paris and called himself Pascin. He was trained in Vienna and Munich and worked for the famous satirical paper *Simplizissimus* before going to Paris in 1905, where he settled soon afterwards. He spent the First World War in the US and became an American citizen, but returned to Paris in 1922 and lived there until he hanged himself on the opening day of his one-man show in 1930. His pictures are all of equivocally young girls in sprawling poses, a sort of Lolita *avant la lettre*, and have much in common with certain French 18th-century painters (BOUCHER) and engravers; perhaps for this reason he is not well represented in public galleries, although there are examples in Paris (Musée d'Art Moderne), Minneapolis, Southampton, and Toledo Ohio. [ill. 1077, p. 425]

Pasmore, Victor (*b.* 1908), was one of the members of the EUSTON Road Group in the late 1930s. He was unable to paint full-time until 1938, but from then until 1947 he painted the most subtle landscapes and interiors seen in England since Steer or Whistler. The later scenes of the Thames were almost Oriental in their tonal subtlety and hinted at the abstraction which he embraced in 1947: since the 1950s he has made constructions in the manner of GABO, usually of simply coloured wood and Perspex. He has been a most influential teacher, first in Newcastle and then in London, of a course based on abstract principles of design. There are works by him in many British and

Commonwealth galleries: he was concerned also with the New Town at Peterlee, Durham. [ill. 980, p. 412]

Pastel is a medium consisting of dry powdered colour mixed with just enough gum (usually gum arabic) to bind it. The mixture is allowed to set in moulds, forming very fragile sticks about the size of a finger. These sticks, when rubbed on paper, disintegrate so that the powder adheres to the paper; but one of the great drawbacks of the medium is the ease with which the powder falls off again or smudges. The softest pastels give an effect which is virtually that of painting, the whole surface of the paper being covered by the pigment layer, but it is also possible to use much harder, grittier pastels (like those commonly used in schools) to get an effect more closely related to drawing. The first method was used by such French masters as Quentin LATOUR or CHARDIN, the second is more usual for making studies instead of finished works. DEGAS, perhaps the greatest of pastellists, tended to use the medium as a form of drawing rather than painting, but he also had various technical tricks (such as soaking the paper in turpentine) which have helped to preserve his pastels, although they incur the wrath of the purists. [Col. pls. 42, 43].

Pastiche, Pasticcio. An imitation or forgery which consists of a number of motives taken from several genuine works by any one artist recombined in such a way as to give the impression of being an independent original creation by that artist.

Patenier, Patinier, or Patinir, Joachim (*d. c.* 1524), is documented in the Antwerp Guild in 1515. Dürer, who owned a picture by him, mentions him as a landscape painter, attended the festivities at his second marriage in 1521, and drew his portrait. His small landscapes have something in common with Antwerp Mannerism in that they are cool in colour and very blue in the distances, and they represent fantastic scenery with jagged mountains, farmlands dotted with villages and ruins, rocky shores, and little figures of saints, hermits, and country people. They offer a wonderful mixture of fantasy and naturalistic detail that presages the more naturalistic landscapes of Bruegel. Sometimes the figures are by others; in one case at least by MASSYS, who became the guardian of Patenier's children in 1524. There are works in Antwerp, Basle, Berlin, Cambridge (Fitzwm), London (NG), Madrid (Prado), Minneapolis, New York (Met. Mus.), Oxford, Paris (Louvre), Philadelphia (Mus. and Johnson), Rome (Borghese), Vienna, York, and elsewhere. [ill. 388, p. 327]

Pater, Jean-Baptiste-Joseph (1695–1736), was an imitator of WATTEAU, whose only pupil he was. Apparently they separated on account of Watteau's extreme irritability, but in his last days Watteau repented of this, sent for Pater, and gave him his final lessons. Pater soon wore out his own talent in repetitions of *fêtes galantes*, typical examples of which are in the Wallace Coll. and at Kenwood, London. [ill. 727, p. 380]

Patina is the greenish incrustation on the surface of old BRONZE. It is esteemed for its own sake, and the word has had its meaning extended to cover all forms of mellowing with age. When a picture has had the dirt cleaned off its surface it is often described as having 'lost its patina'.

Peale, a family of American painters and naturalists. The two earliest members were Charles Willson Peale (1741–1827) and his brother James (1749–1831). Charles was a saddler and wood-carver who had lessons from COPLEY, went to London 1767–9 and worked under WEST, returning to settle in Philadelphia. He painted a number of portraits of the leading figures in the Revolutionary War including the earliest (1772) of Washington. In 1786 he founded the Peale Museum and from then on was principally concerned with the scientific aspect of his museum – e.g. in 1806 he exhibited the skeleton of the first American mastodon. He began to paint again at the age of seventy-four and died at eighty-six, his death being brought on by carrying a trunk for a mile on his way to court his fourth wife. He wrote an autobiography, and his three wives gave him seventeen children who were ambitiously christened, the boys including Raphaelle, Rembrandt, Titian, Rubens, and the girls being christened Angelica Kauffmann, Rosalba Carriera, and Sophonisba (after an Italian woman painter). Raphaelle (1774–1825) painted some very fine and austere still-lifes, not at all Dutch in feeling but far closer to Spanish 17th-century work. He was the best painter of the family, but his attempt with Rembrandt Peale to run the family museum was a failure; he was unhappily married and eventually took to drink. Rembrandt (1778–1860) also painted still-life and some very fine, detailed portraits (*Rubens Peale with a Geranium Plant*). He visited England in 1802–3 and worked under West and painted a number of French statesmen in Paris 1808–10 for his father's museum. He settled in New York in 1822 but revisited Europe in 1829/30, and finally returned to Philadelphia in 1831. He was one of the first American artists to practise lithography and he also painted one of the best-known portraits of Washington, the so-called Port-hole Portrait painted in 1823, twenty-four years after Washington's death. The original is now in the Capitol, Washington, in the Vice-President's room, but about eighty replicas are known. Rubens (1784–1865) and Titian the Elder (1799–1881) were also painters, but less important.

Charles Willson's brother James was a miniaturist in Philadelphia and may have been one of the first painters of still-life in America. He had seven children, five of whom were painters, but they were less eccentrically named than their cousins. There are works by one or other of the Peales in many American museums including Baltimore, New York (Historical Soc.), Philadelphia, Washington (NG), and Worcester. [ills. 854, 855, 913, 914, pp. 397, 403]

Pearce (Pierce), Edward (*d.* 1695), was a prolific and able wood- and stone-carver, who worked on decorative sculpture for country houses and churches, for Wren's City churches (he made the wooden model of the copper dragon for the vane of St Mary-le-Bow), the Guildhall, St Paul's Cathedral, Hampton Court, several City Companies, and Clare College, Cambridge. His bust of Wren (1673: Oxford, Ashmolean) shows him with a gift for the restrained Baroque current in England, and a ready eye for liveliness of character. There are works in the Royal

Collection, and London (NPG, London Mus.). [ill. 862, p. 398]

Pechstein, Max (1881–1955), was one of the leading German Expressionists. He was trained in Dresden and in 1906 became a member of the BRÜCKE group, founded the year before by KIRCHNER, SCHMIDT-ROTTLUFF, and others. In 1907–8 he went to Italy and Paris and in 1914 was able to go to the South Seas, to the island of Palau, where his works were very obviously influenced by GAUGUIN's example. In 1915 he was arrested by the Japanese and sent to Nagasaki, returning to Germany via New York. He served in the German Army until 1918. In 1934 he was expelled from the Prussian Academy and forbidden to exhibit: after 1945, like Schmidt-Rottluff, he became a Professor in Berlin. There are works in several German museums as well as Baltimore, Los Angeles, and Toledo Ohio. His autobiography was published posthumously. [ill. 1017, p. 417]

Pedigree *see* PROVENANCE.

Peinture à l'Essence *see* DEGAS.

Pellegrini, Giovanni Antonio (1675–1741), was a Venetian decorative painter who was a pupil of Sebastiano RICCI and one of the most important of TIEPOLO's predecessors. Like PITTONI, he worked for many foreign patrons and travelled widely. He was first recorded as a painter in 1703 and soon after this he married the sister of Rosalba CARRIERA, who mentions him in her diary on several occasions. In 1707 Lord Manchester went on an embassy to Venice; he commissioned a picture to celebrate the event from CARLEVARIS and brought Pellegrini and Marco Ricci back to London with him in 1708. Pellegrini soon had considerable success and became a Director of Kneller's Academy in 1711. VERTUE says that Pellegrini 'painted prodigious quick, had a very noble and fruitfull invention' which may be seen in the decorations at Kimbolton Castle (now a school), done for Lord Manchester, or in the decorations at Castle Howard (1709: mostly destroyed in 1941). In these decorative series Pellegrini shows that he was a true precursor of Tiepolo in the lightness and gaiety of his touch which contrasts with the duller history painting of Pittoni. In 1713 he went to Germany and Flanders, returning to England in 1719 when, according to Vertue, he was less successful because Marco Ricci had sent for his uncle Sebastiano, who was generally agreed to be a better painter. Pellegrini also painted a splendid ceiling for the Bank of France (since destroyed) in Paris and worked in Prague, Dresden, and Vienna. There is a sketch of 1710 in London (V & A) which may represent his design for the cupola of St Paul's for which, according to Vertue, 'he made several designs and a moddle for painting the Cupulo at St. Paul's, for which he was paid tho' he had not the cupolo to paint'. There are works by him in Berlin, Boston, Dresden, The Hague, Leeds (*Hector* from Kimbolton), London (NG), Paris (Louvre), Vienna, and elsewhere. [ill. 289, p. 315]

Pencil in 18th-century usage means 'brush' and *Pencilling* means BRUSHWORK.

Pencz, Georg (*c.* 1500–50), was a German painter first recorded in the Nuremberg Guild in 1523. He may have been a pupil of DÜRER and, like him, was profoundly influenced by Venetian art. His best works are his portraits, which are very like those of AMBERGER; that is, a combination of Dürer and Venice. Pencz almost certainly visited Italy, and may have studied in Rome, since his mythological pictures show the influence of Raphael, while a ceiling painting in Nuremberg seems to derive from GIULIO Romano's work at Mantua. In the 1540s his portraits are less obviously Italianate and probably owe something to Holbein and Massys, both of whom he is known to have copied. He was also active as an engraver, and some copper engravings signed G.P. are dated between 1534 and 1547. There are pictures by him in Berlin, Brunswick, Cologne, Copenhagen, Darmstadt, Dresden, Florence, and Munich, as well as Nuremberg. [ill. 588, p. 357]

Pentimento (Ital. *pentirsi*, to repent). When a painter changes his mind in the course of a picture and alters, say, the position of a leg, it sometimes happens that the old form will begin to show through in a ghostly way; this ghost is a *pentimento*. It is sometimes inferred that, because there are *pentimenti* visible, a painting must be an original – since it shows the artist changing his mind – and not a copy. The validity of this argument is open to doubt. The word may also be used to denote several attempts to fix a contour with precision in a drawing.

Permeke, Constant (1886–1952), was the leading Belgian Expressionist painter. He was the son of a painter and was trained in Bruges before settling in the village of Laethem-St Martin, which was an artists' colony, where he met several other Expressionists. He was there 1902–12 and was called up in 1914, but was wounded in the same year and spent the rest of the war in England. About 1920 he was slightly influenced by Cubism, but on the whole he was a latter-day MILLET whose deep sympathy for farmers and fishermen is evident in his best work. In 1929 he settled at Jabbeke, near Ostend, where his house is now a museum. Other works by him are in Antwerp, Brussels, London (Tate), Rotterdam, São Paulo, and elsewhere. [ill. 1028, p. 418]

Permoser, Balthasar (1651–1732), was the leading Late Baroque sculptor in Dresden, where he helped to create the Zwinger. He was trained in Salzburg *c.* 1663 before going to Italy for fourteen years. He arrived there *c.* 1675 and went to Venice, Rome, Florence, and other cities; in Florence he carved the façade of S. Gaetano (*c.* 1684) and worked for the Grand Duke Cosimo III, who tried to secure him as Court Sculptor. Permoser, however, went to Dresden as Court Sculptor in 1689. He spent the rest of his life there, except for several trips to Berlin, a visit to Italy in 1697–8 and another in 1725, when, at the age of 74, he walked to Rome. He returned in 1728. As might be expected from his strong Italian leanings, he was much influenced by Bernini, but, like the other Northerners PUGET, DONNER, and SCHLÜTER, he introduced an element of restrained classicism – though this is not very obvious in his most famous work, the *Apotheosis of Prince Eugene* (1718–21: Vienna, Lower Belvedere). Most of his

Dresden works were damaged in 1945, but are now under repair. There are others in Bautzen and Freiberg i. S. [ill. 629, p. 362]

Perréal, Jean (*c.* 1455–1530), used to be identified with the MASTER of MOULINS. He was Court Painter to the Bourbons and later worked for Charles VIII of France and his successors, Louis XII and François I. He was in Italy several times 1499/1505 and in London in 1514, to paint Princess Mary Tudor and supervise her new dresses. He also designed Tombs, notably those (unexecuted) at Brou (1509–12). The most important attributions to him are the *Louis XII of France* in the Royal Coll. and a miniature in London (BM). [ill. 670, p. 372]

Perronneau, Jean-Baptiste (1715?–83), was a French portrait painter in oil and pastel. From *c.* 1755 he journeyed all over Europe, dying in Amsterdam. He was the only rival to LATOUR as a pastellist in the later 18th century, and the popular *Girl with a Kitten* (1745: London, NG) shows his charm. [ill. 738, p. 381]

Perspective. A quasi-mathematical system for the representation of three-dimensional objects in spatial recession on a two-dimensional surface, i.e. for the creation of an independent pictorial space as a microcosm of nature. As normally practised now, perspective is a sophisticated version of the COSTRUZIONE LEGITTIMA invented in the early 15th century, perhaps by Brunelleschi, and improved by Alberti, UCCELLO, and PIERO della Francesca. The basic assumption of all perspective systems is that parallel lines never meet, but that they appear to do so; and that, further, all parallel lines going in any one direction meet at a single point on the horizon known as a Vanishing Point. The early systems were based on a single, central VP; all other parallels were automatically assumed to be parallel to the picture plane and therefore exempt from the assumption that they must meet at some point in the distance. This system is perfectly satisfactory as an aesthetic system, i.e. for the creation of an independent order of reality, a picture-world distinct from the real world; but it is inadequate for an exact representation of physical reality. In order to obtain this greater naturalism – with all the possibilities of illusionism it implies – a system was evolved which uses two VPs on the horizon, and more if necessary to obtain up-hill and down-dale effects. A further refinement is the use of Measuring Points, which allow of the exact representation of objects to scale. All this can be learnt by any moderately mathematically-minded art student in a few hours; for this very reason, many artists are no longer interested in verisimilitude of space and prefer either to renounce the representation of the third dimension altogether (as most abstract artists do), or else they create a spatial illusion of their own, stressing the independence of the world created by the artist from the laws which govern appearance in the physical world.
Aerial Perspective deals with the changes in tone and colour values which are observable in objects receding from the spectator. Owing to the density of the atmosphere all tone contrasts are muted and all colours tend towards blue in proportion to their distance from the observer. Thus, mountains in the background are always bluish. The difference between the atmospheres of Northern Europe and the Mediterranean accounts for the greater interest in aerial perspective to be found in the North, particularly among the Impressionists.

Perugino (*c.* 1445/50–1523) may have been a pupil of PIERO della Francesca late in the 1460s, after which he went to Florence and probably worked in the shop of VERROCCHIO, where, in the early 1470s LEONARDO was also active. He was in Rome in 1479 and is recorded in the 1481 contract for the frescoes in the Sistine Chapel (along with BOTTICELLI, GHIRLANDAIO, and Cosimo Rosselli), where his *Charge to S. Peter* demonstrates his qualities of simplicity, order, and clearly articulated composition. The influence of his friend SIGNORELLI strengthened his draughtsmanship, that of Flemings like MEMLINC suggested the landscape background for his portraits as well as their general composition, and to the persistence of Piero's influence is due the use of architectural and landscape settings for his figure compositions. The *Pietà* (Florence, Accad.) set centrally in a receding arcade, and above all the *Crucifixion with Saints* (Florence, Sta Maria Maddalena de' Pazzi), a fresco of 1496 with an extensive landscape linking the three apparent divisions of the wall, are perfect examples of his quiet, pietistic art; with gentle, rather sentimental figures with drooping postures, tip-tilted heads, and mild rounded faces – a type he repeated all his life with, in his later years, dull and routine repetitiveness.
From *c.* 1500 to *c.* 1504 RAPHAEL was a pupil in his shop. In 1506 Perugino retired to Perugia, since his style was now hopelessly outmoded in Florence; where, however, it had served to counter-balance the confusion of Late Quattrocento style. It was to be the herald of the High Renaissance.
Apart from Rome, Florence, and Perugia there are works by him in Baltimore, Brussels, Cambridge (Fitzwm Mus.), Cerqueto near Perugia (the earliest work, of 1478), Chicago, Edinburgh, Frankfurt, London (NG), Lyons, Munich, Nancy, New York (Met. Mus.), Paris (Louvre), Philadelphia, Vienna, and elsewhere. [ill. 122, p. 289]

Pesellino (*c.* 1422–57) is confused in the old sources with his own grandfather, Giuliano Pesello, who was a painter and probably taught Pesellino; he was certainly influenced by Fra Filippo Lippi and the only documented work by Pesellino, the *Trinity with Saints* (1455–7: London, NG, part on loan from the Royal Coll.) was in fact completed after his death by Fra Filippo's workshop. There are works attributed to him in Berlin, Boston (Gardner), Cambridge Mass. (Fogg), Dresden, Florence (Uffizi, Sta Margherita), Milan (Poldi-Pezzoli), New York (Met. Mus., Hist. Soc.), Paris (Louvre), Philadelphia (Johnson), Toledo Ohio, Washington (NG), Worcester Mass., Yale Univ., and elsewhere. [ill. 79, p. 281]

Pevsner, Antoine (1886–1962), was GABO's elder brother. He was born in Russia and trained in Kiev, where the Byzantine works had a profound effect on him. In 1911 he went to Paris and was influenced by Cubist ideas, but in 1914 he joined his brother in Norway and in 1917 they returned to Revolutionary Russia, hoping for a revolution in the arts. He was made a Professor and worked with

TATLIN and MALEVICH, going on to CONSTRUCTIV-ISM. The growing dissatisfaction of the Soviet authorities with abstract art drove him back to Paris in 1923. There are works by him there (Mus. d'Art Mod.) and also in London (Tate) and New York (M of MA). [ill. 1138, p. 433]

Piazzetta, Giovanni Battista (1683–1754), was a Venetian painter, son of a wood-carver, who studied under G.-M. CRESPI in Bologna and was probably influenced by him to take up genre subjects. He settled in Venice by 1711, and after his death his family petitioned the State for a pension, claiming that his 'constant studies and his pursuit of glory rather than gain had reduced him to poverty and hastened his death'. His works are comparatively few, and though appearing to be executed with speed and facility were the product of careful deliberation and infinite pains. He made many drawings for collectors and as book-illustrations in order to support his family; his work was much influenced by Rembrandt's etchings and his paintings evolve from Baroque contrasts of chiaroscuro towards a freer and more fluid Rococo handling. Piazzetta's influence on the young TIEPOLO was very great and it was Tiepolo who completed the transition to the Rococo. Most of his paintings are in Venice, including his only ceiling decoration, the *Glory of S. Dominic*, painted before 1727 (SS. Giovanni e Paolo). Other works are in Boston, Cologne, Chicago, Cleveland, Detroit, Dresden, Dublin, Florence (Uffizi), London (NG), Milan (Brera), Padua, Vicenza, and elsewhere. [ill. 288, p. 315]

Picabia, Francis (1879–1953), was born in Paris. He has some claim to have painted the first abstract picture – a watercolour of 1908/9, now in Paris, Musée d'Art Moderne – which would antedate KANDINSKY. In 1912 he joined the Section d'Or Cubists, subsequently running through Dadaism and, from 1924, Surrealism: he also painted precisely representational nudes for sale in Algiers. He visited America on several occasions and exhibited at the ARMORY SHOW. There are works in Chicago as well as Paris (Mus. d'Art Mod.). [ill. 1059, p. 422]

Picasso, Pablo Ruiz y, was born in Malaga in 1881, the son of an art teacher. The boy showed exceptional talent at an early age, and the artistic current flowing into Barcelona (where the family had settled) from France and Northern Europe stimulated him into trying out the personal languages of Munch, Toulouse-Lautrec, Renoir, and other Northern lights. In 1900 he visited Paris for a short time, and returned in 1901 to join the cohort of young Bohemians attracted to the capital by the stimulating and exciting atmosphere then prevailing in the arts. Lautrec, Gauguin, van Gogh, Steinlen, Late Impressionism flit across his canvases in a bewildering medley and leave behind a passion for blue, which became the dominant colour for his portrayal of the squalid tragedy of the Paris streets – the beggar, the harlot, the sick child, the hungry. Through this welter of contemporary influences ran the steady current of the things he had grown up with: the elongated forms of Catalan Gothic sculpture and Italian Mannerism, the simplified colour and straightforward approach of Velazquez, Zurbarán, and Goya. These also inform his pictures of actors, mountebanks, and harlequins, whose tender fawns and pinks replace the earlier drab and sad colours.

Until now nothing unusual had transpired: even his interest in Iberian sculpture in 1906, and the radical simplification of form and colour it led to, give little hint of the position when the FAUVE outbreak was at its height. Picasso took no part in this. He was questioning the whole basis of painting and was therefore unable to follow still further the road from Impressionism to the dissolution of form and its translation into colour and imaginative feeling. Picasso's reply to Matisse's 'Composition is the art of arranging in a decorative manner the various elements at the painter's disposal for the expression of his feelings' was to turn to Cézanne, whose *petite sensation* never had any truck with pure decoration and whose composition was based on the rigorous discipline of the relations of form and space on a two-dimensional surface. Picasso's *Les Demoiselles d'Avignon* (New York, M of MA) of 1907 was begun in the vein of his harlequin series, but ended as a semi-abstract composition, in which the forms of the nudes and their accessories are broken up into planes compressed into a shallow space. The influence of Negro sculptures, which first appears in the *Demoiselles*, also fitted in with his quest for the expression of form and helped, by the bizarre nature of their forms, to release him from the tyranny of the representational tradition in art. In 1907 he met BRAQUE, who had drifted into the Fauve circle and out of it again, and in 1909 they found that they faced the same problems and were striving to solve them in the same way. Both rejected decorative arabesques and bright, sensuous colour and were striving to devise a pictorial language which would define volumes and their relationships without destroying the flat surface of the picture, and without descending to the imitation of accidental and superficial appearances. Together they evolved what is now called Analytical Cubism.

By 1912, colour had begun to creep back among the greys, olive-greens, and drab browns, and actual objects – a piece of cane seating, a newspaper heading – were imported so as to stress by their complaisant acquiescence in becoming an element in a design the modest role of Nature in the Ideal, and also to serve as an example of the way in which Nature may be recreated. COLLAGE was a natural extension of this. Objects could be literally reconstituted with bits of wood, wire, paper, and string, their forms distorted by the artist into a flat composition whose inherent third dimension is alluded to at the same time as it is suppressed – although Picasso, having started this hare, did not course it, any more than he did that of SURREALISM, born from the juxtaposition of recognizable objects and reconstituted forms.

At the moment when war broke out in 1914, Braque and Picasso were separated by a quarrel (the breach was never healed) and both had consistently held aloof from the host of minor artists who had by now realized that Cubism was the coming thing and had climbed aboard the bandwagon – Gleizes, Metzinger, Delaunay, Marcoussis, Duchamp-Villon, Picabia, La Fresnaye, and Derain. From 1915 he had shown his interest in Ingres's drawings by precise and restrainedly stylized pencil drawings, and his connection with the Diaghileff Russian Ballet in Rome in 1917 led to works showing a return to traditional vision, with parallel works in a glitteringly sophisticated Cubist idiom. Finally, contact with the Antique and with Roman classicism ushers in a series of paintings and drawings of monumental female nudes, at first almost motionless and then, by 1923, galvanized into terrifying movement which distorts them into frightening caricatures before dissolving them, via calligraphic curves and lines, into the convulsive and repellent distortions of the *Three Dancers* of 1925 (London, Tate). For the next ten years Picasso developed these distorted and disquieting figures through what is generally called the Metamorphic phase, in which he was perhaps somewhat influenced by Miró and Tanguy. By the early 1930s he was rather taking the wind out of Matisse's sails with a series of nudes – odalisques almost – which combine brilliance of colour with flat pattern of a violent intensity; soon after he began the series of bull-fighting subjects which culminated in the imagery present in *Guernica* (1936: on extended loan to M of MA, New York). This huge composition, prompted by the Spanish Civil War, expresses in complicated iconography and personal symbolical language comprehensible after careful study, the artist's abhorrence of the violence and beastliness of war. This dark mood persists in the dislocated forms and frightening imagery of his work during the Second World War. He remained in Paris during the Occupation and gradually acquired by his aloofness the stature of a symbol of resistance. Since the war he has lived chiefly in the South of France, where he devoted himself to ceramics for some time, but he has also painted a large mural for the UNESCO building in Paris.

No man has changed more radically the nature of art. Like Giotto, Michelangelo, and Bernini he stands at the beginning of a new epoch. Most museums of Modern Art throughout the world have examples. [ills. 1038–43, pp. 420–1]

Pickenoy (Picquenoy) *see* ELIAS.

Picture Plane. The extreme front edge of the imaginary space in the picture. It lies immediately behind the glass of the frame and is the plane at which the world of the spectator and of the picture make contact.

Picturesque (Ital. *pittoresco*, pertaining to a painter). Originally (in the 18th century) this meant that a landscape looked as though it came straight out of a picture (by CLAUDE or Gaspar POUSSIN), but the original meaning has been reversed so that it now means that a scene is pictorially worthy to be transferred straight to canvas (it is used in this sense by the sophisticated only with a derogatory implication). In the 18th century, particularly in connection with landscape gardening, there arose a long, complicated, and dreary controversy over The Picturesque (satirized by Jane Austen in 'Sense and Sensibility' and 'Northanger Abbey'), but it served some purpose in that it established a new kind of Beauty, midway between Burke's Sublime and Beautiful (this latter we would call Pretty) and which was dependent for its effect on roughness, irregularity, and a certain amount of deformity. The different types are contrasted in Thomson's 'The Castle of Indolence':

'Whate'er Lorrain light-touched with softening hue,
Or savage Rosa dashed, or learned Poussin drew.'

The idea was much expanded by the Romantics of the 19th century.

Piero di Cosimo (*c.* 1462–1521?) was a pupil of Cosimo Rosselli and probably assisted him on his frescoes in the Sistine Chapel of the Vatican, *c.* 1481. He was much influenced by Signorelli and Leonardo da Vinci and his mature works differ entirely from Rosselli's in that they are mostly rather obscure, but very poetically felt, mythologies. He was famous in his own day as a designer of the *Trionfi* processions, especially for his gruesome *Triumph of Death* of 1511. In his later years he became a recluse. There are pictures by him in Berlin, Chantilly, Florence (Uffizi, Pitti, Horne Mus., Innocenti), The Hague, Hartford Conn., London (NG, Wallace Coll., Dulwich), Munich, New York (Met. Mus.), Ottawa, Oxford, Paris (Louvre), Philadelphia (Johnson), Rome (Borghese, Gall. Naz.), Sarasota Fla, Toledo Ohio, Washington (NG), Worcester Mass., Yale, and elsewhere. [ill. 170, p. 296]

Piero della Francesca (de' Franceschi) (1410/20–92), long neglected, is now probably the most popular painter of the Quattrocento. This is due to the mathematical perfection of his forms and to his superb sense of interval, the whole giving a timeless and serene air to his works, increased by his pale and soft colours. A generation brought up on Cubism and the intellectual rigour of Cézanne has the right to appreciate Piero. He is first recorded in 1439, when he was in Florence with DOMENICO Veneziano, painting frescoes in Sant' Egidio which are now lost. He came from the small town of Borgo San Sepolcro in Umbria, and the experience of Florentine art, in the works of Domenico Veneziano, Andrea del Castagno, Uccello, and Masaccio must have been decisive in his artistic education. In 1442 he was back in Borgo – he had a deep affection for his native place and spent as much time as possible there – and was then serving as a Town Councillor, which would indicate a certain maturity. The Compagnia della Misericordia, a charitable foundation in Borgo, commissioned a polyptych of the *Madonna della Misericordia*, showing the Madonna protecting humanity (and in particular the members of the Compagnia) under her mantle, from him in 1445 for delivery in 3 years: it was not finally paid for until 1462 and the execution may therefore have dragged on for years. Piero always seems to have worked with the greatest deliberation, and other cases are known of his taking several years over a work. The length of time taken over the Borgo *Madonna* makes it difficult to know what his early style was like, but the *Baptism* in London (NG) is accepted as an early work, showing traces of Florentine (and Sienese) influence, yet standing for a calm and classic stillness totally opposed to all that the Florentines then sought. A *S. Jerome* at Berlin, signed and dated 1450, is unfortunately too damaged for use in stylistic comparisons, but a damaged fresco of 1451 in S. Francesco at Rimini, *Sigismondo Malatesta and his Patron Saint*, shows Piero's love of symmetry and of counter-changed patterns in the two dogs. By this time he had probably painted some frescoes, now lost, in Ferrara, the influence of which is discernible in the local School. About 1452 Piero began the work on which his fame chiefly rests, the fresco cycle in the choir of S. Francesco at Arezzo depicting the story of the True Cross. The narrative is highly complicated, being based on several different accounts in the Golden Legend, and it is not made easier to follow by the fact that Piero, presumably for artistic reasons, has treated the story in a cavalier way and arranged, for example, the two battle scenes out of order in the story but facing each other at the bottom of each of the side walls, thus forming one of the symmetries he loved. The frescoes were almost unknown for centuries and suffered from neglect, but at least they were not repainted much and therefore give a good idea of Piero's mature style, and of what he owed to Domenico Veneziano and to Florence. In 1459 Piero was in Rome, by which time the Arezzo frescoes were presumably finished. The work in the Vatican which Piero is known to have done has vanished, but a *S. Luke* in Sta Maria Maggiore is, perhaps optimistically, ascribed to him. The ascription is not made any more plausible by the fact that two of his masterpieces are likely to date from this time – the fresco of *The Resurrection* in Borgo and the diptych with the portraits of his friends and patrons the Duke and Duchess of Urbino (Florence, Uffizi). The portraits have been associated with a poem of 1465, but look stylistically rather later (*c.* 1472?). They show strong influence from Flemish painting in the use of the oil technique, perhaps due to the presence of Flemish pictures in Italy. Later on, JOOS van Ghent worked at Urbino. The curious *Flagellation of Christ*, which again shows Flemish influence, was also painted for Urbino. Various explanations of the subject and date have been advanced. All this time Piero was working on a large altarpiece, parts of which survive. It was commissioned for Borgo San Sepolcro in 1454 and completed fifteen years later: the centre panel was probably a *Madonna* but is now lost; on either side were *SS. Augustine, Michael, John* (?), and *Nicholas of Tolentino* (now in Lisbon, London (NG), New York (Frick Coll.), and Milan (Poldi-Pezzoli)). The last two pictures Piero painted are the *Madonna with the Duke of Urbino as Donor* (Milan, Brera), known as the *Brera Madonna*, which is datable between *c.* 1472 and *c.* 1475, and the unfinished *Nativity* (London, NG). It is sometimes said, on exiguous evidence, that the hand (or even the head) of the Duke in the *Brera Madonna* is by P. BERRUGUETE. In any case, it seems clear that Piero stopped painting in the 1470s – the last document to record him as a painter is of 1478, concerning a lost fresco – although he lived on until 1492. One explanation for this is that he became increasingly interested in perspective and mathematics, for he wrote two treatises, 'De prospectiva pingendi' and 'De quinque corporibus regularibus', and it is also likely that his sight failed, for he seems to have been blind in his last years. His chief pupils were PERUGINO and SIGNORELLI, both of whom reacted against his style. There are other works by him in Arezzo, Borgo San Sepolcro, Boston (Gardner), Monterchi (near Borgo), Perugia, Urbino, Vaduz (Liechtenstein), and Venice (Accad.). [ill. 118, p. 289. Col. pl. 3]

Pietà (Ital. pity). A representation of the Dead Christ supported on His Mother's lap, with or without other mourning figures. The idea originated in 14th-century Germany (Ger. *Vesperbild*) and is an expression of Northern piety which stressed the human relationship between Christ and the Virgin, and which here drew a parallel with the Madonna holding the infant Christ on her lap. The earliest example (*c.* 1320?) is at Veste Coburg. *See* IMAGO PIETATIS.

Pietro Berrettini da Cortona (1596–1669), painter and architect, was one of the founders of the Roman High Baroque, comparable with BERNINI in sculpture. His

first works were painted for the Sacchetti family and are now in the Capitoline Gallery, Rome, along with other works of his, but he was soon taken up by the powerful Barberini family – the family of Urban VIII – for whom he painted frescoes in Sta Bibiana, Rome (1624–6), followed by his greatest work, the Ceiling in the Barberini Palace (now the Galleria Nazionale, Rome). This is a huge fresco representing an *Allegory of Divine Providence and Barberini Power*, begun in 1633 and completed in 1639: a sketch for it is now exhibited with it, but its authenticity is open to doubt. The fresco is a huge illusion, like the ceilings of LANFRANCO or GUERCINO, with the central field apparently open to the sky and scores of figures seen *al di* SOTTO IN SÙ apparently coming into the room itself or floating above it. While working on this Pietro also went to Florence and began a series of similar frescoes in the Pitti Palace; he also began a series of frescoes in the Chiesa Nuova, Rome, which was not finished until 1665 (the *modello* for the cupola is now in Hartford Conn., Wadsworth Atheneum). Towards the end of his life he devoted much of his time to architecture, but he published a Treatise on Painting in 1652 under a pseudonym and in collaboration. He refused invitations to both France and Spain. With the help of numerous pupils, of whom Ciro FERRI was the most important, he painted many other frescoes and easel pictures in Rome and Florence. Outside Italy there are works by him in the Royal Collection, and in Berlin, Bristol, Chatsworth, Madrid, Munich, Paris, Sarasota Fla, Toledo Ohio, and Vienna. [ill. 270, p. 312]

Pigalle, Jean-Baptiste (1714–85), was a French sculptor, a pupil of LEMOYNE, who failed to win a scholarship to Rome, went at his own expense in 1736, nearly starved, and was rescued by G. Coustou II. He returned to France in 1739 and worked for churches and for Mme de Pompadour, for whom he made the *Love and Friendship* (1758) now in the Louvre (the plaster is in Baltimore). His major works include the Tomb of Maréchal de Saxe in S. Thomas, Strasbourg (1753–76) and his *Nude Voltaire* (1776) in the Institut, Paris. He also made the base for BOUCHARDON's equestrian *Louis XV*. [ill. 710, p. 379]

Pilon, Germain (*c.* 1535–90), was a French sculptor who worked in marble and bronze. His early style (e.g. in the Three Graces of the Monument for the Heart of Henri II, 1560: Louvre) is based on the elongated, Mannerist elegance of Primaticcio's plaster decorations at Fontainebleau. Later, his work becomes more fluid and more realist at the same time; his softly flowing forms invest with poignancy the relaxed recumbent marble figures of the dead Henri II and his Queen, Catherine de' Medici, in their tomb, while above on the canopy the living figures of the monarchs are sharply characterized in bronze (1563–70: S. Denis). His marble relief of Valentine Balbiani has a strange rippling quality which stresses the dead woman's angular, skeletal forms beneath the taut skin and the loose curling hair. Pilon seeks to create emotion through the marriage of virtuosity of handling and dramatic intensity. His use of Michelangelo and Pontormo is apparent, but never obvious or derivative. He also made portrait medals and busts, chiefly of the French Royal family, during the 1570s. Most of his works are in

Paris (Louvre and S. Denis) but there is a bronze bust of Charles IX in London, Wallace Coll. [ill. 677, p. 373]

Pintoricchio (Pinturicchio), Bernardino (*c.* 1454–1513), was active in Perugia in 1481, but before that he was probably in Rome assisting Perugino with the frescoes in the Sistine Chapel (1481/2). The influence of Perugino remained dominant for the rest of his life. His principal works are the fresco cycles in the Borgia Apartments in the Vatican (1492–*c.* 1495) and in the Piccolomini Library of the Cathedral of Siena, 1503–8. His numerous works include those in Baltimore (Walters), Berlin, Boston (Mus., Gardner), Cambridge (Fitzwm), and Cambridge Mass. (Fogg), Cleveland Ohio, Dresden, London (NG), New York (Met. Mus.), Oxford, Paris (Louvre), Perugia, Philadelphia (Johnson), Rome (churches), San Marino Cal. (Huntington), Siena (Mus. and Cath.), Spello (Mus. and churches), Spoleto (Cath.), Washington (NG). [ill. 123, p. 289]

Piombo, Sebastiano del, *see* SEBASTIANO.

Piranesi, Giovanni Battista (1720–78), was a Venetian architect who went to Rome in 1740 and became the recorder of Roman antiquities in hundreds of etchings. His feeling for the poetry of ruins, his Romantic archaeology, and his intensely dramatic exploitation of the contrasts of light and shade possible in etching exerted great influence on 18th-century architecture, and even more on the whole visual approach to Antiquity and the Decline and Fall. His most original works are the *Carceri d'Invenzione* (begun *c.* 1745, reworked 1761) of imaginary and megalomaniac prisons, but he was far more famous for his *Vedute,* 137 etchings of ancient and modern Rome, published from 1745 onwards, and for his violent archaeological polemics (pro-Roman and anti-Greek). The *Vedute* continued to be printed long after his death and formed the basis of the mental image of Rome possessed by thousands who never went there, and, with PANINI, he created a lasting picture of Rome, as Canaletto and Guardi created one of Venice. In his lifetime (1771) Horace Walpole spoke of '. . . the sublime dreams of Piranesi, who seems to have conceived visions of Rome beyond what it boasted even in the meridian of its splendour. Savage as Salvator Rosa, fierce as Michael Angelo, and exuberant as Rubens, he has imagined scenes that would startle geometry, and exhaust the Indies to realise'. [ill. 317, p. 317]

Pisanello, Antonio (probably 1395–1455/6), was the major Italian exponent of INTERNATIONAL GOTHIC in succession to GENTILE da Fabriano, who was very probably his master. He was trained in Verona, probably under STEFANO da Verona and then went to Venice where he seems to have succeeded Gentile in painting a series of frescoes in the Doge's Palace (1415/22: all destroyed); he also succeeded Gentile in Rome, at the Lateran Basilica (1431/2: also destroyed). These were probably works in the International style, and the fact that he succeeded Gentile makes it seem likely that he was regarded as his heir. The earliest extant major work by Pisanello is the *Annunciation* (1423/4: Verona, S. Fermo) and in it, as in the later *S. George and the Princess* (1437/8:

Verona, S. Anastasia), his Courtly interests and narrative gifts are clearly shown. In 1438 he made his first datable portrait medal, and it is as a medallist and draughtsman that he is best known. In 1448/9 he made a set of medals of Alfonso of Aragon, King of Naples, and he is known to have been there. The Vallardi Codex (Paris, Louvre) is one of the most important surviving collections of 15th-century drawings, and contains not only Pisanello's own drawings – studies of animals, costume, antiques, sketches for pictures and copies of other drawings – but also what seem to be drawings by pupils and drawings by other artists kept in case they came in handy one day. His wonderful studies of animals reveal how sharp his observation was in this typical International Gothic interest, and his portraits confirm this (Bergamo and Paris), while the closeness of his ties with Burgundy is best demonstrated by the *Profile of a Girl* (Washington, NG) which is still undetermined between him and the Franco-Flemish School *c.* 1420. The only other paintings by him are in London (NG): a good set of his medals is in the V & A Museum. [ill. 143, p. 292]

Pisano, Andrea (*c.* 1290–1348), appears for the first time in 1330, when he began work on the bronze Doors of the Baptistry of Florence. This presumably indicated that he was already a sculptor of some renown, and his name perhaps indicates that he was trained in Pisa. He finished the bronze Doors in 1336, and the type of Gothic relief and the general disposition of the relief fields conditioned the form of GHIBERTI's first Baptistry Doors more than half a century later. The only other work associated with him is a series of reliefs, and possibly some statues on the Campanile of Florence Cathedral, where Andrea succeeded Giotto (*d.* 1337). Giotto may have designed some of the reliefs, and Andrea's bronze Door certainly contains reminiscences of Giotto's work in the Peruzzi Chapel. In 1347 Andrea became head of the works at Orvieto Cathedral, where he was succeeded by his son Nino Pisano (*c.* 1315–68?), also a sculptor, by whom there is a signed *Madonna* in Florence (SM Novella). [ills. 11, 12, p. 270]

Pisano, Nicola (*c.* 1220/5 or earlier–84?) and his son, Giovanni (*c.* 1245/50–after 1314), were the creators of modern sculpture, preceding such painters as GIOTTO in the 'rebirth of the arts'. They are documented between 1258 and 1314 and there is a considerable body of work certainly attributable to them, either individually or in collaboration, including the four great Pulpits which are their main claim to fame. The first of these is the work of Nicola alone and is signed and dated 1260. It stands in the Baptistry at Pisa, and, by its affinity to Antique sarcophagi such as the one in the Campo Santo at Pisa, clearly proclaims that its creator was using Antique art as a model, and was attempting to create a Christian art with the realism and dignity of Late Roman sculpture, thus distinguishing it from the art of the Gothic North of Europe. The place of Nicola's birth is unknown, but there is some evidence for the view that he must have imbibed this feeling for Roman art in South Italy, where the Emperor Frederick II (*d.* 1250) was engaged in a deliberate revival of Roman grandeur. Between 1265 and 1268 Nicola was engaged on the Pulpit in Siena Cathedral, but he had several assistants including ARNOLFO and his own young son Giovanni, who was engaged on the understanding that he would come to Siena and would stay there and be patient in his work. Opinion is divided on the relative shares of these masters, since there is a noticeable increase in French Gothic influence in the relief panels with New Testament scenes and in the rest of the work. Much the same is true of the Fountain in the Piazza at Perugia, which is signed by both and dated 1278. This was Nicola's last major work, the last two pulpits being certainly by Giovanni alone. The French influence in them, as in much of his other work, has led to the hypothesis – for which there is no evidence – that he paid a visit to France at some point in his career. The pulpit in S. Andrea, Pistoia, was completed in 1301 and traditionally took 4 years to make. It shows what is perhaps the highest point of the French influence on Giovanni's style; for the last and greatest of the Pulpits, that in Pisa Cathedral, is considerably closer in spirit to his father and seems to show that Giovanni was working towards a new and personal synthesis of Gothic and classical elements. This pulpit was commissioned in 1302 and completed in 1310, although it is signed and dated 1311. There is also a curious and cryptic inscription alluding to the difficulties and tribulations experienced by Giovanni in the course of the work.

Giovanni was also active as an architect and worked much at Siena Cathedral, where many of the figures on the façade were carved by him (a fragment in London, V & A). As early as 1284 he was exempted from all taxes on account of his work at the Cathedral. Other works by him include an ivory *Madonna* (*c.* 1299) in Pisa Cathedral, and *Madonnas* in Padua (Arena Chapel: *c.* 1305) and Prato Cathedral. [ills. 7, 8, p. 270]

Pisis, Filippo de (1896–1956), was an Italian painter who worked in Ferrara and Paris. He was influenced by CHIRICO and Pittura Metafisica in 1918–19, but he lived in Paris 1920–40 and then based his style on the fluent, quasi-Impressionist brushwork of Manet and GUARDI, whom he especially imitated in his views of Venice and other towns. There are works in the Modern Museums of Florence, Milan, Rome, Turin, and Venice. [ill. 1065, p. 424]

Pissarro, Camille (1831–1903), was born in St Thomas in the West Indies, the son of a Creole mother and a father of Portuguese-Jewish descent. He worked as a clerk in his father's general store until in 1852 he ran away to Venezuela with a Danish painter, after which his reluctant parents resigned themselves to his becoming an artist. He arrived in Paris in 1855, in time to see the great exhibition at the World Fair (when COURBET exhibited his rejected pictures independently). Soon after he met COROT, by whom he was deeply influenced, although by 1866 Corot disapproved of the way that the younger landscape painters were going, and was particularly severe about Pissarro's connection with Courbet and Manet. He met MONET in 1859, and in 1863 several of his pictures were in the SALON des Refusés. From 1866 to 1869 he worked at Pontoise on landscapes painted entirely in the open, but he could sell almost nothing and he and his family lived in the most cruel poverty. In 1870 he fled before the German invasion, first to Brittany and then to London,

where eventually news reached him that his house in Louveciennes had been used as a butchery by the invaders, and his store of 200 to 300 pictures used as duckboards in the muddy garden. In 1872 Cézanne joined him in Pontoise and worked with him, with a radical effect on his own style. In 1874 he took part in the First IMPRESSIONIST Exhibition: he was the only one who exhibited in all eight, and it was he who introduced first Gauguin, then Seurat and Signac into the Impressionist exhibitions, with consequent disruption among the group. He was much influenced from 1884 by Seurat's theories of OPTICAL MIXTURE, which he used until 1888, when he declared that the method 'inhibits me and hinders the development of spontaneity of sensation'. From 1895 the worsening of his eye-trouble forced him to give up working out of doors, and he painted many town views from windows in Paris; he died blind.

His production was enormous and in all techniques – chiefly oil painting, but he also used pastel, gouache, drawing in all media, etching, and lithography. Of all the Impressionists he was the most consistent; he never compromised, he did his best to compose the bitter quarrels which broke out around him, he never blamed any for their defections, intolerance, impatience, and occasional spites. In return, they gave him respect and admiration for his principles as much as for his art. There are paintings by him all over the world, in almost every museum of Modern Art. His son Lucien (1863–1944) followed in his father's stylistic footsteps. He lived in England, where he founded the Eragny Press (named after his father's final home) in 1896 and exerted great influence on book-illustration and printing in this country. His daughter, known as Orovida (*b.* 1893) is also a painter. [ills. 804, 990, pp. 390, 414. Col. pl. 32]

Pitati, Bonifazio de', *see* BONIFAZIO.

Pittoni, Giovanni Battista (1687–1767), was, with PELLEGRINI, one of the principal Venetian Rococo painters on a lower level than TIEPOLO. He was influenced by Tiepolo and by Sebastiano RICCI and was highly regarded by his contemporaries. He entered the Guild in Venice in 1716, and in 1758 succeeded Tiepolo as President of the Venetian Academy. Much of his work was done for German, Polish, and Russian patrons and it is likely that his basic sentimentality and the brightness of his colour appealed to them. There are many works by him in Venice and others in Berlin, Dresden, Florence (Uffizi), Paris (Louvre), and Vicenza. [ill. 286, p. 314]

Plaster Casting is an intermediate stage in the production of a piece of sculpture which is often the last process actually to be carried out by the sculptor himself. Once his model has been cast in plaster it can be regarded as a finished work, rather fragile in nature, or it can be executed in bronze, lead, or any other metal, or, with a POINTING MACHINE, it can be mechanically reproduced in marble or stone.

Any work of sculpture which is not a piece of direct carving in some hard substance is normally carried out in clay or wax. If, say, a head has been modelled in wax it can be left at that; if in clay it will dry up and crumble to pieces unless it is either kept permanently damp or transformed into Terracotta or Plaster. Terracotta is really no more than baking the clay, in the same way as a common flower-pot is produced. The result is the same in texture and usually varies in colour from grey-brown to brick-red. A plaster cast is rather more complicated, but the basic process is simple enough. First, a mould has to be made. The clay head is first divided into two or three parts by strips of zinc, usually stuck like a fringe round the side of the head at ear level (figures and more complex shapes may require multi-part moulds), the purpose being to ensure that the two halves of the mould lift off easily. Some plaster of Paris is now mixed up and tinted with dye, and as soon as it is firm and creamy it is thrown at the head, so that it sticks to the whole surface and forms a coating about $\frac{1}{8}/\frac{1}{4}$ in. thick. This is then thickly coated with untinted plaster and left to harden, the two halves being pulled apart when the plaster has set (the head in clay often gets damaged in this process). The mould is now cleaned out and the inside brushed over with oil and soft soap to prevent the cast from sticking to it. Next, the halves of the mould are reunited and tied together and fresh plaster is poured into it from the open base, swirled around to drive it into all the crevices and then allowed to harden. The mould is now destroyed by chipping it away with mallet and chisel, the purpose of the thin layer of tinted plaster being to warn the sculptor when he is nearing the surface of the cast. When all the plaster has been removed the finished cast is revealed and it can then be left white, painted or bronzed over, or handed to the bronze-founder or mason for reproduction in bronze or marble. *See* BRONZE and POINTING MACHINE.

Plasticity. The quality of appearing three-dimensional. A painting is said to have great plasticity if it gives the impression that the figures are fully modelled and are capable of moving freely in the pictorial space. Plasticity is often obtained by emphasizing the tonal contrasts and by keeping the greater part of the picture in shadow.

Plein Air (Fr. open air). The feeling that a picture really gives the impression of the open air, a quality much sought by the Impressionists. In a more restricted sense it applies to landscapes actually painted out of doors, with the intention of catching this quality. This practice is relatively recent, at least as far as finished pictures are concerned, and it was this concern for a non-aesthetic quality which underlies the remark said to have been made by Degas, that Monet's pictures always made him turn up his coat collar.

Pleydenwurff, Hans (c. 1420–72), was the major Nuremberg painter immediately before WOLGEMUT and DÜRER. He became a citizen in 1457, and introduced the realism of the Netherlands, especially that of BOUTS. In 1462 he completed the altarpiece for the High Altar of S. Elizabeth in Breslau, where fragments still remain. He may also have worked in Cracow. His son Wilhelm (d. 1494) was also a painter and woodcut-maker, and worked in the shop of Wolgemut, who married Pleydenwurff's widow. [ill. 549, p. 353]

Pochade (Fr.). A sketch, usually a small one in oils made in front of some actual landscape with the intention of working up a large picture from it.

Pointillism *see* OPTICAL MIXTURES.

Pointing Machine. A mechanical device for reproducing a PLASTER cast in stone or marble without the exercise of any artistic skill on the part of the carver. It was originally developed by the ancient Greeks but was perfected in the 18th and 19th centuries and became very popular among academic sculptors of the later 19th century, since it allows the sculptor to work in clay or wax and leave all the dirty work to professional masons. The whole idea is repugnant to most modern sculptors, who feel that the form taken by the finished work should be conditioned by the material from which it is carved (e.g. a carving in wood ought to take account of the grain): for this reason most modern sculptors prefer to carve direct, working only from a sketch and not even using a model made of clay, which would be unglyptic.

A pointing machine measures the depth from a given vertical, of, for example, the receding planes of the nose of a plaster cast and transfers the measurements to a hole drilled in the marble block. Scores of measured depths are transferred in this way to the marble, until all that is left for the mason is to cut away surplus stone.

Poliakoff, Serge (b. 1906), was born in Moscow, of a well-off family. He emigrated in 1919 and for many years earned a living as a guitarist, settling in Paris and beginning to paint in 1930. He worked in London at the Slade School 1935–7 and returned to Paris, meeting KANDINSKY in 1937 and DELAUNAY in 1938. From then on he painted abstract pictures, and, later, was influenced by the more mathematical art of MALEVICH. He also makes colour lithographs. [ill. 1102, p. 429]

Pollaiuolo (Pollaiolo, Pollajuolo), Antonio (c. 1432–98) and Piero (c. 1441–96), were brothers who ran one of the most advanced and successful workshops in Florence in the second half of the 15th century. They worked as painters, sculptors, engravers, goldsmiths, and designers of embroidery, and their knowledge of anatomy and the new technique of oil painting, together with the study they made of the problems of representing violent action, placed them at the head of the scientific painters immediately preceding Leonardo. It is now customary to assume that all the best work was done by Antonio, and all the bad by Piero. This view receives considerable support from the fact that the documented work by Piero – a set of *Virtues* in Florence, Uffizi (one other was by BOTTICELLI), and an altarpiece (1483) in San Gimignano – is very poor. On the other hand, a signed engraving by Antonio of a *Battle of the Nude Gods* is of very high quality indeed, and fully justifies the praise which was early lavished on him as a draughtsman and anatomist; yet no painting can be certainly ascribed to him. The influence of DONATELLO and of Andrea del CASTAGNO is paramount in their work, and Piero (not Antonio) is said to have been Castagno's pupil for a short time. Their most ambitious works are the *S. Sebastian* (1475: London, NG) and the Tombs of Popes Sixtus IV (1493) and Innocent VIII (1492–8), both in St Peter's. Other works are in Berlin, Florence (Uffizi, Bargello, Cathedral Mus., S. Miniato, Villa Gallina), London (NG, BM), Milan (Poldi-Pezzoli), Naples, Staggia near Siena,

Turin, Washington (NG: a *Portrait* more usually attributed to Castagno), and Yale. [ills. 77, 80, 81, 89, pp. 280–2]

Pollock, Jackson (1912–56), the chief American exponent of ACTION PAINTING, made studies for his apparently unpremeditated works, done on continuous lengths of canvas tacked to the floor, and later cut up with selective care. He abandoned the use of brushes in 1947, pouring the paint straight on to the canvas, but in 1953 he began to employ brushes again. He said of his paintings (1951): 'I don't work from drawings or colour sketches. My painting is direct. . . . I want to express my feelings rather than illustrate them. . . . When I am painting I have a general notion as to what I am about. I *can* control the flow of paint: there is no accident, just as there is no beginning and no end.' He used metallic paints and ordinary commercial synthetic enamel and plastic paint, with results that are already unfortunate. There are examples in London (Tate), Rio de Janeiro, and many US museums. [ill. 1096, p. 428. Col. pl. 35]

Polychromatic Sculpture is sculpture which, like most sculpture before the 16th century, has been painted in naturalistic colours to heighten its lifelike effect.

Polyptych. A picture or relief, usually an altarpiece, which is made up of two or more panels. Two panels form a diptych, three a triptych, five a pentaptych: more than three are usually called simply a polyptych. A typical Italian 14th–15th-century polyptych consists of a large central panel of the *Madonna*, with perhaps two *Saints* on either side and an *Annunciation* on top. The PREDELLA would then consist of narrative scenes from the Lives of Saints 1 and 2, with a scene from the Life of Christ – perhaps the *Adoration of the Magi* – in the middle and then scenes from the Lives of Saints 3 and 4. [ill. 30, p. 272]

Pontormo, Jacopo (1494–1556), was born at Pontormo, near Empoli. He went to Florence and was influenced by Leonardo, Piero di Cosimo, and Albertinelli, before working under Andrea del Sarto *c.* 1512, when he met ROSSO, with whom he was to be one of the creators of MANNERISM. He was working on his own by about 1513, in Sta Maria Novella and SS. Annunziata in Florence, and in 1518 he painted the *Madonna*, still in S. Michele Visdomini, Florence, which is one of the first Mannerist pictures; profoundly influenced still by Andrea del Sarto, but with a new unease, an agitation which sharply distinguishes it from the complacency of Andrea's Madonnas. Pontormo was a profoundly religious painter and this probably underlies the forms he chose. He came to the notice of the Medici family and was commissioned by them to decorate their Villa at Poggio a Caiano (1521), which he did with a gay and light fresco. His next frescoes were the Passion cycle in the Certosa near Florence (1522–5), disturbing, thoroughly Mannerist, and containing such un-Florentine ideas as borrowings from Dürer, whose angularities of form expressed profound religious ideas. While working on these frescoes Pontormo was assisted by BRONZINO, who was more or less his adopted son, though a totally different kind of artist. What is perhaps his supreme masterpiece, and one of the central pictures in the development of Early Mannerism, is the *Deposition*

painted about 1525 as the altarpiece for a chapel in Sta Felicita, Florence, where there are also frescoes by Pontormo and Bronzino. Here the darkness of the Chapel probably dictated the very light tone and bright colours, but the crowding and agitation of the figures powerfully reinforce the direct emotional effect of the sharp, pale colours. In the drawing the influence of Michelangelo is patent, and this was to become more marked after 1530 when Pontormo was in contact with Michelangelo. Little is known about his later years, principally because the frescoes in S. Lorenzo, on which he worked 1546–56, have all gone and are known only through the drawings. He was a great draughtsman even in an age of great draughtsmen, and there is a huge collection of his drawings in Florence, Uffizi. His character was strange, sensitive, withdrawn, and highly neurotic: his Diary (1555–6) shows him obsessed with his work, his solitariness (often shunning even Bronzino), and above all the state of his bowels. There are works in Amsterdam (Rijksmus.), Baltimore, Cambridge Mass. (Fogg), Carmignano near Florence, Dublin, Florence (Uffizi, Pitti, Accad., Pal. Vecchio, Medici Mus., Innocenti Mus.), Frankfurt, Hanover, London (NG), Lucca, Milan (Castello), Munich, Naples, Oxford (Christ Church), Paris (Louvre, Jacquemart-André), Philadelphia (Johnson), Pontormo, Rome (Borghese, Gall. Naz.), San Francisco, Sansepolcro, Vienna, Washington (NG), and Yale. [ill. 186, p. 299]

Pordenone, Giovanni Antonio (1483/4–1539), was a North Italian painter who was influenced by the Venetians – especially Titian and Giorgione – and also by German art, particularly in its more violent aspects. This fusion leads to a kind of Mannerism in his style as early as the 1520s. He may have gone to Rome *c.* 1515–16, as there is a Raphaelesque phase in his art just then. In 1519/20 he was painting a dome in Treviso in the illusionistic manner introduced by Mantegna, but his dome precedes the one by Correggio, whose influence is, however, discernible in the dome at Piacenza (*c.* 1530). For a brief moment Pordenone presented a serious challenge to the supremacy of Titian himself, and he eventually settled in Venice. His principal works are in Cremona, Piacenza, Treviso, and Venice: others are in the Royal Coll. and in London (NG), Milan (Brera), Philadelphia, Sarasota Fla, and Vienna. [ill. 225, p. 306]

Post-Impressionism is a rather vague term applied to the movement which developed in reaction against both Impressionism and Neo-Impressionism and had as its chief aim either a return to a more formal conception of art or a new stress on the importance of the subject. The most important figures covered by the term are van Gogh, Gauguin, and Cézanne. It was given currency in England by the Exhibition arranged by Roger Fry in the winter of 1910–11, called 'Manet and the Post-Impressionists', which caused much heartburning in London art circles and led to the formation of the LONDON GROUP.

Potter, Paulus (1625–54), one of the most famous Dutch animal painters, was the son of a painter and very precocious – his first works are of 1640, and his most famous picture, the life-size *Bull* (The Hague) is signed and dated

1647. On the whole, however, his smaller pictures are better. There are works by him in the Royal Coll. and in Amsterdam, Berlin, Brussels, Copenhagen, Dresden, Dublin, London (NG and Wallace Coll.), Munich, Paris (Louvre), Philadelphia, and elsewhere. [ill. 494, p. 344]

Pourbus, Pieter (1523–84), worked mainly in Bruges where he followed, in his religious works, the florid Italianizing style of Lancelot Blondeel, whose daughter he married. His portraits are stiff and formal affairs, but equal to those of his contemporaries Mor or Joos van Cleve. There are works in Antwerp, Bruges (Mus. and churches), Brussels, London (Wallace Coll.), New York (Met. Mus.), and elsewhere. [ill. 362, p. 325]
Frans I (1545–81) his son and pupil, painted religious pictures and portraits. He worked mainly in Antwerp, where he was also the pupil of Frans FLORIS, whose niece he married. His religious works are usually in the Italianizing style of Floris, but markedly Reformed Church in content; his portraits are close to the sober style of Mor. There are works in Berlin, Brussels, Dresden, Ghent (Mus. and S. Bavon), London (Wallace Coll.), Rotterdam, Vienna, and elsewhere. [ill. 361, p. 325]
Frans II (1569–1622), son of Frans I, worked for the Court of the Spanish Regents of the Netherlands in Brussels, and in 1600 became Court Painter to the Duke of Mantua, being there at the same time as Rubens. He also worked in Innsbruck, Naples, and Turin, and in 1609 became Painter to Marie de' Medici at the French Court. His is the most international style of any member of the family. There are works in the Royal Collection and in Amsterdam (Rijksmus.), Berlin, Leeds, Madrid (Prado), Munich, Paris (Louvre), Vienna, and elsewhere. [ill. 363, p. 325]

Poussin, Gaspar (1615–75). His name was Dughet but he adopted the name of his illustrious brother-in-law Nicolas, whose pupil he was from *c.* 1630 to 1633. He lived and worked in Rome and its surroundings and attempted, not entirely unsuccessfully, the difficult feat of combining the landscape style and principles of POUSSIN and CLAUDE. He was immensely popular during the 18th century so that most of the older galleries and collections have examples, although these are always attributions, for apart from some frescoes in S. Martino ai Monti in Rome nothing can positively be assigned to him. [ill. 693, p. 375]

Poussin, Nicolas (1594–1665), was born in Normandy and after some training went to Paris about 1612. Little is known about him before 1621 when he was employed with Philippe de CHAMPAIGNE on decorations in the Luxembourg Palace. His style was probably based on the Second School of FONTAINEBLEAU, modified by the Antique and Italian Renaissance works in the French Royal Collection. In 1624 he went to Rome and in his early struggling years there worked in the studio of Domenichino, whose lucid composition and cool colour affected him strongly. In 1628 he obtained a commission for an altarpiece for St Peter's, the *Martyrdom of S. Erasmus* (now in the Vatican), a work painted in competition with Le VALENTIN and not wholly successful since it involved a compromise between Baroque eloquence and Poussin's less dramatic style.

About 1629–30 he had a serious illness. This marks a change in his style, for he now stopped trying to compete with the increasingly popular opulent Baroque and turned to smaller works and to patrons from the upper middle class. He made many experiments in these early Roman years, one being his short interest in Venetian art which led, for instance, in the Louvre *Inspiration of the Poet*, to a combination of classical form and Venetian colour of the most supreme beauty. He turned from religious to classical subjects, to mythologies, and to Tasso. But this elegiac phase was short-lived, and by 1633 he was working on compositions filled with figures grouped in dramatic poses chosen to make the narrative plain; the influence of Venetian colour gave place to a more rigid use of local colour, and Raphael and the Antique are paramount. Poussin used the device of the miniature stage with small draped wax models to try out effects of gesture, grouping, and lighting.
In 1640 he was persuaded to return to Paris to work for the King and Cardinal Richelieu. This brought him into uneasy competition with most of the artists working for the Crown, of whose work he was outspokenly critical, and in particular with VOUET, but the artistic climate of Paris and the conditions of his employment were highly uncongenial and in 1642, after just over 18 months, he made an excuse to return to Rome which he never again left. In 1642 he finished the first set of the *Seven Sacraments*, of which the *Baptism* is now in Washington (NG). His trip to France enabled him to make new contacts among bourgeois patrons, such as Chantelou, for whom he had worked in Rome and who was his host in Paris (as he later was to Bernini) and for whom the second set of the *Seven Sacraments* was painted between about 1644 and 1648. These patrons were highly educated, intellectual men of strict piety, and the classical themes he now chose were the heroic and stoical ones of Roman moral victory and sacrifice paralleling the dramas of Corneille, or dramatic Biblical themes where the action turns on the psychological impact of the moment. The late works are essays in solid geometry, with facial expressions eliminated and immobile figures. By comparison with his early works they are frigid and cerebral, but they are the logical exposition of his theories: a picture must contain the maximum of moral content expressed in a composition which shall convey its intellectual content; the pattern must be pleasing in itself and not conflict with the two-dimensional quality of the picture plane; the colour must offer no sensuous charm to lessen the unity of vision. Nowhere is this severe attitude expressed with more finality than in his landscapes which exemplify his utter dissimilarity to CLAUDE. This doctrine of the subordination of colour led to the quarrel between the Poussinists and the RUBENISTS.
There are works in Berlin, Boston (Mus.), Cambridge Mass. (Fogg), Chantilly, Chicago, Cleveland, Copenhagen, Detroit, Dresden, Edinburgh (NG), Glasgow, Hartford Conn. (Wadsworth) Kansas City, Leningrad, London, (NG, Dulwich, Wallace), Madrid, Minneapolis, Montreal, Munich, New York (Met. Mus.), Ottawa, Paris (Louvre), Philadelphia, Providence RI, Sarasota Fla (Ringling), Stockholm, Toronto, Vaduz (Liechtenstein), the Vatican, Vienna, Washington (NG). [ills. 688–90, pp. 374–5]

Poussinisme *see* RUBÉNISME.

Pozzo, Andrea (1642–1709), was the most skilful of all perspective experts and *quadraturisti*. He was born and trained in the North of Italy and became a Jesuit lay-brother in 1665 (he is often given the courtesy title 'Padre') and wanted to abandon painting but was made to continue by his superiors. From 1681 to 1702 he was in Rome and his masterpiece of illusionism and SOTTO IN SÙ (which only works from one point in the nave) is the ceiling of the Jesuit Church of S. Ignazio (1691–4). This is an allegory of the missionary activity of the Society of Jesus, and Pozzo himself explained it in a letter to Prince Liechtenstein (1694: published as a pamphlet in 1828). In 1702 he went to Vienna, where he died, and he introduced similar ideas there, which were of great importance in the development of Austrian Rococo. His influence was spread by his treatise 'Perspectiva pictorum . . .' (1693–8), which was translated into English in 1693 and is said to have decided Reynolds to become a painter; the book was even translated into Chinese, by Portuguese Jesuits in 1737. [ill. 273, p. 313]

PRB, Pre-Raphaelite Brotherhood. The mysterious initials first appeared following ROSSETTI's signature in an exhibition in 1849. They were the outcome of talks between HUNT and MILLAIS in 1848, although the choice of the expression 'Pre-Raphaelite' was largely fortuitous. It had already been said of the NAZARENER that they sought to emulate the painters earlier than Raphael, and this was more or less the idea of the original Brotherhood (Hunt, Millais, Rossetti, and his brother William, Collinson, Woolner the sculptor, and Stephens) – they knew very little about Italian painting earlier than Raphael, but they did know that they thought Raphael himself over-praised and they did not like Bolognese and Roman 17th-century painting, which they thought insincere. From the first the movement was very literary (a periodical called 'The Germ' ran for four numbers) and the painters insisted on the importance of a serious subject and on a highly elaborated symbolism and freshly thought-out icono-graphy. The technical means, such as bright colour, extreme detail, study of outdoor motives on the spot, and the famous method of working into a wet white ground – all these were no more than means, although they had great influence on later painters who had no connection with the movement, such as Ford Madox BROWN. In 1850 Rossetti revealed the meaning of the initials and at once a great storm broke; the principal accusations being that they set themselves up as better than Raphael, that they were secret Romanists (i.e. linked with the Oxford Movement), and that they were blasphemers. This last point was made – in an exceptionally savage and unperceptive attack – by Dickens, the victim being Millais's *Christ in the House of His Parents*, better known as *The Carpenter's Shop* (RA 1850: London, Tate). In the next year, however, RUSKIN came to their defence and their success was assured. Shortly after this the group, which had never had any avowed theoretical basis, dissolved: Millais to become the typical successful RA and PRA, Rossetti to found a sort of second Brotherhood at Oxford with MORRIS and BURNE-JONES, and Hunt alone, working in Palestine on religious pictures, to maintain the original ideas. From the mid-1850s they were well supported by the new middle-class patrons. There are good collections of their works in Birmingham, Manchester, Oxford, and London (Tate). [ills. 948–52, 954, 955, pp. 408–9. Col. pl. 28]

Predella. An Italian word for the small strip of paintings which form the lower edge or socle of a large altarpiece (*pala*). Such a POLYPTYCH consists of a principal, central panel with subsidiary side and/or top panels, and a *predella*: the *predella* usually has narrative scenes from the lives of the Saints who are represented in the panels above. Because of the small size of *predelle* – they are not usually more than 10–12 inches high, though often relatively very wide – they were frequently used for pictorial experiments that the painter did not wish to risk making in the larger panels. The first datable example seems to be that in Simone Martini's *S. Louis of Toulouse* (1317: Naples).

Preti, Mattia (Il Cavaliere Calabrese) (1613–99), was in Rome *c.* 1630 but had presumably already absorbed the influence of Caravaggio in Naples, since he came from Calabria. His easel pictures are more Caravaggesque than his frescoes, which show the influence of Guercino and Lanfranco, in Rome (1650–1: S. Andrea della Valle and in S. Carlo ai Catinari) and Modena. He was in Naples 1656–60 and spent most of the rest of his life in Malta, where he went in 1661 to decorate the Cathedral in Valletta. Other works are in Aix-en-Provence, Greenville SC, and Naples. [ill. 282, p. 313]

Prévost *see* MASTER OF MOULINS.

Primary Colours are the three colours, red, blue, and yellow, from which, in theory, all others can be obtained. A secondary colour, such as green or orange, is obtained by the mixture of two primaries, and a tertiary colour (and in theory black as well) from three. White and black are not primary colours.

Primaticcio, Francesco (1504/5–70), was the head of the First School of FONTAINEBLEAU and a universal impresario – painter, sculptor, architect, interior decorator. He learned these arts under GIULIO ROMANO in the Palazzo del Tè at Mantua, from 1525/6 until 1532, when he was summoned to France by François I and began to work at Fontainebleau, where he met ROSSO. From 1540 till 1542 he was in Rome buying for François, and on his return he found that Rosso was dead and Cellini had arrived (Cellini later threatened to kill him 'like a dog'). With Niccolò dell'ABBATE he worked on the (lost) decorations of the Galerie d'Ulysse at Fontainebleau, and in 1546 he was again in Rome to get casts made, including Michelangelo's *Pietà* in St Peter's, while in 1563 he revisited Bologna, his native town, and met Vasari there. There are works by him in Barnard Castle (Bowes Mus.), Bologna, Chantilly, Florence (Uffizi), Glasgow, Montpellier, Paris (Louvre, Cluny Mus.), and Pittsburgh, but his main contribution is the combination of painted and high relief stucco decoration evolved at Fontainebleau and still partially preserved there. [ill. 195, p. 302]

Priming. The first coat on which all subsequent paint layers (including the GROUND) are applied. For oil painting on canvas, the sized canvas is usually primed with white lead, either plain or slightly tinted.

Primitive. A word which is now almost meaningless, being applied to (i) painters, particularly of the Netherlandish and Italian Schools, working before *c.* 1500 – i.e. Netherlandish painters of the late 14th and all the 15th centuries, and all Italian painters between Giotto and Raphael. They have no obvious connection with (ii) the naïve, unsophisticated, unspoilt vision consistent with amateur, or 'Sunday' painter, status, admired for its connotations of genuineness and purity of artistic impulse, and freedom from the trammels of professionalism, tradition, technique, and formal training. This type of Primitive varies from the genuine American Primitives of the early 19th century such as Edward Hicks (1780–1849), the Quaker painter of *The Peaceable Kingdom,* to charwomen, peasants, and fishermen in modern Europe. The Douanier ROUSSEAU is their *chef d'école,* but the American 'Grandma' Moses may provide greater thrills for the sophisticated pursuit of the innocent eye. [ills. 916, 1035, pp. 403, 419]

Profil Perdu (Fr. lost profile) is that view of a head in which the profile is lost because the whole head is turned so far away that only the outline of the cheek is visible. By extension, the *profil perdu* of any object is what is seen of it when it is more than half turned away from the spectator.

Proof. Usually this means a print of any kind of engraving, made either by the artist himself or under his supervision and for his own satisfaction or information, before he hands the plate over to a professional printer. Some proofs – e.g. some of Turner's *Liber Studiorum* – were extensively worked on by the artist before he was finally satisfied. A *Proof before all Letters* is one made before an engraving was handed over to the lettering engraver for the title, dedication, etc. to be added: they are naturally rare, and, as they are also supposed to be made while the plate is still very new, they command higher prices than ordinary prints. This has led to the Artist's Proofs racket – i.e. the first 10 or 20 prints of a run, signed or marked in some special way (REMARQUE PROOFS), and sold at advanced prices.

Proportion. The relation of one part to a whole or to other parts. In the arts it usually means a will-o'-the-wisp search for significant mathematical relationships between the parts of the human body. Such a search certainly began in classical times – the evidence is in much Greek sculpture – and the codified rules given in Vitruvius's 'Treatise on Architecture' (early in the 1st century A.D.) led to much theorizing in the Renaissance. Leonardo da Vinci and Dürer were the two artists who devoted the most energy to these studies ('There is no excellent beauty that hath not some strangeness in the proportion. A man cannot tell whether Apelles or Albert Durer were the more trifler; whereof the one would make a personage by geometrical proportions: the other, by taking the best parts out of divers faces to make one excellent': Bacon, 'Of Beauty'). In practice, the normal human body is about 7 or 7½ times as tall as the height of its own head, and the total height is also roughly equal to the width of the outstretched arms. In IDEAL ART, therefore, it is usual to make the height equal to the full width of the arms; and further to gain mathematical harmony by elongating the body so that the total height becomes 8 heads. This gives a body which can be inscribed in squares and circles and also the convenient divisions so beloved of classically-minded artists – e.g. the groin becomes the exact half, the legs can be again halved at the knees, and so on. *See also* GOLDEN SECTION.

Provenance (Fr. source, origin). The provenance of a work of art is its pedigree. A complete record of its ownership is its provenance, and it is the duty of a cataloguer to establish, as far as humanly possible, the provenance of a work of art. In some cases – e.g. the Sistine Ceiling – no doubt is possible, but the exact pedigree of a picture by Vermeer is a matter of great importance, especially to the dealer trying to sell it. The English form 'provenience' is occasionally advocated, but it has a stilted sound and is not usual.

Prud'hon, Pierre-Paul (1758–1823), was born at Cluny. The Bishop of Mâcon sent him to Dijon Academy in 1774 and in 1780 he went to Paris, where he worked for engravers. In 1784 he won the Rome Prize offered by the States of Burgundy; in Italy he became a friend of Canova and did almost no work, but his pictures show the influence of Raphael, Correggio, and Leonardo. In 1787 he returned to Paris and earned a precarious living drawing for engravers and in the provinces painting portraits. He was almost unaffected by the current Neoclassicism in painting – DAVID called him the Boucher of his day – and he became almost the only competitor to David and his pupils, through the warm patronage of both Napoleon's Empresses to whom he was drawing master and Court Painter. He gave his, mostly female, sitters an indefinably romantic and mysterious air, but his faulty technique and free use of bitumen has caused the deterioration of much of his work, particularly his large decorations. He designed all the furniture and decorations for the Empress Marie-Louise's bridal suite, and cradles for the King of Rome, and his considerable influence on interior decoration was, unlike his painting, strongly classicist and Greek revival. From 1803 he found relief from his disastrous marriage, made in haste at 19, in a liaison with his favourite pupil, Constance Mayer, many of whose pictures he designed or worked on, but the shock of her suicide in 1821 eventually killed him.
There are works in Amsterdam (Rijksmus.), Chantilly, Chartres, Dijon, Lille, London (Wallace Coll.), Lyons, Montpellier, New York (Met. Mus., Hist. Soc.), Paris (Louvre, Carnavalet, Jacquemart-André), St Louis, Versailles. [ill. 743, p. 382]

Puget, Pierre (1620–94), was a French sculptor whose controlled Baroque made no appeal to the classicizing taste of Louis XIV, and whose intransigent character was unacceptable to Colbert. He worked much in Italy and was a pupil of PIETRO da Cortona (1640–3). Despite his successful *Milo of Crotona* of 1683, his hopes of Court patronage were frustrated, and other works for the King were refused. There are examples in Toulon (caryatides, Hôtel de Ville, 1656–7), Genoa (SM in Carignano), Marseilles, Paris (Louvre), and Quebec (Laval University). [ill. 708, p. 379]

Punch *see* STONE CARVING.

Purism. In 1918 OZENFANT and Édouard Jeanneret (better known as the architect Le Corbusier) published 'Après le Cubisme', in which they accused the Cubists of turning to mere decoration. Purism, which they therefore invented, was to be an art unsullied by decoration, fantasy, or individuality, and inspired by the machine as a form of creation from which all unnecessary detail has been eliminated. Such is the waywardness of man that this arid doctrine produced no art at all: only to the architecture of Le Corbusier has it proved of any consequence.

Purrmann, Hans (*b.* 1880), studied in Germany before going to Paris in 1906, where he met and greatly admired MATISSE. In 1908 Purrmann organized a school to which Matisse gave his name: it petered out in 1910/11, as Matisse gave less and less time to it. Purrmann also organized several Matisse exhibitions in Germany which greatly influenced the Expressionists. In 1943 he was forced to retire to Switzerland, where he still lives. There are works in Basle, Berlin, Cologne, Karlsruhe, and Munich. [ill. 1009, p. 416]

Putto (Ital. boy) a chubby naked boy: an AMORINO.

Puvis de Chavannes, Pierre (1824–98), attempted to recreate something of the monumental Italian fresco style in his huge decorative canvases painted in oil, but kept flat and pale in colour and simplified in the drawing to give something of the effect of fresco. He decorated many Town Halls and other official buildings in France, the most famous being the Panthéon, Paris (1874–8, 1898, *Life of S. Geneviève*), and the Hôtel de Ville, Paris (1889–93). He was particularly admired by the artists grouped under POST-IMPRESSIONISM and NEO-IMPRESSIONISM as a painter of symbolical and allegorical decorations who respected the plane of the wall and composed his murals in simple areas of colour and with a rhythmic linear pattern. He decorated the Library at Boston in 1893–5, and there are other works by him in Birmingham (Barber Inst.), Chicago, Dresden, Frankfurt (Städel), London (NG), Melbourne, New York (Met. Mus.), Paris (Louvre, Petit Pal., Mus. des Arts Décoratifs, Cluny Mus.), St Louis, Washington (NG), and many French provincial museums. [ill. 787, p. 388]

Pynacker, Adam (1622–73), was a landscape painter from Delft who spent three years in Italy, but was back in Delft by 1649. He moved to Amsterdam *c.* 1658. His landscapes are very like those of BOTH but are often hard and bluish, with silver tree-trunks and blue foliage. There is a particularly fine one in Dulwich which has a curious blue where one would expect green in the foliage; this is due to the use of fugitive yellow pigments which have faded out of the greens. There are examples in Amsterdam, Boston, Copenhagen, Florence (Uffizi), Hamburg, London (Wallace Coll.), Munich, Nottingham, Paris (Louvre), and Vienna (K-H and Akad.). [ill. 424, p. 332]

Pynas, Jan (1583/4–1631), and Jacob (1590–1650 or later), were brothers who were both in Rome *c.* 1605 and returned to Holland with a new kind of history painting, much influenced by Italian ideas and also by ELSHEIMER: their principal importance is that they passed these ideas on to Rembrandt, who may have been Jacob's pupil for a few months. There are works by them in Amsterdam (Rembrandt House), Hartford Conn., Munich, Paris, and Philadelphia (Johnson). [ills. 454, 457, p. 336]

Quadraturista *see* ILLUSIONISM.

Quadro Riportato (Ital. carried picture). A term applied to easel paintings seen in normal perspective, which have been inserted into a ceiling decoration so that the effect is not the same as the ILLUSIONISM of *Quadrature*.

Quarton, Enguerrand (*c.* 1410–66 or later), sometimes wrongly called Charonton, was a French painter working in Avignon. There are two documented works by him, in Chantilly (Musée Condé) and in Villeneuve-lès-Avignon (Hospice): the latter is a large *Coronation of the Virgin*, completed in 1454, which is one of the most important surviving 15th-century French paintings. It is unique in that the contract for it survives and contains the joint theological views of the priest who commissioned it and the painter himself, who reserved the right – which he exercised – to treat the picture as seemed best to him: 'Contract of 25 April 1453 between Dominus Jean de Montagnac and Master Enguerrand Quarton, of the diocese of Laon, painter. (1) There should be the form of Paradise, and in that Paradise should be the Holy Trinity, and there should not be any difference between the Father and the Son; and the Holy Ghost in the form of a dove; and Our Lady in front as it will seem best to Master Enguerrand; the Holy Trinity will place the crown on the head of Our Lady. (2) . . . Item: In paradise below should be all the estates of the world . . . After the heavens, the world in which should be shown a part of the city of Rome . . . the church of S. Peter at Rome . . . On the other side of the sea, will be a part of Jerusalem . . . the cross of Our Lord, and at the foot . . . a praying Carthusian. On the left side will be Hell. . . .'
The greatest of all 15th-century French pictures – the *Pietà* from Villeneuve-lès-Avignon now in the Louvre – has also been attributed to Quarton. [ill. 666, p. 372]

Quattrocento (Ital. four hundred). The 15th century, i.e. the fourteen hundreds. *Quattrocento Mannerism* is a phrase sometimes used to describe the agitated and nervous style of a Botticelli or a Filippino Lippi, the assumption being that it is a 15th-century precursor of MANNERISM.

Quellin, Arnold (1653–86), was the son of Artus I. He was born in Antwerp but settled in London in 1680, where he died at the age of 33. He worked with Grinling GIBBONS (1682–6) and probably did much of the work for which Gibbons was paid – e.g. the *James II*, outside the NG, London. Their major joint work was the Catholic Chapel in Whitehall Palace, designed by Wren in 1685–6 for James II, which Evelyn visited on 29 December 1686:

'Nothing can be finer than the magnificent Marble work and Architecture at the End, where are 4 statues representing st. Joh: st. Petre, st. Paule, and the Church, statues in white marble, the worke of Mr Gibbons. . . .' The Chapel was demolished in 1695, but some fragments survive at Westminster Abbey and in Burnham Church, Somerset. The Thynne Monument (1682/4), in Westminster Abbey, is Quellin's and there are other works in London (Guildhall and Soane Mus.). [ill. 874, p. 398]

Quellin, Artus I (1609–68), was one of the leading sculptors in the Netherlands in the 17th century. He was the son of the sculptor Erasmus Quellin and the father of the sculptors Artus II and Arnold. He studied in Rome, where he was much influenced by the classical Baroque of DUQUESNOY and ALGARDI, and on his return to Antwerp in 1639 he combined these influences with that of Rubens. In 1650 he moved to Amsterdam and spent 14 years working on the Town Hall (now Royal Palace), employing many assistants; this was his major work and many sketches for the decorations there are now in Amsterdam (Rijksmus.). Other works are in Antwerp (S. André), and Brussels (Cath.). [ill. 268, p. 311]

Quercia, Jacopo della (1374/5–1438), was the greatest Sienese sculptor and a contemporary of Ghiberti and Donatello. He took part in the 1401 competition for the First Baptistry Doors (won by Ghiberti) in Florence, but his entry is lost and the earliest work attributed to him is the Tomb of Ilaria del Carretto (*c.* 1406) in Lucca Cath. This is now fragmentary, but it seems to show a knowledge of Northern motives, and it is often said that Jacopo must have had some knowledge of the Burgundian School around SLUTER. The sarcophagus is also decorated with *putti* carrying garlands, perhaps the earliest modern use of a classical Roman motive. In 1408 he was commissioned to make a public fountain, the Fonte Gaia, for his native Siena, and he executed it 1414–19 (he seems always to have been dilatory): it is now dismembered in the Pal. Pubblico, Siena. Between 1417 and 1431 he was working on reliefs for the Baptistry of Siena on which both Ghiberti and Donatello also worked. Indeed, the *Salome* relief by Donatello was originally commissioned from Quercia; in 1425 all three sculptors had to return money advanced to them, on account of their unsatisfactory progress. From 1425 Quercia was also working on another commission, the stone reliefs outside S. Petronio, Bologna, which occupied him until his death. These reliefs in particular show an almost Donatellesque vigour of handling and were much admired by Michelangelo. Other works by Quercia are in Bologna (S. Giacomo), Ferrara (Cath.), Lucca (S. Frediano), and S. Gimignano. [ill. 53, p. 276]

R

Raeburn, Sir Henry (1756–1823), was the portrait painter who has recorded the personalities of the 'Athens of the North', the lawyers and scholars of the great age of Edinburgh, and also some of the more picturesque representatives of the Highland lairds before the depopulations and emigrations. Raeburn was left an orphan at an early age and was apprenticed to a jeweller *c.* 1772, when he probably began to paint miniatures. Very little is known of his early career, but in 1776, at the age of 20, he was commissioned to paint a full-length portrait in oils of George Chalmers, for Dunfermline Town Council (to whom it still belongs). This clearly betrays his lack of professional training; equally, it is an astonishing performance under the circumstances. In 1780 he married a well-off widow and was able to devote himself to painting, but there are few datable works of this period. Traditionally, the *Rev. Robert Walker skating* (Edinburgh, NG) was painted in 1784. In this year Raeburn went to London, where he met Reynolds, and on to Italy. He was back in Edinburgh by 1787, totally uninfluenced by his Italian experience but much influenced by Reynolds, becoming the leading Scots painter. In the course of the 1790s he developed a virtuoso handling of paint, generally drawing straight on to the canvas with his brush (there are no drawings known by him). This executive skill often overreaches itself, and the celebrated 'square touch' which he developed in the first years of the 19th century can render the beefy common sense of one of the great Law Lords (*Lord Newton*, 1806/11), while at other times it is merely insensitive. Perhaps his best-known work is *The Macnab* (1803/13), where the sitter himself was enough to startle any painter out of a rut – particularly in the age of Scott. Hoppner died in 1810 and Raeburn went to London, apparently with the intention of taking over Hoppner's house and practice, but he decided against this and returned to Edinburgh, where he reigned alone. Nevertheless, from 1810 he exhibited regularly at the RA and visited London again in 1815 when he was elected RA. In 1822 George IV made his celebrated State Visit to Edinburgh and Raeburn was knighted and appointed King's Limner for Scotland.

Many of Raeburn's portraits are still in the families for which they were painted, but there are several in Edinburgh (NG and NPG of Scotland, University, and RSA) and in Aberdeen, Baltimore, Boston, Chicago, Cincinnati, Cleveland, Detroit, Glasgow, Kansas City, London (NG, Tate, NPG, RA, Osterley Park (V & A), Courtauld Inst., and Kenwood), Melbourne, Montreal, New York (Met. Mus., Frick Coll., and Brooklyn), San Marino (Huntington), Toronto, Washington (NG, Nat. Coll., and Corcoran), and elsewhere. [ill. 848, p. 397]

Ramsay, Allan (1713–84), was the Scottish counterpart to Reynolds and Gainsborough, with something of the learning of Reynolds and some of Gainsborough's grace. He was the son of the author of 'The Gentle Shepherd' and received his first training in Edinburgh and London; unlike his English contemporaries, however, he underwent a full Italian training as a pupil of Imperiali and SOLIMENA (1736–8). He settled in London and was 'much cried up by the Scotch Gentry': worse, his style was far more elegant and Frenchified than the face-painting practised by Kneller's successors. VERTUE noted in 1739 that: 'Ramsay still accustomes him self to draw the faces in red lines shades &c. finishing the likeness in one red colour or mask before he puts on the flesh Colour, which he proposes as a method to make the flesh clear & transparent – and such a method was used in Italy, by Cavaliere Luti & others. & so did Titian he says. (but is doubted this last) however when the faces are painted 4. 5. or 6 times over little or nothing of that first red is to be seen – certain it is that hitherto. the manner he paints in, neither like the valuable Manner of Dahl Kneller. Lilly [i.e. Lely]. Riley. Dobson Vandyke. Rubens. or Titian – however it is rather lick't than pencilld. neither broad, grand, nor Free, has more of the finishd labourd uncertain – or modish French, German &c. dutch way – his good fortune has been much improvd in this years worke.' His Italian Grand Manner portraits precede Reynolds's by several years but he had not Reynolds's ambition and spent much time in travel – he visited Italy four times – and in conversation, in which Dr Johnson himself admitted his prowess. In 1759 Horace Walpole acutely observed: 'Mr Reynolds . . . is bold and has a kind of tempestuous colouring, yet with dignity and grace; the latter [Ramsay] is all delicacy. Mr Reynolds seldom succeeds in women, Mr Ramsay is formed to paint them.' During the 1760s he was appointed Painter to George III, to Reynolds's chagrin, but he produced only a series of Royal images, mostly executed by assistants, for Government buildings. His best works are in Edinburgh (NG of S, SNPG), including hundreds of the drawings which were the foundations of his pictures, again in contrast with English practice. Other works are in London (NPG, Tate Gall., Courtauld Inst., V & A, Foundling Hospital), Birmingham, Liverpool, Ottawa, and elsewhere. [ill. 832, p. 395]

Raphael (1483–1520), was the youngest of the three great creators of the High Renaissance and was the most eclectic of great artists. He was the son of the painter Giovanni SANTI, and his real name was Raffaello Sanzio. His father died in 1494 and Raphael's earliest years are obscure, but by 1500 he was working in the shop of PERUGINO, probably on the frescoes at Perugia; and in this year he received his first recorded commission, now lost. Probably at this time he painted the *Knight's Dream* (London, NG). He was thus a prodigy, but, what is more extraordinary, in 1500 he was 17 while Leonardo da Vinci was 48 and Michelangelo 25; and yet in less than 10 years the provincial youth, who had not had their advantage in being born and brought up in Florence, was generally admitted to be their equal. The decade 1500–10 not only saw the emergence of Raphael as a great master, it also saw the creation of the High Renaissance, in which Raphael played a leading part and which hardly survived him.

His early works show the influence of Perugino and not much else, as in the *Mond Crucifixion* of *c.* 1502/3 (London, NG), but the *Betrothal of the Virgin* (*Lo Sposalizio*), his first signed and dated work (1504: Milan, Brera), although derived from a Perugino already shows powers of composition and draughtsmanship far in advance of Perugino. At this point in his career Raphael went to Florence, where he must have found that all he knew was old-fashioned and provincial. He began at once to learn all he could from the Florentines, and a whole series of drawings and paintings demonstrates how rapidly he assimilated all they could teach him. From Leonardo's cartoons of the *Virgin and Child with S. Anne* he developed a series of small *Madonnas* (e.g. those in Florence, Paris, and Vienna); from the *Mona Lisa* he learned a new portrait type which he used for his *Maddalena Doni* (Florence, Pitti), while Leonardo's experiments in chiaroscuro are the reason for the dark background in the *Madonna del Granduca* (Florence, Pitti). Michelangelo's influence is principally to be found in a new severity and power in drawing, but the *Deposition* (1507: Rome, Borghese) contains several Michelangelesque motives, not all of them digested. Raphael seems also to have come into close contact with Fra BARTOLOMMEO at this time.

Probably towards the end of 1508 Raphael went to Rome, perhaps because he had heard that the Pope, Julius II, was having new apartments decorated. By 1509 he was certainly employed in the first of these rooms, the Stanza della Segnatura, and he rapidly became the principal master employed in the Vatican, with the sole exception of Michelangelo who was then painting the Sistine Ceiling. At 26 Raphael was in the front rank, and there he remained for the rest of his short life. The Stanza della Segnatura is the first of the series of relatively small rooms, known collectively as the Stanze, which Raphael and his pupils and assistants decorated for Julius II and Leo X. It was painted between 1509 and 1511, the theme of the room being the human intellect. The two principal frescoes represent Philosophy and Theology and are known respectively as the *School of Athens* and the *Disputà*, or *Disputation concerning the Blessed Sacrament*. These two frescoes, balanced and serene, calm, and classically poised, are perhaps the best examples of the High Renaissance at its apogee. The second Stanza, that of Heliodorus (the Stanza d'Eliodoro) has a different theme – Divine intervention on behalf of the Church – and, in keeping with this more dramatic theme, the style is more dramatic and colourful. This may also be due to the fact that the Stanza was painted between 1511 and 1514 and Michelangelo's Sistine Ceiling was unveiled in 1512. The principal sub-

jects are the *Expulsion of Heliodorus from the Temple*, the *Liberation of S. Peter*, and the *Miracle of the Mass at Bolsena*. The remainder of the decorative scheme – the Stanza dell'Incendio and the Sala di Costantino – was almost entirely executed by Raphael's numerous and well-trained assistants, and the exact amount of Raphael's responsibility is a matter of controversy. The principal reason for this is that Raphael was increasingly overwhelmed with work, not only in commissions for pictures from the Pope and from Kings and Princes, but also in that he succeeded Bramante (*d.* 1514) as architect of the new St Peter's, and he was also engaged on innumerable other tasks. The most important of these were the frescoes in the Farnesina, Rome, and the tapestry cartoons designed in 1515–16 and intended to be used for tapestries to hang below the 15th-century frescoes on the walls of the Sistine Chapel. The surviving tapestries are still in the Vatican, and the original cartoons for seven of them are in the V & A, London (loaned from the Royal Coll.). At this time he also supervised the execution of the series of Old Testament scenes in the Loggie of the Vatican: these were completed in 1519, but no more than the general design can be attributed to Raphael. The *Sistine Madonna* (Dresden) probably dates from *c.* 1513 and is unusual in that it is all by Raphael himself and yet it is not known why he should have spent so much trouble on it, apparently for a small religious community in Piacenza. It has been suggested that it was carried at Julius II's funeral. It shows, by comparison with any of his Florentine *Madonnas*, how his style had become larger and simpler and also how the very conception of the Madonna had changed, from the simple naturalism of the 15th century to the superhuman being which the 16th century thought more appropriate to the Mother of God – hence the figure floating in the clouds.

The last major work on which Raphael was engaged was the *Transfiguration* (Vatican), commissioned in 1517 but still unfinished when he died in 1520. It was completed after his death, partly at least by his heir and most important pupil, GIULIO Romano, and it is controversial to what extent the MANNERISM discernible in the picture is due to Giulio. The basic design (including the twisted figure of the woman) and all the drawings, however, are certainly by Raphael and it seems likely that his art was on the point of taking a new direction. When he died at the age of 37 Raphael occupied a unique social position, on terms of friendship with Cardinals and Princes, a position never before attained by an artist. The (baseless) rumour current at his death that the Pope had intended to make him a Cardinal is the most eloquent proof of the change that had come over the status of the artist, a change wrought principally by Leonardo, Michelangelo, and Raphael.

There are pictures by him, in addition to those already mentioned, in Baltimore, Bergamo, Berlin, Bologna, Boston (Gardner Mus.), Brescia, Budapest, Chantilly, Città di Castello, Cracow, Detroit, Dresden, Florence (Pitti and Uffizi), Leningrad, Lisbon, London (NG and Dulwich), Madrid, Milan (Ambrosiana and Brera), Munich, Naples, New York, Paris, Perugia, Princeton NJ (Univ. Gall.), Rome (Borghese and Doria Gall., Accad. di S. Luca, S. Agostino, SM della Pace, SM del Popolo), Vaduz (Liechtenstein Coll.), the Vatican, and Washington. [ills. 174–80, pp. 296–9. Col. pls. 4, 10]

Rayonism (Rayonnism, Rayonnisme), was a short-lived Russian offshoot of CUBISM. 'Rayonism is concerned with the special forms which may arise from the intersection of reflected rays from different objects, forms selected by the artist at will', according to its inventor, the painter Larionov, in 1913.

Rayski, Ferdinand von (1806–90), was trained in Dresden before joining the army in 1825; he served as an officer for four years. He then began to paint portraits of the Saxon nobility, and in 1835 he visited Paris. From 1839 he was settled in Dresden, with a strong connection both for portraits and animals among the local gentry. His style was based on Dutch 17th-century portraits brought up to date by reference to contemporary Frenchmen such as DELACROIX. He visited England in 1862. Most of his works are in Dresden. [ill. 599, p. 359]

Realism as an aesthetic watchword does not go any further back than COURBET, and in the visual arts, as in literature, it generally signifies the search for the squalid and depressing as a means of life-enhancement. It is in fact the total repudiation of IDEAL ART (which in the mid 19th century was necessary). It should not be confused with Naturalism, which is no more than the simple-minded pleasure in being able to make an accurate transcript of nature – 'a speaking likeness' – nor should it be confused with its cousin german SOCIAL REALISM. Some young English painters – notably Bratby, Greaves, and Middleditch – practise a style which some critics have seen fit to call Neo-Realism.

Recession is the name given to the ability to make the objects in a picture appear to recede into the depth of the imaginary picture space. It is most readily obtained by the use of linear and aerial PERSPECTIVE.

Redon, Odilon (1840–1916), created two entirely different types of picture: colourful, semi-Impressionist vases of flowers, animals, or landscapes, and highly imaginative drawings, lithographs, and paintings of fantastic subjects such as plants with human heads, phantoms, and figments from dreams, visions, and nightmares. He maintained stoutly that the fantasy pictures were only possible because of his contact with reality. His work became known in Paris between 1879 and 1882, and he was hailed as one of the principal Symbolist painters, particularly by the literary Symbolists. He was a great friend of Mallarmé. [ill. 788, p. 388]

Refusés *see* SALON.

Relief sculpture is that which is not free-standing, and, in having a background, approximates to the condition of painting. There are several names to indicate the varying depth of projection, ranging from *alto rilievo*, or high relief – which is almost detached from the ground – through *mezzo-rilievo* to bas-relief (*basso-rilievo*) and further still to *rilievo stiacciato* (or *schiacciato*) which is scarcely more than scratched. *Cavo-rilievo* is the same as intaglio, that is, relief in inverse, sunk into the surface instead of embossed upon it.

Remarque Proofs are PROOFS with a scribbled drawing or other mark in the margin to indicate a supposed superiority to ordinary proofs. [ill. 799, p. 389]

Rembrandt van Ryn (1606–69), was born in Leyden, the son of a miller, at the time when Holland became an independent nation. After about a year at Leyden University he was apprenticed for three years to an obscure painter named Swanenburgh, but this was followed by a much more important six months in Amsterdam (1624/5) with Pieter LASTMAN, who was the means of his introduction to the rhetoric of Early Baroque and perhaps also the channel by which the influences of CARAVAGGIO and ELSHEIMER reached him. He may also have spent some time with the PYNAS brothers. In 1625 he returned to Leyden where he set up in company with Jan LIEVENS, an association that lasted until Rembrandt's move to Amsterdam in 1631/2. By 1628 he was sufficiently well known to have DOU as his pupil. The earliest works known to us are dated 1626, and in them – e.g. the *Clemency of Titus* (Utrecht Mus.) – the influence of Lastman is still dominant. Many paintings of the Leyden period show great interest in light and represent scholars in lofty rooms, or are studies of old age; examples are the Melbourne *Scholars disputing*, 1628, the *Scholar in a lofty room* (London, NG), and *Rembrandt's mother as the Prophetess Hannah* (1631: Amsterdam, Rijksmus.). At the end of 1631 or early in 1632 he moved to Amsterdam and set up as a portrait painter, attracting attention in 1632 with the *Anatomy Lesson of Dr Tulp*, a group portrait of the Amsterdam Guild of Surgeons (The Hague, Mauritshuis). This made his name and for the next ten years he prospered, producing highly finished likenesses, often in pairs, such as *Maerten Daey* and his *Wife* (1634: private coll., Paris), *Jan Pellicorne and his son* and his *Wife and daughter* (c. 1635/7, both in London, Wallace Coll.), or the *Unknown Man* of 1641 in Brussels and its pendant, the *Woman with a fan* in the Royal Coll. In 1634 he married Saskia van Uylenborch, who brought him a considerable dowry as well as good connections, and Rembrandt promptly began to live well beyond his means; the *Portrait of himself with Saskia* (c. 1634: Dresden) shows them in a mood of blatant opulence. There are many portraits of Saskia, painted, drawn, and etched (e.g. *Saskia as Flora*, 1635, London, NG), but in 1642 she died, leaving him with a son, Titus. In the same year his great group portrait, the *Company of Capt. Frans Banning Cocq* (Amsterdam, Rijksmus.), better-known as the *Night Watch*, was painted. It was one of several such commemorative groups of the volunteer militia enlisted to defend Amsterdam. Each man paid according to the prominence given to his portrait, some finding themselves subordinated to the exigencies of Rembrandt's art in a way which HELST or KEYSER, or even HALS, would never have attempted.

After 1642 Rembrandt's business declined and the inevitable bankruptcy followed in 1656. It used to be thought that this was because of the revolutionary character of the *Night Watch*, but it now seems certain that Captain Cocq and his men were perfectly content with their picture. Meanwhile he was living with Hendrickje Stoffels, who, with his son Titus 'employed' him from 1660 onwards, thus affording some relief from creditors. During these years he turned to Biblical subjects, creating a Protestant iconography, to landscape, and to studies of the Jews among whom he lived. He had been painting religious subjects from the start of his career, and had painted a series of Passion scenes for Prince Frederick Henry, 1633–9 (now in Munich), and such exuberantly Baroque works as the *Blinding of Samson* of 1636 (Frankfurt), but the later works are deeper in emotional content and far less superficially dramatic. The same contrasts can be seen in his etchings – compare the *Annunciation to the Shepherds* of 1634 with the 'Hundred Guilder Print' (*Christ Healing*) of c. 1649, and the landscapes which he drew and etched in the forties, compared with the romantic ones of the period from c. 1635 when he was much influenced by SEGHERS. His portraits of the fifties and sixties include such masterpieces of psychological penetration painted to please himself as the *Jewish Merchant* of c. 1650 (London, NG), the *Old Jew in an armchair* (1652: London, NG) and the portrait of *Jan Six* (1654: still in the family coll., Amsterdam), as well as portraits like the *Man* (1663: Washington), the *Man with a magnifying glass* (New York, Met. Mus.), and the *Woman with a plume* (Washington), both painted in the sixties and clearly commissioned works.

The long series of self-portraits, datable between 1629 and 1669, records every stage of his career, every moment of disillusion, with ever-deepening self-analysis. In his last years he continued to receive some important commissions, such as the *Anatomy Lesson of Dr Deyman* (1656: Amsterdam, Rijksmus.), or the *Conspiracy of the Batavians*, commissioned in 1661 for the Amsterdam Town Hall but removed at once for alterations (and now in Stockholm, Nat. Mus.); both these now exist only as fragments. In 1662 he completed the group of the *Staal Meesters*, the Syndics of the Guild of Drapers, and this, the greatest of all Dutch group portraits, is now in the Rijksmuseum, Amsterdam. Later still he painted the *Family group* now in Brunswick, and these very late works impressed the aged Hals so much that Rembrandt's influence is perceptible in his last works. It is an influence which has never died out. Rembrandt's output was prodigious, and there are about 650 paintings by him (of which some 60 are self-portraits) as well as about 300 etchings and 1,500–2,000 drawings. He maintained for many years a large teaching studio, and among his numerous pupils were BOL, FLINCK, EECKHOUT, KONINCK, and Aert de GELDER. There are paintings by Rembrandt in the Royal Coll., and in Aix-en-Provence, Amsterdam, Antwerp, Baltimore, Bayonne, Berlin, Boston, Brunswick, Brussels, Cape Town, Cambridge (Fitzwm), Cambridge Mass. (Fogg), Cassel, Chicago, Cincinnati, Cleveland, Cologne, Copenhagen, Detroit, Dublin, Edinburgh, Florence, Frankfurt, Glasgow, The Hague, Kansas City, Leyden, Leningrad, Liverpool, London (NG, Dulwich, Kenwood, V & A, Wallace Coll.), Madrid, Milan, Melbourne, Minneapolis, Munich, New York (Met. Mus., Frick Coll., Historical Soc.), Ottawa, Paris (Louvre, Mus. Jacquemart-André), Philadelphia (Johnson Coll.), Raleigh N. Carolina, Rotterdam, San Francisco, Sarasota Fla (Ringling Mus.), Stockholm, Toledo Ohio, Toronto, Utrecht, Vienna, Washington, Worcester Mass. [ills. 434, 435, 446–9, pp. 334–7. Col. pl. 18]

Renaissance (Fr., or Ital. *Rinascimento*, rebirth). Usually defined as the 'revival of art and letters under the influence of classical models in the 14th–16th century' (OED). As early as 1550 Vasari used the word *rinascita* to describe this rebirth, which he knew to have culminated in his own days, but it probably received the wide currency it now has from Jacob Burckhardt's 'Civilization of the Renaissance in Italy', first published in 1860. In the visual arts the term is now used with some care, if any degree of precision is desirable. It is felt that the influence of classical models is not easy to distinguish in Italy, where the classical tradition is virtually unbroken and a term which can be made to cover Giotto at one end and Titian at the other is too vague to be useful in any discussion of style (the case is even worse in English architectural history, where 'Renaissance' is still made to cover Elizabethan buildings, Wren, and the Adam brothers). It is therefore agreed that Giotto may be said to have begun the Renaissance in the other sense, that of according a new dignity to man and his works, but that the classical ideals hardly came into play before the first years of the 15th century, when the humanist ideals of Alberti were indistinguishable from those of MASACCIO, Brunelleschi, and DONATELLO, and, to a lesser extent, Ghiberti. The period from c. 1420 to 1500 is therefore now generally called the Early Renaissance and the term High Renaissance is reserved for the tiny span of time when a pure, classical, balanced harmony was attained, and when artists of the first rank were in absolute control of their techniques, able to render anything they wanted with the maximum of fidelity to nature. It is this mastery of technique which, with the elimination of superfluous detail, is one of the distinguishing marks between Early and High Renaissance. The High Renaissance lasted from c. 1500 to c. 1527, the date of the Sack of Rome, and it includes the earlier works of MICHELANGELO, all the Roman works of RAPHAEL, and most of LEONARDO's work. The later work of Michelangelo is dedicated to different ideals, and the style of the period 1530/1600 is now generally known as MANNERISM, while the style of the 17th century, in accordance with yet other ideals, is BAROQUE. All these have a passion for classical models as a distinguishing mark, so that the Renaissance style must also have the classical qualities of serenity and harmony – qualities which were lost sight of in the period of the Counter-Reformation or the Thirty Years War.

Reni, Guido (1575–1642), was a Bolognese painter who enjoyed the highest reputation in the 17th and 18th centuries until it was blasted by Ruskin. In spite of his sentimental religiosity his pictures are now returning to favour, on account of the combination of CARAVAGGIO and the CARRACCI. To the surprise of his fellow-countrymen he remained a life-long virgin; this, however, he compensated for by a passionate addiction to gambling. He was a pupil, with Albani and Domenichino, of the Fleming CALVAERT until his conversion to the manner of the Carracci c. 1594. About 1600/3 he went to Rome for the first time, where he was influenced to some extent by the naturalism of Caravaggio (who, typically, is said to have threatened to kill him); his own style, however, depends much more on the Raphaelesque classicism of the Carracci Academy and is best seen in the *Aurora* (1613–14: Rome, Casino Rospigliosi). This is a ceiling fresco that makes no attempt at SOTTO IN SÙ illusionism (cf. GUERCINO's *Aurora* of 1621–3), but is treated exactly as an easel picture seen in the normal way; it also contains some conscious quotations from the Antique. Apart from a trip to Naples in 1622 he worked in Rome, and, mainly, in Bologna. There are many works by him in Bologna and Rome (Capitoline, Borghese, Quirinal Palace, S. Gregorio Magno, and other Roman churches) and others in London (NG and Dulwich), Auckland NZ, Birmingham, Glasgow, Leeds, Munich, Naples, Paris (*Deeds of Hercules* set, 1617/21, in the Louvre, and the *Job*, 1622–36, recently rediscovered in Notre Dame), Sarasota Fla, the Vatican, and Vienna. [ills. 249, 257, pp. 308–9]

Renoir, Pierre-Auguste (1841–1919), was one of the greatest of the painters affected by IMPRESSIONISM. He worked from the age of 13 in a china factory and his early training as a painter on porcelain predisposed him towards the light palette of Impressionism. In 1861 he spent some time in the teaching studio of the academician Gleyre, where he met MONET, BAZILLE, and SISLEY. He also went to the Louvre often, and was particularly interested in Watteau, Boucher, and Fragonard: all his life he was conscious of the need to study art in museums, and dissatisfied with the purely visual aspects of Impressionism. The main influence on his early career was COURBET, until about 1868, and during this time he used heavy impasto and rather dark colour. In 1868 he and Monet worked together on the Seine, and as a result of painting continually out of doors – and of Monet's influence – his colour became lighter and higher in key, and his handling freer, the whole canvas being managed in patches of coloured light and shadow without any definite drawing. He exhibited in the first three Impressionist exhibitions, and then in the seventh; after 1877 he was successful in getting some of his portraits into the Salon, and was unwilling to risk the market that this offered for the sake of the often disadvantageous advertisement provided by the group shows. In 1879 (and again in 1882) he visited North Africa, was in Guernsey in 1880, and made his first of several trips to Italy in the winter of 1881–2; he later travelled widely, visiting London, Holland, Spain, Germany, studying in museums, and he deeply admired Raphael and Velazquez more even than Rubens, to whose art his own was so much indebted. After his first Italian journey his drawing became much firmer, his Impressionism much less the spontaneous result of purely visual stimuli than the conscious use of colour to recreate Nature and form, and this in turn involved departure from Monet's form of Impressionism – direct painting before the object – by the adoption of a more elaborate technique, with preparatory drawings and successive sessions on the canvas while the figure and its setting was worked up: '*Il faut meubler la toile*', was his way of putting it. Where his early works include portraits, landscapes, flowers, and groups of figures in settings of café, dance-hall, boats, or riverside landscapes, his late works are mostly nudes, or near nudes. The warmth and tenderness of pink and pearly flesh entranced him and gave him full scope for his favourite colour schemes of pinks and reds, and the exploitation of a chosen colour-scheme is in itself an un-Impressionist idea: '*Il faut avoir*', he said '*le sentiment des fesses et des tétons.*'

In 1906 he settled in Cagnes in the South of France, but he was already crippled with arthritis, which finally rendered him completely helpless, so that his last pictures were painted with brushes stuck between his twisted fingers. He also 'made' a certain amount of sculpture – 'dictated' rather, since the clay was worked by an assistant who added or removed on his instructions, to create rather Maillol-like figures of impressive simplicity and solidity. In his last years he saw a good deal of Matisse, who lived near by, and he was interested in and sympathetic to the ideas behind Fauvism. He painted about 6,000 pictures: there is a large collection in Paris (Mus. de l'Impressionnisme), and there are works in Berlin, Boston (Mus.), Cambridge Mass. (Fogg), Chicago, Cologne (Wallraf-Richartz), Essen, Glasgow, London (NG, Tate, Courtauld Inst.), São Paulo, Stockholm, Toronto, Washington (NG, Phillips). America is particularly rich in Renoirs, since they were bought there when the artist was still unappreciated in Europe. [ills. 752, 780, 781, 794, pp. 383, 387, 389]

Replica. An exact copy of a picture, made by the painter of the original or at least under his supervision. It is often used to describe two or more paintings, exactly alike, when one is in doubt which (if any) is the prime original.

Repoussoir (Fr. *repousser*, to push back) is used to describe a figure or other object placed in the extreme foreground of a picture, usually at the right or left edge, with the object of deflecting the spectator's eye into the centre of the picture. A *repoussoir* figure often aids in this by gesticulating in the required direction.

Reredos (Retable). The structure behind an altar, sometimes resting on it, like a ledge, and sometimes standing clear of it. The very large groups of carvings, common in medieval Germany, are properly referred to as reredoses or retables, rather than altarpieces, which term is perhaps best reserved for paintings.

Rethel, Alfred (1816–59), was, with CORNELIUS, the major early 19th-century German painter on a monumental scale. He was influenced by the NAZARENER, but worked on a much larger scale. He visited Italy in 1844–5 and again in 1852–3, but his career was cut short by madness in 1853. His major works were the frescoes for the Town Hall, Aachen, projected from 1840, begun in 1847, and left incomplete. He also made a woodcut series of the *Dance of Death* (1849), in imitation of Holbein. [ill. 611, p. 360]

Retroussage is a term used in etching to describe the action of passing a ball of muslin lightly over an inked plate with the intention of dragging some of the ink out of the lines and smearing it across the plate.

Reuwich, E. *See* MASTER OF THE HOUSEBOOK.

Reymerswaele (Roymerswaele) *see* MARINUS.

Reynolds, Sir Joshua (1723–92), is, historically, the most important figure in British painting. He was born at Plympton St Maurice in Devon, where his father was headmaster of the Grammar School and a former Fellow of

Balliol: this is worth mentioning because it shows that Reynolds was born and brought up in an educated family at a time when most English painters were hardly more than ill-educated tradesmen. Reynolds himself became the close friend of Dr Johnson, Goldsmith, Burke, and Garrick, and it is probably true that he did more to raise the status of the artist in England through his learning and personal example than by his actual quality as an artist. He was apprenticed to HUDSON in 1740, in London, but in 1743 he left his master and returned to Devonshire; from 1743 to 1749 he was in practice on his own in London and Devonshire, before leaving for Italy in 1749. As early as 1746 he painted the *Eliot Family Group*, based on a famous van Dyck at Wilton House, and this already shows the fundamental basis of his art – the deliberate use of allusion to the Old Masters or Antique sculpture as a classical allusion might have been used by an 18th-century speaker or writer. This appeal to the educated eye, above and beyond the needs of mere likeness, is the essence of his own style and the reason for the rise in public esteem for the visual arts which is so marked a feature of his age. In 1749 he had the chance to go to Italy with Commodore (later Admiral Viscount) Keppel, who was also to become one of his best friends. Up to this time the main influences on his style had been Hogarth, Ramsay, and to a moderate extent only, Hudson; he now spent two years (1750–2) in Rome, where he made a really prolonged study of the Antique, of Raphael and, above all, of Michelangelo. Here he learned the intellectual basis of Italian art (just as WILSON was doing), and this was something that scarcely any other British painter, with the possible exception of Ramsay, had done up to then, even in Rome itself. In fact, Reynolds's own practice as a portrait painter was more profoundly influenced by the few weeks he spent in Venice on his way home in 1752. He never ceased to exhort his students to master the principles of the Grand Style, and in fact he regarded Venetian art, and portrait painting, as of less importance. In 1753 he set up in London, met Dr Johnson, and began rapidly to make a name. He sought consciously to marry the Grand Style with the needs of face-painting (and earning a living), and he succeeded so well that he was soon employing assistants, although the Kneller School was not converted ('Shakespeare in poetry, and Kneller in painting, damme!' as one of them observed). Only Ramsay and Cotes were rivals of any significance, but by 1768, when the Royal Academy was founded, it was obvious that Reynolds was the only possible choice for the President. He was knighted in 1769 and made DCL at Oxford (an honour that would have been unthinkable for a painter only a generation earlier) and Mayor of his native Plympton in 1772. The works of the years following 1768 show him at his most classical and most learned, determined to use the Academy as an instrument to forge a British School of History painters to stand beside those of Rome or Bologna. To this end he composed and delivered at intervals (1769–90) the fifteen Discourses which are the most lucid and sensible exposition of the Academic position that, by well-directed labour, it is possible to learn the Rules of Art and to use the inventions and ideas of one's predecessors to create a new style of one's own. During these years Reynolds exhibited regularly at the Academy exhibitions and usually showed a skilful blend of large portraits treated in a historical manner, history pictures proper, and some curious combinations of the two, such as *Dr Beattie* (*The Triumph of Truth*) (Aberdeen Univ.) or *Three Ladies adorning a Term of Hymen* (London, NG), both in the RA of 1774. This idea had been exploited by him as early as 1760/1 in his *Garrick between Tragedy and Comedy*, a thoroughly 'learned' picture which he exhibited in 1762 at the Society of Artists, the Academy's precursor. He won the victory in general terms, although many ladies still preferred to be painted in a fashionable gown by Gainsborough to the 'nightgowns' which Sir Joshua insisted on, as less subject to the vagaries of fashion and more nearly classical in type. In 1781 he made a journey to Flanders and Holland and was profoundly influenced by the force and freedom of Rubens's handling and from then until his sight failed in 1789 his works are less consciously classical and painted with greater warmth and feeling. The overwhelming majority of his vast output consists of portraits, which include almost every man and woman of note in the second half of the 18th century. Unlike Gainsborough, he employed many pupils and assistants and his work also differs from Gainsborough's in being frequently badly preserved on account of his bad technical procedures. The faces of his sitters are often deathly pale because the carmine has faded out completely. Most of his sitter-books still exist and thus nearly all his works are documented: practically every major museum in Britain and America contains one or more, and others are as far afield as Leningrad and São Paulo, Dresden and Adelaide, Budapest and Ottawa. [ills. 838, 841, p. 394]

Ribalta, Francisco (1565–1628), was a Catalan painter whose first known work is the *Christ nailed to the Cross* of 1582 (Leningrad, Hermitage). This is a crude work in the Mannerist tradition, but after Ribalta settled in Valencia in 1599 his style seems to have undergone a considerable change. He was one of the first of the 17th-century Spanish realists, and his mature works have an austere, almost grim, sobriety, combined with dramatic lighting which seems to show CARAVAGGIO's influence. It used to be said that he had actually studied in Italy, but this seems improbable and his earliest Caravaggesque paintings are not earlier than 1615, by which date other Spaniards had been influenced by Italian TENEBRISM. In his last works there is an affinity with the style of RIBERA. *The Vision of Father Simon* (1612: London, NG) is a good example of his devotional style, although it does not yet show Caravaggio's influence. His son Juan – who died in the same year, 1628 – was also a painter. There are works in Madrid (Prado) and Valencia. [ill. 637, p. 364]

Ribera, Jusepe or José (1591–1652), was born near Valencia and may possibly have studied under Ribalta before going to Italy, where he travelled, became a member of the Accademia di S. Luca in Rome, and settled in Naples by 1616. The style of his early works shows a blending of Spanish realism with a degree of idealization derived from the Carracci, expressed in the strong chiaroscuro of Caravaggio, of whom in his own day he was considered to be a follower. This invests his often brutal subjects with a powerful but unsubtle forcefulness, now accentuated by the darkening of his colours through his use of bitumen and bolus grounds. His etchings are frequently better composed than his paintings of related subjects in that they are free of these excessive contrasts of light and shadow. By the mid 1630s his style had changed to a greater softness and the blocks of light in a sea of dark gave place to suaver colour and more even handling, perhaps reflecting the influence of Velazquez, who was in Naples in 1630. The tales of his bloodthirsty opposition to the competition in Naples of Guido RENI and DOMENICHINO are probably apocryphal. He enjoyed the patronage of successive Viceroys and his works were very popular in Spain, since they exploited the essentially Spanish subjects of Counter-Reformation painting – half-, or less frequently, full-length figures of strongly characterized male Saints or rapt female ones, occasional mythologies in which even Venus is fully clothed, tender Nativities, scenes from the Passion or the lives of the Saints, full of emotion and devotion. In his late years his reputation was diminished by his reduced output and slowness of execution, due to his ill-health, in turn probably affected by the *éclat* of the seduction of his daughter by Don Juan of Austria, a natural son of Philip IV of Spain, who was sent to Naples to quell the Masaniello Rising in 1647. The large school of Neapolitan Tenebrist painting probably owes more to Ribera than to Caravaggio, since it develops along his lines, to the point that when it is impossible to decide whether a work is Spanish or Italian, the answer is usually to call it Neapolitan.

There are many works by him in Madrid (Prado, Academia), and in Naples (Pinacoteca, Palazzo Reale, Cathedral, Mus. di S. Martino, Mus. Civico), and also in Bilbao, Berlin, Boston (Mus.), Brussels, Budapest, Cambridge Mass. (Fogg Mus.), Dresden, the Escorial, Hartford Conn. (Wadsworth), Leeds, London (Wellington Mus.), Milan (Poldi-Pezzoli), Montreal, New York (Hispanic Soc., Met. Mus.), Paris (Louvre), Philadelphia, Rome (Doria, Gall. Naz.), Salamanca (Immaculate Conception), Toledo Ohio, Vitoria. [ill. 639, p. 365]

Ricci. There were two, Sebastiano and his nephew Marco, both Venetians. Sebastiano (1659–1734) worked in Bologna, Rome, Modena, Florence, and Parma, before going to Vienna, where he worked in the Schönbrunn Palace. In 1712 he went to England with his nephew, and both left in 1716 after Sebastiano failed to get the commissions to decorate the dome of St Paul's and Hampton Court Palace, both of which went to THORNHILL. His major English work is the *Resurrection* painted in the apse of Chelsea Hospital Chapel; it has a light, quick rhythm and a decorative feeling quite new after the ponderous and tasteless works of VERRIO. He left the decoration of Burlington House incomplete (it was finished by KENT) when he returned to Venice, and on the way home he stopped in Paris and visited Watteau, some of whose drawings he copied. There are 21 paintings by Sebastiano in the Royal Collection, including a *Finding of Moses* originally attributed to Veronese. This stresses the fact that Sebastiano had been so well trained in the Veronese tradition that his works could pass as by the 16th-century artist: his stay in London was enlivened by several rows over his abilities as a *pasticheur*. His translations of Veronese into 18th-century style were an important influence on the young TIEPOLO. Marco (1676–1730) was a pupil of Sebastiano's, and probably worked with

him in Florence, 1706–7. He may also have visited Rome and Milan, where he perhaps knew MAGNASCO, who influenced him. He went to England in 1708 with PELLEGRINI, with whom he worked on stage scenery and in 1710 he seems to have gone back to Venice to fetch his uncle. They returned together in 1712, travelling via the Netherlands, and remained for about four years, arriving back in Venice c. 1717. The remainder of his life is ill-documented: he appears to have worked for Sebastiano on landscape backgrounds for large religious works, and to have executed small landscapes in tempera on leather. His landscapes are often *Capricci*; they are usually lively and free in handling.

There is a large number of drawings by both Riccis in the Royal Collection, and many of the older galleries have paintings by them. [ills. 287, 315, pp. 315, 317]

Riccio, Andrea (1470/5–1532), was a Paduan sculptor who is supposed to have been a pupil of Bellano, who was himself an assistant of DONATELLO. Riccio was trained as a goldsmith, which may account for the very delicate handling of his small bronzes. He was working in Padua by 1496/7 and his most famous work is the Paschal candlestick in the Santo at Padua of 1507/15. His bronze statuettes are in most major museums, and reflect the humanist tastes of Padua in the 15th and 16th centuries. [ill. 153, p. 294]

Richards, Ceri (*b.* 1903), is a Welsh painter whose abstract pictures are often based on themes taken from poetry (Dylan Thomas: 'Do not go gentle into that good night . . .') or music (Debussy, *La Cathédrale engloutie*), or based on earlier paintings, such as the *Lion Hunt*, after Delacroix. He undertook a huge decoration for the Shakespeare Festival in 1964. There are works by him in Aberdeen, Cardiff, London (Tate), Manchester (Whitworth), Ottawa, Swansea (Gallery and Parish Church), and Toledo Ohio. [ill. 1107, p. 428]

Richardson, Jonathan (1665–1745), a pupil of Riley, *c.* 1688–91, and inheritor of his teacher's stiff and solemn manner, was the principal portrait painter of the period between Kneller and Hudson. In 1711 he and Kneller founded the St Martin's Lane Academy, from which eventually sprang the RA Schools. He had a considerable influence through his books 'The Theory of Painting', 1715, and the guide-book widely used by Grand Tourists, which he wrote with his son, Jonathan the Younger (1694–1771), in 1722. His son also painted, but is better known for his writings on connoisseurship.

There are works in Oxford and Cambridge Colleges, Edinburgh (NPG), Leeds, London (NPG), and elsewhere. [ill. 822, p. 393]

Richier, Germaine (1904–59), was a French sculptress, who also made engravings, book-illustrations, and ceramics. She worked with BOURDELLE 1925–9 and then, under the influence of Surrealism, she began to make spindly figures similar to those by GIACOMETTI (who had also been a pupil of Bourdelle). She lived in Switzerland 1939–45, but in 1950 was commissioned to make a crucifix for the new and controversial church at Assy (Haute-Savoie), which has works by Braque, Matisse,

Lipchitz, and other leading artists. There are works in museums in Amsterdam, Basle, Brussels, London (Tate), Minneapolis, Paris, Rome, Stockholm, and Zürich. [ill. 1147, p. 433]

Riemenschneider, Tilman (c. 1460–1531), was, with STOSS, the leading German sculptor of the Late Gothic style. From 1483 he worked in Würzburg where he kept a very large shop which produced scores of carvings, mostly in wood, of dramatic and emotional subjects such as the Lamentation over the Dead Christ. He also worked in stone. Apart from Würzburg, there are examples in Berlin, Cleveland Ohio, London (V & A), Munich, Providence RI, and many German churches. [ill. 624, p. 361]

Rigaud, Hyacinthe (1659–1743), was awarded the Prix de Rome in 1682 but did not go to Italy. He was the principal official painter to the Court of Louis XIV and also worked under Louis XV: like his friend and rival LARGILLIERRE he expresses the pomp of *le Roi Soleil* in his great State portraits, and occasionally the character of his sitters. His non-official portraits show the influence of Rembrandt. He had a very active studio and few of his pictures – on the evidence of his account books – can be wholly his own work. There are examples in Versailles, Paris (Louvre), and French provincial museums and in Dresden, Florence (Uffizi), London (NG, NPG, Wallace Coll., Dulwich, Kenwood), Melbourne, Munich, Naples, New York (Met. Mus.), Ottawa, Stockholm, Vienna, and elsewhere. He painted an average of 35 portraits a year for 62 years. [ill. 699, p. 376]

Riley, John (1646–91), was the leading English portrait painter in the short interval between the dominations of Lely and Kneller. Nothing is known of Riley's work before 1680, but by 1688 his fame was so well grounded that he was appointed Principal Painter to William and Mary jointly with Kneller; nevertheless, his best works may well be the portraits of humble people, such as the *Bridget Holmes, a nonagenarian Housemaid*, in the Royal Coll., or the *Scullion* at Christ Church, Oxford. There are other pictures by him in the Royal Coll., London (Tate), and Oxford (Ashmolean and Bodleian Library). [ill. 813, p. 392]

Rilievo see RELIEF.

Riopelle, Jean Paul (b. 1923), is the leading Canadian abstract painter, although he has lived in Paris since 1947. His work shows the influence of Kandinsky, Miró, and Pollock. There are pictures in London (Tate) and New York (Guggenheim). [ill. 1100, p. 428]

Rivera, Diego (1886–1957), was a Mexican painter who worked in Paris during the years that brought Cubism to birth, and he knew most of the principal artists in that movement. He held aloof from it, however, and eventually returned to Mexico (in 1921), where, like OROZCO, he was powerfully affected by politics. His first teacher, in Mexico City, had been a pupil of Ingres and Rivera's art was always more revolutionary in content than in style. His 'Mexican' art is largely dependent on a vocabulary evolved from a mixture of Gauguin with Aztec and Mayan sculpture. In his large commissions for the

decoration of public buildings Rivera used *buon fresco*, a technique that he revived, as he also revived the use of ancient encaustic methods. His mural in the Rockefeller Center, New York, was replaced by one by BRANGWYN on account of the introduction of a portrait of Lenin rather than for any objection to the style. [ill. 1072, p. 425]

Robbia, Luca della (1400–82), was ranked by contemporaries as one of the great innovators at the beginning of the 15th century, along with Ghiberti and Donatello, who were much older, and Masaccio, who was his contemporary but had a very short life instead of Luca's very long one. His first major work was the Cantoria or Singing Gallery for the Cathedral in Florence (1431–8: now in the Cath. Mus.), which was commissioned from him before its companion was ordered from Donatello. This shows his use of Antique examples, but it has also his warm and cheerful humanity, quite unlike the drama and grandeur of Donatello. Much later, between 1464 and 1469, he made the bronze doors of the Cathedral Sacristy, and again the comparison with Donatello's Sacristy in S. Lorenzo can hardly be avoided. Early in his career – perhaps even before 1430 – Luca discovered a means of applying the vitrified lead glazes used by potters to sculpture in terracotta, and he exploited this discovery in a number of smallish works with figures in white against a clear blue background. He was also able to use a large number of colours in this way, but he restricted them to architectural and decorative works (e.g. the entrance of the Pazzi Chapel, Florence). To some extent this discovery was the ruin of his art (but not so much as is commonly supposed), for he was able to found a flourishing family business which later undertook some very large and highly coloured commissions. His nephew, Andrea della Robbia (1435–1525), carried on the business and is best known for the *Foundling Children* on the façade of the Spedale degli Innocenti, Florence (1463–6). His sons, Giovanni (1469–after 1529) and Girolamo (1488–1566), and other sons for a short time as well, all carried on the tradition well into the 16th century.
There are works by Luca in Berlin, Florence (Bargello, Cath., Campanile, Sta Trinita, Sta Croce (Pazzi Chapel), and other churches and palaces), Impruneta, London (V & A), New York (Met. Mus.), Paris (Louvre, Cluny Mus., Jacquemart-André), Peretola near Florence, Pescia, Toledo Ohio, Urbino (S. Domenico), Vienna, and Washington (NG). [ill. 64, p. 279]

Robert, Hubert (1733–1808), went to Rome in 1754 and spent 11 years in Italy, where he became a friend of PIRANESI and PANINI, whose type of Romantic ruin-painting he introduced into France. In 1761 he went to South Italy and Sicily with FRAGONARD and the Abbé de Saint-Non, and he and Fragonard influenced each other profoundly in style, though not in subject-matter. He returned to Paris in 1765, became a member of the Academy and painted his decorative compositions for a number of great houses; later, his range widened and he painted views and street-scenes in Paris. He became Keeper of Louis XVI's pictures and was later one of the first Curators of the Louvre. He is represented in the Louvre and many French provincial museums and also in Baltimore, Barnard Castle (Bowes Mus.), Boston, Bristol, Cambridge

(Fitzwm), Chicago, Detroit, New York (Met. Mus.), and elsewhere. [ill. 754, p. 384]

Roberti, Ercole d'Antonio de' (*c.* 1448/55–96), was active in Ferrara from 1479 and from 1486 was Court Painter to the Este family there. He may have been a pupil of COSSA and worked with him in Bologna before settling in Ferrara, but he was also influenced by the Ferrarese Tura and above all by Giovanni Bellini, although he is not known to have had any contacts with Venice. The only work reasonably certainly his is a large altarpiece of 1480/1 (Milan, Brera) by 'Ercole', but his highly personal style, with its nervous sensibility and deep pathos in such works as the Liverpool *Pietà*, is easily recognizable: nevertheless, much confusion has been caused by the introduction of Ercole di Giulio Cesare de' Grandi, who is said to have died in 1531. This man may well have existed and even have been a Bolognese painter, and was conceivably influenced by Ercole Roberti – only there is no evidence at all for any work by him. Other works by Roberti are in Berlin, Bologna (Pinacoteca, University), Chicago, Dresden, Ferrara, London (NG), Paris (Louvre), Philadelphia (Johnson), the Vatican, and Washington (NG). [ills. 132, 133, p. 291]

Rococo. Immediately after the death of Louis XIV of France in 1715 there was a reaction of relief against the excessive splendours and pomps of Versailles and the whole ceremonial *Roi Soleil* way of life. One of the results was to transfer the centre of French life back to Paris and to build new town houses which were both smaller and much more comfortable than the Baroque palaces. Rococo – which comes from a French word *rocaille*, meaning rock-work – is basically a style of interior decoration, and consists principally in the use of C scrolls and counter-curves, and, in its fullest form around 1730, asymmetrical arrangements of curves in panelling and elsewhere. Porcelain and gold and silversmiths' work of the first half of the 18th century exemplify the tendencies admirably. The characteristics of small curves, prettiness, and gaiety can also be found in painting and sculpture of the period – Watteau and Boucher, and even, in a very modified form, in Hogarth. Nevertheless, England did not take to Rococo and in France it fell out of fashion in the 1740s to be decisively superseded by the earnest ideals and Republican Roman virtue of NEOCLASSICISM, which was largely propagated by Germans. Yet the one country in which the Rococo produced numerous great works of art (and not merely amusing interiors) was Germany, or rather, Germany and Austria. There, in the Catholic South, the style produced scores of absurdly beautiful churches and statues, by artists like Ignaz GÜNTHER, which are elegant, modish, and deeply moving. Guardi, Tiepolo, and Goya all produced masterpieces, but Rococo had relatively little currency in Italy and Spain.

Rodin, Auguste (1840–1917), was the most celebrated sculptor of the late 19th century, achieving during his lifetime a fame which has done much to obscure his real qualities. He worked as a mason from about 1864, and in 1871 was sent to Brussels to do the decorative figures on the new Stock Exchange building, on which he eventually worked as a free-lance. He supplemented his technical training by studying in museums and became interested in

Michelangelo, to whom he was probably led by his admiration for PUGET. In 1875 he visited Italy, and soon after began working on his first independent free-standing figure, *Bronze Age* (1877). Its lifelike quality, accuracy of proportion and anatomy, and rendering of movement gave rise to the tale that it had been made from a cast taken from a live model. Though the absurd accusation was later dropped, the figure received no real recognition until it was shown in London in 1884. This put Rodin into much the same position of anti-academism as the Impressionists and their successors, although he never had to face opposition as vehement and entrenched as they did. Most of his public commissions were unlucky: the base of the *Claude Lorraine* monument in Nancy was altered to suit the town council; the town council of Calais refused to erect his *Burghers* (1884–6; replica outside the Houses of Parliament, London) according to his design; his only equestrian statue, *General Lynch*, was destroyed before erection in Santiago by a Chilean revolution (a small bronze of the model is now in Santiago); his *Thinker* was not erected as he wished and was savaged by a vandal with a chopper; his *Hugo* was produced in several versions to meet endless objections and was finally not put up as planned; his *Balzac* monument was refused by the commissioning committee in 1893 and only erected much later; his *Gate of Hell*, commissioned in 1880 as a door for the École des Arts Décoratifs, Paris, was still unfinished at his death.

This door, inspired by Ghiberti's so-called *Gates of Paradise* for the Baptistry in Florence, contained a large number of figures which provided him with a fount of ideas which he used over and over in larger independent statues and groups in bronze and marble. He employed many marble-cutters and cast-makers to make replicas, which he often completed himself. He was the creator of a new form in sculpture – the fragment as a finished work, usually a head and trunk, but sometimes a pair of hands only – and he also employed a variant of Michelangelo's unfinished figures, giving to some parts a waxy delicacy of finish, while leaving others parts buried in the hardly touched block. His great influence was through the possibilities opened up by his use of fragments, through his expression of emotion and movement, his use of symbolism and distortion, and the amazing sensitiveness of his modelling. This is seen particularly in his male portraits which combine vivid characterization with a deliberately free handling.

There is little point in listing museums containing works, since there are, for instance, 150 or more replicas of the *Bronze Age*, but the Musée Rodin in Paris and the Tate Gall., London have perhaps the most examples. There is also a Rodin Mus. in Philadelphia. [ill. 1118, p. 430]

Rohlfs, Christian (1849–1938), was the son of a farmer, but a leg injury enabled him to study art at Weimar, where he lived until *c.* 1900, painting in an Impressionist manner. An exhibition of works by van Gogh (his younger contemporary) at Hagen in 1902 was a major influence on him, as was his friendship with NOLDE from *c.* 1905. He then began to practise a gentle form of Expressionism, and, like MÜLLER, he abandoned oil paint in favour of tempera and watercolour (from 1911). He painted several series of buildings – the church at Soest and Erfurt Cathedral – but his finest works are the delicate flowerpieces, mostly painted when he was nearing 80. Many of these were painted at Ascona, on Lake Maggiore, where he spent most of the years 1927–37. There are works by him in Cologne, Dresden, Essen, Hagen in Westphalia, Harvard University, Karlsruhe, Mannheim, and Paris (Mus. d'Art Mod.). [ill. 1013, p. 417]

Romanists were the Northern artists who went to Italy and returned filled with the idea of rivalling Raphael and/ or Michelangelo. The name is principally given to painters of the first half of the 16th century, such as MABUSE, van ORLEY, or Maerten van HEEMSKERCK, all of whom imported a quasi-Renaissance style into Northern Europe.

Romano, Giulio, *see* GIULIO.

Romantic *see* CLASSIC.

Rombouts, Theodor (1579–1637), was an Antwerp painter who became a Master in the Guild there in 1601, but he went to Rome *c.* 1616 and stayed until *c.* 1625; there he immediately became strongly influenced by Caravaggio. Like the members of the UTRECHT School he took his Caravaggism home to the Netherlands, but on settling in Antwerp again he changed his style under the fresh influence of Rubens and van Dyck. There are pictures in Antwerp, Ghent, Karlsruhe, Lawrence (Kansas Univ. Mus.), Lille, Madrid, Munich, Paris, Vaduz (Liechtenstein Coll.). [ill. 406, p. 329]

Romney, George (1734–1802), was, with Gainsborough and Reynolds, the most famous English portrait painter of the later 18th century, before the rise of Lawrence. He was, however, artistically very inferior to any of these, even as a portrait painter. He was born in Lancashire and practised in the North until 1762, when he moved to London. He visited Paris in 1764 and in 1773 he took the serious step of abandoning his London practice (Reynolds was then at the height of his powers, and Gainsborough arrived in London in 1774) to go to Italy, where he stayed till 1775. In Rome he was infected with a longing for the Grand Style, and much of the rest of his life was spent in making sketches for vast historical pictures, some of which were begun on canvas, and painting prosaic portraits, which he did with skill if without passion. He is best known for his Lady Hamilton pictures. He met her in 1781 and seems to have had some kind of liaison with her (his wife having been left in the North), and he could paint portraits of her in more or less *déshabille*, imagining them to be history pieces if called *Lady Hamilton as Circe* or some such title. Many hundreds of his execrable drawings exist, mostly scribbles for historical compositions or illustrations to the poems of Hayley, with whom he was in close contact: in this way he had some importance as a Neoclassic and as a link with FLAXMAN, FUSELI, and BLAKE. He rarely exhibited his works, and never at the RA. In his last years he became senile and returned to his wife to die. At one time his pictures were popular in America and many are in museums there: representative works are in Boston, Edinburgh (NG), London (NG, Tate, NPG, Wallace Coll., Courtauld Inst., Dulwich, and Kenwood), Manchester, New York (Met. Mus.), Ottawa, San Marino Calif., and Washington (NG). [ill. 834, p. 395]

Rosa, Salvator (1615–73), painter, etcher, poet, actor, and musician, is the 19th century's idea of the Romantic artist. He was traditionally a bandit for a while, but this story, unfortunately, seems to have been invented in the 19th century. He was very precocious as a painter of landscapes near his native Naples and of battle-pieces, and is said to have attracted the notice of LANFRANCO. He went to Rome in 1635 but contracted malaria, and had to return to Naples in 1636; in 1639 he returned to Rome and settled there, painting battles, marines, and landscapes: in the same year, however, he was rash enough to compose and recite a lampoon on Bernini. He arrived safely in Florence in 1640 and did not go back to Rome until 1649, when he set up as a religious and historical painter but met with less success. His landscapes are infused with the Pathetic Fallacy, thus having a 'poetic' quality quite different from that of Poussin or Claude, and one that appealed deeply to the Age of Reason, so that he was immensely popular in England in the 18th and 19th centuries: indeed the celebrated lines

> 'What'er Lorrain light-touched with softening hue,
>   Or savage Rosa dashed, or learned Poussin drew'

(Thomson, 'The Castle of Indolence') more or less sum up the 18th-century connoisseur's equipment.
He began etching only in 1660 but was very successful and completed over 100 plates. His very numerous pictures are in all older galleries, but there are good examples in Florence (Pitti), Glasgow, London (NG and Wallace Coll.), New York (Met. Mus.), Paris (Louvre), Rome (Gall. Naz.), and Sarasota Fla. [ill. 311, p. 317]

Roslin, Alexandre (1718–93), was a Swedish portrait painter who worked much in Paris and who is stylistically indistinguishable from a French painter. He arrived in Paris in 1752, revisited Stockholm in 1774, going in 1775 to St Petersburg and returning to Paris, via Warsaw and Vienna, in 1779. There are pictures by him in London (NG), Paris (Louvre), and Stockholm. [ill. 740, p. 381]

Rosselli, Cosimo (1439–1507), was a Florentine painter who ran an important workshop despite his being one of the most uninspired and pedestrian of the better-known painters of his day, and gifted particularly in irrelevant and trivial details. Part of the contract for the 1481 fresco cycle in the Sistine Chapel in the Vatican was with him, and he appears to have been given a large share of the work. Among his pupils were Piero di Cosimo and Fra Bartolommeo. There are works by him in Baltimore (Walters), Berlin, Boston (Mus.), Cambridge (Fitzwm), Florence (Accad., Uffizi, Mus. di S. Marco, and churches), Liverpool (Walker), Lucca (Cath.), Oxford (Ashmolean), Paris (Louvre), Philadelphia (Johnson), San Marino (Huntington), and elsewhere. [ill. 104, p. 285]

Rossellino, Bernardo (1409–60) and Antonio (1427–*c.* 79), were brothers. Bernardo was active as an architect as well as a sculptor, and both seem to have done a certain amount of decorative work. Bernardo's principal work is the Tomb of the Florentine Chancellor Leonardo Bruni (1444/50: Florence, Sta Croce), which derives directly from the Tomb of John XXIII by DONATELLO and in its turn sets the type of Tomb in a niche which was normal for the rest of the century. There are other works by him in Florence and in Empoli and Forlì. Antonio was his pupil and was also much influenced by Donatello, although, like MINO, DESIDERIO, and BENEDETTO da Maiano, he rejected the rugged side of Donatello and concentrated on grace and beauty of line. He is best known for his Madonna reliefs, but he also made portrait busts and a Tomb which derives from his brother's, but is a grander affair: it is that of the Cardinal-Prince of Portugal (1461–6: Florence, S. Miniato al Monte). There are works by him in Berlin, Empoli, Faenza, Florence (Bargello, Sto Spirito), London (V & A), Naples, New York (Met. Mus.), Pistoia (Cath.), Prato (Cath.), Vienna, Washington (NG), and elsewhere. [ills. 84, 93, p. 282]

Rossetti, Dante Gabriel (1828–82), poet and painter, was the son of an Italian political refugee in London. He was taught drawing by Cotman and after a few unsuccessful months with Ford Madox BROWN he went to Holman HUNT in 1848. Under his guidance he painted his first major work, the *Girlhood of Mary Virgin*, the first picture exhibited (March 1849) with the initials of the PRB. His adherence to the tenets of the Brotherhood was, however, very short-lived. His subjects were drawn mostly from Dante and from a medieval dream world also reflected in his verse. In 1850 he met Elizabeth Siddal, who also posed for Hunt and MILLAIS, and from 1852 onwards she developed under his inspiration into an artist of poetic and neurotic intensity. His best work was produced during the years of their uneasy association. They married in 1860; in 1862 she died of narcotics and he became virtually a recluse and eventually a chloral addict. In 1857 he was concerned (with MORRIS, BURNE-JONES, and others) in the decoration of the Oxford Union and he did one painting directly on a whitewashed wall. It perished immediately. His poor technique and his use of studio assistants are obvious in many of his later works. Birmingham, Cambridge (Fitzwm), Cambridge Mass. (Fogg), Dublin, Liverpool, London (NG, NPG, Tate, V & A), Manchester, and Wilmington Delaware have examples. [ill. 950, p. 409]

Rosso, Giovanni Battista ('Rosso Fiorentino') (1494–1540), was a friend and contemporary of PONTORMO and, like him, worked under Andrea del Sarto, and was one of the founders of MANNERISM. He worked in Florence from 1513 to 1523, when he went to Rome and stayed there until the Sack (1527), after which he wandered around Italy until 1530 when he went to Venice and then, in the same year, to France for François I. He worked at Fontainebleau with PRIMATICCIO and was thus one of the founders of the Fontainebleau style and had a great influence on French painting. According to Vasari he committed suicide, which would have been in keeping with his neurotic temperament, but he seems in fact to have died a natural death. His *Deposition* (Paris, Louvre) was painted in France and its dead Christ with His greenish body and reddish hair is typical of his later emotional style. There are works by him in Arezzo, Berlin, Florence (Uffizi, Pitti, SS. Annunziata, S. Lorenzo), Frankfurt, Liverpool, London (NG), Los Angeles, Naples, Pisa, Rome (Borghese), Siena, Volterra, and Washington (NG). [ill. 185, p. 298]

Rosso, Medardo (1858–1928), was one of the leading Italian sculptors of the late 19th century, although he was

a painter until 1883 and only turned to sculpture as a result of reading Baudelaire's 'Curiosités esthétiques'. He was fascinated by the play of light on surfaces – an essentially Impressionist preoccupation – and, like RODIN, he translated this into sculpture, although he differed from Rodin in preferring the single viewpoint. His favourite medium was wax, since this has a colouristic effect as well as allowing very slight modulations of the surface. He did, in fact, exert some influence on Rodin as well as on later Italian sculptors (e.g. MANZÙ), but his fame has been largely confined to Italy, since his stay in Paris (1884–6) was disastrous. There are works by him in Paris (Petit Palais and Mus. Rodin) as well as in Italian museums, particularly Rome (Gall. Naz. d'Arte Moderna) and the Rosso Museum in Barzio. [ill. 1123, p. 430]

Rothko, Mark (*b.* 1903), was born in Russia but went to America in 1913. He began painting in 1926 and is now known for his large abstract pictures which consist of horizontal bands of colour with muzzy edges. There are examples in London (Tate), New York (M of MA), and other American museums. [ill. 1111, p. 429]

Rottluff, Karl Schmidt, *see* SCHMIDT.

Rottmayr, Johann Michael (1654–1730), was the leading Austrian Baroque painter. According to his own account, he went to Venice in 1675 and worked there for thirteen years in the studio of Johann Carl Loth (known in Italy as Carlo Lotti): no works of his are known from this period, but his style is certainly Italianate (PITTONI and Correggio) with a trace of French influence. He returned to Salzburg *c.* 1688 and lived in Vienna from 1696, but was often away painting ceilings all over Austria. His large ceiling in the Karlskirche, Vienna (1726–30), is very close to Correggio, but other late works show some influence from Rubens. There are many ceilings still in existence in Vienna, Melk, and elsewhere, and paintings in Munich, Nuremberg, Passau Cathedral, Sarasota Fla., and Vienna (Oesterreichische Gal.). [ill. 589, p. 358]

Rouault, Georges (1871–1958), had already completed his apprenticeship to a stained-glass window maker when he entered, in 1891, the École des Beaux-Arts, where he was a pupil of MOREAU from 1892 to 1895. He became the first Curator of the Musée Moreau in 1898. His early works show Moreau's influence, but by 1903 he had abandoned his dark and overworked oil-paintings of Biblical subjects for the series of *Prostitutes*, *Clowns* (from 1904, 1907, and again during the 1930s), and *Judges* (from 1908). These usually have heavy dark contours enclosing areas of violent colour, and express the painter's loathing of vice, hypocrisy, cruelty, and complacency. Although he exhibited at the famous FAUVE show in 1905, he remained aloof from all groups and systems of aesthetics, and developed one of the purest forms of Expressionism. Before 1908 he worked mostly in watercolour and gouache, only returning to oil painting after about 1918: he also executed a large amount of graphic work. His series of etchings, originally made for two books *Guerre* and *Miserere* from 1916 to 1927, were eventually published in 1948 under the title *Miserere*, and he also made lithographs and coloured etchings. His themes remained within the limits of his three series, religious subjects – chiefly of the Passion (Rouault was a devout Catholic) – landscapes of bleak and hostile country, and an occasional bouquet of flowers. He worked for the Diaghileff Ballet in 1929, executed tapestry cartoons in 1933, and in 1945 designed stained-glass windows for the Church of Plateau d'Assy. There are works in most museums of Modern Art. [ill. 1026, p. 418]

Roubiliac, Louis-François (?1705–62), was born in Lyons. He came to England *c.* 1732, and in 1737 carved the statue of Handel for Vauxhall Gardens (terracotta at Cambridge, Fitzwm) which made his name. From 1745 he taught sculpture at the St Martin's Lane Academy, precursor of the Royal Academy Schools, and he worked for a short time as a modeller at the Chelsea china factory *c.* 1750. His was probably the finest sculpture done during the 18th century in England: his busts have a vivid look of life, allied to a great style in presentation and a superb technique. His monument to Lady Elizabeth Nightingale (1761: Westminster Abbey) has been decried as theatrical; despite its allusions to the circumstances of her death, the skeletal figure of Death issuing from the tomb to strike at the living owes much to Bernini's monument to Alexander VII in St Peter's in Rome, although he did not visit Italy until 1752. He executed a number of other tombs in Westminster Abbey (including the very fine and influential one of the Duke of Argyll, 1745–9), a statue of Newton, and a large series of fine busts for Trinity College, Cambridge, and there are other works in the Royal Collection, Greenwich (Nat. Marit. Mus.), Leeds, London (BM, NPG, RA, V & A), and elsewhere. [ill. 864, p. 399]

Rousseau, Henri, called 'le Douanier' (1844–1910), was an amateur or 'Sunday' painter with a direct, simple, and hauntingly naïve vision who painted often unusually large and complicated pictures of elaborately fanciful and picturesquely exotic subjects in a matter-of-factly pedestrian technique and strong colour. He served as a Regimental bandsman – according to his own account, in Mexico in 1861–7, which provided him with his fantastic settings – and as a Sergeant in the Franco-Prussian War of 1870–1. He entered the Paris municipal Customs service (hence 'le Douanier'), and began painting about 1880, exhibiting at the Indépendants from 1886. A dinner in his honour was given in Picasso's studio in 1908, and this gesture has played its part in the transmogrification of 'le Douanier' into a symbol of sophisticated interest in the pseudo-Primitive and in the opening of the floodgates of both the psychological and the sentimental school of writers on art. He seems to have combined a certain peasant shrewdness and bland self-esteem with gullible simple-mindedness; he kept a school where he taught elocution, music, and painting, wrote two plays, got himself involved, though guiltlessly, in a trial for fraud, and finally died, it is said, as a result of a disappointment in love in pursuit of a third wife. There are works in London (Tate, Courtauld Inst.), New York (M of MA), Paris (Louvre), Zürich, and elsewhere. [ill. 1035, p. 419]

Rousseau, Théodore (1812–67), was a French landscape painter who was a friend of MILLET and DIAZ. He settled at BARBIZON in 1844. The Dutch 17th-century masters influenced him and, from 1863, he was deeply

interested in Japanese art. There are pictures in Boston, Glasgow, London (NG, V & A, and Wallace Coll.), New York (Met. Mus.), Ottawa, and many French and US museums. [ill. 762, p. 385]

Rowlandson, Thomas (1756–1827), was the finest of the draughtsmen and caricaturists who portrayed life and manners in 18th- and early-19th-century England. He was born in London, went to Paris for two years at 16 and studied there, and was at the RA Schools before and after his stay abroad. He started as a painter of serious subjects and portraits, but was an inveterate gambler and, after dissipating the fortune inherited from his French aunt, earned a living and paid his debts with a flood of drawings of popular and low-life subjects, full of rollicking humour and an outsize sense of the ridiculous. His gift for exuberant and flowing line is more French – and Rococo – than English, but his handling of tone is typically English in the delicacy of its effects, which often enhance by contrast the robustness of his subjects. Much of his work was produced for the print-publisher Ackermann. Most English museums have examples. [ill. 905, p. 403]

Royal Academy *see* ACADEMY.

Rubénisme was the most important artistic movement in France at the end of the 17th century, reaching a climax in the work of WATTEAU. In 1671–2 there was a violent argument in the Academy of Painting (known as the Quarrel of Colour and Design), concerning the relative importance of colour in painting. The Poussinistes regarded it as a mere decorative adjunct to the formal essentials of drawing and design, as typified in the works of Raphael, the Carracci, and the Frenchman Poussin (thus cunningly introducing a patriotic note). The strong suit of the Colourists was naturalism: painting is an imitation of appearances, and, they said, colour was the most convincing means of imitation. This theory depends on Titian as much as Rubens, but the fact of the existence in Paris of the great Rubens cycle of the *Life of Marie de' Medici* coupled with the undoubted naturalism of most Flemish painting led to the Party of Colour becoming transformed into Rubénistes. In 1672 LEBRUN himself had officially settled the matter once and for all: 'The function of colour is to satisfy the eyes, whereas drawing satisfies the mind' – that is, he merely repeated the classic theory of DISEGNO. The critic Roger de Piles published a Life of Rubens in 1677; in 1699 he was elected an Honorary Member of the Academy, thus marking the final victory of Rubénisme, and he then republished his earlier 'Dialogue sur le Coloris' (1st ed. 1673). Thus, by the beginning of the 18th century the way was prepared for Watteau and also for the new ideas in ROCOCO.

Rubens, Sir Peter Paul (1577–1640), was born at Siegen in Westphalia. He came of an Antwerp family which returned there by 1589 and in 1591 he became for six months the pupil of a landscape and decorative painter called Verhaecht, who had been to Italy. He was then, for four or five years, in the studio of Adam van Noort before becoming a pupil of Otto van Veen, a travelled and scholarly painter, until 1599. He entered the Guild in 1598 and in 1600 went to Italy and became Court Painter to Vincenzo Gonzaga, Duke of Mantua. In 1603 he accompanied an embassy taking horses and pictures from Mantua to Philip III in Madrid, where he admired the Titians and Raphaels in the Spanish Royal Collection. From 1604 to 1608 he was in Mantua, Rome, Genoa, and Milan, and was working in Rome when he received news of his mother's illness. He reached Antwerp too late, and was about to return to Mantua when he was appointed Court Painter to the Spanish Governors of the Netherlands, an appointment he held to his death. He settled in Antwerp, where he built himself an Italianate palace, married Isabella Brandt in 1609, and started on what was perhaps the most energetic and fruitful career in the history of art and one which made him the most important artist in Northern Europe and the greatest Northern exponent of the Baroque.

In Italy he had studied the artists of the High Renaissance, particularly Titian and Michelangelo, and after his return to Flanders his first works show how deeply he was influenced by Caravaggio. After the success of the *Raising of the Cross* (1610), he evolved in the *Descent from the Cross* (1611–14: both Antwerp Cathedral) a less passionately dramatic style so that numerous assistants could work under him to fulfil the multitude of commissions that poured in. His letters prove how carefully he controlled the execution of his designs, and in most cases he did the final work on a picture himself to restore to it something of the unity of the first sketch; the amount of personal execution was a question of price. His chief assistants were of the first ability; the young van DYCK entered his studio about 1617, and JORDAENS and SNYDERS were for many years employed by him. Without the methods he devised for the division of labour his vast output over so many years could never have been achieved, much less maintained, at so high a standard. His practice was to make smallish sketches, very free in handling, usually on panels with a light streaky buff or grey ground, the loose drawing touched in with indications of the local colours. Some of his tapestry designs are larger, more closely worked out, and more fully coloured.

His major commissions include the decoration, begun in 1620, of the Jesuit Church in Antwerp, calling for 39 ceiling paintings and three altarpieces, which last alone survive, the rest having been burnt in 1718: the Medici cycle painted for the Luxembourg Palace in Paris (1622–5: now in the Louvre); the ceiling of the Banqueting House in Whitehall (his only surviving ceiling) completed for Charles I in 1635; the huge scheme of decoration for the Torre de la Parada commissioned by Philip IV of Spain, on which he was working at his death. Besides these there were countless altarpieces, portraits, hunting scenes, landscapes, religious pictures, scenes from classical mythology and history, allegories, tapestry designs, book illustrations, and designs for triumphal processions.

He was employed on diplomatic missions by the Governors of the Netherlands – to Holland in 1627 (when he visited Utrecht and met HONTHORST), to Spain in 1628 (when he made copies of the Titians he had admired in 1603, and became friendly with Velazquez), to England in 1629 (when he was knighted by Charles I), and these missions served as a distraction after the death of Isabella Brandt in 1626. In 1630 he married again. The sixteen-year-old Hélène Fourment became the theme and inspiration of his late mythologies and the subject of many portraits. Since gout was now limiting his activity in the workshop he

could devote more time to the personal side of his art in which his domestic life, hitherto kept in the background, played a dominant part. After his death, his widow wanted to destroy some of his more intimate portraits of her, such as the one in a fur cloak, now in Vienna.

Almost all the older galleries, and most of the more recent ones, contain works attributed to Rubens, which may be entirely autograph or more or less autograph workshop productions. [ills. 403, 411–14, pp. 329–31. Col. pl. 20]

Rude, François (1784–1855), was the major French sculptor of the early 19th century, whose principal work is the relief of the *Volunteers of 1792* (better known as the *Marseillaise*), on the Arc de Triomphe in Paris (1833–6). The romanticism of Delacroix is coupled in his work with the classical outlook as well as the Napoleonic enthusiasm of DAVID, whom he accompanied to Brussels 1814–27. His bust of David (1831) is in the Louvre, and his wife Sophie (1797–1867) was a painter and pupil of David. Rude went to Italy in 1842. His works are in Brussels and Paris and in a Rude Museum in his native Dijon. [ill. 723, p. 379]

Ruisdael, Jacob van (1628/9–82), was the greatest of the Dutch realist landscape painters and exerted a huge influence on the development of European landscape painting in the 19th century, although in his own day he was less popular than Italianate painters such as BERCHEM (who may occasionally have painted figures in Ruisdael's landscapes). He was born in Haarlem, where the realist landscape was first developed in the early 17th century, and may have been a pupil of his father, Isack, about whom little is known. Later he probably worked with his uncle Salomon van RUYSDAEL (whose son, also a landscape painter, was also named Jacob). His early works represent views in the neighbourhood of Haarlem with great fidelity, so that many are still recognizable. About 1650 he travelled in East Holland and probably in Western Germany as well, where he saw mountains for the first time. He settled in Amsterdam c. 1655 and lived there until his death, although he was buried in Haarlem. In 1676 he took a medical degree at Caen and he seems to have practised as a surgeon in Amsterdam while continuing to paint, but the latest date on any of his pictures is 1678. It is now known that the story of his poverty and death in the Haarlem Poorhouse refers to Jacob Salomonsz. RUYSDALE.

His later works have a much more Romantic approach and are more dramatic in handling; some even imitate the kind of mountain landscape popularized by A. van EVERDINGEN. His finest works, however, are generally agreed to be the typical Dutch panoramas with the sun breaking fitfully through the clouds and lighting up patches of the duneland. It has been said that 'he never painted a hot day', and his temper was indeed melancholic and grave; yet unlike his uncle or Jan van GOYEN who sought breadth and used monochromatic effects to get it, he employs strong local colours and gains his atmospheric effects by means of the luminosity of his skies and the vast sweep of his clouds. HOBBEMA was the most important of his many pupils and imitators. He is thought to have painted well over a thousand pictures, so that practically every major gallery has one, but the best collection is in the NG, London. [ill. 484, p. 343]

Runge, Philipp Otto (1777–1810), was a German painter who studied in Copenhagen 1799–1801. After this he went to Dresden where he became the most important early German Romantic painter. In Dresden he met FRIED-RICH and Goethe, who was interested in Runge's theory of colour. He began a series of *The Times of Day* which reflect his highly subjective and emotional approach to landscape as a revelation of Nature. He was a naïve, almost primitive, painter and his rather austere Romanticism was influenced by English artists, principally FLAXMAN and BLAKE. It is therefore sharply distinguished from the (by comparison) voluptuousness of the later French Romantics. There is a biography of him by his elder brother which gives an account of his ideas. Most of his works are in Hamburg, but there are others in Berlin, Hartford Conn,. and Vienna. [ill. 597, p. 358]

Ruskin, John (1819–1900), was the most influential art critic of 19th-century England. He was the son of well-off parents, who encouraged his precocious artistic and literary gifts, and he was able to travel all over Europe between 1833 and 1888. He met TURNER in 1840, and in 1843 published the first volume of 'Modern Painters', a work designed to establish Turner's supremacy over all other landscape painters. The remaining four volumes, published at intervals up to 1860, were less single-minded and contain a highly personal aesthetic. His many other books deal with architecture, politics, social reform, mineralogy, and other subjects, but his advocacy of Gothic – particularly Venetian Gothic – architecture had results so horrible that he himself bitterly repented it: 'there is scarcely a public-house near the Crystal Palace but sells its gin and bitters under pseudo-Venetian capitals copied from the church of the Madonna of Health or of Miracles . . . my present house . . . is surrounded everywhere by the accursed Frankenstein monsters of, indirectly, my own making'. His view of art as an expression of morality, his identification of good art with medieval art, his violent diatribes against Palladian architecture, his powerful and timely support of the Pre-Raphaelites, his sensational attack on Whistler leading to the libel suit, his disastrous marriage to Effie Gray in 1848 and its annulment in 1854 (after which she married Millais), as well as his Utopian agricultural schemes and his hatred of industrialism – all illustrate his complex and many-sided character. He became very famous, and his involved, contradictory, and highly emotional prose gave his art criticism an impact so enduring that not only is he still a folk-memory in the English attitude to the arts, but there has lately been a revival of interest in his theories. He died insane.
He was a meticulous draughtsman, particularly of architecture and plant forms, and there are large collections of his drawings in Oxford (where he was the first Slade Professor) and at Bembridge School. Many British and American museums possess examples. [ill. 938, p. 406]

Ruysch, Rachel (1664–1750), was a Dutch woman painter of flowers and still-life. There are works by her in Amsterdam, Brussels, Dresden, Florence (Uffizi and Pitti), Glasgow, The Hague, London (NG), Melbourne, Munich, New York (Met. Mus.), Oxford, Preston, and Vienna (Akad.). [ill. 476, p. 341]

Ruysdael, Salomon van (*c.* 1600/2–70), was one of the leading Dutch realist landscape painters of the first half of the 17th century, the brother of Isack and uncle of Jacob van RUISDAEL (the fully signed pictures always have this difference in spelling). He is first recorded in the Haarlem Guild in 1623 but the earliest dated picture is of 1627 (Vienna), and the early works are all of the simplest landscape themes, many of them approaching very closely to the work of Jan van GOYEN, especially those with ferry-boats, an expanse of water, and a few trees on the bank in an even grey light. He lived in Haarlem, was a Mennonite, prosperous and esteemed: his son, Jacob Salomonsz. (1629/30–81), was also a landscape painter who is known to have worked up to at least 1668 and who died in the Haarlem Poorhouse. There are representative pictures by Salomon in the Royal Coll. and in Amsterdam, Antwerp, Baltimore, Barnard Castle (Bowes Mus.), Basle, Berlin, Brussels, Cambridge (Fitzwm) and Cambridge Mass. (Fogg Mus.), Cologne, Copenhagen, Detroit, Dresden, Dublin, Frankfurt, Grenoble, The Hague (Mauritshuis and Bredius Mus., which has a *Still-life* of 1662), Hamburg, Leicester, Leipzig, Leningrad, Liverpool, London (NG), Melbourne, Merion Pa (Barnes Foundation), Minneapolis, Munich, New York (Met. Mus.), Oslo, Ottawa, Paris (Louvre and Mus. des Arts Décoratifs), Philadelphia, Providence RI, Rotterdam, Sarasota Fla (Ringling Mus.), Stockholm, Strasbourg, Vienna, Worcester Mass., and York. There is a picture by Jacob Salomonsz. in London (NG), but the few signed works bear only a monogram JvR which can lead to confusion with Jacob's pictures. [ills. 488, 489, p. 343]

Ryder, Albert Pinkham (1847–1917), was the most original and poetic late-19th-century American Romantic painter, and the counterpart to Edgar Allen Poe, whom he admired. He was born in New Bedford, Mass., a whaling port from the world of 'Moby Dick,' and all his life he was haunted by the sea, although he actually lived in squalor in New York. His marine and landscape paintings have a visionary and brooding quality and were very fine in colour, but his deficient technique and the loading of layers of rich, enamel-like pigment have caused them to deteriorate badly. He travelled to Europe, but seems to have been unaffected by it. There are works by him in many American museums, including Chicago, Cleveland, Detroit, New York (Met. Mus.), St Louis, Toledo Ohio, and Washington (NG, Corcoran, and Phillips): it is said that many forgeries also exist. [ill. 964, p. 411]

Rysbrack, John Michael (1694–1770), was the son of an Antwerp landscape painter, Peter, who worked for a time in England. Rysbrack worked first for Gibbs the architect, but from about 1730 he shared with ROUBILIAC the position of most eminent sculptor in England, until the advent of SCHEEMAKERS in 1741 somewhat affected his business. In 1747 he began his celebrated *Hercules* (the marble, now at Stourhead, Wilts., is signed and dated 1756) which embodied a variant of the theory of ideal beauty, in that the artist composed it by using as models boxers and wrestlers, from whom he selected the best parts. He executed a number of tombs in Westminster Abbey, and there are works by him in the Royal Collection, Cambridge (Senate House), London (NPG, Wallace Coll., BM, V & A, Nat. Marit. Mus., St Martin-in-the-Fields), Oxford (Radcliffe, Christ Church, Ashmolean). [ill. 863, p. 399]

S

Sacchi, Andrea (1599–1661), was the chief representative of the classic strain of ALGARDI and POUSSIN in Roman Baroque painting. He was a native Roman, trained first under ALBANI and then, while still in his teens, in Bologna he came under the influence of Lodovico CARRACCI. Back in Rome he was patronized by the great Barberini family, for whom he painted the *Divine Wisdom* in the Barberini Palace (*c.* 1629–33) in a much less Baroque style than PIETRO da Cortona's ceiling in the same Palace. Sacchi's *Vision of S. Romuald* (1640: Vatican) is still more classic in feeling and this classicism was handed down to the 18th century through his chief pupil, MARATTA. Apart from Rome there are works by him in Berlin, Dresden, Madrid, Philadelphia, and Vienna. [ill. 250, p. 308]

Sachlichkeit, Die neue, *see* NEUE SACHLICHKEIT.

Sacra Conversazione (Ital. holy conversation) is the name given to a representation of the Madonna and Child with Saints, in which the sacred personages are aware of each other or are united by some common action. This type of representation replaced the earlier form of altarpiece in which each figure occupied one panel of a POLYPTYCH: in a *Sacra Conversazione* the barriers have been broken down and all the figures have moved into a single, unified space. The earliest examples occur in the work of Fra ANGELICO and his contemporaries, Fra Filippo LIPPI and DOMENICO Veneziano. [ills. 72–4, pp. 278–9]

Saenredam, Pieter (1597–1665), was a Haarlem painter who specialized in church interiors, rendered in cool silvery tones with an occasional gleam of sunlight. He never went to Italy, but a few of his pictures were painted from the drawings made in Rome in 1532/5 by Maerten van HEEMSKERCK. He seems to have made very elaborate preparatory drawings, including fully worked out perspective projections and diagrams. There are examples in Amsterdam (Rijksmus.), Glasgow, Haarlem (Hals Mus. and Bisschoppelijk Mus.), Hamburg, London (NG), Munich, Orleans, Philadelphia (Johnson), Rotterdam, Utrecht, Worcester Mass., and elsewhere. [ill. 479, p. 340]

Salon. During the 17th century exhibitions of works by members of the French Royal Academy were held in the Salon d'Apollon in the Louvre, hence the name. Originally occasional, it was biennial from 1737 to the Revolution, and then annual, being thrown open to all artists and the jury abolished, although it was soon re-established to limit the huge entry. Since there was no other public Exhibition of any standing, the jury (composed almost exclusively of members of the Institut) obtained a stranglehold, using its enormous power to exclude any painter of whom it did not approve. In 1863 the scandal and the protests over the number of works refused were so great that Napoleon III ordered a special exhibition of them, known as the *Salon des Refusés*. So bitter was the official opposition and so uncomprehending was the mass of the public, incapable of independent judgement, that no such exhibition was held again, nor was the rigour of the jury modified. Among the principal exhibitors were MANET, BOUDIN, FANTIN-LATOUR, JONGKIND, PISSARRO, WHISTLER, while CÉZANNE also exhibited and COURBET had the distinction of being rejected from both exhibitions. The present huge yearly Salon is organized by the Société des Artistes Français and has been since 1881, but there are now several other 'Salons' – e.g. d'Automne, des Indépendants – which cater for different types of art.

Salviati, Francesco (1510–63), was a Florentine Mannerist and a close friend of Vasari. He worked on various decorative schemes in Rome, Venice, and Florence and went to France in 1554. He was a pupil of Andrea del Sarto and was much influenced by Michelangelo, Pontormo, and the Venetians: out of this mixture he was able to produce some fine portraits as well as allegories. There are works in Florence (Uffizi, Pitti), London (NG), New York (Met. Mus.), Paris (Louvre), Turin, Vienna, Washington (NG), and elsewhere. [ill. 199, p. 303]

Sánchez Coello, Alonso (1531/2–88), was the pupil and successor of MOR as Court Portrait Painter to Philip II of Spain. He received his education in Flanders and Portugal, and his style is based upon the withdrawn dignity with which Mor invested his sitters; but he was also much influenced by TITIAN (who was Philip II's favourite painter). He began his career in Portugal and painted a few altarpieces, but he is principally known for his portraits, and he worked for the Court at Valladolid from 1557. His portraits, especially the full-lengths, became models for imitation since they perfectly express the rigidity of Spanish Court etiquette, or at least the more pleasing side of it. The dignity and gravity of his style was admirably adapted to these royal icons which were sent as presents to the numerous connections of the Hapsburgs. He is said to have painted S. Ignatius Loyola in 1585, but this, which would have been a fascinating document, is unfortunately lost. There are four pictures by him in the Royal Collection, and others in Bamberg, Berlin, Boston (Gardner Mus.), Brussels, Dublin, the Escorial, Madrid (Prado), New York (Hispanic Soc.), San Diego

Calif., Vienna (K-H), and Wisconsin University. [ill. 642, p. 364]

Sandby, Paul (1725–1809), and his brother Thomas (1721–98), were topographical draughtsmen employed by the Crown, and Paul was sent to the Highlands of Scotland to work on the Ordnance Survey made after the 1745 Rising. He portrayed landscape not only with accuracy and feeling, but also with a sensitive eye for atmosphere. He studied figure drawing, etched, and introduced aquatint into England. From about 1752 he lived in London, and he worked a good deal at Windsor, where Thomas was Deputy Ranger of Windsor Forest. He was a Founder-Member of the RA. From 1770, he visited Wales several times, and was one of the first watercolour painters to appreciate Welsh scenery. He usually painted in transparent washes, and often drew in watercolour as distinct from tinting a pencil drawing; he also painted in gouache, and many of his large series of Windsor (in the Royal Library) use this medium, which in his hands almost rivals oil paint. Gainsborough referred to him as 'the only man of genius' who had painted 'real views from Nature in this country'; that is, who did not rearrange the material into picturesque compositions *à la* Gaspar or Claude, or work up his topography (for instance, at Windsor) according to the example of Canaletto's views. Besides the unrivalled series in the Royal Collection, there are examples in the BM, the V & A, and the Tate in London. Thomas was also a Founder-Member of the RA, and its first Professor of Architecture. He painted many watercolours, very similar to Paul's, but was also the designer of Virginia Water, near Windsor. [ill. 929, p. 404. Col. pl. 49]

Sandrart, Joachim von (1606–88), was a German painter who lived in Italy 1628–35, where he met most of the famous artists of the day. His paintings are forgotten but his book, 'Teutsche Akademie' (1675–9, Latin ed. 1683), was the first of a long line of German art-historical books and is a source of great importance for many 17th-century painters. [ill. 408, p. 329]

Sanguine. A reddish-brown chalk used for drawing.

Sansovino, Andrea (*c.* 1460–1529), was a Florentine sculptor who was trained under Antonio POLLAIUOLO and BERTOLDO but developed under the influence of Raphael and the Antique. He went to Portugal in 1491, sent by Lorenzo de' Medici, worked on the Baptistry in Florence 1493–6, and returned to Portugal until 1499: nothing is known of his activity there. On his return to Italy he worked in Rome 1505–12 and his most famous works are the two large and complex Tombs in Sta Maria del Popolo to Cardinal Ascanio Sforza (1505) and Cardinal Girolamo della Rovere (1507). These large wall-tombs with recumbent effigies and standing figures of Virtues set the type of monument normal in the 16th century. Most of his later years were spent in Loreto. His *Baptism* (1502–5: Florence, Baptistry) was completed by DANTI after 1568. Other works are in Berlin, Florence (Bargello), and Genoa (Cath.). [ill. 164, p. 294]

Sansovino, Jacopo (1486–1570), was the pupil of Andrea Sansovino and took his name. He worked as a sculptor and architect in Florence and Rome before going to Venice in 1527, where he became City Architect and is principally famous as the designer of the Library of S. Mark and other buildings. His most famous work in sculpture is the pair of gigantic statues of *Mars* and *Neptune* at the head of the steps in the Doge's Palace. Other works are in Venice and Florence (Bargello) and elsewhere. [ill. 159, p. 294]

Santi, Giovanni (*c.* 1430/40–94), is important for two reasons, neither connected with his pictures. First, he was the father of Raphael; second, he wrote a rhymed Chronicle which mentions a number of 15th-century artists. There are pictures by him in Urbino, where he worked, and in Berlin, London, Milan, the Vatican, and elsewhere. [ill. 120, p. 289]

Saraceni, Carlo (1579–1620), was a Venetian painter who went to Rome *c.* 1598, where he later came under the influence of CARAVAGGIO and ELSHEIMER; in particular, he imitated Elsheimer's effects of light in small-scale pictures (often on copper) so that they have been confused. Elsheimer and Caravaggio both died in 1610, and Saraceni seems to have succeeded to their market. It was Saraceni who replaced Caravaggio's rejected *Death of the Virgin*. By 1613 he was working for the Mantuan Court, and, *c.* 1619, he went to Venice, where he began a painting for the Doge's Palace, completed after his death by a pupil. There are works by him in Berlin, Bologna, Detroit, Dresden, Munich, Naples, Padua, Rome (Capitoline and churches, especially his masterpiece, *The Miracle of S. Benno,* 1618, in SM dell' Anima), and Venice (Accad. and Redentore). [ill. 239, p. 309]

Sargent, John Singer (1856–1925), was an American virtuoso portrait painter who settled in London and painted High Society in Edwardian and Georgian times. He was born in Italy of American expatriate parents and was trained in Florence and Paris, settling in London in 1884/5 and continuing the *bravura* tradition of LAWRENCE, crossed with Velazquez. He visited the US frequently and painted some large-scale decorations in Boston Public Library (1890) and the Museum of Fine Arts (1916–25), but he is best known for his portraits, and for his brilliant watercolours. In 1880 he had visited Spain and the technical skill and simple colour schemes of most of his portraits reflect Velazquez, seen through the eyes of MANET and Courbet: Sargent's *Mme Gautreau,* painted in Paris in 1884, shows all this, but was a *succès de scandale* and was one of the causes of his leaving Paris for London. His huge output means that his portraits are almost everywhere in Britain and America. His superficial brilliance is very like that of BOLDINI. [ill. 958, p. 409]

Sarto, Andrea del, *see* ANDREA.

Sartorius, John N. (*c.* 1755–1828), was a British painter of fox-hunts and horse-races. There is a typical example in San Marino Cal. [ill. 899, p. 402]

Sassetta, Stefano di Giovanni (*c.* 1400, perhaps 1392–1450), was with GIOVANNI di Paolo, the major Sienese 15th-century painter. Like all his Sienese contemporaries, he was quite happy to continue the style of the 14th-century masters, but he was also aware of new trends coming from the North, and the INTERNATIONAL Gothic style makes itself felt in his work and is perceptible in the influence on him of painters like MASOLINO or GENTILE da Fabriano. He is first recorded as painting an altarpiece in 1423–6 (parts of it survive, in Siena, Barnard Castle (Bowes Mus.), Budapest, and the Vatican): it has a sense of space that is not improperly associable with the work then being painted in Florence, even with MASACCIO's Brancacci Chapel. Sassetta did not develop into a realistic painter, as that would have been understood in Florence, but his essentially mystic character uses the new forms to give a blend of tradition and modern actuality. The best example of this is the altarpiece painted in 1437–44 for S. Francesco, Sansepolcro (where PIERO della Francesca would have seen it). The altarpiece is now dismembered, the central panel of *S. Francis in Glory* belonging to the Berenson Coll. in Florence, but the greater part of it is in London (NG) and Paris (Louvre). An altarpiece dated 1436 in the Chiesa dell' Osservanza, Siena, is now thought to be the work of an imitator, known as the Osservanza Master (there is another work by him in London, NG). Other pictures by Sassetta are in Berlin, Boston, Chantilly (part of the *S. Francis Altar*), Cortona (S. Domenico), Detroit, London (NG), New York (Met. Mus., Frick Coll.), Siena, Washington (NG), Yale Univ., and elsewhere. [ill. 110, p. 288]

Savoldo, Giovanni Girolamo (active 1508–after 1548). He was a Brescian who worked mainly in Venice, where he was deeply influenced by GIORGIONE and TITIAN, yet he is first recorded in the Guild at Florence, in 1508; he may also have worked in Milan *c.* 1532/35. His works have a wonderful sense of light effect, and his night scenes are half a century earlier than CARAVAGGIO. The writer Pino was his pupil and records that he painted but few works. In 1548 Aretino referred to him as 'decrepit', and he probably died soon afterwards. There are pictures by him in the Royal Coll. and in Amsterdam, Berlin, Brescia, Cleveland, Dublin, Florence (Uffizi), London (NG, Courtauld Inst.), Milan (Brera), New York (Met. Mus.), Paris (Louvre), Rome (Borghese and Capitoline), Turin, Venice, Vienna, and Washington. [ill. 231, p. 306]

Schadow, Gottfried (1764–1850), was one of the leading German Neoclassic sculptors. He was in Rome 1785–7 and was much influenced by his friend CANOVA before returning to Berlin, to become Court Sculptor in 1788. He spent the rest of his life there. His works include many monuments in Berlin churches, the first major one being to the boy Graf von der Marck (1790). He also made the Quadriga on the Brandenburg Gate and numerous busts, including one of Goethe (who had earlier criticized Schadow for his excessive realism), and others for the Bavarian Valhalla. His monuments to Frederick the Great (1793) and Blücher (1819) are at Stettin and Rostock, but his projected equestrian Frederick the Great was never realized. His son Rudolf (1786–1822) was also a sculptor – there is a work at Chatsworth, Derbyshire – and another son, Wilhelm (1788–1862), was a painter and a member of the NAZARENER. [ill. 631, p. 362]

Schäuffelein, Hans Leonhard (*c.* 1483–1539/40), was a painter and designer of woodcuts. As a painter he was

much influenced by DÜRER, his master, but his woodcuts are both more original and more important than his pictures. He often signed his works HS and a little shovel (*Schäuffelein*). There are paintings by him in Basle, Berlin, Chatsworth, Dresden, Gateshead, Hamburg, Munich, Nuremberg, Vienna, and Nördlingen, where he lived from 1515. [ill. 566, p. 355]

Scheemakers, Peter (1691–1781), was the son of an Antwerp sculptor, and first worked in Cologne, but was so determined to get to Rome that he walked there. After a short stay he went to London, where he worked for BIRD, and he was then in partnership with DELVAUX, with whom, in 1728 he went again to Rome. His first success was in 1740 with his Shakespeare Monument in Westminster Abbey, and the reputation he gained somewhat obscured RYSBRACK's. Scheemakers gave his works a very detailed finish and a high polish which, aided by his habit of undercutting his rivals' prices, brought him much business. He began to retire in 1753, but worked here until 1771, when he returned to Antwerp.
There are many tombs by him in Westminster Abbey, in parish churches all over England, and one in Boston Mass. There are also works in many of the greater houses and gardens in England, and some busts at the Trinity Colleges of Cambridge and Dublin. [ill. 878, p. 398]

Schiele, Egon (1890–1918), was an Austrian Expressionist painter, the contemporary of KOKOSCHKA, and, like him, influenced by KLIMT, as well as by HODLER. He began to exhibit early and was profoundly affected by Freudian psychology, which he endeavoured to apply to portrait painting. He died in the influenza epidemic of 1918. There are works in Vienna (Oesterreichische Gal.), The Hague, and Minneapolis. [ill. 1014, p. 417]

Schildersbent *see* BENTNAME.

Schlemmer, Oskar (1888–1943), was a pupil of HÖLZEL. He taught at the BAUHAUS, 1920–9, where he had a great influence. He taught in Breslau and Berlin until 1933, after which he had to live in retirement until his death. He did a great deal of theatrical design, and his paintings have the slightly desiccated air of those Bauhaus products that were emphatically machine-made. There are paintings in Basle, Cologne, Harvard University, and New York (M of MA). [ill. 1070, p. 424]

Schlüter, Andreas (1660/4–1714), was the leading North German Baroque architect and sculptor, whose position in Berlin was in its way analogous to that of Bernini in Rome. He arrived in Berlin from Poland in 1694 and, after short trips to France (1695) and Italy (1696) he began the decorative sculpture for the Zeughaus (largely executed by others) and also his masterpiece, the equestrian statue of the Great Elector. This was begun in 1696, cast in bronze in 1700, set up in 1703, and completed by the *Slaves* made by others from his designs, in 1708/9. It is strongly influenced by similar Italian works, such as the Farnese monuments in Piacenza by MOCHI, and the TACCA *Four Moors* in Leghorn. The monument is now in Berlin-Charlottenburg. His statue of Friedrich III was begun in

1697, and cast in 1698, but was not set up (in Königsberg) until 1802. Early in the 18th century Schlüter was engaged in several architectural undertakings, but these were attended by misfortune and he was sacked in 1706. He accepted an invitation to St Petersburg in 1714, but died there soon after his arrival. There are several works in sculpture by him in Berlin (churches and public buildings) and also in Homburg-Hessen. [ill. 627, p. 362]

Schmidt-Rottluff, Karl (*b.* 1884), was born Karl Schmidt in the village of Rottluff in Saxony. He became one of the leaders of German Expressionism, especially in the graphic arts (there are some 700 engravings and lithographs by him). He studied architecture in Dresden, where he met KIRCHNER, and in 1906 he met NOLDE. In 1905 he was one of the founders of the BRÜCKE. He went to Norway in 1911 and settled in Berlin in that year, where he met FEININGER. During the 1920s his art became rather more naturalistic, although still much influenced by Negro art and by Cubism and with great stress on the outline. He was particularly persecuted by the Nazis, being expelled from the Prussian Academy in 1933 and, in 1941, forbidden to paint at all and supervised by the Nazi police. He now lives in East Germany and is once more a Professor in Berlin. There are pictures by him in London (Tate) and New York (M of MA), and once again in German galleries (Berlin, Hamburg). [ill. 1018, p. 417]

Schnorr von Carolsfeld, Julius (1794–1872), was a German painter and illustrator who was in Italy 1818–25 and joined the NAZARENER in their decoration of the Casa Massimo in Rome (1819). His contribution consisted of a combination of 15th-century Italian frescoes and Raphael but it was successful enough to get him a commission in Munich from the King in 1825. This, and later commissions, occupied him until 1867. He became a Professor in Dresden in 1846 and was also Director of the Dresden Gallery. His Bible illustrations were also published in an English edition in 1860. Many German galleries have examples. [ill. 610, p. 360]

Schongauer, Martin (first recorded 1465–*d.* 1491), was a Colmar painter and engraver who was much influenced by Roger van der WEYDEN and other Netherlandish painters. His only reasonably certain painting is the *Madonna of the Rosehedge* (1473: Colmar, S. Martin), an over-life-size figure which shows the influence of his Flemish models. There are 115 engravings by him, all signed MS, and these were of great importance in the development of the art in Germany: it is well known that Dürer went to visit him, only to find that he had died. Some fragments of a wall-painting of the *Last Judgement* have been discovered in S. Stephan, Breisach, where Schongauer lived from 1488/9. There are pictures ascribed to him in Basle, Berlin, Boston (Gardner), Colmar (Mus.), Frankfurt (Städel), London (NG), Munich, and Vienna. [ills. 546–7, p. 352]

School. This word is susceptible of a variety of meanings and no precise demarcation between them is commonly accepted. In its widest sense – Italian School, British School – it means no more than that an experienced eye

can detect the country of origin of a particular picture without being able to identify the painter, or indeed to give more than a vague explanation of the processes by which this conclusion was reached. A more limited sense attaches to the term when it is applied to a smaller territorial area, usually in Italy: in this sense an experienced eye can again distinguish with considerable accuracy and speed between a work painted in Florence, say in the 15th century, and one of the same approximate date painted in Venice. The characteristics of such Schools–whether of Florence, Siena, Naples, or of Bruges and Antwerp – are recognizable and could perhaps be imprecisely formulated in words. There seems no point in trying to do so here, as the essential marks of such stylistic varieties are purely visual. Anyone who wishes to distinguish Florentine from Sienese pictures can do so in one way and one way only – looking at them as often and as hard as possible. A more easily defined use of the word occurs in connection with a painter instead of a place, e.g. School of Raphael. This can be sub-divided into two meanings, according to the intention of the person using it; a good and useful meaning being that a picture has all the characteristics of one by Raphael except genius. In this case, it is licit to assume that it was painted by assistants in Raphael's studio, more or less under his supervision (and probably according to the amount the buyer was offering). A less valid use of the word is as a synonym for 'copy after' or 'imitation of'. It has been suggested in recent years (e.g. in the National Gallery Catalogues) that *School* is best reserved for a geographical designation, while *Style of . . .* should be used to indicate relationship to a particular painter and this distinction would help to clarify the term.

Schutterstuk *see* DOELENSTUK.

Schwind, Moritz von (1804–71), was an Austrian Romantic painter, influenced by CORNELIUS and Nazarene ideas. He painted the German Middle Ages, with Teutonic Knights in armour, and also designed for the crafts. His frescoes in Karlsruhe Gallery date from 1840. In 1857 he visited London and Manchester (for the great Old Master Exhibition) and later designed stained glass for Glasgow Cathedral and for S. Michael, Paddington, London. There are pictures by him in many German galleries. [ill. 613, p. 361]

Schwitters, Kurt (1887–1948), was a poet and abstract painter, best known as the inventor of *Merz*, a form of DADA. He was influenced by KANDINSKY and the Dadaists, and, after studying in Dresden, he began to experiment with abstract pictures in 1918, using COLLAGES with pieces of torn-up paper attached to them. One such piece had the letters MERZ in red capitals torn from the advertisement of a Bank (*Commerz und Privatbank*) and from this circumstance he described his assemblages as Merz, and *c.* 1920 he began his first Merzbau, a huge construction which expanded so that it nearly filled a house (it was destroyed in 1943). He was particularly fond of rubbish – bits of lino, bus tickets, worn-out shoe soles – as a typical Dadaist gesture in creating art from non-art: in a rather Wagnerian way he said: 'my ultimate object is to combine art and non-art in a *Merzgesamtweltbild*'. In 1929 he first visited Norway, and in 1937 he emigrated there and made his second Merzbau (destroyed 1951). In 1940 he escaped from Norway to Britain, where he died leaving a third Merzbau unfinished at Ambleside, Westmorland. There are works by him in London (Tate) and New York (M of MA) and there is to be a Schwitters Museum in Oslo. [ill. 1061, p. 423]

Scorel, Jan van (1495–1562), was trained in Amsterdam but had gone to Utrecht by 1517. In 1519 he set off on a journey to Germany and went to Nuremberg and visited Dürer. By 1520 he was in Carinthia, where he painted a triptych still in Obervellach Parish Church. He went on to Venice, where he was influenced by Giorgione and Palma Vecchio, and then on to Jerusalem with a pilgrimage, returning to Venice in 1521 and going down to Rome where he had the good fortune to arrive during the Pontificate of Hadrian VI, the Utrecht Pope. He was appointed Inspector of the Belvedere, painted the Pope, was made Canon of Utrecht, and was deeply influenced by Michelangelo and Raphael. After Hadrian died Scorel went back to Utrecht (1524) and Haarlem, where HEEMS-KERCK was his pupil in 1527. In 1540 he went to France and in 1550 restored the Ghent Altar. Many of his large religious works were destroyed by the Iconoclasts in the 16th century, but there are works in Haarlem and Utrecht (including group portraits of *Pilgrims to Jerusalem*) and in Amsterdam (Rijksmus.), Basle, Berlin, Birmingham, Bloomfield Hills Mich., Bonn, Breda, Brussels, Cassel, Detroit, Florence (Pitti), Lisbon, Padua, Palermo, Rome (Gall. Naz., Spada), Rotterdam, Stuttgart, Venice (Cà d'Oro), Vienna, and York. His portrait by his pupil MOR hung over his tomb: it now belongs to the Society of Antiquaries in London. [ills. 360, 361, p. 325]

Scorzo, Iscorzo. An Italian word for a figure in sharp FORE-SHORTENING. [ill. 128, p. 291]

Scott, Samuel (c. 1702–72), was one of the earliest English marine and topographical painters. He worked in the manner of the van de VELDES, painting naval battles, colonial forts, and Thames shipping until CANALETTO's success in London (he arrived in 1746) caused Scott to work in his manner on similar views. There are several scenes by the two men which are nearly identical and it seems that, at least once, Canaletto worked from Scott's drawings. There are pictures in London (Guildhall, Tate, and Nat. Maritime Mus.), and Bath. [ill. 922, p. 404]

Scott, William (b. 1913), was born in Scotland but trained in Belfast and then at the Royal Academy. He visited Italy and lived in France before the Second World War, when he served in the Royal Engineers and learned lithography. In 1953 he went to America, where he met POLLOCK, KLINE, and ROTHKO; as a result his work, described before 1951 as hermetically sexually symbolic, is now more abstract and greyer in colour. In 1958–61 he painted a mural for Londonderry Hospital and many galleries have pictures, including Belfast, Edinburgh, London (Tate and V & A), Paris (Mus. d'Art Mod.), and Rome. [ill. 1112, p. 428]

Scrots (or Stretes), Guillim, a Netherlander, was appointed painter to Mary of Hungary, Regent of the Netherlands, in

1537, and was employed by Henry VIII from 1545/6 to 1553. His portraits, which are Italianate and Mannerist in type, are important in the development of the full-length portrait – a form which became commoner in England than it was on the Continent at the same period. *Henry Howard, Earl of Surrey* (Parham Park, Sussex; Knole and elsewhere), dated 1546 but probably painted after his execution in 1547, is reasonably attributed to Scrots. [ill. 366, p. 325]

Sculp. (Lat. *sculpsit*, he engraved it) on an engraving refers to the name of the engraver. In 17th-century English 'sculptures' means engravings: cf. Evelyn's 'Sculptura, or the History and Art of Chalcography and Engraving in Copper' . . . 1662. *Incidit* also refers to the engraver.

Sculpture is the art of creating forms in three dimensions or in RELIEF. Basically, there are two opposed conceptions of sculptural form: glyptic, which means carved, and consists essentially in removing waste material until the form is freed from the matter in which it was imprisoned (this Neo-Platonic conception was Michelangelo's) and its opposite, in which form is created from nothing, by building up in some plastic material. Carving and modelling are thus two separate and complementary aspects of sculpture, the present tendency being to exalt direct carving and the feel of the material at the expense of modelling, which involves using clay or wax as a preliminary material for translation into plaster, bronze, lead, or even stone (*see* BRONZE, PLASTER, POINTING MACHINE, STONE CARVING).

Scumbling is the opposite of GLAZING. It consists of working an opaque layer of oil paint over another layer of a different colour or tone so that the lower layer is not entirely obliterated, giving an uneven, broken effect. The two processes of glazing and scumbling together demonstrate the range of effects, from transparency to opacity, possible in the oil medium; effects which ensured its universal adoption. [Col. pls. 29, 34, 35]

Sebastiano del Piombo (c. 1485–1547), was a Venetian painter who was perhaps trained under Giovanni BELLINI but was certainly deeply influenced by GIOR-GIONE. When Giorgione died (1510) Sebastiano may have completed some of his unfinished works: his style at this date can be seen in his *Salome* (1510: London, NG). In 1511 he went to Rome and began working in the Villa Farnesina, in contact with the Raphael circle. He seems to have quarrelled with Raphael and soon became a partisan of Michelangelo, who influenced him deeply and even provided him with drawings to work from (e.g. the *Pietà* in Viterbo and the *Flagellation* in S. Pietro in Montorio, Rome). His gigantic *Raising of Lazarus* (1517–19: London, NG) shows the Michelangelo influence at its height and was painted in more or less open competition with Raphael's *Transfiguration*. In 1531 he received a Papal sinecure (known as 'il Piombo', hence his name) and he painted rather less, but continued to produce admirable portraits which combine the virtues of his Venetian training with the Roman discipline in form. There are other works by him in Arezzo, Basle, Berlin, Cambridge (Fitzwm), Dublin, Florence (Uffizi, Pitti), London (NG),

Madrid, Naples, New York (Met. Mus.), Paris (Louvre), Parma, Philadelphia (Johnson), Rome (SM del Popolo) Sarasota Fla, Venice (Accad. and churches), and Vienna. [ill. 181, p. 299]

Section d'Or *see* GOLDEN SECTION.

Segantini, Giovanni (1858–99), was an Italian painter of Alpine landscapes and subject pictures. He used a method not unlike that of NEO-IMPRESSIONISM to get the maximum effect of the bright mountain light. There is a Segantini Museum in St Moritz. [ill. 323, p. 318]

Seghers, Hercules (1589/90–1638 or earlier), a Dutch landscape painter and etcher, was a pupil of G. van CONINXLOO in Amsterdam and continued the fantastic mountain landscapes of Momper and Savery, but in a far more realistic and at the same time romantic way. Some of his landscapes represent actual places and it has been argued that he must have been to Italy and in the Alps. He was much influenced by ELSHEIMER and was himself probably the most important influence on Rembrandt's landscapes. Rembrandt owned eight of his paintings and actually reworked an etching of his. Seghers was a virtuoso etcher and frequently used coloured paper or tinted the proofs to increase the romantic light effects. There are over 50 etchings known; his rare paintings include those in Amsterdam, Berlin, Detroit, Florence, The Hague (Bredius Mus.), London, Philadelphia (Johnson Coll.), and Rotterdam. [ill. 492, p. 343]

Seicento (Ital. six hundred). The 17th century, i.e. the sixteen hundreds.

Seisenegger, Jakob (1505–67), painted portraits of the Emperor Charles V in 1530 and again in 1532 in Bologna, where the copy made by Titian so excelled the original full-length that Titian henceforth painted the Emperor's State portraits. There are pictures by him in Vienna and one in London (NG). [ill. 586, p. 357]

Sepia. A brown pigment, like BISTRE, made from cuttlefish.

Séraphine (i.e. Séraphine Louis) (1864–1934) was a domestic servant at Senlis, near Paris, whose talent was discovered in 1912 by the German critic Wilhelm Uhde, who had a special interest in modern primitives. Unlike most of them, however, she was not a naïve realist (like VIVIN, whom Uhde also discovered), but painted only plants and flowers of the greatest complexity and richness of colour, reminiscent of Indian Numdah rugs and Persian miniatures, as well as the stained-glass windows that were certainly familiar to her. She became insane in 1930 and died in an asylum. There is a characteristic example in Paris (Mus. d'Art Mod.). [ill. 1037, p. 419]

Serigraphy, or Silk Screen printing, is not, strictly speaking, a technique of ENGRAVING. The basic principles are those of a stencil, in that it is a method by which paint is brushed over a screen so that the colour penetrates those parts of the screen that have not previously been masked. By using successive masks on the same screen it is possible to produce prints in several colours, and also to obtain colour mixtures by printing one colour over another – for instance, printing blue over yellow to make a green. The screen itself is made of fairly fine silk, and the masks are usually either of paper, or made by painting an impervious lacquer on the screen itself; paint is brushed on and soaks through the silk in the parts which have not been masked. The process was originally developed for commercial purposes, since it is possible to use unskilled labour to make prints once the masks have been prepared. In recent years, however, first in America and later in Europe, the technique has been greatly developed as a method of making large numbers of artist-produced prints which can be sold at fairly low prices, although each print is, like a lithograph, an original work of art. One of the advantages to the artist is that by very slight, but easily – even accidentally – made changes in mask or paint density, variations are achieved in the prints which can remove serigraphy from the more mechanical processes of printing such as those employed in lithography.

Sérusier, Paul (1863–1927). The year of his birth is sometimes given as 1864 or 1865. He met GAUGUIN in Brittany in 1888, and was deeply influenced by the ideas of SYNTHETISM: Gauguin gave him one lesson – 'How do you see those trees? They are yellow? Well, paint them yellow. That shadow is bluish? Make it pure ultramarine. . . . Red leaves? Use vermilion.' In Paris, Sérusier was, with DENIS, BONNARD and VUILLARD, one of the founders of the NABIS. He visited Italy and Germany, and, in 1897, went to the Benedictine monastery at Beuron in Germany, where he was much influenced by their theories of religious art. His own 'ABC de la Peinture' was first published in 1921. There are works in London (Tate), Ottawa, Paris (Mus. d'Art Mod.), Stuttgart, and Warsaw. [ill. 993, p. 415]

Settecento (Ital. seven hundred). The 18th century, i.e. the seventeen hundreds.

Settignano, Desiderio da, *see* DESIDERIO.

Seurat, Georges (1859–91), studied at the École des Beaux-Arts, when he read Chevreul's book on the theory of colour (first published in 1839, and republished in 1889). Later he studied the paintings of Delacroix at S. Sulpice in Paris, and Delacroix's theory as it is ascertainable from his Diaries, for precedents for the theories he was himself elaborating. He was also much influenced by the aesthetic theories based on the observations of a scientist, Charles Henry, and the conclusions of David Sutter's writings on the phenomena of vision, published in 1880. These led him to evolve first the theory of Divisionism (*see* OPTICAL MIXTURES) and then a method of painting by the use of colour contrasts in which the areas of shadow are broken down into the complementaries of adjacent areas of light, the light itself being broken down into local colour, the colour of the light and of reflections, so that for instance, bright yellow-green grass will contain reflections from the sky and from other near-by objects, and shadows in it will tend towards reddish-purple; or the shadows in a reddish-orange dress will be preponderantly greenish-blue. He also evolved a formal type of composition, based on the Golden Section, on the proportion and relation of objects within the picture space to one another and to the size and shape of the picture, on the balance of verticals and horizontals, and on figures placed across the picture plane or at right angles to it. Where the Impressionists stressed the flickering quality of light and figures caught in movement, Seurat aimed at a static quality. His *Bathers at Asnières* (*La Baignade*: London, NG), exhibited in 1884 at the Salon des Artistes Indépendants in Paris, was not so thorough-going an exposition of his theories as the *Sunday on the Island of La Grande Jatte* (Chicago) exhibited in 1886 at the last Impressionist Exhibition, and the term NEO-IMPRESSIONISM was established for Seurat and the group round him by 1886. He was for long opposed to any popularization of his theories, since he believed that by robbing them of novelty it would also rob them of their effect, but in 1890 he consented to the publication of a *résumé* of his theory. His early death, however, meant that his ideas were developed only by followers and imitators.

There are works in Brussels, Chicago, Glasgow, Indianapolis, Liverpool, London (NG, Tate, Courtauld Inst.), Merion Pa (Barnes Fdn), New York (M of MA), Otterlo (Kröller-Müller), Paris (Louvre), and elsewhere. [ill. 988, p. 414. Col. pl. 33]

Severini, Gino (*b.* 1883), was living in Paris when the original FUTURIST Manifesto appeared in 1910. He signed it, but thought that it showed his fellow-countrymen in a provincial light and induced them to pay more attention to Cubism. He himself was much influenced by Seurat and Neo-Impressionist theories. In recent years he has decorated several churches in Switzerland with frescoes and mosaics in a more Neoclassical manner. [ill. 1033, p. 419]

Sezession (Ger. secession). The *Sezessionen* were groups of artists in Germany and Austria who resigned from established academic bodies and exhibiting societies in order to forward the aims of various modern (usually Impressionist) movements. The most important were those of Munich (1892), Berlin, headed by LIEBERMANN and partly due to the scandal over the MUNCH Exhibition of 1892 (1899), Vienna (1897), and Darmstadt. In due course the Expressionists seceded in their turn.

Sfumato (Ital. evaporated, cleared like mist) is a word used to describe the transitions of colour or, especially, tone from light to dark by stages so gradual as to be imperceptible. LEONARDO attached great importance to this as a means of obtaining that effect of relief which he regarded as essential to the art of painting, and in some of his works the softness of contour and the darkness of the shadows have now combined to spoil much of the effect intended. In his notes on painting he says that light and shade should blend 'without lines or borders, in the manner of smoke'. [Col. pl. 12]

Sgraffito (Ital. scratched). A decorative technique in which tinted plaster is covered with a thin layer of white plaster (or vice versa), the top layer then being scratched with a design, revealing the lower layer. The technique was employed for arabesques and similar decorations in 16th-century Italy, but it can usually be seen in a rudimentary form on any whitewashed wall, and has been exploited in this sense by modern painters such as DUBUFFET. A much earlier form of the technique, found in Italian panel paintings, consists of a gold ground with opaque colour over it, so that scratching the surface provides gold lights.

Shahn, Ben (*b.* 1898), was born in Lithuania, but went to the US in 1906 and became a characteristically American exponent of SOCIAL REALISM. His use of photographic realism of detail and some of the technical devices of advertising set him apart from most modern American painters, but his art has always been a vehicle for ideas. The Sacco and Vanzetti case (when two immigrant anarchists were judicially murdered) led to the production of a series (1931–2) of biting comments, mostly drawings. Naturally, he was much influenced by ROUAULT and RIVERA, collaborating with the latter on the Radio City murals in 1933. Other murals are in the Bronx Post Office, New York (1938–9), and the Social Security Building, Washington (1940–2). He has also written on art. [ill. 1075, p. 425]

Shop Work *see* WORKSHOP PRODUCTION.

Sickert, Walter Richard (1860–1942), was, with Wilson STEER, the most important of the British Impressionists – and it is highly characteristic of him that he can hardly be included in any definition of Impressionism, since he worked at the bottom of the tone scale, and his light effects gleam out from sombre colours and tones. Towards the end of his life his palette lightened considerably, when he painted scenes (never on the spot) in Bath and Brighton and also made a series of pictures based either on newspaper and other photographs or on Victorian magazine illustrations. He was profoundly influenced by Whistler and Degas, sharing something of their dispassionate wit, and was equally far from being a typical Impressionist. He was at various times connected with the stage and most of his best works are scenes of London music halls and their audiences, although he also had great feeling for the shabbier parts of London, Dieppe, and Venice. The open air and the countryside had no appeal for him. In 1911 he founded the CAMDEN TOWN GROUP (with Islington it was one of his favourite boroughs) and he later belonged to the LONDON GROUP (which absorbed the Camden Town one), the NEAC, and the RA, from which he resigned resoundingly. He was one of the few modern painters to make extensive use of studio assistants and his technical procedures are very like those of the Old Masters. He also etched and wrote a great deal (not all of it sense). He is well represented in London (Tate, Courtauld Inst. and Islington Public Library) as well as Rouen, many British provincial galleries (especially Liverpool), and Dieppe, Melbourne, New York (M of MA), Ottawa, Sydney, and Toledo Ohio. [ill. 966, p. 410]

Signac, Paul (1863–1935), was a follower of SEURAT, whose ideas he enthusiastically advocated, and whose style he imitated with more energy than perception. He was the most vocal theorist among the Neo-Impressionists and his book 'De Delacroix au Néo-Impressionnisme' published in 1899, is the text-book of the movement. [ill. 989, p. 414]

Significant Form. A phrase invented by Clive Bell to define the specifically aesthetic element in a work of art. That is aesthetically valid ('significant') which is an expression of form: that is formally effective which is significant. A neat example of arguing in a circle.

Signorelli, Luca (*c.* 1441/50–1523), was traditionally a pupil, with PERUGINO, of PIERO della Francesca. He is first documented in 1470 and some fragments in Città di Castello, of 1474, are his earliest datable works. Although his earliest works (including two sides of a processional banner in the Brera, Milan) show some influence from Piero they already show the very marked influence of the POLLAIUOLI in the use of figures with exaggerated muscular development in violent action. This Florentine stress on outline as a means of conveying drama, and the use of characteristic gesture, link him with Donatello on the one hand and Verrocchio on the other; as may be seen in his frescoes in the Casa Santa at Loreto. He was in Rome in the early 1480s and probably worked on the Sistine Chapel frescoes with Perugino, Botticelli, Rosselli, and others. His masterpiece is the fresco cycle in Orvieto Cathedral, begun by Fra Angelico in 1447, which he was commissioned to complete in 1499. The frescoes depict with vivid realism the End of the World, the Coming and Fall of Anti-Christ, and the Last Judgement. His gifts as a draughtsman are fully revealed in the sharp fore-shortenings of the figures, their strained poses, the illusionistic perspective, the hardness of outline, and the imaginative power with which, for example, he peoples Hell, not with pathetically grotesque creatures half-beast, half-fantasy, but with vigorous, muscular devils, passion-ately engaged in fiendish cruelties and entirely human in form, though with the hideous colour of rotting flesh. His use of the nude figure for dramatic ends, his interest in classical antiquity, and his *terribilità* presage, and influenced, Michelangelo. His later works never again reach this pitch of intensity, probably because the Orvieto frescoes were painted at the time of the French invasions and while Savonarola's threats of doom and the coming of Anti-Christ were in all men's minds. He was in Rome again *c.* 1508, and again in 1513, but he stood no chance against Raphael and Michelangelo and he settled in Cortona as a good, provincial master with a large shop, producing hard, repetitive, and old-fashioned altarpieces. Vasari claimed to be his great-nephew. There are works in Altenburg, Arezzo, Baltimore (Walters), Bergamo, Berlin, Borgo San Sepolcro, Boston (Mus.), Cortona (Mus. and churches), Detroit, Florence (Uffizi, Horne Mus.), Liverpool, London (NG), Milan (Brera, Poldi-Pezzoli), Monte Oliveto Maggiore, Munich, Naples, New York (Met. Mus.), Orvieto (Cath., Mus., Library, S. Rocco), Paris (Louvre, Mus. Jacquemart-André), Perugia (Mus., Cath.), Phila-delphia (Johnson), Umbertide (Sta Croce), Urbino, Venice (Cà d'Oro), Washington, and elsewhere. [ill. 105, p. 285]

Signorini, Telemaco (1835–1901), was an Italian painter and etcher who was a representative of *Verismo*, the Italian form of the Realist movement of the 19th century. He joined the MACCHIAIOLI and was also much influenced by the French Impressionists. He met COROT in Paris in 1861, and travelled to London and Edinburgh with De NITTIS – like his friend he was much influenced by DEGAS and Toulouse-Lautrec. His Memoirs (1893) are the chief source of information about the Macchiaioli. There are works by him in Florence, Milan, Rome, Turin, and Venice. [ill. 320, p. 318]

Silk-Screen *see* SERIGRAPHY.

Silver Point. A technique of drawing much favoured in the 15th and 16th centuries but now almost entirely disused. The drawing is made on a sheet of paper which has been prepared by coating it with opaque white (to which a slight tint of colour is usually added), with a piece of silver wire held in wood like the lead in a modern pencil. The silver point produces a silver-grey indelible mark which will not smudge and the drawing can be heightened, if desired, with Chinese white. Gold or lead may be used in place of silver, all giving the effect of a modern pencil but rather more subtle and with the advantage of indelibility, which makes the draughtsman think before he puts down a line. [ill. 108, p. 287]

Simone Martini *see* MARTINI.

Sinopia, a reddish-brown earth colour often used for the under-drawing of a FRESCO. Frequently used to mean the drawing itself. [ill. 71, p. 279. Col. pl. 7]

Sisley, Alfred (1839–99), was a French Impressionist painter of English descent. With MONET he was one of the purest of the IMPRESSIONISTS and was practically exclusively a landscape painter: unlike Monet, however, he did not dissolve the forms of the landscape into a sort of coloured mist in his search for colour and light. In 1856–7 he was sent to England to learn the language and to begin a commercial career but in 1862 he entered the École des Beaux-Arts, where he met Monet, Renoir, and Bazille. He exhibited at the SALON des Refusés in 1863 and at the First Impressionist Exhibition (1874) and some of the later ones. During the Franco-Prussian War he went to England (1871) and he returned in 1874, when he painted at Hampton Court and in the London suburbs. There are pictures by him in most modern museums, including Aberdeen, Boston, London (Tate Gall., Courtauld Inst.), Paris (Mus. de l'Impressionnisme), and Washington (NG). [ill. 803, p. 390]

Size colour. A method of painting in which the powdered pigment is mixed with hot glue-size. It is quick and simple but easily damaged and is now used almost exclusively for scene-painting. Ordinary distemper is a form of size colour.

Sketch. A sketch is the rough draught of a composition or part of a composition, made in order to satisfy the artist himself on certain points of scale, composition, lighting, etc. It is the trial run – or one of many – for the full-scale work but it must be carefully distinguished from a

STUDY. A sketch by a landscape painter is usually a small and rapid note of the effect of light on a given scene, and it is intended for future reference and reworking if necessary. The quality of some artists' sketches is, however, so high that what they would have considered their important works are now often undervalued: Rubens and Constable are examples. Constable's sketches, in particular, have been responsible for many subsequent artists painting such rapid notations – and then exhibiting them as works of art. Rubens's sketches were often made as guides to his assistants in the layout and first stages of a grand composition. These compositions were often executed almost entirely by the assistants, hence the preference now accorded to the original sketches. [ills. 411, 933, pp. 330, 406]

Slevogt, Max (1868–1932), was, with CORINTH and LIEBERMANN, one of the leading German Impressionists. He was trained in Munich before going to Paris in 1889 and then to Italy; later he travelled widely in Denmark, Holland, and Egypt (1913–14, where he painted landscapes filled with blazing light). His Impressionist style began c. 1900, at the same time as he made a name as an illustrator. He worked for 'Simplizissimus' and the Art Nouveau periodical 'Jugend', as well as illustrating many books. His most famous paintings are the series of the singer *D'Andrade as Don Giovanni* (c. 1902–3), but his last work, a fresco of Golgotha in the Friedenskirche at Ludwigshafen (1932) may be his masterpiece. He painted other frescoes and there are pictures by him in many German museums. [ill. 620, p. 361]

Sluter, Claus (active c. 1380–d. 1406), was the greatest realist sculptor of Northern Europe at the turn of the 15th century and preceded both Jan van Eyck and Donatello, the two 15th-century artists most akin to him in spirit. He worked exclusively for the Dijon Court of Philip the Bold, Duke of Burgundy, but he was himself of Dutch origin and probably worked in Brussels before arriving in Dijon, where he was assistant to the Duke's sculptor, Jean de Marville, 1385–9, when he became Court Sculptor himself. He worked on the sculptural decoration of the Duke's foundation, the Chartreuse de Champmol, 1391–6/7 and from 1395 was engaged on his masterpiece the *Well of Moses*, a well-head with six full-length Prophets around it. This survives, but the upper part, a *Calvary*, is known only from a fragment of the *Crucified Christ* (Dijon, Musée Archéologique). The grandeur of style of the *Moses* and its sharply characterized pose and features mark it as something quite new and totally different from the INTERNATIONAL Gothic or SOFT STYLE then current. Sluter also worked on the Tomb of Philip the Bold, but this had been begun under his predecessor in 1384 and was continued by his own successor, his nephew Claus de Werve (d. 1439), who completed it in 1411. The most famous part of it is the series of Pleurants or Weepers, small mourning figures round the sides, of the greatest realism. One of these is in Cleveland (Mus.); the surviving parts of the Tomb are in Dijon (Mus.). [ill. 332, p. 320]

Smet, Gustave De (1877–1943), was, with PERMEKE, one of the leading Belgian Expressionists. He was trained in Ghent and settled at the artists' colony of Laethem-Saint-Martin in 1901. Up to 1914 he painted in an Impressionist manner, but became an Expressionist while a refugee in Holland. There are works in Amsterdam (Stedelijk), Antwerp, Basle, Brussels, Ghent, Grenoble, The Hague, Liège, and Rotterdam. [ill. 1027, p. 418]

Smibert, John (1688–1751), was an Edinburgh painter who worked in Italy 1717–20 and went to America with Berkeley (later Bishop Berkeley) in 1728. In 1730 he settled in Boston and painted portraits which recall those of Jervas – i.e. they are not very good imitations of the KNELLER style. There are works in Edinburgh (NPG), London (NPG), and many American museums, including Boston. [ill. 829, p. 394]

Smith, Sir Matthew (1879–1959), first went to Paris in 1910 and was in contact with Matisse for a month or two, at Matisse's school, which closed in 1911. The influence of the FAUVE movement was decisive and he spent much time in France up to 1939; the richness of his colour and the opulence of his forms have always made him seem more of a French than an English painter. There are pictures by him in Leeds (Temple Newsam), London (Tate), Manchester, Ottawa, and other museums. [ill. 1005, p. 416]

Snyders, Frans (1579–1657), was a pupil of Pieter Bruegel the Younger. He travelled in Italy in 1608–9 and on his return settled in Antwerp, where he was much employed by RUBENS on the still-life and animal parts of his hunting and other pictures. He also worked with JORDAENS, and on his own account produced many vigorous hunting scenes and large still-life subjects of great complexity. He married a sister of the de VOS brothers. There are examples in the Royal Collection, and in Antwerp, Berlin, Boston (Mus.), Brussels, Cape Town, Dresden, Edinburgh (NG), The Hague, London (NG, Kenwood), Madrid, Munich, Ottawa, Paris (Louvre), Toronto, and elsewhere. [ill. 419, p. 331]

Social Realism is the painting of the contemporary scene, usually from a Leftish viewpoint. The movement probably goes back to COURBET (and owes much to literary examples, e.g. Zola): it is now fairly current in the US (SHAHN, the ASHCAN School) and in Britain (Bratby, Jack Smith, and the New, or 'Kitchen Sink', Realists). GUTTOSO is perhaps the leading European exponent. It must be distinguished from *Socialist Realism*, which is the official Party Art of the USSR and the Communist Party generally. This is the dreariest kind of academic art, glorifying the Party or the Peasant and other stock figures. A victim has said of it: 'Impressionism is painting what you see, Expressionism is painting what you feel, and Socialist Realism is painting what you hear.'

Sodoma. Giovanni Antonio Bazzi, called 'Il Sodoma' (1477–1549), was one of the best-known Sienese painters of the early 16th century. He was born at Vercelli and trained under the minor Lombard G. M. Spanzotti (1490–7) and was probably in Milan between 1497 and 1501, when he arrived in Siena. He must have seen the work of Leonardo da Vinci in Milan and again in Florence *c.* 1504. Between 1505 and 1508 he completed a series of 31 frescoes in the Benedictine Monastery of Monte Oliveto, near Siena, where Signorelli had begun the scenes from the Life of S. Benedict. Sodoma became the leading artist of Siena, but Vasari – who is very severe on Sodoma's general beastliness – points out that this was not really deserved and much of his work is very uninspired. The obvious interpretation of his nickname seems to be belied by the tax-return (perhaps not wholly serious) that he filled in *c.* 1531: 'I have an ape and a talking raven, which I keep in a cage so that he can teach a theological ass to talk . . . I possess three beastly she-animals, which are women, and I have also thirty grown-up children, which is a real encumbrance . . . and as twelve children exempt a man from taxation I recommend myself to you. Farewell.' In recent years it has come to be realized that the great Sienese artist of the period is not Sodoma but BECCA-FUMI. Sodoma painted in the Vatican in 1508 (part of the ceiling of the Stanza della Segnatura, subsequently given to Raphael to complete) and some fine frescoes in the Villa Farnesina in Rome in 1512. He is well represented in Siena and Florence and in London, Paris, New York, and many other galleries. [ill. 187, p. 299]

Soest, Konrad von, *see* KONRAD.

Soft Ground Etching *see* ENGRAVING.

Soft Style is a name given to the style found principally in Germany at the end of the 14th and beginning of the 15th centuries. It is very closely related to INTERNATIONAL GOTHIC, and, as the name implies, is characterized by soft and gentle rhythms, especially in the flow of drapery, and by a sweet and playful sentiment. The principal subject is the Madonna playing with the Christ Child and these are sometimes called *Schöne Madonnen* – 'Beautiful Madonnas'. The earliest woodcuts and sculpture show the style even more clearly than painting. [ills. 538–9, 541, pp. 351–2]

Solimena, Francesco (called L'Abate Ciccio) (1657–1747), was the major Late Baroque painter in Naples and was extremely famous in the 18th century, being described in 1733 as 'by universal consent the greatest painter in the world'. He acquired great wealth, lived in a Palace, became a Baron, and was in constant demand by Kings and Princes. He was a celebrated teacher, and his pupils included such diverse artists as CONCA and Allan RAMSAY, although his style was most faithfully continued by Francesco de Mura. He formed his style on that of Luca GIORDANO but modified it profoundly by the classical tendencies of MARATTA and Pietro da Cortona, as well as Lanfranco and Mattia Preti. He settled in Naples in 1674 and his principal works there are in the churches (all damaged in 1939/45) of S. Paolo Maggiore (1689–90), the Gesù Nuovo (1725), and S. Domenico Maggiore. Many of his best works are the sketches for large compositions in Naples (Mus.) and there are many others in Neapolitan churches as well as in Abingdon Berks., Dresden, Florence (Uffizi), The Hague, Leeds, Liverpool, Madrid, Milan (Brera), New York (Met. Mus.), Northampton, Oxford, Paris (Louvre), Rome (Gall. Naz.),

the Vatican, Venice (Accad.), Vienna, York. [ill. 275, p. 313]

Somer, Paul van (*c.* 1577/8–1622), was an Antwerp painter who settled in London in 1616. He was, with MYTENS and JOHNSON, one of the best portrait painters in England before the arrival of van Dyck. He soon began to work for the Court, and his earliest datable work, *Queen Anne of Denmark with her horse and dogs* (1617: Royal Coll.) is perhaps also his best. There are others in London (NPG and Tate). [ill. 521, p. 348]

Sopra Porte, Superporte – grand words for overdoors; i.e. paintings, usually landscapes, specially composed to fit the space above a doorway.

Sotto in Sù (Ital. from below upwards). A term applied to the extreme of illusionistic perspective which shows figures painted on a ceiling so foreshortened as to appear actually floating in space above the spectator. It is first found in a developed form in MANTEGNA (1474) and was taken up by CORREGGIO and Roman Baroque painters such as LANFRANCO and PIETRO da Cortona and, later, POZZO. [ill. 126, p. 290]

Soulages, Pierre (*b.* 1919), is, with HARTUNG, one of the leading abstract painters of the School of PARIS. He has travelled in the US and Japan and is well represented in American museums. His paintings have no titles, but are referred to by the date of completion – e.g. *23 mai 1953* (London, Tate). [ill. 1095, p. 428]

Soutine, Chaïm (1894–1943), was born near Minsk but managed to get to Paris in 1913, where he met MODI-GLIANI, CHAGALL, and other *peintres maudits*. He was much influenced by EXPRESSIONISM and developed a style depending greatly on impasto; this is most noticeable in his slaughterhouse pieces. There are many works in America – Dr Barnes bought 100 in 1923 – including the M of MA, New York, and Washington (NG and Phillips). The Barnes pictures are now in Merion, Pa. [ill. 1031, p. 418]

Spencer, Sir Stanley (1891–1959), was one of the most original of modern painters; original in iconography rather than formally, with a kind of naïve religious feeling that is probably closer to Blake than to anyone else. He was trained at the Slade School 1908–12 and served in Macedonia in the First World War from 1915 to 1918: his experiences in the RAMC were to be transformed in the next decade into the series of mural decorations in Burghclere Chapel, Berks. He made designs for such a series of pictures, culminating in a *Resurrection of the Soldiers* as an altarpiece, in 1922–3, and in 1926–7 a chapel was built as a memorial to a man killed in the War, and the paintings carried out between 1926 and 1932: at this time he was also painting his huge *Resurrection, Cookham* (1922–7: London, Tate), Cookham being his native village, where he spent most of his life. During the Second World War he painted a series of *Shipyards*, officially commissioned, in Port Glasgow. After 1945 he returned to the Resurrection theme in a series of large-scale religious works. He was elected ARA in 1932, but resigned in 1935 after a controversy over two of his more imaginative pictures. In 1950 he returned as RA and in 1959, just before his death, he was knighted. There are pictures by him in Aberdeen, Belfast, Birmingham, Cambridge (Fitzwm), Hull, Leeds, London (Tate, Imperial War Mus.), Manchester, New York (M of MA), Ottawa, Sheffield, Southampton, Toronto, and elsewhere. [ill. 1080, p. 426] His brother Gilbert (b. 1892) is also a painter.

Spinello Aretino (active 1373–d. 1410/11), came, as his name implies, from Arezzo but was probably trained in Florence, perhaps under Agnolo GADDI. So far from being the last flicker of the Giotto tradition Spinello seems to have returned, about the end of the Trecento, to the massive style of Giotto and was thus a precursor of Masaccio. There are works by him in Arezzo (Mus. and churches), Budapest, Cambridge Mass. (Fogg), Chicago, Copenhagen, Florence (Uffizi, Accad., churches), Liverpool, London (NG), New York (Met. Mus.), Oxford (Christ Church), Paris (Louvre, École des Beaux-Arts), Pisa (Mus., churches), Providence RI, St Louis, Siena, the Vatican, Washington (NG), and elsewhere. His son, Parri Spinelli (d. 1452), worked with him. [ill. 47, p. 274]

Spitzweg, Carl (1808–85), was perhaps the most characteristic BIEDERMEIER painter. He was self-taught and worked as a newspaper illustrator before becoming a painter: it was probably this training which prevented him from falling into the pretentiousness which afflicted his friend SCHWIND. He travelled extensively – Italy, Paris, London, Antwerp – and was deeply impressed by both DELACROIX and the BARBIZON painters, but was not tempted into the Grand Style. His *Poor Poet*, of which three versions exist, is a good example of his homely, anecdotic, style. There are pictures in Berlin, Berne, Hamburg, Hanover, and Munich. [ill. 614, p. 360]

Spolvero, a kind of auxiliary CARTOON (from Ital. *spolvero*, fine dust). The purpose of the *spolvero* was to preserve the cartoon for the guidance of the assistants working on the final painting, since the *spolvero* was pricked through and pounced with charcoal dust. For this reason it is doubtful whether any have survived.

Spranger, Bartholomeus (1546–1611), was an Antwerp painter who worked in Paris (c. 1565) at the same time as PRIMATICCIO and N. dell' ABBATE, and in Rome (c. 1567–75) as an assistant to Taddeo ZUCCARI, and in Vienna, for the Emperor Maximilian II, in 1575. He later worked for Rudolf II in Prague, where he died. He was a typical representative of Late Mannerism, using numerous nude figures in unlikely attitudes to fill his compositions, which derive ultimately from Correggio and Parmigianino. The engravings of GOLTZIUS made his works very widely known. He is well represented in the Vienna Gallery, but there are other examples in Antwerp, Brussels, Chicago, Cleveland, Munich, Paris, and elsewhere. [ill. 383, p. 326]

Squarcione, Francesco (1397–1468), was a Paduan, first recorded as a painter in 1429. Although he seems to have been active as a painter all his life, he is principally famous on account of his pupils. It is said that he had 137, some of whom he seems to have adopted. The most famous was MANTEGNA who quarrelled violently with him and left his house in 1448. ZOPPO was also a pupil. He is said to

have had a house full of casts of Antique sculpture and to have made journeys to Rome and even to Greece in pursuit of antiquities. Only two works are known by him, a polyptych of 1449–52 in Padua (Mus.) and a signed *Madonna* in Berlin. Both demonstrate the extreme dryness of his style and his archaeological interests, and the link with Donatello goes far to explain Mantegna's early style. [ill. 124, p. 290]

Squared (for transfer). A drawing is said to be squared (up) when it has been covered with a network of squares. These squares can be numbered, and the same number of squares of a larger size can then be drawn on a wall or canvas: the contents of each small square can then be rapidly transferred to the corresponding large one, thus giving an enlarged version of the original drawing, more or less mechanically. [ill. 69, p. 278]

Stabile. Sculpture that keeps still. The opposite of MOBILE.

Staël, Nicholas de (1914–55), was born in St Petersburg but was brought up and educated in Brussels. He went to Paris in 1933 and became one of the leading abstract painters, coming under the influence of BRAQUE, whom he met during the Second World War. His later works mark a return to a kind of representation in which the forms, though mostly abstract, were recognizably landscapes, still-life, or other real objects. He committed suicide in 1955. There are works by him in Edinburgh, New York (M of MA), London (Tate), Ottawa, and Paris (Mus. d'Art Mod.). [ill. 1101, p. 429]

Staffage. This word, pronounced as French, is used in both English and German to describe the figures and animals which animate a picture intended essentially as a landscape or *veduta*; in other words, figures which are not really essential and could be added by another painter. In the highly specialized world of the Dutch painters of the 17th century this was very often the case, so that a landscape painter like WYNANTS never did his own *staffage*; whereas a CANALETTO or a GUARDI always did.

Stained Glass consists of designs or figure subjects made from pieces of coloured glass held together by strips of lead, which themselves form the outlines of a design partly independent of the coloured patches. It was apparently a Byzantine invention but soon became a distinctively Western and medieval art, the earliest surviving windows being the early-11th-century ones at Augsburg. By 1100 the French were leading exponents and the art was introduced to England in the second half of the 12th century. Splendid examples of the early period exist at Canterbury, while York has the best later windows. The coloured glass was made in one of two ways; by adding metallic oxides to molten glass, thus causing it to be coloured all through, or by fusing thin layers of coloured glass on to plain. The former is called 'pot metal' and the latter 'flashed'. Ruby-red was usually obtained by flashing: pot metal varies very much in colour according to the temperature, and great variations often exist in the same window. Details were painted in matt enamel on the glass and then fused to it by reheating. In the later Middle Ages much *grisaille* glass was produced; that is, plain glass with

enamel drawing on it and sometimes silver-stain was
added. This is a strong yellow obtained by painting on a
silver preparation and then heating it. It was introduced
soon after 1300 and was often used to obtain the most
elaborate patterns. The art continued to flourish until well
into the 16th century (King's College Chapel, Cambridge)
in England and on the Continent, especially in Germany
and Switzerland, but it gradually gave way to the bastard
form of painted glass, which is simply a translation of oil
painting. The windows by Sir Joshua Reynolds at New
College, Oxford, are good examples. The medieval
methods have been used for the new Coventry Cathedral.
CHAGALL has also made a series of twelve important
stained-glass windows for a Synagogue in Jerusalem.
[Col. pl. 37]

Stanze. The suite of rooms in the Vatican decorated by
RAPHAEL.

Stanzione, Massimo (1585/6–1656), was one of the leading
Neapolitan painters of the Caravaggio School. He was
working in Rome by 1617, where he would have seen the
Farnese Gallery by Annibale CARRACCI. His style is
similar to that of SARACENI in that it is a more graceful
and elegant form of Caravaggism than that practised by his
fellow-Neapolitan RIBERA, although Ribera exerted some
influence on him. Stanzione has been called the Neapolitan
Guido RENI which aptly summarizes his semi-Bolognese
classicism. Most of his pictures are in Naples, but there are
works in Dresden, Florence (Uffizi), Frankfurt (Städel),
and London (NG). [ill. 240, p. 309]

State is the name given to the stages in the development of
an engraving or etching. When the artist has finished his
work and pulls the first proofs these constitute the first
state; if he decides to add a line here or burnish one out
there then each successive alteration will constitute a
fresh state. Many of Rembrandt's etchings run to seven
or eight, each marking some definite artistic change, but
it is an unfortunate temptation for cataloguers to invent
new states, and for artists to meet the demand by introducing meaningless alterations. It should be noted that the
twentieth state is not necessarily a poor impression, if only
two or three prints have been pulled of each of the preceding states; equally, a plate can be worn out in its first
state. *See* PROOF, REMARQUE.

Steel Engraving, Steel-faced. The comparative softness
of copper limits the number of prints that can be taken
from an engraving, and, in the second quarter of the 19th
century, steel plates came into use. These, however, are
very hard on the engraver and a satisfactory solution was
soon found by steel facing the completed copper plates.
This is done by electrolysis, depositing a microscopic
film of steel on the surface of the plate, which hardens it
sufficiently to allow the printing of large editions, without
interfering with the finest work on the plate.

Steell, Sir John (1804–91), was a Scottish sculptor who
studied in Rome. Chantrey urged him to settle in London,
but he preferred to stay in Scotland, where he soon
became the foremost sculptor, received a Court appointment in 1838, and was knighted in 1876. His *Scott* in the
Scott Monument was probably the first marble statue

commissioned in Scotland from a Scot. He also introduced
bronze-founding into Scotland and his large equestrian
Wellington in Edinburgh was aptly described as 'The Iron
Duke in bronze by Steell'. There are many other works in
Edinburgh, and in London (Nat. Marit. Mus.). [ill. 876,
p. 399]

Steen, Jan (1626–79), was a Dutch painter of humorous
subjects from the life of the peasantry and middle classes
in a variety of styles, like those of BROUWER, OSTADE,
and DOU. Even his Biblical subjects are treated as
incidents in 17th-century Holland, but his pictures mostly
represent tavern scenes or visits to respectable households.
He worked in The Hague and Delft, where he leased a
brewery, Haarlem, and Leyden, where he kept a tavern.
He was the son-in-law of van Goyen, in whose manner he
painted a few landscapes, and he also painted some
portraits. About 700 paintings by him exist and most
galleries have one. [ill. 508, p. 347]

Steenwyck *see* STILL-LIFE.

Steer, Wilson (1860–1942), was the son of a portrait
painter. He studied in Paris, 1882–3, and in the late
1880s discovered Degas and the Impressionists, particularly
Monet. From then on his work reflects these influences,
which are very strong in his landscapes, these being
Constable revivified by Impressionist technique, although
he made occasional excursions into Gainsborough. There
are works in Aberdeen, Bradford, Cambridge (Fitzwm),
Leeds, Liverpool, London (Tate), Manchester (City and
Whitworth), Ottawa, Southampton, and elsewhere.
[ill. 975, p. 411]

Stefano da Zevio (or da Verona) (c. 1375–1451), was the
principal Veronese painter in the INTERNATIONAL
Gothic style. He was much influenced by GENTILE da
Fabriano and was probably the master of PISANELLO,
continuing a sort of proto-Pisanello style as late as 1435
in his signed and dated *Adoration of the Magi* (Milan,
Brera): on the other hand, the *Madonna of the Quail*
(Verona) may be by him or by Pisanello. Most of his
works are in Verona (Mus. and churches), but there are
others in Rome (Pal. Venezia) and Worcester Mass.
[ill. 144, p. 292]

Stevens, Alfred (1817–75), was born in Blandford
Forum, Dorset, the son of a decorator. He was befriended
by a clergyman who lent him things to copy, so that at
15 he was a competent portraitist in the Reynolds tradition.
His patron collected £60 and approached Landseer, but
Landseer's premium was £500, so in 1833 the boy was
put on a ship for Naples. No arrangements had been made
for him and no further funds were provided; he knew no
Italian, got involved in political intrigues, and fell among
thieves. He spent 18 months in and around Naples, and in
1835 walked to Rome, keeping himself by painting and
drawing portraits. He found Rome in an uncongenial
political uproar, so went on to Florence, where he remained
four years, copying in the Uffizi for a living and producing
for dealers what were virtually forgeries. In 1839 he was
in Milan and Venice, studying Titian, and in 1840 was in
Rome, where he met Thorwaldsen and worked in his

studio until he returned to England in 1842. He failed even to get a mention in the 1842 Houses of Parliament Competition, worked for industrialists on products exhibited in the 1851 Great Exhibition, and in 1856 had his first success with the Wellington Monument in St Paul's Cathedral, although the equestrian statue of the Duke was not erected until 45 years after the artist's death. He worked in houses now destroyed and on mosaics in St Paul's Cathedral (finished 1864). He painted occasional portraits, but his principal surviving works are drawings, chiefly in sanguine, the main inspiration for which was Raphael.

There are large collections of his work in Liverpool and London (Tate) with most of his surviving paintings and sculpture, and Cambridge (Fitzwm), Oxford, and Sheffield have many drawings. [ill. 872, p. 399]

Stiacciato *see* RELIEF.

Stijl, De, was a Dutch magazine (1917–28) devoted to boosting MONDRIAN and Neo-Plasticism in general; it subsequently sank into the hands of DADAISTS. The ideas advocated by it are also sometimes called De Stijl, and these have had a marked influence on the architecture of Gropius and others of the BAUHAUS movement, and on commercial art – poster designing, packaging, printing – particularly in Germany at first, but later spreading all over the world.

Still-life does not emerge as a subject in its own right until the 16th century; before that it appeared in religious pictures and portraits as part of the setting. It is a Northern rather than a Southern art form, with its greatest currency in Flanders and Holland and its least in England. After the Reformation, when religious painting virtually disappeared in the Protestant North, it became popular and was developed along various lines, the chief being the *Vanitas* type, a collection of objects chosen and arranged to remind the spectator of the transience and uncertainty of life; the symbolic type, where the objects portrayed have a significance beyond their individual appearance, and one heightened by their association; into this latter category come many still-life subjects which at first sight appear no more than members of the third type – collections of objects arranged to display the painter's virtuosity. The *Vanitas* is named from Ecclesiastes (i. 2). 'Vanitas Vanitatum . . .' and is easily recognized – hour-glasses, skulls, mirrors, butterflies, flowers, guttering candles, books, speak an immediate and universal language. The type was probably derived from the *Memento Mori* representations of S. Jerome, popular in Utrecht, whereas in the theological University city of Leyden the still-life alone could be made to carry the moral. The second type is more difficult but usually contains bread in some form, wine, water, and other recondite references to the Passion, the Trinity, the iconography of Saints or the Virgin. The last category is self-evident, but often difficult to distinguish from the symbolical one.

This also applies to flower-pieces. Many are merely luxuriant bouquets; many are also composite works containing flowers blooming at different times of the year, thus suggesting Time or the Seasons; many of the flowers may have hidden religious or literary meanings.

There are also large still-life pieces of the 'furniture picture' type – kitchen interiors, with quantities of raw and cooked food, flowers, guns, dogs, and cookmaids. The earliest flower-piece seems to be the vase of flowers on the back of a portrait by Memlinc in the Thyssen Coll., though this probably had a devotional emblematical meaning; and the earliest dated pure flower-piece is German, of 1562. The type seems to have developed from Herbals in the mid 16th century. The earliest known still-life is by the Venetian-trained Jacopo de' Barbari, dated 1504, in Munich, but there is a *Madonna* of *c.* 1470, by a follower of Roger van der Weyden, which has a niche containing still-life objects painted on the back (Rotterdam); this, however, is almost certainly symbolic in intent, since the objects are those often associated with the Annunciation. The towel, basin, and ewer all figure in the *Annunciation* on the back of the Ghent Altar. Even earlier is a similar still-life by T. Gaddi. Still-life hardly appears in Italian painting independently of a subject, except for the small baskets of fruit by Caravaggio, done early in his career. It is, however, an essential feature of the pictures in wood veneers known as *intarsie* and marble panels inlaid with *pietre dure* – onyx, lapis lazuli, etc., and also bulks large in Bassano's genre subjects, being, in fact, usually allied to such pictures. Spain produced a rather austere form, known as BODEGÓNES, and in France the 17th and 18th centuries saw, with Oudry and Chardin, highly developed forms of the Northern furniture pictures and the virtuoso still-life, though Oudry verges on animal painting and Chardin eschews *objets de luxe* in favour of kitchen utensils and simple arrangements of food and drink. [ills. 224, 341, 378–9, 419, 465–70, 658, 706–7, pp. 306, 320, 326, 331, 338–9, 369, 377. Col. pls. 16, 17, 36, 50]

Stippled Drawing is one modelled in light and shade by hundreds of tiny dots and flecks, sometimes also STUMPED, an elaborate technique giving a result not unlike a photograph and consequently very popular in 19th-century art schools. Stipple engraving *see* ENGRAVING.

Stomer, Matthias (1600–after 1650), was a Dutch Caravaggesque, whose style has much in common with the UTRECHT School. He was born in Amersfoort and was a pupil of HONTHORST, presumably soon after 1620. He was in Naples in 1631 and seems to have spent the rest of his life in Sicily and South Italy, never returning to Holland. There are pictures by him in Baltimore, Berlin, Birmingham, Brussels (Musée de S. Jean), Caccamo in Sicily (S. Agostino: dated 1641), Catania, Copenhagen, Darmstadt, Greenville SC, The Hague (Bredius Mus.), Madrid, Monreale, Munich, Naples, Padua, Palermo (SM del Rosario and palaces), Paris, Stockholm, Turin, Vaduz (Liechtenstein Coll.), Valetta Malta, and Worcester Mass. [ill. 463, p. 338]

Stone Carving is of incalculable antiquity, and the basic tools employed by the modern sculptor are fundamentally the same as those used by the Greeks of the 6th century B.C. It is possible to reproduce a model made in wax or plaster mechanically by means of the POINTING MACHINE, but many sculptors have always preferred direct carving, since the material conditions the final form. A block of stone is usually more or less rectilinear, and the outlines are first drawn on all the faces of it as a rough guide. The first blocking-out of the form is done with a stonemason's hammer, or *boucharde*, which has a heavy steel head covered with pyramidal points. Next, a punch, which is simply a pointed bar of steel, is used with a mallet to knock off large chips of stone. The forms are then defined with more precision by means of a claw chisel, which has three, four, or more teeth, giving a furrow-like effect to the surface of the stone. When the statue is virtually complete, but still furrowed all over by the claw marks, the sculptor takes an ordinary cold chisel and begins to define the forms as closely as possible. If a polished surface is desired it can be obtained by using files and abrasive powders. A drill is often used, and was particularly popular with Baroque sculptors to produce small points of shadow, in the hair or in an eyeball, to give vivacity to the expression.

Stopping Out *see* ENGRAVING.

Stoss, Veit (1440/50–1533), was, with RIEMENSCHNEIDER, the leading German Late Gothic sculptor. He went to Cracow in Poland (where he is known as Wita Stwosza) in 1477, where he carved his masterpiece, the High Altar for the Church of S. Mary (1477–89), an enormously complicated shrine, full of figures and some forty feet high. He also worked in stone, and other works by him are in the Cathedral and Museum at Cracow. In 1496 he returned to Nuremberg, and in 1503 attempted to exculpate himself from a criminal charge by forging a document, as a result of which he was sentenced to be branded on both cheeks and forbidden to leave Nuremberg. He also made some engravings and was active as a painter. Other works are in Nuremberg and Florence (SS. Annunziata). [ill. 623, p. 360]

Streeter (Streater), Robert (1624–80), appointed Sergeant-Painter to Charles II in 1663, is best known for his ceiling (*c.* 1669) of the Sheldonian Theatre, Oxford, painted with an elaborate allegory of the Triumph of Truth and the Arts. It is the most high-flown Baroque composition painted by an Englishman before Thornhill, and it inspired the immortal lines: '... future Ages must confess they owe To Streeter more than Michael Angelo' (R. Whitehall, 'Urania', 1669). [ill. 891, p. 401]

Stretes *see* SCROTS.

Strigel, Bernhardin (*c.* 1460/61–1528), was a German painter mainly of portraits who became Court Painter to the Emperor Maximilian I. All attributions to him are based on the *Cuspinian Family* (private coll.) which has an inscription dated 1520 and giving Strigel's name. There are, however, two pictures (Vienna, K-H) of *Maximilian and his Family* and the *Virgin and Child with S. Anne and other Saints* which are apparently of about 1515 but came from the same complex as the *Cuspinian Family*. Other pictures are in Baltimore, Berlin, Boston, Denver Col., Munich, New York (Met. Mus.), Nuremberg, Stuttgart, Vienna (K-H), Washington (NG), and York. [ill. 585, p. 357]

Strozzi, Bernardo (1581–1644), was a Genoese painter who became a Franciscan friar at the age of 17 (hence his nicknames 'Il Cappuccino' and 'Il Prete Genovese'). From 1607 his art was powerfully affected by Rubens, who was in Genoa then. In 1610 he left his convent to support his mother and spent the rest of his life as a painter although he was made a Monsignor in 1635. From 1630 he lived in Venice and Venetian art was the other great influence on his work. There are pictures by him in the Royal Collection and in Baltimore, Berlin, Cardiff, Cincinnati, Cleveland, Dresden, Dublin, Florence (Uffizi), Genoa, Greenville SC, Hartford (Wadsworth Atheneum), Kansas City, London (NG), Milan (Brera), New York (Met. Mus.), Ottawa, Oxford (Ashmolean and Christ Church), Paris (Louvre), Rome (Gall. Naz.), St Louis, Venice, Vienna, Washington, Worcester Mass., and elsewhere. [ill. 281, p. 313]

Stuart, Gilbert (1755–1828), was born in America but went to Scotland *c.* 1770. After returning to America he came back to London in 1775 and studied under his fellow-countryman WEST. After escaping from his creditors by working in Dublin 1787–93 he returned to America and became famous as a portrait painter. His *Washington* exists in three main types, versions being in every major American collection. The Tate Gallery, London, has his *West* and others, and the NPG also has portraits. [ill. 847, p. 396]

Stubbs, George (1724–1806), painted portraits for a living while studying anatomy in York, where he lectured to medical students. His earliest works are illustrations for a textbook of midwifery (1751). In 1754 he went to Rome, not to study Italian art but to prove to himself that this was unnecessary, since 'Nature is superior to art.' Returning via Ceuta he saw a lion devouring a horse, a sight which haunted him for the rest of his life and which became one of his most admired subjects. He then lived in a desolate Lincolnshire farmhouse, dissecting horses and drawing them, but during the 1760s he lived in London and worked as an animal painter while preparing his 'Anatomy of the Horse', published in 1766. In 1780 he became an ARA, but was never elected RA because of a dispute with the Academy. From 1795 until his death he worked on a book on the comparative anatomy of Man, Tiger, and Fowl. The text and 125 drawings were discovered in 1957 in the Public Library, Worcester Mass.
Most of his paintings are oils on canvas, but from 1770 he experimented with enamel, fired on copper plates, or on Wedgwood china plaques. Stubbs is far more than an animal painter or a horse portraitist: all nature was his field, and his amazing accuracy of representation is the servant of a highly developed pictorial imagination. There are examples in Bath (Holburne Mus.), Glasgow (Hunterian), Leeds, Liverpool, London (NG, BM, Tate, RA), Melbourne, Port Sunlight, Yale, and elsewhere. [ill. 896, p. 402]

Study. A drawing or painting of a detail, such as a figure, a hand, or a piece of drapery, made for the purpose of study or for use in a larger composition. A study should never be confused with a SKETCH, which is a rough draught of the whole, whereas a study may be very highly wrought but does not usually embrace more than a part of the composition.

Stump. A cigar-shaped roll of paper, sharply pointed at each end, which was used to rub charcoal or chalk drawings so as to obtain very delicate transitions of tone.

A stumped drawing looks very like a photograph, hence the decay of the technique.

Style Criticism requires an exact knowledge of the characteristics of any given School as well as the personal style of any particular artist. Given such a knowledge, it is possible to analyse the style of a work of art so that a convincing attribution may be made to a specific artist and even to a particular moment in his career. Further, given a precise knowledge of many works by many masters of any one country or period, it is possible to make general deductions about the style of that country or period as reflected in its practitioners. The proper practice of stylistic analysis is more difficult than it is sometimes made to seem.

Sully, Thomas (1783–1872), was born in England but went to America as a child. He studied under STUART in Boston before working with WEST in London in 1809. He returned to America and settled in Philadelphia in 1810 but revisited England in 1837–8 to paint Queen Victoria at the request of the St George's Society of Philadelphia. Sully painted her at Buckingham Palace and said that 'she was very affable, like a well-bred lady of Philadelphia or Boston'. This finished picture is still in Philadelphia but the original study is in New York (Met. Mus.) and another version is in London (Wallace Coll.). Sully kept an index of his works from 1801 which runs to 2,631 items, most of which are in America. His 'Hints to Young Painters' was published posthumously. [ill. 852, p. 397]

Super-Realism *see* SURREALISM.

Suprematism was a hyper-orthodox form of CUBISM, invented in 1913/15 by MALEVICH (who later wrote a book about it) as an absolutely pure geometrical abstract art. To the uninitiated it is scarcely distinguishable from analytical Cubism: to the really initiated it must be distinguished from CONSTRUCTIVISM and from the abstract paintings of MONDRIAN.

Surrealism, which was born of a union between the COLLAGE and CONSTRUCTIVIST aspects of CUBISM, and the nihilism of DADA, claims a long artistic ancestry in the art of Bosch, Arcimboldi, Fuseli, Goya, Redon, and any other artist who has expressed the weird and fantastic. After the demise of Dada in 1922, André Breton gathered up the remnants of the group, took over the word *surréaliste* from Apollinaire (who had used it in 1917), and defined it as 'Pure psychic AUTOMATISM, by which it is intended to express verbally, in writing or in any other way, the true process of thought. It is the dictation of thought, free from the exercise of reason, and every aesthetic or moral pre-occupation.' The object was to free artists from the normal association of pictorial ideas and from all accepted means of expression, so that they might create according to the irrational dictates of their subconscious mind and vision. Surrealism developed in two directions: pure fantasy, and the elaborate reconstruction of a dream-world. The first produced FOUND OBJECTS, either alone or composed – a bottle dryer, a bicycle wheel, or a birdcage filled with sugar-cubes and a thermometer, a random assortment of bric-à-brac – automatic drawing, Ernst's FROTTAGES and abstract works

charged with meaning by a strange title – Klee's *Twittering machine*, or Picabia's *Catch as catch can*. The second took the form of highly detailed likenesses of objects, straight or distorted, or three-dimensional abstractions, in a fantastic and unexpected juxtaposition, or in a setting of a hallucinatory kind: CHIRICO, Tanguy, DALI, Man Ray's photographs, and much of Picasso's painting and sculpture from the late 1920s develop this type, the feverish search for the unexpected being well rendered by Lautréamont's simile: 'Beautiful as the chance encounter of a sewing machine and an umbrella on an operating table.'
In 1925 the fifth number of 'La Révolution Surréaliste', edited by Breton, associated the movement with Communism, but the Communists, as a political party, would have none of it. The movement has had as much currency in literature and drama as in the visual arts, and despite its own particular strait-jacket, has had a liberating influence. Its ideas of strange juxtapositions have been widely commercialized – particularly in sophisticated window-dressing – and, its initial force now spent and its edge dulled by surfeit, it survives as a respectable ghost of hauntingly incoherent incantations, and even threatens to become academic.

Sutherland, Graham, OM (*b.* 1903), one of the best known of living British painters, began as an etcher and engraver and painted little before 1935. He was appointed an Official War Artist in 1941 and his semi-abstract scenes of desolation after bombing exactly expressed the atmosphere of such a scene. He is primarily a painter of the mood of landscape, but exceptions are the *Crucifixion* and the related subjects and studies of about 1946, and his portraits. The *Crucifixion* was commissioned by Canon Hussey for S. Matthew's, Northampton, where there is also a Henry Moore statue of the *Madonna and Child*, and his religious works have become more important with the huge tapestry for Coventry Cathedral (1962: most of the studies are in Coventry Mus.) and the *Crucifixion* for S. Aidan's, East Acton, London, of 1963. Sutherland's portraits include the *Maugham* (1949), *Beaverbrook* (1951), and the *Churchill*, not so far seen in public. There are pictures in Birmingham, Darlington, Hull, London (Tate, Imperial War Mus.), Manchester, Melbourne, Nebraska Univ., New Brunswick, New York (M of MA), Ottawa, Paris (Mus. d'Art Mod.), Southampton, Toronto, and elsewhere. [ill. 978, p. 412]

Sweerts, Michael (1624–64), was a Brussels painter who went to Rome in or before 1646, when he was a member of the Academy, charged with the difficult task of collecting the dues owed to the Guild by the Netherlandish immigrant painters. He remained in Rome until 1651 at least, and in 1656 opened a school in Brussels. In 1661, as a lay-brother, he began a journey to the East with an unsuccessful religious mission. He died in Goa. His Roman works are good examples of BAMBOCCIATE, but after his return north his works approximated more closely to Dutch genre painting as practised by Pieter de HOOCH, or portraits similar to those by VERMEER. There are works by him in Amsterdam, Detroit, Haarlem, The Hague, Hartford Conn., Milan (Castello), Munich, Oberlin Ohio, Paris (Louvre), Rome (Capitoline and Accad.), Rotterdam, and Worcester Mass. [ill. 516, p. 346]

Synthetism, or Cloisonnism, is synonymous with Symbolism. The movement was originally a literary one, starting in 1886 with Rimbaud's 'Illuminations'. In 1889 GAUGUIN and other artists from Pont-Aven exhibited their works as 'Synthetist' painters, their object being the expression of ideas, mood, and emotion and the complete rejection of naturalistic representation. Their pictures were painted in brilliant colours, separated by black lines, and sought to be both decorative and the abstractions, or syntheses, of the ideas which inspired them. The chief members of the group were Gauguin, Émile BERNARD (who claimed to have invented Synthetism), and Paul SÉRUSIER; Odilon REDON developed the purely personal and fantastic side of Symbolism and strongly influenced the NABIS. Linked with the group, though not part of it, were Gustave MOREAU and PUVIS de Chavannes.

T

Tacca, Pietro (1577–1640), was a pupil of Giovanni da BOLOGNA and succeeded him as Sculptor to the Tuscan Grand Dukes. He also finished his master's equestrian statues in Madrid and Paris (*Henri IV*, destroyed 1792). His masterpiece is *The Four Moors* (1615–24) on the base of the Monument to the Grand-Duke Ferdinand I in Leghorn. He also made an equestrian monument to Philip IV in Madrid and monuments in Florence (S. Lorenzo, Chapel of the Princes). [ill. 166, p. 295]

Tachisme (Fr. *tache* blot, stain) is very similar to ACTION PAINTING. The most notable exponent was POLLOCK, who now has a host of followers on both sides of the Atlantic, but KANDINSKY painted remarkably similar pictures before the First World War.

Tactile Values. An illusion of tangibility. The inventor of the phrase, Bernhard Berenson, claimed that the representation of three-dimensional objects on a two-dimensional surface in such a way that one received a strong impression of physical tangibility is 'life-enhancing'. It is not clear why.

Taille-Douce (Fr.). Line ENGRAVING.

Tamayo, Rufino (*b.* 1899), is a Mexican painter who has, like RIVERA, founded his style on a mixture of his native prehistoric art and modern European art, chiefly Expressionism and Surrealism. He has worked a good deal in America, and in 1943 executed frescoes for Smith College Library, Northampton Mass. His use of sophisticated foreign elements has made him something of a prophet in his own land. [ill. 1073, p. 425]

Tanguy, Yves (1900–55), was a French Surrealist, who began life as a merchant seaman and took up painting in 1924 after seeing a Chirico. From 1939 he lived in the US. There are works by him in Basle, Buffalo, Chicago, Hartford Conn. (Wadsworth), New York (Met. Mus., M of MA, Whitney), Paris (Mus. d'Art Mod.), and Philadelphia. [ill. 1053, p. 423]

Tapiès, Antonio (*b.* 1923), studied law before becoming the leading Spanish abstract painter. He began to paint in 1946 and went to Paris in 1950: his works mostly consist of puddled sand and paint, often with incised dashes, giving an effect not unlike the sea-shore after the tide has ebbed. There are examples in London (Tate) and New York (M of MA). [ill. 1114, p. 428]

Tatlin, Vladimir (1885–1953?), was a Russian painter who, in 1913, switched to sculpture and founded CONSTRUCTIVISM. In the same year he met Picasso in Paris. Unlike many other Russian artists – GABO, PEVSNER, CHAGALL – he remained after the Soviet authorities abandoned their brief flirtation with 'advanced' art. Tatlin worked as a designer, especially for film and stage sets, but it is significant that the date of his death is difficult to ascertain. It was probably 1953, but 1956 is also given in reference books, and some writers speak of him as still alive [ill. 1136, p. 432]

Tectonic *see* ARCHITECTONIC.

Tempera. This word really means any kind of binder which will serve to 'temper' powder colour and make it workable: in practice, however, it is confined to egg tempera, which was the commonest technique of painting until the late 15th century for the production of easel pictures. If you take a panel well prepared with GESSO and paint on it with powder colour which is mixed with fresh egg-yolk thinned with water the result will be a paint film which dries almost instantaneously (making reworking difficult) and is also tough and permanent. It dries several tones lighter than the wet paint. There are many modifications of this basic recipe, and some painters used the whole egg; illuminators of MSS often used only the white. From very early times it was noticed that powder colour could be mixed with some form of drying oil and would then form a rich and transparent film which could be used to modify the semi-opaque tempera layer. Probably the earliest use of this oil GLAZE was to shade off burnished gold- or silver-leaf, but from this the whole technique of OIL PAINTING developed. For many years it was usual to paint most of a picture in tempera – which dries in minutes – and then to apply only the final touches in oil. One good reason for this is the fact that tempera, because of the speed with which it dries, has to be hatched and cross-hatched to obtain modelling: a final glaze of oil colour will spread a unifying film, or, as painters say, 'pull it together'. No one really knows how long this 'Mixed Method' continued – it was certainly still practised by Rubens – but it is plain that the oil medium has such attractive qualities of its own, notably in IMPASTO, that it became the dominant partner. Rembrandt, whose lifetime overlaps with Rubens, seems always to have used oil alone. In the last few years a small number of painters have returned to the pure tempera medium (the paints can now be bought ready mixed), but a judicious use of the Mixed Method offers great scope for technical virtuosity and could well be revived. [Col. pls. 40, 41]

Tenebrism (from Ital. *tenebroso*, murky) is the name given to painting in a very low key, specifically to the works of those early-17th-century painters, mostly Neapolitan and Spanish, who were much influenced by CARAVAGGIO. They did not form any kind of organized group and the *Tenebristi* did not call themselves by that name. [Col. pl. 24]

Teniers, David I (1582–1649), was a painter of religious pictures, influenced by Rubens, and some landscapes with peasants similar to those by his son David II (1610–90), the most famous member of the family. Teniers the Younger became a Master in Antwerp in 1632/3 and worked there until 1651, when he settled in Brussels. He was the Court Painter to the Archduke Leopold Wilhelm, Regent of the Netherlands and one of the greatest of collectors, and Teniers became Keeper of his pictures. He was also Court Painter to the next Regent and was the main founder of the Antwerp Academy, opened in 1665. He painted almost every kind of picture, but predominantly genre scenes of peasant life. His earliest are in the manner of BROUWER, but he developed his own style and produced most of his best works in the decade 1640–50, before moving to Brussels. Many of his later works are largely by assistants, since the demand was enormous. He painted a few religious subjects and some of Witches' Sabbaths, and even apes and cats dressed up as humans, but historically the most interesting are the interiors of picture galleries, showing recognizable pictures in their 17th-century settings. As an art historian he made many copies of the Archduke Leopold Wilhelm's pictures, 244 of which were engraved in 1660 under the title 'Theatrum Pictorium': most of the originals are now in Vienna and have thus an established history back to the mid 17th century. More than 2,000 pictures are attributed to him, and there are good examples in the Royal Coll. and in Amsterdam, Antwerp, Berlin, Brussels, Dresden, Edinburgh (NG), Glasgow, The Hague, Leningrad, London (NG, Wallace Coll. (an example of almost every kind of picture he painted), Dulwich, Wellington Mus.), Madrid, Munich, New York (Met. Mus.), Paris (Louvre), and Vienna (K-H). His son David III (1638–85) was also a painter and often imitated him. [ills. 395, 396, 398, p. 328]

Ter Borch (Terburg, Terborch), Gerard (1617–81), was the son of a minor painter and was very precocious. He was in Amsterdam and Haarlem 1632/4, when Rembrandt was making his name and Hals was working in Haarlem; in 1635 he visited England; in 1640 he was in Italy; he returned to Holland probably via France, and in 1646 he went to Münster in Westphalia (presumably to paint portraits of the dignitaries at the Congress of the Peace of Westphalia), and in 1648 he accompanied the Spanish Envoy to Madrid, returning to Holland in 1650. On account of these travels Ter Borch must have had first-hand knowledge of almost all the great 17th-century artists – Rembrandt, Hals, Velazquez, Bernini – and yet his style betrays no hint of this, for he is content to paint small portraits and genteel genre scenes, diligent in style, paying particular attention to the rendering of silk and satin. His most famous is the *Peace of Münster, 15 May 1648* (London, NG), a group portrait of all the dignitaries at full length, on copper, $17\frac{1}{2}$ by $22\frac{1}{2}$ inches: all his other pictures are small portraits and portrait groups, usually full-length, and scenes of well-to-do Dutch family life or else guard-room scenes. Most of his figures have a curious doll-like charm and the costumes and accessories recur so often in his portraits, even down to identical folds, that it is possible he painted the pictures in advance and simply added heads and hands when necessary. His works are often similar to those of his junior, METSU, but his subtle treatment of colour and light were far exceeded by VERMEER. There are works by him in the Royal Coll. and in Aix, Amsterdam, Antwerp, Berlin, Boston (Gardner), Bremen, Budapest, Cape Town, Chicago, Cincinnati, Cologne, Copenhagen, Detroit, Deventer (Town Hall), Dresden, Dublin, Florence (Uffizi), Frankfurt (Städel), Haarlem, The Hague, Hamburg, Indianapolis, London (NG, V & A, and Wallace Coll.), Munich, New York (Met. Mus., Frick Coll., and Hist. Soc.), Paris (Louvre and Petit Palais), Philadelphia, Richmond Va, Rotterdam, Vaduz (Liechtenstein Coll.: *Portrait of van Goyen*), Vienna, Washington (NG), and Wellesley College Mass. [ill. 513, p. 347]

Terbrugghen, Hendrick (1588–1629), was born in Deventer and became a pupil of BLOEMAERT before going to Italy 1604–14. He settled in Utrecht by 1616 and became one of the leading members of the UTRECHT School, but his style shows almost no influence of his master Bloemaert and, strictly speaking, little of that of Caravaggio except in the predilection for strong contrasts of light and shadow – and even that disappears in his later works, for the *Jacob and Laban* (1627: London, NG) is painted in much lighter and clearer colours and looks forward to VERMEER, who also turned *Caravaggismo* upside-down. Some of Terbrugghen's religious subjects are taken from Caravaggio – the *Incredulity of S. Thomas* and the *Calling of S. Matthew* are reworkings of Caravaggio themes – but the iconography of others goes back to such Northern artists as e.g. Dürer. More typical works are nearer to MANFREDI, e.g. the *Lute Players* and the harlot and the clown of the *Duet* and similar pictures. There are pictures by him in the Royal Coll. and in Amsterdam (Rijksmus.), Augsburg, Basle, Berlin, Bordeaux, Cambridge Mass. (Fogg), Cassel, Cologne, Copenhagen, Deventer (Town Hall), Edinburgh (NG), Gotha, Gothenborg, Greenville SC, Le Havre, London (NG), New York (Met. Mus.), Oberlin Ohio, Oxford (Ashmolean), Paris (Louvre), Rome (Gall. Naz.), Sacramento Cal., Schwerin, Stockholm, Utrecht, and Vienna (K-H). [ill. 460, p. 339. Col. pl. 24]

Terracotta (Ital. baked earth) *see* PLASTER.

Terribilità (Ital. terribleness), a word usually applied to Michelangelo and, by extension, to any art of austere and tragic grandeur.

Tesserae. The cubes used in MOSIAC. [Col. pl. 39]

Theodoric of Prague (active 1343?–68), was recorded in the Prague Painters' Guild in 1348. He was Painter to the Emperor Charles IV by 1359 and executed over 100 paintings for his Castle at Karlstein in Bohemia by 1365. He was the greatest of the Bohemian painters of the 14th century and began a severe and realistic style that influenced much later German and Bohemian painting. [ill. 537, p. 351]

Thoma, Hans (1839–1924), spent a few weeks in Paris in 1868 and was profoundly impressed by the Realist ideas of COURBET and the BARBIZON painters. In the 1870s he met LEIBL and BÖCKLIN and in 1874 he went to Italy, where he met MARÉES, and the Romanticism of these latter influenced his work in the direction of what now seems a deplorable sentimentality. He is very well represented in German museums, especially Karlsruhe (where he was Director), and there are other pictures in New York (Met. Mus.), Stockholm, Vienna, and Zürich. [ill. 615, p. 360]

Thornhill, Sir James (1675/6–1734), was the only English decorator in the grand Baroque tradition. In the Dome of St Paul's (1715–17) incidents from the Saint's life appear in eight grisaille panels picked out in gold, and the decoration does not obtrude on the painted architectural setting. His work at Greenwich Hospital, lasting from 1708 to 1727, includes the immense Painted Hall, the lower Hall, and Vestibule, and set him the problem of treating modern history subjects in a grand allegorical setting, which he solved with a display of the most Italianate illusionism. He does not appear to have had any direct contact with Verrio or Laguerre, yet both influenced him, though his ceiling of Queen Anne's Bedroom at Hampton Court (1715) is finer than anything of theirs. He travelled in the Netherlands in 1711, and in France 1717; was knighted and made Sergeant-Painter in 1720, Member of Parliament for his native town of Melcombe Regis in Dorset in 1722, Fellow of the Royal Society in 1723, and Master of the Painter-Stainer's Company. These offices and honours gave him a very different position from that usually accorded to artists and not reached again until the advent of Reynolds. He appeared at a time when grand decoration was required, and reaped the advantage of being the only English painter able to compete with the many foreigners then seeking work in England (Pellegrini, the Riccis, and Amigoni, besides Verrio and Laguerre) at a moment when anti-foreign feeling prevailed. His son-in-law, Hogarth, is an excellent example of this. His only big failure was when Kent was given the job of decorating Kensington Palace, through the influence of his patron, Lord Burlington.
There are also works at Chatsworth, Easton Neston, London (Tate, NPG), and elsewhere. [ill. 893, p. 401]

Thorwaldsen, Bertel (1768–1844), was the only Danish artist to attain international fame. From 1797 to 1838 he lived in Rome, where he was one of the best-known exponents of Neoclassic sculpture and was ranked rather below CANOVA and above GIBSON. His works are calm and noble, or insipid copies of the Antique according to taste: there is a complete collection of them, originals, casts, and copies, in the Thorwaldsen Mus. in Copenhagen, but there are also some in Naples and Rome, especially in St Peter's (Tomb of Pius VII). [ill. 870, p. 399]

Tibaldi, Pellegrino (1527–96), was a painter, sculptor, and architect who was one of the leading Italian Mannerists of the late 16th century and whose work in Spain helped to

spread the style there. His earliest painting is the large *Adoration of the Shepherds* (1548 not 49: Rome, Borghese) painted when he was twenty-one. This shows the influence of Michelangelo and his followers, but Tibaldi was also influenced by PARMIGIANINO and Niccolo dell' ABBATE. He was in Rome by 1549/50, but returned to Bologna in 1553 when he began a series of frescoes of the story of Odysseus (Pal. Poggi, now the University) and the decorations in S. Giacomo Maggiore. From 1560 Tibaldi was connected with S. Charles Borromeo, Archbishop of Milan, for whom he also worked as an architect. In 1585 he was invited to Spain by Philip II, but he did not go until 1587. There he supervised the building and decoration of the Escorial, painting forty-six frescoes in the cloister alone. In 1596, rich and ennobled, he returned to Milan where he died. There are other works by him in Amsterdam, Ancona, Bologna, Leningrad, Milan (Brera), and Vaduz (Liechtenstein Coll.: replica of the Borghese *Adoration*). [ill. 201, p. 303]

Tiepolo, Giovanni Battista (Giambattista) (1696–1770), was the last of the great Venetian decorators, the purest exponent of the Italian ROCOCO, and arguably the greatest painter of the 18th century. He was trained under an obscure painter named Lazzarini but was really formed by the study of Sebastiano RICCI and PIAZZETTA among living painters and VERONESE among the older masters. He was received into the Fraglia (Guild) in 1717 but had already painted the *Sacrifice of Abraham* (1715/16: Venice, Ospedaletto), a dark picture very much in the manner of Piazzetta and the 17th century generally. In 1719 he married the sister of Guardi and at about this time his own lighter and looser style began to form. His first great commission for fresco decorations came in 1725, when he began the work in the Archbishop's Palace at Udine (completed 1728). These already show the virtuosity of his handling, the light tone and pale colours necessitated by fresco obviously helping him to break free from the dark Piazzettesque models he had previously followed. The Udine frescoes also show him developing as the creator of a world in steep perspective beyond the picture plane, with the architecture receding into dizzy distances. The highly specialized work of painting these architectural perspectives was done by Mengozzi-Colonna, who did this work for Tiepolo for most of his life. Following the Udine frescoes Tiepolo travelled widely in N. Italy, painting many more frescoes in palaces and churches, as well as altarpieces in oil which culminate in the gigantic *Gathering of the Manna* and *Sacrifice of Melchizedek* (c. 1735–40: Verolanuova, Parish Church), each of which is about 30 feet high. The frescoes of this period culminate in the *Antony and Cleopatra* series in the Palazzo Labia, Venice, which were probably finished just before 1750, when he left Venice for Würzburg. He was invited to decorate the ceiling of the Kaisersaal in the Residenz at Würzburg by the Prince-Bishop, Karl Phillip von Greiffenklau, and Tiepolo and his sons Giandomenico and Lorenzo arrived in Würzburg at the end of 1750 and remained there until 1753. He painted the staircase with frescoes, some overdoors, and some altarpieces as well as the Kaisersaal, and both his sons, as well as several other assistants, helped in the gigantic task. The Palace itself is a superb example of German Rococo architecture and the combination of

architecture and painting into one vast and airy allegory –
apparently referring to the Prince-Bishop as a patron, but
including Barbarossa and German history – is perhaps the
most successful even in Tiepolo's career. In 1755, after his
return to Venice, he was elected first President of the
Venetian Academy and in 1761 he was invited to Spain to
decorate the Royal Palace in Madrid by Charles III. He
arrived in 1762, with his sons and assistants, and painted
the huge ceilings in the Palace in 4 years. In 1767 Charles
commissioned seven altarpieces for Aranjuez but Tiepolo's
last years in Spain were embittered by intrigues on behalf
of MENGS, the representative of that Neoclassicism which
was soon to condemn his kind of splendid and carefree
painting as frivolous. He died suddenly in Madrid. His
enormous output of frescoes and altarpieces was partly due
to his habit of painting small *modelli* which, when approved
by the client, could be carried out by his skilled assistants
under his own supervision. Scores of these *modelli* and
sketches survive, together with hundreds of drawings. He
painted very few portraits – the best known is the so-
called *Querini* in the Querini Gall., Venice, but this may,
in fact, be by his son Domenico. He also etched many
plates. There are works in many churches, palaces, and
galleries in Venice and in Amsterdam, Barnard Castle
(Bowes Mus.), Bergamo (Cath., Accad.), Berlin, Boston
(Mus. and Gardner), Budapest, Cambridge Mass. (Fogg),
Chicago, Detroit, Dresden, Edinburgh (NG), Este,
London (NG, Dulwich), Melbourne (NG), Milan (Brera
and Poldi-Pezzoli), Montreal, Munich, New York (Met.
Mus.), Ottawa, Paris (Louvre), Philadelphia (Johnson),
Rovigo, St Louis, Stockholm (Nat. Mus. and Univ. Mus.),
Strà (Villa Pisani), Stuttgart, Verona, Vicenza (Villa
Valmarana), Vienna (K-H, Akad.), Washington (NG), and
many other places. [ills. 297–9, p. 314. Col. pl. 9]
His son Giovanni Domenico (1727–1804) was also a considerable painter in his own right, as well as his father's
assistant and imitator. His frescoes in the Villa Valmarana
(one is now known to be dated 1757) show that he had a
different approach from his father's, less allegorical and
more sardonic and matter-of-fact, with a delight in the
activities of clowns and mountebanks. There are some
pictures by him in London (NG), but there is a tendency
to ascribe works to him which are not quite good enough
for his father: if they are not really good enough for
Domenico they get ascribed to Lorenzo (1736–76), about
whose style little is known. He made some etchings after
his father's pictures. [ill. 300, p. 315]

Tino di Camaino (*c.* 1285–1337) was a Sienese sculptor,
perhaps the pupil of Giovanni PISANO. He was working
in Pisa by 1311 and became head of the works at the
Cathedral in 1315, when he was commissioned to make a
Tomb for the Emperor Henry VII, parts of which survive
in the Cathedral. In 1319–20 Tino was head of the works
at Siena Cathedral and later worked in Florence before
going to Naples in 1323/4 to make Monuments for the
Angevin rulers. He stayed in Naples until his death, and
he seems to have been in close touch with Giotto, who was
Court Painter in Naples 1329–33, and also with the
Sienese painter Pietro Lorenzetti, who became guardian of
Tino's child: Tino's grave, but rather clumsy, figures have
much in common with Lorenzetti's. There are works in
Florence, Naples, Pisa, Siena, and in Berlin, Detroit,

Frankfurt, London (V & A), Paris (Louvre), and Turin.
[ill. 10, p. 270]

Tintoretto, Jacopo (1518–94), was born in Venice. Little
is known of his early years; he claimed to have been a
pupil of Titian, and was probably associated with Schiavone
and Paris BORDONE. He was a Master in 1539, but no
work can certainly be ascribed to him before about 1545.
Titian was his model, and he aimed at the Mannerist conception of the ideal through a synthesis of Michelangelo's
drawing with Titian's colour, which in his case succeeded,
chiefly because his drawing is nothing like Michelangelo's
and his colour is nothing like Titian's.
In his early works he composes his figures across the picture
in a frieze, with elegant elongated forms and all the devices
of placing the principal incident deep into the picture, dis-
persing the interest over the whole canvas, or using *repoussoir* figures in front and at the sides, opposing diagonals
and contrasts of light on dark and dark on light. He made
his reputation in 1548 with the *S. Mark rescuing a slave*
(Venice, Accad.), a large and crowded composition with
daring foreshortening, brilliant colour, and a concentration
on one moment and incident. Later he evolved compositions based on an exploding centre or on rapidly receding
diagonals, full of figures in violent movement. After the
fires in the Doge's Palace in 1574 and 1577, Tintoretto and
Veronese were the principal artists commissioned to
renew the interior, and for this Tintoretto painted the
gigantic *Paradise* for the main hall.
Like Titian, Tintoretto kept a huge workshop, his chief
assistants being his sons Domenico and Marco, and his
daughter Marietta. The system in the Tintoretto workshop
differed from that in use in the Titian and Veronese
workshops in that instead of limiting his assistants to close
versions, copies, or preparatory work on a commission, he
employed them mainly on enlargements and extensively
altered variants of his original compositions. Besides his
work for the State, he worked for most of the larger
Confraternities and he began his long association with the
Scuola di S. Rocco in 1564, becoming a member in 1565.
In 1576 he contracted with the Confraternity for a regular
stipend (which was paid; his State pension was often in
arrears) in return for which he undertook to complete the
decoration of the entire building. This was finished in
1588. The Scuola di S. Rocco consists of a huge lower hall
with paintings over 12 feet high illustrating the Life of the
Virgin, an upper hall of the same size with paintings over
16 feet high of the Life of Christ, with a further large
room adjoining it with scenes from the Passion. They
display to the full his extraordinary use of the unexpected
viewpoint, contrasts of scale, unusual movement, and
visionary effects of colour and flickering light. Vasari disapproved of him, and tempered his admiration by saying
that Tintoretto treated art as a joke – which is a measure
of the difference between Central Italian Mannerism and
the Venetian kind.
There are few mythologies in his *œuvre*, for he had none
of Titian's classical interest, neither does he approach
Titian's range and inventiveness in portraits. After his
death, painting in Venice dwindled to an insignificant
place, not to revive until Piazzetta nor to see similar glories
until Tiepolo.
Most of the major galleries of the world possess an

example, but it is impossible to see him properly except in Venice, and in particular in the Scuola di S. Rocco. [ills. 220, 223, p. 305. Col. pl. 15]

Tischbein, Johann Heinrich Wilhelm (1751–1829), was one of a family of painters and was the pupil of his uncles in Hamburg. He went to Holland in 1771 and began to work as a portrait painter, having a great success at the Court in Berlin after 1777. He became dissatisfied with portraiture and went to Munich where he studied Dürer and the early German painters, going on to Italy in 1779. In 1783 he was in Rome for the second time and began to paint history pictures, but in 1786 he met Goethe, and in 1786/88 he painted the *Goethe in the Campagna* (Frankfurt, Städel) on which his reputation chiefly rests. In 1789 he became Director of the Naples Academy and from 1791 supervised the engravings of the Greek vases belonging to Sir William Hamilton which were so important in the spread of NEOCLASSICISM. He returned to Germany in 1799. There are works by him in Berlin, Hamburg, Weimar, and other German museums. [ill. 596, p. 358]

Tissot, James (1836–1902), was born in Nantes but settled in England after the Franco-Prussian War of 1870. He spent 10 years in Palestine, working on his pictures of the Life of Christ, but he is now remembered as the most charming illustrator of Victorian life. There are good examples of this in London (Tate). [ill. 965, p. 410]

Titian (Tiziano Vecelli) (*c.* 1487/90–1576), was the greatest of Venetian painters and, in some senses, the founder of modern painting. Traditionally he lived to be 99; but this is highly improbable, since it makes him born in 1477 and therefore older than GIORGIONE who seems to have been the decisive innovator in the early years of the 16th century. Certainly Giorgione is the only painter mentioned in the documents concerning the frescoes on the Fondaco dei Tedeschi (1508), although Titian traditionally painted those on the less important façade. All these frescoes have now perished, but Titian's earliest style is certainly involved with Giorgione's. Titian seems to have been a pupil first of Gentile BELLINI and then of his brother Giovanni; but long before Giovanni's death in 1516 Titian had been decisively influenced by Giorgione, who, though not his master in any strict sense, was his real teacher. Giorgione's early death, in 1510, led to the completion of some of his works by Titian and SEBASTIANO del Piombo, and to consequent critical confusion: the Dresden *Venus* and the *Noli Me Tangere* (London, NG) may be two such Giorgione/Titians. In 1511 Titian was painting frescoes in Padua, but the unexpected death of Giorgione and the removal of Sebastiano to Rome in 1511 left Titian without a rival in Venice except the very aged Giovanni Bellini: on his death in 1516 Titian succeeded him as Painter to the Republic, and in the same year he began his *Assumption* for the Frari Church in Venice. This was completed in 1518 and laid the foundations of his fame. It is an enormous picture, in the 'modern' style, and marks the beginning of the High Renaissance in Venice. The *Pesaro Altar* (1519–26), in the same church, contains further innovations and shows Titian now firmly established and in possession of a fully developed personal style. In 1532 he met the Emperor Charles V at Bologna, where he painted a copy

(1532–3: Madrid, Prado) of a full-length portrait of Charles by his Austrian Court Painter SEISENEGGER, as a result of which he was ennobled and made Court Painter in 1533. Subsequently Titian became a personal friend of the Emperor – an unheard-of honour for a painter of the 16th century, comparable only with Michelangelo's relationship with the Popes. During the 1540s Michelangelo's influence on Titian can be noted and some Mannerist elements infiltrate into his style – these, and also a new interest in classical antiquity are partly attributable to his visit to Rome in 1545–6, when he painted a shatteringly revealing portrait of Paul III and his nasty Farnese grandsons apparently engaged in a family quarrel (Naples). He visited the Imperial Court at Augsburg in 1548–9 and again in 1550–1 and his portraits of these years established the type of official portrait which was later to be exploited by Rubens, van Dyck, and many others. After the abdication of Charles V in 1555 Titian continued to work for his successor, Philip II of Spain, who, however, employed him less as a portraitist than as a painter of *poesie* (Titian's own word); that is, more or less erotic mythologies which, at first sight, accord ill with the Counter-Reformation ideals of Philip II. During these years the old painter developed a very free handling, almost anticipating Impressionism in its disregard for contours and its concentration on the rendering of form as patches of colour. In the 1560s there were many criticisms of his failing powers, but in fact he was developing a sublime late style, best seen in the *modelli* he produced and from which his numerous assistants (who included his son Orazio) fabricated 'finished pictures'. The *Entombment* (Venice, Accad.) was left unfinished at his death and was completed by PALMA Giovane, who has left the following description of Titian's technique: 'He laid in his pictures with a mass of colour which served as a groundwork for what he wanted to express. I myself have seen such vigorous underpainting in plain red earth [*terra rossa,* probably Venetian red] for the half-tones, or in white lead. With the same brush dipped in red, black, or yellow he worked up the light parts and in four strokes he could create a remarkably fine figure. . . . Then he turned the picture to the wall and left it for months without looking at it, until he returned to it and stared critically at it, as if it were a mortal enemy. . . . If he found something which displeased him he went to work like a surgeon. . . . Thus, by repeated revisions he brought his pictures to a high state of perfection and while one was drying he worked on another. This quintessence of a composition he then covered with many layers of living flesh. . . . He never painted a figure *alla prima,* and used to say that he who improvises can never make a perfect line of poetry. The final touches he softened, occasionally modulating the highest lights into the half-tones and local colours with his finger; sometimes he used his finger to dab a dark patch in a corner as an accent, or to heighten the surface with a bit of red like a drop of blood. He finished his figures like this and in the last stages he used his fingers more than his brush.'
There are works in the Royal Collection and in Ancona, Antwerp, Baltimore, Berlin, Besançon, Boston (Mus. and Gardner Mus.), Brescia, Cambridge (Fitzwm), Cassel, Chicago, Cincinnati, Cleveland, Copenhagen, Detroit, Dresden, Dublin, Edinburgh (NG: loan from Lord Ellesmere), the Escorial, Florence (Pitti and Uffizi), Indianapolis, Kansas City, Kremsier, Leningrad, Lentiai

near Belluno, Lille, London (NG and Wallace Coll.), Madrid (Prado), Melbourne, Milan (Brera, Ambrosiana, and Castello), Minneapolis, Munich, Naples, New York (Met. Mus., Frick Coll.), Omaha Nevada, Ottawa, Padua (Scuola del Santo and Mus.), Paris (Louvre), Philadelphia, Rome (Mus. Naz., Borghese, Capitoline), Rotterdam, San Diego Cal., San Francisco, St Louis, São Paulo, Treviso (Cath. and Mus.), Urbino, the Vatican, Venice (Accad. and widely elsewhere), Verona (Cath. and Mus.), Vienna (Akad. and K-H), Washington (NG, Nat. Coll., and Corcoran), Yale, and elsewhere. [ills. 217, 219, 221, 222, pp. 304–5. Col. pl. 14]

Tobey, Mark (*b.* 1911), was born in Centerville Wis., and originally worked as a commercial artist. He taught at Dartington Hall School, in England, 1931–8, but visited Japan and China in 1934. He was much influenced by Chinese calligraphy (taking lessons from a Chinese artist) and was also one of the first American intellectuals to become interested in Zen. From 1935 he painted abstract pictures in what is called 'white writing', based on Chinese calligraphy: the effect is reminiscent of, but more fastidious than, the calligraphy of POLLOCK. These white squiggles have been described by an admirer as: 'looping over layers of interpenetrating space . . . holding icons in a shifting web'. Since 1939 he has lived in Seattle. There are works in London (Tate) and New York (M of MA). [ill. 1092, p. 427]

Tocqué, Louis (1696–1772), was a French portrait painter who was the pupil and son-in-law of NATTIER. He admired Rigaud and Largillierre and adapted their styles, and Nattier's, to the requirements of his own time. He worked in Paris except for a trip to St Petersburg and Copenhagen (1756–9), and a second trip to Copenhagen in 1769. There are examples in Boston, Copenhagen, London (NG), Paris (Louvre), and Versailles. [ill. 735, p. 380]

Tondo (Ital. round). A circular picture. They became fashionable in Italy in the mid 15th century, although earlier examples are known.

Tone Values *see* VALUES.

Torrigiano, Pietro (1472–1528), was a Florentine sculptor who, in youth, broke the nose of Michelangelo and for this has been hated by all Florentines ever since. Cellini tells how Torrigiano, who worked in England 1511–18 on the Tombs of Lady Margaret Beaufort, Elizabeth of York, and Henry VII in Westminster Abbey, returned to Florence *c.* 1519 and offered him a job in England. 'He had stories every day of his brave deeds among those brutes of Englishmen', but in spite of the prospects Cellini, after hearing how Torrigiano broke Michelangelo's nose 'felt such a hatred for him that far from wanting to go to England with him I could not bear to look at him'. Torrigiano did return to England – his masterpiece is the Tomb of Henry VII – and then went to Seville. There, according to Vasari (who also hated him for breaking Michelangelo's nose), he fell into the hands of the Inquisition and starved himself to death from sheer spleen. There is a bust of *Henry VII* in London (V & A). [ill. 158, p. 295]

Torso. The trunk of the human body. Usually applied to a statue which lacks head, arms, and legs: the *Belvedere Torso* is a celebrated Antique statue in the Vatican.

Totentanz *see* DANCE OF DEATH.

Toulouse-Lautrec, Henri-Marie-Raymond de (1864–1901), had the misfortune to break both his legs in childhood, as a result of which he was stunted in his growth. In 1882 he began to study art seriously in Paris, and by 1885 had a studio in Montmartre. He exhibited at the Salon des Indépendants from 1889 and with Les XX in Brussels, and in 1891 his first posters brought him immediate recognition. He made his first colour prints in 1892, and held a one-man show in Paris in the following year. In 1894 he went to Brussels, and in 1895 made his first of several visits to London, where he knew Oscar Wilde and Beardsley. He held a second exhibition in 1896, and visited Holland, Portugal, and Spain, but in 1898 his health began to suffer from drink. In 1899 he spent three months in a clinic recovering from an attack of DTs, and during his convalescence he worked on a series of drawings of the circus. After his recovery, he resumed his old life, but in 1901 he broke down completely and was taken to his mother's country house, where he died.

His first teacher had encouraged him to paint animals, particularly horses; after he began studying in Paris he met Émile Bernard and van Gogh, and he was deeply influenced by the technique and subject-matter of Degas, and by Japanese prints, the influence of which was all-pervasive in Impressionist circles. His subject-matter was centred narrowly round the life he led: some portraits, many painted out of doors, scenes from dance-halls and cafés in Montmartre, such as the Moulin Rouge, or from Aristide Bruant's cabaret 'Le Mirliton', figures of actresses, female clowns, circus artists seen backstage, and a great number of nudes, either *à la* Degas – washing, dressing – or seen sitting around in brothels, waiting for customers. He loathed posed models; these naked women just walking or sitting about provided him with models in movement and under no restraint either in pose or behaviour, and to study them he lived for some time in *maisons closes*.

His technical range was very wide. He was a superb draughtsman with a gift for conveying rapid movement and the whole atmosphere of a scene with a few strokes. Most of his paintings are in spirit-thinned oil paint on unprimed cardboard, using the neutral buff tone of the board as an element in the design. He executed a large number of posters in lithography, with masterly handling of highly simplified line, large areas of flat colour, and a unique concentration on the eye-catching quality of the design. He also made small lithographs, either for menu-heads, programmes, book-covers or the like, or as single prints or series from his usual subject-matter. Occasionally he used watercolour and pastel, and towards the end of his life his use of oil paint tended to become heavier, more impasted, with more solidly painted backgrounds. He was not interested in light as were the Impressionists, but only in form and movement, and most of his works are devoid of chiaroscuro; for him, light illuminated, never enveloped. He subscribed to no theories, was a member of no artistic or aesthetic movement, and the works in which he records what he saw and understood contain no hint of comment – no pity, no sentiment, no blame, no innuendo.

There are works in most museums of Modern Art; Albi (his birthplace) has a notable collection, and the following may be particularly mentioned: London (Tate, Courtauld Inst.), Paris (Mus. de l'Impressionnisme), and Washington (NG). [ills. 778, 799, pp. 386, 389]

Tour, de la, *see* LATOUR.

Traini, Francesco, was first recorded in 1321. He was a Pisan painter much influenced by the Sienese LORENZETTI and by Giovanni PISANO's pulpit in Pisa Cathedral. He signed an altarpiece (Pisa Mus.) in 1345, and a *Glory of S. Thomas Aquinas* in Sta Caterina, Pisa, may be the picture referred to in a document of 1363. Much the most important work attributed to him is the *Triumph of Death*, a series of frescoes in the Campo Santo in Pisa. These were almost entirely destroyed in 1944, but the destruction of the top layer exposed the SINOPIE which have a strength of draughtsmanship reminiscent of Giotto. [ill. 32, p. 273]

Trecento (Ital. three hundred). The 14th century, i.e. the thirteen hundreds.

Triptych. A tripartite POLYPTYCH. Usually the central panel is twice the width of the wings, so that they can be folded over it to protect it. A common form of triptych, as an object of private devotion, is to have a *Madonna* as the centre and one's patron Saints on the wings: the backs of the wings, which become visible when the triptych is shut, usually bear the owner's coat of arms.

Trompe-l'œil (Fr. deceive the eye) *see* ILLUSIONISM.

Troy, Jean-François de (1679–1752), was a French painter, first of classical subjects like LE MOYNE, then of *fêtes galantes* and hunting scenes, and of the elaborate breakfasts and picnics that accompanied them. He also designed two large series of Gobelins tapestries – the *History of Queen Esther* and *Jason and Medea* – and painted some religious subjects, such as Susanna, that afforded opportunities for the nude. He was the son of François de Troy (1645–1730), a Toulouse portrait painter who sent him to Italy at the age of 14. The influence of Venice was permanent. From 1738 to 1751 he was Director of the French Academy in Rome, and, when he was replaced, died of grief at the thought of leaving a young Roman woman with whom he had just fallen in love. His style incorporates the colour and realism of Rubens's hunts, Snyders's animals and still-life, with the pastoral quality of the best Watteau followers – i.e. he is a particularly good example of RUBÉNISME. There are pictures in Paris (Louvre, Carnavalet, and S. Étienne du Mont), Toulouse, Versailles, and other French provincial museums, Florence (Uffizi), Leningrad, London (NG, V & A, Wallace Coll.), New York (Met. Mus.), and Rotterdam. [ill. 704, p. 377]

Trumbull, John (1756–1843), was an American artist who fought in the War of Independence, after which (1780) he travelled to London and Paris and worked with WEST. He painted principally portraits and historical pictures of the War of Independence, well represented in American museums. His *Battle of Bunker's Hill, 1775,* was painted in London in the studio of the loyalist West; rather to his surprise no English engraver would reproduce it. His 'Autobiography' was published in 1841 (and again in 1953). [ill. 890, p. 400]

Tura, Cosmè (Cosimo) (before 1431–95), was the first great Ferrarese painter. He worked there from 1451 for the Este Court, but much of his production has been lost. The main influence on his style was MANTEGNA, and perhaps also Mantegna's own inspirer Donatello, and the wiry quality of the forms and the austerity of feeling persists in all the Ferrarese painters of the 15th century – Cossa, Costa, and above all Ercole ROBERTI. Curiously, the very different world of Piero della Francesca also plays a strong part in Tura's stylistic evolution, most probably through the frescoes, now lost, which Piero painted in Ferrara some time before 1450. His brittle and metallic sense of form hardly changed during his lifetime, but he was succeeded as Court Painter by Roberti in 1486 and died poor. There are works in Ajaccio, Bergamo, Berlin, Boston (Gardner), Caen, Cambridge (Fitwm), and Cambridge Mass. (Fogg), Ferrara (Pinac. and Cath.), Florence (Uffizi), London (NG), Milan (Brera, Poldi-Pezzoli), Modena, Nantes, New York (Met. Mus.), Paris (Louvre), Philadelphia (Johnson), San Diego Cal., Venice (Accad., Correr), Vienna, and Washington (NG). [ill. 129, p. 290]

Turner, Joseph Mallord William (1775–1851), was the son of a barber and born in Maiden Lane, Covent Garden. His talent was precocious. He was admitted to the Royal Academy Schools in 1789 and first exhibited at the RA in 1791: throughout his life he was much indebted to the RA, which recognized his genius and supported him against many of the arbiters of taste. He became an ARA in 1799, RA in 1802 – at the age of 27 – Professor of Perspective in 1807, and Deputy President in 1845. His extremely good head for business caused him to be appointed to audit the finances for many years. In 1792 Turner made the first of the sketching tours that were to take up so much of his time for the next half-century. Soon after this, for three years in the mid 90s he worked with GIRTIN at Dr MONRO's house, Girtin drawing the outlines and Turner washing in the effects. After the death of Girtin Turner is said to have remarked 'If Tom Girtin had lived I should have starved': apart from the element of exaggeration in this, it is probably true that, at this stage, Girtin was the leader and Turner imitated him so closely that it is not always possible to distinguish the watercolours of the one from those of the other. Up to *c.* 1796 Turner was exclusively a watercolourist, working in the topographical tradition, but in 1796 or 1797 he exhibited his first oil-paintings at the RA; the two which he showed in 1797 being markedly influenced by Dutch 17th century marine painting (the *Millbank, moonlight,* now in the Tate Gall., is close to the moonlight scenes of A. van der Neer). This influence was almost immediately succeeded by that of Wilson and Claude, and, early in the 1800s, he was composing in a Grand Manner learned ultimately from Claude. In 1802, with scores of other artists, he went to see the pictures looted by Napoleon which were then exhibited in the Louvre, and there he particularly admired Poussin. His next major work, however, was the *Calais Pier* of 1803 (now in the NG), which is very unlike Poussin, is thoroughly Romantic, and was generally condemned as unfinished. For many years after this Turner was bitterly attacked, principally by Sir George Beaumont, the artistic dictator of the day, and warmly defended, by Sir Thomas LAWRENCE among others. These attacks led to a decline in sales in his larger oil-paintings (*Crossing the Brook*, 1815: London, NG is a case in point) and in 1816 his landscapes were actually called 'pictures of nothing, and very like'. Turner himself, in one of his few recorded epigrams, is said to have remarked of painting in general that it was 'a rum thing', but between 1806 and 1819 he did take steps to defend himself by publishing a series of engravings of different kinds of landscape under the title 'Liber Studiorum' (*see* LIBER VERITATIS). The series was not successful, principally because Turner was always very close with his money and underpaid the engravers. In 1819, encouraged by Lawrence, he made his first visit to Italy and from then on his oil-paintings tend more and more to the pale brilliance of colour which he had already achieved in watercolour and he begins to think in terms of coloured light, or, in Constable's phrase, 'tinted steam'. He returned to Italy in 1828 and to Venice in 1835 and again in 1840, the late Venetian watercolours and gouaches being among the most magical effects of light even in his work. By this time he was rather out of favour and public interest was turning to the detailed approach that culminated in the Pre-Raphaelites, when, rather to his surprise, Ruskin came to his defence with the first volume of 'Modern Painters' in 1843 (the full title is: 'Modern Painters: their superiority in the art of landscape painting to all the ancient masters proved by examples of the True, the Beautiful, and the Intellectual, from the works of modern artists, especially from those of J. M. W. Turner, Esq., RA'). By his will Turner left nearly 300 paintings and nearly 20,000 watercolours and drawings to the nation: his conditions have been scandalously disregarded but the principal collections remain those in London (NG, Tate Gall., and BM), with others in the V & A, Nat. Marit. Mus., and Kenwood, and in Auckland NZ, Boston (Mus.), Cambridge (Fitzwm), and Cambridge Mass. (Fogg Mus.), Cardiff, Chicago, Cleveland, Dublin, Dunedin, Edinburgh (NG), Hartford Conn. (Wadsworth Atheneum), Indianapolis (Herron), Manchester (City Art Gall., and Whitworth), Melbourne, New York (Met. Mus., Frick Coll.), Ohio, Ottawa (NG), Oxford, Philadelphia, Sheffield, Washington (NG, Corcoran), and elsewhere. [ills. 932, 935, 936, pp. 405, 407. Col. pl. 47]

U

Uccello, Paolo (1396/7–1475), is celebrated in the early sources as a master of perspective; indeed, the invention of it is sometimes wrongly credited to him. What is clear is that he became absorbed in the study of perspective (and, still more, foreshortening) and that it modified his style in his middle years, but he never used it for the naturalist purposes envisaged by MASACCIO and others. Uccello is first recorded as a *garzone* in 1407, in the shop where GHIBERTI's First Baptistry Doors were being made and this semi-Gothic style was to remain the foundation of his own. In 1415 he entered the Painters' Guild, but nothing is known of any paintings by him for about another 15 years. In 1425 he went to Venice and worked on mosaics in S. Mark's for about 5 years. He was certainly in Florence again in 1431, but he had been out of the city during the years when Masaccio created the new, naturalistic style which was later to influence him in a rather superficial way. In 1436 he was commissioned by the city to paint the fresco in imitation of an equestrian statue to the English mercenary soldier Sir John Hawkwood, known in Italy as Giovanni Acuto. This fresco is still in the Cathedral of Florence, but it was repainted by Uccello himself, since the first version failed to please. In it we see for the first time the intensive study of the new science of foreshortening, since the intention is to deceive the eye into thinking that the painted statue is a real one: in fact, Uccello never really carried out the full implications of a perspective setting, since the plinth and the effigy are seen from two disparate viewpoints, and this inconsistency is usual in all his works. He was able to make another experiment in foreshortening in the *Four Prophets* (1443) round the clockface in the Cathedral, and between 1443 and 1445 he designed stained-glass windows for it. About 1445 he went to Padua, and the *Giants* he painted there are supposed to have influenced MANTEGNA, but they are now lost. On his return, *c.* 1445, he painted his most famous work, *The Deluge* in the Chiostro Verde of Sta Maria Novella, Florence, where he had already painted some Creation scenes (from *c.* 1431). The *Deluge* (recently restored, previously almost lost) shows the impact of the new ideas on perspective at their most powerful, and it is often related to the treatise on painting by the humanist Alberti ('Della Pittura', 1435), where a system of perspective construction is explained and several subjects are suggested which are to be found in the *Deluge*. Similar ideas on foreshortening may be found in the three *Battles* (1454/7: Florence (Uffizi), London (NG), and Paris (Louvre)), which he painted for the Medici, but here the decorative aspect is far more important and in all his later works the decorative side of his early training comes back strongly. His last documented work is the *predella* for an altarpiece, commissioned by an Urbino Confraternity of the Holy Sacrament (1465–9: Urbino), see JOOS van Gent: a *Hunt* (Oxford, Ashmolean) which is equally decorative in character and fairy-tale in atmosphere is probably of the same date. In 1469, in filling in his tax return he said: 'I am old, infirm, and unemployed, and my wife is ill.'

Other works are in Chambéry, Dublin, Florence (S. Martino alla Scala), London (NG), Paris (Louvre, Mus. Jacquemart-André), and Washington (NG). [ills. 67–9, p. 278]

Ugolino da Siena (active 1317–27), was a close follower of DUCCIO. He painted the High Altar of Sta Croce, Florence, now dispersed: parts of it are in London (NG) and Berlin and Philadelphia (Johnson). Other pictures attributed to him are in Birmingham (Barber Inst.), Cleveland Ohio, London (Courtauld Inst.), St Louis, Siena, and Washington. [ill. 38, p. 275]

'Ugolino-Lorenzetti'. An invented name for an unknown artist midway between the styles of UGOLINO da Siena and the LORENZETTI. Also known as the Ovile Master, he has been tentatively identified with Bartolommeo Bulgarini (active 1345, *d.* 1378), who is known to have been a painter. [ill. 39, p. 275]

Underpainting is the preliminary lay-in, usually in GRISAILLE, in which the drawing, composition, and tone values of a picture are worked out. It may sometimes include an indication of colour, but the purpose of underpainting is to get the design and tonal values established before tackling the colouristic problems, particularly if many GLAZES are envisaged. The underpainting of a specific area can mean, in a narrower sense, the preparation for a glaze – e.g. a solid yellow which is to be glazed with red and purple to get a richer effect of shot colours and in shadows. [ill. 106, p. 286. Col. pl. 41]

Utrecht School. This is a fairly precisely defined moment in Dutch painting, early in the 17th century, when the influence of CARAVAGGIO made its impact on a whole circle of Utrecht painters, of whom the most important were BABUREN, HONTHORST, and TERBRUGGHEN. All three were in Rome in the period 1610/20, at the moment immediately after Caravaggio's death when his influence was at its highest and was then being exploited by MANFREDI. All three returned to Utrecht by the 1620s. They painted religious pictures – Utrecht is a Catholic centre – and also genre scenes of the Five Senses and brothel pictures, unlike Caravaggio's work (but like Manfredi's), though stemming from his relentless realism.

Towards the end of the 1620s the effect began to wear off and Terbrugghen in particular began to lighten his palette (e.g. *Jacob and Laban*, 1627: London, NG) and to study light effects in a totally un-Caravaggesque way. Bylert, Bor, and Stomer were more or less influenced by Utrecht ideas, although Bylert changed his style and Stomer remained in Italy. The spread of Caravaggism through the Utrecht School was such that even Hals, Vermeer, and Rembrandt were affected by it. [ills. 458–64, pp. 338–9]

Utrillo, Maurice (1883–1955), was the son of Suzanne Valadon, herself a talented painter who was encouraged by Renoir, Degas, and Toulouse-Lautrec, for whom she posed as a model. He early developed into a confirmed drunkard and drug addict, spent many years in clinics and sanatoria, and his drinking bouts often ended in the police station. His mother made him learn to paint as a distraction and a form of therapy. His art shows nothing of this wild and melodramatic background. His paintings are almost all town views, often painted from picture-postcards; they show a sensitive understanding of tone, are delicate and almost monochromatic in colour, with precise drawing and a strange feeling for the atmosphere of a particular street or building. His best works were produced between 1908 and 1916: success made him repeat himself. Most museums of Modern Art have an example. [ill. 791, p. 388]

Uytewael *see* WTEWAEL.

V

Valdés Leal, Juan de (1622–90), was a painter active in Seville where he helped to found the Academy in 1660. He was President 1663–6, but his difficult temperament made it impossible for him to get on with his fellow-artists. His style is dramatic and emotional to the point of morbidity and is seen at its best in VANITAS subjects such as the *Triumph of Death* and the *Sic Transit Gloria Mundi*, with their decomposing corpses. There are works by him in Cordova and Seville, and in Barnard Castle (Bowes Mus.), Dresden, Dublin, Grenoble, Hartford Conn., Kansas City, London (NG), Madrid (Prado), New York (Hispanic Soc.), Paris (Louvre), Washington (NG), and York. [ill. 645, p. 365]

Valentin, Le (Moïse Valentin, Valentin de Boullogne) (*c.* 1591 or 1594–1632), was a French painter, born at Coulommiers, but was perhaps the son of an Italian (neither his Christian name Moïse nor the de Boullogne seems to be correct); certainly he was, like Finsonius, more of an Italian than a Northern painter. He was in Rome perhaps as early as 1612/13, certainly by 1614, and was there strongly influenced by VOUET, whose pupil he may have been, and perhaps even more by MANFREDI and the Caravaggio influence he represents. Valentin became a friend of Poussin and his only documented work, the *Martyrdom of SS. Processus and Martinian* (1629/30: Vatican) was a pendant to Poussin's *S. Erasmus* in St Peter's. There are pictures attributed to him in Besançon, Cambridge (Fitzwm), Cologne, Dresden, Gateshead, London (NG), Munich, Paris (Louvre), Poughkeepsie NY (Vassar College), Rome (Gall. Naz.), Toulouse, Versailles, and Vienna. [ill. 407, p. 329]

Values (Fr. *valeurs*) are the gradations of tone from light to dark observable in any solid object under the play of light. Tone values are independent of local colour and are best perceived by half-closing the eyes so that colour effects are diminished (a photograph is an example of pure tonal effect). Since it is impossible to match the range from light to dark in nature with pigments ranging only from white to black, the greatest skill is necessary to determine where the transitional tones shall be modified, suppressed, or exaggerated so as to maintain pictorial unity. The problem is complicated by Colour Values, when the relative importance to the composition as a whole of each patch of colour has to be determined simultaneously with its tonal value, one often interacting on the other. 'Keeping' is an old-fashioned word, frequent in 18th-century criticism, signifying success in this operation.

Vandyke *see* DYCK.

Vanishing Point *see* PERSPECTIVE.

Vanitas *see* STILL-LIFE.

Vanloo *see* LOO.

Vansomer *see* SOMER.

Variant. Generally used to mean a version of a picture which has slight differences, perhaps intended by the artist. The assumption is that a variant is at least from the studio of the painter of the prime original, but it is often a convenient euphemism for a copy.

Varley, John (1778–1842), was an English watercolour painter of the transitional period between the topographical drawing and the painting in watercolours. He was helped at the beginning of his career by Dr MONRO, and in his turn helped and taught many other artists: he was also a close friend of Blake. He seems to have been very credulous and he wrote on astrology, in which he firmly believed. There are works in London (BM, Tate, and V & A). His brothers Cornelius (1781–1873) and William (*c.* 1785–1856) were also painters and are represented in the V & A. [ill. 924, p. 405]

Vasari, Giorgio (1511–74), was born in Arezzo and trained in Florence in the circle of Andrea del Sarto and his pupils Rosso and Pontormo, and where, above all, he became a Michelangelo idolater. He spent his busy and productive life as a painter between Florence and Rome, but he was really a superb impresario rather than a painter himself, and perhaps because of his gifts in this direction his work as an architect ranks much higher than his painting. His principal paintings are in Florence (Pal. Vecchio frescoes and in galleries) and Rome (Sala Regia in the Vatican, and the so-called 100 days fresco in the Cancelleria), as well as in his own house in Arezzo, which is now a museum. Above all, however, his fame rests solidly on his book 'Le Vite de' più eccellenti Architetti, Pittori, et Scultori Italiani . . .' first published in 1550 and issued in a second, much enlarged, edition in 1568. This 1568 edition has been translated into most languages and is perhaps the most important book on the history of art ever written, both as a source-book and as an example for all the later Italian historiographers. By comparison the 1550 edition is little-known, but the differences between it and the second edition are not all in the latter's favour; in the first edition the plan is much clearer, for in it Vasari's intention is plain – to show how the arts died in the Dark Ages, after having been brought to a high pitch in Ancient Rome, and were then revived under Giotto the Tuscan, to progress in a steady rise in Tuscany, until the ultimate perfection was reached in his own day in the hands of the Tuscan Michelangelo. In the 1550 edition MICHELANGELO is the climax of the story and his is the only biography of a living artist. The later edition is less sure in design and includes a number of living artists, including Vasari's own autobiography. [ill. 197, p. 302]

Vecchietta (1412–80), was a Sienese sculptor who also worked as a painter and architect. He was a pupil of SASSETTA and the teacher of MATTEO di Giovanni. His style is expressive, naturalistic, and linear, with strong Florentine influences. His works are mostly in Siena, but there are others in Florence (Uffizi), Liverpool, New York (Frick), Paris (Louvre, Cluny Mus.), Pienza (Cath.), and Rome (SM del Popolo). [ills. 91, 114, pp. 283, 288]

Veduta (Ital. view). A painting or drawing of a place, usually a town e.g. Venice or Rome. The accuracy of the delineation varies greatly: a *veduta ideata* is an imaginary view, while a CAPRICCIO is often architecturally accurate but fantastic in its juxtapositions. PANINI and PIRANESI, CANALETTO and GUARDI are the best-known *vedutisti*, but the genre was probably invented by Northern artists working in Italy, e.g. BRILL.

Vehicle is synonymous with MEDIUM, as something to bind pigment or to thin stiff paint.

Velazquez, Diego Rodriguez de Silva (1599–1660), was born in Seville but was of Portuguese origin. Any training he may have had before entering PACHECO's Academy in Seville in 1613 may be disregarded; in 1617 he became an independent master and in 1618 married Pacheco's daughter. He worked in Seville until 1622 and his early paintings show his interest in the naturalistic representation of things seen in strong light. In 1622 he visited Madrid, and in 1623 returned there to become Court Painter. He was a slow worker, with a deliberate technique without bravura, sober colour rather low in tone, and used a plain background for many of his portraits so that the figure stands out as a silhouette. His Court appointment gave him few opportunities for religious painting; mythologies were rare in Spain and only occasionally did he execute subject pictures, except during his Italian journeys. He was little influenced by other artists, though he profited from the Titians in the Spanish Royal Collection and the visit of Rubens in 1628, which was his first contact with a great living painter, who was also a Court Painter, though one with an entirely different vision, temperament, and artistic education. Whether or not it was Rubens who inspired him to visit Italy, it was due to Rubens's influence that he obtained permission to go. He left in August 1629, visited Genoa, Venice, Rome, and Naples (where he met Ribera) and returned to Madrid in 1631. The *Topers* (*Los Borrachos*; in the Spanish Royal Collection by July 1629), with its character heads and still-life detail, suggests the influence of RIBERA's realism, and the subject pictures painted in Italy (*Joseph's coat brought to Jacob*, Escorial, and the *Forge of Vulcan*, Prado) show his preoccupation with the male nude and his fuller range of colour. The main effect of his Italian

journey was to increase his breadth of vision, but without affecting its fundamentally realistic basis.

The surrender of Breda – an incident in the Dutch Wars of Independence – took place in 1625. In 1634, Velazquez recorded the moment when the Marchese Spinola (whom he had known in Italy in 1629) received the surrender from Justin of Nassau, as one of a series of victory pictures (others were by Maino and Zurbarán) intended to accompany his equestrian portraits of Philip, his Queen, and his heir, Don Balthasar Carlos. Velazquez's composition may owe something to Tempesta's engravings after van Veen in the 'Bataviorum cum Romanis Bellum' of Tacitus, published in Antwerp in 1612, but his brilliant colour, panoramic landscape background, and heightened realism transcend any derivation. Portraits painted after his return possibly owe their more brilliant colour to their being the record of the only joyous years in the King's dreary reign – the portrait of the King called *The Fraga Philip* (1644: Frick Collection, New York) has a richness reminiscent of Rubens.

In 1648 Velazquez accompanied the Embassy travelling to Italy to escort the new Queen, Marianna of Austria. He again visited Genoa, Venice, Rome, and Naples, and returned to Madrid in June 1651. His object had been to buy pictures for the Royal Collection, and he also executed several works during his stay: the portrait of Pope Innocent X (Doria Coll., Rome), and his only female nude, the so-called *Rokeby Venus* (London, NG), were the most outstanding. The finest of the portraits painted after the second Italian journey is that of the little Infanta Margareta Teresa with her retinue of ladies and dwarfs, called *Las Meninas* (1656: Prado), and in this work he reaches perhaps his highest point in the blending of realism with atmosphere and a deeply sensitive appreciation of character. During the 1630s and 1640s he had painted a series of portraits of the Court dwarfs, playmates of the Royal children, for they interested him as character studies much as old age, wrinkles, and rags interested him in his imaginary portraits of *Aesop* and *Menippus* (both in the Prado), and as did, too, the ageing face of his sick and gloomy King, whom he painted all through his long reign, and who acknowledged the greatness of his painter by making him a Knight of the Order of Santiago in 1658. His chief assistant was his son-in-law MAZO, but he was far from his equal, and after Velazquez's death his position was held by a succession of dim foreigners, mostly French, until, late in the 18th century, Mengs and Tiepolo were followed by Goya.

There are unrivalled collections in Spain – in the Prado in Madrid and in the Escorial – but most major galleries have an example including Berlin, Boston (Mus. and Gardner Mus.), Budapest, Chicago, Cincinnati, Detroit, Dresden, Florence (Pitti), Kansas City, London (NG, Wallace Coll., Wellington Mus.), Montreal, New York (Met. Mus., Hispanic Soc., Frick Coll.), Paris (Louvre), São Paulo, San Diego Calif., Toledo Ohio, Vienna, and Washington (NG). [ills. 653–8, p. 368. Col. pl. 17]

Velde, Adriaen van de (1636–72), was the son of Willem I van de Velde, the brother of Willem II, and probably the nephew of Esaias. He was trained under his father and under WYNANTS and POTTER. It is doubtful whether he ever went to Italy, but he uses Italian motives and landscapes (e.g. in the Wallace Coll. *Jacob and Laban*); he also painted a few religious subjects without landscape (e.g. the *Annunciation* in Amsterdam), but most of his works are pastoral landscapes with figures or simply the figures in the landscapes of other painters. He painted figures for his elder brother Willem II, for his master Wynants, and for Ruisdael, Hobbema, and others, especially van der Heyden. This last died in 1712, yet nearly all his works are described as having Adriaen's figures, although dated pictures painted after Adriaen's early death prove that van der Heyden was quite capable of adding his own figures. There are pictures in the Royal Coll. and in Amsterdam, Antwerp, Berlin, Boston, Cambridge (Fitzwm), Dresden, Florence (Uffizi), Frankfurt, Glasgow, The Hague, Leipzig, London (NG, Wallace Coll., Dulwich), Munich, New York (Hist. Soc.), Paris (Petit Pal.), Philadelphia, Rotterdam, Vienna, and Washington. [ill. 432, p. 333]

Velde, Esaias van de (*c.* 1591–1630), was a painter of genre and battle pictures, but is best known for his realistic landscapes which presage those of his great pupil Jan van GOYEN. He worked in Haarlem 1610–18 and then in The Hague, where he was Court Painter to the Princes Maurits and Frederik Hendrik, until his death. There are pictures in Amsterdam (Rijksmus.), Berlin, The Hague, Leipzig, London (NG), Munich, Rotterdam, Stockholm, and elsewhere. [ill. 497, p. 344]

Velde, Willem I van de (1611–93), and his son Willem (1633–1707), both arrived in London in 1672 and remained there as official marine artists. It is extremely difficult to separate the works of the two, and a document of 1674 which provides for regular payment to the father for drawing sea-fights and to his son for colouring them suggests that they worked together. There are, however, some elaborate grisaille drawings on a large scale that are certainly the elder man's work, while there are over 600 pictures of marine subjects attributed to the younger, who is generally recognized as the greatest marine painter of the Dutch School as well as the father of all English marine painting. Most of their records of sea-fights were done from drawings made under fire from a small boat in the thick of the action: there is a very large and important collection of these in the Nat. Marit. Mus., London, which also has paintings. Other paintings are in the Royal Coll. and in Amsterdam (Rijksmus.), and London (NG, Wallace Coll., Kenwood, and Ham House). [ills. 499, 501, p. 345]

Veneziano, Domenico, *see* DOMENICO.

Vermeer, Jan (1632–75), of Delft, was the most calm and peaceful of all the Dutch masters and the recognition of his greatness has been long delayed. Very little is known of his life and his pictures were completely forgotten until the mid 19th century. He was certainly influenced by Carel FABRITIUS, and may have been his pupil before becoming a Master himself in the Delft Guild in 1653. He married in the same year, was Dean of the Guild in 1663 and 1670 and died in 1675, leaving a widow and eleven children and an enormous debt to the baker, who held two pictures of his. In 1676 his widow tried to get them

back, offering to pay off the debt over twelve years. Later that year she was declared bankrupt. It is certain that she and the children were Catholics, and this may explain the relative obscurity in which Vermeer lived. He was obviously a very slow worker, for only about 40 pictures are generally accepted as his and most of them are quite small. They usually represent domestic interiors with one or two figures writing, doing housework, or playing musical instruments; in reproduction they look exactly like works by Maes or Pieter de Hooch, but in the originals the splendour of the colour and the play of light, falling in little pearls of paint on everything in the picture, transform the everyday scenes into poetry totally unlike the sober prose of the average Dutch master. There are some pictures, such as the *Allegory of Faith* (New York, Met. Mus.) or the *Allegory of Painting* (Vienna, K-H Mus.), which represents the painter in his studio, that go beyond the domestic interior and these form a link with a small group of totally different scenes. One, the *Procuress* (Dresden), is signed and dated 1656 and is the only dated work by him. This is clearly an early work and shows a link – though not a very strong one – with the UTRECHT School, as does the *Christ in the House of Martha and Mary* (Edinburgh, NG), presumably also early. The third and most puzzling is the *Diana and her Companions* (The Hague, Mauritshuis) which is unlike all his other works and has, accordingly, been attributed to another Vermeer, an Utrecht painter (*c.* 1630–88) who had been in Italy. (The signature on it, partially visible in 1895 is now almost illegible.) There are pictures by him in the Royal Coll., and in Amsterdam (Rijksmus.), Berlin, Boston (Gardner), Brunswick, Dresden, Edinburgh, Frankfurt (Städel), The Hague, London (NG, Kenwood), New York (Met. Mus., Frick Coll.), Paris (Louvre), Vienna (K-H Mus.), and Washington (NG). [ills. 519, 520, p. 347. Col. pl. 23]

Vermeyen, Jan Cornelisz. (*c.* 1500–59), was a Dutch painter and tapestry designer who was probably a pupil of MABUSE. About 1525 he became Court Painter to Margaret of Austria, Regent of the Netherlands, at Malines and in 1535 he accompanied the Emperor Charles V to Tunis. This journey supplied him with scenes for later works, including tapestries designed 1545/8 for the Regent, Mary of Hungary. At present many portraits are ascribed to him on very little evidence, as an alternative to SCOREL, HEEMSKERCK, or LUCAS van Leyden. There are pictures in Amsterdam, Brussels, Florence, Haarlem, New York, Vienna (tapestry designs), and (as Style of 'Vermeyen') London, and elsewhere. [ills. 357, 358, p. 324]

Vernet. A family of French painters of whom the best known were: Claude-Joseph (1714–89) who painted landscapes in a sub-Claude manner and worked for many years in Italy, where he was a friend of Wilson. He was commissioned by Louis XV to paint the *Ports of France*, of which he executed 16. He also painted dramatic shipwrecks of a highly romantic and rather theatrical kind. His father and three brothers were also painters. Carle, son of Joseph (1758–1836), specialized in horses, racing, and battle scenes, the latter principally for Napoleon. Horace, son of Carle (1789–1863), also painted horses and battle scenes, as popular and facile as his father's. He remained an ardent Bonapartist, and his chief work was the huge Gallery of Battles at Versailles, painted for Louis-Philippe. His sister married the costume-history painter Paul Delaroche. [ills. 753, 767, 768, pp. 384, 386]

Verona, Stefano da, *see* STEFANO.

Veronese, Bonifazio, *see* BONIFAZIO.

Veronese, Paolo (*c.* 1528–88), was born in Verona and trained under several minor artists, but the chief influence on him was Titian although such diverse artists as Michelangelo, Giulio Romano, and Parmigianino all contributed to his formation. He worked in Venice, probably from 1553 onwards, when he began his ceilings for the Doge's Palace, with daring SOTTO IN SÙ perspective and Mannerist nude figures in complicated poses filling up the picture space. He is thought to have gone to Rome for the first time in 1560, and it was probably after this that he painted the frescoes in the Villa Maser (near Vicenza), with their brilliant mixture of illusionism with Palladio's simple architecture. They are also important in the history of Venetian landscape painting.

He specialized mainly in huge pictures of Biblical, allegorical, or historical subjects which permitted of the introduction of vast crowds of accessory figures, filling the scene with light and colour, with splendid golden-haired women dressed in the height of fashion, with horses, dogs, apes, courtiers, musicians, soldiers, and magnificent buildings, but devoid of religious or dramatic content. His gorgeous pageantry is redolent of the magnificence and richness of 16th-century Venice; but the licence he took with sacred subjects (e.g. the *Feast in the House of Levi*, Venice, Accad.) got him into trouble with the Inquisition, which in 1573 called him to account for the profane incidents – dogs, German soldiers, and such things – introduced into a religious picture. His repudiation of any impropriety and his claim to an absolute right of pictorial licence has remained one of the classic defences of the artist against the Philistine (even though the Inquisitor seems to have out-argued him). Most of his works are in Venice, but other examples are in the Royal Coll. and Amsterdam, Baltimore (Mus. and Walters Gall.), Berlin, Boston (Mus. and Gardner Mus.), Brussels, Caen, Cambridge (Fitzwm) and Cambridge Mass. (Fogg Mus.), Chicago, Cleveland, Detroit, Dresden, Dublin, Edinburgh, the Escorial, Florence (Pitti and Uffizi), Greenville SC, Hartford Conn., Kansas City, Leningrad, London (NG, Courtauld Inst., Dulwich, Westminster Hospital), Madrid, Melbourne, Milan (Brera), Modena, Munich, New York (Met. Mus. and Frick Coll.), Ottawa, Oxford, Padua, Paris (Louvre), Philadelphia, Rome (Borghese, Capitoline), San Francisco, St Louis, Sarasota Fla (Ringling), Verona, Vicenza, Vienna, Washington (NG), and elsewhere. [ills. 233, 235, p. 307]

Verrio, Antonio (1639–1707), was a Neapolitan painter who was an Agréé of the French Academy in 1671, and probably came to England in the next year. From about 1675 to 1684 he worked at Windsor and Whitehall (though little survives), and succeeded Lely as Court Painter in 1684. After 1688 he worked chiefly at Chatsworth and Burghley, but from 1699 he was employed extensively at Hampton Court and Windsor by Queen Anne. His decora-

tions are gaudy and banal; they represent the tail-end of a Baroque tradition sufficiently novel in England to impress through pretentiousness, and blatant enough to dazzle eyes ignorant of the real thing. His greatest immortality is in Pope's 'On painted ceilings you devoutly stare, Where sprawl the saints of Verrio and LAGUERRE'. [ill. 276, p. 313]

Verrocchio, Andrea del (*c.* 1435–88), was a Florentine painter, goldsmith, and sculptor. He was perhaps a pupil of Donatello, after whose death he ranked as the principal sculptor in the city. He executed many works for the Medici. His style as a sculptor is clearly established and is markedly different from that of Donatello, for Verrocchio is intent upon lightness, grace, and elegance of pose and highly finished craftsmanship, completely missing the tragic power of Donatello. The *David* (before 1476: Florence, Bargello), if compared with Donatello's bronze *David* shows this difference; even more is it visible in Verrocchio's last work, the equestrian monument to Bartolommeo Colleone in Venice (commissioned *c.* 1479, completed after Verrocchio's death), where all his effort has been directed to the rendering of movement and of a sense of strain and energy. The Donatello monument to Gattamelata in Padua was obviously the model he sought to surpass, but he misses the air of calm command. Verrocchio ran a large and prosperous shop, accepting orders for paintings as well as sculpture and goldsmith's work. In later years his principal assistant in painting was Lorenzo di CREDI, but he was also the master (and probably employer) of LEONARDO da Vinci, who is supposed to have painted an Angel in the *Baptism* (Florence, Uffizi). There are works by him, in painting or sculpture, in Berlin, Budapest, Florence (Bargello, Cathedral Mus., Orsanmichele, S. Lorenzo, and the Pal. della Signoria), London (NG, V & A), New York (Met. Mus.), Paris (Louvre), Pistoia (Cath.), Sheffield (Ruskin Mus.), and Washington (NG). [ills. 95, 98, pp. 283–4]

Vertue, George (1684–1756), was an engraver and antiquary who is now remembered as the father of English art history. His voluminous, ill-written, and rambling notes on the arts in England, especially on his immediate predecessors and his contemporaries, are our principal source and have now been published *in extenso*. They were originally bought by Horace Walpole, and, reduced to order, served as the basis of his 'Anecdotes of Painting in England' (1762–71). [ill. 828, p. 393]

Vesperbild *see* PIETÀ.

Vien, Joseph (1716–1809), was a French painter who was in Rome 1743–50; he probably knew the young MENGS at that time, when all Rome was excited by the Antique Roman paintings newly discovered in Herculaneum and Pompeii, and by Greek classical architecture at Paestum. This revival of interest in the Antique made him the more receptive to Winckelmann's Neoclassicist ideas on their publication in 1755 and 1764, an influence reinforced by his long and close association with the amateur archaeologist, the Comte de Caylus. His cold, prim, classical genre subjects, depict Greek maidens of whom Diderot remarked that they induced 'no desire to be their lover, only their father or brother', yet he achieved enormous prestige, and was the chief teacher of the period; his most celebrated pupil was DAVID. [ill. 741, p. 382]

Vigée-Lebrun, Louise Élisabeth (1755–1842), one of the most successful of all women painters, was the daughter of a pastellist named Vigée and married the dealer Lebrun. She was trained by her father and influenced by GREUZE, and got her great chance when she was summoned to Versailles in 1779 to paint Marie-Antoinette. She became her friend as well as Painter to the Queen, was elected to the Academy in 1783, and kept a famous Salon. She was in fact a charming woman. She left France in 1789, at the outbreak of the Revolution, and went to Italy, Vienna, Prague, Dresden, and was in Russia 1795–1800 before returning to Berlin and, in 1802, to Paris. She had received permission to return but disliked society under Napoleon and left at once for England, where she stayed until 1805, before going to Switzerland and so back to France. In all these countries she had great success as a portraitist, excelling in portraits of women and children. She wrote her Memoirs, which give a picture of the times as well as an account of her works (they were first published in 1835–7: two English translations exist). Her portraits may be found in most of the places she worked in and there are other examples in London (Wallace Coll. and NG) and in New York (Met. Mus.). [ill. 737, p. 381]

Villon, Jacques (1875–1963). His full name was Gaston Duchamp-Villon, and he was the brother of Marcel DUCHAMP and Raymond DUCHAMP-VILLON. He went to Paris in 1895 and became a friend of Toulouse-Lautrec, making satirical drawings for illustrated papers (later he earned his living as an engraver). He became a Cubist in 1911, and in 1912 organized the Section d'Or Exhibition (see GOLDEN SECTION) with GLEIZES, METZINGER, LÉGER, and La Fresnaye. He visited the US in 1935 and began gradually to make a name, but in 1940, when he fled to the Tarn in Southern France, he began painting landscapes which, though abstract, have a feeling for locality. Big exhibitions in 1951 and 1961 in Paris established his reputation. There are works in Paris (Mus. d'Art Mod.). [ill. 1050, p. 422]

Villon, Raymond Duchamp-Villon, *see* DUCHAMP-VILLON.

Vinci, Leonardo da, *see* LEONARDO.

Vingt, Les ('Les XX'), were 20 painters, including ENSOR, who formed an exhibiting society in Brussels in 1884 which lasted for ten years and showed non-Belgian artists such as Seurat (1887, *Grande Jatte*), Gauguin (1889), Cézanne, and van Gogh (1890), but rejected Ensor in 1889.

Vischer. A Nuremberg family of bronze-workers and sculptors, the most celebrated of whom, Peter I and II, were Dürer's contemporaries. The family workshop was started by Hermann (*d.* 1488), who was the father of Peter I (*c.* 1460–1529). Peter was trained by his father and became a Master in 1489, after which he travelled to Heidelberg and Cracow, but not to Italy, although the influence of Renaissance ideas can be seen in his work, though far less powerfully than in Dürer. The real problem concerns the exact shares of the various members of the family in their masterpiece, the Shrine of S. Sebaldus in Nuremberg. The first design (now in Vienna, Akad.) is signed by Peter I and dated 1488, but the actual work was begun, on a new design, in 1508, worked on for four years and then completed 1514–19. After 1512, Peter I was working on a Tomb at Innsbruck for the Emperor Maximilian, and it is likely that his sons, Hermann and Peter II, took an increasing share in the Sebaldus Shrine, especially in the second phase: nevertheless, the *Apostles* may be by him. The most important of his sons was Peter II (1487–1528), who may have visited Italy and who did the statuettes on the Sebaldus Shrine. [ill. 625, p. 361]

Vittoria, Alessandro (1525–1608), was the pupil of Jacopo SANSOVINO and the most important sculptor in Venice in the late 16th century. He did a great deal of decorative work in the Doge's Palace after the 1577 fire and there are religious works in Sta Maria de' Frari and other Venetian churches, but he is best known for his portrait busts, many in Venetian galleries. With his friends Titian and Tintoretto, and with the great architect Palladio, Vittoria was one of the leading artists of the Venetian Renaissance. Other works are in Berlin, Chicago, London (NG, V & A), New York (Met. Mus.), Oxford, Rotterdam, Vienna, and Washington (NG). [ill. 156, p. 294]

Vivarini. A family of Venetian painters, consisting of Antonio (active 1440–*d.* 1476/84), his brother Bartolommeo (active 1450–99), and Antonio's son Alvise (alive in 1457–*d.* 1503/5). Antonio was the partner of his brother-in-law, Giovanni d'Alemagna, whose name may imply that he was a German. Antonio signed a picture in 1440 (Parenzo, province of Pola) by himself, but he seems to have worked with Giovanni until 1450 (when Giovanni probably died), and then he went into partnership with his brother Bartolommeo. The pictures produced by both partnerships were influenced first by Gentile da Fabriano and then by Mantegna and Giovanni Bellini – i.e. the successive leaders of Venetian painting. There is a picture signed by Antonio alone and dated 1464 in the Vatican; one signed by Bartolommeo alone and dated 1459 in Paris, Louvre, as well as others up to 1491: it is doubtful whether it is worth the trouble to distinguish further. Alvise was the son of Antonio but perhaps the pupil of Bartolommeo: the important influences on him were ANTONELLO da Messina and Giovanni BELLINI. He was alive in 1457, but the earliest signed and dated work is of 1475; from 1488 he was employed by the State, and an altarpiece in Sta Maria de' Frari, Venice, was completed after his death by another Bellinesque, Marco Basaiti. There are examples of one or more of the family in London (NG, Courtauld Inst.), New York (Met. Mus.), and Washington (NG), as well as in the Accademia and the churches of Venice. [ills. 138, 145, 146, pp. 292–3]

Vivin, Louis (1861–1936), was a French modern primitive who worked in the Post Office, 1879–1922, and first exhibited at the Post Office Art Club in 1889. He was – like Séraphine – discovered by the German critic Uhde, in 1925. His works consist largely of naïvely realist townscapes, and often seem to be inspired by picture-postcard views. There are works in Paris (Mus. d'Art Mod.). [ill. 1036, p. 419]

Vlaminck, Maurice (1876–1958), was one of the FAUVE group, and shared a studio with Derain. He wrote, played the violin, was a racing cyclist, loved speed, crowds, and popular amusements. He admired van Gogh in 1901, Negro sculpture about 1904, Cézanne in 1907, and denounced CUBISM as over-intellectual and sterile. He painted chiefly landscapes of stormy weather, where the feeling is Expressionist and the dark shadows, strong light effects, and wild skies are rendered in a technique whose slashing brush-stroke and heavy impasto are largely derived from Courbet – an artist whom he resembled in many ways. Most museums of Modern Art have examples. [ill. 1007, p. 416]

Vlieger, Simon de (c. 1600–53), was one of the leading Dutch marine painters of the first half of the 17th century. He was a pupil of W. van de VELDE the Elder and the teacher of W. van de VELDE the Younger, and he also exerted a great influence on CAPPELLE who owned 1300 drawings and nine paintings by him. His principal paintings are of the sea and are representative of the period of Dutch marine painting which concentrated on the rendering of light effects in subdued local colours. He also made twenty etchings of landscapes and animals. He painted a great many pictures, and most museums have examples. [ill. 502, p. 345]

Vorticism. A variety of CUBISM, exclusive to England, invented by Wyndham LEWIS.

Vos, Cornelis de (1584–1651), was an Antwerp portrait painter who occasionally worked for Rubens; some of his portraits have been mistaken for those of Rubens or van Dyck. He also painted large historical and allegorical works. There are examples in Antwerp, Berlin, Brussels, London (Wallace Coll.), Madrid, Munich, Philadelphia (Mus.), San Francisco (Legion of Honor), Vienna, York, and elsewhere. [ill. 379, p. 328]
His brother Paul (1596–1678) was a painter of lively hunting scenes and large still-life subjects with dead game, fruit, and live birds and animals. Their sister married SNYDERS, with whose art Paul's has much in common, and they were close friends of van Dyck. [ill. 418, p. 331]

Vos, Marten de (1531/2–1603), was an Antwerp painter of the last generation of Italianizers (see SPRANGER). He spent six years in Italy, in Rome and then in Venice, where he is said to have worked as a landscape assistant to Tintoretto. He brought the Venetian style back to Antwerp, where he returned in 1558, and there painted many altarpieces (especially after the destruction caused in the Spanish Fury of 1576) as well as some portraits. There are works in Amsterdam, Antwerp, Berlin, Brussels, Florence (Uffizi), The Hague, Paris (Louvre), Stockholm, and Vienna. [ill. 380, p. 326]

Vouet, Simon (1590–1649), was in Italy between 1613 and 1627, when he returned to France to enjoy a successful career as a painter of large decorations and smaller, highly decorative religious and allegorical works. He derived from his years in Rome, and his visits to Venice, Naples, Genoa, and elsewhere, a form of temperate and classicized Baroque which he infused into French painting, and he also adapted to his own uses the cool colour of CHAMPAIGNE, the classical composition of POUSSIN, and the richness of Venetian handling. Poussin's return to Paris in 1640 put him on his mettle (particularly in view of Louis XIII's malicious remark which Poussin records with disingenuous satisfaction, and which may be freely translated as 'Here's one in the eye for Vouet'), but after 1642 his position remained unchallenged.
There are works in the Royal Collection and Berlin, Brussels, Chatsworth, Dresden, Florence (Uffizi), Fontainebleau, Genoa, Glasgow, Leningrad, London (NG), Madrid, Naples, Ottawa, Oxford, Paris (Louvre and many churches), Rome (S. Francesco a Ripa, S. Lorenzo in Lucina, Corsini), Sarasota Fla, Versailles, Washington (NG), and many French provincial museums. [ill. 678, p. 373]

Vries, Adriaen de (c. 1560–1626), was one of the leading Late Mannerist sculptors, whose career well exemplifies the internationalism of the period: he was born in The Hague, trained in Italy, and worked mainly in Prague. He was trained as a bronze-worker under Giovanni BOLOGNA (a Fleming in spite of his name) and, from 1593, he worked for the Emperor Rudolf II in Prague, but he also made two Fountains in Augsburg (*Mercury*, completed 1599, and *Hercules*, 1602) and works for Bückeburg and Stadthagen. There are also examples in London (V & A), Paris (Louvre), Stockholm, and Vienna. [ill. 626, p. 361]

Vuillard, Édouard (1868–1940), was an Intimist painter and decorator whose career closely paralleled that of his friend BONNARD. There are pictures by him in Boston, Bristol, Cleveland, Glasgow, London (Tate and Courtauld Inst.), Manchester (Whitworth), New York (M of MA), Northampton Mass. Smith College, Paris (Mus. d'Art Mod. and Petit Palais), Toronto, and Washington (Phillips), and decorations in Paris (Comédie des Champs-Élysées, Palais de Chaillot) and Geneva (League of Nations). [ill. 994, p. 415. Col. pl. 44]

W

Waldmüller, Ferdinand Georg (1793–1865), was the leading Austrian artist of the early 19th century, painting BIEDERMEIER portraits and landscapes, which later approached the *plein-air* works of the BARBIZON group. He was trained at the Vienna Academy, and from 1829 was a Professor there, but he was bitterly opposed to the teaching methods of his colleagues and wrote many pamphlets on the subject. For a time he was put on half-pay. He visited Italy in 1829 (the first of many visits), Paris in 1830, and in 1856 he started out for Philadelphia, but stopped in London, where, through the intervention of the British Ambassador in Vienna, he succeeded in selling 31 pictures to Queen Victoria, Prince Albert, and the Court. The best collection of his works is in Vienna (Oesterreichische Gal.), but many other Austrian and German galleries have examples; the pictures sold in London seem to have disappeared. [ill. 606, p. 359]

Walker, Robert (*c.* 1605/10–56/8), is chiefly known for his portraits of Cromwell and his circle. The usual way of putting it is that DOBSON painted the Royalists and Walker the Parliamentarians. There are works in Leeds, London (NPG), Oxford (Ashmolean), and elsewhere. [ill. 814, p. 393]

Wall-Painting, or mural, is a term used to describe any kind of wall decoration: it is not interchangeable with FRESCO.

Wanderjahre (Ger. wander years). In the North of Europe it was common for a young artist to complete his apprenticeship in his home town and then to spend several years as a JOURNEYMAN, wandering from one famous master's shop to another and working for a while in each until he returned home, submitted his masterpiece (in the literal sense) to his GUILD, married, and settled down. 'The Cloister and the Hearth' gives a picture of this life and Dürer's career affords another.

Ward, James (1769–1859), was a British landscape and animal painter whose early work was influenced by that of his brother-in-law George MORLAND. In 1803 his style was much affected by Rubens's *Château de Steen* (London, NG). His best work is the vast *Gordale Scar, Yorkshire*, which is one of many works by him in the Tate Gallery, London. [ill. 908, p. 403]

Warm Colour, Tone. Those colours and tones which are red, orange, or purplish in general effect. Not necessarily HOT, but the opposite of COLD.

Watercolour. The technique of painting with colour ground up with water-soluble gums (Gum Arabic, etc.). When moistened with plain water a transparent stain is obtained which is then applied in washes to white or tinted paper. The classical English method – and pure watercolour is almost an English monopoly – is to use the white paper as the highest lights and to apply transparent washes one over another to obtain gradations of colour and of tone: to the purists of this school the use of any form of BODY COLOUR is Frenchified and anathema. Nevertheless, the four greatest practitioners – J.R. COZENS, GIRTIN, COTMAN, and TURNER – all used procedures which vary from the norm defined above. The watercolours of Cozens are perhaps nearest to this norm, but he retained the monochromatic underpainting used by the earliest exponents as a legacy from oil technique. Turner not only used body colour freely, but also wiped partially dry colour with rags and sponges and scratched the surface of the paper with a knife to get extra lights: this last practice is now regarded with peculiar horror. [Col. pls. 46–50]

Watteau, (Jean) Antoine (1684–1721), was born in Valenciennes, a Flemish town which had recently become French. To a contemporary Watteau was *Vato, peintre flamand*, and this Flemish background probably explains his admiration for (and obscure affinity with) Rubens, whose healthy vitality expressed everything Watteau could only envy. He went to Paris *c.* 1702 and worked as a hack painter before going to Gillot, a painter of theatrical scenes, in 1704/5. By then he had probably already contracted tuberculosis and was already exhibiting the symptoms of chronic restlessness which dominated the rest of his short life. By 1707/8 he had moved on to the decorative painter Claude Audran, who, as Keeper of the Luxembourg Palace, was able to give him access to the great Rubens cycle of the *Life of Marie de' Medici*: this was the main influence in the formation of his style, and the drawings he then made were used over and over again. In 1709 he revisited Valenciennes and painted a few military scenes in a Flemish manner, but on his return to Paris he was able to study the great Venetians, especially Veronese, and he then merged all these influences into a completely personal form of RUBÉNISME. In 1712 he was made an Agréé of the Academy and he should then have submitted a Diploma Work, but he delayed this until 1717 when he presented the *Embarkation for the Island of Cythera* (now in the Louvre: a later version in Berlin) and was received as a painter of *fêtes galantes*, the first to be so described. The difficulty felt by the Academy in classifying him is understandable, for, like Giorgione's, his pictures have a mood for a subject, a fleeting and melancholy sense of the transitoriness of all pleasure and all life. In 1719–20 Watteau was in London, perhaps to seek medical advice, but a London winter completed the ruin of his constitution and he returned to Paris to die. One of the last pictures he painted, the *Halt in the Chase* (London, Wallace Coll.) is in the same style as his previous works but the shop-sign he painted in 1720–1 for his friend the dealer Gersaint (known as the *L'Enseigne de Gersaint*, now in Berlin) shows a new stylistic trend. The sign is bigger than his usual small size, and it represents the interior of Gersaint's shop, full of customers and assistants, with a greater degree of realism than was usual with Watteau. The new style was in fact a return to Flemish naturalism, owing much to Teniers (who had also influenced his early military scenes), but his death prevented any further development along these lines. His theatrical subjects are far less realistic, although they derive from the painstaking representations of Gillot. They usually show figures from the Italian or French Comedy in more or less melancholy and reflective attitudes. All Watteau's pictures – except the *Enseigne* – were composed by taking the required number of figures from the big bound volumes in which he kept hundreds of his superb drawings. Studies of figures, heads, hands, draperies were made in three-colour crayon – black, red, and white for the highlights – and were then used when needed. Many hundreds of these still exist, usually in better condition than most of his paintings, which have suffered badly from his atrocious technique. Because the same drawing may have been used over and over again all his pictures have a strong family likeness, increasing the sense of half-attained intimacy. LANCRET and PATER were his principal imitators, but neither was gifted with his exquisite sensibility and his tender amorousness coarsens under their hands. There are several pictures by Watteau in the Wallace Coll., and others in Berlin, Birmingham (University, Barber Inst.), Boston, Chantilly, Cleveland, Dresden, Edinburgh (NG), Glasgow, Hartford Conn., Leningrad, London (NG, Soane Mus., and Dulwich Coll.), Madrid, New York (Met. Mus.), Paris (Louvre), Stockholm, Troyes, and Washington (NG). [ills. 725, 726, pp. 380, 381].

His nephew and great-nephew, Louis-Joseph (1731–98), and François-Louis-Joseph (1758–1823), were both known as 'Watteau de Lille'. Louis was born in Valenciennes but went to Lille in 1755 and taught drawing from the nude there: this caused such scandal that he had to resign and did not return until 1775. He did not always imitate his uncle's works, often painting histories or religious pictures. His son worked in a style closer to his great-uncle's, and, like him, was influenced by Teniers. Lille has examples of both men.

Watts, George Frederic (1817–1904), first exhibited, with success, at the RA in 1837, and in 1843 won a £300 prize in one of the competitions for the decoration of the Houses of Parliament. He left at once for Florence, where he stayed until 1847, leading the sheltered life of a tame genius in the household of the British Minister at the Tuscan Court, Lord Holland. In 1847 he again won a prize in a Houses of Parliament competition, this time for £500, and he started to paint large allegorical pictures while earning his living as a portraitist. His portraits of beauties and celebrities make a real attempt at more than a successful superficial likeness; in his series of famous men he strove to portray the whole man – character, personality, and appearance, and for this reason would only paint men he could like or admire. His decorations are either frankly decorative stories, such as his *Tales from Boccaccio* (1843–4: Tate), with areas of crude, warring colour, applied flatly within a strongly marked contour, or huge turgid allegories, expressing in trite, rather literary symbolism such moral imponderables as *Mammon, Progress, Destiny, Chaos, Love and Death*. The best known of these is probably *Hope*, which, it has been objected, could as easily portray *Despair*. He attempted to revive fresco painting, of which he had no proper knowledge, and in his allegories often used appalling technical methods which have resulted in considerable deterioration. He also executed some large pieces of sculpture; the best known are the *Physical Energy* in Kensington Gardens, and the huge *Tennyson* monument at Lincoln. He became an RA in 1867, twice refused a baronetcy, but accepted the Order of Merit in 1902. Watts was one of the last grand allegorical history painters in the Haydon tradition of 'High Art': a type of picture based on high-minded generalities or abstractions, expressed with idealized forms, and a striving for sublime feeling that results in a numbing divorce from reality, physical and intellectual.

There are examples in the Royal Collection, Bristol, Compton near Guildford (Watts Museum in his former house), Dublin (Municipal Gall.), Edinburgh (NG), Leicester, Liverpool (Walker), London (Tate, NPG, V & A, Leighton House), Manchester, Munich, New York (Met. Mus.), Northampton, Ottawa, and elsewhere. A large mural, *Justice*, is in the New Hall, Lincoln's Inn, London (1853–9). [ill. 955, p. 408]

Weenix, Jan Baptist (1621–before Nov. 1663), was a pupil of BLOEMAERT who was in Italy 1642–6 and returned, calling himself 'Giovanni Battista', to Holland to paint Italianate landscapes with ruins of ancient buildings and figures in modern dress, very reminiscent of the work of BERCHEM. Later in life he changed his style entirely and painted still-life and some portraits, his very detailed style being continued by his son Jan. There are typical works in Amsterdam, Antwerp, Berlin, Dresden, Glasgow, Hartford Conn., London (NG, Wallace Coll., Kenwood), New York (Met. Mus.), Paris (Louvre), Rotterdam, Utrecht (including a *Descartes*), and Vienna. [ill. 433, p. 333]

Weenix, Jan (1640–1719), was the son of Jan Baptist Weenix, and was his father's pupil with his cousin Hondecoeter. He never visited Italy, but he painted Italianate scenes like his father's and pursued more single-mindedly the still-life with flowers, animals, and dead game subjects which he also took over from his father. He worked mainly in Amsterdam, but also at Bensberg and Düsseldorf for the Elector Palatine, for whom he executed a huge series of still-lifes (1702–16). There are works in Amsterdam (Rijksmus.), Augsburg, Cape Town, Dresden, The Hague, London (NG, Wallace Coll., Dulwich), Munich, Oxford, Toronto, and elsewhere. [ill. 474, p. 341]

Weepers. Small mourning figures on a tomb.

Weicher Stil *see* SOFT STYLE.

West, Benjamin (1738–1820), came of Pennsylvania Quaker stock, and learned to paint in America. In 1760 he went to Italy, and spent three years in Rome, Florence, Bologna, and Venice. He enjoyed the prestige of novelty – American painters were unknown and the blind Cardinal Albani asked if he were not a Red Indian. He was much influenced by the Neoclassical style of Mengs and Gavin Hamilton, and evolved, partly through them and partly because of his lack of academic training, history pictures on a smallish scale (what Haydon dubbed 'Poussin size'). He set up as a portrait painter in London in 1763, working in a style close to Mengs, was a Founder-Member of the RA, and in 1769 began his long, and highly profitable, association with George III. His *Death of Wolfe* (RA 1771: Ottawa and many versions) marked a turning-point in the painting of modern history pieces in England since West, whose picture is, in fact, historically inaccurate, imposed a classical composition on figures in contemporary dress. He carried the idea further in his pictures of medieval history subjects, and established a fashion not only popular in England but widely imitated in France. Such was his prestige and his favour with George III, that he succeeded Reynolds as President of the RA in 1792, but refused a knighthood because of his Quaker principles.
There are works in the Royal Collection, Leeds, London (Tate, V & A, Foundling Hospital, Nat. Marit. Mus.), and a great number of American museums. [ill. 889, p. 400]

Westmacott, Sir Richard (1775–1856), was the son of a sculptor, whose pupil he was before he went to Rome, where he worked under CANOVA. He was in Italy from 1793 to 1797, and on his way home was robbed and wounded by bandits. He enjoyed a large and successful practice in London, working for Queen Charlotte and at Brighton Pavilion for the Prince Regent, executing panels for the Marble Arch, the *Achilles* in Hyde Park as a memorial to Wellington, and the pediment of the British Museum. He became an RA in 1811, succeeded Flaxman as Professor of Sculpture at the RA Schools, and was knighted in 1837. He made a number of tombs in Westminster Abbey, including those of Fox (1810: Canova praised the Negro highly) and Pitt the Elder, and in countless parish churches all over England. [ill. 869, p. 399]

Weyden, Roger van der, or Rogier de le Pasture (1399/1400–64), was the major artist of the mid 15th century in Flanders. He was a pupil of Robert CAMPIN in Tournai, 1427–32, and develops from Campin's direct, realistic, and plebeian style towards one imbued with more emotion, warmth, and sensitiveness. Technically, he achieves the same triumphs of luminosity and observation as Jan van EYCK, but in Roger these *tours de force* are subordinated to the deeper considerations of religious feeling and human sympathy. Where Jan develops his composition in depth, creating a miniature world as a stage for his figures (e.g. in the *Rolin Madonna*, Louvre), Roger arranges the parts of his composition so that the eye is held by the significance of the action rather than by the realistic quality of the representation (e.g. in the Vienna *Crucifixion* or the *Adoration of the Magi*, Munich, known as the

S. Columba Altarpiece). Also, his colour is cooler, more *recherché* in its juxtapositions, and far more emotional than Jan's. It is because of these warmer and more human qualities that so much of Flemish 15th-century painting derives from Roger's influence, and his great altarpiece of the *Deposition*, Madrid, probably of 1435, became, with the van Eyck Ghent Altar, the most influential 15th-century work.
Roger married a Brussels woman c. 1426, and after completing his apprenticeship with Campin, settled in Brussels. He became, before 1436, the City Painter, and achieved a great reputation and a solid fortune. In 1450, the year of the Jubilee, he probably visited Rome and also Florence, since the *Entombment* (Uffizi), once in the Medici Collection, has strong affinities not only with Italian art generally but with Fra Angelico specifically, and the *Madonna with four Saints* (Frankfurt, Städel) not only bears the Medici arms, contains the Medici patron saints, Cosmas and Damian, and SS. John Baptist and Peter, name saints of Cosimo's two sons, but also reflects in its composition the Italian SACRA CONVERSAZIONE type of Domenico Veneziano's S. Lucy Altar. Roger never held a Court appointment, as Jan did, but he nevertheless worked for many members of the Burgundian Court, such as Chancellor Rolin, for whose foundation, the Hospice de Beaune, he painted the *Last Judgement*, c. 1446 (still there); Peter Bladelin, Duke Philip's controller of finances and founder of Middelburg, for whose church the triptych of the *Nativity* (c. 1452: Berlin) was painted; Jean Chevrot, Bishop of Tournai (the *Seven Sacraments*, Antwerp, c. 1453). He also painted superb and sensitive portraits, *Charles the Bold* (Berlin), *Le Grand Bâtard* of Burgundy (Brussels), *Francisque d'Este* (New York, Met. Mus.). He appears to have invented the type of diptych with a Madonna and Child on one wing facing a praying portrait on the other, and though none survives intact, the *Phillipe de Croy* (Antwerp) and *Madonna* (San Marino Cal., Huntington) and *Laurent Froiment* (Brussels) and *Madonna* (Caen) may be cited. This type of diptych became very popular and perhaps the best complete example is that by his pupil MEMLINC of *Martin Nieuenhoven*, while many were executed in the BOUTS workshop. His most closely datable work is the unusual *Braque Triptych* (c. 1452: Louvre) which displays all his characteristics of colour, feeling, and technique.
Other works are in Berlin, Boston, Brussels, Chicago, Detroit, Granada (Capilla Real), London (NG, and two silverpoint drawings in the BM), Paris (Louvre), Philadelphia (Johnson), Washington (NG), and elsewhere. [ills. 339, 341, pp. 320–1]

Wheatley, Francis (1747–1801), may have been a pupil of Zoffany, and began as a painter of small portraits and conversation pieces. From 1779–83/4 he worked in Dublin, and after his return to London gave up his small group portraits in favour of adaptations to the English taste of Greuze's type of genre subject, with overtones of the picturesque and deserving poor. His *Mr Howard relieving prisoners* (1787) and his celebrated *Cries of London*, engraved in 1795, are instances of this skilful blend of moral feeling and popular sentiment, and also show his clear, rather pale colour and his free, sensitive handling. [ill. 884, p. 400]

Whistler, James Abbott McNeill (1834–1903), was born in Lowell, Mass., and attended West Point Military Academy, 1851–4. Failing there, he worked as a Navy cartographer, which at least taught him the technique of etching, before going to Paris to study painting in 1855. There he met Fantin-Latour and Degas and was influenced by COURBET, as may be seen in *Au piano*, rejected by the Salon in 1859 and exhibited privately by Whistler, following Courbet's example. In 1859 he moved to London, but he continued to visit Paris frequently as well as going – for no known reason – to Valparaiso in 1866. In 1876/7 he had a quarrel (in which he was entirely in the wrong) over the decoration of the 'Peacock Room' in a London house (now in Washington, Freer Gallery) and in 1877 Ruskin wrote of his *Nocturne in Black and Gold* (now in Detroit) as 'flinging a pot of paint in the public's face'. Whistler sued him and won, in 1878, damages of a farthing but his own costs ruined him and he went to Venice in 1879 and 1880 to make a series of etchings, for his mastery of etching was never disputed even by bitter critics of his paintings and he hoped to recoup himself in this way. He lived as a dandy and had a deserved reputation as a mordant wit, well able to keep up with his friend Oscar Wilde: after one sally Wilde is supposed to have said admiringly 'I wish I had said that.' Whistler replied 'You will, Oscar, you will!'

The early influence of Fantin-Latour and Courbet was succeeded to some extent by that of Manet, who was one of Whistler's fellow-exhibitors in the Salon des Refusés of 1863, but an even more marked influence in the 1860s was that of Japanese art, then finding its way to Europe and being discovered by the more advanced Parisians. Strangely, there is also some influence discernible from English academic painters like Albert Moore, particularly in the colour 'arrangements' which are really studies in the juxtaposition of closely related tones and colours. Whistler liked to emphasize the aesthetic nature of his pictures in conscious reaction against the dominance of the subject in Victorian painting, hence his choice of titles like *Symphony* or *Nocturne*. The best collections of his work are in Washington (Freer Gall.) and Glasgow University; other pictures are in Glasgow (Gall.), London (Tate), Paris (Louvre), and several American museums. His etchings are well represented in the Royal Coll., and London (BM and V & A). [ills. 956, 957, p. 409]

Wilhelm, Master (active 1358–*d.* 72/8), was a Cologne painter by whom no works are known but who has been built up into a legendary figure to whom even LOCHNER's *Dombild* has been ascribed. He may have been identical with a painter named Wilhelm von Herle, but the legend was begun in the German Romantic era, and, though now dead in Germany, is still active in British and American auction rooms and elsewhere.

Wiligelmo was the sculptor responsible for most of the decoration of Modena Cathedral, in a very classical style, between *c.* 1099 and *c.* 1106. Similar sculpture at Cremona Cathedral is strongly influenced by his work but is probably not actually his. Wiligelmo's low-relief style is characterized by stocky, expressive, figures of great narrative force. [ill. 2, p. 269]

Wilkie, Sir David (1785–1841), was the son of the minister of Cults, Fifeshire, and studied in Edinburgh. His first important work, painted when he was nineteen, was *Pitlessie Fair* (1804: Edinburgh, NG) which is an accomplished essay in the manner of Teniers. In 1805 he entered the RA Schools in London and exhibited his *Village Politicians* in the RA of 1806. This made his name and led to his treating similar subjects in the style of Ostade or Teniers for some 20 years. He was elected ARA in 1809, RA in 1811, succeeded Lawrence as Painter to the King in 1830, and was knighted in 1836. He was a friend of HAYDON – although he had the sense not to attempt Haydon's High Art – and they went to Paris together in 1814 to see the pictures looted by Napoleon. Because of ill-health he spent 1825–8 in Italy, Austria, Germany, and Spain, and his new experience of Italian and Spanish art led to a great style change; Velazquez and Murillo being the principal influences on the new, broader, manner and change of subject-matter, which included several histories. In 1840 he went to the Near East and died at sea on the way home: his burial at sea is the subject of an imaginative composition by Turner. There are examples in the Royal Coll. and in Cupar Town Hall, Edinburgh (NG, NPG), London (Tate, Wallace Coll., Wellington Mus.), Munich, New York (Met. Mus.), and elsewhere. [ill. 911, p. 403]

Wilson, Benjamin (1721–88), was an English portrait painter, whose chief claim to fame lies in the easy confusion of his name with Richard Wilson's. Zoffany may have worked for him until *c.* 1762, perhaps on theatrical scenes. From about 1770 Wilson seems to have devoted himself principally to science. There are examples in Leeds and London (NPG and Dulwich Coll.). [ill. 826, p. 393]

Wilson, Richard (1713 (or 14)–82), was the son of a Welsh clergyman who gave him a good classical education. This was probably decisive in his approach to landscape painting, which, for Wilson, has the classic overtones of the Italy of Claude and Gaspar Poussin. These two, with Cuyp, were acknowledged by Wilson as his inspiration. He came to London in the 1740s and soon built up a practice as a portrait painter (there are portraits by him in London (NPG, Tate Gall., and Nat. Marit. Mus.). and in Edinburgh), but he was certainly painting landscapes by 1746, when he painted two for the Foundling Hospital which are still there. The real turning-point in his career was his Italian period, when he decided to devote himself exclusively to landscape; a decision which may have been influenced by ZUCCARELLI and C.-J. VERNET. He was in Venice in 1750 and spent most of his Italian years in Rome and the Campagna, which left its mark on him as on so many other landscapists from Claude and Gaspar Poussin onwards. He returned to England, probably in 1757, and continued to paint Italian landscapes, which, considering their classicism of subject as well as of handling, should have been much more popular among the Grand Tourists than they were. The remainder of his output consisted of views in England and Wales treated in a markedly Italian and classical way (so much so, that it is not always possible to be sure what the scene represented is), and of commissioned views of country houses. His *Niobe* was exhibited at the Society of Artists in 1760 and during the 1760s he seems to have painted a series of Grand Manner mythologies, perhaps as an equivalent to the Grand Manner portrait then being introduced by Reynolds, whose success was in marked contrast to Wilson's neglect. He was one of the Founder-Members of the Royal Academy in 1768 and was appointed Librarian in 1776, when he had almost ceased to paint and was in need. At his best, in such designs as the *Snowdon* (Liverpool and Nottingham), Wilson achieved a pure classicism which depends on the austere beauty of the design and informs it with a glow of light learned from the Dutch as well as from Claude. These designs are of such nobility that they can stand numerous repetitions, which they often received, and their poetry is indeed Roman in inspiration: there could hardly be a greater contrast to the naturalness of Constable. Wilson's pictures often exist in many versions, so that most English galleries have at least one. The largest collection is in Cardiff (Nat. Mus. of Wales), and there are others in Adelaide, Auckland NZ, Baltimore, Berlin, Boston, Buffalo, Cambridge Mass. (Harvard Univ.), Chicago, Detroit, Dublin, Dunedin, Edinburgh (NG and NPG), Glasgow, Hanover, London (NG, NPG, Tate Gall., V & A, Royal Academy, Nat. Marit. Mus., Dulwich Coll., and Foundling Hosp.), Manchester, Melbourne, Minneapolis, Montreal, New York (Met. Mus.), Ottawa, Philadelphia, San Marino Cal., Stockholm, Vancouver, Washington (Nat. Coll.), and Worcester Mass. [ills. 824, 920, pp. 392, 405]

Wilton, Joseph (1722–1803), was the son of a prosperous maker of ornamental plasterwork. After studying sculpture with Delvaux in Belgium, he went to Paris in 1744, where he was a pupil of Pigalle. In 1747 he went to Rome with Roubiliac, travelled widely in Italy, and worked in Florence from 1751 to 1753. He returned to London in 1755 with Chambers the architect and soon had a considerable practice, in which he was helped by Chambers, who often employed him to carve the ornamental detail and chimney-pieces in his buildings (notably at Somerset House). Wilton was a Founder-Member of the RA. He retired in 1786, and was appointed Keeper of the RA in 1790, having dissipated the large fortune inherited from his father, and that won by his own work. There are several tombs by him in Westminster Abbey (including General Wolfe's), and works in Edinburgh (NPG), London (V & A), and New York (Hist. Soc.). [ill. 879, p. 398]

Winckelmann, Johann Joachim (1717–68), was the first of the great German art historians and one of the founders of NEOCLASSICISM. He published his 'Gedanken über die Nachahmung der griechischen Werke . . .' ('On the Imitation of Greek Works . . .') in 1755, and later that year he moved from Dresden to Rome. The 'Gedanken' contains the phrase which sums up all his teachings about Greek art (which he scarcely knew from the originals, most of them being still undiscovered): *edle Einfalt und stille Grösse*, noble simplicity and calm grandeur. In 1764 he published his very influential history of ancient art, soon translated into French and English, and in 1768 he was murdered in Trieste for some medals he carried. His theories profoundly influenced many artists, but the one closest to him was MENGS. [*see* ill. 595, p. 358]

Wint, Peter De, *see* DE WINT.

Witte, Emanuel de (1607 or 1615/17–92), was a Dutch painter of church and house interiors and market scenes. His interiors usually stress shafts of light falling on pillars, tombs, or parquetry floors, and his open-air scenes have still-life detail in the foreground, as in his various *Fish-Market* scenes. Despite the beauty of his interiors they brought him little success, and his life ended in suicide. There are works in Amsterdam (Rijksmus.), Berlin, Brussels, Cape Town, The Hague, Hartford Conn., London (NG, Wallace Coll.), Rotterdam, Toledo Ohio, and elsewhere. [ill. 480, p. 340]

Witz, Konrad (1400/10–44/6), was the greatest Swiss painter before Holbein. He entered the Basle Guild in 1434, but he came from Germany and may have been attracted to Basle by the Church Council which convened there in 1431. About 1435 he probably began his major work, the large Altarpiece of the Redemption (*Heilspiegelaltar*), parts of which are still missing. His only signed and dated work is the *Christ walking on the Waters* (1444: Geneva), which contains one of the earliest certainly datable views in modern art. The landscape is recognizably that of a particular point on the Lake of Geneva, not just a Swiss scene. His extremely realist style shows that he must have been in contact with his immediate predecessors in Flanders, Jan van Eyck and the Master of Flémalle, and with them he substituted a strongly realistic style for the Soft Style hitherto practised in Germany. His few known works are in Basle (Mus. and Mus. of History), Berlin, Dijon, Geneva, Naples, Nuremberg, and Strasbourg. [ill. 548, p. 353]

Wolgemut, Michael (1434–1519), a Nuremberg painter and designer of woodcut book-illustrations, was the master of Dürer. He probably went to Flanders *c.* 1450, as the influence of BOUTS and Roger van der WEYDEN seems to have come to Nuremberg through him. Only two paintings can be given to him: the altarpiece in Zwickau (1476–9) and the one in Schwabach (1506–8), but the central panel of a triptych in Brighton is signed MW, and he also designed the woodcuts for two of the most famous 15th-century books, the 'Schatzbehalter' of 1491 and Schedel's 'Weltchronik' (1491–3). [ill. 564, p. 355]

Wols (i.e. Alfred Otto Wolfgang Schulze) (1913–51) was born in Berlin and studied at the Bauhaus under MOHOLY-NAGY before going to Paris in 1933. He made a living as a photographer until he was interned in 1939, when he began to paint. He lived in desperate poverty in the South of France, 1940–5, and began to paint in oils only in 1946. His spiky abstractions are Tachiste in style. [ill. 1093, p. 428]

Woodcut (Wood Engraving) *see* ENGRAVING.

Wootton, John (d. 1756), was one of the earliest English exponents of landscape in the style of Claude and Gaspar, and introduced this form into England after his visit to Italy during the 1720s. He combined his landscapes – which are often very large – with horse portraits, hunting scenes, and sporting conversation pieces, and occasionally even portrayed battles. There is a fine and representative hunt picture in London (Tate), a *Battle of Dettingen* in the

National Army Mus., and a landscape in Manchester. [ill. 895, p. 402]

Workshop Production or a 'Shop Work' are descriptions of works of art which are produced by relatively unskilled or insensitive assistants from drawings or cartoons by a major artist, and more or less under his supervision. There are, for example, two *tondi* of the *Madonna and Child*, one in the NG, London, and one in the Chigi Coll., Rome, which are painted from the same cartoon by Botticelli – but which nevertheless betray the hands of two men, neither of whom was Botticelli.

Wotruba, Fritz (*b.* 1907), is a Viennese sculptor whose work is based on the human figure, but treated in an abstract way. He usually employs coarse stone and works direct, but some of his work is in lead or bronze. He emigrated to Switzerland, 1939–45, but now teaches at the Vienna Academy. There are works by him in London (Tate), Vienna (City and State Galleries), Winterthur, and Zürich. [ill. 1154, p. 434]

Wouwerman, Philips (1619–68), was a Haarlem painter who was a pupil of Hals but who painted genre scenes of horsemen, battles, and camp life much more akin to BAMBOCCIATE. He frequently disposed dozens, even hundreds, of small figures in his canvases and he had a special fondness for white horses. He often painted figures in the landscapes of other painters – e.g. Wynants, Ruisdael. There are about 1,200 pictures recorded, some of the largest collections being in Dresden, Leningrad, London (NG and Dulwich), and Vienna. His brothers Jan (1629–66) and Pieter (1623–82) were also landscape painters. [ill. 486, p. 342]

Wright, John Michael (?1617–1700). Wright, whose first name is uncertain, was born in London but apprenticed to Jamesone in Edinburgh in 1636 and seems to have gone to Italy by 1647: in 1648 he became a member of the Roman Academy of S. Luke, the only British member in the 17th century. In Rome he became an antiquarian and later worked as such for that great patron of the arts, the Archduke Leopold Wilhelm, Governor of the Netherlands. It is clear that he was a Catholic, yet he returned to Commonwealth England in 1656/8 and painted many portraits in a Dobsonesque manner, the most important being a series (of which only two survive) for the City of London; of which Evelyn observed in 1673 that 'Most of them are very like the persons they represent, though I never took Wright to be any considerable artist' and Pepys had earlier (1662) compared him with Lely, remarking 'Lord! the difference': Wright was, nevertheless, Painter to Charles II. He returned to Rome with an Embassy to the Pope in 1686, while Kneller built up his practice in London, and Wright died apparently in poverty. There are pictures by him in the Royal Coll., and in Aberdeen (University), Edinburgh (NPG), London (Tate, NPG, Guildhall, and Ham House), Manchester, Nottingham, and Oxford (Magdalen College). [ill. 815, p. 393]

Wright, Joseph (1734–97), usually called Wright of Derby, was a pupil of Hudson. He established himself at Derby where, except for a visit to Liverpool in 1769, he remained until he travelled in Italy in 1773–5. All his life he specialized in lighting effects and his candlelight pictures show affinities with those of Honthorst and others of the Utrecht School, and his moonlit landscapes recall Aert van der Neer as well as the contemporary Vernet. In Derby he found admirers among the pioneers of science allied to industry: Wedgwood and Arkwright were his patrons, and among his completely new subjects were representations of experiments made by candlelight, such as *The Orrery* (1766: Derby) and the *Experiment with an Air Pump* (1768: London, Tate).

In Italy he was not interested in the grandest art, but was deeply impressed by a fireworks display at Castel S. Angelo and an eruption of Vesuvius, both of which he painted on his return. He also evolved moonlit landscapes, first of Vesuvius, then of the Derbyshire countryside, his main interest being as much in the quality of the light as in the picturesque effect. He tried to replace Gainsborough at Bath in 1775, but in 1777 returned to Derby where he had a prosperous portrait connection and opportunities for painting landscapes and subject pictures which eventually decline into sentimental genre. His best portraits were painted in the early 1780s, and *Sir Brooke Boothby* (1781: London, NG), lying reading Rousseau in a woody glade, is an adroit but sympathetic blend of Batoni with the new literary influences from France. [ill. 885, p. 400]

Wtewael, Joachim (1566–1638), was one of the leading Mannerists in Utrecht at the time of BLOEMAERT. He spent four years in Italy and France (St Malo 1588–90). His religious pictures and portraits are well represented in Utrecht, and there are others in Gateshead, London (NG), Ottawa, Oxford, and Vienna. [ill. 385, p. 326]

Wynants, Johannes (*c.* 1625–84), was a Haarlem landscape painter who also kept an inn, but was still always in debt. His rather limited art consisted of landscapes with low hills in the background and a sandy road in the foreground winding past trees in the middle distance. There is usually a dead tree in the foreground as well as a figure group. These figures are never by Wynants himself, but usually by Wouwerman, Lingelbach, or Wynants's own pupil Adriaen van de Velde. Some of his early works were painted in collaboration with a specialist in wildfowl, and it is a nice point whether they are landscapes or animal pieces: otherwise, his charming views run to type and were much collected in the 18th and 19th centuries so that most galleries have one or more. [ill. 487, p. 342]

X Y Z

XX, Les, *see* VINGT, Les.

Xylography *see* ENGRAVING.

Yeats, Jack B. (1871–1957), was the son of a painter and brother of the poet W. B. Yeats. He began his career as a watercolour painter and illustrator for the family press (later known as the Cuala Press). He began to paint in oil about 1915 and evolved an intensely romantic, occasionally rather slapdash, landscape style which, in his last works, approaches ABSTRACT IMPRESSIONISM. It has been said that 'Irish romance is not easily exportable' but Yeats's works have been admired by painters like Kokoschka. There are examples in Cork, Dublin (Municipal Gall.), and London (Tate). [ill. 1032, p. 418]

Ysenbrandt *see* ISENBRANDT.

Zadkine, Ossip (*b.* 1890), was born in Russia, came to London in 1907, and studied in Paris from 1911 where he met and was influenced by the Cubists. His works, in wood and stone, usually deal with figures from Greek mythology and are quasi-representational. Many of his wooden figures are very large, and have ingenious effects of silhouette obtained by cut-out shapes. There are examples in Antwerp, Edinburgh, Glasgow, Paris (Mus. d'Art Mod.) Philadelphia, as well as a memorial to the destruction of Rotterdam made in 1952–3. [ill. 1132, p. 431]

Zais, Guiseppe (1709–84), was a Rococo landscape painter active in Venice. His early style was probably influenced by Marco RICCI, but his later landscapes have the brightness and prettiness of the style usually associated with ZUCCARELLI. There are characteristic examples in Venice and London (NG). [ill. 314, p. 317]

Zandomeneghi, Federigo (1841–1917), was born in Venice, the son of a sculptor. He was in Sicily with Garibaldi in 1860, but from 1862 to 1866 was in Florence in contact with the MACCHIAIOLI. From 1874 until his death he lived in Paris, often exhibiting with the Impressionists, although he was closest to DEGAS and the works of the two men have occasionally been confused. There are pictures by him in Florence, Milan, Piacenza, Philadelphia (Drexel Inst.), and Venice. [ill. 322, p. 318]

Zevio, Stefano da, *see* STEFANO.

Zick, Januarius (1730–97), was one of the leading German Rococo painters. He was trained in Munich and then went to Paris, where he copied WATTEAU, after which (rather inappropriately) he went to Rome and worked in MENGS's studio (1757–8). In 1758 he returned to Germany and began his prolific career as a painter of altarpieces and decorative frescoes, the best of them being those at Mainz, Coblenz, and Wiblingen (1778–80), in the Klosterkirche. Many German museums have works and there is one in Kansas (University). [ill. 591, p. 358]

Zoffany, Johann (1733?–1810), was a painter of portraits, conversation pieces, and theatrical scenes, who was born in Germany, studied in Italy, and worked mainly in England. He arrived about 1761 and was a Founder-Member of the RA (1768): in 1772, at the expense of George III, he went to Florence and spent some years there. One result of this was *The Tribuna of the Uffizi Gallery, Florence* (1772–80: Royal Coll.). He returned to England in 1779 but went to India and painted many portraits there 1783–9. He painted many theatrical scenes, usually representing an actual moment in a play and many of them include portraits of Garrick – his first success was in 1762 with *Garrick in 'The Farmer's Return'* – and in this he was probably following HOGARTH, whose *Garrick as Richard III* was painted in 1746. There are works by him in Birmingham, Burnley, Edinburgh (NG), Glasgow, London (NG, NPG, Tate), Ottawa, and elsewhere. [ill. 840, p. 394]

Zoppo, Marco (*c.* 1433–*c.* 1478), was a Bolognese painter who was probably originally a pupil of TURA, but went, at the age of twenty-one, to work for SQUARCIONE whose adopted son he became in 1455. In the same year he went to Venice and subsequently to Bologna. His style is a slightly softer version of the angular manner of both his masters and may reflect the influence of Giovanni Bellini. His main works are in Berlin and Bologna (San Clemente), but there are others in London and Oxford. [ill. 130, p. 290]

Zuccarelli, Francesco (1702–88), was a Florentine landscape painter who worked principally in Venice and England. He met Richard Wilson in Venice in 1751 and they exchanged paintings: in 1752 he went to London and remained until 1762. He returned to London in 1765 and stayed until 1771, being elected a Founder-Member of the Royal Academy in 1768. His light and facile style of landscape painting, with picturesque peasantry, was very popular in England and was preferred to the graver style of Wilson. There are several works at Windsor Castle and others in Cambridge (Fitzwm), Glasgow, London (NG), Venice, and elsewhere. [ill. 313, p. 317]

Zuccari (Zuccaro, Zuccheri), Taddeo (1529–66), and Federico (c. 1540/3–1609), were brothers and represent the end of the MANNERIST tradition in Rome. Taddeo was the chief exponent of the style of the mid 16th century and his principal works were the fresco cycles in the Sala Regia of the Vatican and the *Farnese Deeds*, in the Villa Farnese at Caprarola, near Viterbo. So far as is known, there are no easel pictures by him. The two fresco cycles were completed by his younger brother, after which Federico went, in 1574, to France and Antwerp and, late in the year, to England. There he certainly made two drawings, one of Queen Elizabeth (both are in London, BM), but he was back in Italy by October 1575, so he cannot have painted all (or perhaps even any) of the portraits attributed to him in English houses. The *Queen Elizabeth* in Siena is certainly an Italian picture and the only one with a reasonable claim to be regarded as his, but the attribution is still controversial. Federico also worked in the Vatican, completed the frescoes of the dome of Florence Cathedral left incomplete by Vasari in 1574, and went to Spain in 1585, remaining until 1589 but finding little favour at the hands of Philip II, who was accustomed to the works of Titian. In 1593 he established the ACADEMY of S. Luke in his own Palazzo in Rome, becoming Principe of it in 1598, and devoting much thought in his last years to the theory of art and particularly of DISEGNO. Like the Cavalier d'Arpino, he was an eclectic Mannerist who lived on into a new era. Among the many pictures attributed to him are those in Florence (Uffizi, Pitti), Glasgow, Minneapolis, Milan (Brera), New York (Hist. Soc.), Rome (Borghese), and Vienna. His treatise 'L'Idea de' Scultori, Pittori e Architetti' was published in 1607, and his collected writings in 1961. [ills. 198, 200, pp. 302–3]

Zurbarán, Francisco de (1598–1664), was born near Bádajoz and was apprenticed in Seville in 1614 to a craftsman painter of devotional images. By 1617 he had settled in Llerena in Southern Spain, but established himself in Seville at the invitation of the City Council in 1629. In 1634 he visited Madrid to paint a *Siege of Cadiz* for the King, to hang with Velazquez's *Surrender of Breda* and Maino's *Recovery of the Bay of S. Salvador*. He was back in Seville in 1635 to enter on his most productive and successful decade, during which he worked for monasteries and churches all over the south-west of Spain. He also painted pictures, some in long series, for religious houses in the Spanish colonies in the New World, and exported them as articles of trade possibly through members of his second wife's family, established in Peru. Much of this production was shop work, but the argosies were not always successful, for there are many records of his difficulties in collecting the monies due to him. In 1658 he moved to Madrid in search of business, and renewed contact with Velazquez, for whom he was a witness in the proceedings that admitted him to the Order of Santiago. He died in Madrid.

The bleak, austere piety of his early pictures of Saints, painted for the more severe religious Orders, made him the ideal painter of simple doctrinal altarpieces, expressed in clear, sober colour, with figures of massive solidity and solemnity, and with a Tenebrism owing but little to Caravaggio or Ribera, but developed straight out of Southern Spanish traditions of unidealized representation. He probably never saw a painting by Ribera until the mid 1630s, but he certainly knew his etchings. His ability to portray rather arid scenes from saintly lives, with a perfect union of the mystical and the realistic, accords well with Counter-Reformation theories of the purpose of paintings in churches and with the importance of subjects expressing the 'witness' aspect of a Saint's life. The first journey to Madrid opened his eyes to other styles, and shows in something of a stronger feeling for Baroque magnificence. He still retains his hold on pure realism, but the splendour of his colour and the clarity and solidity of the masses in, for example, the *Adoration of the Shepherds* (1638: Grenoble) shows how well he absorbed lessons learnt from Italian art. The rise of Murillo in the 1640s forced Zurbarán to compete with his softer, sweeter expression and more fused, smooth technique, and to abandon his own austerity of vision and colour, and impasted handling. His Saints become more romantic in their devotion, his Madonnas ape the sentiment of Italian Mannerist painting, and in this competition with something entirely alien to him his own personality and individuality were lost.

Many of his works are in the churches and religious houses of Spain and Spanish America for which they were painted, but museums in Berlin, Boston (Mus., Gardner), Cadiz, Chicago, Cincinnati, Dresden, Edinburgh (NG), Hartford Conn. (Wadsworth), Indianapolis, Lisbon, London (NG), Madrid (Prado and Acad.), Munich, New York (Hispanic Soc., Met. Mus.), Paris (Louvre), Philadelphia, St Louis, San Diego, São Paulo, Seville, and Washington (NG) also have examples. [ill. 640, p. 365]

THE MAJOR TECHNIQUES
IN COLOUR

1 GIOTTO. Detail from the *Funeral of S. Francis*, fresco, *c.* 1320? Florence, Sta Croce. About ½ original size.

MASACCIO. Detail of the head of S. John from the
Tribute Money, fresco, *c.* 1425/28. Florence, Sta Maria del
Carmine. About actual size.
PIERO DELLA FRANCESCA. Detail of the head of Adam
from the *Death of Adam*, fresco, *c.* 1452. Arezzo, S.
Francesco. About ½ actual size.

The Masaccio detail shows how close to oil painting fresco
can come, in the rendering of form by tone alone. The
Piero detail is closer to the Giotto, in that it is simpler and
more linear in conception.

4 RAPHAEL. Detail of Plato from *The School of Athens*, fresco, 1508/11. Vatican, Stanza della Segnatura. About actual size.

5 CORREGGIO. *Angel Musicians* from the fresco of *The Assumption*, c. 1526/30. Parma, Cathedral. Much reduced.

Correggio's soft fresco technique seems to owe much to both Raphael and Michelangelo. The Raphael figures have a freedom and force of expression that demonstrate the *buon fresco* technique at its most developed, with only the slightest reliance on the cartoon, as indicated by the stylus marks.

6 MICHELANGELO. Detail of '*Mors stupebit . . .*' from the
Last Judgement. Vatican, Sistine Chapel, fresco, 1536/41.
About ⅓ actual size.

7 SINOPIA and FRESCO of *Geometry* by an unknown
painter, *c.* 1420/25. Foligno, Palazzo Trinci. Much reduced
from the original fragment.

This clearly demonstrates the way in which the *sinopia*
conditions the upper, fresco layer: the Michelangelo is
painted with far greater freedom, and probably had no
more than the slightest underpainting. The use of a
sinopia made it much easier to employ skilled assistants.

8 GOYA. Detail from *The Miracle of S. Antony of Padua*,
   fresco, 1798. Madrid, San Antonio de la Florida. About
   ½ actual size.
9 TIEPOLO. Detail of *Asia* from the fresco cycle in the
   Residenz, 1753. Würzburg, Germany. Reduced.

These are the finest frescoes painted in the 18th century,
and probably the last of their kind. The Goya is painted
impressionistically with sponges and rags, as well as
brushes, rather thickly; the Tiepolo is painted more traditionally, but the thin paint has a luminous quality typical
of Tiepolo, adding to the lightness and gaiety of the whole.

II DISTEMPER ON PAPER

10 RAPHAEL. Head of S. Peter, detail from the cartoon for the tapestry of *The Miraculous Draught of Fishes*, distemper on paper, 1515/16. The Royal Collection (on loan to the Victoria and Albert Museum, London). About ½ actual size.

III OIL PAINTING

11 EL GRECO. *Modello* for the *Adoration of the Name of Jesus*, c. 1578. London, National Gallery. Actual size $22\frac{3}{4} \times 13\frac{11}{16}$ ins.

12 LEONARDO DA VINCI. Detail of the Angel from the *Virgin of the Rocks*, c. 1483/1506. London, National Gallery. About actual size.

13 GIORGIONE (?). Detail of the *Adulteress brought before Christ*, c. 1505/10. Glasgow, Art Gallery. About actual size.

Both these are among the earliest examples of oil painting
used to obtain soft and *sfumato* effects: Vasari makes it clear
that they were both regarded as pioneers, but it is evident
that Leonardo was still much influenced by the Florentine
tradition of draughtsmanship.

14 TITIAN. Head from the *Vendramin Family*, c. 1543.
London, National Gallery. About ½ actual size.
15 TINTORETTO. Detail of *Vincenzo Morosini*, c. 1580.
London, National Gallery. About ⅔ actual size.

th details show the rough Venetian canvas with the paint dragged
er the surface, but the Tintoretto seems also to have been painted
er a foundation of tempera. This is noticeable in the details of the
dscape and also perhaps of the stole.

16 CARAVAGGIO. Still-life detail from the *Supper a* *Emmaus, c.* 1598. London, National Gallery. About actual size.

17 VELAZQUEZ. Detail from the *Old Woman Frying Eggs* 1618. Edinburgh, National Gallery of Scotland. Abou ⅔ actual size.

Caravaggio's influence is clearly shown in the fascinatior which still-life detail exerted on many painters of the early 17th century. The Spanish type is known as *Bodegón*, and the domestic scene shown here is typical of the degree o realism obtainable with oil paint.

18 REMBRANDT. Detail from *Jacob Trip*, *c.* 1661. London, National Gallery. About ½ actual size.

19 FRANS HALS. *Unknown Man*, 1633. London, National Gallery. About ¾ actual size.

The fluent brushwork of the Hals is due to the *alla prima* handling (although it may, in fact, have taken more than one sitting to achieve): by comparison, the Rembrandt is a patient accretion of layers of oil paint. (Compare the handling of van Gogh and Cézanne, plates 30, 31.)

20 RUBENS. Detail from *Le Chapeau de Paille*, *c.* 1620.
London, National Gallery. About ½ actual size.

21 GAINSBOROUGH. Detail from *Lady Howe*, *c.* 1760/65.
London, Kenwood, Iveagh Bequest. About ⅓ actual size.

The Rubens is a superb example of the technique of
underpainting in cool monochrome and then glazing with

translucent films of warm colour to obtain an effect of
luminosity in the skin; by comparison the Gainsborough
appears like porcelain. Gainsborough used very thin films
of paint, almost like watercolour, but they are applied to
a warm neutral ground, so that the full range of contrasts
exploited by Rubens cannot be obtained.

22 JAN VAN EYCK. Detail from the *Arnolfini Marriage Portrait*, 1434. London, National Gallery. About actual size.

23 VERMEER. Detail from *A Young Woman Standing at a Virginal*, c. 1670/75. London, National Gallery. About $\frac{1}{2}$ actual size.

Both details show the use of a very smooth paint film with blobs of white to render the highest lights. The van Eyck – which may be underpainted in tempera – shows the amount of detail which can be rendered in oil.

24 TERBRUGGHEN. Detail of Salome from the *Decollation of S. John the Baptist, c.* 1617/20. Edinburgh, National Gallery of Scotland. About ¾ actual size.

25 DEGAS. Detail from *Woman at a Window, c.* 1871/72. London, Courtauld Institute Galleries. About actual size.

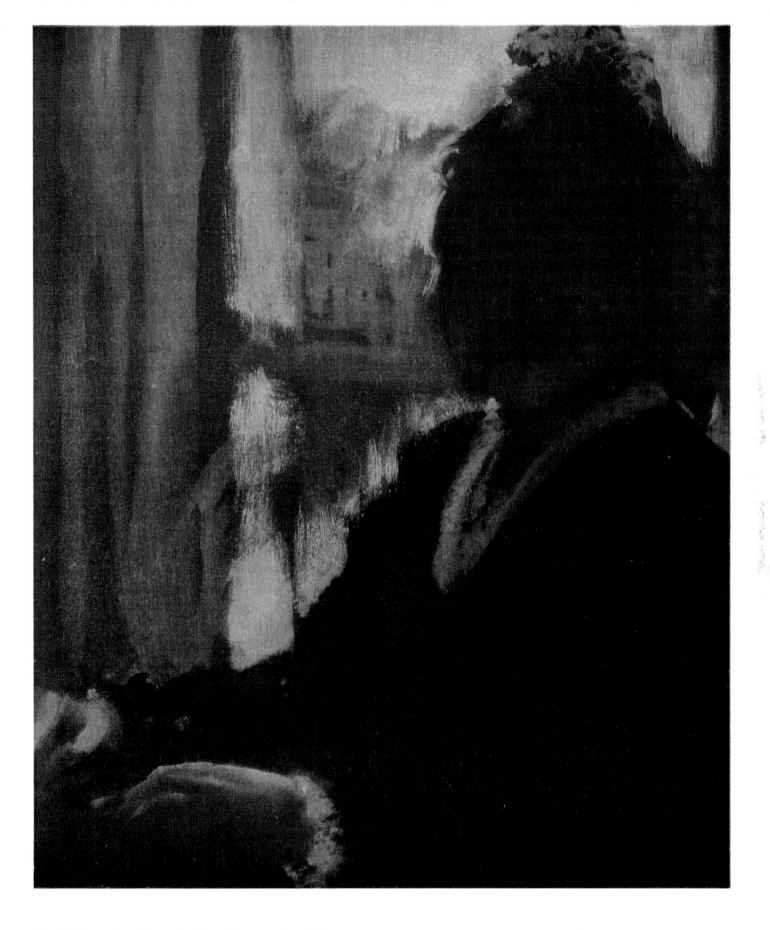

The Terbrugghen shows the Tenebrist use of a dark
ground with a single brightly lit feature to give relief. The
Degas is in thinned oil-paint on paper (*peinture à l'essence*)
and also uses a dark, warm ground as the basis for the
tonal modelling of the head, seen in a *contre-jour* effect.

26 INGRES. Detail from *Madame Moitessier*, 1856. London, National Gallery. About ⅓ actual size.

27 DELACROIX. Detail from the *Women of Algiers*, 1834. Paris, Louvre. About ⅓ actual size.

The Romantic artist revelled in the sensuous qualities of
oil paint, but Ingres confined himself to an even, enamel-
like surface and meticulous detail: compare plate 28 for
a different means of obtaining detail.

28 MILLAIS. Detail from *The Blind Girl*, 1856. Birmingham,
    City Museum and Art Gallery. About actual size.
29 MANET. Detail from *The Waitress*, 1879. London,
    National Gallery. About ¾ actual size.

The Pre-Raphaelite technique of painting into wet white, over a brilliantly white ground, gave luminosity as well as clarity of detail. Manet was one of the great *alla prima* painters, but he used wet-in-wet (top right) to contrast with dry scumbles (the blue streaks on the tankard).

30 VAN GOGH. Detail from *Self-portrait with his Ear cut off*, 1889. London, Courtauld Institute Galleries. About $\frac{2}{3}$ actual size.

31 CÉZANNE. Detail from *Man smoking a Pipe, c.* 1892. London, Courtauld Institute Galleries. About $\frac{2}{3}$ actual size.

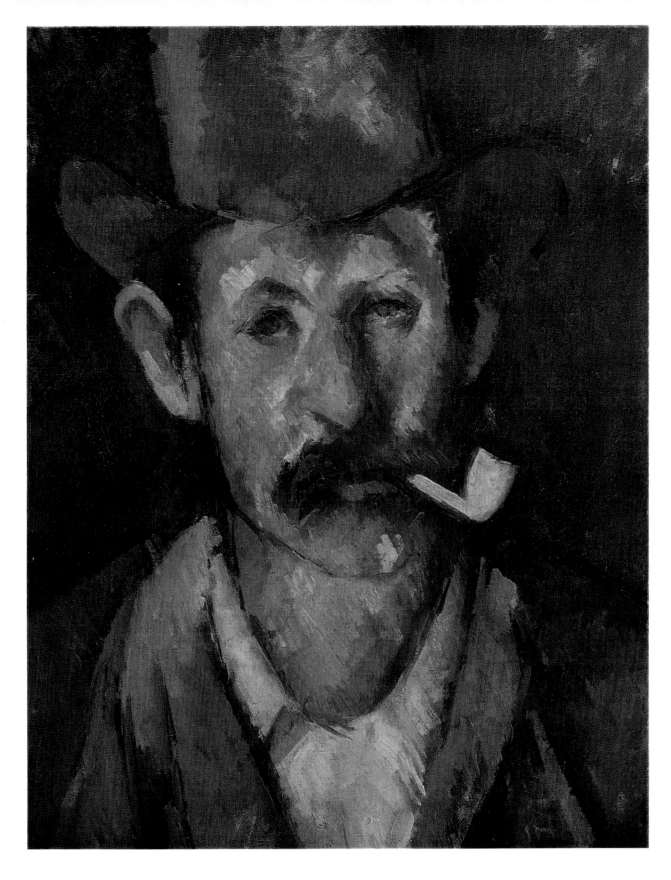

The van Gogh was painted between the 9th and 17th January 1889, probably at one sitting, in thickly impasted oil paint, which may have been made thicker by removing some of the oil; by contrast, the Cézanne is built up of layer on layer of semi-transparent paint, so that the overlapping strokes give the richest colouristic effects, contrasting with the occasional patch of bare canvas.

32 CAMILLE PISSARRO. Detail from the *Côte des Bœufs, near Pontoise,* 1877. London, National Gallery. About ½ actual size.
33 SEURAT. Detail from *Sunday Afternoon on the Island of La Grande Jatte,* 1884/86. Courtesy of the Art Institute of Chicago. About ½ actual size.

The breaking up of colour into patches, according to
Neo-Impressionist theory, can be seen in the Seurat, but
the technique of a broken surface is seen earlier in the
Pissarro.

34 MONET. Detail from *Water Lilies, c.* 1919/26. Cleveland Ohio, Museum (John L. Severance Collection). About $\frac{1}{4}$ actual size.

35 POLLOCK. Detail from *Gothic*, 1944. Collection of Lee Krasner Pollock. About $\frac{1}{2}$ actual size.

These details show how Abstract Impressionism has developed from the apparent formlessness of Monet's very late works: in fact, however, the Monet is an enormous picture, 14 feet wide, which gives the overall impression of a shimmering pool of water with flowers floating on the surface – *i.e.* the effect of space and form is still rendered.

36 BRAQUE. Detail from *The Pedestal Table*, 1929. Washington, Phillips Collection. About ⅔ actual size.

37 CHAGALL. Detail from *Naphtali*, one of the Twelve Tribes of Israel, a stained-glass window in the Synagogue of the Hadassah (Hebrew University) Medical Centre, Jerusalem, 1959/61. This detail is actually over 6 feet across.

IV STAINED GLASS,
CERAMIC TILE MOSAIC
AND MOSAIC

The effects of texture, so much sought after in recent years, are obtained by Braque by the use of sand mixed into the paint, especially in contrast with patches of bare canvas. Chagall's windows are made of glass which was specially coloured and was then painted, etched and scratched in addition.

38 MIRÒ. Detail from a mural in ceramic tiles, 1960. Cambridge Mass., Harvard Graduate Center. Actual size of each tile 8¾ × 14½ ins. Whole mural approximately 20 feet wide.

39 GIOTTO. *Angel*. Detail from the Navicella mosaic formerly in St Peter's. Soon after 1300. Rome, St Peter's. About ½ actual size.

V TEMPERA PAINTING

40 DUCCIO. Detail of Christ healing the Blind Man from the *Maestà*, 1308/11. London, National Gallery. About ½ actual size.

41 CIMA DA CONEGLIANO. Detail from *The Madonna and Child with Saints*, an unfinished tempera painting. Edinburgh, National Gallery of Scotland. About ⅔ actual size.

The Duccio shows the traditional 14th-century technique, including the use of gold. The Cima shows the under-painting in monochrome and most of the paint layers, except that it may perhaps have been intended to finish the picture in oil glazes.

VI PASTEL   42 CHARDIN. Detail from the *Self-portrait*, 1775. Paris, Louvre. About ¾ actual size.

43 DEGAS. Detail from *Duranty*, 1879/80. Glasgow Art Gallery (Burrell Collection). About ½ actual size.

The Chardin is one of the finest 18th-century pastels, in
a very simple technique. The Degas is much more sophisticated in technique, since the ground is canvas and the
pastels are reinforced with tempera.

VII COLOUR PRINTING

44 VUILLARD. *The Gallery*, 1900. London, British Museum.
About actual size.
45 BLAKE. Detail from *The Ancient of Days*, frontispiece to
Europe, 1794. Actual size. Nearly complete picture.

The Vuillard is a colour lithograph produced in the traditional way from five stones, carefully overprinted. The Blake is based on a print from a 'relief etching' (*i.e.* printed like a woodcut), which was then hand-coloured by Blake himself in watercolour.

46 DÜRER. *House on an island: 'Weier Haws'*, *c.* 1497. London, British Museum. Actual size about $8\frac{1}{4} \times 8\frac{3}{4}$ ins.

47 TURNER. *Bellinzona*, 1841. London, British Museum. Actual size about 9×13 ins.

48 COTMAN. *Greta Bridge*, 1805. London. British Museum. Actual size about 9×13 ins.

49 SANDBY. *Windsor Castle from Bishopsgate*. London, British Museum. Actual size $7\frac{3}{4} \times 10\frac{1}{2}$ ins.

The Cotman shows the classic technique of pure watercolour, with a dark underpainting and a few, simple washes of colour. The lights are normally reserved by leaving the paper untinted. The Sandby is in gouache (body-colour), allowing light tones to be painted over darks, as in oil painting: these are the two extremes of technique, but as early as the 1490s Dürer had used pure watercolour heightened and strengthened by judicious use of solid body-colour. This is handled with supreme virtuosity by Turner, in search of ever more subtle light effects.

50 CÉZANNE. *Still-life, c.* 1905. London, Courtauld Institute Galleries. Actual size $17\frac{1}{2} \times 23\frac{1}{4}$ ins.

In this Cézanne returns to the pure watercolour technique, with great use of reserved lights.

IX MINIATURE PAINTING

51 HILLIARD. *The Artist's Wife Alicia,* 1578. London, Victoria and Albert Museum. Actual diameter $2\frac{5}{16}$ ins.

52 COSWAY. *Unknown Lady,* 1798. London, Victoria and Albert Museum. Sight size $2\frac{7}{8} \times 2\frac{9}{32}$ ins.

Both these miniatures are enlarged. The Hilliard shows the earlier technique, derived from illuminated manuscripts, with opaque watercolour used on parchment, usually stuck on card; the Cosway is on ivory and painted with thinner, transparent or semi-transparent watercolour, so that the ivory forms a luminous ground.

A VISUAL HISTORY OF ART

ITALY

1

2

The beginnings of Italian art

1 BONANUS. *Adam and Eve with their Children*. Signed 1185. Monreale, Cathedral.
2 WILIGELMO. *Creation*. Signed. *c*. 1099–*c*. 1106. Modena, Cathedral.
3 BARISANUS. *Deposition*. Signed. Trani, Cathedral.
4 ANTELAMI. *Deposition*. Signed 1178. Parma, Cathedral.
5 COSMATI. Tomb of Cardinal Rodriguez (*d*. 1299) Signed by Johannes Cosmati. Rome, Sta Maria Maggiore.
6 MARGARITONE. *Madonna Enthroned and other scenes*. Signed. London, National Gallery.

3

4

5

6

7

8

9

10

11

12

7 PISANO, NICOLA. *Nativity*. Detail from pulpit. Signed 1260. Pisa, Baptistery.

8 PISANO, GIOVANNI. *Nativity*. Detail from pulpit. Signed 1311. Pisa, Cathedral.

9 ARNOLFO DI CAMBIO. Tomb of Cardinal de Braye (*d.* 1282). Detail. Signed. Orvieto, S. Domenico.

10 TINO DI CAMAINO. *Madonna,* from the Orso Monument. Monument signed. Florence, Bargello.

11 PISANO, ANDREA. *Naming of the Baptist*. Detail from bronze doors. Signed 1330 (cast 1336). Florence, Baptistry.

12 PISANO, NINO. *Madonna*. Signed. Florence, Sta Maria Novella.

13 BERLINGHIERO. *Crucifix*. Signed. Lucca, Pinacoteca.

14 GIUNTA PISANO. *Crucifix*. Signed. Bologna, S. Domenico.

15 CAVALLINI. *Birth of the Virgin*. Mosaic. Formerly signed and perhaps dated 1291. Rome, Sta Maria in Trastevere.

13

14

15

16

17

Sculpture and painting up to Giotto

16 CIMABUE. *Sta Trinita Madonna*. Traditionally attributed. Florence, Uffizi.

17 GIOTTO. *Ognissanti Madonna*. Traditionally attributed. Florence, Uffizi.

18 CIMABUE. *S. John*. Mosaic detail. Documented 1302. Pisa, Cathedral.

19 MASTER OF S. CECILIA. *S. Cecilia Altarpiece*. Florence, Uffizi.

18

19

20

24

25

26

27

29

30

3

21

22

23

Giotto and his followers

20 GIOTTO. *Lamentation over the Dead Christ.* Documented before 1313. Padua, Arena Chapel.

21 GIOTTO. *S. Francis receiving the Stigmata.* Traditionally attributed. Assisi, S. Francesco.

22 GIOTTO. *S. Francis receiving the Stigmata.* Signed (but perhaps by assistants). Paris, Louvre.

23 GIOTTO. *S. Francis receiving the Stigmata.* Traditionally attributed. Florence, Sta Croce, Bardi Chapel.

24 GIOTTINO. *The S. Remigio Deposition.* Attributed. Florence, Uffizi.

25 DADDI. *Madonna and Saints.* Signed 1328. Florence, Uffizi.

26 GADDI, TADDEO. *Madonna.* Centre of polyptych. Documented *c.* 1353. Pistoia, S. Giovanni Fuorcivitas.

27 GADDI, AGNOLO. *Ascension.* Detail of polyptych. Documented 1393–6. Florence, S. Miniato.

28 MASO DI BANCO. *S. Sylvester restores two clerks to life.* Traditionally attributed. Florence, Sta Croce.

29 ORCAGNA AND JACOPO DI CIONE. *S. Matthew Altarpiece.* Begun 1367 by Orcagna, finished by Jacopo 1368. Florence, Uffizi.

30 ORCAGNA. *The Strozzi Altarpiece.* Signed 1357. Florence, Sta Maria Novella.

31 BARONZIO. *Madonna and Scenes from the Life of Christ.* Polyptych. Signed 1345. Urbino, Galleria Nazionale.

32 TRAINI. *Scenes from the Life of S. Dominic.* Detail of altarpiece. Signed and documented 1345. Pisa, Sta Caterina, Seminario.

33 BARNABA DA MODENA. *Coronation of the Virgin.* Signed 1374. London, National Gallery.

34 ALTICHIERO (AND AVANZO). *Soldiers casting lots.* Detail of fresco. Documented 1379. Padua, Il Santo.

35 ORCAGNA. *Inferno.* Detail of fresco. Traditionally attributed to Nardo di Cionc. Florence, Sta Maria Novella.

28

35

32

33

34

36

**Thirteenth to fifteenth-century painting
in Siena, Venice and Arezzo**

36 GUIDO DA SIENA. *Madonna*. Signed (?1221). Siena, Palazzo Pubblico.

37 DUCCIO. *Maestà* (front). Documented 1308–11. Siena, Museo dell'Opera del Duomo.

38 UGOLINO. *Deposition*. Part of signed altarpiece. London, National Gallery.

39 'UGOLINO-LORENZETTI'. *Madonna*. Siena, S. Pietro Ovile.

40 LORENZETTI, P. *Birth of the Virgin*. Signed 1342. Siena, Museo dell'Opera del Duomo.

41 LORENZETTI, A. *Presentation in the Temple*. Signed 1342. Florence, Uffizi.

37

42 LORENZETTI, A. *Good Government in the Country*. Part of fresco cycle. Signed 1337–9. Siena, Palazzo Pubblico.

43 MARTINI. *Christ returning to His Parents*. Signed 1342. Liverpool, Walker Art Gallery.

44 BARNA. *Raising of Lazarus*. Traditionally attributed. S. Gimignano, Collegiata.

45 BARTOLO DI FREDI. *Mary returns to her home*. Part of the Montalcino Altarpiece. Signed 1388. Siena, Pinacoteca Nazionale.

44

45

46

4

38

39

40

41

42

43

46 LORENZO MONACO. *Coronation of the Virgin*. From polyptych. Signed 1413 (1414 modern style). Florence, Uffizi.

47 SPINELLO ARETINO. *Madonna*. Triptych. Signed 1391. Florence, Accademia.

48 JACOBELLO DEL FIORE. *Madonna of Mercy*. Triptych. Signed 1436. Venice, Accademia.

49 GIAMBONO. *Madonna*. Signed. Rome, Galleria Nazionale.

50 PAOLO VENEZIANO. *Dormition of the Virgin*. From polyptych. Signed 1333. Vicenza, Museo Civico.

50

48

49

51

53

54

52

55

**International Gothic and
early fifteenth-century Florentine art**

56

51 GHIBERTI. *Road to Calvary*. First doors. Documented 1403–24. Florence, Baptistry.
52 GHIBERTI. *Solomon and the Queen of Sheba*. Second doors. Documented 1425–52. Florence, Baptistry.
53 QUERCIA. *Madonna*. From the Trenta Altar. Signed 1422. Lucca, S. Frediano.
54 GENTILE DA FABRIANO. *Madonna*. From the Quaratesi Altarpiece. 1425 (altarpiece formerly signed). Royal Collection.
55 GENTILE DA FABRIANO. *Strozzi Adoration of the Magi*. Signed 1423. Florence, Uffizi.
56 MASOLINO. *Nativity*. Detail of lower half. Signed. Castiglione d'Olona, Lombardy, Collegiata.

57

58

60

61

62

59

57 MASACCIO. *Madonna*. From the Pisa Polyptych. Documented 1426. London, National Gallery.

58 MASACCIO. *S. Peter's shadow healing the sick*. From fresco cycle traditionally attributed. Florence, Sta Maria del Carmine.

59 'DESCO DA PARTO'. Attributed to Masaccio. Berlin, Staatliche Museen.

60 NANNI DI BANCO. *Isaiah*. Documented 1408. Florence, Cathedral.

61 DONATELLO. *'Lo Zuccone', a prophet*. Inscribed and documented, probably 1423/5. Florence, Museo dell'Opera del Duomo.

62 DONATELLO. *Judith*. Signed. Florence, Piazza della Signoria.

63

67

68

69

63 DONATELLO. *S. Antony and the mule*. Documented 1447. Padua, Il Santo.

64 ROBBIA, LUCA DELLA. *Trumpeters*. From the Cantoria. Documented 1431–8. Florence, Museo dell' Opera del Duomo.

65 AGOSTINO DI DUCCIO. *A Virtue*. Documented 1457–62. Perugia, S. Bernardino, Oratory.

66 MICHELOZZO. *S. John the Baptist*. From the Silver Altar. Commissioned 1452. Florence, Museo dell' Opera del Duomo.

67 UCCELLO. *The Deluge*. Traditionally attributed. Florence, Sta Maria Novella.

68 UCCELLO. *Sir John Hawkwood*. Signed 1436. Florence, Cathedral.

69 UCCELLO. *Sir John Hawkwood*. Squared drawing. Florence, Uffizi.

70 CASTAGNO. *Niccolò da Tolentino*. Documented 1456. Florence, Cathedral.

71 CASTAGNO. *Sinopia* of the *Risen Christ*. Florence, Museo Castagno.

72 ANGELICO. *Madonna enthroned with eight Saints*. Fresco from cycle recorded in the 15th century. Florence, Museo di S. Marco.

73 DOMENICO VENEZIANO. *S. Lucy Altarpiece*. Signed. Florence, Uffizi.

74 LIPPI, FRA FILIPPO. *Barbadori Altarpiece*. Documented 1437. Paris, Louvre.

72

64

65

66

Mid fifteenth-century Florentine art

70

71

Sacre Conversazioni

73

74

75

76

77

Florence: later fifteenth century

75 LIPPI, FRA FILIPPO. *Funeral of S. Stephen*. Fresco. Signed 1460. Prato, Cathedral.

76 GOZZOLI. *Procession of the Magi*. Detail of fresco with Piero de' Medici. Signed. Begun 1459. Florence, Medici Palace Chapel.

77 POLLAIUOLO, P. *Coronation of the Virgin*. Signed 1483. S. Gimignano, Collegiata.

78 GHIRLANDAIO, DOMENICO. *Visitation*. From fresco cycle. Documented 1485–90. Florence, Sta Maria Novella.

79 PESELLINO. *Trinity with Saints*. Documented 1455–7. London, National Gallery.

80 POLLAIUOLO. *Martyrdom of S. Sebastian*. Attributed to Antonio and Piero. Formerly dated 1475. London, National Gallery.

81 POLLAIUOLO, A. *Battle of the Nude Gods*. Engraving. Signed. London, British Museum.

82 BALDOVINETTI. *The Virgin Annunciate*. Detail. Documented after 1466. Florence, S. Miniato al Monte.

83 'ALUNNO DI DOMENICO'. *Lamentation*. Predella to Ghirlandaio's *Adoration*.

79

80

81

82

83

281

Fifteenth-century sculpture

84 ROSSELLINO, B. *Monument to the Beata Villana*. Documented 1451. Florence, Sta Maria Novella.
85 DESIDERIO DA SETTIGNANO. Tomb of Carlo Marsuppini. Traditional attribution. After 1453. Florence, Sta Croce.
86 MINO DA FIESOLE. Tomb of Conte Ugo. Documented 1471. Florence, Badia.
87 LOMBARDO, P. AND T. Tomb of Doge P. Mocenigo. Documented 1476/81. Venice, SS. Giovanni e Paolo.

88 LAURANA. *Madonna*. Signed 1471. Noto, Sicily, Chiesa del Crocifisso.
89 POLLAIUOLO. Tomb of Sixtus IV. Signed by Antonio 1493. Rome, Museo Petriano.
90 BUON. *Justice*. Documented 1438–42. Venice, Doges' Palace, Porta della Carta.
91 VECCHIETTA. *Risen Christ*. Signed 1476. Siena, Sta Maria della Scala.

92 MINO DA FIESOLE. *Piero de' Medici*. Signed. Datable 1453. Florence, Bargello.
93 ROSSELLINO, A. *Matteo Palmieri*. Signed 1468. Florence, Bargello.
94 BENEDETTO DA MAIANO. *Pietro Mellini*. Signed 1474. Florence, Bargello.
95 VERROCCHIO. *Monument to Bartolommeo Colleone*. Detail. Documented. Venice.
96 BERTOLDO. *Bellerophon and Pegasus*. Signed. Vienna, Kunsthistorisches Museum.

84

88   89

92   93   9

85

86

87

90

91

5

96

97

98

Late Quattrocento art

97 LIPPI, FILIPPINO. *Mystic Marriage of S. Catherine*. Signed 1501. Bologna, S. Domenico.

98 VERROCCHIO. *Incredulity of S. Thomas*. Documented 1467–83. Florence, Orsanmichele.

99 BOTTICELLI. *Fortitude*. Documented 1470. Florence, Uffizi.

100 BOTTICELLI. *Mystic Nativity*. Signed 1500. London, National Gallery.

101 BOTTICINI. *S. Andrew*. Detail. Documented 1484–91. Empoli, Galleria della Collegiata.

102 CREDI. *Madonna and two Saints*. Documented 1494. Paris, Louvre.

103 'AMICO DI SANDRO'. *Adoration of the Kings*. London, National Gallery.

104 ROSSELLI. *Procession of the Relics*. Documented 1484–6. Florence, S. Ambrogio.

105 SIGNORELLI. *Devils and Damned*. Detail from fresco cycle. Documented 1499–1504. Orvieto, Cathedral.

101

10

99

100

103

104

105

Leonardo da Vinci

106 LEONARDO DA VINCI. *The S. Donato Adoration*. Documented 1481. Florence, Uffizi.
107 LEONARDO DA VINCI. *Virgin of the Rocks*. Commissioned 1483. London, National Gallery.
108 LEONARDO DA VINCI. *Head of an Angel*. Silverpoint drawing for the *Virgin of the Rocks*. Turin, Library.
109 LEONARDO DA VINCI. *Last Supper*. Recorded 1497. Milan, Sta Maria delle Grazie.

107

108

109

110

111

112

113

114

110 SASSETTA. *Death of S. Francis*. Documented 1437–44. London, National Gallery.
111 GIOVANNI DI PAOLO. *Presentation in the Temple*. Documented 1447–8. Siena, Accademia.
112 FRANCESCO DI GIORGIO. *Nativity*. Signed commissioned 1475. Siena, Accademia.
113 MATTEO DI GIOVANNI. *Madonna and four Angels*. Signed (damaged) 1470. Siena, Accademia.
114 VECCHIETTA. *Assumption*. Signed. Pienza, Cathedral.
115 'CASSONE'. The Morelli-Nerli Cassone. Documented 1472. London, Courtauld Institute Galleries.
116 FOPPA. *Crucifixion*. Signed 1456. Bergamo, Accademia Carrara.
117 BORGOGNONE. *Crucifixion*. Signed 1490. Pavia, Certosa.

**Fifteenth-century painting in
Siena, Lombardy and Florence**

118 PIERO DELLA FRANCESCA. *Flagellation of Christ*. Signed. Urbino, Galleria Nazionale.
119 MELOZZO DA FORLÌ. *Platina appointed Vatican Librarian*. Documented 1477. The Vatican, Museums and Galleries.
120 SANTI. *Madonna and Saints*. Signed. Fano, S. Croce.
121 FRANCIA. *Felicini Madonna*. Signed 1494. Bologna, Pinacoteca.
122 PERUGINO. *Crucifixion with Saints*. Fresco. Documented 1493–6. Florence, Sta Maria Maddalena de' Pazzi.
123 PINTORICCHIO. *Aeneas Silvius Piccolomini at the Court of Scotland*. Documented 1503–8. Siena, Biblioteca Piccolomini.

115

116

117

118

19

120

121

Fifteenth-century painting in Central Italy

122

123

124

125

126

Painting in Padua in the fifteenth century:
Mantegna

Fifteenth-century painting in Ferrara and the Marches

129

130

13

127

124 SQUARCIONE. *Madonna*. Signed. Berlin, Staatliche Museen.
125 MANTEGNA. *Madonna and Saints*. Documented *c.* 1456/9. Verona, S. Zeno.
126 MANTEGNA. Ceiling. Signed 1474. Mantua, Castello, Camera degli Sposi.
127 MANTEGNA. *Agony in the Garden*. Signed. London, National Gallery.
128 MANTEGNA. *Dead Christ*. Probably the *Cristo in scurto* recorded in Mantegna's studio after his death. Milan, Brera.

128

129 TURA. *S. George and the Dragon*. Organ doors, detail. Documented 1469. Ferrara, Museo dell'Opera del Duomo.
130 ZOPPO. *Madonna and Four Saints*. Signed 1471. Berlin, Staatliche Museen.
131 COSSA. *Madonna and two Saints*. Signed 1474. Bologna, Pinacoteca.
132 ROBERTI. *Pietà*. Attributed. Liverpool, Walker Art Gallery.
133 ROBERTI. *Madonna and Saints*. Documented (as by 'Ercole') 1481. Milan, Brera.
134 COSTA. *Madonna and Saints*. Signed 1505. London, National Gallery.
135 CRIVELLI, C. *Annunciation*. Signed 1486. London, National Gallery.

133

134

135

132

136   137   138   139

143   144   145

Fifteenth-century Venetian painting

136 BELLINI, JACOPO. *Madonna*. Signed 1448. Milan, Brera.
137 ANTONELLO DA MESSINA. Fragment of the S. Cassiano Altarpiece. Documented 1475/6. Vienna, Kunsthistorisches Museum.
138 VIVARINI, ALVISE. *Madonna*. Signed. London, National Gallery.
139 BELLINI, GIOVANNI. *Madonna*. Signed. London, National Gallery.
140 CATENA. *Madonna and three Saints with a Donor*. Signed. Liverpool, Walker Art Gallery.
141 CIMA. *Madonna*. Signed. London, National Gallery.

149   150

140

141

142

146

147

148

142 BASAITI. *Madonna.* Signed. London, National Gallery.

143 PISANELLO. *SS. Antony and George with a Vision of the Madonna and Child.* Signed. London, National Gallery.

144 STEFANO DA ZEVIO. *Adoration of the Magi.* Signed 1435. Milan, Brera.

145 VIVARINI, ANTONIO. Polyptych with *Imago Pietatis and Saints.* Signed 1464. The Vatican, Museums and Galleries.

146 VIVARINI, BARTOLOMMEO. *S. Martin Triptych.* Signed 1491. Bergamo, Accademia Carrara.

147 BELLINI, GIOVANNI. *Madonna and Saints.* Signed 1505. Venice, S. Zaccaria.

148 MONTAGNA. *Madonna and four Saints.* Signed. Vicenza, Museo Civico.

149 CARPACCIO. *Leavetaking of the English Ambassadors.* Signed. Venice, Accademia.

150 BELLINI, GENTILE. *Recovery of the Relic of the True Cross.* Signed 1500. Venice, Accademia.

151 BELLINI, GIOVANNI. *Feast of the Gods.* Signed 1514. Washington D.C., National Gallery of Art (Widener Collection).

152 BELLINI, GIOVANNI. *Doge Loredano.* Signed. London, National Gallery.

151

152

153

153 RICCIO. *Christ in Limbo*. Paschal candlestick. Documented 1507/15. Padua, Il Santo.
154 LOMBARDO, T. *Miracle of the Miser's Heart*. Signed 1525. Padua. Il Santo.
155 FERRARI. *Crucifixion*. Traditionally attributed. Varallo, Sacro Monte, Cappella della Crocifissione.
156 VITTORIA. *Francesco Duodo*. Documented 1596. Venice, Accademia.
157 ARCIMBOLDI. *Summer*. Signed 1563. Vienna, Kunsthistorisches Museum.
158 TORRIGIANO. *Angel*. Detail from tomb of Henry VII. Documented 1512. London, Westminster Abbey.
159 SANSOVINO, J. *Neptune*. Signed 1554–67. Venice, Doges' Palace.

Italian sculpture of the sixteenth and early seventeenth centuries

154

159

155

156

164

157

Arcimboldi

160 Bandinelli. *Hercules and Cacus*. Documented 1534. Florence, Piazza della Signoria.
161 Cellini. *Perseus*. Signed 1553 but actually completed 1554. Florence, Loggia dei Lanzi.
162 Ammanati. *Neptune*. Documented 1575. Florence, Piazza della Signoria.
163 Bologna, Giovanni da. *Samson slaying a Philistine*. Signed. London, Victoria and Albert Museum.
164 Sansovino, A. *Baptism of Christ*. Documented 1502–after 1505. Florence, Baptistry.
165 Danti. *Decollation of S. John Baptist*. Documented 1571. Florence, Baptistry.
166 Tacca. *The Four Moors*. Documented 1620/3. Leghorn.

158

60

161

162

163

65

166

167   168   169

170   171   172

173

The High Renaissance in Florence: Raphael

17

167 BARTOLOMMEO, FRA. *God the Father with SS. Mary Magdalen and Catherine of Siena.* Documented 1509. Lucca, Pinacoteca.

168 BARTOLOMMEO, FRA. *Madonna and Saints.* Begun 1510. Florence, Museo di S. Marco.

169 ALBERTINELLI. *Madonna and Saints.* Signed. Florence, Accademia.

170 PIERO DI COSIMO. *Visitation, with SS. Nicholas of Bari and Antony Abbot.* Recorded in Vasari. Washington D.C., National Gallery of Art (Samuel H. Kress Collection.)

171 GHIRLANDAIO, RIDOLFO. *Translation of the Body of S. Zenobius.* Datable 1517, described by Vasari. Florence, Uffizi.

172 GRANACCI. *Madonna and four Saints.* Documented 1521. Montemurlo, Parish Church.

173 FRANCIABIGIO. *David and Bathsheba.* Signed monogram 1523. Dresden, Gemäldegalerie.

174 RAPHAEL. *Lo Sposalizio (Betrothal of the Virgin).* Signed 1504. Milan, Brera.

175 RAPHAEL. *'La Belle Jardinière'.* Signed 1507. Paris, Louvre.

176 RAPHAEL. *School of Athens* cartoon. Detail of Anaxagoras. Milan, Ambrosiana.

177 RAPHAEL. *School of Athens.* Documented 1508–11. The Vatican, Stanze.

174

175

177

178

179

**Raphael and his followers,
Sebastiano del Piombo
and Tuscan Mannerism**

183

184

185

178 RAPHAEL. *Baldassare Castiglione*. Probably recorded in a letter of 1516. Paris, Louvre.

179 RAPHAEL. '*Feed my Sheep*'. Tapestry cartoon. Documented 1515–16. London, Victoria and Albert Museum (on loan from the Royal Collection).

180 RAPHAEL. *Transfiguration*. Begun 1517, unfinished at Raphael's death. The Vatican, Museums and Galleries.

181 SEBASTIANO DEL PIOMBO. *Raising of Lazarus*. Signed 1517–19. London, National Gallery.

182 GIULIO ROMANO. *Fall of the Giants*. Documented. Mantua, Palazzo del Tè.

180   181   182

183 BRONZINO. *Ugolino Martelli*. Signed. Berlin, Staatliche Museen.

184 ANDREA DEL SARTO. *Madonna delle Arpie*. Signed 1517. Florence, Uffizi.

185 ROSSO. *Deposition*. Signed 1521. Volterra, Pinacoteca.

186 PONTORMO. *Deposition*. Recorded in Vasari. Florence, Sta Felicita.

187 SODOMA. *S. Sebastian*. Documented 1525–6. Florence, Pitti.

188 BECCAFUMI. *Birth of the Virgin*. Recorded in Vasari. Siena, Accademia.

186   187   188

Michelangelo

189 MICHELANGELO. *Adam*. Drawing. London, British Museum.
190 MICHELANGELO. *Creation of Adam*. Documented 1508–12. The Vatican, Sistine Chapel.
191 MICHELANGELO. *Jonah*. Documented 1508–12. The Vatican, Sistine Chapel.
192 MICHELANGELO. *Last Judgement*. Detail of S. Laurence. Documented 1536–41. The Vatican, Sistine Chapel.
193 MICHELANGELO. *Pietà*. Signed *c.* 1500. Rome, St Peter's.
194 MICHELANGELO. *Pietà*. Documented *c.* 1550. Florence, Cathedral.

189

191

192

190

193

194

195   196   197   198

195 PRIMATICCIO. Stucco decoration, with figures. Documented *c.* 1541–5. Fontainebleau, Chambre de la Duchesse d'Etampes.
196 ABBATE, N. DELL'. *Martyrdom of SS. Peter and Paul.* 1547. Recorded in Vasari. Formerly Dresden. (Destroyed.)
197 VASARI. *Temptation of S. Jerome.* 1541. Described by Vasari himself. Florence, Pitti.
198 ZUCCARI, F. *Barbarossa and Alexander III.* Signed 1582, reworked 1603. Venice, Doges' Palace.
199 SALVIATI. *Ranuccio Farnese receiving Arms.* Fresco recorded in Vasari. Rome, Palazzo Farnese.
200 ZUCCARI, T. *Conversion of S. Paul.* 1566. Recorded in Vasari. Rome, S. Marcello in Corso.
201 TIBALDI. *Adoration of the Shepherds.* Signed 1548. Rome, Galleria Borghese.
202 BANDINELLI. *Bandinelli's Academy in Rome.* 1531. Engraving by Agostino Veneziano. London, British Museum.

203   204

203 BOLTRAFFIO. *S. Barbara.* Documented 1502. Berlin, Staatliche Museen.
204 LUINI. *Madonna with SS. Anthony Abbot and Barbara.* Fresco. Signed 1521. Milan, Brera.
205 LOTTO. *Madonna Enthroned.* Detail of central panel. Signed 1508. Recanati, Pinacoteca.
206 LOTTO. *Andrea Odoni.* Signed 1527. Hampton Court, Royal Collection.
207 MORETTO. *Madonna with S. Elizabeth and Two Donors.* Signed 1541. Berlin, Staatliche Museen.
208 MORONI. *Man.* Signed 1563. Florence, Uffizi.

209   210   211

199

200

201

202

205

206

207

208

209 CORREGGIO. *Assumption*. Detail, group of angels. Documented 1522. Parma, Cathedral.
210 CORREGGIO. *Madonna of S. Jerome*, '*Il Giorno*'. Documented 1523/8. Parma, Galleria.
211 PARMIGIANINO. *Madonna of S. Zachary*. Documented *c*. 1530. Florence, Uffizi.
212 BAROCCI. *La Madonna del Popolo*. Signed 1579. Florence, Uffizi.
213 CRESPI, G.B. *Nativity*. Signed. Turin, Pinacoteca.
214 CRESPI, DANIELE. *Pietà*. Signed. Madrid, Prado.

Sixteenth-century and Mannerist painting in Italy

212

213

214

High Renaissance and Mannerism in sixteenth-century Venice

215

216

217

215 GIORGIONE. *The Tempest*. Recorded by Michiel in 1530. Venice, Accademia.

216 PALMA VECCHIO. *The Three Graces*. Recorded by Michiel in 1525. Dresden, Gemäldegalerie.

217 TITIAN. *Danäe*. Recorded in a letter of 1553. Madrid, Prado.

218 GIORGIONE. *Laura*. Inscribed as by Giorgione and dated 1506. Vienna, Kunsthistorisches Museum.

219 TITIAN. *Man* ('*Ariosto*'). Signed. London, National Gallery.

220 TINTORETTO. *Self-portrait*. Engraved in 1588. Paris, Louvre.

221 TITIAN. *Pesaro Altar*. Documented 1519–26. Venice, Sta Maria dei Frari.

222 TITIAN. *Jacopo Strada*. Signed *c.* 1567/8. Vienna, Kunsthistorisches Museum.

223 TINTORETTO. *Flight into Egypt*. Documented 1583–7. Venice, Scuola di S. Rocco.

218

219

220

221

222

223

224

225

226

227

228

229

Venice, Cremona, and Ferrara in the sixteenth century

224 BARBARI. *Dead Bird*. Signed 1504. Munich, Alte Pinakothek.
225 PORDENONE. *Christ nailed to the Cross*. Fresco. Documented 1520/21.
Cremona, Cathedral.
226 BONIFAZIO. *Madonna and Saints*. Signed 1533. Venice, Accademia.
227 BASSANO, JACOPO AND FRANCESCO. *Christ at Bethany*. Signed by both.
Greenville SC, Bob Jones University Collection.
228 BORDONE. *A Man aged 27*. Signed 1540. Paris, Louvre.
229 BASSANO, LEANDRO. *Man with statuette of Hercules*. Signed. Hampton
Court, Royal Collection.
230 DOSSI, DOSSO AND BATTISTA. *The Nativity*. Documented 1536.
Modena, Pinacoteca.

230

231

232

233

231 SAVOLDO. *Madonna with SS. Peter, Dominic, Paul and Jerome*. Signed. Milan, Brera.
232 BASSANO, JACOPO. *Adoration of the Shepherds*. Signed 1568. Bassano, Museo Civico.
233 VERONESE. *Mars and Venus*. Signed. New York, Metropolitan Museum of Art (Kennedy Fund, 1910).
234 PALMA GIOVANE. *Venice crowned by Victory*. Documented 1578/84. Venice, Doges' Palace, Sala del Maggior Consiglio.
235 VERONESE. *Feast in the House of Levi*. Documented 1573. Venice, Accademia.

234

235

Caravaggio and his followers

236 CARAVAGGIO. *Una Musica.* Documented. New York, Metropolitan Museum of Art (Rogers Fund, 1952).
237 CARAVAGGIO. *Martyrdom of S. Matthew.* Documented. Rome, S. Luigi dei Francesi.
238 CARAVAGGIO. *Entombment.* Documented 1602. The Vatican, Museums and Galleries.
239 SARACENI. *S. Raymond preaching.* Engraved 1614. Rome, S. Adriano.
240 STANZIONE. *S. Bruno.* Signed 1631. Naples, Museo di S. Martino.
241 GENTILESCHI, O. *SS. Cecilia, Valerian and Tibertius.* Signed 1620. Milan, Brera.
242 CARACCIOLO. *Annunciation.* Signed monogram. Courtesy of the Wadsworth Atheneum, Hartford Conn.
243 CAVALLINO. *S. Cecilia.* Signed initials 1645. Property of the Italian Government.
244 MANFREDI. *The Fortune Teller.* Attributed. Rome, Galleria Nazionale.

The Carracci and their followers

239

240

241

242

243

244

245 CARRACCI, L. *Madonna dei Bargellini*. Signed 1588. Bologna, Pinacoteca.
246 CARRACCI, ANNIBALE. *Madonna with SS. John Evangelist and Catherine.* Signed 1593. Bologna, Pinacoteca.
247 CARRACCI, AGOSTINO. *Last Communion of S. Jerome.* Signed. Bologna, Pinacoteca.
248 DOMENICHINO. *Last Communion of S. Jerome.* Signed 1641. The Vatican, Museums and Galleries.
249 RENI. *La Pietà dei Mendicanti.* Documented 1614–16. Bologna, Pinacoteca.
250 SACCHI. *S. Romuald recounting his Vision.* Documented. The Vatican, Museums and Galleries.
251 DOLCI. *Martyrdom of S. Andrew.* Signed 1646. Florence, Pitti.
252 GUERCINO. *Erminia and the Shepherds.* Signed 162–. Birmingham, City Museum and Art Gallery.
253 GUERCINO. *Madonna.* Signed 1651. Turin, Pinacoteca.
254 CARRACCI, ANNIBALE. Gallery. 1597–1604. Rome, Palazzo Farnese.
255 CARRACCI, ANNIBALE. *Polyphemus.* Rome, Palazzo Farnese.
256 GUERCINO. *Aurora.* Documented 1621–3. Rome, Casino Ludovisi.
257 RENI. *Aurora.* Documented 1613–14. Rome, Casino Rospigliosi.
258 ALBANI. *Triumph of Diana.* Documented 1622. Rome, Galleria Borghese.

256

254

257

255

258

309

259

260

263

264

265

Bernini and Baroque sculpture

259 BERNINI. *Neptune and Triton.* Documented 1620. London, Victoria and Albert Museum.
260 BERNINI. Tomb of Urban VIII. Documented 1628–47. Rome, St Peter's.
261 BERNINI. *Ecstasy of S. Teresa.* Documented 1645–52. Rome, Sta Maria della Vittoria.
262 BERNINI. *Louis XIV.* Bozzetto. Documented after 1669. Rome, Galleria Borghese.
263 BERNINI. *Gabriele Fonseca.* Documented 1668–75. Rome, S. Lorenzo in Lucina.

264 ALGARDI. *Attila repulsed by Leo the Great.* Documented 1646–53. Rome, St Peter's.
265 ALGARDI. Tomb of Leo XI. Documented 1634–52. Rome, St Peter's.
266 MOCHI. *S. Veronica.* Documented finished 1640. Rome, St Peter's.
267 BOLGI. *S. Helena.* Documented 1629–39. Rome, St Peter's.
268 QUELLIN, ARTUS I. *S. Peter.* Documented 1658. Antwerp, S. Andreaskerk.
269 DUQUESNOY. *S. Susanna.* Documented 1629–33. Rome, Sta Maria di Loreto.

261

262

266

267

268

269

270

271

Baroque decoration

270 PIETRO BERRETTINI DA CORTONA. *Allegory of Divine Providence and Barberini Power*. Ceiling. Documented 1633–9. Rome, Palazzo Barberini.

271 LANFRANCO. Ceiling, S. Gennaro Chapel. Documented 1641–3. Naples, Cathedral.

272 BACICCIA. Ceiling. Documented 1668–85. Rome, Il Gesù.

273 POZZO. *Allegory of the Jesuit Missions*. Documented 1691–4. Rome, S. Ignazio.

274 FERRI. Ceiling, Sala di Saturno. Documented 1659/64. Florence, Pitti.

275 SOLIMENA. *Expulsion of Heliodorus*. Signed 1725. Naples, Gesù Nuovo.

276 VERRIO. *The Caesars*. Documented. The King's Staircase. Hampton Court.

Seventeenth-century painting in North and Central Italy

277 CASTIGLIONE. *The Angel appearing to the Shepherds*. Signed. Birmingham, City Museum and Art Gallery.

278 ARPINO. *Annunciation*. Signed 1606. The Vatican, Museums and Galleries.

279 CRESPI, G.M. *S. John Nepomuk confessing the Queen of Bohemia*. Signed monogram. Turin, Pinacoteca.

280 FETI. *David with the Head of Goliath*. Documented. Hampton Court, Royal Collection.

278

279

280

277

312

272

273

274

275

276

281 STROZZI. *Sculpture*. Documented 1635. Venice, Biblioteca Marciana.
282 PRETI. *S. Andrew crucified*. Fresco. Documented 1650/1. Rome, S. Andrea della Valle.
283 MARATTA. *Madonna with SS. Francis and James*. Documented 1686. Rome, Sta Maria di Montesanto.
284 GIORDANO. *Mars, Venus and Cupid*. Signed. Sarasota Fla, John and Mabel Ringling Museum of Art.

281

282

283

284

285

286

291   292   293

Eighteenth-century painting

285 CONCA. *Madonna of the Rosary.* Signed 1714. Rome, S. Clemente.
286 PITTONI. *Nero and the Corpse of Seneca.* Signed 1718/21. Dresden, Gemäldegalerie.
287 RICCI, S. AND M. *Adoration of the Magi.* Documented 1726. The figures are by Sebastiano, the background by Marco. Hampton Court, Royal Collection.
288 PIAZZETTA. *SS. Vincent Ferrer, Hyacinth and Louis Beltran.* Documented before 1740. Venice, Church of the Gesuati (S. M. del Rosario).
289 PELLEGRINI. *The Education of Cupid by Painting and Drawing.* Reception piece for Academy, 1733. Paris, Louvre.
290 GIAQUINTO. *Glory of Constantine.* Commissioned 1744. Rome, Sta Croce in Gerusalemme.

297

298

29

287   288   289   290

294   295   296

291 GHISLANDI. *Self-portrait*. Signed 1732. Bergamo, Accademia Carrara.

292 LONGHI, A. *Bartolommeo Ferracina*. Signed. Venice, Museo Correr.

293 CARRIERA. *The Dancer Barbarina Campani*. Documented. Dresden, Gemäldegalerie.

294 LONGHI, P. *The Quack*. Signed 1757. Venice, Ca' Rezzonico.

295 AMIGONI. *Metastasio, Teresa Castellini, Farinelli, Amigoni and a Page*. Signed 1750/2. Melbourne, National Gallery of Victoria.

296 BATONI. *Peter Beckford*. Signed 1766. Copenhagen, Statens Museum.

297 TIEPOLO, G.B. *S. Thecla delivering the City of Este from the Plague*. Signed 1758–9. Este, Cathedral.

298 TIEPOLO, G.B. *S. Thecla delivering the City of Este from the Plague*. Modello for painting in the cathedral at Este. Datable 1758. New York, Metropolitan Museum of Art (Rogers Fund, 1937).

299 TIEPOLO, G.B. *Apollo conducting Beatrice of Burgundy*. Documented 1751. Würzburg, Residenz.

300 TIEPOLO, G.D. *Carnival Scene*. Signed 1757. Vicenza, Villa Valmarana, Foresteria.

301 GUARDI, G.A. *Death of S. Joseph*. Signed. Berlin, Staatliche Museen. (Destroyed).

302 BIBIENA. Etching from *Varie Opere*. Inscribed 'Franceso Bibiena'. Datable 1703/8.

300   301   302

315

303

304

305

Eighteenth-century Venetian Veduta painting

303 CARLEVARIS. *The Reception in Venice of the Earl of Manchester as British Ambassador, 22 September 1707.* Signed initials. Birmingham, City Museum and Art Gallery.

304 MARIESCHI. *Venice, the Rialto Bridge.* Signed monogram. Bristol, City Art Gallery.

305 BELLOTTO. *The University Square, Vienna.* Painted for the Imperial Collection 1759/60. Vienna, Kunsthistorisches Museum.

306 CANALETTO. *St Paul's from the Gardens of Somerset House.* Documented. Royal Collection.

307 GUARDI, F. *The Bacino, Venice.* Signed. Waddesdon Manor (National Trust, Rothschild Bequest).

308 CANALETTO. *Horses of St Mark's.* Signed (?1743). Royal Collection.

309 CANALETTO. *Piazza S. Marco, St Mark's and the Campanile, Venice.* Documented. Royal Collection.

310 GUARDI, F. *Pius VI's visit to Venice.* Commissioned 1782. Oxford, Ashmolean Museum.

306

307

310

308

309

Picturesque and classical landscape

311 ROSA. *S. John in the Wilderness*. Signed monogram. Glasgow, Art Gallery and Museum.

312 MAGNASCO. *Landscape with S. Anthony*. Signed AMP. Formerly Dresden, Gemäldegalerie. (Destroyed.)

313 ZUCCARELLI. *Landscape with Figures bathing and fishing below a Waterfall*. Documented before 1762. Royal Collection.

314 ZAIS. *Landscape*. Signed. London, National Gallery.

315 RICCI, M. *Landscape*. Tempera on leather. Documented. Royal Collection.

316 PANINI. *View of the Forum*. Signed 1747. Baltimore Md, Walters Art Gallery.

317 PIRANESI. *The Basilica of Maxentius*. Etching. London, British Museum.

318

Nineteenth and early twentieth-century painting and sculpture

318 CANOVA. *Pauline Bonaparte Borghese as Venus Victrix*. Signed 1808. Rome, Galleria Borghese.

319 FATTORI. *The Rotonda at Leghorn*. Signed 1866. Florence, Galleria d'Arte Moderna.

320 SIGNORINI. *View in Leith, near Edinburgh*. Florence, Galleria d'Arte Moderna.

321 LEGA. *The Pergola*. Signed 1868. Milan, Brera.

322 ZANDOMENEGHI. *Place d'Anvers, Paris*. Signed 1880. Piacenza, Museo Ricci-Oddi.

323 SEGANTINI. *The Punishment of Luxury*. Signed 1891. Liverpool, Walker Art Gallery.

324 NITTIS. *The English Girl*. Signed on back. Rome, Galleria Nazionale d'Arte Moderna.

325 BOLDINI. *Self-portrait*. Signed 1911. Ferrara, Museo Boldini.

319

320

321

322

323

324

325

II

HOLLAND AND FLANDERS

EARLY NETHERLANDISH PAINTING

326

327

328

331

329

330

326 LIMBOURG BROTHERS. *May*. From 'Très Riches Heures du Duc de Berri'. Documented before 1416. Chantilly, Musée Condé.

327 HOURS OF TURIN. *Mass for the Dead*. Turin, Museo Civico.

328 BROEDERLAM. *Presentation and Flight into Egypt*. Documented 1392–9. Dijon, Musée de la Ville.

329 JACQUEMART DE HESDIN. *The Duke of Berri and his Patron Saints*. From 'Très Belles Heures du Duc de Berri'. Documented *c*. 1402. Brussels, Bibliothèque Royale.

330 BELLECHOSE. *Martyrdom of S. Denis*. From the S. Denis Altarpiece. Attributed. Datable 1416. Paris, Louvre.

331 MALOUEL. *Trinity with the Virgin and S. John Evangelist*. Attributed. Paris, Louvre.

319

332

333

334

337

338

341

332 SLUTER. *The Well of Moses*. Detail. Documented 1402. Dijon, Puits de Moïse.

333 DARET. *Visitation with a Donor*. Documented 1433–5. Berlin, Staatliche Museen.

334 EYCK, JAN VAN. *The Arnolfini Marriage*. Signed 1434. London, National Gallery.

335 EYCK, JAN VAN. *The Ghent Altar*. Closed. Ghent, S. Bavon.

336 EYCK, JAN VAN. *The Ghent Altar*. Open. Documented 1432. Ghent, S. Bavon.

337 MASTER OF FLÉMALLE. *Crucified Thief*. Frankfurt, Städelsches Kunstinstitut.

338 MASTER OF FLÉMALLE. *The Mérode Altar*. New York, Metropolitan Museum of Art (Cloisters Collection, Purchase).

339 WEYDEN. *Deposition*. Traditionally attributed. Madrid, Prado.

340 CHRISTUS. *Annunciation, Nativity and Last Judgement*. Diptych. Signed 1452. Berlin, Staatliche Museen.

341 WEYDEN SCHOOL. *Still-life*, on reverse of *Madonna*. c. 1460. Rotterdam, Boymans-van Beuningen Museum.

335

336

339

**The early fifteenth century:
The Eyckian style, Roger van der Weyden**

340

342   343   344

342 BOUTS, A. *Assumption*. Signed with A and two Bolts. Brussels, Musées Royaux.

343 BOUTS, D. the Elder. *Last Supper*, from the 'Mystic Meals' altarpiece. Documented 1464–8. Louvain, S. Pierre.

344 OUWATER. *Raising of Lazarus*. Traditionally attributed. Berlin, Staatliche Museen.

345 GEERTGEN. *Julian the Apostate burning the Bones of S. John Baptist*. Traditionally attributed. Vienna, Kunsthistorisches Museum.

346 MASTER OF THE VIRGO INTER VIRGINES. *Virgo inter Virgines*. Amsterdam, Rijksmuseum.

347 BOSCH. *Temptation of S. Anthony*. Signed. Lisbon, Museu Nacional de Arte Antiga.

348 MEMLINC. *Madonna and the two SS. John*. Triptych. Inscribed with Memlinc's name. 1479. Bruges, Hôpital.

349 DAVID, G. *Virgo inter Virgines*. Documented 1509. Rouen, Musée des Beaux-Arts.

350 ISENBRANDT. *Madonna of the Seven Sorrows*. Attributed. Bruges, Notre Dame.

351 MASTER OF MOULINS. *Madonna*. Moulins, Cathedral.

352 MARMION. *Scenes from the Life of S. Bertin*. Attributed. Berlin, Staatliche Museen.

353 MASTER OF S. GILES. *The Mass of S. Giles*. London, National Gallery.

354 JOOS VAN GENT. *The Institution of the Eucharist*. Documented 1473–4. Urbino, Galleria Nazionale.

355 GOES. *The Portinari Altarpiece. SS. Anthony and Thomas and donors*. Traditionally attributed. Florence, Uffizi.

356 GOES. *The Portinari Altarpiece. SS. Mary Magdalen and Margaret and donors*. Traditionally attributed. Florence, Uffizi.

Fifteenth and early sixteenth-century painting in

348

35

352

345

346

the Netherlands and Northern France

347

349

350

351

354

355

356

The sixteenth century

357

358

359

357 VERMEYEN. *Cardinal Erard de la Marck*. Engraving. Signed 'Jo. Maiu'. London, British Museum.

358 VERMEYEN, Style of. *Man*. Vienna, Akademie der bildenden Künste.

359 JOOS VAN CLEVE. *Man*. Attributed. 1526. Cassel, Gemäldegalerie.

360 SCOREL. *Agatha van Schoonhoven*. Signed 1529. Rome, Galleria Doria–Pamphilj.

361 HEEMSKERCK. *Self-portrait with the Colosseum in the background*. Signed 1553. Cambridge, Fitzwilliam Museum.

362 POURBUS, P. *J. van der Gheenste, Échevin of Bruges*. Signed 1583. Brussels, Musées Royaux.

363 POURBUS, FRANS II. *Man aged 32*. Signed 1591. Leeds, Temple Newsam House.

364 MOSTAERT. *Man*. Attributed. Liverpool, Walker Art Gall.

365 MOR. *Queen Mary Tudor*. Signed 1554. Madrid, Prado.

366 SCROTS. *Henry Howard, Earl of Surrey*. Parham Park, Sussex (By permission of the Hon. Clive Pearson).

367 EWORTH. *Lord Darnley and his Brother*. Signed monogram 1563. Royal Collection.

368 GHEERAERTS. *Duke of Württemberg*. Signed c. 1608. Hampton Court, Royal Collection.

369 MASTER OF THE DEATH OF THE VIRGIN. *Dormition of the Virgin*. Cologne, Wallraf-Richartz Museum.

370 MASSYS. *The S. Anne Altar*. Centre panel. Signed 1509. Brussels, Musées Royaux.

371 SCOREL. *The Holy Kinship*. Signed 1520. Obervellach Church, Carinthia.

372 ORLEY. *The Job Altar*. Signed 1521. Brussels, Musées Royaux.

373 ANTWERP MANNERIST. *Calling of S. Matthew. c.* 1525. Royal Collection.

374 LUCAS VAN LEYDEN. *Conversion of S. Paul*. Engraving. Signed 'L' 1509. London, British Museum.

375 LUCAS VAN LEYDEN. *Moses striking the Rock*. Signed 'L' 1527. Courtesy of the Museum of Fine Arts, Boston Mass.

376 MABUSE. *Neptune and Amphitrite*. Signed 1516. Berlin, Staatliche Museen.

377 MARINUS. *Banker and his Wife*. Signed 1538. Madrid, Prado.

369

370

374

375

360

361

362

363

364

365

366

367

368

371

372

373

376

377

378

379

380

381

382

383

384

385

386

378 BUECKELAER. *Christ in the House of Martha and Mary*. Signed monogram 1565. Brussels, Musées Royaux.

379 AERTSEN. *Christ in the House of Martha and Mary*. Signed monogram 1553. Rotterdam, Boymans-van Beuningen Museum.

380 VOS, M. DE. *Christ on the Sea of Tiberias*. Signed monogram 1589. Berlin, Staatliche Museen.

381 POURBUS, FRANS I. *S. Matthew and the Angel*. Signed 1573. Brussels, Musées Royaux.

382 FLORIS. *Last Judgement*. Signed monogram 1565. Vienna, Kunsthistorisches Museum.

383 SPRANGER. *Allegory of Rudolf II*. Signed monogram 1592. Vienna, Kunsthistorisches Museum.

384 GOLTZIUS. *Adam and Eve*. Signed monogram 1608. Leningrad, Hermitage.

385 WTEWAEL. *The Temptation of Adam*. Signed 1614. Gateshead, Shipley Art Gallery.

386 MANDER. *Adoration of the Magi*. Signed monogram. Courtesy of the Wadsworth Atheneum, Hartford Conn.

387 MOSTAERT. *Landscape in the West Indies*. Haarlem, Frans Hals Museum.

388 PATENIER. *S. Jerome*. Signed. Madrid, Prado.

389 BRUEGEL, PIETER I. *Dulle Griet*. Signed (?) 1562 (?). Antwerp, Musée Mayer van den Bergh.

390 BRUEGEL, PIETER I. *The Dark Day*. Signed 1565. Vienna, Kunsthistorisches Museum.

391 BRUEGEL, PIETER II. *The Misanthropist*. Signed 1599. Antwerp, Koninklijk Museum voor Schone Kunsten.

392 CONINXLOO, G. VAN. *Midas in a Landscape*. Signed monogram 1588. Dresden, Gemäldegalerie.

393 BRUEGEL, JAN, the Elder. *Landscape with a Fishing Village*. Signed 1604. Toledo Ohio, Museum of Art (Gift of Edward Drummond Libbey).

394 HOLLAR. *View of Richmond*. Signed 1638. Royal Collection.

387

388

391

**Landscape
and fantasy**

389

392

390

393

394

395

399

396

400

397

401

398

402

395 TENIERS, D. I. *Pan with Nymphs and Satyrs*. Signed 1638. Vienna, Kunsthistorisches Museum.

396 TENIERS, D. II. *Boors carousing*. Signed 1644. London, Wallace Collection.

397 VOS, C. DE. *Family Group*. Signed 1631. Philadelphia, Museum of Art.

398 TENIERS, D. II. *Archduke Leopold Wilhelm in his Gallery in Brussels*. Documented. Vienna, Kunsthistorisches Museum.

399 BRIL, M. *Procession of Gregory XIII, 1580*. Documented 1580/3. The Vatican, Museums and Galleries.

400 BRIL, P. *Campo Vaccino, Rome*. Signed. Amsterdam, Rijksmuseum.

401 BLOEMAERT. *Prodigal Son*. Signed. Leamington Spa, Museum.

402 ELSHEIMER. *Flight into Egypt*. Signed on back 1609. Munich, Alte Pinakothek.

403 RUBENS. *Deposition*. Documented 1611–14. Antwerp, Cathedral.

404 FINSON. *Decollation of the Baptist*. Signed. Brunswick, Herzog Anton Ulrich Museum.

405 CALVAERT, D. *Danäe*. Signed 1614. Lucca, Pinacoteca.

406 ROMBOUTS. *The Musicians*. Signed. Lawrence, University of Kansas, Museum of Art.

407 VALENTIN. *Martyrdom of SS. Processus and Martinian*. Documented 1629/30. The Vatican, Museums and Galleries.

408 SANDRART. *Good Samaritan*. Signed 1632. Milan, Brera.

409 LISS. *The Inspiration of S. Jerome*. Documented. Venice, S. Niccolò dei Tolentini.

410 JORDAENS. '*As the Old sing, so the Young pipe*'. Signed 1646. Munich, Alte Pinakothek.

403

404

405

406

407

408

409

410

411

Rubens and his contemporaries

411 RUBENS. *Coronation of Marie de Médicis.*
Sketch. Munich, Alte Pinakothek.
412 RUBENS. *Coronation of Marie de Médicis.*
Documented 1622/5. Paris, Louvre.
413 RUBENS. *Caspar Gevartius.* Engraved, as by
Rubens, soon after 1637. Antwerp, Koninklijk Mus.
voor Schone Kunsten.
414 RUBENS. *Landscape with S. George.* Documented
1629/30. Royal Collection.

415 DYCK. *Five Children of Charles I.* Signed 1637.
Royal Collection.
416 DYCK. *Charles I on Horseback.* Documented.
London, National Gallery.
417 DYCK. *Cupid and Psyche.* Documented. Hampton
Court, Royal Collection.

418 VOS, P. DE. *Stag Hunt.* Signed. Brussels, Musées
Royaux.
419 SNYDERS. *Still-life with Cats and Monkeys.*
Signed. Sarasota Fla, John and Mabel Ringling
Museum of Art.
420 CHAMPAIGNE. *Mère Agnès and Soeur Catherine
de Ste-Susanne.* Signed 1662. Paris, Louvre.

415

416
417

330

412

413

414

18

419

420

331

SEVENTEENTH-CENTURY
DUTCH PAINTING

Italianate landscape, Cuyp and Calraet

421 BOTH, J. AND A. *Figures in the Roman Forum.* Signed ('Both' only). Amsterdam, Rijksmuseum.

422 CALRAET. *Scene on the Ice outside Dordrecht.* Signed initials. London, National Gallery.

423 LINGELBACH. *Mediterranean Seaport.* Signed 1668. Glasgow, Art Gallery and Museum.

424 PYNACKER. *Landscape with Sportsmen and Dogs.* Signed. London, Dulwich College Gallery.

425 ASSELYN. *Bentvueghels.* Drawing. Signed. Berlin, Kupferstichkabinett.

426 ASSELYN. *Beggars at a Monastery.* Signed 1647. Dresden, Gemäldegalerie.

427 BERCHEM. *Mountainous Landscape.* Signed 1658. London, National Gallery.

428 BAMBOCCIO. *Outside the Inn.* Signed 1635. Brunswick, Herzog Anton Ulrich Museum.

429 BOTH, J. *Peasants with Mules and Oxen.* Signed. London, National Gallery.

430 CUYP, A. *View of Dordrecht.* Signed. London, Kenwood, Iveagh Bequest.

431 DUJARDIN. *Woman and Boy with Animals at a Ford.* Signed 1657. London, National Gallery.

432 VELDE, ADRIAEN VAN DE. *Jacob and Laban.* Signed 1663. London, Wallace Collection.

433 WEENIX, J.B. *Seaport in Italy.* Signed. London, Kenwood, Iveagh Bequest.

421

422

423

42.

425

426

427

428

429

430

431

432

433

434 REMBRANDT. *Anatomy Lesson of Dr Tulp.* Signed 1632. The Hague, Mauritshuis.

435 REMBRANDT. *The Staal Meesters.* Signed 1661 and 1662. Amsterdam, Rijksmuseum.

436 BACKER. *Governors of the Nieuwezijds Huiszittenhuis.* Signed. Amsterdam, Rijksmuseum.

437 BOL. *Governors of the Leper Hospital.* Signed 1649. Amsterdam, Rijksmuseum.

438 ELIAS. *Governors and Secretary of the Workhouse.* Signed monogram 1628. Amsterdam, Rijksmuseum.

439 EECKHOUT. *Officers of the Amsterdam Coopers' Guild.* Signed 1657. London, National Gallery.

440 DUJARDIN. *Regents of the Women's Prison in Amsterdam.* Signed 1669. Amsterdam, Rijksmuseum.

441 DOU. *Man with a Pipe.* Signed. London, National Gallery.

434

436

437

438

442 HELST. *A Dutch Burgomaster.* Signed 1647. New York, Metropolitan Museum of Art (Purchase, 1871).

443 FABRITIUS, B. *Young Man.* Signed 1650. Frankfurt, Städelsches Kunstinstitut.

444 FABRITIUS, C. *Man in a Fur Cap.* Signed 1654. London, National Gallery.

445 FLINCK. *Portrait of Rembrandt.* Signed 1639. London, National Gallery.

446 REMBRANDT. *Self-portrait.* Signed monogram 1629. Boston Mass., Isabella Stewart Gardner Museum.

447 REMBRANDT. *Self-portrait.* Signed 1659. Washington D.C., National Gallery of Art (Mellon Collection).

441

442

443

444

435

439

440

**Rembrandt:
his contemporaries
and followers**

446

447

445

448

450

451

452

453

45

455

456

45

448 REMBRANDT. *The Night Watch* (*The Company of Captain Cocq*). Signed 1642. Amsterdam, Rijksmuseum.
449 REMBRANDT. *The Deposition.* Signed 165– (perhaps 1653). Washington D.C., National Gallery of Art (Widener Collection).
450 KEYSER. *Constantine Huyghens and his Secretary.* Signed monogram 1627. London, National Gallery.
451 MAES. *Woman scraping Parsnips.* Signed 1655. London, National Gallery.
452 KONINCK, S. *Solomon's Idolatry.* Signed 1644. Amsterdam, Rijksmuseum.

453 LASTMAN. *Juno discovering Jupiter with Io.* Signed 1618. London, National Gallery.
454 PYNAS, JACOB. *Adoration of the Magi.* Signed 1617. Courtesy of the Wadsworth Atheneum, Hartford Conn.
455 LIEVENS. *Raising of Lazarus.* Signed initials 1631. Brighton, Art Gallery.
456 GELDER. *Christ taken captive in the Garden.* Signed. Amsterdam, Rijksmuseum.
457 PYNAS, JAN. *Crucifixion.* Signed ('J. Pynas') 1610. Amsterdam, Rembrandthuis.

458

459

463

458 BABUREN. *The Procuress*. Signed 1622.
Courtesy of the Museum of Fine Arts, Boston
Mass.
459 HONTHORST. *The Procuress*. Signed 1625.
Utrecht, Centraal Museum.
460 TERBRUGGHEN. *Duet*. Signed 1629. Rome,
Galleria Borghese.
461 BOR. *Soothsayer*. Signed 1641. Utrecht,
Centraal Museum.
462 BYLERT. *Sutler*. Signed. Utrecht, Centraal
Museum.
463 STOMER. *Miracle of S. Isidore*. Signed 1641.
Caccamo, Sicily, S. Agostino.
464 EVERDINGEN, C. VAN. *Diogenes searching
for an honest Man*. Signed 1652. The Hague,
Mauritshuis.

465

465 HEEM, D. DE. *Still-life of Fruit*. Signed.
Oxford, Ashmolean Museum.
466 *Vanitas Still-life*, by Steenwyck (1612–
after 1656). Signed. London, Nat. Gallery.
467 HEDA, G. *Still-life*. Signed 1642.
Amsterdam, Rijksmuseum.
468 KALF. *Still-life*. Signed. Glasgow, Art
Gallery and Museum.
469 HEEM, C. DE. *Still-life with Fruit and
Oysters*. Signed. Oxford, Ashmolean Museum.
470 HEDA, W. *Still-life*. Signed 1634. Munich,
Alte Pinakothek.
471 HEEM, J.D. DE. *Man at a Table*
('*Melancholia*'). Signed 1628. Oxford, Ashmolean
Museum.

Still-life

467

468

469

460

461

462

464

466

470

471

Still-life and flower painting

472 HONDECOETER. *A Cock and other Birds*. Signed. London, Wallace Collection.

473 FERGUSON, W. *Dead Game*. Signed 1684. Edinburgh, National Gallery.

474 WEENIX, JAN. *Still-life with dead Hare*. Signed 1703. Toronto, Art Gallery (Gift of Miss L. Aileen Larkin, 1945).

475 MONNOYER. *Still-life*. Academy reception piece 1665. Montpellier, Musée Fabre.

476 RUYSCH. *Flowerpiece*. Signed 1687. Oxford, Ashmolean Museum.

477 HUYSUM, JAN VAN. *Flowerpiece*. Signed 1726. London, Wallace Collection.

478 HUYSUM, JUSTUS VAN. *Flowerpiece*. Signed. Schwerin, Staatliches Museum.

472

475

Veduta painters

479 SAENREDAM. *Interior of the Buurkerk at Utrecht*. Signed 1644. London, National Gallery.

480 WITTE, E. DE. *Church Interior*. Signed. Toledo Ohio, Museum of Art (Gift of Edward Drummond Libbey, 1958).

481 BERCKHEYDE, G. *The Market Place and Groote Kerk at Haarlem*. Signed 1674. London, National Gallery.

482 HEYDEN. *Martelaarsgracht at Amsterdam*. Signed. Amsterdam, Rijksmuseum.

479

480

473

474

476

477

478

481

482

341

483

Landscape

483 HOBBEMA. *The Travellers*. Signed 1664.
Washington D.C., National Gallery of Art
(Widener Collection).
484 RUISDAEL, J. *Landscape with Watermill*.
Signed 1661. Amsterdam, Rijksmuseum.
485 GAINSBOROUGH. *Road through a Wood*.
Signed 1747. Philadelphia, Museum of Art
(Wilstach Collection).

486

487

490

491

484

485

486 WOUWERMAN. *Courtyard with a Farrier.*
Signed monogram. London, Dulwich College.
487 WYNANTS. *Landscape with a dead Tree.*
Signed 1659. London, National Gallery.
488 RUYSDAEL, S. *River with Ferry-Boat.*
Signed 1650. Liverpool, Walker Art Gallery.
489 RUYSDAEL, J.S. *Landscape.* Signed ('JvR')
1665. Rotterdam, Boymans-van Beuningen Mus.

490 EVERDINGEN, A. *Rocky Landscape with
Sawmill.* Signed. London, National Gallery.
491 KONINCK, P. *Landscape.* Signed 1676.
Amsterdam, Rijksmuseum.
492 SEGHERS. *Landscape.* Signed. Rotterdam,
Boymans-van Beuningen Museum.
493 NEER, A. VAN DER. *A River by Moonlight.*
Signed monogram. London, National Gallery.

488

489

492

493

494

495

496

497

498

344

499

500

501

Landscape and marines

494 POTTER, PAULUS. *The Young Bull*. Signed
1647. The Hague, Mauritshuis.
495 GOYEN. *Emmerich on the Rhine*. Signed 1645.
Cleveland Ohio, Museum of Art (John L. Severance
Fund).
496 AVERCAMP. *Winter Scene*. Signed monogram.
London, National Gallery.
497 VELDE, E. VAN DE. *Winter Landscape*. Signed
1623. London, National Gallery.
498 OSTADE, ISACK VAN. *Winter Scene*. Signed.
London, Kenwood, Iveagh Bequest.

499 VELDE, W. VAN DE, the Elder. *Dutch Ships
coming to Anchor*. Grisaille. Signed ('W.V. Velde')
1654. London, National Maritime Museum.
500 CAPPELLE. *A Dutch Yacht firing a Salute*.
Signed 1650. London, National Gallery.
501 VELDE, W. VAN DE, the Younger. *Coast
Scene, Calm*. Signed 1661. London, National
Gallery.
502 VLIEGER. *View of an Estuary*. Signed. London,
National Gallery.
503 BACKHUYSEN. *Boats in a Storm*. Signed 1696.
London, Dulwich College Gallery.

502

503

504

505

506

509

510

515

516

Genre painters

504 BROUWER. *Smokers*. Signed. New York, Metropolitan Museum of Art (Michael Friedsam Collection, 1931).
505 BOTH, A. *Boors carousing*. Signed 1634. Utrecht, Centraal Museum.
506 CUYP, B.G. *Three Peasants*. Signed. Amsterdam, Rijksmuseum.
507 OSTADE, A. VAN. *Peasants playing Shuffleboard at an Inn*. Signed 1677. London, Apsley House, Wellington Museum.
508 STEEN. *Wedding*. Signed 1667. London, Apsley House, Wellington Museum.

517

518

507

508

511

512

513

514

509 HALS, D. *Party at Table*. Signed 1626. London, National Gallery.

510 MOLENAER. *The Painter's Workshop*. Signed 1631. Berlin, Staatliche Museen.

511 LEYSTER. *Boy playing the Flute*. Signed monogram (JL*). Stockholm, Nationalmuseum.

512 METSU. *The Sick Child*. Signed. Amsterdam, Rijksmus.

513 TER BORCH. *Lady writing a Letter*. Signed initials. The Hague, Mauritshuis.

514 NEER, E. VAN DER. *Girl with Dog*. Signed. Karlsruhe, Staatliche Kunsthalle.

515 DOU. *The Poulterer's Shop*. Signed. London, National Gallery.

516 SWEERTS. *Studio of a Painter*. Signed 1652. Courtesy of the Institute of Arts, Detroit, Michigan.

517 HOOCH. *Courtyard of a House in Delft*. Signed monogram 1658. London, National Gallery.

518 OCHTERVELT. *Music Party*. Signed. London, N.G.

519 VERMEER. *Lady seated at the Virginals*. Signed. London, National Gallery.

520 VERMEER. *Christ in the House of Martha and Mary*. Signed. Edinburgh, National Gallery of Scotland.

519

520

521

522

523

Portraits

521 SOMER. *Queen Anne of Denmark with her horse and dogs*. Signed 1617. Royal Collection.
522 MYTENS. *The First Duke of Hamilton*. Signed 1629. Edinburgh, National Gallery of Scotland (on loan from the present Duke of Hamilton).
523 HONTHORST. *Charles I and Henrietta Maria with the Liberal Arts*. Documented 1628. Hampton Court, Royal Collection.
524 HALS, F. *Banquet of the Civic Guard of S. Adrian*. Signed monogram 1622/7. Haarlem, Frans Hals Museum.

524

525

525 HALS, F. *De Heer Bodolphe*. Signed monogram 1643. New Haven Conn., Yale University Art Gallery (Bequest of Stephen C. Clark).
526 JAMESONE. *Self-portrait*. Traditionally attributed. Edinburgh, National Portrait Gallery of Scotland.
527 CUYP, A. *Bearded Man*. Signed 1649. London, National Gallery.
528 MAES. *Elderly Man*. Signed 1666. London, National Gallery.
529 LIEVENS. *Self-portrait*. Signed initials. London, National Gallery.
530 BRAY, J. DE. *Regents of the Children's Hospital*. Signed 1663. Haarlem, Frans Hals Museum.

526

527

528

529

530

531

532

533

534

531 MIEREVELD. *Woman aged fifty*. Signed 1636. Manchester, City Art Gallery.
532 CUYP, J.G. *Young Woman*. Signed 1636. Cambridge, Fitzwilliam Museum.
533 BRAY, S. DE. *Young Woman in a Straw Hat*. Signed 1635. Dresden, Gemäldegalerie.
534 JOHNSON. *Unknown Woman*. Signed 1655. London, National Gallery.
535 HALS, F. *Woman Governors of the Old Men's Almshouse in Haarlem*. Documented *c.* 1664. Haarlem, Frans Hals Museum.

Portraits

535

III

GERMANY, AUSTRIA BOHEMIA AND SWITZERLAND

The soft style

536 BERTRAM, MASTER. *Grabow Altar.* Attributed. *c.* 1379/83. Hamburg, Kunsthalle.
537 THEODORIC, MASTER. *S. Theodore.* Documented before 1365. Karlstein, Castle Chapel.
538 MASTER OF WITTINGAU. *Entombment,* from the Wittingau (Třeboň) altar. Prague, National Gallery.
539 FRANCKE, MASTER. *Entombment,* from the St Thomas à Becket Altar. Documented 1424. Hamburg, Kunsthalle.

536

537

538

539

540

541

542

543

544

545

546

547

540 LOCHNER. *Patron Saints of Cologne* ('*Das Dombild*'), detail. Attributed. Cologne, Cathedral.
541 KONRAD VON SOEST. *Altarpiece* (detail). Signed 1404(?). Niederwildungen, Parish Church.
542 HORTUS CONCLUSUS. *Paradise Garden*. Anonymous. Frankfurt, Städelsches Kunstinstitut.
543 MOSER. *Magdalen Altar*. Signed 1431. Tiefenbronn, Parish Church.
544 MULTSCHER. *Dormition of the Virgin*, Wurzach altar. Signed 1437. Berlin, Staatliche Museen.
545 MASTER OF THE HOUSEBOOK. *Two Lovers*. Engraving. Amsterdam, Prentenkabinet.

546 SCHONGAUER. *Nativity*. Engraving. Signed initials. London, British Museum.
547 SCHONGAUER. *Madonna of the Rosehedge*. Traditionally attributed. 1473. Colmar, S. Martin.
548 WITZ. *Christ walking on the Waters*. Signed 1444. Geneva, Musée d'Art et d'Histoire.
549 PLEYDENWURFF. *Deposition*. Documented 1462. Nuremberg, Germanisches Nationalmuseum.
550 NOTKE. *Ecce Homo*, from the High Altar. Documented 1478–9. Aarhus, Cathedral.
551 PACHER. *Christ driving the Traders from the Temple*, from an altarpiece. Documented 1471–81. Inscribed on frame 'Michaelem Pacher 1481'. Salzkammergut, S. Wolfgang.

548

549

550

551

552

552 MASTER OF S. BARTHOLOMEW.
SS. John and Margaret. Part of the
S. Bartholomew altarpiece. Munich,
Alte Pinakothek.
553 MASTER OF THE LIFE OF MARY.
Birth of the Virgin. From the Life of
the Virgin Altarpiece. Munich, Alte
Pinakothek.
554 FRUEAUF, R. the Elder. *The Agony
in the Garden.* Part of signed altarpiece,
1490–1. Vienna, Österreichische Galerie.
555 FRUEAUF, R. the Younger. *Boar Hunt.*
Scene from the Life of S. Leopold, series
signed initials 1507. Klosterneuberg,
Stiftsmuseum.

553

554

555

556

557

558

560

559

561

562

563   564   565   566

567

568

556 DÜRER. *Self-portrait*. Signed monogram 1498. Madrid, Prado.

557 DÜRER. *Adam and Eve*. Engraving, Signed monogram 1504. London, British Museum.

558 DÜRER. *Assumption*. Woodcut. Signed monogram. 1510. London, British Museum.

559 DÜRER. *Four Apostles: SS. John, Peter, Paul, and Mark*. Signed monogram 1526. Munich, Alte Pinakothek.

560 WOODCUT. *St Christopher*. 1423. Manchester, John Rylands Library.

561 ARS MORIENDI. *The Dying Man tempted to show Impatience*. Woodcut. *c.* 1470. London, British Museum.

562 DOTTED PRINT. *Events of the Day of the Resurrection*. London, British Museum.

563 BALDUNG. *Mercenary Love*. Signed 1527. Liverpool, Walker Art Gallery.

564 WOLGEMUT. *Nativity*, from the altarpiece. Documented 1476–9. Zwickau, Marienkirche.

565 KULMBACH. *Martyrdom of S. Catherine*, from the altarpiece. Signed monogram. Dated 1514 and 1515. Cracow, S. Mary.

566 SCHÄUFFELEIN. *Agony in the Garden*. Signed monogram 1516. Munich, Alte Pinakothek.

567 GRAF. *The Soldier's Farewell*. Signed monogram 1516. Basle, Kupferstichkabinett.

568 GRÜNEWALD. *Crucifixion*, from the Isenheim altarpiece. Reasonably documented. ?1515. Colmar, Musée Unterlinden.

569   570   571   572

The Danube School

569 CRANACH, L. *Katherine, wife of Henry the Pious.* Signed 1514. Dresden, Gemäldegalerie.

570 CRANACH, L. *Luther.* Signed 1525. Bristol, City Art Gallery.

571 CRANACH, L. *Rest on the Flight.* Signed 1504. Berlin, Staatliche Museen.

572 CRANACH, L. *Venus.* Signed 1529. Paris, Louvre.

573 ALTDORFER. *S. George in the Forest.* Signed monogram 1510. Munich, Alte Pinakothek.

574 ALTDORFER. *Recovery of the Body of S. Florian.* Signed monogram. Nuremberg, Germanisches National-museum.

575 HUBER. *The Danube Valley.* Signed initials 1529. Berlin, Kupferstichkabinett.

Holbein and his contemporaries

576   577

581   582   583   584

573

574

575

576 HOLBEIN, HANS I. *Martyrdom*, from S. Sebastian Altar. Documented 1515/17. Munich, Alte Pinakothek.
577 HOLBEIN, HANS II. *Noli Me Tangere*. Documented. Hampton Court, Royal Collection.
578 HOLBEIN, HANS II. *The Ambassadors*. Signed 1533. London, National Gallery.
579 HOLBEIN, HANS II. *The Monk* ('Dance of Death'). London, British Museum.
580 HOLBEIN, HANS II. *The Family of S. Thomas More*. Drawing. Documented 1527. Basle, Kupferstichkabinett.
581 BREU. *Madonna with SS. Barbara and Catherine*. Signed monogram 1512. Berlin, Staatliche Museen.
582 BURGKMAIR. *S. John Evangelist*. Signed 1518. Munich, Alte Pinakothek.

583 APT. *Crucifixion* (centre of triptych). Signed. Augsburg, Galerie.
584 BRUYN. *S. Helena with the relic of the True Cross*. Documented 1529–34 (this panel datable 1534). Xanten, S. Victor.
585 STRIGEL. *The Emperor Maximilian and his family*. Part of diptych, with contemporary ascription to Strigel, dated 1520, but of *c.* 1515. Vienna, Kunsthistorisches Mus.
586 SEISENEGGER. *The Emperor Charles V*. Formerly monogram 1532. Vienna, Kunsthistorisches Museum.
587 AMBERGER. *The Emperor Charles V*. Inscribed 'aetatis 32'. Signed (damaged) on back. *c.* 1532. Berlin, Staatliche Museen.
588 PENCZ. *Portrait of Jörg Herz*. Signed monogram 1545. Karlsruhe, Staatliche Kunsthalle.

578

579

580

585

586

587

588

589   590   591

594   595   596   597

602   603   604

589 ROTTMAYR. *Tarquin and Lucretia*. Signed 1692. Vienna, Österreichische Nationalgalerie.

590 MAULBERTSCH. *The Assumption*. Sketch for documented fresco of 1764 (destroyed 1944/5). Vienna, Barockmuseum.

591 ZICK. *S. Charles Borromeo giving Communion to the Plague-stricken*. Signed 1787. Berlin, Staatliche Museen.

592 MENGS. *Parnassus*. Signed 1761. Rome, Villa Albani.

593 CARSTENS. *Eteocles setting out for battle*. Cartoon in chalk and water-colour. Signed 1797. Weimar, Staatliche Kunstsammlungen.

594 LIOTARD. *Self-portrait*. Inscribed 1744 and documented. Florence, Uffizi.

595 KAUFFMANN. *Winckelmann*. Inscribed and dated 1764. Documented by letter of Winckelmann. Zurich, Kunsthaus.

596 TISCHBEIN. *Goethe in the Campagna*. Documented 1786/8. Frankfurt, Städelsches Kunstinstitut.

597 RUNGE. *The Hülsenbeck Children*. Documented. 1805/6. Hamburg, Kunsthalle.

598 GRAFF. *Self-portrait*. Signed 1809. Leipzig, Museum der Bildenden Künste.

599 RAYSKI. *Portrait of Graf Hans Haubold von Einsiedel*. Signed monogram 1855. Berlin, Staatliche Museen.

600 LENBACH. *Bismarck*. 1894. Munich, Städtische Galerie.

601 LIEBERMANN. *Self-portrait*. Signed 1934. London, Tate Gallery.

602 KRÜGER. *Prince Wilhelm out riding, accompanied by the Artist*. Signed 1836. Berlin, Staatliche Museen.

603 FRIEDRICH. *Abbey under Oak Trees*. Documented. Berlin, Staatliche Schlösser und Gärten.

604 KOCH. *Heroic landscape with rainbow*. Signed initials (1805). Karlsruhe, Staatliche Kunsthalle.

592

593

598

599

600

601

605

606

607

608

605 BLECHEN. *Ravine near Amalfi.* Signed
1831. Berlin, Staatliche Museen.
606 WALDMÜLLER. *Homecoming.* Signed
1859. Hamburg, Kunsthalle.
607 BÖCKLIN. *The Island of the Dead.* 1880
version. Basle, Kunstmuseum.
608 CORINTH. *Walchensee.* Signed 1924.
Cologne, Wallraf-Richartz Museum.

609

610

611

612

614

615

616

617

609 OVERBECK. *Madonna with SS. John and Elizabeth*. Signed initials 1825. Munich, Neue Pinakothek.
610 SCHNORR. *The Flight into Egypt*. Signed monogram 1828. Düsseldorf, Kunstmuseum.
611 RETHEL. *Kaiser Maximilian's Guardian Angel*. Fresco. 1845. Frankfurt, Städelsches Kunstinstitut.
612 CORNELIUS. *Wise and Foolish Virgins*. Documented. Düsseldorf, Kunstmuseum.
613 SCHWIND. *Consecration of Freiburg Cathedral*. Fresco. 1841–2. Karlsruhe, Kunsthalle.
614 SPITZWEG. *The Poor Poet*. Signed 1839. Munich, Neue Pinak.

615 THOMA. *Sunday Peace*. Signed 1876. Hamburg, Kunsthalle.
616 FEUERBACH. *Paolo and Francesca*. Signed 1864. Munich, Schackgalerie.
617 LEIBL. *Three Women in Church*. Signed 1881. Hamburg, Kunsthalle.
618 MARÉES. *The Hesperides*. 1885; centre of polyptych, 1884–7. Munich, Neue Pinakothek.
619 MENZEL. *Plans for Travel*. Signed 1875. Essen, Folkwang Museum.
620 SLEVOGT. *D'Andrade in the rôle of Don Giovanni*. Signed 1902. Stuttgart, Staatsgalerie.

621

622

623

613

The Nazarenes and nineteenth-century painting

618

619

620

German sculpture

624

621 GERHART. Crucifix. Signed 1467. Baden-Baden, Old Cemetery.
622 ERHART. *S. John Evangelist*. Detail of altarpiece. Attributed 1493. Blaubeuren, Klosterkirche.
623 STOSS. *High Altar* (detail). Documented 1477–89. Cracow, S. Mary.
624 RIEMENSCHNEIDER. *Adoration*. Probably from documented altarpiece. 1505–6. London, British Museum.
625. VISCHER. *Hercules*, from the Tomb of S. Sebaldus. Documented 1508–19. Nuremberg, S. Sebaldus.
626. VRIES. Figure from the Hercules Fountain. Documented 1602. Augsburg.

625

626

627

628

629

630

627 SCHLÜTER. *The Great Elector*. Documented 1698–1703. Berlin, Schloss Charlottenburg.
628 DONNER. *S. Martin*. Documented 1735. Pressburg, Cathedral.
629 PERMOSER. *S. Augustine*. Documented *c*. 1725. Bautzen, Stadtmuseum.
630 GÜNTHER. *Annunciation*. Documented. 1764. Weyarn, Bavaria.
631 SCHADOW. Tomb of Graf von der Marck. Signed and dated 1790. Berlin, Doretheenkirche.
632 HILDEBRAND. The Wittelsbach Fountain. Detail of right section. 1891–4. Munich.

631

632

IV

SPAIN AND PORTUGAL

633

634
635

Fifteenth-century Spanish and Portuguese art

633 BERMEJO. *Pietà with S. Jerome and a Donor*. Signed 1490. Barcelona, Cathedral.
634 BERRUGUETE, P. *Apparition of the Virgin to a Dominican Community*. Attributed. From S. Tomas, Avila. Madrid, Prado.
635 GONÇALVES. *S. Vincent Altar*. Attributed. Lisbon, Museu Nacional de Arte Antiga.

636   637   638

Spanish painting and sculpture: the sixteenth and seventeenth centuries

636 BERRUGUETE, A. *Abraham and Isaac*. Documented 1527–32. Valladolid, Museum.

637 RIBALTA. *The Vision of Father Simon*. Signed 1612. London, National Gallery.

638 MORALES. *Pietà*. Attributed. Madrid, Academia de S. Fernando.

639 RIBERA. *S. Peter Repentant*. Signed 1628. Glasgow, Art Gallery and Museum.

640 ZURBARÁN. *S. Serapion*. Signed 1628. Courtesy of the Wadsworth Atheneum, Hartford Conn.

641 COELLO, CLAUDIO. *S. Catherine of Alexandria*. Signed 1683. London, Apsley House, Wellington Mus.

642 SÁNCHEZ COELLO. *Anne of Austria, Queen of Spain*. Signed 1571. Vienna, Kunsthistorisches Mus.

643 MAZO. *Queen Mariana of Spain in Mourning*. Signed 1666. London, National Gallery.

644 PACHECO. *Man*. Signed 1626. Williamstown Mass., Williams College Museum of Art.

645 VALDÉS LEAL. *Immaculate Conception, with two Donors*. Signed monogram 1661. London, Nat. Gall.

646 CANO. *Annunciation*. Documented 1652–6. Granada, Cathedral.

647 MURILLO. *Madonna and Child in Glory*. Documented 1673. Liverpool, Walker Art Gallery.

642   643   644

639

640

641

645

647

646

648

649

650

651

El Greco

648 EL GRECO. *View of Toledo*. Signed. New York, Metropolitan Museum of Art (Bequest of Mrs H.O. Havemeyer, 1929. The H.O. Havemeyer Collection).
649 EL GRECO. *Assumption*. Signed 1577. Courtesy of the Art Institute of Chicago (Gift of Nancy Atwood Sprague in memory of Albert Atwood Sprague).
650 EL GRECO. *El Espolio*. Documented 1577–9. Toledo, Cathedral.
651 EL GRECO. *Baptism of Christ*. Signed 1596–1600. Madrid, Prado.
652 EL GRECO. *Cardinal Niño de Guevara*. Signed datable 1596/1601. New York, Metropolitan Museum of Art (Bequest of Mrs H.O. Havemeyer, 1929. The H.O. Havemeyer Collection).

652

653

Velazquez

654

655

656

657

658

653 VELAZQUEZ. *Los Borrachos* (*The Topers*). Bought in 1629. Madrid, Prado.
654 VELAZQUEZ. *Las Meninas*. Documented 1656. Madrid, Prado.
655 VELAZQUEZ. *Conde-Duque de Olivares*. Documented 1624. São Paulo, Museu de Arte.

656 VELAZQUEZ. *Philip IV* (The Fraga Philip). Documented 1644. Courtesy of the Frick Collection, New York.
657 VELAZQUEZ. *Innocent X*. Signed 1650. Rome, Galleria Doria-Pamphilj.
658 BODEGÓN. Velazquez. *Old Woman frying eggs*. 1618. Edinburgh, National Gallery of Scotland.

659

Goya

659 GOYA. *El Pelele* (*The Manikin*). Tapestry cartoon, 1791 or 1792. Madrid, Prado.
660 GOYA. *Family of Charles IV*. Documented 1800. Madrid, Prado.
661 GOYA. *Madrid, 3 May 1808*. Documented *c.* 1814. Madrid, Prado.
662 GOYA. *Tal para qual* (*Two of a kind*). From *Los Caprichos*. Aquatint engraving.
663 BAYEU, F. *Picnic in the Country*. Tapestry cartoon, 1784. Signed. Madrid, Prado.

660

661

662

663

664

664 GISLEBERTUS. *The Three Magi.*
Part of a signed cycle. After 1120.
Autun, S. Lazare.

665

666

669

670

671

672

673

The fifteenth to seventeenth centuries

674

675

676

667

668

665 MASTER OF THE AIX ANNUNCIATION. *Annunciation.*
Aix-en-Provence, Église des Prêcheurs.
666 QUARTON. *Coronation of the Virgin.* Documented
1453–4. Villeneuve-lès-Avignon, Hospice.
667 FROMENT. *Mary in the Burning Bush.* Detail.
Documented completed 1476. Aix-en-Provence, Cathedral.
668 FOUQUET. *The Clemency of Cyrus.* From 'Antiquités
Judaïques'. Documented. Paris, Bibliothèque Nationale.
669 MASTER OF 1456. *Portrait of a Man.* 1456. Vaduz,
Liechtenstein Collection.
670 PERRÉAL. *Louis XII of France.* Attributed. Royal
Collection.
671 CORNEILLE DE LYON. *The Earl of Hertford*(?).
Attributed. London, Wallace Collection.
672 CLOUET, FRANÇOIS. *Pierre Quthe.* Signed 1562.
Paris, Louvre.
673 CLOUET, JEAN II. *Guillaume Budé.* Drawing.
Attributed. Chantilly, Musée Condé.
674 GOUJON. *Nymph.* From the *Fontaine des Innocents.*
Documented as existing 1549. Paris, Louvre.
675 FONTAINEBLEAU, CHÂTEAU DE. Escalier d'Honneur.
676 FONTAINEBLEAU, SECOND SCHOOL OF. Toussaint
Dubreuil: *Lady at her Toilet.* Attributed. Paris, Louvre.
677 PILON. Tomb of Valentine Balbiani. Detail.
Documented. Paris, Louvre.
678 VOUET. *Diana.* Signed 1627 (or 37). Hampton Court,
Royal Collection.
679 LA TOUR, G. DE. *S. Joseph and the Angel.* Signed.
Nantes, Musée des Beaux-Arts.
680 LE NAIN, A. *The Village Piper.* Signed 'Lenain' 1644.
Courtesy of the Institute of Arts, Detroit Michigan.
681 LE NAIN, L. *Old Woman.* Signed 'Lenain' 1644.
Avignon, Musée Calvet.
682 CALLOT. *Robbers hanged from a Tree.* Etching from
Grandes Misères de la Guerre. 1633. London, British
Museum.

678

679

680

681

677

682

The seventeenth century: Claude and Poussin

683 LE NAIN, M. *Adoration of the Shepherds*. Attributed. Paris, Louvre.
684 LE NAIN, L. AND M. *Venus at the Forge of Vulcan*. Signed 'Lenain' 1641. Rheims, Musée.
685 BLANCHARD. *Charity*. Signed 1637. London, Courtauld Institute Galleries.
686 BOURDON. *Martyrdom of S. Peter*. Documented 1643. Paris, Notre Dame.
687 LE SUEUR, E. *Death of S. Bruno*. Documented 1645/8. Paris, Louvre.
688 POUSSIN, N. *Holy Family on the Steps*. Documented 1648. Washington D.C., National Gallery of Art (Samuel H. Kress Collection 1949).
689 POUSSIN, N. *Annunciation*. Signed 1657. London, National Gallery.
690 POUSSIN, N. *The Inspiration of the Poet*. Documented. Paris, Louvre.
691 MILLET. *Landscape with Lightning*. Attributed. London, National Gallery.
692 CLAUDE. *Classical Landscape*. Signed 1645. Birmingham, Barber Institute of Fine Art.
693 POUSSIN, G. *Elias*. Fresco 1644–50. Rome, S. Martino ai Monti.

683

684

685

686

688

689

690

687

691

692

693

375

694

695

696

697

694 LEBRUN, C. *Hercules and the Horses of Diomedes.*
Signed before 1641. Nottingham, Mus. and Art Gallery.
695 LARGILLIERRE. *Charles Lebrun.* Documented. 1686.
Paris, Louvre.
696 COYSEVOX. *Charles Lebrun.* Terracotta model.
Documented 1676. London, Wallace Collection.
697 MIGNARD. *The Marquise de Seignelay as Thetis.*
Signed 1691. London, National Gallery.

698 COYPEL, CHARLES. *Perseus freeing Andromeda.* Documented 1727.
Paris, Louvre.
699 RIGAUD. *Family Group.* Signed 1699. Ottawa, National Gallery of
Canada.
700 VAN LOO, J.B. *The Rt Hon. Thomas Winnington.* Signed. Worcester
City Corporation.
701 COYPEL, ANTOINE. Ceiling of the Royal Chapel. Documented as
finished 1708. Versailles.

698

699

700

701

702

703

704

702 LE MOYNE, F. *Time revealing Truth*. Documented 1737. London, Wallace Collection.
703 LAGUERRE. Wall paintings on the staircase. Documented after 1714. Petworth, Sussex.
704 TROY, J.F. DE. *The Alarm*. Signed 1723. London, Victoria and Albert Museum.
705 VAN LOO, C. *The Grand Turk giving a concert to his Mistress*. Signed 1737. London, Wallace Collection.
706 OUDRY. *The Dead Wolf*. Signed 1721. London, Wallace Collection.
707 CHARDIN. *Still-life with Rib of Beef*. Signed 1739. Oberlin College, Ohio, Allen Art Museum.

707

705

706

708

709

711

712

713

714

715

719

720

721

710

French sculpture

708 PUGET. *Caryatids*. Signed 1656–7. Toulon, Hôtel de Ville.
709 GIRARDON. *Apollo and the Nymphs of Thetis*. Commissioned 1666. Versailles.
710 PIGALLE. *Love and Friendship*. Plaster. Documented 1758. Courtesy of the Walters Art Gallery, Baltimore Md.
711 ADAM, L.S. *Neptune calming the Waves*. Documented. 1737. Paris, Louvre.
712 BOUCHARDON. *Cupid*. Signed 1750. Paris, Louvre.
713 CLODION. *Faun and Bacchante*. Signed 1770. Paris, Louvre.
714 FALCONET. *Baigneuse*. Exhibited 1757. Paris, Louvre.
715 HOUDON. *Diana*. Signed 1780. Lisbon, Gulbenkian Foundation.
716 LEMOYNE, J.B. *Montesquieu*. Signed 1761. Bordeaux, Musée des Beaux-Arts.
717 PAJOU. *J.B. Lemoyne*. Signed 1758. Paris, Louvre.
718 COUSTOU, G., II. *Marguérite Le Comte*. Signed. London, Victoria and Albert Museum.
719 COUSTOU, G., I. *Cheval de Marly*. Documented 1740/5. Paris, Champs Élysées.
720 FALCONET. *Equestrian monument to Peter the Great*. Documented 1766/78. Leningrad.
721 HOUDON. *Washington*. Signed 1788, documented as completed by 1791. Richmond Va, Capitol.
722 BARYE. *Jaguar devouring a Gazelle*. Signed. Edinburgh, National Gallery of Scotland.
723 RUDE. '*La Marseillaise*'. Completed 1836. Paris, Arc de Triomphe de l'Étoile.
724 CARPEAUX. *The Dance*. Stone. 1865–9. Paris, Opéra façade (now Louvre).

716

717

718

722

723

724

725

727

728

The eighteenth century: Rococo, Watteau, portraits

725 WATTEAU. *Embarkation for the Island of Cythera*. Documented 1717. Paris, Louvre.
726 WATTEAU. *L'Enseigne de Gersaint*. Documented 1720–1. Berlin, Staatliche Schlösser und Gärten.
727 PATER. *Soldiers revelling*. Documented 1728. Paris, Louvre.
728 FRAGONARD. *The Meeting*, from *The Progress of Love*. Documented c. 1771. Courtesy of the Frick Collection, New York.
729 BOUCHER. *Visit of Venus to Vulcan*. Signed 1754. London, Wallace Collection.

732

733

734

73

726

729

730

731

730 LANCRET. *Youth*. Engraved in 1735. London, National Gallery.

731 GREUZE. *L'Accordée de Village*. Salon 1761. Paris, Louvre.

732 AVED. *Mme Crozat*. Signed 1741. Montpellier, Musée Fabre.

733 NATTIER. *Queen Marie Lesczinska*. Signed 1748. Versailles.

734 DROUAIS. *Mme Favart*. Signed 1757. New York, Metropolitan Museum of Art (Mr and Mrs Isaac D. Fletcher Collection. Bequest of Isaac D. Fletcher, 1917).

735 TOCQUÉ. *The Marquis de Marigny*. Signed 1755. Versailles.

736 LOO, L.M. VAN. *Diderot*. Signed 1767. Paris, Louvre.

737 VIGÉE-LEBRUN, LOUISE. *The Artist and her Daughter*. Documented 1789. Paris, Louvre.

738 PERRONNEAU. *The Engraver Laurent Cars*. Signed 1750. Ann Arbor, University of Michigan, Museum of Art.

739 LATOUR, M.Q. DE. *Mlle Fel*. Sketch for 1757 Salon portrait. Saint-Quentin, Musée A. Lécuyer.

740 ROSLIN. *The Artist's Wife with a Fan*. Signed 1762. Stockholm, Nationalmuseum.

736

737

738

739

740

741

742

743

744

745

746

The eighteenth and nineteenth centuries:
David, Ingres, portraits up to Renoir

747

748

749

750

751

741 VIEN. *La Marchande d'Amours*. Salon of 1763. Fontainebleau.
742 DAVID, J.L. *The Oath of the Horatii*. Signed 1785. Paris, Louvre.
743 PRUD'HON. *The Empress Josephine*. Signed. Paris, Louvre.
744 DAVID, J.L. *Mme. de Verninac*. Signed 1799. Paris, Louvre.
745 GÉRARD. *J.B. Isabey and his Daughter*. Signed 1795. Paris, Louvre.
746 GIRODET. *J.B. Belley, Député de S. Domingue*. Signed 1797. Versailles.
747 INGRES. *M. Bertin l'Aîné*. Signed 1832. Paris, Louvre.

748 CHASSÉRIAU. *Le Père Lacordaire*. Signed 1840. Paris, Louvre.
749 FANTIN-LATOUR. *L'Atelier aux Batignolles*. Signed 1870. Paris, Louvre.
750 COROT. *Woman in Studio*. Signed. Washington D.C., National Gallery of Art (Widener Collection).
751 DEGAS. *Roman Beggar Woman*. Signed 1857. Birmingham, City Museum and Art Gallery.
752 RENOIR. *Mme Charpentier and her Children*. Signed 1878. New York, Metropolitan Museum of Art (Wolfe Fund, 1907).

752

753

754

753 VERNET, CLAUDE JOSEPH. *Italian Landscape.* Signed. London, Dulwich College Gallery.

754 ROBERT, HUBERT. *Architectural Composition with Temple and Obelisk.* Signed 1768. Barnard Castle, Bowes Museum.

755 MILLET. *The Winnower.* Signed 1848. Paris, Louvre.

756 COURBET. *Les Demoiselles de la Seine.* Signed 1857. Paris, Petit Palais.

757 COROT. *The Forum, Rome.* Signed 1826. Paris, Louvre.

758 DAUBIGNY. *St Paul's from the Surrey side.* Signed 1873. London, National Gallery.

759 MICHEL. *Landscape with a Mill.* Signed. Leningrad, Hermitage.

760 BOUDIN. *Gravelines.* Signed 1888. University of Glasgow, Art Collections.

761 JONGKIND. *The Sea at Étretat.* Signed 1853. Birmingham, City Museum and Art Gallery.

762 ROUSSEAU, THÉODORE. *Forest of Clairbois.* Signed. Glasgow, Art Gallery and Museum.

763 DIAZ. *Woodland Scene.* Signed. Birmingham, City Museum and Art Gallery.

764 COROT. *Road at Ville d'Avray.* Signed 1874. Lisbon, Gulbenkian Foundation.

765 LÉPINE. *Rue de Norvins, Montmartre.* Signed. Glasgow, Art Gallery and Museum.

766 HARPIGNIES. *Summer.* Signed 1898. Toledo Ohio, Museum of Art (Gift of Arthur J. Secor, 1922).

755

756

757

758

759

760

761

762

763

764

765

766

767

768

The nineteenth century: Delacroix and Ingres to Renoir

767 VERNET, CARLE. *Triumph of Paulus Aemilius.*
Signed 1789. New York, Metropolitan Museum of Art (Gift of
Darius O. Mills, 1906).
768 VERNET, HORACE. *Battle of Montmirail in 1819.*
Signed 1822. London, National Gallery.
769 GROS. *The Battle of Nazareth.* Signed 1801. Nantes,
Musée des Beaux-Arts.
770 GÉRICAULT. *Raft of the Medusa.* Salon 1819. Paris,
Louvre.
771 GÉRICAULT. *The Mad Woman.* Documented 1821/4.
Lyons, Musée des Beaux-Arts.
772 DELACROIX. *Massacre at Chios.* Signed (Salon 1824).
Paris, Louvre.
773 DELACROIX. *Medea.* Signed 1862. Paris, Louvre.

774 DELACROIX. *Arab Horses fighting.* Signed 1860. Paris,
Louvre.
775 INGRES. *Baigneuse de Valpinçon.* Signed 1808. Paris,
Louvre.
776 INGRES. *Two Nudes*, study for *The Golden Age* (1842–9).
Signed drawing. Courtesy of the Fogg Art Museum, Harvard
University (Grenville L. Winthrop Collection).
777 COUTURE. *A Roman Feast.* Signed monogram 1843.
London, Wallace Collection.
778 TOULOUSE-LAUTREC. *Au Salon* (*rue des Moulins*).
Signed monogram 1895. Albi, Musée Toulouse-Lautrec.
779 DEGAS. *Le Tub.* Pastel. Signed 1886. Paris, Louvre.
780 RENOIR. *Baigneuse au Griffon.* Signed 1870. São Paulo,
Museu de Arte.
781 RENOIR. *Bather.* Signed 1912. Toledo Ohio, Museum
of Art (Gift of Mrs C. Lockhart McKeloy, 1955).

775

776

777

778

779

769

770

771

772

773

774

780

781

782

783

784

785

786

787

788

789

790

791

782 DAUMIER. *Le dernier Conseil des Ministres*. Signed initials 1848. Paris, Bibliothèque Nationale.

783 DAUMIER. *Third-class Railway Carriage*. Signed. Ottawa, National Galle[ry] of Canada.

784 GUYS. *In the Streets of Constantinop[le]*. Documented 1854. London, B.M.

785 FORAIN. *The Court*. Signed 1908. London, Tate Gallery.

786 MOREAU, GUSTAVE. *Salome*. Wat[er]colour. Signed. Paris, Louvre.

787 PUVIS DE CHAVANNES. *S. Genevi[eve] watching over Paris*. Signed 1898. Paris, [Panthéon.

788 REDON. *Les Yeux clos*. Signed 189[ ] Paris, Louvre.

789 MERYON. *S. Étienne-du-Mont, Pa[ris]*. Pencil drawing. 1850–2. Toledo Ohio, Museum of Art (Winthrop E. Percy Fu[nd] 1948).

790 MERYON. *S. Étienne-du-Mont, Pa[ris]*. Etching. Toledo Ohio, Museum of Art (Winthrop E. Percy Fund, 1948).

791 UTRILLO. *L'Impasse Cottin*. Sign[ed] c. 1910. Paris, Musée National d'Art Moderne.

388

792

793

794

795

796

797

98

799

792 BAZILLE. *The Pink Dress*. Signed 1864. Paris, Musée de l'Impressionnisme.

793 MORISOT. *The Cradle*. 1st Impressionist Exhibition 1874. Paris, Louvre.

794 RENOIR. *La Loge*. Signed 1874. 1st Impressionist Exhibition. London, Courtauld Institute Galleries.

795 DEGAS. *The Dancing Class*. 1st Impressionist Exhibition 1874. Signed. Paris, Louvre.

796 MANET. *Le Déjeuner sur l'Herbe*. Salon des Refusés 1863. Signed 1863. Paris, Louvre.

797 MANET. *The Bar at the Folies Bergère*. Signed 1882. London, Courtauld Institute Galleries.

798 DEGAS. *Pianist and Chanteur*. Pastel on monotype. Courtesy of Paul Brame and C. de Hauke, Paris.

799 TOULOUSE-LAUTREC. *La Revue Blanche*. Coloured lithograph: 1st state of poster, with *Remarque*. Signed monogram 1895. Baltimore Md, Museum (Collection of Mr and Mrs Nelson Gutman).

800

801

803

802

804

VI

BRITAIN AND
AMERICA

805

Miniatures

805 HILLIARD. *Self-portrait, aged 30*. Signed monogram 1577. London, Victoria and Albert Museum.
806 OLIVER, I. *Unknown Man* (wrongly called *Sir Philip Sidney*). Signed monogram. Royal Collection.

806

807

811

808

812

809

813

810

824

807 HOSKINS. *Young Man with a View of London.* Signed 1647. London, Victoria and Albert Museum.

808 COOPER, A. *Man.* Signed. London, Victoria and Albert Museum.

809 COOPER, S. *Self-portrait.* Signed 1657. London, Victoria and Albert Museum.

810 COSWAY. *William Calcraft.* Signed on back 1793. London, Victoria and Albert Museum.

811 DOBSON. *Unknown Girl.* Signed 1645. Birmingham, City Museum and Art Gallery.

812 CRITZ. *Hester Tradescant and her Stepson John.* Attributed. 1645. Oxford, Ashmolean Museum.

813 RILEY. *Bridget Holmes, a nonagenarian Housemaid.* Signed 1686. Royal Collection.

814 WALKER. *Self-portrait.* Signed. Oxford, Ashmolean Museum.

815 WRIGHT, J. M. *Colonel John Russell.* Signed 'Io. MRitus/P.1659'. London, Victoria and Albert Museum (Ham House).

816 LELY. *Sir Jeremy Smith.* Documented *c.* 1666. London, National Maritime Museum.

817 FULLER. *Self-portrait.* Signed 1670. Oxford, Bodleian Library.

818 MEDINA. *Self-portrait.* Signed. Providence RI, School of Design.

819 KNELLER. *Samuel Pepys.* Signed 1689. London, National Maritime Museum.

820 DAHL. *Self-portrait.* Signed 1691. London, National Portrait Gallery.

814

815

816

817 818 819 820

English and Scottish
portraiture in the eighteenth century

821 AIKMAN. *Allan Ramsay, senior*. Documented 1723. Edinburgh, Scottish National Portrait Gallery.

822 RICHARDSON. *George Vertue*. Documented 1738. London, National Portrait Gallery.

823 HONE. *Self-portrait*. Signed monogram 1778. Manchester, City Art Gallery.

824 WILSON, RICHARD. *Captain Michael Everitt, RN*. Signed *c*. 1747/8. Melbourne, National Gallery of Victoria.

825 HUDSON. *Gentleman*. Signed 1750. London, Dulwich College Gallery.

826 WILSON, BENJAMIN. *The Fourth Earl of Chesterfield*. Signed 1752. Leeds, City Art Gallery.

827 COTES. *Benjamin Vaughan*. Signed 1768. Courtesy of the Museum of Fine Arts, Boston Mass.

828 VERTUE. *Self-portrait*. Drawing. Signed 1741. London, British Museum.

821 822 823

825 826 827 828

829

830

831

836

837

838

English and American group portraits

840 ZOFFANY. *Charles Towneley in his Gallery*. Exhibited RA 1790. Burnley, Towneley Hall.
841 REYNOLDS. *Lady Smith and her Children*. Exhibited RA 1787. New York, Metropolitan Museum of Art (Bequest of Collis P. Huntington, 1925).

840

841

842

32   833   834   835

39

829 SMIBERT. *Mrs Elizabeth Ferne*. Signed 1724. Worcester Mass., Art Museum.

830 HOGARTH. *Mrs William James*. Signed 1744. Worcester Mass., Art Museum.

831 KNAPTON. *Miss Lucy Ebberton*. Engraved as by Knapton. London, Dulwich College Gallery.

832 RAMSAY. *The Artist's Wife*. Documented. Edinburgh, National Gallery of Scotland.

833 HOPPNER. *Princess Mary*. Exhibited RA 1785. Royal Collection.

834 ROMNEY. *Mrs Wilbraham Bootle*. Documented 1781. Edinburgh, National Gallery of Scotland.

835 DOWNMAN. *Mrs Siddons*. Drawing. Signed 1787. London, National Portrait Gallery.

836 DEVIS, ARTHUR. *The Love Song*. Signed 1749. London, Victoria and Albert Museum.

837 KETTLE. *Charles and John Sealy*. Signed 1773. London, Courtauld Institute Galleries.

838 REYNOLDS. *The Triumph of Truth (Dr Beattie)*. Exhibited RA 1774. Aberdeen, Marischal College.

839 GAINSBOROUGH. *General Honywood*. Exhibited Society of Artists 1765. Sarasota Fla, John and Mabel Ringling Museum of Art.

842 COPLEY. *The Copley Family*. Exhibited RA 1777. Washington D.C., National Gallery of Art (Purchase Fund, Andrew W. Mellon Gift).

843 DUNLAP. *The Artist Showing his Picture of a Scene from 'Hamlet' to his Parents*. 1788. Exhibited National Academy 1833. Courtesy of the New-York Historical Society, New York City.

844 EARL. *Chief Justice Ellsworth and his Wife*. Signed 1792. Courtesy of the Wadsworth Atheneum, Hartford Conn.

43   844

845

846

84

845 GAINSBOROUGH. *The Hon. Mrs Graham*. Exhibited RA 1777. Edinburgh, National Gallery of Scotland.

846 BEECHEY. *Queen Charlotte*. Documented. London, Courtauld Institute Galleries.

847 STUART. *William Grant skating*. Exhibited RA 1782. Washington DC, National Gallery of Art.

848 RAEBURN. *Colonel Alastair Macdonnell of Glengarry*. Exhibited RA 1812. Edinburgh, National Gallery of Scotland.

849 LAWRENCE. *Pope Pius VII*. Documented 1819. Windsor Castle, The Waterloo Chamber (Royal Collection).

850 GEDDES. *George Sanders*. Signed 1816. Edinburgh, National Gallery of Scotland.

851 MORSE. *Lafayette*. Documented 1825–6. Courtesy of the Art Commission of the City of New York. Brooklyn Mus., New York.

852 SULLY. *Queen Victoria*. Signed initials 1838. New York, Metropolitan Museum of Art.

853 ABBOTT. *Nelson*. Documented. London, N.P.G.

854 PEALE, C. W. *Self-portrait with a Mastodon Bone*. Documented 1824. Courtesy of the New-York Historical Society, New York City.

855 PEALE, REMBRANDT. *George Washington*. Signed. Washington D.C., National Gallery of Art (Gift of Mr and Mrs George Davison).

856 HAYMAN. *May Day*. Documented *c.* 1737. London, V. & A

857 HOGARTH. Engraving from the *Harlot's Progress*. 173 London, British Museum.

858 HOGARTH. *The Lady's Last Stake, or, Virtue in Danger* Documented 1759. Buffalo NY, Albright-Knox Art Gallery.

859 HIGHMORE. *Pamela tells a Nursery Story*. Engraved in 174 Cambridge, Fitzwilliam Museum.

860 GRAVELOT. *Scene from 'Pamela'*. Drawing. Engraved i reverse for 6th ed., 1742. London, British Museum.

856

8

848

849

850

851

852

853

854

855

860

English Genre painting in the eighteenth century

858

859

861 LE SUEUR, H. *Charles I*. Detail. Signed 1633. London, Charing Cross.

862 PEARCE. *Sir Christopher Wren*. 1673. Oxford, Ashmolean Museum.

863 RYSBRACK. *Sir Robert Walpole*. Terracotta. Documented 1738. London, N. P. Gal.

864 ROUBILIAC. *Martin Folkes*. Terracotta. Marble signed 1749. London, British Museum.

865 NOLLEKENS. *Lord Mansfield, L.C.J.* Signed 1779. London, Kenwood, Iveagh Bequest.

866 CHANTREY. *George Crabbe*. Signed 1828. London, Victoria and Albert Museum.

867 BUSHNELL. *Sir Thomas Gresham*. Documented 1671. London, Old Bailey.

868 BACON, J. *Samuel Johnson Monument*. Signed 1796. London, St Paul's.

869 WESTMACOTT. *Monument to Charles James Fox*. Detail of negro slave. Documented 1810. London, Westminster Abbey.

870 THORWALDSEN. *S. Paul*. Documented 1820–8. Copenhagen, Frukirke.

871 GIBSON. *Hylas and the Nymphs*. Signed 1826. London, Tate Gallery.

872 STEVENS. *Valour and Cowardice*. Model for part of the Wellington Monument, *c*. 1860. London, Tate.

873 CIBBER. *Raving Madness*, from Bedlam. *c*. 1680. Recorded in Vertue. London, Guildhall.

874 QUELLIN, ARNOLD. *Boy with Censer*, from the Whitehall Chapel by Quellin and Gibbons. 1685–6. Burnham Church, Somerset. Photo: Country Life.

875 DELVAUX. Detail of Pulpit. Documented 1745. Ghent, S. Bavon.

876 STEELL. *Equestrian Monument to the Duke of Wellington*. 1852. Edinburgh, Princes Street.

877 BIRD. *Dr Richard Busby Monument*. Documented after 1695. London, Westminster Abbey.

878 SCHEEMAKERS. *Shakespeare Monument*. Designed by Kent. Signed 1740. London, Westminster Abbey.

879 WILTON. *Dr Stephen Hales Monument*. Documented 1761. London, Westminster Abbey.

880 FLAXMAN. *Agnes Cromwell Monument*. Signed 1798. Chichester, Cathedral.

881 BANKS. *Penelope Boothby Monument*. Signed. Model in RA 1793. Ashbourne, Derbyshire.

882 GILL. *Christ before Pilate*, from *The Stations of the Cross*. Documented 1913–18. London, Westminster Cathedral.

861

862

867

868

873

874

877

878

879

863 864 865 866

869 870 871 872

875 876

Sculpture from Charles I to the twentieth century

880

881

882

I. JESUS IS CONDEMNED TO DEATH

883

884

885

886

887

888

889

890

Genre and history painting in the eighteenth century

883 ALLAN. *The Origin of Painting*. Documented 1773. Edinburgh, National Gallery of Scotland.
884 WHEATLEY. *The Return from Market*. Signed initials 1786. Leeds, Temple Newsam House.
885 WRIGHT OF DERBY. *The Orrery*. Exhibited Society of Artists 1766. Derby, Art Gallery.
886 OPIE. *The Murder of Rizzio*. Exhibited RA 1787. London, Guildhall Museum.
887 HAMILTON. *Rape of Helen*. Signed 1784. Rome, Museo di Roma.
888 NORTHCOTE. *Richard II and Bolingbroke entering London*. Documented 1793. Exeter, Royal Albert Memorial Museum.
889 WEST. *The Death of Wolfe*. Signed 1770. Exhibited RA 1771. Ottawa, National Gallery of Canada.
890 TRUMBULL. *The Battle of Bunker's Hill, 1775*. Signed 1786. New Haven Conn., Yale University Art Gallery.

891

892

893

894

Decorative painting

891 STREETER. Ceiling. Documented *c.* 1669. Oxford, Sheldonian Theatre.
892 KENT. Ceiling. Signed 1725. London, Kensington Palace.
893 THORNHILL. Ceiling of the Painted Hall. Documented 1717. Greenwich, Royal Naval College.
894 BARRY. *Triumph of Modern Commerce.* Documented 1777–83. London, Royal Society of Arts.

895 WOOTTON. *Members of the Beaufort Hunt.* Signed 1744. London, Tate Gallery.
896 STUBBS. *White Horse frightened by a Lion.* Signed 1770. Liverpool, Walker Art Gal.
897 GILPIN, S. *Horses in a Thunderstorm.* Signed 1798. London, Royal Academy.
898 MORLAND. *The Farrier's Forge.* Signed 1793. Manchester, City Art Gallery.
899 SARTORIUS. *A Match at Newmarket, no. 1.* Signed 1790. San Marino Cal., Henry E. Huntington Library and Art Gallery.
900 MARSHALL. *Sam with Sam Chifney, Jr., up.* Signed 1818. San Marino Cal., Henry E. Huntington Library and Art Gallery.
901 FERNELEY. *Squire Osbaldeston and Sir Francis Holyoake-Goodricke.* Signed 1830. Melbourne, National Gallery of Victoria.
902 BEWICK. *The Tame Goose.* Wood engraving from 'British Birds', 1804.
903 LANDSEER. *Shoeing the Mare.* Documented 1844. London, Tate Gallery.
904 HERRING. *Feeding the Horses.* Signed 1858. Nottingham, Castle Museum.
905 ROWLANDSON. *Skating on the Serpentine.* Watercolour. Signed 1786. London Mus.
906 BLAKE. *Nebuchadnezzar.* Colour print. Signed 1795. London, Tate Gallery.
907 MARTIN. *Zadak in search of the Waters of Oblivion.* Signed 1812. Southampton, Art Gal.
908 WARD. *Gordale Scar.* Oil sketch for large picture exhibited RA 1815. London, Tate Gal.
909 FUSELI. *Death of Oedipus.* Documented. Liverpool, Walker Art Gallery.
910 HAYDON. *Lazarus.* Documented 1821–2. London, Tate Gallery.
911 WILKIE. *The Waterloo Dispatch.* Signed 1822. London, Wellington Mus., Apsley House.
912 ETTY. *Pandora.* Exhibited RA 1824. Leeds, City Art Gallery.
913 PEALE, RAPHAELLE. *Still-Life with Peaches.* Signed 1821. Courtesy of the Brooklyn Museum, New York.
914 PEALE, JAMES. *Still-Life.* Signed 1825. Worcester Mass., Art Museum.
915 COPLEY. *Brook Watson and the Shark.* Replica of picture in RA 1778. Courtesy of the Museum of Fine Arts, Boston Mass.
916 HICKS. *The Peaceable Kingdom. c.* 1833. Buffalo NY, Albright-Knox Art Gallery.
917 CURRIER AND IVES. *The Burning of the 'Lexington'.* Lithograph. 1840. Museum of the City of New York (Harry T. Peters Collection).

895

896

897

898

899

900

901

902

903

904

905

906

907

Late eighteenth and nineteenth-century subject painters in England and America

908

909

910

911

912

915

916

917

913

914

918

919

918 COZENS, A. *Landscape with Distant High Hill*. Blot drawing reworked as book illustration. Cambridge, Fitzwilliam Museum.
919 COZENS, J. R. *The Lake of Nemi*. Watercolour. Signed 1778. London, Victoria and Albert Museum.
920 WILSON, RICHARD. *Lake Albano and Castelgandolfo*. Signed monogram RW (drawing is 1754). Port Sunlight, Lady Lever Art Gallery.

921 FARINGTON. *Worcester Cathedral and the Canons' Houses*. Watercolour. Signed 1789. London, V. & A.
922 SCOTT. *Old London Bridge*. Documented. London, Bank of England.
923 DE WINT. *Westminster Palace, Hall and Abbey*. Documented. London, Victoria and Albert Museum.
924 VARLEY. *Chiswick from Barnes*. Watercolour. Signed 1816. Birmingham, City Museum and Art Gallery.

922

923

927

928

929

930

920

921

English landscape painting in oil and watercolour in the eighteenth and nineteenth centuries

925 CROME. *The Yarmouth Water-Frolic.* 1821. Completed by J. B. Crome. London, Kenwood, Iveagh Bequest.
926 CROME. *Silver Birches.* Watercolour. Signed. Norwich, Castle Museum.
927 GIRTIN. *Durham Cathedral.* Watercolour. Signed 1799. Manchester, Whitworth Art Gallery.
928 COTMAN. *Greta Bridge.* Watercolour. Signed 1810. Norwich, Castle Museum.

929 SANDBY. *Bishopsgate Entrance to Windsor Great Park.* Gouache. Signed 1801. Royal Collection.
930 MONRO. *Clearing in a Wood.* From album documented 1814. London, Courtauld Institute (Witt Coll.).
931 GAINSBOROUGH. *Rocky Landscape.* Exhibited RA 1783. Edinburgh, National Gallery of Scotland.
932 TURNER. *Salisbury Cathedral.* Watercolour. Signed *c.* 1802. London, Victoria and Albert Museum.

924

925

926

931

932

933

934

937

938

939

940

941

English and American landscape
in the nineteenth century

935

936

933 CONSTABLE. Sketch for *The Hay Wain*. London, Victoria and Albert Museum.

934 CONSTABLE. *The Hay Wain*. Signed 1821. London, National Gallery.

935 TURNER. *Dido building Carthage*. Signed 1815. London, National Gallery.

936 TURNER. *Burning of the Houses of Parliament*. Exhibited RA 1835. Cleveland Ohio, Museum of Art (John L. Severance Collection).

937 BONINGTON. *Column of S. Mark, Venice*. Signed. London, Tate Gallery.

938 RUSKIN. *End of the Façade of the Doges' Palace, Venice*. Wash drawing. 1852. Oxford, Ashmolean Museum.

939 CALVERT. *The Cyder Feast*. Wood engraving. Signed 1828. London, British Museum.

940 PALMER. *Ruth*. Chalk and wash. Exhibited RA 1829. London, Victoria and Albert Museum.

941 MÜLLER. *Bristol Cathedral*. Signed 1835. Bristol, City Art Gallery.

942 COX. *Rhyll Sands*. Signed 1854–5. Birmingham, City Museum and Art Gallery.

943 LINNELL. *Noonday Rest*. Signed 1865. London, Tate Gallery.

944 ALLSTON. *Italian Landscape*. Signed 1814. Toledo Ohio, Museum of Art.

945 COLE. *View of the White Mountains*. 1828. Courtesy of the Wadsworth Atheneum, Hartford Conn.

946 DURAND. *View Towards the Hudson Valley*. Signed 1851. Courtesy of the Wadsworth Atheneum, Hartford Conn.

942

943

944

945

946

947

948

949

**The Pre-Raphaelites
and their contemporaries**

953

954

955

947 DYCE. *Madonna.* Signed 1845. Royal Collection.
948 MILLAIS. *Lorenzo and Isabella.* Signed 1849.
Liverpool, Walker Art Gallery.
949 HUNT. *The Hireling Shepherd.* Signed 1851. Manchester, City Art Gallery.
950 ROSSETTI. *Wedding of S. George and the Princess.*
Watercolour. Signed monogram 1857. London, Tate Gallery.
951 MORRIS. *La Belle Iseult.* 1858. London, Tate Gallery.
952 BURNE-JONES. *Pygmalion and the Image.* Signed 1868–78. Birmingham, City Museum and Art Gallery.
953 FRITH. *Many Happy Returns of the Day.* Signed 1856. Harrogate Art Gallery.
954 BROWN. *Work.* Signed 1852–65. Manchester, City Art Gallery.
955 WATTS. *Hope.* Documented 1885. London, Tate Gall.

956 WHISTLER. *Nocturne in Black and Gold.* Documented. Courtesy of the Institute of Arts, Detroit Mich.
957 WHISTLER. *The White Girl.* Signed 1862. Washington D.C., National Gallery of Art (Harns Whittemore Collection, 1943).
958 SARGENT. *Vernon Lee.* Signed *c.* 1881. London, Tate Gallery.
959 CASSATT, MARY. *The Loge.* Signed. Washington D.C., National Gallery of Art (Chester Dale Collection).

950

951

952

956

957

958

959

960   961   962

965

Nineteenth and twentieth-century American and British painting

960 BINGHAM. *The Trappers' Return*. Signed 1851. Courtesy of the Institute of Arts, Detroit Michigan.

961 HOMER. *Breezing Up*. Signed 1876. Washington D.C., National Gallery of Art (Gift of the W.L. and May Mellon Foundation, 1943).

962 EAKINS. *The Gross Clinic*. 1875. Philadelphia, Jefferson Medical College.

963 BELLOWS. *Stag at Sharkey's*. 1909. Cleveland Ohio, Museum of Art (Hinman B. Hurlbut Collection).

964 RYDER. *Death on a Pale Horse*. Signed. Cleveland Ohio, Museum of Art.

965 TISSOT. *The Captain's Daughter*. Signed 1873. Southampton, Art Gallery.

966 SICKERT. *The Old Bedford Music Hall*. Signed. Ottawa, National Gallery of Canada.

967 BRANGWYN. *Bridge of Sighs, Venice*. Etching. London, B.M.

968 BONE. *The Ruins of London from S. Bride's*. Drawing. Signed 1940. London, Imperial War Museum.

969 GORE. *Nude Woman on a Bed*. Signed 1910. Bristol, City Art Gallery.

970 NICHOLSON, W. *Mushrooms*. Signed 1940. London, Tate Gallery.

971 JOHN, GWEN. *Self-Portrait*. Signed *c.* 1900. London, Tate Gallery.

972 GILMAN. *Mrs Mounter*. Signed. Liverpool, Walker Art Gallery.

973 LEWIS, W. *The Artist's Wife*. Signed 1937. Glasgow Art Gallery and Museum.

974 JOHN, AUGUSTUS. *Matthew Smith*. Signed *c.* 1946. London, Tate Gallery.

975 STEER. *The Horseshoe Bend of the Severn*. Signed 1909. Aberdeen, Art Gallery.

976 INNES. *Canigou in Snow*. Signed 1911. Cardiff, National Museum of Wales.

966

967   968

963

964

969

970

971

972

973

974

975

976

977

978

979

980

977 HITCHENS. *Damp Autumn*. Signed *c*. 1940.
London, Tate Gallery.
978 SUTHERLAND. *Devastation 1941: East End
Street*. Signed 1941. London, Tate Gallery.
979 NASH. *Pillar and Moon*. Signed 1932–42.
London, Tate Gallery.
980 PASMORE. *The Thames at Chiswick*. 1946–7.
Melbourne, National Gallery of Victoria.

VII

MODERN ART

981

982
983

981 CÉZANNE. *Woman with Coffee-pot*. Documented. Paris, Louvre.
982 CÉZANNE. *La Maison du Pendu*. 1st Impressionist Exhibition 1874. Signed. Paris, Louvre.
983 CÉZANNE. *La Montagne Ste Victoire*. Signed. London, Courtauld Institute Galleries.

984

985

986

987

984 VAN GOGH. *Outdoor Café at Night, Arles*. Documented 1888. Otterlo, Rijksmuseum Kröller-Müller.
985 VAN GOGH. *Portrait of the Artist with his Ear cut off*. Documented 1889. London, Courtauld Institute Galleries.
986 GAUGUIN. *The Haystacks*. Signed 1889. London, Courtauld Institute Galleries.
987 GAUGUIN. *Nevermore*. Signed 1897. London, Courtauld Institute Galleries.

988

988 SEURAT. *Bathers at Asnières*. Signed 1884. London, National Gallery.
989 SIGNAC. *Palace of the Popes, Avignon*. Signed 1900. Paris, Musée National d'Art Moderne.
990 PISSARRO, L. *Snow Scene*. Signed monogram 1917. Bristol, City Art Gallery.

989

990

991

992

993

994

995

991 BERNARD. *Breton Women under Umbrellas*. Signed 1892. Paris, Musée National d'Art Moderne.
992 DENIS. *April*. Signed monogram 1892. Otterlo, Rijksmuseum Kröller-Müller.
993 SÉRUSIER. *Landscape, Pont-Aven*. Signed 1890. Ottawa, National Gallery of Canada.
994 VUILLARD. *Interior at l'Étang-la-Ville*. Signed 1893. Northampton Mass., Smith College.
995 BONNARD. *The Table*. Signed 1925. London, Tate Gallery.

996

997

996 MUNCH. *The Sick Child*. Signed 1906–7. London, Tate Gallery.
997 ENSOR. *Death and the Masks*. Signed 1897. Liège, Musée des Beaux-Arts.
998 BEARDSLEY. *Messalina and her Companion*. Drawing. 1895. London, Tate Gallery.
999 KLIMT. *Mme Fritsa Riedler*. Signed 1906. Vienna, Oesterreichische Galerie.
1000 HODLER. *Day*. Signed 1900. Berne, Kunstmuseum.

998

999

1000

1001

1002

1003 1004 1005

1006

1007

1001 MATISSE. *Nu au Canapé Jaune*. Signed 1926. Ottawa, National Gallery of Canada.

1002 MATISSE. *Portrait of Derain*. Signed initials 1905. London, Tate Gallery.

1003 DONGEN. *Dancer*. Signed 1907. Paris, Musée National d'Art Moderne.

1004 MARQUET. *Matisse painting a Nude in Manguin's Studio*. Signed (1905). Paris, Musée National d'Art Moderne.

1005 SMITH. *Nude, Fitzroy Steet No. 1*. Signed monogram 1916. London, Tate Gallery.

1006 DERAIN. *Portrait of Matisse*. Signed 1905. London, Tate Gallery.

1007 VLAMINCK. *The Painter's House at Valmondois*. Signed 1920. Paris, Musée National d'Art Moderne.

1008 DUFY. *Paddock at Deauville*. Signed 1930. Paris, Musée National d'Art Moderne.

1009 PURRMANN. *Landscape near Lacco Ameno*. Signed 1956. Wuppertal, Von der Heydt Museum.

1009

1008

1010   1011   1012

1013   1014   1015

1010 KOLLWITZ. *Killed in Action*. Pencil drawing for lithograph. Signed.
Baltimore Md, Museum of Art (Gift of Mr and Mrs Albert Lion).

1011 MODERSOHN-BECKER. *Self-portrait with Camellia*. Signed monogram. 1907.
Essen, Folkwang Museum.

1012 NOLDE. *Young Woman and Old Men*. Signed. Cologne, Stadtmuseum.

1013 ROHLFS. *Narcissi*. Watercolour. Signed initials 1937. Dresden,
Kupferstichkabinett.

1014 SCHIELE. *Paris von Gütersloh, the Painter's Biographer*. Detail. Signed 1918.
Minneapolis, Institute of Arts (Gift of the P. D. McMillan Land Company).

1015 KOKOSCHKA. *Auguste Forel*. Signed initials. 1910. Mannheim, Kunsthalle.

1016 HECKEL. *Two Men at a Table* (*to Dostoievsky*). 1912. Hamburg, Kunsthalle.

1017 PECHSTEIN. *Red Girl at Table*. Signed initials 1910. Essen, Folkwang Museum.

1018 SCHMIDT-ROTTLUFF. *Dr Rosa Schapire*. Signed 1919. London, Tate
Gallery.

1019 MÜLLER. *Two Nude Girls*. Signed initials *c*. 1919. Cologne, Wallraf-Richartz
Museum.

1020 KIRCHNER. *The Painters of the Brücke Group*. Signed (on back) 1925. Cologne,
Wallraf-Richartz Museum.

1016

1017   1018   1019   1020

1021

1022

1023

1024

1025

1026

1027

1028

1029

1031

1030

1032

1033

1034

1021 KANDINSKY. *Battle*. Signed 1910.
London, Tate Gallery.
1022 MACKE. *Woman in a Green Jacket*.
Signed 1913. Cologne, Wallraf-Richartz
Museum.
1023 MARC. *Large Blue Horses*. 1911.
Minneapolis, Walker Art Centre.
1024 JAWLENSKY. *Astonishment*. 1919.
Pasadena Cal., Art Museum (Bequest of Galka
E. Scheyer).
1025 CAMPENDONK. *In the Forest*. Courtesy of
the Institute of Arts, Detroit Michigan.

1026 ROUAULT. *Head of a Clown*. Signed
1940–8. Courtesy of the Museum of Fine Arts,
Boston Mass.
1027 SMET. *Girl in Blue*. Signed 1935.
Brussels, Musées Royaux.
1028 PERMEKE. *Les Fiancés*. Signed 1923.
Brussels, Musées des Beaux Arts.
1029 BUFFET. *Portrait de l'Artiste*. Signed
1954. London, Tate Gallery.
1030 MARIN. *Street Crossing, New York*.
Watercolour. Signed 1928. Washington D.C.,
Phillips Collection.
1031 SOUTINE. *Flayed Ox*. Signed.
Amsterdam, Stedelijk Museum.
1032 YEATS. *The Two Travellers*. Signed 1942.
London, Tate Galllery.

1033 SEVERINI. *Black Cat*. Signed 1911.
Ottawa, National Gallery of Canada.
1034 BALLA. *Girl running on a Balcony*.
Signed 1912. Milan, Galleria Civica d'Arte
Moderna.
1035 ROUSSEAU LE DOUANIER. *The Dream*.
Signed 1910. New York, Museum of Modern
Art (Gift of Nelson A. Rockefeller).
1036 VIVIN. *Notre Dame*. Signed *c.* 1933. Paris,
Musée National d'Art Moderne.
1037 SÉRAPHINE. *The Tree of Paradise*. Signed
c. 1929. Paris, Musée National d'Art Moderne.

1035

1037

1036

1038

1039

1040

1042

1043

1045

1044

1038 PICASSO. *La Belle Hollandaise*. Signed 1905. Brisbane, Queensland Art Gallery.

1039 PICASSO. *Woman in White*. Signed 1923. New York, Metropolitan Museum of Art (Rogers Fund, 1951; from the Museum of Modern Art, Lillie P. Bliss Collection).

1040 PICASSO. *Les Demoiselles d'Avignon*. 1906–7. New York, Museum of Modern Art (Lillie P. Bliss Bequest).

1041 PICASSO. *Guernica*. 1937. New York, Museum of Modern Art (on extended loan from the artist).

1042 PICASSO. *Toad*. 1936. Sugar aquatint for Buffon, 'Histoire Naturelle' published 1942.

1043 PICASSO. *Goat's Skull, Bottle and Candle*. Signed 1952. London, Tate Gallery.

1044 LÉGER. *The Great Parade*. 1954. New York, Solomon R. Guggenheim Museum.

1045 BRAQUE. *Violon et Cruche*. 1910. Basle, Oeffentliche Kunstsammlung.

1046 GRIS. *The Sunblind*. Signed 1914. London, Tate Gallery.

1047 METZINGER. *Still-life*. 1916. Courtesy of the Museum of Fine Arts, Boston Mass.

1048 DELAUNAY. *The Eiffel Tower*. Signed 1924. Paris, Musée National d'Art Moderne.

1049

1050

1051

1052

1060

1058

1059

1053

1054

1055

1056

1057

1049 FEININGER. *Church at Gelmerode*. Signed 1929. Providence, Rhode Island School of Design, Museum of Art.
1050 VILLON. *Between Toulouse and Albi*. Signed 1941. Paris, Musée National d'Art Moderne.
1051 GLEIZES. *Le Port*. Signed 1912. Toronto, Art Gallery (Gift from the Junior Women's Committee Fund, 1955).
1052 OZENFANT. *Vie*. Signed 1931–8. Paris, Musée National d'Art Moderne.

1053 TANGUY. *Lazy Days*. Signed 1937. Paris, Musée National d'Art Moderne.
1054 DALI. *Christ of S. John of the Cross*. 1951. Glasgow, Art Gallery and Museum.
1055 MAGRITTE. *The Domain of Lights*. Signed 1954. Brussels, Musées Royaux.
1056 LAM. *The Jungle*. Gouache. 1943. New York, Museum of Modern Art.
1057 ERNST. *Europe after the Rain*. Signed 1940–2. Courtesy of the Wadsworth Atheneum, Hartford Conn.

1061

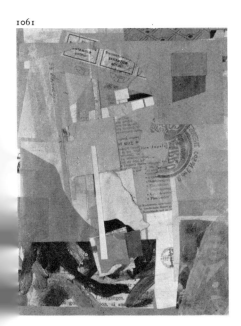

1058 HÖLZEL. *Colour Composition*. Pastel. Stuttgart, Galerie.
1059 PICABIA. *Edtaonisl*. Signed 1913. Courtesy of the Art Institute of Chicago.
1060 DUCHAMP. *Nude descending a Staircase, No. 2*. Signed 1912. Philadelphia, Museum of Art (Louise and Walter Arensberg Collection).
1061 SCHWITTERS. *Opened by Customs*. Collage. c. 1937–9. London, Tate Gallery.

1062

1063

1064

1065

1066

1067

1068

1069

1070

424

1071

1072

1073

1074

1075

1062 CHIRICO. *The Painter's Family*. Signed 1926. London, Tate Gallery.
1063 CARRÀ. *Boy on Horseback*. Signed 1936. Rome, Galleria Nazionale d'Arte Moderna.
1064 MORANDI. *Still-life*. Signed (1946). London, Tate Gallery.
1065 PISIS. *Red House on the Lido, Venice*. Signed 1945. Turin, Galleria Civica d'Arte Moderna.
1066 BECKMANN. *Odysseus and Calypso*. Signed 1943. Hamburg, Kunsthalle.
1067 DIX. *The Artist's Parents*. 1924. Hanover, Landesgalerie.
1068 GROSZ. *Man and Wife*. Signed 1930. London, Tate Gallery.
1069 HOFFER. *Head of a Girl*. Signed initials 1937. Courtesy of the Institute of Arts, Detroit Michigan.
1070 SCHLEMMER. *Roman (Four figures in space)*. 1925. Basle, Kunstmuseum.

1071 OROZCO. *The Caudillo Zapata*. Signed 1930. Courtesy of the Art Institute of Chicago (The Joseph Winterbotham Collection).
1072 RIVERA. *The Making of a Fresco*. 1931. San Francisco, Art Institute.
1073 TAMAYO. *Women of Tehuantepec*. Signed 1939. Buffalo NY, Albright-Knox Art Gallery.

1074 GUTTOSO. *The Discussion*. Signed. London, Tate Gallery.
1075 SHAHN. *Cherubs and Children*. Tempera 1944. New York, Whitney Museum of American Art.
1076 MODIGLIANI. *Nude*. Signed. London, Courtauld Institute Galleries.
1077 PASCIN. *Seated Girl*. Signed. Toledo Ohio, Museum of Art (Gift of Edward Drummond Libbey).

1076

1077

1078

1081

1079

1082

1080

1083

1084

1078 LURÇAT. *Summer*. Tapestry. Designed 1939; woven at Aubusson 1942. Paris, Mobilier National.

1079 CHAGALL. *The Poet Reclining*. Signed 1915. London, Tate Gallery.

1080 SPENCER. *The Betrayal*. 1922. Belfast, Ulster Museum and Art Gallery.

1081 KLEE. *The Golden Fish*. Signed 1925. Hamburg, Kunsthalle.

1082 BAUMEISTER. *Polished Stones*. Signed 1947. Cologne, Wallraf-Richartz Museum.

1083 MIRÒ. *Painting, 10 June 1933*. Courtesy of the Wadsworth Atheneum, Hartford Conn.

1084 GORKY. *Engagement II*. Signed 1947. New York, Whitney Museum of American Art.

1085

1086

1087

1088

1089

1090

1091

1092

1085 KANDINSKY. *Yellow Accompaniment, No. 269*. Signed initials. 1924. New York, Solomon R. Guggenheim Museum.

1086 MONDRIAN. *Composition*. Signed initials. 1940–2. Buffalo NY, Albright-Knox Art Gallery.

1087 MALEVICH. *Suprematist Composition: White on White*. 1918. New York, Museum of Modern Art (on extended loan).

1088 NICHOLSON, B. *Au Chat Botté*. 1932. Manchester, City Art Gallery.

1089 DOESBURG. *Composition IX*. Signed monogram. 1917. The Hague, Municipal Museum.

1090 KUPKA. *Vertical and diagonal plane*. Signed 1955. Paris, Musée National d'Art Moderne.

1091 MAGNELLI. *Face au large*. Signed 1955. Essen, Museum Folkwang.

1092 TOBEY. *Northwest Drift*. Signed 1958. London, Tate Gallery.

1093 WOLS. *Composition*. Signed 1947. Hamburg, Kunsthalle.
1094 HARTUNG. *Painting T 54-16*. Signed 1954. Paris, Musée National d'Art Moderne.
1095 SOULAGES. *23 mai 1953*. Signed. London, Tate Gallery.
1096 POLLOCK. *Cathedral*. Signed 1947. Dallas Texas, Museum of Fine Arts (Gift of Mr and Mrs Bernard Reis, 1950).
1097 MOTHERWELL. *Personage with Yellow Ochre and White*. 1947. New York, Museum of Modern Art.
1098 KOONING. *Woman I*. 1950–2. New York, Museum of Modern Art.
1099 KLINE. *Abstraction*. 1955. Baltimore Md, Museum of Art (Thomas E. Benesch Memorial Collection).
1100 RIOPELLE. *Perspective*. Signed 1956. London, Tate Gallery.
1101 STAËL. *The Roofs*. Signed 1952. Paris, Musée National d'Art Moderne.
1102 POLIAKOFF. *Composition 1959*. Signed. London, Tate Gallery.
1103 AFRO. *Composition in black and green*. Signed 1959. Berlin, Staatliche Museen.
1104 APPEL. *Amorous Dance*. Signed 1955. London, Tate Gallery.

1105 BAZAINE. *June Night*. Signed 1950. Oslo, Nasjonalgalleriet.
1106 MANESSIER. *Crown of Thorns*. Signed 1950. Paris, Musée National d'Art Moderne.
1107 RICHARDS. *La Cathédrale engloutie*. Aberdeen, Art Gallery.
1108 DUBUFFET. *Man with a Hod*. Collage. Signed 1956. London, Tate Gallery.
1109 NAY. *Stars*. Signed 1963. Münster, Landesmuseum.
1110 FRANCIS. *The Over Yellow*. Stuttgart, Staatsgalerie.
1111 ROTHKO. *Light Red over Black*. London, Tate Gallery.
1112 SCOTT. *White, sand and ochre*. 1961. London, Tate Gallery.
1113 BURRI. *Composition*. 1953. New York, Solomon R. Guggenheim Museum.
1114 TAPIÈS. *Green and Black*. 1957. London, Tate Gallery.
1115 NOLAN. *Glenrowan*. Signed 1957. London, Tate Gallery.
1116 BACON. *Seated Man with Turkey Rug*. 1961. London, Tate Gallery.
1117 MATTA. *Yo-U*. 1950. Courtesy of the Art Institute of Chicago.

1101

1102

1103

1108

1109

1110

1111

1115

1116

1117

1118

1119

1118 RODIN. *The Kiss*. Signed 1904. London, Tate Gallery.

1119 MEŠTROVIČ. *Torso*. London, Tate Gallery.

1120 MILLES. *Europa and the Bull*. 1923–4. London, Tate Gallery.

1121 MAILLOL. *The Three Nymphs*. Signed initials 1930–8. London, Tate Gallery.

1122 BOURDELLE. *The Virgin of Alsace*. Bronze study. Signed. Edinburgh, N.G. of Scotland.

1123 ROSSO, M. *Yvette*. Wax. 1935. Rome, Galleria Nazionale d'Arte Moderna.

1124 GAUDIER-BRZESKA. *Alfred Wolmark*. Bronze. Signed 1913. Liverpool, Walker Art Gallery.

1125 DESPIAU. *Antoinette Schulte*. Bronze. Signed 1934. London, Tate Gallery.

1126 EPSTEIN. *Einstein*. Bronze. 1933. London, Tate Gallery.

1127 LEHMBRUCK. *Kneeling Woman*. Bronze. Signed 1911. Duisburg, Museum.

1128 LAURENS. *Bather*. Bronze. 1931. London, Tate Gallery.

1129 ARCHIPENKO. *Woman combing her Hair*. 1914. London, Tate Gallery.

1130 DUCHAMP-VILLON. *Horse*. Bronze, 1914. Paris, Musée National d'Art Moderne.

1131 GONZÁLES. *Cactus man*. Bronze. 1939/40. Hamburg, Hamburger Kunsthalle.

1132 ZADKINE. *Dancers*. *c.* 1953. Edinburgh, Gallery of Modern Art.

1133 LIPCHITZ. *Study for a Monument*. Signed 1953. London, Tate Gallery.

1134 BOCCIONI. *Single Form of Continuity in Space*. Bronze. 1913. Milan, Galleria Civica d'Arte Moderna.

1123

1124

1125

1129

1130

1131

1128

1120

1121

1122

1126

1127

1134

1132

1133

1135

1136

1137

1141

1142

1143

1144

1145

1146

1138

1139

1140

1135 BRANCUSI. *Bird in Space.* 1919. New York, Museum of Modern Art.

1136 TATLIN. *Relief.* 1917. Moscow, Tretyakov Gallery.

1137 GABO. *Linear Construction 1942–3.* London, Tate Gallery.

1138 PEVSNER. *Maquette for a Monument symbolising the Liberation of the Spirit.* Signed 1952. London, Tate Gallery.

1139 ARP. *Hybrid Fruit called Pagoda.* 1934. London, Tate Gallery.

1140 HEPWORTH. *The Cosdon Head.* Blue marble. 1949. Birmingham, City Museum and Art Gallery.

1141 CALDER. *Black Crescent.* 1960. Toronto, Art Gallery (Gift of Mr and Mrs H.R. Jackman, 1962).

1142 MOHOLY-NAGY. *Plexiglass and chromium-rod Sculpture.* 1946. New York, Solomon R. Guggenheim Museum.

1143 BARLACH. *The Doubter.* Wood. 1937. Güstrow, Barlachhaus.

1144 MANZÙ. *Two Saints.* Detail from bronze doors. Completed 1958. Salzburg, Cathedral.

1145 GRECO. *Seated figure.* Bronze. Signed 1951. London, Tate Gallery.

1146 MARINI. *Horseman.* Bronze. Signed 1947. London, Tate Gall.

1147 RICHIER. *L'Eau.* Bronze. Signed 1953–4. London, Tate Gall.

1148 GIACOMETTI. *Man Pointing.* Bronze. Signed 1947. London, Tate Gallery.

1149 MOORE. *Family Group.* Bronze. Signed 1949. London, Tate Gallery.

1147

1148

1149

1150

1151

1152

1154

1153

1155

1156

1150 CHADWICK. *Dragonfly*. Iron mobile. 1951. London, Tate Gallery.

1151 ARMITAGE. *Sibyl III*. Bronze. Signed initials 1961. London, Tate Gallery.

1152 BUTLER. *Girl*. Bronze. 1953–4. London, Tate Gallery.

1153 CÉSAR. *L'Homme de Saint-Denis*. Welded iron. 1958. London, Tate Gallery.

1154 WOTRUBA. *Seated Figure*. Stone. 1949. Vienna, Österreichische Galerie.

1155 BILL. *Construction from one Ring*, 1942–44, granite version 1963. Buffalo N.Y., Albright-Knox Art Museum.

1156 KRICKE. '*Grosse Kasseler*'. Stainless steel. 1958–9. Leverkusen, Schloss Morsbroich Museum.

BIBLIOGRAPHIES

The place of publication of all books is given, and the language in which the book is written is that of the place of publication unless otherwise stated: thus, a book published in Rome is in Italian unless (*in Eng.*) appears, in which case the book is in English. We have tried to be careful to note the language in cases such as Antwerp or Berne, where more than one language is current. We have often given the place of publication as London, but many books are published simultaneously in London and New York, and others are published in several languages at the same time: obviously, we have used the most convenient edition. The date of publication is also given, but it is not necessarily that of the latest edition. In a few cases, also, where the date is not given in the book itself we have added it in brackets, thus: (1950), since it seems to us useful to know the approximate date of a book.

In the Alphabetical Bibliography we have often given references in an abbreviated form, e.g. Friedländer, *Altniederländische Malerei*, xi. This refers to the Classified Bibliography, where the title, date, and place of publication can be found in full.

Finally, it should be noted that there are some deliberate omissions in the Alphabetical Bibliography, where no monograph exists and no single book seemed to us to give more than can be found in the usual works of reference.

CLASSIFIED BIBLIOGRAPHY

BIBLIOGRAPHIES, DICTIONARIES, ENCYCLOPAEDIAS

Chamberlin, M., *Guide to Art Reference Books*, Chicago 1959 (2500 entries, but excludes monographs).

Lucas, E. L., *Books on art; a foundation list*, Harvard, 2nd ed. 1938. *The Harvard List of Books on Art*, Harvard 1952.

Schlosser, J. von, *La letteratura artistica*, 2nd Italian ed. with additions by O. Kurz, Florence 1956.

Thieme-Becker, *Allgemeines Lexikon der bildenden Künstler von der Antike bis zur Gegenwart*, 37 vols., Leipzig 1908–50.

Vollmer, H. (ed.), *Allgemeines Lexikon der bildenden Künstler des XX. Jahrhunderts*, 6 vols., Leipzig 1953–62.

Darmstaedter, R., *Künstlerlexikon*, Berne, Munich, 1961.

Encyclopedia of World Art, London and New York, 8 vols. so far (of 15 planned), 1959 in progress. An Italian version is also published in Florence.

Holt, E., *A Documentary History of Art*, 2 vols., New York 1957–8.

CATALOGUES

London, National Gallery, *Catalogues:*
   Summary Catalogue, 1958.
   Earlier Italian Schools, 1961.
   16th Century Italian Schools, 1962.
   16th Century Venetian School, 1959.
   18th Century Italian Schools, 1956.
   Early Netherlandish School, 1955.
   Dutch School, 1960.
   French School, 1957.
   British School, 1959.
   German School, 1959.
   Spanish School, 1952.
British Museum, *Catalogues of Drawings:*
   Italian Drawings, XIV and XV centuries: A. E. Popham and Philip Pouncey, 2 vols., 1950, and supplement 1952.
   Italian Drawings: Michelangelo and his Studio: Johannes Wilde, 1953.
   Italian Drawings: Raphael and his Circle: Philip Pouncey and J. A. Gere, 2 vols., 1962.
   A Catalogue of British Drawings: *XVI and XVII centuries:* Edward Croft-Murray and Paul Hulton, with a supplement on foreign artists' drawings con-

nected with Great Britain by Christopher White, vol. I (2 parts), 1960.

Pictures in the Collection of H.M. the Queen. A complete catalogue is in preparation: Part I by O. Millar, 1963, Part II by M. Levey, 1964.

Windsor Castle, *Catalogues of Drawings in the Royal Collection*, 14 vols. so far, London 1942–60 in progress.

PERIODS AND STYLES

Chastel, A., *The Age of Humanism: Europe 1480–1530*, London 1963.

Benesch, O., *The Art of the Renaissance in Northern Europe*, Harvard 1945.

Murray, Peter and Linda, *The Art of the Renaissance*, London 1963.

Schönberger, A., and H. Soehner, *The Age of Rococo*, London 1960.

Pauli, G., *Die Kunst des Klassizismus und der Romantik*, Berlin 1925.

Brion, M., *Romantic Art*, London 1960.

Novotny, F., *Painting and Sculpture in Europe, 1780–1880*, London 1960 (Pelican History of Art).

Raymond, M., *From Baudelaire to Surrealism*, New York 1949 (Documents of Modern Art, 10).

Cassou, J., E. Langui, and N. Pevsner, *The Sources of Modern Art*, London 1962.

Langui, E., *Fifty Years of Modern Art*, London 1959 (based on Exhibition at Brussels World Exhibition, 1958).

Rosenblum, R., *Cubism and Twentieth Century Art*, New York and London 1960.

Bihalji-Merin, O., *Modern Primitives*, London 1961.

Haftmann, W., *Painting in the Twentieth Century*, 2 vols., London 1960 (revised from earlier German eds.).

Read, Sir H., *A Concise History of Modern Painting*, London 1959.

Lake, C., and R. Maillard, *Dictionary of Modern Painting*, London, 3rd ed. 1964.

Berckelaers, F., and M. Seuphor, *A Dictionary of Abstract Painting*, London 1958.

Kahnweiler, D., *The Rise of Cubism*, New York 1949 (Documents of Modern Art, 9).

Barr, A., *Cubism and Abstract Art*, New York (Museum of Modern Art) 1936. *Fantastic Art, Dada, Surrealism*, New York (Museum of Modern Art) 1946.

Motherwell, R., *The Dada Painters and Poets*, New York 1951 (Documents of Modern Art, 8).

Seuphor, M., *Abstract Painting, from Kandinsky to the Present*, London 1962.

Giedion-Welcker, Carola, *Contemporary Sculpture*, London and New York (revised ed.) 1961.

Maillard, R. (ed.), *A Dictionary of Modern Sculpture*, London 1962.

Read, Sir H., *A Concise History of Modern Sculpture*, London 1964.

Ritchie, A. C., *Sculpture of the Twentieth Century*, New York (Museum of Modern Art) 1952.

Selz, J., *Modern Sculpture, its Origins and Evolution*, New York 1963.

Seuphor, M., *The Sculpture of this Century*, London 1959.

Trier, E., *Sculpture of the Twentieth Century*, London 1962.

TECHNIQUES

Gettens, R., and G. Stout, *Painting Materials*, London and New York 1947.

Thompson, D. V., *The Materials of Medieval Painting*, London 1936.

Constable, W. G., *The Painter's Workshop*, Oxford 1954.

Vasari, G., ed. G. Baldwin Brown, *Vasari on Technique*, London 1907, and reprint New York and London 1960.

Eastlake, C., *Materials for a History of Oil Painting*, 2 vols., London 1847–69, and reprint London and New York 1960.

Jensen, L., *Synthetic Painting Media*, London 1964.

Rich, J., *The Materials and Methods of Sculpture*, New York 1947.

Percy, H. M., *New Materials in Sculpture*, London 1962.

Seitz, W., *The Art of Assemblage*, New York (Museum of Modern Art) 1961.

Meder, J., *Die Handzeichnung: Ihre Technik und Entwicklung*, Vienna, 2nd ed. 1923.

Tolnay, C. de, *History and Technique of Old Master Drawings*, New York 1943.

Watrous, J., *The Craft of Old-Master Drawings*, Madison, Wis. 1957.

Lehrs, Max, *Geschichte und kritischer Katalog des deutschen, niederländischen und französischen Kupferstichs im XV. Jahrhundert*, 18 vols., Vienna 1908–34.

Bartsch, A. von, *Le peintre-graveur. . .* , 21 vols., Würzburg 1920 (1st ed. Vienna 1803–21; up to the end of the 17th century).

Delteil, L., *Le peintre-graveur. . .* , 31 vols., Paris 1906–30 (19th and 20th century, mostly French, but includes Goya).

Ivins, W., *How Prints Look*, Boston 1958.

COUNTRIES
arranged in alphabetical order

BRITAIN AND AMERICA

Groce, G., and D. Wallace, *The New York Historical Society's Dictionary of Artists in America, 1564–1860*, Yale University Press 1964.

Walpole Society. Annual volumes (1912 in progress) dealing with British art. Contains the Notebooks of G. Vertue (q.v.).

Saxl, F., and R. Wittkower, *British Art and the Mediterranean*, Oxford 1948.

Mercer, E., *English Art, 1553–1625*, Oxford 1962 (Oxford History of English Art, vii).

Waterhouse, E. K., *Painting in Britain, 1530–1790* (Pelican History of Art), London 1953.

Whinney, M., and O. Millar, *English Art, 1625–1714*, Oxford 1957 (Oxford History of English Art, viii).

Walpole, H., *Anecdotes of Painting in England*, 4 vols., London 1762–71: the 5th vol. published by Yale University Press 1937 consists of unpublished addenda. Walpole based his work on Vertue's notebooks.

Edwards, E., *Anecdotes of painters. . .* , London 1808 (Continuation of Walpole).

Murray, E. Croft-, *Decorative Painting in England*, London 1962 (only 1 vol. of 2, so far).

Whitley, W., *Artists and their Friends in England, 1700–99*, 2 vols., London 1928; *id., 1800–20*, Cambridge 1928; *id., 1821–37*, Cambridge 1930.

Redgrave, R. and S., *A Century of British Painters*, London 1866; new, illustrated, ed. 1948.

Boase, T. S. R., *English Art, 1800–1870*, Oxford 1959 (Oxford History of English Art, x).

Hunt, W. Holman, *Pre-Raphaelitism and the Pre-Raphaelite Brotherhood*, 2 vols., London 1905.

Ironside, R., and J. Gere, *Pre-Raphaelite Painters*, London 1948.

Long, B., *British Miniaturists*, London 1929.

Reynolds, G., *English Portrait Miniatures*, London 1952.

Winter, C., *Elizabethan Miniatures*, London (revised ed.) 1949.

Binyon, L., *English Watercolours*, London 1944.

Roget, J. L., *History of the Old Water Colour Society*, 2 vols., London 1891.

Williams, I. A., *Early English Watercolours. . .* , London 1952.

Sparrow, W. S., *A Book of Sporting Painters*, London 1931. *British Sporting Artists*, London 1922.

Taylor, B., *Animal Painting in England*, London 1955.

Gunnis, R., *Dictionary of British Sculptors, 1660–1851*, London 1953.

Whinney, M. D., *Sculpture in Britain, 1530–1830* (Pelican History of Art), London 1964.

Dunlap, W., *History of the Rise and Progress of the Arts of Design in the United States*, 2 vols., New York 1834.

Richardson, E. P., *Painting in America*, London 1956.

Belknap, W., *American Colonial Painting. . .* , Harvard 1959.

Wehle, H., *American Miniatures, 1730–1850*, New York 1937.

Soby, J. T., and D. C. Miller, *Romantic Painting in America*, New York (Museum of Modern Art) 1943.

Goodrich, L., and J. Baur, *American art of the 20th century*, London 1962.

Ritchie, A. C., *Abstract Painting and Sculpture in America*, New York (Museum of Modern Art) 1951.

FRANCE

Sterling, Charles (also known as Charles Jacques), *Les Peintres du Moyen Âge (La Peinture Française)*, Paris 1941.

Ring, G., *A Century of French Painting, 1400–1500*, London 1949.

Blunt, Sir Anthony, *Art and Architecture in France, 1500–1700* (Pelican History of Art), London 1953.

Isarlo, G., *La peinture en France au XVIIᵉ siècle*, Paris 1960.

Réau, L., *Histoire de la peinture française au 18ᵉ siècle*, 2 vols., Paris 1925–6.

Dimier, L. (ed.), *Les peintres français du 18ᵉ siècle*, 2 vols., Paris and Brussels 1928–30.

Goncourt, E., and J. de, *L'Art du XVIIIᵉ Siècle*, 3 vols., Paris 1906. English ed., *French XVIIIth Century Painters*, London 1948 (parts only of French ed.).

Locquin, J., *La peinture d'histoire en France, 1747–1785*, Paris 1912.

Friedländer, W., *David to Delacroix*, Harvard 1952.

Rewald, J., *The History of Impressionism*, New York (Museum of Modern Art) 1946, revised ed. 1961. *Post-Impressionism*, New York (Museum of Modern Art) 1956.

Duthuit, G., *The Fauvist Painters*, New York 1950 (Documents of Modern Art, 11).

Apollinaire, G., *The Cubist Painters* (1913), New York 1949 (English translation ed. by R. Motherwell: Documents of Modern Art, 1).

Lami, S., *Dictionnaire des sculpteurs de l'école française*, 8 vols., Paris 1898–1921.

Robert-Dumesnil, A., *Le peintre-graveur français. . .* , 11 vols., Paris 1835–71.

GERMANY, CZECHOSLOVAKIA, HUNGARY, RUSSIA

Dehio, G., *Geschichte der deutschen Kunst.*, 5 vols., Berlin and Leipzig, 3rd ed. 1923–34.

Fischer, O., *Geschichte der deutschen Malerei*, Munich, 2nd ed. 1943.

Stange, A., *Deutsche Malerei der Gotik*, 9 vols., Munich and Berlin 1934–58.

Heidrich, E., *Die altdeutsche Malerei*, Jena 1941.

Winkler, F., *Altdeutsche Tafelmalerei*, Munich 1941.

Sandrart, J. von, *Teutsche Academie. . .* , 2 vols., Nuremberg 1675–79; Latin ed. 1683; modern ed. Munich 1925.

Hempel, E., *Baroque Art and Architecture in Central Europe* (Pelican History of Art), London 1965.

Benz, R., *Die Kunst der deutschen Romantik*, Munich 1939.

Myers, B. S., *Expressionism: A Generation in Revolt*, London, 2nd ed. 1957.

Selz, P., *German Expressionist Painting*, University of California 1957.

Haendler, G., *German Painting in Our Time*, Berlin 1956.

Ritchie, A. C. (ed.), *German Art of the Twentieth Century*, with contributions by W. Haftmann, A. Hentzen and W. S. Liebermann, New York 1957.

Röthel, H., *Modern German Painting*, London 1958.

Feulner, A., and T. Müller, *Geschichte der deutschen Plastik*, Munich 1953.

Müller, T., *Deutsche Plastik der Renaissance*, Königstein 1963.

Hollstein, F., *German engravings, etchings and woodcuts, c. 1400–1700*, 7 vols. (of about 22), Amsterdam 1954–62 in progress.

Matějček, A., and J. Pešina, *Czech Gothic Painting, 1350–1450*, Prague 1950.

Pešina, J., *Painting of the Gothic and Renaissance Periods, 1450–1550*, Prague 1958.

Radocsay, D., *Gothic Panel Painting in Hungary*, Budapest 1963.

Dvořáková, V., J. Krása, A. Merhautova, K. Stejskal, *Gothic Mural Painting in Bohemia and Moravia 1300–1378*, London 1964.

Gray, C., *The Great Experiment: Russian Art 1863–1922*, London 1962.

ITALY

Vasari, G., *Lives of the . . . Painters, Sculptors and Architects*. First (Italian) eds. 1550 and 1568. The standard Italian ed. is G. Milanesi's (9 vols., 1878–85); there are several English eds., the best being G. de Vere's (10 vols., London 1912–15).

Venturi, A., *Storia dell'arte italiana*, 11 vols. (bound as 25 parts), Milan 1901–40.

Chastel, A., *Italian Art*, London 1963.

Blunt, Sir Anthony, *Artistic Theory in Italy*, Oxford 1940.

Crowe, J. A., and G. B. Cavalcaselle, *A History of Painting in Italy*, 6 vols., London 1903–14. *A History of Painting in North Italy*, 3 vols., London 1912.

Marle, R. van, *The Development of the Italian Schools*, 19 vols., The Hague 1923–36.

De Wald, E. T., *Italian Painting, 1200–1600*, New York, 1961.

Garrison, E., *Italian Romanesque Panel Painting*, Florence 1949.

Sinibaldi, G., and G. Brunetti, *Pittura italiana del Duecento e Trecento* (Commemorative Catalogue of Mostra Giottesca, 1937), Florence 1943.

Toesca, P., *Il Trecento*, Turin 1951.

Oertel, R., *Die Frühzeit der italienischen Malerei*, Stuttgart 1953.

Wölfflin, H., *Classic Art*, London 1952.

Gould, C., *Introduction to Italian Renaissance Painting*, London 1957.

Freedberg, S. J., *Painting of the High Renaissance in Rome and Florence, 1475–1521*, 2 vols., Harvard 1961.

Voss, H., *Die Malerei der Spätrenaissance in Rom und Florenz*, 2 vols., Berlin 1920.

Briganti, G., *Italian Mannerism*, London 1962.

Golzio, V., *Seicento e Settecento*, 2 vols., 2nd ed., Turin 1961.

Wittkower, R., *Art and Architecture in Italy, 1600–1750* (Pelican History of Art), London 1958.

Mahon, D., *Studies in Seicento Art and Theory*, London 1947.

Waterhouse, E. K., *Italian Baroque Painting*, London 1962.

Brizio, A. M., *Ottocento e Novecento*, Turin 1945.

Comanducci, A., *Dizionario illustrato dei pittori e incisori italiani moderni (1800–1900)*, 2 vols., Milan, 2nd ed. 1945.

Ballo, G., *Modern Italian Painting*, London 1958.

Mazzariol, G., *Pittura italiana contemporanea*, Bergamo 1958.

Soby, J. T., and A. Barr, *Twentieth Century Italian Art*, New York (Museum of Modern Art) 1951.

Berenson, B., *Pitture italiane del Rinascimento*, Milan 1936. *Italian Painters of the Renaissance*, London 1953. *Italian Pictures of the Renaissance, Venetian School*, 2 vols., London 1957. *Italian Pictures of the Renaissance, Florentine School*, 2 vols., London 1963.

Sandberg-Vavala, E., *Uffizi Studies*, Florence 1948. *Sienese Studies*, Florence 1953. *Studies in the Florentine Churches*, Florence 1959.

Longhi, R., *Officina Ferrarese*, Florence 1934, 2nd ed. 1956.

Nicolson, B., *The Painters of Ferrara*, London 1950.

Antal, F., *Florentine Painting and its Social Background*, London 1947.

Meiss, Millard, *Painting in Florence and Siena after the Black Death*, Princeton 1951.

Offner, R., *A Corpus of Florentine Painting*, 10 vols., New York 1931–62 in progress.

Becherucci, L., *Manieristi Toscani*, Bergamo 1944.

Rinaldis, A. de, *Neapolitan Painting of the Seicento*, Florence, Paris, and New York 1929.

Fokker, T. H., *Roman Baroque Art*, 2 vols., Oxford 1938.

Mahon, D., and D. Sutton, *Artists in 17th Century Rome* (Catalogue, Exhibition at Wildenstein's), London 1955.

Voss, H., *Die Malerei des Barock in Rom*, Berlin n.d. (1924).

Carli, E., *Sienese Painting*, London 1956.

Edgell, G., *A History of Sienese Painting*, New York 1932.

Cecchi, E., *Trecentisti Senesi*, Milan 1948.

Weigelt, C., *Sienese Painting of the Trecento*, New York and Florence 1930.

Pope-Hennessy, J., *Sienese Quattrocento Painting*, London 1947.

Godfrey, F., *Early Venetian Painters, 1415–95*, London 1954.

Donzelli, C., *Pittori Veneziani del Settecento*, Florence 1957.

Levey, M., *Painting in XVIII Century Venice*, London 1959.

Crichton, G. H., *Romanesque Sculpture in Italy*, London 1954.

Pope-Hennessy, J., *Italian Gothic Sculpture*, London 1955. *Italian Renaissance Sculpture*, London 1958. *Italian High Renaissance and Baroque Sculpture*, 3 vols., London 1963.

Faldi, I., *La Scultura barocca in Italia*, Milan 1958.

Hind, A. M., *Early Italian Engraving. . .*, 7 vols., London 1938–48 (see also Engraving).

Baudi di Vesme, *Le peintre-graveur italien*, Milan 1906.

NETHERLANDS

Bautier, P., R. Cazier, and R. Delevoy, and others, *Dictionnaire des Peintres*, Arts en Belgique series, Brussels n.d. (c. 1950).

Gelder, H. E. van, and others, *Guide to Dutch Art*, 3rd ed., The Hague 1961.

Hall, H. van, *Repertorium voor de geschiedenis der Neder-landsche schilder- en graveer-kunst. . .*, 2 vols., The Hague 1936–49.

Corpus des Primitifs Flamands:
Series I. *Corpus de la peinture des anciens Pays-Bas méridionaux au 15e siècle*, Antwerp and Brussels, 6 vols so far, in 9 parts, 1951–63 in progress. Some volumes also available in English.

Mander, C. van, *Het Schilderboek. . .*, Haarlem 1604 and Amsterdam 1946 (French translation Paris 1884, English ed. New York 1936).

Friedländer, M. J., *Die altniederländische Malerei*, 14 vols., Leyden 1923–37. *From van Eyck to Brueghel*, London 1956.

Panofsky, E., *Early Netherlandish Painting*, 2 vols., Harvard 1953.

Hoogewerff, G., *De Bentvueghels*, The Hague 1952.

Schneider, A. van, *Caravaggio und die Niederländer*, Marburg 1933.

Utrecht Exhibition Catalogue: Caravaggio en de Neder-landen, Utrecht and Antwerp 1952 (with English summaries).

Gerson, H., and E. Ter Kuile, *Art and Architecture in Belgium, 1600–1800* (Pelican History of Art), London 1960.

Hofstede de Groot, C., and others, *A Catalogue Raisonné of the Works of the Most Eminent Dutch Painters of the Seventeenth Century, based on the Work of John Smith*, London, vols. 1–8, 1907–27 in English ed.; Stuttgart and Paris, vols. 9–10, 1926–28 in German only.

Bernt, W., *Die niederländische Maler des XVII. Jahr-hunderts*, 3 vols., Munich 1948, and *Supplement*, Munich 1962.

Bode, W., *Great Masters of Dutch and Flemish Painting*, London 1926.

Plietzsch, E., *Holländische und Flämische Maler des XVII. Jahrhundert*, Leipzig 1960.

Bengtsson, A., *Studies on the Rise of Realistic Landscape Painting in Holland, 1610–25*, Uppsala 1952.

Bergström, I., *Dutch Still-life Painting in the 17th Century*, London 1956.

Warner, R., *Dutch and Flemish Flower and Fruit Painters of the 17th and 18th Centuries*, London 1928.

Hollstein, F., *Dutch and Flemish etchings, engravings and woodcuts, c. 1450–1700*, 15 vols., Amsterdam 1949–62 in progress (expected to be 25 vols. and index).

Bernt, W., *Die niederländischen Zeichner des 17. Jahr-hunderts*, 2 vols., Munich 1957–58.

SPAIN, PORTUGAL, AND LATIN AMERICA

Kubler, G., and M. Soria, *Art and Architecture in Spain and Portugal, and their American Dominions* (Pelican History of Art), London 1959.

Post, C. R., *A History of Spanish Painting*, 12 vols. in 18, Cambridge Mass. 1930–58.

Gudiol, J., *Spanish Painting*, Toledo Ohio 1941.

Harris, E., *Spanish Painting*, London 1938.

Jedlicka, G., *Spanish Painting*, London 1963.

Lafuente Ferrari, E., *Breve historia de la pintura española*, Madrid, 4th ed. 1953.

Weisbach, W., *Spanish Baroque Art*, Cambridge 1941.

Myers, B. S., *Mexican Painting in Our Time*, New York 1956.

ALPHABETICAL BIBLIOGRAPHY

The arrangement of this part of the Bibliography is alphabetical, following the order of the Dictionary itself. Thus, for a monograph on 'Correggio', a history of 'Impressionism', or a handbook on 'Engraving' it is necessary only to look under those names. Obviously, the lists are as short as possible and no periodical literature is quoted; this may seem a great omission, but we think that the monographs listed will almost always provide the necessary references and our aim has been simply to provide a starting-point for further study. The monographs themselves are not of equal value; of some of them the best that can be said is that they are the best we have. We have tried to give those that we think most helpful – which may sometimes mean that an excellent, long, study in very difficult German has been omitted and a shorter work in English quoted, but we have tried to give a reasonable amount of choice and we have also included as many very recent works as we could find, since they will usually have references to earlier studies. Other omissions are probably due to ignorance rather than malice.

A

ABBATE. See L. Dimier, *Le Primatice*, Paris 1928; and Cat. of Exh., *Fontainebleau e la Maniera*, Naples 1952. See also Venturi, *Storia*, ix.

ABBOTT. See Waterhouse, *Painting in Britain*.

ABSTRACT ART. See A. Heath, *Abstract Painting; its origin and meaning*, London 1953; Berckelaers and Seuphor, *A Dictionary of Abstract Painting*; A. C. Ritchie, *Abstract Painting and Sculpture in America*, Cat. of Exh., M of MA, New York 1951; also see under PERIODS AND STYLES in Classified Bibliography.

ABSTRACT IMPRESSIONISM. Cat. of Exh., Arts Council, London 1958.

ACADEMY. N. Pevsner, *Academies of Art, Past and Present*, Cambridge 1940.

ADAM. Monograph by H. Thirion, Paris 1885 (on the Adams and Clodion). See also Lami, *Dictionnaire des Sculpteurs*.

AERTSEN. Monograph by J. Sievers, Leipzig 1908. See also Friedländer, *Altniederländische Malerei*, xiii.

AFRO. Monograph by J. J. Sweeney, Rome 1961 (in Eng.). See also Haftmann, *Painting in the Twentieth Century*.

AGOSTINO DI DUCCIO. Monograph by A. Pointner, Strassburg 1909 (in German). See also Pope-Hennessy, *Italian Sculpture*, ii.

AIKMAN. See Waterhouse, *Painting in Britain*.

ALBANI. See Wittkower, *Art and Architecture in Italy*.

ALBERTINELLI. Monograph by G. Gruyer, Paris 1886

(on A. and Fra Bartolommeo). See also Freedberg, *High Renaissance*; and Venturi, *Storia*, ix.

ALGARDI. See Pope-Hennessy, *Italian Sculpture*, iii; and Wittkower, *Art and Architecture in Italy*.

ALLAN. Monograph by T. Crouther Gordon, privately printed 1951.

ALLSTON. Monograph by E. P. Richardson, Chicago 1948.

ALTDORFER. Monographs by O. Benesch, Vienna 1939 and 1943; M. J. Friedländer, Berlin n.d.; F. Winzinger, Munich 1952 (on his drawings), and Munich 1963 (on his graphic work).

ALTICHIERO and AVANZO. Monograph by L. Bronstein, Paris 1932. See also Crowe and Cavalcaselle, *Painting in Italy*; Toesca, *Trecento*; van Marle, *Italian Schools*, iv.

'ALUNNO DI DOMENICO'. See van Marle, *Italian Schools*, xiii.

AMBERGER. Monograph by Haasler, Königsberg 1894.

'AMICO DI SANDRO'. C. Gamba in *Miscellanea di Storia dell'Arte in Onore di I. B. Supino*, 1933. See also K. Neilson, *Filippino Lippi*, Cambridge Mass. 1938.

AMIGONI. See Levey, *Venice*; and Donzelli, *Pittori Veneziani*.

AMMANATI. See Pope-Hennessy, *Italian Sculpture*, iii.

ANDREA DEL SARTO. Monographs by S. J. Freedberg, 2 vols., Harvard 1963; and J. Shearman, 2 vols., Oxford 1965.

ANGELICO. Monographs by J. Pope-Hennessy, London 1952; G. C. Argan, Lausanne 1955 (in Eng.); S. Orlandi, Florence 1964.

ANTELAMI. Monograph by G. de Francovich, 2 vols., Milan and Florence 1952; see also Crichton, *Romanesque Sculpture in Italy*.

ANTONELLO. Monographs by J. Lauts, Vienna 1940; and G. Vigni, Milan 1952 and London 1963. See also Cat. of Exh., Messina 1953.

ANTWERP MANNERISTS. See Friedländer, *Altniederländische Malerei*, xi.

APPEL. Monograph by H. Claus, London 1963.

APT. See Stange, *Deutsche Malerei der Gotik*, viii.

ARCHIPENKO. Monograph by A. and others, *Fifty Creative Years, 1908–58*, New York 1960. See also Selz, *Modern Sculpture*.

ARCIMBOLDI. Monograph by F. C. Legrand, Paris 1955.

ARMITAGE. Monograph by N. Lynton, London 1962.

ARMORY SHOW. M. Brown, *The Story of the Armory Show*, London and New York 1963.

ARNOLFO DI CAMBIO. Monograph by V. Mariani, Rome 1943. See also Pope-Hennessy, *Italian Sculpture*, i.

ARP. Monographs by C. Giedion-Welcker, London, New York and Stuttgart 1957; J. T. Soby (ed.), New

York (M of MA) 1958; and M. Seuphor, London 1961. See also A., *On my way: poetry and essays, 1912–47*, New York 1948, and Cat. of Exh., Kunsthalle, Basle 1962.

ARPINO. See Voss, *Die Malerei der Spätrenaissance*.

ARS MORIENDI. See A. M. Hind, *An Introduction to a History of Woodcut*, 2 vols, London 1935 (republ. 1963).

ART NOUVEAU. Monographs ed. by P. Selz and M. Constantine, New York (M of MA) 1959; and R. Schmutzler, London 1963. See also Cassou, Langui, and Pevsner, *Sources of Modern Art*.

AVANZO. See under ALTICHIERO.

AVED. Monograph by G. Wildenstein, Paris 1922.

AVERCAMP. Monograph by C. J. Welcker, Zwolle 1933. See also Bernt, *Niederländische Maler*.

B

BABUREN. Monograph by L. Slatkes, Utrecht 1965 (in Eng.). See also Cat. of Exh., Utrecht 1952.

BACICCIA. Monograph by R. Enggass, Pennsylvania 1964. See also Waterhouse, *Italian Baroque Painting*; and Wittkower, *Art and Architecture in Italy*.

BACKER. Monograph by K. Bauch, Berlin 1926.

BACKHUYSEN. See Hofstede de Groot, *Dutch Painters*, vii.

BACON, F. Monograph by R. Alley, London 1964. See also Cat. of Exh., Tate Gall., London 1962.

BACON, J. See Gunnis, *Dictionary of British Sculptors*; and Whinney, *Sculpture in Britain*.

BALDINUCCI. *Notizie de' Professori del Disegno da Cimabue in quà. . . ,* Florence 1681–1728, 6 vols.; the Life of Bernini is included in later eds, e.g. the complete ed. publ. in Milan in 14 vols., 1811–12.

BALDOVINETTI. Monograph by R. Kennedy, New Haven 1938.

BALDUNG. Monograph by O. Fischer, 2nd ed. Munich 1943. See also Cat. of Exh., Staatliche Kunsthalle, Karlsruhe 1959.

BALLA. See J. C. Taylor, *Futurism*, New York (M of MA) 1961, and catalogue publ. Turin, Galleria Civica d'Arte Moderna, 1963.

BAMBOCCIATA/BAMBOCCIO. See Hoogewerff, *Bentvueghels*; Wittkower, *Art and Architecture in Italy*; and Cat. of Exh., *I Bamboccianti*, Rome 1950.

BANDINELLI. See Pope-Hennessy, *Italian Sculpture*, iii; and Venturi, *Storia*, x.

BANKS. *Annals of Thomas Banks*, ed. by C. Bell, Cambridge 1938. See also Gunnis, *Dictionary of British Sculptors*; and Whinney, *Sculpture in Britain*.

BARBARI. Monographs by A. de Hevesy, Paris and Brussels 1925; and L. Servolini, Padua 1944.

BARBIZON SCHOOL. Monographs by D. C. Thompson, London 1890; M. de Forges, Paris 1962; and A. Billy, *Les beaux jours de Barbizon*, Paris 1947. See also Cat. of Exh., *Barbizon revisited*, with essay by R. Herbert, San Francisco; Toledo Ohio; Cleveland and Boston 1962.

BARISANUS. See A. Boeckler, *Die frühmittelalterlichen Bronzetüren*, iv, Berlin 1953; H. Leisinger, *Romanesque Bronzes*, London 1956. See also under BONANUS.

BARLACH. Autobiographies, Berlin 1928 and 1948; and monograph by F. Schuldt, Hamburg 1959. See also Cat. of Exh., Berlin 1951–2; and Selz, *Modern Sculpture*.

BARNA DA SIENA. See E. Cecchi, *The Sienese Painters of the Trecento*, London and New York 1931, and *Trecentisti Senesi*. See also Venturi, *Storia*, v.

BARNABA DA MODENA. See Venturi, *Storia*, v; van Marle, *Italian Schools*, iv; and P. Rotondi, *Il polittico di Barnaba da Modena a Lavagnola*, Genoa 1955.

BAROCCI. Monograph by H. Olsen, Copenhagen 1962 (in Eng.).

BARONZIO. See Toesca, *Trecento*; van Marle, *Italian Schools*, iv; and Cat. of Exh. (by C. Brandi), Rimini 1935.

BAROQUE. See Wittkower, *Art and Architecture in Italy*; Waterhouse, *Italian Baroque Painting*; Blunt, *Art and Architecture in France*; Gerson and Ter Kuile, *Art and Architecture in Belgium*; W. Weisbach, *Die Kunst des Barock*, Berlin 1924.

BARRY. See *The Works of James Barry*, 2 vols., London 1809; and Waterhouse, *Painting in Britain*.

BARTOLO DI FREDI. See van Marle, *Italian Schools*, ii.

BARTOLOMMEO, FRA. Monograph by H. von der Gabelentz, 2 vols., Leipzig 1922. See also Freedberg, *High Renaissance*.

BARYE. Monographs by R. Ballu, Paris 1890; and G. Saunier, Paris 1925. See also Selz, *Modern Sculpture*; and Cat. of Exh., Louvre, Paris 1956–7.

BASAITI. See Venturi, *Storia*, viii; and Berenson, *Venetian School*.

BASSANO. Monographs by W. Arslan, 2 vols., 2nd ed. Milan 1960; P. Zampetti, Rome 1958 (in Eng.). See also Cat. of Exh., Venice 1957.

BATONI. Monograph by E. Emmerling, Darmstadt 1932. See also Wittkower, *Art and Architecture in Italy*.

BAUHAUS. W. Gropius, *The New Architecture and the Bauhaus*, London 1955.

BAUMEISTER. Monograph by W. Grohmann, Cologne 1963, and Paris 1931. See also the artist's *Das Unbekannte in der Kunst*, Stuttgart 1947.

BAYEU. Monograph by V. de Sambricio, Madrid 1955. See also Lafuente Ferrari, *Breve historia*.

BAZAINE. Monograph by A. Maeght, Paris 1953. See also B.'s *Notes sur la peinture d'aujourd'hui*, 2nd ed., Paris 1953; and Haftmann, *Painting in the Twentieth Century*.

BAZILLE. Monograph by F. Daulte, Geneva 1952 (in French). See also Rewald, *Impressionism*.

BEARDSLEY. Monograph by A. E. Gallatin, New York 1945. See also the artist's letters to L. Smithers, ed. by R. A. Walker, London 1937.

BECCAFUMI. Monograph by M. Gibellino-Krascenninikowa, Siena 1933. See also Cat. of the Pontormo Exh., Florence 1956; Becherucci, *Manieristi Toscani*; Venturi, *Storia*, ix; and Sandberg-Vavala, *Sienese Studies*.

BECKMANN. Monographs by B. Reifenberg and Hausenstein, Munich 1949; L. Buchheim, Feldafing 1959; and G. Busch, Munich 1960. See also L. Buchheim, *The Graphic Art of German Expressionism*, Feldafing 1960.

BEECHEY. Monograph by W. Roberts, London 1907.

BELLECHOSE. See Ring, *Century of French Painting*; and Sterling, *Les Peintres du Moyen Âge*.

BELLINI. Monographs on Giovanni by L. Dussler, Frankfurt 1935 and Vienna 1949; P. Hendy and L. Goldscheider, London 1945; G. Fiocco, London 1960; and F. Heinemann, 2 vols., Venice 1962. See also Cat. of Exh., Venice 1949. Monograph on Jacopo by C. Ricci, Bergamo 1908; and also V. Goloubew, *Les dessins de J. B. au Louvre et au British Museum*, 2 vols., Brussels 1912–13 (facsimile ed.); and V. Moschini, *Disegni di J.B.*, Bergamo 1943. See also Venturi, *Storia*, viii; and Berenson, *Venetian School*.

BELLOTTO. Monograph by H. Fritzsche, Burg b. M. 1936. See also Levey, *Venice*; Donzelli, *Pittori Veneziani*; and Cat. of Exh., Whitechapel Gallery, London 1957, and Albertinum, Dresden 1963–4.

BELLOWS. Cat. of Retrospective Exh., NG, Washington 1957.

BENEDETTO DA MAIANO. Monograph by L. Dussler, Munich 1924. See also Pope-Hennessy, *Italian Sculpture*, ii.

BENTNAME. See Hoogewerff, *Bentvueghels*.

BERCHEM. Monograph by I. von Sick, Berlin 1930. See also Hofstede de Groot, *Dutch Painters*, ix.

BERCKHEYDE. See Bernt, *Niederländische Maler*.

BERLINGHIERO. See Garrison, *Italian Romanesque Panel Painting*; and Sinibaldi and Brunetti, *Mostra Giottesca Catalogue*.

BERMEJO. See Post, *Spanish Painting*, v and xii; and Lafuente Ferrari, *Breve historia*.

BERNARD. Monograph by P. Mornand, Geneva 1957. See also Rewald, *Post-Impressionism*.

BERNINI. Monograph by R. Wittkower, London 1955. See also Pope-Hennessy, *Italian Sculpture*, iii.

BERRUGUETE, A. Monograph by R. de Orueta, Madrid 1917. See also Cat. of Pontormo Exh., Florence 1956.

BERRUGUETE, P. See Cat. of Exh., *Juste de Gand, Berruguete et la Cour d'Urbino*, Ghent 1957; and also Post, *Spanish Painting*, ix, part 1; and Lafuente Ferrari, *Breve historia*.

BERTOLDO. Monograph by W. Bode, Freiburg 1925. See also Pope-Hennessy, *Italian Sculpture*, ii.

BERTRAM, MEISTER. Monographs by A. Dorner, Berlin 1937; and F. A. Martens, Berlin 1934.

BEWICK. Memoir by himself, 1st publ. 1862 (also 1961); monographs by R. Stone, London 1949; and C. M. Weekley, London 1953. Memorial ed. of his works in 5 vols., London 1885–7.

BIBIENA. Monograph by A. H. Mayor, New York 1945. See also G. Galli-B., *Architectural and Perspective Designs* (ed. A. Hyatt Mayor), New York 1964.

BIEDERMEIERSTIL. Monograph by P. F. Schmidt, *Biedermeier Malerei*, 2nd ed. Munich 1923.

BILL. Monograph by T. Maldonado, Buenos Aires 1955 (in Eng., French, and German). See also B.'s *Mathematische Denkweise in der Kunst unserer Zeit* (in Cat. of Exh.) Zürich 1949; and his essay in *Kandinsky*, Basle 1949. Also Haftmann, *Painting in the Twentieth Century*; and Giedion-Welcker, *Contemporary Sculpture*.

BINGHAM. Monograph by A. Christ-Janer, New York 1940. See also Richardson, *Painting in America*.

BIRD. See Gunnis, *Dictionary of British Sculptors*; and Whinney, *Sculpture in Britain*.

BLAKE. Monographs by A. Gilchrist, 2 vols., London 1863 (republ. ed. by Ruthven Todd, 1945); M. Wilson, London 1948; and Sir A. Blunt, New York 1959. See also Catalogue, Tate Gall., London 1957 (by M. Butlin).

BLANCHARD. See Blunt, *Art and Architecture in France*.

BLAUE REITER. Monographs by L. Grote, Munich 1949; and L. G. Buchheim, Feldafing 1959. See also

Cat. of Exhs, Harvard University 1955, and Edinburgh Festival 1960.

BLECHEN. Monograph by P. O. Rave, Berlin 1940.

BLOCK-BOOK. See H. T. Musper, *Die Urausgaben des holländischen Blockbuchs. . .*, Munich 1961; and A. M. Hind, *An Introduction to a History of Woodcut*, 2 vols., London 1935 (republ. New York 1963).

BLOEMAERT. Monograph by G. Delbanco, Strassburg 1928 (in German). See also Cat. of Exh., *Caravaggio en de Nederlanden*, Utrecht 1952.

BOCCIONI. Monographs by G. C. Argan, Rome 1953; and G. Ballo, Milan 1962. See also the artist's own writings republ. Rome 1958–60; Selz, *Modern Sculpture*; and under FUTURISM.

BÖCKLIN. Monographs by G. Floerke, Munich 1921; H. A. Schmid, 4 vols., 1892–1901, 2nd ed. Munich 1922. See also Autobiography ed. F. Runkel, Berlin 1910; M. Huggler and A. M. Cetto, *Schweizer Malerei im 19. Jhr.*, Basle n.d.; and Cat. of Exh., Basle 1951.

BOL. See N. Maclaren, *Cat. of Dutch School*, NG, London 1960.

BOLDINI. Monograph by D. Cecchi, Turin 1962. See also Cat. of Exh., Ferrara and Paris 1963.

BOLGI. See Wittkower, *Art and Architecture in Italy*.

BOLOGNA. Monograph by E. Dhanens, Brussels 1956 (in Flemish). See also J. Pope-Hennessy, *Samson and a Philistine*, London (V & A) 1954, and *Italian Sculpture*, iii.

BOLTRAFFIO. See W. Suida, *Leonardo und sein Kreis*, Munich 1929.

BONANUS. Monograph by A. Boeckler, Berlin 1953. See also H. Leisinger, *Romanesque Bronzes*, London 1956; and under BARISANUS.

BONE. See Cat. of Exh., Arts Council, London 1955.

BONIFAZIO. Monograph by D. Westphal, Munich 1931. See also Venturi, *Storia*, ix.

BONINGTON. Monograph by A. Shirley, London 1940.

BONNARD. Monographs by J. Rewald, New York (M of MA) 1948, and 1962; and D. Sutton, London 1957.

BOR. See Cat. of Exh., *Caravaggio en de Nederlanden*, Utrecht 1952.

BORDONE. Monographs by L. Bailo and G. Biscaro, Treviso 1900; and G. Canova, Venice 1964.

BORGOGNONE. Monographs by N. Aprà, Milan 1945; and F. Mazzini, Brescia 1948.

BOSCH. Monographs by C. de Tolnay, Basle 1937 (in French); J. Combe, London 1946; C. Linfert, London 1959; and L. Baldass, London 1960.

BOTH, A. and J. See Hoogewerff, *Bentvueghels*; and Hofstede de Groot, *Dutch Painters*, ix (for Jan).

BOTTICELLI. Monographs by H. Horne, London 1908; J. Mesnil, Paris 1938; R. Salvini, 2 vols., Milan 1958 and 1962.

BOTTICINI. See van Marle, *Italian Schools*, xiii; and *Cat. of Earlier Italian Schools*, NG, London 1961.

BOUCHARDON. See Lami, *Dictionnaire des Sculpteurs*.

BOUCHER. Monograph by A. Michel (with cat. by E. Soulié and Ch. Masson), Paris 1907. See also E. and J. de Goncourt, *French 18 c. Painters*.

BOUDIN. Monograph by R. L. Benjamin, New York 1937. See also Rewald, *Impressionism*.

BOURDELLE. Monographs by F. Monod, Brussels 1928;

and E. Auricoste, Paris 1955. See also the sculptor's own *Écrits sur l'art. . .* , Paris 1955; *Hommage à Bourdelle*, Introd. by R. Cogniat, Paris 1961; and Selz, *Modern Sculpture*.

BOURDON. Monograph by C. Ponsonhailhe, Paris 1883.

BOUTS. Monograph by W. Schöne, Berlin and Leipzig 1938. See also Panofsky, *Early Netherlandish Painting*; and Cat. of Exh., *Dieric Bouts*, Brussels and Delft 1957–8.

BOZZETTO. See A. E. Brinckmann, *Barock-Bozzetti*, 4 vols., Frankfurt am Main 1923–5 (in German and Eng.).

BRANCUSI. Monographs by C. Giedion-Welcker, Basle and Stuttgart 1958, and New York 1960; and I. Jianou, London 1963 (with cat. raisonné). See also Selz, *Modern Sculpture*.

BRANGWYN. Monograph by W. de Belleroche, London 1948. See also W. de Belleroche, *Brangwyn Talks*, London 1944; and Cat. of Exh., RA, London 1952.

BRAQUE. Monographs by H. Hope, New York (M. of MA) 1949; J. Richardson, London 1959; J. Russell, London 1959; J. Leymarie, Lausanne 1961 (in Eng.). See also W. Hoffmann, London 1962, for his graphic work; and Cats. of Exhbs. in Edinburgh and London 1956, and Munich 1963 (Introds. by D. Cooper).

BRAY, J. DE. See Bernt, *Niederländische Maler*.

BRAY, S. DE. See Bernt, *Niederländische Maler*.

BREU. See E. Buchner and K. Feuchtmayr, *Beiträge zur Geschichte der deutschen Kunst*, ii, Augsburg 1928.

BRIL, P. Monograph by R. Baer, Munich 1930.

BROEDERLAM. See Panofsky, *Early Netherlandish Painters*; Ring, *Century of French Painting*.

BRONZE. See J. Montagu, *Bronzes*, London 1963.

BRONZINO. Monographs by A. McComb, Cambridge Mass. 1928; A. Emiliani, Busto Arsizio 1960. See also Becherucci, *Manieristi Toscani*; and Cat. of the Pontormo Exh., Florence 1956.

BROUWER. Monograph by G. Knuttel, The Hague 1962 (in Eng.). See also Hofstede de Groot, *Dutch Painters*, iii; and Gerson and Ter Kuile, *Art and Architecture in Belgium*.

BROWN. Monograph by F. M. Hueffer, London 1896. See also Ironside and Gere, *Pre-Raphaelite Painters*.

BRÜCKE. Monographs by H. M. Wingler, Feldafing 1954; and L. G. Buchheim, Feldafing 1956. See also Arts Council Exh. Cat., Tate Gall., London 1964.

BRUEGEL, JAN I. Monograph by F. Klauner, Uppsala 1952 (in German). See also J. Denucé, *Brieven en documenten betreffend Jan Brueghel I en II*, Antwerp 1934; and Gerson and Ter Kuile, *Art and Architecture in Belgium*.

BRUEGEL, PIETER I. Monographs by C. de Tolnay, Brussels 1935; and F. Grossmann, London n.d. (1955 in progress). See L. Münz, London 1961 and C. de Tolnay, London 1952, for his drawings.

BRUEGEL, PIETER II. See Gerson and Ter Kuile, *Art and Architecture in Belgium*.

BRUYN. See H. J. Tümmers, *Die Altarbilder des älteren B.B.*, Cologne 1964; and Cat. of Exh., Wallraf-Richartz Museum, 2nd enlarged ed., Cologne 1955.

BUECKELAER. See van Mander, *Het Schilderboek*; and Bautier, Cazier et al., *Dictionnaire*.

BUFFET. Monographs by J. Giono, Paris 1956; and by M. Druon and A. Buffet, Paris 1964.

BUON. See Pope-Hennessy, *Italian Sculpture*, i: and Venturi, *Storia*, vi.

BURGKMAIR. Monographs by K. Feuchtmayr, Augsburg 1931; and A. Burkhard, Leipzig 1934.

BURNE-JONES. Monographs by M. Bell, London 1901; and G. Burne-Jones, 2 vols., London 1906.

BURRI. Monograph by C. Brandi, Rome 1963 (in Eng.).

BUSHNELL. See Gunnis, *Dictionary of British Sculptors*; and Whinney, *Sculpture in Britain*.

BUTLER. See the artist's *Creative Development: Five lectures to Art Students*, London 1962; and Seuphor, *Sculpture of this Century*.

BYLERT. See Cat. of Exh., *Caravaggio en de Nederlanden*, Utrecht 1952.

C

CALDER. Monograph by J. J. Sweeney, New York (M of MA) 1943, revised ed. 1951. See also Cat. of Retrospective Exh., Guggenheim Mus., New York 1964.

CALLOT. Monographs by J. Lieure, 5 vols., Paris 1927–9; and D. Ternois, 2 vols. (with cat. of drawings), Paris 1962.

CALRAET. See N. Maclaren, *Cat. of Dutch School*, NG, London 1960.

CALVAERT. Monograph by S. Bergmans, Brussels 1931 and 1934.

CALVERT. Monographs by S. Calvert (the artist's son), London 1893; and R. Lister, London 1962. See also L. Binyon, *The Followers of William Blake*, London 1925; and A. H. Palmer, *Catalogue of . . . Drawings . . . by Samuel Palmer. . .* , London (V & A) 1926.

CAMERA OTTICA. See T. Pignatti, *Il Quaderno di Disegni del Canaletto alle Gallerie di Venezia*, Venice 1958; J. Meder, *Die Handzeichnung*.

CAMPENDONK. Monograph by M. Engels, Recklinghausen, 1958. See also Myers, *Expressionism*; and Haftmann, *Painting in the Twentieth Century*.

CAMPIN. See under MASTER OF FLÉMALLE.

CANALETTO. Monographs by W. G. Constable, 2 vols., Oxford 1962; F. Watson, London 1949; V. Moschini, London 1955; and Sir K. Parker, London 1948 (for C.'s drawings).

CANO. Monograph by H. E. Wethey, Princeton 1955.

CANOVA. Monographs by E. Bassi, Bergamo 1943; and A. Muñoz, Rome 1957. See also Cat. of Exh. (ed. by L. Coletti), Treviso 1957.

CAPPELLE. See Hofstede de Groot, *Dutch Painters*, vii.

CARACCIOLO. See Wittkower, *Art and Architecture in Italy*.

CARAVAGGIO. Monographs by R. Hinks, London 1953; and W. Friedländer, Princeton 1955. See also Cat. of Exh., Milan 1951; and Wittkower, *Art and Architecture in Italy*.

CARLEVARIS. Monograph by F. Mauroner, Padua 1945.

CARPACCIO. Monographs by G. Ludwig and P. Molmenti, Milan 1906, Eng. trans. London 1907; T. Pignatti, Lausanne 1958 (in Eng.); G. Perocco, Milan 1960; and J. Lauts, London 1962.

CARPEAUX. Monographs by E. Chesneau, Paris 1880; and Mme L. Clément Carpeaux, 2 vols., Paris and Nemours, 1934–5. See also Cat. of Exh., Petit Palais, Paris 1955–6; and Selz, *Modern Sculpture*.

CARRÀ. Monograph by R. Longhi, 2nd ed. Milan 1945.

CARRACCI. See Cat. of Exh., Bologna 1956, and Cat. of Exh. of C.'s Drawings, Bologna 1956. See also R. Wittkower, *Drawings of the C.*, London 1952, and *Art and Architecture in Italy*; H. Bodmer, monograph on Ludovico, Burg b. M., 1939; and J. Martin, *The Farnese Gallery*, Princeton 1965.

CARRIERA. See Rosalba's *Diary* (of her stay in Paris), French ed. with notes by A. Sensier, Paris 1865. See also Levey, *Venice*; and Donzelli, *Pittori Veneziani*.

CARSTENS. Monographs by C. L. Fernow, Leipzig 1806 and 2nd ed. Hanover 1867; and A. Kamphausen, Neumünster 1941

CARTOON. See Meder, *Die Handzeichnung*.

CASSATT. Monographs by M. Breuning, New York 1944; and A. Breeskin, New York 1948. See also F. Sweet, *Sargent, Whistler and M. C.*, Chicago 1954; and Rewald, *Impressionism*.

CASSONE. P. Schubring, *Cassoni*, 2 vols., Leipzig 1915, and suppls. Leipzig 1923, and Vienna 1930.

CASTAGNO. Monographs by G. Richter, Chicago 1943; A. M. Fortuna, Florence 1957; and M. Salmi, Florence 1957. See also Cat. of Exh., *Quattro Maestri del Primo Rinascimento*, Florence 1954.

CASTIGLIONE. Monograph by Sir A. Blunt (on the drawings of C. and Stefano della Bella), London 1954. See also Waterhouse, *Italian Baroque Painting*.

CATENA. Monograph by G. Robertson, Edinburgh 1954.

CAVALLINI. Monographs by E. Lavagnino, Rome 1953; and P. Toesca, London 1959. See also Oertel, *Die Frühzeit der italienischen Malerei*.

CAVALLINO. Monograph by A. de Rinaldis, Rome 1921. See also Wittkower, *Art and Architecture in Italy*.

CELLINI. *Autobiography*, trans. by G. Bull, London 1956. Monographs by E. Plon, Paris 1883, with new appendix, Paris 1884; and E. Camesasca, Milan 1955. *The Treatises*, originally publ. Florence 1568, ed. and trans. by C. R. Ashbee, London 1898.

CENNINI. Edition of the *Libro* by D. V. Thompson, London 1932–3, 2 vols. including original Ital. text, and later ed. (n.d.) with Eng. trans. only. See also Thompson, *The Materials of Medieval Painting*.

CÉSAR. Monograph by D. Cooper, Amriswil 1960 (in Eng. and French). See also Giedion-Welcker, *Contemporary Sculpture*.

CÉZANNE. Monographs by R. Fry, 2nd ed. London 1952; L. Venturi, 2 vols., Paris 1936; B. Dorival, London 1949; and J. Rewald, London 1950.

CHADWICK. Monographs by J. Hodin, London 1961; and A. Bowness, London 1962.

CHAGALL. His autobiography, Paris 1931 and 1957, and London 1965. Monographs by J. Sweeney, New York 1946; F. Meyer, London 1964; and J. Leymarie (on the Jerusalem windows), Monte Carlo 1962 (in Eng.). See also Cat. of Exh., Musée des Arts Décoratifs, Paris 1959.

CHAMPAIGNE. Monograph by A. M. de Poncheville, Paris 1938. See also Blunt, *Art and Architecture in France*; and Cat. of Exh., Orangerie, Paris 1952.

CHANTREY. Monograph by J. Holland, Sheffield 1851. See also Whinney, *Sculpture in Britain*; Boase, *English Art*; and Gunnis, *Dictionary of British Sculptors*.

CHARDIN. Monographs by A. Pascal and R. Gaucheron, Paris 1931; G. Wildenstein, Paris 1933, 2nd ed. Zürich 1963 (in French); and P. Rosenberg, Lausanne 1963 (in Eng.).

CHASSÉRIAU. Monographs by V. Chevillard, Paris 1893; H. Marcel and J. Laran, Paris 1911; and L. Bénédite, 2 vols., Paris 1932. See also Cats. of Exhs., Orangerie, Paris 1933; and Louvre, Paris 1957.

CHIRICO. Monograph by J. T. Soby, New York (M of MA) 1955.

CHRISTUS. See Panofsky, *Early Netherlandish Painting*; Friedländer, *Altniederländische Malerei*, i, and *Van Eyck to Brueghel*.

CIBBER. Monograph by H. Faber, Oxford 1926. See also Whinney, *Sculpture in Britain*; and Gunnis, *Dictionary of British Sculptors*.

CIMA. Monograph by L. Coletti, Venice 1959. See also Cat. of Exh., Treviso 1962.

CIMABUE. Monographs by R. Salvini, Rome 1946; A. Nicholson, Princeton 1934; and E. Battisti, Milan 1963. See also Garrison, *Italian Romanesque Panel Painting*.

CLAUDE. Monographs by P. Courthion, Paris 1932; W. Friedländer, Berlin 1921; M. Rothlisberger, 2 vols., Yale 1961; and A. M. Hind (for the drawings), London 1925. See also Blunt, *Art and Architecture in France*.

CLODION. Monograph by H. Thirion, Paris 1885 (on Clodion and the Adams). See also Lami, *Dictionnaire des sculpteurs*.

CLOUET. Monograph by E. Moreau-Nélaton, 3 vols., Paris 1924 (on the family and their followers). See also Blunt, *Art and Architecture in France*.

COELLO, C. Monograph by J. A. Gaya Nuño, Madrid 1957. See also Kubler and Soria, *Art and Architecture in Spain*.

COLE. Monographs by L. L. Noble, New York 1853 (new ed. by E. Vesell, Cambridge Mass. 1964); and E. I. Seaver, Hartford Conn. 1948. See also Soby and Miller, *Romantic Painting in America*.

COLLAGE. See Seitz, *The Art of Assemblage*.

CONCA. See Wittkower, *Art and Architecture in Italy*.

CONINXLOO. See Gerson and Ter Kuile, *Art and Architecture in Belgium*.

CONSTABLE. Monograph by C. R. Leslie, London 1843 (and many later eds, e.g. A. Shirley's, London 1937, and 1944 abridged). See also Cat. of the C. Collection, V & A, London 1960, by G. Reynolds; and Boase, *English Art*.

CONSTRUCTIVISM. K. Malevich, *Die gegenstandslose Welt*, Dessau 1927 (Eng. trans. as *The Non-Objective World*, Chicago 1959). N. Gabo, J. L. Martin, and B. Nicholson, *Circle: International Survey of Constructive Art*, London 1937; N. Gabo, 'On Constructive Realism;' (Chapter in *Three Lectures on Modern Art*), New York 1949. See also Cat. of Gabo-Pevsner Exh., M of MA, New York 1948, ed. by Sir H. Read.

CONVERSATION PIECE. Monograph by R. Edwards, London 1954.

COOPER, S. and A. See Long, *British Miniaturists*; and Reynolds, *English Portrait Miniatures*.

COPLEY. Monograph by J. T. Flexner, Boston 1948.

CORINTH. His own *Selbstbiographie*, Leipzig 1926. Monograph by G. von der Osten, Munich 1955; and œuvre cat. by C. Berend-Corinth, Munich 1958. See also Cat. of Exh., Arts Council, Tate Gall., London 1959.

CORNEILLE DE LYON. See Blunt, *Art and Architecture in France.*

CORNELIUS. See K. K. Andrews, *The Nazarenes,* Oxford 1964.

COROT. Monographs by A. Robaut, 4 vols., Paris 1905, and suppl., Paris 1948 (with œuvre cat.); also G. Bazin, Paris 1951. See also *Corot raconté par lui-même. . .*, 2 vols., Geneva 1946.

CORREGGIO. Monographs by A. E. Popham (the drawings), London 1957; P. Bianconi (the paintings), Milan 1953; and S. Bottari, Milan 1961. See also S. de Vito-Battaglia, *Correggio, Bilbiografia,* Rome 1934.

COSMATI. Monograph by E. Hutton, London 1950.

COSSA. Monographs by A. Neppi, Milan 1958; E. Ruhmer, Munich 1959; S. Ortolani, *Cosmé Tura, Francesco del Cossa, Ercole de' Roberti,* Milan 1941. See also Longhi, *Officina ferrarese,* with *Ampliamenti,* Florence 1940, and *Nuovi ampliamenti,* Florence 1956; and Nicolson, *Painters of Ferrara.*

COSTA. See Longhi, *Officina ferrarese*; and Nicolson, *Painters of Ferrara,* as for Cossa; and Venturi, *Storia,* vii, part 3.

COSTRUZIONE LEGITTIMA. See Alberti, *On Painting,* ed. J. R. Spencer, London 1956; J. Pope-Hennessy, *Uccello,* London 1950; and J. White, *The Birth and Rebirth of Pictorial Space,* London 1957.

COSWAY. Monograph by G. C. Williamson, London 1905. See also Long, *British Miniaturists*; and Reynolds, *Portrait Miniatures.*

COTES. See Waterhouse, *Painting in Britain.*

COTMAN. Monographs by S. Kitson, London 1937; and V. Rienaecker, Leigh-on-Sea 1953. See also Boase, *English Art.*

COURBET. Monograph by G. Mack, New York and London 1951. See also *C. raconté par lui-même,* 2 vols., Geneva 1948–50; and Cat. of Exh., Philadelphia and Boston 1959–60.

COUSTOU I and II. See Lami, *Dictionnaire des sculpteurs.*

COUTURE. See his own *Méthodes et entretiens d'atelier,* Paris 1868, Eng. trans., New York 1879; and *Paysage,* Paris 1869.

COX. Monograph by Trenchard Cox, London 1947.

COYPEL family. See C. A. Coypel, *Discours sur la peinture,* Paris 1752. See also P. Marcel, *La peinture française au début du 18ᵉ siècle, 1690–1721,* Paris 1906; Dimier, *Les peintres français du 18ᵉ siècle*; and H. Lapauze, *Histoire de l'Académie de France à Rome,* 2 vols., Paris 1924.

COYSEVOX. Monograph by G. Keller-Dorian, Paris 1920 (with cat.). See also Lami, *Dictionnaire des sculpteurs.*

COZENS, A. and J. R. Monograph by A. P. Oppé, London 1952 (includes A. C.'s *A New Method . . .*). See also C. F. Bell and T. Girtin, *The Drawings and Sketches of J. R. C.,* Walpole Soc., xxiii, Oxford 1935.

CRANACH. Monographs by M. Friedländer and J. Rosenberg, Berlin 1932; H. Posse, Vienna 1942; and E. Ruhmer, London 1963. For his drawings and graphic work, see J. Jahn, Leipzig 1955; and J. Rosenberg, Berlin 1960.

CREDI. See van Marle, *Italian Schools,* xiii; and Venturi, *Storia,* vii.

CRESPI, D. Monograph by G. Nicodemi, 2nd ed. Busto Arsizio 1930.

CRESPI, G. B. See Cat. of Exh., Novara 1964; and Wittkower, *Art and Architecture in Italy.*

CRESPI, G. M. Monograph by H. Voss, Rome 1921. See also Wittkower, *Art and Architecture in Italy*; and Cat. of Exh., Bologna 1948.

CRIVELLI, C. Monograph by P. Zampetti, Milan 1963; and A. Bovero, Milan 1961. See also Cat. of Exh., Venice 1961.

CROME. Monograph by C. H. Collins Baker, London 1921. See also W. F. Dickes, *The Norwich School of Painting,* London 1905; and Boase, *English Art.*

CUBISM. Monographs by A. Gleizes and J. Metzinger, London (Eng. ed.) 1913; J. Golding, London 1959; and R. Rosenblum, London 1960.

CURRIER AND IVES. Monographs by H. T. Peters, 2 vols., New York 1929–31; and C. Simkin (ed.), New York 1952. On Currier alone, see N. C. White, Cambridge Mass. 1936.

CUYP. See Hofstede de Groot, *Dutch Painters,* ii; and Bode, *Dutch and Flemish Painting.*

D

DADA. Monographs by W. Verkauf, Teufen 1961; H. Richter, London 1965; A. H. Barr, *Fantastic Art, Dada, Surrealism*; R. Motherwell, *The Dada Painters and Poets: an anthology,* New York 1951; and G. Huguet, *L'Aventure Dada, 1916–22,* Paris 1957.

DADDI, B. Monographs by G. Vitzthum, Leipzig 1903; and R. Offner, New York 1930. See also Offner, *Corpus of Florentine Painting,* iii, part 3.

DAHL. See W. Nisser, *M. D. and the contemporary school of Swedish painting,* Uppsala 1927.

DALI. Monographs by A. R. Morse and M. Tapié, Greenwich Conn. 1958; and J. T. Soby, New York (M of MA) 1941, 2nd ed. 1946.

DANCE OF DEATH. See J. M. Clark, *The Dance of Death by Hans Holbein,* London 1947.

DANTI. See Venturi, *Storia,* x, part 2; and Pope-Hennessy, *Italian Sculpture,* iii.

DANUBE SCHOOL. See H. Voss, *Der Ursprung des Donaustils,* Leipzig 1907.

DARET. See Panofsky, *Early Netherlandish Painting*; Friedländer, *Altniederländische Malerei,* ii, and *Van Eyck to Brueghel.*

DAUBIGNY. Monographs by J. Laran, Paris 1913; and E. Moreau-Nélaton, Paris 1925.

DAUMIER. Monographs by J. Adhémar, Paris 1954; and K. Fuchs, 2nd ed. Munich 1930; R. Lejeune, Berlin n.d. (c. 1960, reproduces lithographs). See also Delteil, *Le peintre-graveur* (10 vols. on Daumier); and Cat. of Exh., Arts Council, London 1961.

DAVID, GERARD. Monographs by W. Weale, London 1895; E. von Bodenhausen, Munich 1905; and K. G. Boon, Amsterdam n.d. (c. 1945). See also Friedländer, *Altniederländische Malerei,* vi, and *Van Eyck to Brueghel.*

DAVID, J. L. Monographs by J. J. David, 2 vols., Paris 1880–2; R. Cantinelli, Paris 1930; K. Holma, Paris 1940; D. L. Dowd, *Pageant Master of the Republic,* Nebraska University 1948; A. Maurois, Paris 1948; L. Hautecœur, Paris 1954.

DEGAS. Monographs and œuvre cats. by P. Lemoisne, 4 vols., Paris 1946–9, and abridged ed. Paris 1954; P.

Cabanne, Paris 1958 (Eng. ed.); J. Fevre, Geneva 1949; J. Rewald, *Works in Sculpture*, 2nd ed. London 1957; D. Cooper, *Pastels. . .*, London 1953. See also *Lettres . . .*, ed. by M. Guérin, Paris 1931, Eng. ed. Oxford 1947; D. Rouart, *D. à la recherche de sa technique*, Paris 1945; L. Browse, *D. dancers*, London 1949, and J. S. Boggs, *Portraits by D.*, University of California Press 1962.

DELACROIX. Monographs by R. Escholier, 3 vols., Paris 1926–9; L. Johnson, London 1963; R. Huyghe, London 1963. See also his *Diary*, ed. by A. Joubin, 3 vols., Paris 1950, Eng. eds. (selection) ed. by H. Wellington, London 1951; and W. Pach, New York 1937; and his *Letters*, ed. by A. Joubin, 5 vols., Paris 1936–8; and *Lettres intimes*, ed. by A. Dupont, Paris 1954.

DELAUNAY. Monograph by F. Gilles de la Tourette, Paris 1950. See also D. himself, *Du cubisme à l'art abstrait*, ed. by P. Francastel, with cat. by G. Habasque, Paris 1957; and Cat. of Exh., Museo Civico, Turin 1960.

DELVAUX. Monograph by G. Willame, Brussels 1914. See also Gerson and Ter Kuile, *Art and Architecture in Belgium*; and Gunnis, *Dictionary of British Sculptors*.

DENIS. Monograph by S. Barazetti, Paris 1945. See also D.'s *Théories*, 2nd ed. Paris 1920; *Nouvelles Théories*, Paris 1922; *Histoire d'art religieux*, Paris 1939; *Sérusier, sa vie, son œuvre*, Paris 1943; and A. Humbert, *Les Nabis*, Geneva 1954; and Haftmann, *Painting in the Twentieth Century*.

DERAIN. Monograph by D. Sutton, London 1959.

DESIDERIO. Monographs by I. Cardellini, Milan 1962; and L. Planiscig, Vienna 1942. See also Pope-Hennessy, *Italian Sculpture*, ii.

DESPIAU. Monograph by W. George, London 1958. See also Selz, *Modern Sculpture*.

DEVIS. Monograph by S. H. Pavière, Leigh-on-Sea 1950. See also Cat. of Exh., Harris Museum, Preston 1937 and (for Anthony Devis) 1956.

DE WINT. Monograph by C. G. E. Bunt, Leigh-on-Sea 1948. See also Cat. of Exh., Usher Art Gallery, Lincoln 1937; and Binyon, *English Watercolours*.

DIAZ. Monograph by R. Ballu, Paris 1877.

DIDEROT. *Oeuvres esthétiques*, ed. by P. Vernière, Paris 1959. *Salons*, ed. by J. Seznec and J. Adhémar, Oxford, vols. i, 1957, ii, 1960, iii, 1962 (in French).

DISEGNO. See Blunt, *Artistic Theory in Italy*.

DIX, OTTO. Monographs by O. Conzelmann, Hanover 1959; and F. Loeffner, Dresden 1960. See also his own *Der Krieg* (publ. in 1924 as original etchings), East Berlin 1963, as 50 repr. of etchings, with introd. and some drawings; Myers, *Expressionsim*.

DOBSON. See Whinney and Millar, *English Art*; Waterhouse, *Painting in Britain*; and Cat. of Exh., Tate Gall., London 1951.

DOELENSTUK. See A. Riegl, *Das holländische Gruppenporträt*, Vienna 1931.

DOESBURG. See H. Jaffé, *De Stijl*, Amsterdam 1956 (in Eng.).

DOLCI. Monograph by G. Hay, London 1908 (largely a translation of BALDINUCCI). See also Waterhouse, *Baroque Painting*.

DOMENICHINO. Monograph by L. Serra, Rome 1909. See also J. Pope-Hennessy, *The Drawings of D. at Windsor Castle*, London 1948; and Wittkower, *Art and Architecture in Italy*.

DOMENICO VENEZIANO. Monograph by M. Salmi, *Uccello, Castagno, D. V.*, Milan 1938, and Paris 1939. See also van Marle, *Italian Schools*, x.

DONATELLO. Monograph by H. W. Janson, 2 vols., Princeton 1959. See also Pope-Hennessy, *Italian Sculpture*, ii.

DONGEN. Monograph by P. Fierens, Paris 1927. See also Haftmann, *Painting in the Twentieth Century*.

DONNER. Monographs by A. Pigler, Vienna 1929, and K. Blauensteiner, Vienna 1944 (and 1947). See Hempel, *Baroque Art . . . in Central Europe*.

DOSSI. Monograph by H. Mendelsohn, Munich 1913. See also Nicolson, *Painters of Ferrara*.

DOTTED PRINT. See Lehrs, *Geschichte und kritischer Katalog*.

DOU. Monographs by W. Martin, 2nd ed., London 1908; and Stuttgart and Berlin 1913. See also Hofstede de Groot, *Dutch Painters*, i.

DOWNMAN. Monograph by G. C. Williamson, London 1907. See also Waterhouse, *Painting in Britain*.

DROUAIS. See Réau, *Histoire de la peinture française*.

DUBUFFET. Monograph by P. Selz, New York (M of MA) 1962 (with three statements by the artist). See also Cat. of Exh., Louvre, Paris 1960–1.

DUCCIO. Monographs by E. Carli, Milan 1961; and C. Brandi, Florence 1951. See also Garrison, *Italian Romanesque Panel Painting*.

DUCHAMP. Monograph by R. Lebel, London 1959. See also the artist's own *The Bride stripped bare by her Bachelors, even*, New York 1960; *Marchand du sel*, Paris 1958; and Barr, *Fantastic Art, Dada, Surrealism*.

DUCHAMP-VILLON. Monograph by W. Pach, Paris 1924. See also Haftmann, *Painting in the Twentieth Century*; Selz, *Modern Sculpture*; and Giedion-Welcker, *Contemporary Sculpture*.

DUFY. Monograph by R. Ben Sussan and M. Brion, London 1959.

DUJARDIN. See Bernt, *Niederländische Maler*, and Hofstede de Groot, *Dutch Painters*, ix. His complicated chronology is discussed in the *Cat. of the Dutch School*, NG, London 1960.

DUNLAP. See his *History of the . . . Arts of Design in the US*, and his *Diary*, ed. D. Barck, 2 vols., New York 1931. See also Richardson, *Painting in America*.

DUQUESNOY. Monograph by M. Fransolet, Brussels 1942. See also Gerson and Ter Kuile, *Art and Architecture in Belgium*; Wittkower, *Art and Architecture in Italy*; and Pope-Hennessy, *Italian Sculpture*, iii.

DURAND. Monograph by his son (John D.), New York 1894. See also Richardson, *Painting in America*.

DÜRER. Monograph by E. Panofsky, 2 vols., Princeton 1948, and abridged ed. in 1 vol. 1955. Dürer's own writings, *Schriftlicher Nachlass*, ed. by H. Rupprich, Berlin 1956 (in progress; 1 vol. so far); *Records of the Journey. . .*, ed. by R. Fry, Boston 1913; and *The Literary Remains. . .*, ed. M. Conway, London 1889, reprint 1958. See also W. Kurth, *Complete Woodcuts. . .*, New York 1946; and K. A. Knappe, *Complete Woodcuts, Engravings and Etchings*, London 1965.

DYCE. See K. K. Andrews, *The Nazarenes*, Oxford 1964; Boase, *English Art*.

DYCK, VAN. Monographs by G. Glück, Stuttgart (KdK) 1931; and L. van Puyvelde, Brussels 1950. See also M. Mauquier-Hendrickx, *L'Iconographie d'A. van D., Cat. Raisonné*, 2 vols., Brussels 1956; Cat. of Exh., Antwerp 1960, by R.A. d'Hulst and H. Vey; and Gerson and Ter Kuile, *Art and Architecture in Belgium.*

E

EAKINS. Monographs by L. Goodrich, New York 1933; and F. Porter, New York 1959.

EARL. See Cat. of Exh. (Whitney Mus.), New York, and Worcester Mass. 1946.

ELSHEIMER. Monograph by H. Weizsäcker, Berlin, 2 vols., 1936 and 1952 (part i in 2 vols., ii in 1). See Hempel, *Baroque Art . . . in Central Europe.*

ENCAUSTIC WAX. See A. P. Laurie, *Greek and Roman methods of painting*, Cambridge 1910.

ENGRAVING. See A. M. Hind, *History of Engraving and Etching*, 3rd ed. London 1923, and *An Introduction to a History of Woodcut* (2 vols.), London 1935 (republ. 1963). See also S.W. Hayter, *About Prints*, Oxford 1962; S.T. Prideaux, *Aquatint Engraving*, London 1909; D.P. Bliss, *History of Wood Engraving*, London 1928; C. Davenport, *Mezzotints*, London 1904; B. Gray, *The English Print*, London 1937; E. Dacier, *La gravure française*, Paris 1944.

ENSOR. Monograph by P. Haesaerts, London 1960. See also Cat. of Exh., Musée National de l'Art Moderne, Paris 1954.

EPSTEIN. Two *Autobiographies*, London 1940 and 1955. Monograph by R. Buckle, London 1963. See also Cat. of Memorial Exh., Arts Council, London 1961; and Selz, *Modern Sculpture.*

ERHART. Monograph by G. Otto, Berlin 1943.

ERNST. Monographs by P. Waldberg, Paris 1958; and W. S. Lieberman (ed.), New York (M of MA) 1961. See also his own *Beyond Painting*, ed. R. Motherwell, New York 1948.

ETTY. Monographs by A. Gilchrist (2 vols.), London 1855; and D. Farr, London 1958.

EUSTON ROAD. See Sir J. Rothenstein, *British Art since 1900*, London 1962.

EVERDINGEN. See *Cat. of Dutch School*, NG, London 1960; and Schneider, *Caravaggio und die Niederländer* (for Caesar).

EWORTH. See Mercer, *English Art.*

EXPRESSIONISM. Monographs by B. S. Myers, London 1957; and P. Selz, Berkeley and Los Angeles 1957.

EYCK, VAN. Monograph by L. Baldass, London 1952. See also P. Coremans et al., *L'Agneau mystique au laboratoire. . .*, Antwerp 1953.

F

FABRITIUS, B. Monograph by D. Pont, Utrecht 1958.

FABRITIUS, C. Monograph by K. E. Schuurman, Amsterdam n.d. (*c.* 1945). See also Hofstede de Groot, *Dutch Painters*, i.

FALCONET. Monograph by L. Réau, 2 vols., Paris 1922. See also Lami, *Dictionnaire des Sculpteurs.*

FANTIN-LATOUR. Monographs by A. Jullien, Paris 1909; and F. Gibson, London 1924. See also Mme F.-L., *Cat. de l'Oeuvre . . .* (complete cat.), Paris 1911.

FARINGTON. His *Diary* ed. by J. Grieg, London 1922–8 (8 vols.).

FATTORI. Monographs by O. Ghiglia, Florence 1913; A. Franchi (on F., Lega, Signorini), Milan 1953; G. Malesci (Cat.), Novara 1961; and M. de Micheli (incl. autobiographical writings), Busto Arsizio 1961. See also Comanducci, *Dizionario.*

FAUVE. Monographs by G. Duthuit, New York 1950; and J. Leymarie, Geneva 1959 (Eng. ed.). See also Cat. of Exh., Berne 1950 (in German).

FEININGER. Monograph by H. Hess, London 1961, with an œuvre cat. by F.'s widow. See also Cat. of Exh., New York 1944.

FERNELEY. Monograph by G. Paget, London 1931. See also Sparrow, *A Book of Sporting Painters*; and Taylor, *Animal Painting in England.*

FERRARI. Monograph by E. Halsey, London 1904 and 1908. See also Cat. of Exh., Vercelli 1956.

FERRI. See Voss, *Die Malerei des Barock in Rom.*

FETI. See Wittkower, *Art and Architecture in Italy*; and Waterhouse, *Italian Baroque Painting.*

FEUERBACH. His Autobiography, pub. Vienna 1882. Monographs by H. Uhde-Bernays, Stuttgart-Leipzig (KdK), 1929.

FINE MANNER. See under ENGRAVING (A.M. Hind).

FINSON. See Schneider, *Caravaggio und die Niederländer*; and Voss, *Die Malerei des Barock in Rom.*

FLAXMAN. Monograph by W. G. Constable, London 1927. See also F.'s own *Lectures on Sculpture*, 2nd ed. London 1838; and Whinney, *Sculpture in Britain.*

FLINCK. See Hofstede de Groot, *Dutch Painters*, vi; and Bernt, *Die niederländischen Maler.*

FLORIS. Monograph by D. Zuntz, Strassburg 1929 (in German).

FONTAINEBLEAU. Monograph by S. Béguin, Paris 1960. See also Cat. of Exh., *Fontainebleau e la Maniera Italiana*, Naples 1952; and Blunt, *Art and Architecture in France.*

FOPPA. Monograph by F. Wittgens, Milan 1949.

FORAIN. See M. Guérin, *Cat. raisonné* (lithographs), Paris 1909; and M. Salaman, London 1925.

FORESHORTENING. See J. White, *The Birth and Rebirth of Pictorial Space*, London 1957.

FOUND OBJECT. See Seitz, *The Art of Assemblage.*

FOUQUET. Monographs by T. Cox, London 1931; K. Perls, London 1940; and P. Wescher, Basle (Eng. ed.) 1947. See also Ring, *A Century of French Painting.*

FRAGONARD. Monographs by L. Réau, Paris 1956; and G. Wildenstein, London 1960.

FRANCESCO DI GIORGIO. Monograph by A. S. Weller, Chicago 1943.

FRANCIA. Monographs by G. Williamson, London 1901; and G. Lipparini, Bergamo 1913.

FRANCIABIGIO. See Freedberg, *High Renaissance*; and Venturi, *Storia*, ix.

FRANCIS. See Haftmann, *Painting in the Twentieth Century.*

FRANCKE. Monographs by A. Lichtwark, Hamburg 1899; and B. Martens, 2 vols., Hamburg 1929.

FRESCO. See Thomson, *The Materials of Medieval Painting*; R. Mayer, *The Artist's Handbook of Materials and Techniques*, London 1957; U. Procacci, *La Tecnica degli Antichi Affreschi.* . . , Florence 1958, and also *Sinopie ed Affreschi*, Milan 1961. Also Eve Borsook, *The Mural Painters of Tuscany*, London 1960.

FRIEDRICH. Monographs by H. von Einem, Berlin 1938, and 3rd ed. 1950; and I. Emmrich, Weimar 1964.

FRITH. See *My Autobiography and Reminiscences*, 3 vols., London 1887–8 and extracts ed. by N. Wallis, London 1957.

FROMENT. See L. Chamson, *N.F. et l'École Avignonnaise au XVe Siècle*, Paris 1931. See also Ring, *A Century of French Painting*.

FRUEAUF, Rueland I and II. See L. von Baldass, *Conrad Laib und die beiden R. F.*, Vienna 1946.

FULLER. See Whinney and Millar, *English Art*; also Waterhouse, *Painting in Britain*.

FUSELI. Monographs by J. Knowles, 3 vols., London 1831; E. Mason, London 1951; and F. Antal, London 1956. For F.'s drawings see P. Ganz, London 1949; and C. N. Powell, London 1951.

FUTURISM. Monographs by R. Carrieri, Milan 1961; J. C. Taylor, New York (M of MA) 1961; and R. T. Clough, New York 1964. See also Cat. of Exh., Bologna 1951; *Archivio del F.*, ed. G. Argan, F. Bellonzi et al., 2 vols., Rome 1958–62. J. T. Soby and A. Barr, *Twentieth Century Italian Art*, New York (M of MA) 1951.

G

GABO. Monograph by Sir H. Read and L. Martin, London 1957. See also A. Pevsner, *a biographical sketch of my brothers n. g. and a. pevsner*, Amsterdam 1964 (in Eng.); and Gabo's own Mellon Lectures (1959) pub. as *Of Divers Arts*, New York and London 1962. Also Gabo/Pevsner, *Constructivist Manifesto*, Moscow 1920; and Cat. of Exh., M of MA, New York 1948; Selz, *Modern Sculpture*.

GADDI, A. Monograph by R. Salvini, Florence 1936.

GADDI, T. See van Marle, *Italian Schools*, iii; and Toesca, *Trecento*.

GAINSBOROUGH. Monograph by E. K. Waterhouse, London 1958.

GAUDIER-BRZESKA. Monographs by H. S. Ede, London 1930, and London 1931; and E. Pound, Hessle 1960 (in Eng.). See also Selz, *Modern Sculpture*.

GAUGUIN. Monograph by J. Rewald, London 1949; and (œuvre cat.) by G. Wildenstein, vol. i only, Paris 1964. See also *Intimate Journals of P. G.*, London (Eng. ed.) 1931; and Rewald, *Post-Impressionism*.

GEERTGEN. Monograph by W. Vogelsang, 2nd ed. Amsterdam 1950.

GELDER. Monograph by K. Lilienfeld, The Hague 1914 (in German).

GENRE. See M. J. Friedländer, *Landscape, Portrait, Still-Life*, Oxford 1949.

GENTILE DA FABRIANO. Monograph by L. Grassi, Milan 1953.

GENTILESCHI A. and O. See Wittkower, *Art and Architecture in Italy*; Voss, *Die Malerei des Barock in Rom*, Berlin n.d. (1924); and Waterhouse, *Italian Baroque Painting*. See also Cat. of Caravaggio Exh., Milan 1951.

GÉRARD. Monograph by C. Lenormant, 2nd ed., Paris 1847. See also H. Gérard, *Oeuvres.* . . , Paris 1852–7.

GERHAERT. Monographs by O. Wertheimer, Berlin 1929; and L. Fischel, Munich 1944.

GÉRICAULT. Monograph by K. Berger, Paris 1952 (in French). See also *G. par lui-même*, Geneva 1947.

GESSO. See Thompson, *The Materials of Medieval Painting*; also Constable, *The Painter's Workshop*.

GHEERAERTS. See Mercer, *English Art*.

GHIBERTI. Monograph by R. Krautheimer and T. Krautheimer-Hess, Princeton 1956.

GHIRLANDAIO. Monograph by J. Lauts, Vienna 1943.

GHISLANDI. Monograph by A. Milesi, Bergamo 1945.

GIACOMETTI. Monographs by J. Dupin and E. Scheidegger, Paris 1962; and P. Bucarelli, Rome 1962 (in Ital., but with Eng. and French trans.).

GIAMBONO. See Berenson, *Venetian School*; van Marle, *Italian Schools*, viii.

GIAQUINTO. Monograph by Mario d'Orsi, Rome 1958.

GIBBONS. Monograph by D. Green, London 1964. See also Gunnis, *Dictionary of British Sculptors*; Whinney and Millar, *English Art*; and Whinney, *Sculpture in Britain*.

GIBSON. Monograph by Lady Eastlake, London 1870. See also Gunnis, *Dictionary of British Sculptors*.

GILL. Monograph by J. Thorp and C. Marriott, London 1929. His *Autobiography* pub. London 1940; the *Letters* ed. W. Shewing, London 1948. See also Cat. of Engravings, 2 vols., V & A, London 1963.

GILMAN. See Cat. of Exh., Arts Council, London 1954.

GILPIN, S. See Taylor, *Animal Painting*; and Sparrow, *British Sporting Artists*.

GILPIN, W. Monograph by C. P. Barbier, Oxford 1962.

GIORDANO. Monographs by E. Petraccone, Naples 1919; and O. Benesch, Vienna 1923. See also Wittkower, *Art and Architecture in Italy*; and Waterhouse, *Italian Baroque Painting*.

GIORGIONE. Monographs by G. M. Richter, Chicago 1937; L. Coletti, Milan 1955 and London 1962; and L. Baldass, London 1965. See also Cat. of Exh., Venice 1955.

GIOTTESCHI. See Meiss, *Painting in Florence after the Black Death*. See also Toesca, *Trecento*; and Antal, *Florentine Painting and its Social Background*.

GIOTTINO. Monograph by O. Sirén, Leipzig 1908.

GIOTTO. Monographs by C. Gnudi, London 1959; and R. Salvini, Milan 1962, 2nd ed. London 1963, 2 vols. See also Salvini, *Giotto, Bibliografia*, Rome 1937.

GIOVANNI DI PAOLO. Monographs by J. Pope-Hennessy, London 1937; and C. Brandi, Florence 1947.

GIRARDON. Monograph by P. Francastel, Paris 1928. See also Lami, *Dictionnaire des Sculpteurs*.

GIRODET. Monograph by P. A. Coupin, Paris 1829. See also R. Escholier, *La Peinture Française au 19e Siècle: De David à Géricault*, Paris 1941.

GIRTIN. Monographs by J. Mayne, Leigh-on-Sea 1949; and D. Loshak and T. Girtin, London 1954.

GISLEBERTUS. Monograph by D. Grivot and G. Zarnecki, London 1961.

GIULIO ROMANO. Monograph by F. Hartt, 2 vols., Yale 1958.

GIUNTA PISANO. See Garrison, *Italian Romanesque Panel Painting*.

GLAZING. See Constable, *The Painter's Workshop*.

GLEIZES. See J. Cassou et al., *Hommage*, Lyons 1954; Gleizes-Metzinger, *Du Cubisme*, Paris 1912 and 1947, Eng. ed. London 1913; and Cats. of Exhs, Grenoble 1963; and Mus. d'Art Moderne, Paris 1964; Guggenheim Mus., New York 1964.

GOES. Monographs by J. Destrée, Brussels 1914; J. B. Knipping, Amsterdam n.d. (*c*. 1945); and F. Winkler, Berlin 1964.

GOGH, VINCENT VAN. Monographs by A. Barr, New York (M of MA) 1934; and C. Nordenfalk, London 1953. The complete Eng. ed. of *Letters*, London 1959 (3 vols.); selection ed. by M. Roskill, London 1963.

GOLTZIUS. Monographs by O. Hirschmann, The Hague 1916; and E. K. J. Reznicek, Utrecht 1961, 2 vols. (in German, on drawings).

GONÇALVES. Monograph by R. dos Santos, London 1955.

GONZALEZ. Monographs by A. C. Ritchie, New York (M of MA) 1956; L. Degand, London 1958; and V. Cerni, Rome 1962. See also Giedion-Welcker, *Contemporary Sculpture*.

GORE. See Cat. of Exh., Arts Council, London 1955.

GORKY. Monographs by E. Schwabacher, New York 1957; and H. Rosenberg, New York 1962. See also Cat. of Exh., Arts Council, Tate Gall., London 1965.

GOUACHE. See Constable, *The Painter's Workshop*.

GOUJON. Monograph by P. du Colombier, Paris 1949. See also Blunt, *Art and Architecture in France*.

GOYA. Monographs by A. de Beruete y Moret, 3 vols., Madrid 1915–18; F. J. Sanchez Cantón, French trans. Paris 1930; F. D. Klingender, London 1948; A. Malraux, London 1957; and F. X. Desparmet FitzGerald, 4 vols., Paris 1928–51. See also E. Lafuente Ferrari, *Frescoes in San Antonio*, New York and Lausanne 1955 (in Eng.); E. Trapier (portraits), New York 1955; and T. Harris, *Complete Cat. of G.'s Engravings and Lithographs*, 2 vols., Oxford and London 1964.

GOYEN. Monograph by H. van de Waal, Amsterdam 1941. See also Hofstede de Groot, *Dutch Painters*, viii; and Bode, *Great Masters of Dutch and Flemish Painting*.

GOZZOLI. Monographs by G. Hoogewerff, Paris 1930; and M. Lagaisse, Paris 1934.

GRAF. Monograph by E. Major and E. Gradmann, London 1947.

GRAFF. Monograph by O. Waser, Frauenfeld 1926. See also Cat. of Exh., Nationalgalerie, Berlin 1963.

GRANACCI. See Freedberg, *High Renaissance*.

GRAPHIC ARTS. As for ENGRAVING, also Meder, *Die Handzeichnung: Ihre Technik und Entwicklung*; and Watrous, *The Craft of Old-Master Drawings*.

GRAVELOT. Monograph by V. Salomons, London 1911.

GRECO, EL. Monograph by H. Wethey, 2 vols., Princeton 1962. See also E. du G. Trapier, *El G.'s Early Years at Toledo 1576–86*, New York 1958.

GRECO. Monographs by B. Degenhart, Munich 1959; and D. Grassi, Munich 1959. See also Langui, *Fifty Years of Modern Art*.

GREUZE. Monograph by L. Hautecœur, Paris 1913.

GRIS. Monographs by D. H. Kahnweiler, trans. D. Cooper, London 1947; and J. T. Soby, New York (M of MA) 1958. See also *Letters of J. G. 1913–27*, collected by D. Kahnweiler, trans. and ed. by D. Cooper, London 1956 (privately printed).

GROS. Monograph by J. Tripier le Franc, Paris 1880. See also Cat. of Exh., Petit Palais, Paris 1936.

GROSZ. Monograph by J. Baur, New York 1954; see also his *Autobiography*, (Eng.) New York 1946, (German) Hamburg 1955. Also Cat. of Exh., Arts Council, London 1963.

GROUND. See Constable, *The Painter's Workshop*.

GRÜNEWALD. Monographs by N. Pevsner and M. Meier, London 1958; W. Zülch, Munich 1938 (abridged ed. 1949); and J. K. Huysmans and E. Ruhmer, London 1958.

GUARDI, F. Monographs by G. Fiocco, Florence 1923; J. Byam-Shaw (drawings) London 1951; and V. Moschini, London 1957. See also Levey, *Venice*; Donzelli, *Pittori Veneziani*, and Cat. of Exh., Venice 1965.

GUARDI, G. A. Monograph by F. de Maffeis, Verona 1951.

GUERCINO. Monographs by M. Marangoni, Milan 1959; and N. Grimaldi, Bologna n.d. (*c*. 1961). See also Wittkower, *Art and Architecture in Italy*; and Mahon, *Studies in Seicento Art and Theory*.

GUIDO DA SIENA. Monograph by J. Stubblebine, Princeton NJ 1964. See also Garrison, *Italian Romanesque Panel Painting*; and Oertel, *Die Frühzeit der italienischen Malerei*.

GUILD. See Constable, *The Painter's Workshop*.

GÜNTHER. Monograph by A. Schoenberger, Munich 1954. See Hempel, *Baroque Art . . . in Central Europe*.

GUTTOSO. Monograph by G. Marchiori, Milan 1952.

GUYS. Monographs by G. Geffroy, Paris 1904 (limited ed.); G. Grappe, Berlin n.d., French trans. Paris n.d.; and C. Hall, London 1945. See also P. G. Konody, *The Painter of Victorian Life . . .* (incl. Baudelaire's account), London 1930.

H

HALS, F. Monograph by N. S. Trivas, 2nd ed., London 1949. See also Cat. of Exh., Haarlem 1962 (Eng. ed.); and Hofstede de Groot, *Dutch Painters*, iii.

HAMILTON. See Waterhouse, *Painting in Britain*.

HARTUNG. Monographs by M. Rousseau, J. Sweeney and O. Domnick, Stuttgart n.d. (*c*. 1950) (Text in Eng./Fr./German); also R. Gindertael, Paris and New York 1961 (French and Eng. eds.).

HAYDON. Monographs by E. George, Oxford 1948; and C. Olney, Athens Georgia 1952. See also *Autobiography*, London 1853 and many later eds. (e.g. 2 vols. 1926); and *Diary* ed. by W. Pope, 5 vols., Harvard 1960–3.

HAYMAN. See Cat. of Exh., Kenwood, London 1960. Also Waterhouse, *Painting in Britain*.

HECKEL. Monographs by P. O. Rave, E. Berlin 1949; H. Köhn, Berlin 1948; L. Thormaehlen, Karlsruhe 1953. See also Haftmann *Painting in the Twentieth Century*; Röthel, *Modern German Painting*; and Myers, *Expressionism*.

HEDA, WILLEM CLAESZ. See H. E. van Gelder, *W. C. H., Abr. van Beyeren, en W. Kalff*, Amsterdam n.d. See also Bergström, *Dutch Still-Life Painting in the 17 c.*, and Cat. of Still-Life, Oxford (Ashmolean Mus.).

HEEM family. See Bergström, *Dutch Still-Life Painting in the 17 c.*

HEEMSKERCK. See Friedländer, *Altniederländische Malerei*, xiii; also C. Huelsen and H. Egger, *Die Römischen Skizzenbücher*, Berlin 1913–16.

HELST. Monograph by J. J. de Gelder, Rotterdam 1921.

HEPWORTH. Monographs by J. Hodin and A. Bowness, London 1961; and Sir H. Read, London 1952 (with autobiog. writings).

HERRING. See Sparrow, *A Book of Sporting Painters*, and *British Sporting Artists*.

HEYDEN. See Hofstede de Groot, *Dutch Painters*, viii.

HIGHMORE. See Cat. of Exh., Kenwood, London 1963. Also Waterhouse, *Painting in Britain*.

HILDEBRAND. Monographs by A. Heilmeyer, Munich 1922; and W. Hausenstein, Munich 1947. See also H.'s *Problem der Form*, Strassburg 1893 (and many later eds., including Eng. trans., New York 1945).

HILLIARD. Monograph by E. Auerbach, London 1961. See also G. Reynolds, Cat. of Exh., V & A., London 1947; and Winter, *Elizabethan Miniatures*.

HISTORY PAINTING. See bibliographies for BARRY, HAYDON, and REYNOLDS.

HITCHENS. Monograph by P. Heron, London 1955 (Penguin Modern Painters). See also Cat. of Exh., Tate Gall., London 1963.

HOBBEMA. Monograph by G. Broulhiet, Paris 1938. See also Hofstede de Groot, *Dutch Painters*, iv.

HODLER. Monographs by C. Loosli, 9 vols., Zürich and Berne 1918–24; and W. Hugelshofer, Zürich 1952 (in German). See also M. Huggler and A. M. Cetto, *Schweizer Malerei im 19. Jhr.*, Basle n.d. (*c.* 1945).

HOFER. Monograph by A. Jannasch, Potsdam 1948. See also H.'s Autobiography, Berlin 1952 and 1953, and *Über das Gesetzliche in der bildenden Kunst*, Berlin 1956; and Haftmann *Painting in the Twentieth Century*; Myers, *Expressionism*; and Röthel, *Modern German Painting*.

HOGARTH. Monographs by R. Beckett, London 1949; and F. Antal, London 1962. For drawings see A. P. Oppé, London 1948. See also Waterhouse, *Painting in Britain*.

HOLBEIN, HANS I. Monograph by N. Lieb and A. Stange, Munich 1960. See also Cat. of Exh., Basle (H. family) 1960.

HOLBEIN, HANS II. Monographs by H. Schmid, 3 vols., Basle 1945–8 (in German); and P. Ganz, London 1950. For drawings see Sir K. Parker, London and Oxford 1945. See also under DANCE OF DEATH.

HOLLAR. Monograph by F. Sprinzels, Vienna 1938 (in German and Eng.). See also Cat. of Exh., City Art Gallery, Manchester 1963 (by F. Grossmann).

HÖLZEL. See H.'s *Gedanken und Lehren*, Stuttgart 1953; Haftmann, *Painting in the Twentieth Century*; Myers, *Expressionism*; and Cat. of Exh., Stuttgart 1953.

HOMER, W. Monograph by L. Goodrich, New York 1944 and 1959. See also Cat. of Retrospective Exh., NG, Washington and Met. Mus., New York 1958–9.

HONDECOETER. See Bernt, *Die niederländischen Maler*; and N. Maclaren, *Cat. of Dutch School*, NG, London 1960.

HONE. See Waterhouse, *Painting in Britain*. See also Whitley, *Artists and their Friends in England, 1700–99*.

HONTHORST. Monograph by J. R. Judson, The Hague 1959 (in Eng.). See also Cat. of Exh., Utrecht 1952.

HOOCH. Monographs by C. H. Collins Baker, London 1925; W. Valentiner, Stuttgart 1930; and F. van Thienen,

Amsterdam n.d. (*c.* 1945). See also Hofstede de Groot, *Dutch Painters*, i.

HOPPNER. Monograph by W. McKay and W. Roberts, London 1909. See also Waterhouse, *Painting in Britain*.

HOSKINS. See Reynolds, *English Portrait Miniatures*; Long, *British Miniaturists*; and Whinney and Millar, *English Art*.

HOUDON. Monographs by G. Giacometti, Paris 1918–19 in 3 vols. and Paris 1928 in 2 vols.; L. Réau, Paris 1930 (new ed. announced 1964). See also Lami, *Dictionnaire des Sculpteurs*, and Cat. Exh., Worcester Mass. 1964 (long introduction by H. Avnason).

HOURS OF TURIN. See under VAN EYCK.

HUBER. Monographs by M. Weinberger, Leipzig 1930; and E. Heinzle, Innsbruck n.d. [1953].

HUDSON RIVER SCHOOL. See F. A. Sweet, *The Hudson River School and the Early American Landscape Tradition*, Chicago 1945. Also Richardson, *Painting in America*.

HUDSON, T. See Waterhouse, *Painting in Britain*.

HUNT. For his autobiography see Classified Bibliography. See also Ironside and Gere, *Pre-Raphaelite Painters*; and Boase, *English Art*.

HUYSUM, JACOB VAN. Monograph by M. Grant, Leigh-on-Sea 1950.

HUYSUM, JAN VAN. See Hofstede de Groot, *Dutch Painters*, x. Also Bergström, *Dutch Still-Life Painting in the 17 c.*; and Warner, *Dutch and Flemish Flower and Fruit Painters*.

I

ICONS. Monograph by K. Onasch, Eng. ed. revised by D. Talbot Rice, London 1963.

IMPRESSIONISM. See J. Rewald, *The History of Impressionism*, M of MA, New York 1946, 2nd French ed. Paris 1955, 2nd enlarged Eng. ed. 1961. Also L. Venturi, *Les Archives de l'Impressionnisme*, 2 vols., Paris 1939.

INGRES. Monographs by G. Wildenstein, London 1956 (2nd ed.); and L. Fröhlich-Bume, London 1926. Also *I. par lui-même*, 2 vols., Geneva 1947–8; and N. Schlenoff, *I.: ses Sources Littéraires*, and *Ses Cahiers Inédits*, 2 vols., Paris 1956.

INNES. Monograph by J. Fothergill, London 1946.

ISENBRANDT. See Friedländer, *Altniederländische Malerei*, xi.

J

JACOBELLO DEL FIORE. See Berenson, *Venetian School*; also van Marle, *Italian Schools*, vii.

JACQUEMART. See Panofsky, *Early Netherlandish Painting*; also Ring, *A Century of French Painting*.

JAMESONE. Monograph by M. W. Brockwell, London 1939 (privately printed). See also Waterhouse, *Painting in Britain*.

JAWLENSKY. Monograph by C. Weiler, Cologne 1959. See also Röthel, *Modern German Painting*.

JOHN. Monograph by Sir J. Rothenstein, London 1944. See also his Autobiography, London 1952 and 1964.

JOHNSON, C. See Waterhouse, *Painting in Britain*. See also Whinney and Millar, *English Art*.

JONGKIND. Monograph by M. Hennus, Amsterdam n.d. (c. 1945/50).

JOOS VAN CLEVE. Monograph by L. Baldass, Vienna 1925. See also Friedländer, *Van Eyck to Brueghel*, and *Altniederländische Malerei*, ix.

JOOS VAN GENT. Monograph by J. Lavalleye, Louvain and Rome 1936 (in French). See also Cat. of Exh. *Juste de Gand, Berruguete et la Cour d'Urbino*, Ghent 1957.

JORDAENS. Monographs by M. Rooses, Antwerp and Paris 1906, London 1908; and L. van Puyvelde, Brussels 1953 (in French). See also Cat. of Exh., Utrecht 1952; and Gerson and Ter Kuile, *Art and Architecture in Belgium*.

K

KALF. See H. E. van Gelder, *W. C. Heda, Abr. van Beyeren en W. Kalff*, Amsterdam n.d. (c. 1945/50); and Bergström, *Dutch Still-Life Painting in the 17 c.*

KANDINSKY. Monographs by W. Grohmann, London 1959; Sir H. Read, London 1959; and L. D. Ettlinger, Oxford 1961. See also K.'s *Concerning the Spiritual in Art*, New York 1947 (1st German ed. 1912); *Point to Line and Plane*, New York 1947; and essays: *Über Kunst und Künstler*, ed. M. Bill, Teufen 1955.

KAUFFMANN. Monographs by G. de Rossi, Florence 1810; Lady V. Manners and G. C. Williamson, London 1924; and A. Hartcup, London 1954. See also Cat. of Exh., Kenwood, London 1955.

KENT. Monograph by M. Jourdain, London 1948. See also Waterhouse, *Painting in Britain*.

KETTLE. See Waterhouse, *Painting in Britain*.

KEYSER. Monograph by R. Oldenbourg, Leipzig 1911.

KIRCHNER. Monograph by W. Grohmann, London and New York 1961.

KLEE. Monographs by W. Haftmann, London 1954; and W. Grohmann, 2nd ed. London 1957. See also K.'s *On Modern Art*, London 1948; *Das Bildnerische Denken*, Basle 1956; *Pedagogical Sketchbook*, New York and London 1953; *Tagebücher von P. K.*, Cologne 1957; and *The Thinking Eye*, ed. J. Spiller, London and New York 1961.

KLIMT. Monographs by M. Eisler, Vienna 1920; E. Pirchau, Vienna 1956; H. Dobai, Vienna 1959.

KLINE. See Langui, *Fifty Years of Modern Art*; and Haftmann, *Painting in the Twentieth Century*.

KNAPTON. See Waterhouse, *Painting in Britain*.

KNELLER. See Whinney and Millar, *English Art*; also Waterhouse, *Painting in Britain*.

KOCH. Monographs by O. von Lutterotti, Berlin 1940 and (abridged) Innsbruck 1944. See also Cat. of Exh., Nationalgalerie, Berlin 1939.

KOKOSCHKA. Monographs by E. Hoffmann, London 1947; H. M. Wingler, London 1958; and B. Bultmann, London 1962. See also Cat. of Exh., Arts Council, London 1962.

KOLLWITZ. Monographs by F. Schmalenbach, Berne 1948; and C. Zigrosser, New York 1945. See also *Schriften 1907-55*, ed. H. Kollwitz, Munich 1956; and *Diaries and Letters of K. K.*, ed. H. Kollwitz, Chicago 1955.

KONINCK, PH. Monograph by H. Gerson, Berlin 1936.

KONINCK, S. See Hofstede de Groot, *Dutch Painters*, vi.

KONRAD VON SOEST. Monographs by K. Steinbart, Vienna 1946; and R. Fritz, Munich 1954.

KOONING. Monographs by T. Hess, New York 1959; and H. Janis and R. Blesch, New York and London 1960.

KRICKE. Monograph by J. Thwaites, London 1964. See also Giedion-Welcker, *Contemporary Sculpture*.

KRÜGER. Monograph by W. Weidmann, Berlin 1927.

KULMBACH. Monograph by F. Winkler, Kulmbach 1959.

KUPKA. Monograph by J. Cassou and D. Fedit, London 1965. See also K.'s *La Création dans l'art plastique*, Prague n.d.; Haftmann, *Painting in the Twentieth Century*; and Cat. of Exh., Mus. d'Art Moderne, Paris 1958.

L

LAGUERRE. See Whinney and Millar, *English Art*; and Croft-Murray, *Decorative Painting*.

LAM. See Haftmann, *Painting in the Twentieth Century*.

LANCRET. Monograph by G. Wildenstein, Paris 1924.

LANDSEER. Monograph by F. G. Stephens, London 1881. See also Cat. of Exh., RA, London 1961; and Boase, *English Art*.

LANFRANCO. See Waterhouse, *Italian Baroque Painting*; and Wittkower, *Art and Architecture in Italy*.

LARGILLIERRE. Monograph by G. Pascal, Paris 1928.

LASTMAN. Monograph by K. Freise, Leipzig 1911. See also Cat. of Exh., *Caravaggio en de Nederlanden*, Utrecht 1952.

LA TOUR, G. DE. Monographs by G. Pariset, Paris 1948; S. Furness, London 1949; V. Bloch, Amsterdam 1950. See also Blunt, *Art and Architecture in France*.

LATOUR, M.-Q. DE. Monograph by A. Besnard and G. Wildenstein, Paris 1928.

LAURANA. See Pope-Hennessy, *Italian Sculpture*, ii.

LAURENS. Monograph by C. Goldscheider, London 1958. See also Giedion-Welcker, *Contemporary Sculpture*.

LAWRENCE. Monograph by K. Garlick, London 1954, and ed., Cat. Raisonné in Walpole Society, xxxix, 1964. See also Cat. of Exh., RA, London 1961.

LE BRUN. See Cat. of Exh., Versailles 1963. See also Blunt, *Art and Architecture in France*.

LEGA. Monograph by A. Franchi (on Fattori, L., Signorini), Milan 1953. See also Memoir by T. Signorini, Florence 1896; Comanducci, *Dizionario*; and Cat. of Exh. by P. Bucarelli, *I Macchiaiuoli*, Rome 1956.

LÉGER. Monographs by D. Cooper, London 1949; F. Descargues, Paris 1955; R. Delevoy, Lausanne 1962 (in Eng.). See also Cat. of Exh., Mus. des Arts Décoratifs, Paris 1956.

LEHMBRUCK. Monographs by W. Hofmann, London 1958; P. Westheim, 2nd. ed. Potsdam 1922; J. Abbot (Lehmbruck and Maillol), New York (M of MA) 1930. See also Selz, *Modern Sculpture*.

LEIBL. Monographs by K. Römpler, Dresden (1955) (based on Cat. of Exh., Berlin 1914 by E. Waldmann); A. Langer, Leipzig 1961.

LELY. Monograph by R. Beckett, London 1951. See also

Waterhouse, *Painting in Britain*; and Whinney and Millar, *English Art*.

LE MOYNE, F. See Dimier, *Les peintres français du 18ᵉ siècle*.

LEMOYNE, J.-B. Monograph by L. Réau, Paris 1927. See also Lami, *Dictionnaire des sculpteurs*.

LE NAIN family. Monograph by P. Fierens, Paris 1933. See also Blunt, *Art and Architecture in France*.

LENBACH. Monographs by A. Rosenberg, 5th ed. Bielefeld and Leipzig 1911, and H. Kehrer, Munich 1937.

LEONARDO. Monographs by Sir K. Clark, 2nd ed. London 1952, and 1958 (Penguin); L. Heydenreich, London 1954. On his drawings: A.E. Popham, London 1946 (paperback 1964). His writings: ed. by J. Richter, 2 vols., Oxford 1939; E. McCurdy, 2 vols., London 1938; A. Chastel, Paris 1952. See also C. Pedretti, *Leonardo da Vinci on Painting. A Lost Book (Libro A)*, London 1965.

LE SUEUR, EUSTACHE. Monograph by G. Rouchès, Paris 1923. See also Blunt, *Art and Architecture in France*.

LE SUEUR, HUBERT. See Whinney and Millar, *English Art*.

LEWIS, W. Monograph by C. Handley-Read and E. Newton, London 1951. See also Cat. of Exh., Tate Gall., London 1956.

LEYSTER. See Cat. of Exh., *Caravaggio en de Nederlanden*, Utrecht 1952.

LIBER STUDIORUM. Monographs by W. G. Rawlinson, London 1878; and C. F. Bell, London n.d. See also under TURNER.

LIEBERMANN. Monographs by M. J. Friedländer, Berlin n.d. (1924); and K. Scheffler, Wiesbaden 1953. See also his own *Gesammelte Schriften*, Berlin 1922.

LIEVENS. Monograph by H. Schneider, Haarlem 1932 (in German).

LIMBOURG BROTHERS. See Panofsky, *Early Netherlandish Painting*; and Ring, *A Century of French Painting*.

LINNELL. Monograph by A. Story, 2 vols., London 1892. See also Boase, *English Art*.

LIOTARD. Monographs by E. Humbert, A. Revilliod; and J. Tilanus, Amsterdam 1897 (in French); and F. Fosca, Lausanne and Paris 1956.

LIPCHITZ. Monographs by H. R. Hope, New York (M of MA) 1954; R. Goldwater, London 1954; A. Hammacher, London 1964. See also Cat. of Exh., Tate Gall., London 1959; and Selz, *Modern Sculpture*.

LIPPI, FRA FILIPPO. Monographs by R. Oertel, Vienna 1942; and M. Pittaluga, Florence 1949.

LIPPI, FILIPPINO. Monographs by A. Scharf, 2nd ed. Vienna 1950; and K. Neilson, Harvard 1938.

LISS. Monographs by K. Steinbart, Berlin 1940, and Vienna 1946. See Hempel, *Baroque Art . . . in Central Europe*.

LOCHNER. Monograph by O. Foerster, Bonn 1952.

LOMBARDO FAMILY. See Pope-Hennessy, *Italian Sculpture*, ii.

LONGHI, A. See his own *Compendio delle Vite de' Pittori Veneziani storici. . .*, Venice 1762; Donzelli, *Pittori Veneziani*; and Levey, *Venice*.

LONGHI, P. Monograph by V. Moschini, Milan 1956.

See also Donzelli, *Pittori Veneziani*; and Levey, *Venice*.

VAN LOO FAMILY
Carle: Monograph by Dandré-Bardon, Paris 1765 (new ed. Aix 1920).
J.-B.: Monograph by Dandré-Bardon, Paris 1779.
L.-M.: See Locquin, *Peinture d'histoire*.

LORENZETTI BROTHERS
Both: Monograph by G. Sinibaldi, Siena 1933.
Pietro: Monograph by E. De Wald, Harvard 1930.
Ambrogio: Monograph by G. Rowley, 2 vols., Princeton 1958.

LORENZO MONACO. Monograph by V. Golzio, Rome 1931.

LOTTO. Monographs by B. Berenson, London 1956; and P. Bianconi, Milan 1955, and 2 vols. London 1963. See also Cat. of Exh. by P. Zampetti, Venice 1953.

LUCAS VAN LEYDEN. Monographs by M. J. Friedländer, Berlin 1963; and N. Beets, Amsterdam n.d. For his engravings see Hollstein, x (c. 1954).

LUINI. Monograph by A. Ottino Della Chiesa, Milan 1956.

LURÇAT. Monograph by J. Marcenac, Zürich 1952 (in French). See also his own writings, including *Designing Tapestry*, London 1950.

M

MABUSE. Monographs by M. Gossart, Lille 1902; and E. Weiss, Parchim (Germany) 1913. See also Friedländer, *Altniederländische Malerei*, viii.

MACCHIAIOLI. Monographs by R. de Grada, Milan 1963; and E. Cecchi and M. Borgiotti, Florence 1963. See also Cat. of Exh., Rome 1956 (by P. Bucarelli).

MACKE. Monographs by W. Holzhausen, Munich 1956; and G. Vriesen, 2nd ed. Stuttgart 1957. See also under EXPRESSIONISM.

MAES. Monograph by W. Valentiner, Stuttgart 1924. See also Hofstede de Groot, *Dutch Painters*, vi; and W. Bode, *Dutch and Flemish Painting*.

MAGNASCO. Monographs by B. Geiger, the latest being Bergamo 1949.

MAGNELLI. Monograph by M. Mendes, Rome 1964 (text in French, Eng., and Ital.). See also Haftmann, *Painting in the Twentieth Century*.

MAGRITTE. Monographs by E. Mesens, Brussels 1947 (in French), and L. Scutenaire, Antwerp 1948 (in French and Flemish). See also Haftmann, *Painting in the Twentieth Century*.

MAILLOL. Monographs by J. Abbott, New York (M of MA) 1930; J. Rewald, London and New York 1939, and Paris 1950; W. George, London 1965. See also Cat. of Exh., Musée d'Art Moderne, Paris 1961; and Selz, *Modern Sculpture*.

MALEVICH. K. Malevich, *The Non-Objective World*, Chicago 1959. See also Cat. of Exh., Whitechapel Gall., London 1959; and Gray, *The Great Experiment*.

MALOUEL. See Ring, *Century of French Painting* and Sterling, *Peintres du Moyen Age*.

MANDER. K. van Mander, *Het Schilderboek*, Haarlem 1604, 2nd ed. (with Life of van Mander), Amsterdam 1618; modern ed. Amsterdam 1946; French ed. by H. Hymans, Paris 1884; and Eng. ed. by C. van de

Waal, New York 1936. Monograph by E. Valentiner, Strassburg 1930 (in German).

MANESSIER. Monograph by J. Cayrol, Paris 1955.

MANET. Monographs by E. Moreau-Nélaton, 2 vols., Paris 1926; A. Tabarant, Paris 1947; J. Richardson, London 1958; P. Courthion, London 1962. See also Manet on himself: *Manet raconté par lui-même*, Geneva 1953, and Eng. ed. 1960; and G. Hamilton, *Manet and his critics*, Yale and London 1954.

MANFREDI. See Voss, *Malerei des Barock in Rom.*

MANNERISM. See Becherucci, *Manieristi Toscani*; W. Friedländer, *Mannerism and Anti-Mannerism in Italian Painting*, New York 1957; Briganti, *Italian Mannerism*; F. Würtenberger, *Mannerism*, London 1963.

MANTEGNA. Monographs by P. Kristeller, London 1901; E. Tietze-Conrat, London 1955; R. Cipriani, Milan 1956, and London 1963. See also Cat. of Exh., Mantua 1961.

MANZÙ. Monographs by A. Pacchioni, Milan 1948; C. L. Ragghianti, 2nd ed. Milan 1957. See also Giedion-Welcker, *Contemporary Sculpture*; and Cat. of Exh., Arts Council, Tate Gall., London 1960.

MARATTA. See *Le vite inedite del Bellori . . . Vita di Carlo Maratta*, ed. by M. Piacentini, Rome 1942. See also Wittkower, *Art and Architecture in Italy*; Voss, *Barock*; Waterhouse, *Italian Baroque Painting*; and Cat. of Exh., *Il Settecento a Roma*, Rome 1959.

MARC. Monograph by K. Lankheit, Berlin 1950. See his own writings: *Briefe, Aufzeichnungen und Aphorismen*, 2 vols., Berlin 1920, and *Briefe aus dem Felde*, Berlin 1956. On his drawings and watercolours see K. Lankheit, London 1960. See also Cat. of Exh., Lenbachhaus, Munich 1963; and under BLAUE REITER.

MARÉES. Monographs by K. Fiedler, Munich 1889; and J. Meier-Graefe, 3 vols., Munich 1909. On the Naples frescoes see B. Degenhart, Munich 1958.

MARGARITO(NE). Monograph by A. del Vita, Arezzo 1910. See also Garrison, *Italian Romanesque Panel Painting*.

MARIESCHI. See Donzelli, *Pittori Veneziani*; and Levey, *Venice*.

MARIN. Monograph by M. Helm, Boston 1948. See also Cat. of Exh., Arts Council, London 1956.

MARINETTI. See under FUTURISM.

MARINI. Monographs by E. Trier, on the sculpture, London 1961; and by F. Russoli, London 1965, on his paintings and graphic work.

MARINUS VAN REYMERSWAELE. See Friedländer, *Altniederländische Malerei*, xii.

MARMION. See Ring, *Century of French Painting.*

MARQUET. Monograph by F. Jourdain, Paris 1959.

MARSHALL. Monograph by W. Shaw-Sparrow, London 1929. See also Taylor, *Animal Painting in England.*

MARTIN. Monographs by T. Balston, London 1947; and J. Seznec, London 1964 (Martin in France).

MARTINI. Monograph by G. Paccagnini, London 1957, and 2nd ed. Milan 1963.

MASACCIO. Monographs by U. Procacci, 2nd ed. Milan 1952, and Eng. ed. London 1962; and L. Berti, Milan 1964.

MASO. See Sinibaldi and Brunetti, *Mostra Giottesca Catalogue.*

MASOLINO. Monograph by E. Micheletti, Milan 1960. See also under MASACCIO.

MASSYS. Monographs by J. de Bosschère, Brussels 1907; and K. Boon, Amsterdam (*c.* 1945). See also Friedländer *Altniederländische Malerei*, vii.

MASTER OF THE AIX ANNUNCIATION. See Ring, *Century of French Painting.*

MASTER OF S. BARTHOLOMEW. Monograph by K. vom Rath, Bonn 1941. See also K. Reiners, *Die Kölner Malerschule*, München-Gladbach 1925; and M. Levey, *Cat. of German School*, NG, London.

MASTER OF S. CECILIA. See Offner, *Corpus*, i, part 3.

MASTER OF THE DEATH OF THE VIRGIN. See JOOS van Cleve.

MASTER OF FLÉMALLE. Monograph by C. de Tolnay, Brussels 1939. See also Friedländer, *Altniederländische Malerei*, ii and xiv; and Panofsky, *Early Netherlandish Painting.*

MASTER OF S. GILES. See Ring, *Century of French Painting*; and Sterling, *Peintres du Moyen Age.*

MASTER OF THE HOUSEBOOK. Monograph by A. Stange, Baden-Baden 1958 (with catalogue). For a facsimile of the Housebook, see H. Bossert and W. Storck, Leipzig 1912.

MASTER OF THE LIFE OF MARY. See H. Reiners, *Die Kölner Malerschule*, München-Gladbach 1925; and M. Levey, *Cat. of German School*, NG, London.

MASTER OF MOULINS. See Ring, *Century of French Painting*; and Sterling, *Peintres du Moyen Âge.*

MASTER OF THE VIRGO INTER VIRGINES. See Friedländer, *Altniederländische Malerei*, v.

MASTER OF WITTINGAU. Monograph by A. Matějček, Prague 1937. See also Matějček and Pešina, *Czech Gothic Painting*; and Stange, *Deutsche Malerei der Gotik*, ii.

MATISSE. Monographs by A. Barr, New York 1951; and J. Lassaigne, Lausanne 1959 (in Eng.). See also W. S. Lieberman, *Matisse: Fifty years of his graphic art*, London 1957; and M. Wheeler, *The Last Works of Henri Matisse*, New York (M of MA) 1961.

MATTA. Monograph by W. Rubin, New York (M of MA) 1957. See also Haftmann, *Painting in the Twentieth Century.*

MATTEO DI GIOVANNI. Monograph by G. Hartlaub, Strassburg 1910 (in German). See also Pope-Hennessy, *Sienese Quattrocento Painting.*

MAULBERTSCH. Monograph by K. Garas, Vienna and Budapest 1960 (in German). See Hempel, *Baroque Art . . . in Central Europe.*

MAZO. See Kubler and Soria, *Art and Architecture in Spain.*

MEDINA. See Waterhouse, *Painting in Britain.*

MELOZZO DA FORLI. Monographs by R. Buscaroli, Rome 1938, and Bologna 1955.

MEMLINC. Monograph by L. von Baldass, Vienna 1942. See also Friedländer, *Altniederländische Malerei*, vi; and Panofsky, *Early Netherlandish Painting.*

MENGS. Monograph by K. Gerstenberg, Halle a/S 1929. See also his own writings, *Opere*, ed. by d'Azara, Parma 1780; U. Christoffel, *Der Schriftliche Nachlass des A.R.M. . .*, Basel 1918; and Cat. of Exh., Madrid 1929, by F. J. Sánchez Cantón.

MENZEL. Monographs by K. Scheffler, Munich 1955; H. Knackfuss, Wiesbaden 1900; and E. Waldmann, 3rd ed. Vienna 1944.

MERYON. Monographs by C. Dodgson, London 1921; G. Ecke, Leipzig 1923, and L. Delteil, London 1928. See also Delteil, *Peintre-Graveur*, ii.

MEŠTROVIĆ. Monographs by E. Collings, London 1919; J. Kljakovich and M. Curtchin, Syracuse (USA) 1948; and Z. Grum, Zagreb 1960. See also Selz, *Modern Sculpture*.

METSU. See Hofstede de Groot, *Dutch Painters*, i; and Bode, *Dutch and Flemish Painting*.

METZINGER. See A. Gleizes and J. Metzinger, *Du Cubisme*, Paris 1912, Eng. ed. London 1913, and new ed. Paris 1947.

MICHEL. Monographs by A. Sensier, Paris 1873; and L. Larguier, Paris 1927.

MICHELANGELO. Monographs by J.A. Symonds, 2 vols., 3rd ed. London 1925; C. de Tolnay, Princeton 1943 (in progress: 5 vols. so far); L. Goldscheider, London 1953 (reproducing the complete works); C. Holroyd, London 1911 (with trans. of the *Life* by Condivi); Condivi is also in P. d'Ancona and others, Milan 1964. For his drawings, see J. Wilde, *Cat. of Drawings in the British Museum*, London 1953; and L. Dussler, Berlin 1959. His *Letters* have been trans. and ed. by E. Ramsden, 2 vols., London 1963. See also C. de Tolnay, *Art and Thought of Michelangelo*, New York 1964; and E. Steinmann and R. Wittkower, *Michelangelo-Bibliographie*, Leipzig 1927.

MICHELOZZO. Monograph by O. Morisani, Turin 1951.

MIGNARD. See Blunt, *Art and Architecture in France*.

MILLAIS. Monograph by J. G. Millais, 2 vols., London 1899. See also Sir W. James, *The Order of Release*, London 1947; and Ironside and Gere, *Pre-Raphaelite Painters*.

MILLES. Monograph by M. Rogers, Yale and London 1940. See also Selz, *Modern Sculpture*; and H. Cornell, *Carl Milles and the Milles Gardens*, Stockholm 1957.

MILLET, FRANCISQUE. See *Biographie Nationale Belge*, xiv (1897).

MILLET, JEAN-FRANÇOIS. Monographs by A. Sensier, Paris and London 1881; E. Moreau-Nélaton, 3 vols., Paris 1921; F. Gsell, Paris and London 1928; L. Thompson, London 1927.

MINIATURE. See T.H. Colding, *Aspects of miniature painting: its origins and development*, Copenhagen 1953; Long, *British Miniaturists*; Wehle, *American Miniatures*; and Cat. of Exh., *Five centuries of miniature painting*, Brooklyn Inst. of Arts and Sciences 1936.

MINO DA FIESOLE. See Pope-Hennessy, *Italian Sculpture*, ii.

MIRÒ. Monographs by J.T. Soby, New York (M of MA) 1959; and J. Dupin, London 1962.

MOBILE. See J. Lynch, *Mobile Sculpture, New Forms, New Techniques*, New York 1957. See also under CALDER.

MOCHI. Monograph by A. Pettorelli, Piacenza 1926. See also Wittkower, *Art and Architecture in Italy*; and Pope-Hennessy, *Italian Sculpture*, iii.

MODERSOHN-BECKER. Monograph by O. Stelzer, Berlin 1958.

MODIGLIANI. Monographs by J.T. Soby, New York (M of MA) 1951; A. Pfannstiel, Paris 1956 (with Cat. Raisonné); A. Ceroni, Milan 1958 and 1965 (in French). See also Cat. of Exh., Arts Council, London 1963.

MOHOLY-NAGY. Monograph by S. Moholy-Nagy, New York 1950. See also M-N.'s *The New Vision*, New York 1946 and *Vision in Motion*, Chicago 1947; and Selz, *Modern Sculpture*; Giedion-Welcker, *Contemporary Sculpture*; and Haftmann, *Painting in the Twentieth Century*.

MOLENAER. See N. Maclaren, *Cat. of the Dutch School*, NG, London 1960.

MONDRIAN. Monographs by J. Sweeney, New York 1948; and M. Seuphor, London 1957. See also M.'s *Plastic Art and Pure Plastic Art* (ed. R. Motherwell), New York (M of MA) 1947; and H. Jaffé, *De Stijl*, Amsterdam 1956 (in Eng.).

MONET. Monographs by D. Rouart, Lausanne 1958; and W. Seitz, London 1960. See also Rewald, *Impressionism*; and Cats. of Exhs., Edinburgh and London 1957 (by D. Cooper) and M of MA, New York 1960 (by W. Seitz).

MONNOYER. See Waterhouse, *Painting in Britain*.

MONOTYPE. See H. Rasmussen, *Printmaking with monotype: a guide to transfer techniques*, Philadelphia and London 1961; S.W. Hayter, *About Prints*, London 1962; W. M. Ivins, *How Prints Look*, New York (Met. Mus.) 1943, reprinted Boston 1958.

MONRO. See Cat. of Exh. of Drawings . . . by Monro, V & A, London 1917. See also Boase, *English Art*; Roget, *Old Water Colour Society*; Bell, in Walpole Society, xxiii, 1935; and references in Farington's *Diary* (see under FARINGTON).

MONTAGNA. Monograph by L. Puppi, Venice 1962.

MOORE. Monographs by Sir H. Read, London 1944–55, 2 vols. so far; and W. Grohmann, London 1965.

MOR. Monograph by L.C.J. Frerichs, Amsterdam [1949]. See also Friedländer, *Altniederländische Malerei*, xiii

MORALES. Monographs by E. du G. Trapier, New York 1933; J. Gaya Nuño, Madrid 1961; I. Bäcksbacka, Helsinki 1962 (in Eng.).

MORANDI. Monographs by L. Vitali, Turin 1957 (on graphic work only), Milan 1964 (on his paintings); C. Brandi, 2nd ed. Florence (1952?).

MOREAU. Monograph by R. von Holten (Paris) 1960. See also monograph on Redon, Moreau, Bresdin, by J. Rewald, D. Ashton, and H. Joachim, New York (M of MA) 1961; and Cat. of Exh., Louvre, 2nd ed. Paris 1961.

MORETTO. Monograph by G. Gombosi, Basle 1943 (in German).

MORISOT. Monographs by M. Angoulvent, Paris (1933); E. Mongan and others, London 1961. Oeuvre catalogue by M. Bataille and G. Wildenstein, Paris 1962. See also Cat. of Exh., Arts Council, London 1950.

MORLAND. Monograph by G. Williamson, London 1907. See also Cat. of Exh., Arts Council at Tate Gall., London 1954.

MORONI. Monographs by G. Lendorff, Winterthur 1933; and D. Cubini, Bergamo 1939.

MORRIS. Monograph by J. W. Mackail, London 1899 and Oxford 1950 (with introd. by Sir S. Cockerell). His *Collected Works*, London 1910–15.

MORSE. Monographs by H. Wehle, New York 1932; and O. Larkin, Boston 1954. His *Collected Works* (includ. Diary), 24 vols., London 1910–15.

MOSAIC. See H.P. L'Orange and P. Nordhagen, *Mosaik von der Antike bis zum Mittelalter*, Munich 1960; L. Jenkins and B. Mills. *The Art of making Mosaics*, Princeton 1957; J. Young, *Mosaics: Principles and Practice*, New York 1963.

MOSER. Monographs by K. Bauch, Berlin 1940; and J. von Waldburg-Wolfegg, Berlin 1939.

MOSTAERT. Monograph by S. Pierron, Brussels and Paris 1912. See also Friedländer, *Altniederländische Malerei*, x.

MOTHERWELL. See his own eds of *Documents of Modern Art Series*, New York, from 1951; his *Collages 1958–60*, Paris 1961; and Haftmann, *Painting in the Twentieth century*.

MÜLLER, OTTO. Monograph by E. Troeger, Freiburg-im-Breisgau 1949. See also Röthel, *Modern German Painting*; Myers, *Expressionism*; and Haftmann, *Painting in the Twentieth Century*.

MÜLLER, WILLIAM JAMES. Monographs by N. Solly, London 1875; and C. Bunt, Leigh-on-Sea 1948.

MULTSCHER. Monograph by N. Rasmo, Bozen (Bolzano) 1963 (in German).

MUNCH. Monographs by J. Langaard and R. Revold (on Oslo Mus. material), Stuttgart 1963; F. Deknatel, Boston and London 1950; O. Benesch, London 1960; J. P. Hodin, Stockholm 1948 (in German).

MURILLO. Monographs by A.L. Mayer, 2nd ed. Stuttgart (KdK) 1923; and S. Montoto, Seville 1923 and 1932.

MYTENS. See Whinney and Millar, *English Art*; and Waterhouse, *Painting in Britain*.

N

NABIS. Monograph by A. Humbert, Geneva 1954 (in French).

NANNI DI BANCO. Monographs by L. Planiscig, Florence 1946; and P. Vaccarino, Florence 1950. See also Pope-Hennessy, *Italian Gothic Sculpture*.

NASH. *Outline, an Autobiography*, London 1949. Monograph by M. Eates (ed.), *A Memorial Volume*, London 1948. See also H. Read in Penguin Modern Painters series, London 1944.

NATTIER. Monograph by P. de Nolhac, London 1905 (in Eng. and French). See also Dimier, *Les peintres français du 18ᵉ siècle*.

NAY. Monographs by W. Haftmann, Cologne 1960; and (on watercolours) by F. Usinger, Munich 1956. See also N.'s *Vom Gestaltwert der Farbe*, Munich 1955; and Röthel, *Modern German Painting*.

NAZARENER. Monograph by K. Andrews, Oxford 1964.

NEAC. A. Thornton, *Fifty years of the NEAC*, London 1935 (privately printed).

NEER, AERT VAN DER. See Hofstede de Groot, *Dutch Painters*, vii; and Bode, *Great Masters of Dutch and Flemish Painting*.

NEER, EGLON H. VAN DER. See Hofstede de Groot, *Dutch Painters*, v.

NEOCLASSICISM. See P. Murray in *New Cambridge Modern History*, viii, 1965.

NEO-IMPRESSIONISM. See Rewald, *Post-Impressionism*; P. Signac, *De Delacroix au Néo-Impressionnisme*, Paris 1899 and 1964.

NEUE SACHLICHKEIT. See Myers, *Expressionism*.

NICHOLSON, B. Monograph by Sir H. Read, 2 vols., London 1955–6. Also monographs by Sir J. Summerson, London 1948; and D. Baxandall, London 1962.

NICHOLSON, W. Monographs by R. Nichols (Penguin Modern Painters), London 1948; and L. Browse, London 1956.

NITTIS. Monographs by E. Blémont, Paris 1884; V. Pica, Milan 1914; M. Cassandro, Barletta 1934; M. Pittaluga and E. Piceni, Milan 1963. See also Comanducci, *Dizionario*; and P. Bucarelli, *I Macchiaioli*, Rome 1956.

NOLAN. Monograph by B. Robertson, C. MacInnes, and Sir K. Clark, London 1961.

NOLDE. Autobiography: 2nd ed. Flensburg 1949. Monographs by W. Haftmann, London 1959 and 1965; and P. Selz, New York 1963. See also Myers, *Expressionism*; and L. Buchheim, *Die Künstlergemeinschaft Brücke*, Feldafing 1956.

NOLLEKENS. Monograph by J. T. Smith, London 1828 (also London 1949). See also Gunnis, *Dictionary of British Sculptors*; and Whinney, *Sculpture in Britain*.

NORTHCOTE. See W. Hazlitt, *Conversations of N.*, London 1830. *Conversations of N. with J. Ward*, ed. Fletcher, London 1901; *Memorials of an 18c. Painter*, ed. Gwynn, London 1898; also Waterhouse, *Painting in Britain*.

NORWICH SCHOOL. Monographs by W. F. Dickes, London 1905; and G. Barnard, Norwich 1950.

NOTKE. Monograph by W. Paatz, 2 vols., Berlin 1939 and Vienna 1944.

O

OCHTERVELT. See *Cat. of Dutch School*, NG, London 1960.

OIL PAINTING. See under TECHNIQUES (Classified Bibliography).

OLIVER. Monograph by G. Reynolds; Cat. of Exh., V & A, London 1947. See also Winter, *Elizabethan Miniatures*; and Long, *British Miniaturists*.

OPIE. See ed. of Opie's *Lectures on Painting*, London 1809. Monographs by J. Rogers, London 1878; and A. Earland, London 1911. See also Cat. of Arts Council Exh., London 1962–3.

OPTICAL MIXTURES. See P. Signac, *De Delacroix. . .*, Paris 1899 and 1964.

ORCAGNA, NARDO and JACOPO DI CIONE. Monograph by H.D. Gronau, Berlin 1937. See also Meiss, *Painting in Florence and Siena after the Black Death*; and Offner, *A Corpus of Florentine Painting*, iv.

ORLEY. Monograph by A. Wauters, Paris 1893. See also Friedländer; *Altniederländische Malerei*, viii.

OROZCO. Autobiography (Eng. ed.), Austin Texas 1962. Monograph by A. Reed, New York 1956.

ORPHIC CUBISM. See DELAUNAY, CUBISM.

OSTADE, A. VAN. Monograph by A. Rosenberg, Leipzig 1900. See also Hofstede de Groot, *Dutch Painters*, iii.

OSTADE, I. VAN. Monograph by A. Rosenberg, Leipzig 1900. See also Hofstede de Groot, *Dutch Painters*, iii.

OUDRY. Monograph by N. Hennique, Paris 1926; J. Locquin, *Cat. Raisonné d'O.*, Paris 1912.

OUWATER. See Friedländer, *Altniederländische Malerei*, iii.

OVERBECK. Monographs by J. Atkinson, London 1882; and C. G. Heise, Munich 1928. See also K. Andrews, *The Nazarenes*, Oxford 1964.

OZENFANT. See O.'s *Art*, Paris 1929 and his diary, *Journey through Life*, London 1939. See also Barr, *Cubism and Abstract Art*; and Haftmann, *Painting in the Twentieth Century*.

P

PACHECO. See his *Arte de la Pintura*, Seville 1649 and new ed. by F. J. Sánchez Cantón, 2 vols., Madrid 1956. See also Kubler and Soria, *Art and Architecture in Spain and Portugal*.

PACHER. Monographs by J. von Allesch, Leipzig 1931; E. Hempel, Vienna 1931 (6th. ed. 1952).

PAJOU. Monograph by H. Stein, Paris 1912. See also Lami, *Dictionnaire des Sculpteurs*.

PALMA VECCHIO. Monographs by G. Gombosi, Stuttgart (KdK) 1937; and A. Spahn, Leipzig 1932.

PALMER. Monographs by A. H. Palmer, London 1892; and G. Grigson, London 1947. See also Cat. of Exh., V & A, London 1926.

PANINI. Monograph by L. Ozzola, Turin 1921. See also Voss, *Barock*; and Wittkower, *Art and Architecture in Italy*.

PAOLO VENEZIANO. See Berenson, *Venetian School*; and Toesca, *Trecento*.

PARMIGIANINO. Monograph by S. J. Freedberg, Cambridge Mass. 1950. For drawings see A. E. Popham, London 1953.

PASCIN. Monographs by P. Morand, Paris 1931; A. Warnod, Monte Carlo, 1954; and A. Werner, London 1962.

PASMORE. Monographs by C. Bell, London 1945 (Penguin Modern Painters); and J. Reichardt, London 1962. See also Haftmann, *Painting in the Twentieth Century*.

PASTEL. See under TECHNIQUES (Classified Bibliography).

PATENIER. See Friedländer, *Altniederländische Malerei*, ix, and *Van Eyck to Brueghel*.

PATER. Monograph by F. Ingersoll-Smouse, Paris 1928.

PEALE FAMILY. Monograph by C. C. Sellers on C. W. P., 2 vols., Philadelphia 1947. See also Cat. of Exh., Cincinnati 1954.

PEARCE. See Whinney, *Sculpture in Britain*; and Gunnis, *Dictionary of British Sculptors*.

PECHSTEIN. Monograph by G. Biermann, 2nd ed. Leipzig 1920—with autobiog. See also *Erinnerungen*, ed. L. Reidemeister, Wiesbaden 1960 (written 1945–6); and L. G. Buchheim, *Die Künstlergemeinschaft Brücke*, Feldafing 1956.

PELLEGRINI. See Cat. of Exh., Venice 1959; Levey, *Venice*; and Donzelli, *Pittori Veneziani*.

PENCZ. Monograph by A. Kurzwelly, Leipzig 1895.

PERMEKE. Monograph by R. Avermaete, Brussels 1958 (in French). See also Cat. of Arts Council Exh., Tate Gall., London 1957.

PERMOSER. Monographs by E. Michalski, Frankfurt am Main 1927; W. Boeck, Burg 1938; W. Boeckelmann, Traunstein 1951. See Hempel, *Baroque Art . . . in Central Europe*.

PERRÉAL. See Ring, *A Century of French Painting*.

PERRONNEAU. Monograph by L. Vaillat and P. Ratouis de Limay, 2nd ed. Paris 1923.

PERSPECTIVE. See J. White, *The Birth and Rebirth of Pictorial Space*, London 1957.

PERUGINO. Monographs by F. Canuti, 2 vols., Siena 1931; and E. Camesasca, Milan 1959.

PESELLINO. See W. Weisbach, *F. P. und die Romantik der Renaissance*, Berlin 1901.

PEVSNER. See Cat. of Exh., M of MA, New York 1948; also Selz, *Modern Sculpture*, and A. Pevsner, *a biographical sketch of my brothers naum gabo and antoine pevsner*, Amsterdam 1964.

PIAZZETTA. Monographs by A. Pallucchini, Bologna 1934, and Milan 1956. See also Levey, *Venice*; and Donzelli, *Pittori Veneziani*.

PICABIA. Monograph by M. Sanouillet, Paris 1964. See also P.'s *Poèmes et dessins de la fille née*, Lausanne 1918.

PICASSO. Monographs by A. Barr, New York 1946, and Cat. of Exh., New York 1957 (as supplement). Also R. Penrose, London 1958. See also Sir A. Blunt and P. Pool, London 1962. C. Zervos (Complete Works of P.), Paris 1932 in progress.

PICTURESQUE. See C. Hussey, *The Picturesque*, London 1927; also C. Barbier, *William Gilpin*, Oxford 1962.

PIERO DI COSIMO. Monograph by R. Langton Douglas, Chicago 1946.

PIERO DELLA FRANCESCA. P.'s own *De Prospectiva Pingendi*, ed. G. Nicco Fasola, Florence 1942. Monographs by Sir K. Clark, London 1951; P. Bianconi, Milan 1957 and London 1962; and R. Longhi, 3rd ed. Florence 1963.

PIETRO DA CORTONA. Monograph by G. Briganti, Florence 1962; and Cat. of Exh., Rome 1956. See also Wittkower, *Art and Architecture in Italy*; Waterhouse, *Italian Baroque Painting*; and Voss, *Barock*; Pietro's own *Trattato della Pittura e Scultura* was pub. under the pseudonyms Odomenigio Lelonotti and Britio Prenetteri (i.e. P. da C. and G. Ottanelli, S.J.), Florence 1652.

PIGALLE. Monograph by L. Réau, Paris 1950. See also Lami, *Dictionnaire des Sculpteurs*.

PILON. Monographs by J. Babelon, Paris 1927; and C. Terrasse, Paris 1930.

PINTORICCHIO. Monograph by E. Carli, Siena-Milan 1960.

PIRANESI. Monographs by A. Giesecke, Leipzig n.d. (1911); A. M. Hind, London 1922; H. Thomas (the drawings), London 1954; A. H. Mayor, New York 1952. See also Cat. of Exh., Smith College, Northampton Mass. 1961.

PISANELLO. Monographs by G. F. Hill, London 1905 (for his medals); B. Degenhart, Vienna 1940 and Turin 1941; and R. Brenzoni, 2nd ed. Florence 1952.

PISANO, A. Monograph by I. Falk, Hamburg 1940. See also Pope-Hennessy, *Italian Gothic Sculpture*.

PISANO, G. Monographs by A. Venturi, Paris 1928 (in Eng.); and H. Keller, Vienna 1942. See also E. Carli, *Il Pulpito di Siena*, Bergamo 1943; G. Nicco Fasola, *La Fontana di Perugia*, Rome 1951, and Pope-Hennessy, *Italian Gothic Sculpture*.

PISANO, NICOLA. Monographs by G. H. and E. R. Crichton, Cambridge 1938; and G. Swarzenski,

Frankfurt 1926. See also E. Carli and G. Nicco Fasola as above; and Pope-Hennessy, *Italian Gothic Sculpture*.

PISANO, NINO. See I. Toesca, *Andrea e Nino Pisano*, Florence 1950.

PISIS. Monograph by G. Raimondi, Florence 1952. See also de Pisis's own *Prose e articoli*, Milan 1947.

PISSARRO, C. Monographs by L. R. Pissarro and L. Venturi, 2 vols., Paris 1939; and by J. Rewald, London 1963. See also P.'s *Letters to his Son Lucien*, New York and London 1944.

PISSARRO, L. Monograph by W. Meadmore, London 1962. See also Cat. of Arts Council Exh., London 1963.

PITTONI. Monograph by L. Pittoni, Florence 1921. See also Levey, *Venice*; and Donzelli, *Pittori Veneziani*.

PLASTER CASTING. See Rich, *The Materials and Method of Sculpture*.

PLEYDENWURFF. See Stange, *Deutsche Malerei der Gotik*, ix.

POLIAKOFF. Monograph by D. Vallier, Paris 1959. See also Cat. of Exh., Whitechapel Gall., London 1963.

POLLAIUOLO, ANTONIO AND PIERO. Monographs on Aontonio by M. Cruttwell, London 1907; G. Colacicchi, Florence 1943; and S. Ortolani, Milan 1948. For both Antonio and Piero see A. Sabatini, Florence 1944.

POLLOCK. Monographs by S. Hunter, New York (M of MA) 1956; and by B. Robertson, London 1960.

PONTORMO. Monographs by F. Clapp, Yale 1916; and E. Toesca, Rome 1943. For his drawings see J. C. Rearick, 2 vols., Harvard 1964. See also Cat. of Exh., Florence 1956. P.'s own *Diario 1554-6*, ed. E. Cecchi, Florence 1956.

PORDENONE. Monograph by G. Fiocco, Udine 1939.

POST-IMPRESSIONISM. See Rewald, *Post-Impressionism*.

POTTER. Monograph by E. Michel, Paris 1907. See also Hofstede de Groot, *Dutch Painters*, iv; and Bode, *Great Masters of Dutch and Flemish Painting*.

POURBUS, FRANS I. See Gerson and Ter Kuile, *Art and Architecture in Belgium*.

POURBUS, FRANS II. See Gerson and Ter Kuile as above entry.

POURBUS, PIETER. Monograph by K. de Volkaersbeke, Ghent 1870 (in French, and all three Pourbus). See also Friedländer, *Altniederländische Malerei*, xi.

POUSSIN, G. See Waterhouse, *Italian Baroque Painting*; and Wittkower, *Art and Architecture in Italy*.

POUSSIN, N. Monographs by O. Grautoff, 2 vols., Munich 1914; W. Friedländer, Munich 1914; and D. Mahon, London 1962. W. Friedländer, Sir A. Blunt, and R. Wittkower (drawings), London 1939 in progress: 3 vols. so far. See also Cat. of Exh., Louvre, Paris 1960.

POZZO. Monograph by R. Marini, Trento 1959 (in Ital.). See also Wittkower, *Art and Architecture in Italy*.

PRB. See Holman Hunt, *Pre-Raphaelitism and the Pre-Raphaelite Brotherhood*; and Ironside and Gere, *Pre-Raphaelite Painters*.

PREDELLA. See R. Salvini and L. Traverso, *The Predella from the XIII to XVIth centuries*, London 1960.

PRETI. Monographs by A. Frangipane, Milan 1929; and C. R. Taschetta, Brindisi 1961. See also Wittkower, *Art and Architecture in Italy*; and Waterhouse, *Italian Baroque Painting*.

PRIMATICCIO. Monograph by L. Dimier, Paris 1928. See also Blunt, *Art and Architecture in France*.

PRIMITIVE. See J. Lipman, *American Primitive Painting*, New York 1942; and Bihalji-Merin, *Modern Primitives*.

PROOF. See ENGRAVING.

PROPORTION. See E. Panofsky, *Meaning in the Visual Arts*, New York 1955.

PRUD'HON. Monographs by J. Guiffrey, Paris 1924; and R. Regamey, Paris 1928. See also Cat. of Exh., Musée Jacquemart-André, Paris 1958.

PUGET. Monographs by F. Alibert, Paris 1930; and M. Brion, Paris 1930. See also Blunt, *Art and Architecture in France*.

PURISM. See A. Ozenfant, *Après le Cubisme*, Paris 1918 and also his *Foundations of Modern Art*, New York 1952. See also Berckelaers and Seuphor, *Dictionary of Abstract Painting*.

PURRMANN. Monograph by E. Hausen, Berlin 1950. See also Röthel, *Modern German Painting*; and Haftmann, *Painting in the Twentieth Century*.

PUVIS DE CHAVANNES. Monographs by A. Michel, London 1912; L. Werth, Paris 1926; and C. Mauclair, Paris 1928. See also Rewald, *Post-Impressionism*.

PYNACKER. See Hofstede de Groot, *Dutch Painters*, ix (in German only).

PYNAS. See Cat. of Exh., Utrecht 1952.

Q

QUARTON. See C. Sterling, *Le Couronnement de la Vierge par E. Q.*, Paris 1939; also Ring, *Century of French Painting*.

QUELLIN FAMILY. (i) Artus 1: Monograph by J. Gabriels, Antwerp 1930 (in Flemish). See also Gerson and Ter Kuile; *Art and Architecture in Belgium*. (ii) Arnold: see Gunnis, *Dictionary*; also Whinney and Millar, *English Art*; and Whinney, *Sculpture in Britain*.

QUERCIA. Monographs by L. Biagi, Florence 1946; and O. Morisani, Milan 1962. See also A. Hanson, *J. della Q.'s Fonte Gaia*, Oxford 1965.

R

RAEBURN. Monographs by W. Armstrong, London 1901; and J. Grieg, London 1911. See also Cat. of Exh., Edinburgh 1956.

RAMSAY. Monograph by A. Smart, London 1952. See also Cat. of Exh., Kenwood, London 1958.

RAPHAEL. Monographs by A. P. Oppé, London 1909; O. Fischel, 2 vols., London 1948; and E. Camesasca, 2 vols., Milan 1956 (Eng. ed. 4 vols., London 1963). For original sources see V. Golzio, *R. nei documenti. . .*, Vatican City 1936. See also Pouncey and Gere, *The Drawings of Raphael and his Circle* (BM catalogue).

RAYONISM. See Gray, *The Great Experiment: Russian Art 1863-1922*.

RAYSKI. Monographs by M. Goeritz, Berlin 1942; and M. Walter, Bielefeld-Leipzig 1943.

REALISM. For COURBET see G. Boase (ed.), *Courbet and the Naturalistic Movement*, Baltimore 1938.

REDON. Monograph by R. Bacou, 2 vols., Geneva 1956 (in French). See also monograph on R., Moreau, and Bresdin by J. Rewald, D. Ashton, and H. Joachim, New York (M of MA) 1961.

REMBRANDT. There are general monographs on R. by

A. M. Hind, London 1938; and J. Rosenberg, 2 vols., London 1948 (2nd ed. 1 vol. 1964). For original sources see S. Slive, The Hague 1953. There is also a volume in Hofstede de Groot's *Dutch Painters* (vi). For R.'s paintings see A. Bredius, London 1937 and 1942 (2 vols.); for his etchings there are monographs by A. M. Hind, 2 vols., London 1912, L. Münz, London 1952 (2 vols.), and G. Bürkhund, Stockholm 1955 (Eng.); and for his drawings see O. Benesch, London 1954–7 (6 vols.).

RENAISSANCE. See W. K. Ferguson, *The Renaissance in Historical Thought*, Cambridge Mass. 1948; and E. Panofsky, *Renaissance and Renascences in Western Art*, 2 vols., Uppsala 1960. See also Freedberg, *High Renaissance*; and P. and L. Murray, *The Art of the Renaissance*.

RENI. Monograph by C. Gnudi and G. Cavalli, Florence 1955. See also Cat. of Exh., Bologna 1954; and Wittkower, *Art and Architecture in Italy*.

RENOIR. Monographs by M. Drucker, Paris 1944 and London 1950; W. Gaunt, London 1952; and D. Rouart, Lausanne 1954 (in Eng.). See also J. Renoir, *My Father, Pierre Renoir*, London 1962.

RETHEL. Monograph by J. Ponten, Stuttgart-Leipzig (KdK) 1911 and Stuttgart 1922.

REYNOLDS. Monographs by C. Leslie and T. Taylor, 2 vols., London 1856; E. K. Waterhouse, London 1941. Early *Lives* include those by E. Malone, 2nd ed. London 1798 and J. Northcote, 2nd ed. London 1818. Modern eds. of his literary works include the *Discourses*, ed. by R. Wark, San Marino Cal. 1959; *Letters* ed. by F. Hilles, Cambridge 1929; and *The Literary Career of Sir J. R.*, by F. Hilles, Cambridge 1936. W. Cotton, *Sir J. R. and his Works*, London 1856, and *Notes and Observations*, London 1859, contain much original material. The standard catalogue of his works is A. Graves and W. Cronin, 4 vols., London 1899–1901.

RIBALTA. Monographs by D. Fitz Darby, Cambridge Mass. 1938; and C. Espresati, Barcelona 1948.

RIBERA. Monograph by E. du G. Trapier, New York 1952. See also Wittkower, *Art and Architecture in Italy*.

RICCI, M. See Cat. of Exh., Bassano 1963, revised ed. 1964. For drawings by both Ricci see Sir A. Blunt, *Venetian Drawings at Windsor Castle*, London 1957. See also Donzelli, *Pittori Veneziani*; and Levey, *Venice*.

RICCI, S. Monograph by J. Derschau, Heidelberg 1922. See also Donzelli, *Pittori Veneziani*; Levey, *Venice*; and Wittkower, *Art and Architecture in Italy*.

RICCIO. Monograph by L. Planiscig, Vienna 1927. See also Pope-Hennessy, *Italian Sculpture*, iii.

RICHARDS. Monograph by D. Thompson, London 1963.

RICHARDSON. See *The Works of J. R.*, new ed. Strawberry Hill 1792; and Waterhouse, *Painting in Britain*.

RICHIER. Monograph by J. Cassou, London 1961. See also Giedion-Welcker, *Contemporary Sculpture*.

RIEMENSCHNEIDER. Monographs by J. Bier, 6th ed. Vienna 1948; M. von Freeden, 2nd ed. Munich 1959; and K. Gerstenberg, 5th ed. Munich 1962.

RIGAUD. See *Livre de Raison du Peintre H. R.*, ed. J. Roman, Paris 1919.

RILEY. See Waterhouse, *Painting in Britain*; and Whinney and Millar, *English Art*.

RIOPELLE. See Langui, *Fifty Years of Modern Art*; and Haftmann, *Painting in the Twentieth Century*.

RIVERA. Monographs by B. D. Wolfe, New York 1939; A. Rodriguez, Mexico 1948; and H. F. Secker, Dresden 1957. Cat. of Exh., M of MA, New York 1931. See R.'s own *Portrait of America*, New York and London 1935. Also B. Myers, *Mexican Painting in Our Time*, New York 1956.

ROBBIA DELLA, FAMILY. See A. Marquand, *The Brothers of Giovanni d. R.*, Princeton 1928.

ROBBIA, LUCA DELLA. Monographs by A. Marquand, Princeton 1914; and L. Planiscig, Florence 1948. See also Pope-Hennessy, *Italian Sculpture*, ii.

ROBERT, H. Monographs by C. Gabillot, Paris 1895; and P. de Nolhac, Paris 1910. See also Cat. by L. Hautecœur, Orangerie, Paris 1933.

ROBERTI. Monograph by M. Salmi, Milan 1960. See also Nicolson, *The Painters of Ferrara*.

ROCOCO. See Schönberger and Soehner, *The Age of Rococo*.

RODIN. Monographs by S. Story, London 1939; R. M. Rilke (Eng. ed.), London 1946; and A. Elsen, New York (M. of MA) 1963. See also G. Grappe, *Cat. du Musée R.*, Paris 1945; and Selz, *Modern Sculpture*. See also R.'s own *Entretiens sur l'art*, ed. P. Gsell, Lausanne 1946.

ROHLFS. Monographs by P. Vogt, Cologne 1956 and Recklinghausen 1958. See also Röthel, *Modern German Painting*; Myers, *Expressionism*; and Haftmann, *Painting in the Twentieth Century*; and Cat. of Exh., Arts Council, London 1956.

ROMBOUTS. See Cat. of Exh., Utrecht 1952. Also Gerson and Ter Kuile, *Art and Architecture in Belgium*.

ROMNEY. Monographs by H. Ward and W. Roberts, 2 vols., London 1904; and A. Chamberlain, London 1911. See also Cat. of Exh., Kenwood, London 1961; and Waterhouse, *Painting in Britain*.

ROSA. Monograph by L. Salerno, Milan 1963. See also Lady (S.) Morgan, London 1824; and U. Limentani (R.'s poetry and letters), Florence 1950 and *Bibliografia . . .*, Florence 1955. Also Wittkower, *Art and Architecture in Italy*; and Waterhouse, *Italian Baroque Painting*.

ROSLIN. Monograph by G. W. Lundberg, 3 vols., Malmö 1957 (with French Summary).

ROSSELLI, COSIMO. Monograph by A. Lorenzoni, Florence 1921. See also van Marle, *Italian Schools*, xi.

ROSSELLINO. Monograph by L. Planiscig, Vienna 1942. See also Pope-Hennessy, *Italian Sculpture*, ii.

ROSSETTI. Monographs by H. C. Marillier, London 1899; and O. Doughty, London 1949. For R.'s literary work see A. C. Benson, London 1904; for his art see L. Pissarro, London 1907.

ROSSO. Monographs by K. Kusenberg, Paris 1931; and P. Barocchi, Rome 1950. See also Becherucci, *Manieristi Toscani*; and Cat. of Pontormo Exh., Florence 1956.

ROSSO, MEDARDO. Monographs by M. Borghi, Milan 1950; and M. Barr, New York (M of MA) 1963. See also Selz, *Modern Sculpture*.

ROTHKO. See Cats. of Exhs., Whitechapel Gall., London 1961, and Basle, Kunsthalle 1962. See also Seuphor, *Abstract Painting, from Kandinsky to the Present*.

ROTTMAYR. See Hempel, *Baroque Art and Architecture in Central Europe*.

ROUAULT. Monographs by L. Venturi, Paris 1949; J. T. Soby, 3rd ed. New York (M of MA) 1947; and P. Courthion, London 1962. See also Cat. of Exh., Cleveland and New York (M of MA) 1953.

ROUBILIAC. Monograph by K. Esdaile, Oxford 1928. See also Gunnis, *Dictionary of British Sculptors*; and Whinney, *Sculpture in Britain*.

ROUSSEAU (LE DOUANIER). Monographs by D. C. Rich, New York (M of MA) 1942; D. Cooper, London and Paris 1951; and J. Bouret, London 1961.

ROUSSEAU, THÉODORE. Monographs by A. Sensier, Paris 1872; and P. Dorbec, Paris 1910.

ROWLANDSON. Monographs by A. P. Oppé, London 1923; F. G. Rowe, Leigh-on-Sea 1947; and A. Bury, London 1949.

RUBÉNISME. See A. Fontaine, *Les Doctrines d'Art en France*, Paris 1909; and L. Hourticq, *De Poussin à Watteau*, Paris 1921.

RUBENS. Bibliography up to 1960 in Gerson and Ter Kuile, *Art and Architecture in Belgium*. Monographs by M. Rooses, Antwerp, 5 vols. (in French), 1886–92, and in one vol. Antwerp 1903 (Eng. ed. 1904); R. Oldenbourg, Berlin-Leipzig (KdK) 1921; For R.'s drawings see J. Held, 2 vols., London 1959 and L. Burchard and R. d'Hulst, 2 vols., Brussels 1963 (in Eng.).

RUDE. Monographs by M. Legrand, Paris 1856; and R. Garraud, Dijon 1876. See also Cat. of Centenary Exh., Dijon 1955; Selz, *Modern Sculpture*; and Lami, *Dictionnaire des Sculpteurs*.

RUISDAEL, J. VAN. Monograph by J. Rosenberg, Berlin 1928. See also Hofstede de Groot, *Dutch Painters*, iv; and Bode, *Great Masters of Dutch and Flemish Painting*.

RUNGE, P. O. Monographs by Daniel Runge, ed. of P. O. R.'s writings, 2 vols., Hamburg 1840–1; and P. Schmidt, 2nd ed. Wiesbaden 1956. R.'s *Farbenkugel* was reprinted Stuttgart 1959.

RUSKIN. R.'s *Works*, ed. by Cook and Wedderburn, 39 vols., London 1903–12; and his *Diaries*, ed. by J. Evans and J. Whitehouse, 3 vols., Oxford 1956–9. Monographs include those by R. Wilenski, London 1933; J. Evans, Oxford 1954; Q. Bell, London 1963; and Sir K. Clark, London 1964. See also J. Whitehouse, *R. the Painter*, London 1938.

RUYSCH. Monograph by M. H. Grant, Leigh-on-Sea 1956. See also Hofstede de Groot, *Dutch Painters*, x; and Bergström, *Dutch Still-Life Painting in the 17 c.*

RUYSDAEL, SALOMON VAN. Monograph by W. Stechow, Berlin 1938. See also Bode, *Great Masters of Dutch and Flemish Painting*.

RYDER. Monograph by L. Goodrich, New York 1959. See also Richardson, *Painting in America*.

RYSBRACK. Monograph by M. Webb, London 1953. See also Gunnis, *Dictionary of British Sculptors*; and Whinney, *Sculpture in Britain*.

S

SACCHI. Monograph by H. Posse, Leipzig 1925. See also Wittkower, *Art and Architecture in Italy*; and Waterhouse, *Italian Baroque Painting*.

SAENREDAM. Monograph by P. Swillens, Amsterdam 1935. See also complete Cat. of Exh., Utrecht 1961 (in Eng.).

SALON. See K. W. Luckhurst, *The Story of Exhibitions*, London 1951. See also J. J. Guiffrey, *Salons du XVIIIᵉ Siècle . . . Notes sur les Anciennes Expositions. . .*, Paris 1873.

SALVIATI. See Briganti, *Italian Mannerism*; and Voss, *Die Malerei der Spätrenaissance in Rom und Florenz*.

SÁNCHEZ COELLO. Monograph by F. de B. San Román y Fernández, Lisbon 1938. See also Cat. of New York Hispanic Society, New York 1930.

SANDBY. Monograph by W. Sandby, London 1902. See also *Catalogue of S. Drawings at Windsor Castle*, by A. P. Oppé, Oxford 1947; and Addenda in *English Drawings at Windsor Castle*, also by A. P. Oppé, London 1950.

SANDRART. See ed. of *Teutsche Academie*, ed. by R. A. Peltzer, Munich 1925. See also Cat. of Exh., Utrecht 1952.

SANSOVINO, A. Monograph by G. H. Huntley, Cambridge Mass. 1935. See also Pope-Hennessy, *Italian Sculpture*, iii.

SANSOVINO, J. Monographs by H. R. Weirauch, Strasburg 1935 (in German: sculpture only); and G. Mariacher, Milan 1962 (incl. architecture). See also J. Pope-Hennessy, *Italian Sculpture*, iii.

SANTI. See *Cronaca Rimata*, ed. Holzinger, Stuttgart 1897.

SARACENI. Monograph by A. Porcella, Venice 1928. See also Waterhouse, *Italian Baroque Painting*; Wittkower, *Art and Architecture in Italy*; and V. Golzio, *Seicento e Settecento*, 2 vols., 2nd ed. Turin 1961.

SARGENT. Monographs by C. M. Mount, New York 1955; and D. McKibben, Boston 1956 (with check-list of portraits). See also F. Sweet, S., *Whistler and Mary Cassatt*, Chicago 1954.

SARTORIUS. See Sparrow, *A Book of Sporting Painters*.

SASSETTA. Monographs by J. Pope-Hennessy, London 1939; B. Berenson, Florence 1946 (in Eng.); and E. Carli, London 1957. See also Pope-Hennessy, *Sienese Quattrocento Painting*.

SAVOLDO. Monograph by A. Boschetto, Milan 1963.

SCHADOW. Monographs by H. Mackowsky, Berlin 1927 and 1951.

SCHÄUFFELEIN. For drawings see F. Winkler, *Die Zeichnungen Hans Süss von Kulmbachs und Hans Leonhard Schäuffeleins*, Berlin 1942.

SCHEEMAKERS. See Gunnis, *Dictionary of British Sculptors*; and Whinney, *Sculpture in Britain*.

SCHIELE. Monographs by P. Gütersloh, Vienna 1915; O. Nirenstein, Vienna 1930; A. Koessler, 2nd ed. Vienna 1948; O. Benesch (S. as a draughtsman – in Eng.), Vienna 1951.

SCHLEMMER. Monograph by H. Hildebrandt, Munich 1952. See also S.'s Letters and Diaries, Munich 1958; and Röthel, *Modern German Painting*.

SCHLÜTER. Monographs by H. Ladendorf, Berlin 1935 and 1937. See Hempel, *Baroque Art. . . in Central Europe*.

SCHMIDT-ROTTLUFF. Monograph by W. Grohmann, Stuttgart 1956 (with cat.).

SCHNORR VON CAROLSFELD. Monograph by H. W. Singer, Bielefeld and Leipzig 1911. See also his Letters from Italy, ed. F. Schnorr von Carolsfeld, Gotha 1886; his Writings, ed. by F. Schnorr von Carolsfeld, Leipzig

1909; and his Diaries 1849–61, Dresdener Geschichts-bibliothek, vols. ivff.

SCHONGAUER. Monographs by J. Baum, Vienna 1948; and W. E. Flechsig, Strassburg 1951 (in German). For his paintings see monograph by E. Buchner, Berlin 1941.

SCHWIND. Monograph by O. Weigmann, Stuttgart-Leipzig (KdK) 1906.

SCHWITTERS. Monographs by H. Bergruen, Paris 1954; and S. Themerson, London 1958. See also Barr, *Fantastic Art, Dada, Surrealism*; and Haftmann, *Painting in the Twentieth Century*.

SCOREL. Monographs by G. Hoogewerf, La Haye 1923 (in French); and J. C. H. De Jonge, Amsterdam (*c.* 1945). See also Friedländer, *Altniederländische Malerei*, xii; and Cat. of Exh., Centraal Museum, Utrecht 1955.

SCOTT, SAMUEL. See Cat. of Exh., Guildhall Art Gallery, London 1955. See also Waterhouse, *Painting in Britain*.

SCOTT, WILLIAM. Monograph by A. Bowness, with M. Ragon and W. Schmalenbach, London 1964.

SCROTS. See E. Auerbach, *Tudor Artists*, London 1954.

SEBASTIANO. Monographs by L. Dussler, Basel 1942 (in German); and R. Pallucchini, Milan 1944.

SEGANTINI. See his own *Scritti e Lettere*, Turin 1910. Monographs by G. Segantini, last ed. Trent 1955 (in German); G. Nicodemi, Milan 1956; and L. Budigna, Milan 1962. See also Cat. of Exh., Kunst-museum, St Gall 1956.

SEGHERS. Monographs by G. Knuttel, Amsterdam (1949); and L. C. Collins, Chicago 1953. For engravings see W. Fraenger, Munich 1922.

SEISENEGGER. Monograph by K. Löcher, Munich and Berlin 1962.

SÉRAPHINE. See W. Uhde, *Fünf primitive Meister*, Zürich 1947; Haftmann, *Painting in the Twentieth Century*; and Bihalji-Merin, *Modern Primitives*.

SERIGRAPHY. Monograph by J. Biegeleisen and M. Cohn, New York 1958.

SÉRUSIER. See S.'s *A.B.C. de la peinture*, Paris 1921, 1942 (with Life of S. by M. Denis), and 1950; Rewald, *Post-Impressionism*, and A. Humbert, *Les Nabis*, Geneva 1954.

SEURAT. Monographs by H. Dorra and J. Rewald, Paris 1959; C. de Hauke and P. Brame, 2 vols. (with cat.) Paris 1963; E. Seligmann, New York 1947 (on drawings); and J. Russell, London 1965. See also W. Homer, *Seurat and the Science of Painting*, Cambridge Mass. 1964.

SEVERINI. See his Autobiography, Milan 1946. Monograph by B. Wall, London 1946. See also Cat. of Exh., Rome 1961.

SEZESSION. See H. Bahr, *Secession*, 2nd ed. Vienna 1900.

SHAHN. Monograph by J. T. Soby, 2 vols., New York 1963 (smaller ed. London 1947). His own writings include *Paragraphs on Art*, New York 1952; *The Shape of Content*, New York 1960, and *Love and Joy about Letters*, London 1963.

SICKERT. Monographs by R. B. Emmons, London 1941; L. Browse and R. Wilenski, London 1944; and L. Browse, London 1960. See also Cat. of Arts Council Exh., Tate Gall., London 1960. Sickert's collected essays were published as *A Free House!*, London 1947.

SIGNAC. Monograph by G. Besson, Paris 1950. See also Signac's *De Delacroix au Néo-Impressionisme*, Paris 1899 and 1964. Exh. Cats.: Musée d'Art Moderne, Paris 1951; Louvre, Paris 1963–4. See also Rewald, *Post-Impressionism*.

SIGNIFICANT FORM. See Clive Bell, *Art*, London 1914.

SIGNORELLI. Monographs by L. Dussler, Stuttgart 1927; and M. Salmi, Novara 1953. See also Cat. of Exh., Cortona 1953.

SIGNORINI. Monographs by U. Ojetti, Rome 1901; and A. Franchi, Milan 1953. See also his own *Caricaturisti e Caricaturati* (1893), 2nd ed. Florence 1952; and Comanducci, *Dizionario*.

SILVER POINT. See Watrous, *The Craft of Old Master Drawings*; Meder, *Die Handzeichnung: Ihre Technik und Entwicklung*; and Thompson, *The Materials of Mediaeval Painting*.

SINOPIA. See under FRESCO.

SISLEY. Monographs by F. Daulte, Paris and Lausanne 1959; and P. du Colombier, Brussels 1965. See also Rewald, *Impressionism*.

SLEVOGT. Monograph by E. Waldmann, Berlin 1923. See also Myers, *Expressionism*.

SLUTER. Monographs by G. Troescher, Freiburg-im-Breisgau 1932; A. Liebreich, Brussels 1936; and H. David, Paris 1951.

SMET. Monograph by L. van Puyvelde, Antwerp (in French) 1949.

SMIBERT. Monograph by H. Foote, Cambridge Mass. 1950.

SMITH. Monograph by F. Halliday and J. Russell, London 1962. See also Cats. of Exhs, Tate Gall., London 1953, and RA 1960.

SNYDERS. See Gerson and Ter Kuile, *Art and Architecture in Belgium*.

SOCIAL REALISM. See Aragon, *Pour un Réalisme Socialiste*, Paris 1935.

SODOMA. Monograph by R. H. Cust, London 1906. See also Sandberg-Vavalà, *Sienese Studies*; and Cat. of Exh., Vercelli-Siena 1950.

SOLIMENA. Monograph by F. Bologna, Naples 1958. See also Wittkower, *Art and Architecture in Italy*; and Waterhouse, *Italian Baroque Painting*.

SOMER. See Waterhouse, *Painting in Britain*; and Mercer, *English Art*.

SOULAGES. Monograph by H. Juin, Paris 1959. See also Haftmann, *Painting in the Twentieth Century*.

SOUTINE. Monographs by W. Wheeler, New York (M of MA), 1950; and J. Leymarie, London 1965.

SPENCER, STANLEY. Monograph by E. Rothenstein, London 1945. See also Cat. of Exh., Tate Gall., London 1955 (with preface by the artist).

SPINELLO ARETINO. Monograph by G. Gombosi, Budapest 1926 (in German).

SPITZWEG. Monographs by H. Uhde-Bernays, 10th ed. Munich 1935; A. Elsen, Vienna 1948; E. Kalkschmidt, 2nd ed. Munich 1949; and G. Roennefahrt, Munich 1960.

SQUARCIONE. Monograph by P. E. Selvatico, Padua 1839. See A. Moschetti, *Mantegna*, Venice 1931; and Crowe and Cavalcaselle, *Painting in North Italy*.

STABILE. See J. Lynch, *Metal Sculpture: New Forms, New Techniques*, New York 1957.

STAËL. Monographs by D. Sutton, London and New York 1960; and D. Cooper, London 1961.

STAINED GLASS. See J. L. Fischer, *Handbuch der Glasmalerei*, Leipzig 1914; G. Marchini, *Italian Stained Glass Windows*, London 1955; J. Baker, *English Stained Glass*, London 1960 (these last have technical sections); and E. L. Armitage, *Stained Glass*, London 1959.

STANZIONE. Monograph by H. Schwanenberg, Bonn 1937. See also Wittkower, *Art and Architecture in Italy*.

STEEL-ENGRAVING. See A. M. Hind, *The Processes and Schools of Engraving*, 4th ed. London 1952.

STEELL. See Gunnis, *Dictionary of British Sculptors*.

STEEN. Monographs by F. Schmidt-Degener and H. E. van Gelder, London 1927; A. Bredius, Amsterdam 1927; and W. Martin, Amsterdam 1954. See also Hofstede de Groot, *Dutch Painters*, i.

STEER. Monographs by R. Ironside, London 1943; and D. S. McColl, London 1945.

STEFANO DA ZEVIO. See Cat. of Exh., Verona 1958.

STEVENS. Monograph by K. R. Towndrow, London 1939, and Liverpool 1951. See also his Cat. of Stevens in Tate Gall., London 1950.

STIJL, DE. Monograph by H. L. C. Jaffé, Amsterdam 1956 (in Eng.). See also under DOESBURG and MONDRIAN.

STILL-LIFE. See Cat. of the Ward Bequest, Ashmolean Mus., Oxford, with introd. on Still-Life painting in the Netherlands, by J. G. van Gelder, Oxford 1950; M. J. Friedländer, *Landscape, Portrait, Still-Life*, Oxford 1949; Bergström, *Dutch Still-Life Painting in the 17th Century*; and C. Sterling, *La Nature Morte*, Paris 1952, and Eng. ed. (revised) Paris 1959.

STOMER. See Cat. of Exh., Utrecht 1952. See also Schneider, *Caravaggio und die Niederländer*.

STOSS. Monographs by E. Lutze, Berlin 1952; P. Skubis-zewski, Warsaw 1957; and A. Jaeger, Nuremberg 1958. See also Feulner and Müller, *Geschichte*.

STREETER. See Whinney and Millar, *English Art*.

STRIGEL. Monograph by G. Otto, Berlin 1964. See also Stange, *Deutsche Malerei*, viii.

STROZZI. Monograph by G. Fiocco, Rome 1921. See also Wittkower, *Art and Architecture in Italy*.

STUART. Monographs by L. Park, 4 vols., New York 1926; C. M. Mount, New York 1964. See also Richardson, *Painting in America*.

STUBBS. Monographs by Sir W. Gilbey, London 1898; and W. S. Sparrow, London 1929 (Stubbs and B. Marshall). See also Cat. of Exh., Whitechapel Art Gall., London 1957; and Taylor, *Animal Painting in England*.

SULLY. Monograph by E. Biddle and M. Fielding, Philadelphia 1921. See also Cat. of Exh., Pennsylvania Academy 1922; and Sully's own *Hints to Young Painters*, Philadelphia 1873.

SUPREMATISM. See under MALEVICH.

SURREALISM. Monographs by M. Nadeau, 2nd ed. Paris 1945–8, another ed. Paris 1958; and P. Waldberg, London 1965. See also Sir H. Read (ed.) *Surrealism*, London 1936; A. Breton, *Manifeste du Surréalisme*, Paris 1929; and *Second Manifeste du Surréalisme*, Paris 1930. Also Barr, *Fantastic Art, Dada, Surrealism*. For a bibliography see H. Edwards, Chicago 1956.

SUTHERLAND. Monograph by D. Cooper, London 1961.

SWEERTS. Exh. Cats.: Museum Boymans, Rotterdam 1958; Palazzo Venezia, Rome 1958. See also Gerson and Ter Kuile, *Art and Architecture in Belgium*.

SYNTHETISM. See H. Rookmaaker, *Synthetist Art Theories*, Amsterdam 1959.

T

TACCA. See Wittkower, *Italy*; and Pope-Hennessy, *Italian Sculpture*, iii.

TACTILE VALUES. See Berenson, *Italian Painters of the Renaissance*.

TAMAYO. Monographs by R. J. Goldwater, New York 1947; and R. Cogniat, Paris 1951. See also B. Myers, *Mexican Painting in Our Time*, New York 1956.

TANGUY. Monograph by J. T. Soby, New York (M of MA) 1955.

TAPIÈS. Monograph by M. Tapié, Paris 1956.

TATLIN. See Gray, *The Great Experiment*; and Selz, *Modern Sculpture*.

TEMPERA. See Thompson, *The Materials of Medieval Painting*; and Constable, *The Painter's Workshop*.

TENIERS, DAVID II. Monograph by A. Rosenberg, Bielefeld 1895. See also Gerson and Ter Kuile, *Art and Architecture in Belgium*.

TER BORCH. Monograph by S. Gudlaugsson, 2 vols., The Hague 1959–60 (in German). See also Hofstede de Groot, *Dutch Painters*, v.

TERBRUGGHEN. Monograph by B. Nicolson, London 1958. See also Cat. of Exh., Utrecht 1952.

THEODORIC OF PRAGUE. Monographs by J. Loriš, Prague 1938; and A. Friedl, Prague (1956?) (in Eng.). See also Matějček and Pešina, *Gothic Painting in Bohemia, 1350–1450*.

THOMA. Monographs by H. Thode, Stuttgart-Leipzig (KdK) 1909; and H. Busse, 3rd ed. Berlin 1939.

THORNHILL. See Whinney and Millar, *English Art*; Waterhouse, *Painting in Britain*; and Croft-Murray, *Decorative Painting*.

THORWALDSEN. Monographs by J. Thiele, 4 vols., Copenhagen (in Danish) 1831–50; also later Danish eds., and German trans.; abridged Eng. ed. London 1865; A. Rosenberg, Leipzig 1896, 2nd ed. 1901; and P. O. Rave, Berlin 1947.

TIBALDI. Monograph by G. Briganti, Rome 1945.

TIEPOLO, G. B. Monograph by A. Morassi, 2 vols., London 1955 and 1962. See also Cat. of Exh., Venice 1951; Levey, *Venice*; and Donzelli, *Pittori Veneziani*.

TIEPOLO, DOMENICO. Monograph by J. Byam-Shaw, London 1962 (on drawings).

TINO DI CAMAINO. Monographs by E. Carli, Florence 1934; and W. R. Valentiner, Paris 1935 (in Eng.). See also Pope-Hennessy, *Italian Sculpture*, i.

TINTORETTO. Monographs by M. Pittaluga, Bologna 1925; E. von der Bercken, 2 vols., Munich 1942; H. Tietze, London 1948; and E. Newton, London 1952. See also Cat. of Exh., Venice 1937.

TISCHBEIN. Monograph by F. Landsberger, Leipzig 1908. See also T.'s Autobiography, ed. K. Mittelstädt, Berlin 1956.

TISSOT. Monograph by J. Laver, London 1936.

TITIAN. Monographs by H. Tietze, London 1950 and

F. Valcanover, 2 vols., Milan 1960. See also Cat. of Exh., Venice 1935.

TOBEY. See Cats. of Exhs., Whitehapel Gall., London 1962; and *Modern Art in the US*, Tate Gall., London 1956. See also Langui, *Fifty Years of Modern Art*; and Haftmann, *Painting in the Twentieth Century*.

TOCQUÉ. Monograph by A. Doria, Paris 1929.

TORRIGIANO. See Pope-Hennessy, *Italian Sculpture*, ii.

TOULOUSE-LAUTREC. Monographs by M. Joyant, 2 vols., Paris 1926–7; F. Jourdain and J. Adhémar, Paris 1952; and D. Cooper, London 1955 and 1963. See also Rewald, *Post-Impressionism*.

TRAINI. See Toesca, *Trecento*.

TROY DE. See Réau, *Histoire de la peinture française au 18ᵉ siècle*, and Dimier, *Les peintres français du 18ᵉ siècle*.

TRUMBULL. Monograph by T. Sizer, New Haven 1950. See also T.'s *Autobiography*, ed. T. Sizer, New Haven 1953.

TURA. Monographs by M. Salmi, n.p., 1957 (in Ital.); E. Ruhmer, London 1958; and P. Bianconi, Milan 1963. See also Nicolson, *The Painters of Ferrara*.

TURNER. Monographs by J. Ruskin, in *Modern Painters*, i, London 1843; A. Finberg, 2nd ed. Oxford 1961; and Sir J. Rothenstein and M. Butlin, London 1964. See also M. Butlin, *T. Water Colours*, London 1962; and A. J. Finberg, *Cat. of T. Drawings in B.M.*, 2 vols., London 1909.

U

UCCELLO. Monographs by J. Pope-Hennessy, London 1950; P. d'Ancona, London 1960; and E. Carli, London 1963.

UGOLINO DA SIENA. See Sandberg-Vavalà, *Sienese Studies*; and M. Davies, *Cat. of Early Italian Schools*, NG., 2nd ed. London 1961.

'UGOLINO-LORENZETTI'. See Berenson, *Pitture italiane; del Rinascimento*.

UNDERPAINTING. See L. Lamb, *Preparation for Painting*, Oxford 1954; and Constable, *The Painter's Workshop*.

UTRECHT SCHOOL. See A. von Schneider, *Caravaggio und die Niederländer*; and Cat. of Exh., *C. en de Nederlanden*, Utrecht, Antwerp 1952 (with summaries in Eng.).

UTRILLO. Monograph by W. George, London 1960. See also Oeuvre Cat. by P. Petrides, Paris 1959, in progress.

V

VALDÉS, LEAL. Monograph by E. du G. Trapier, New York 1960. See also Kubler and Soria, *Art and Architecture in Spain*.

VALENTIN. See Voss, *Malerei des Barock in Rom*; and Blunt, *Art and Architecture in France*.

VARLEY. Monograph by A. Bury, Leigh-on-Sea 1946. See also Williams, *Early English Watercolours*; and Roget, *History of the Old Water Colour Society*.

VASARI. Monographs by R. Carden, London 1910; E. Rud, London 1964; and P. Barocchi, Milan 1964. For eds. of the *Vite*, see Classified Bibliography.

VECCHIETTA. Monograph by G. Vigni, Florence 1937. See also Pope-Henessy, *Sienese Quattrocento Painting*.

VELAZQUEZ. Monographs by A. L. Mayer, London 1936; E. Lafuente Ferrari, Oxford 1943; E. du G. Trapier, New York 1954; and J. Lopez-Rey, London 1963.

VELDE, ADRIAEN VAN DE. Monograph on the family by K. Zoege von Manteuffel, Bielefeld-Leipzig 1927. Also Bode, *Great Masters of Dutch and Flemish Painting*; and Hofstede de Groot, *Dutch Painters*, iv.

VELDE, ESAIAS VAN DE. See A. Bengtsson, *Studies on the Rise of Realistic Landscape Painting in Holland, 1610–25*, Uppsala 1952; and K. Zoege von Manteuffel, Bielefeld-Leipzig 1927 (on the family).

VELDE, WM. VAN DE, I and II. Monograph by M. Robinson (Nat. Marit. Mus. Cat.), Cambridge 1958. See also H. Baard, *Wm. van de Velde de Oude en W.v.d.V. de Jonge*, Amsterdam n.d.; Hofstede de Groot, *Dutch Painters*, vii; and K. Zoege von Manteuffel, Bielefeld-Leipzig 1927 (on the family).

VERMEER. Monographs by A. de Vries (Eng. ed.), London 1948; P. Swillens, Utrecht-Brussels 1950 (in Eng.); L. Gowing, London 1952; L. Goldscheider, London 1958; and V. Bloch, London 1963. See also Cat. of Exh., Utrecht 1952; and Hofstede de Groot, *Dutch Painters*, i.

VERMEYEN. See Friedländer, *Altniederländische Malerei*, xii, and *From van Eyck to Brueghel*.

VERNET. Monographs by A. Durande, Paris 1863; A. Dayot (Les Vernet), Paris 1898 and (Carle Vernet only), Paris 1925. See also F. Ingersoll-Smouse, 2 vols. (Joseph V.), Paris 1926.

VERONESE. Monographs by G. Fiocco, Bologna 1928 and Rome 1934; R. Pallucchini, 2nd ed. Bergamo 1943; and A. Orliac, London 1948. See also Cat. of Exh., Venice 1939.

VERRIO. See Whinney and Millar, *English Art*; and Waterhouse, *Painting in Britain*; and Croft-Murray, *Decorative Painting in England*.

VERROCCHIO. Monograph by L. Planiscig, Vienna 1941. See also Pope-Hennessy, *Italian Sculpture*, ii.

VERTUE. Notebooks are vols. xviii, xx, xxii, xxiv, xxvi, and xxix (Index) and xxx (with its own index) of the Walpole Soc., London 1930–55.

VIEN. See Locquin, *La Peinture d'Histoire en France*.

VIGÉE-LEBRUN. Monographs by W. Helm, London 1916; and L. Hautecœur, Paris 1917. Her *Memoirs* first issued as *Souvenirs*, 3 vols., Paris 1835–7; Eng. trans. London 1904 and London 1927.

VILLON, J. Monographs by P. Éluard, Paris 1948; and W. S. Lieberman (on Graphic work), New York 1953. See also Haftmann, *Painting in the Twentieth Century*.

VINGT, LES. See Cat. of Exh., Otterlo 1962 (in French).

VISCHER. Family: Monograph by S. Meller, Leipzig 1925. Peter II: Monograph by H. Stafski, Nuremberg 1962. Sebaldus Shrine: see A. Feulner, *Peter Vischers Sebaldusgrab in Nürnberg*, Munich 1924.

VITTORIA. Monograph by F. Cessi, 4 vols., Trent 1960–2. See also Pope-Hennessy, *Italian Sculpture*, iii; Wittkower, *Art and Architecture in Italy*; and Venturi, *Storia dell'Arte Italiana*, x, part 3.

VIVARINI. Monograph by R. Pallucchini, Venice n.d. (1962).

VIVIN. See W. Uhde, *Fünf primitive Meister*, Zürich

1947; Haftmann, *Painting in the Twentieth Century*; and Bihalji-Merin, *Modern Primitives*.

VLAMINCK. Monographs by K. Perls, New York 1941; M. Sauvage, Geneva 1956 (French); and J. Selz, Paris n.d. (1963). See also Autobiography 1929 (French) and trans. as *Dangerous Corner*, London 1961.

VLIEGER. See N. Maclaren, *Cat. of Dutch School*, NG, London 1960.

VORTICISM. See Cat. of Exh., Tate Gall., London 1956. See also under LEWIS.

VOS, C. DE. Monograph by E. Greindl, Brussels 1944 (in French). See also Gerson and Ter Kuile, *Art and Architecture in Belgium*.

VOS, MARTEN DE. See Gerson and Ter Kuile, *Art and Architecture in Belgium*.

VOUET. Monograph by W. Crelly, Yale and London 1962. See also Blunt, *Art and Architecture in France*.

VRIES, A. DE. Monograph by C. Buchwald, Leipzig 1899.

VUILLARD. Monograph by A. C. Ritchie, New York (M of MA) 1954.

W

WALDMÜLLER. Monographs by A. Roessler and G. Pisko, 2 vols., Vienna 1908; and B. Grimschitz, Salzburg 1957.

WALKER. See Whinney and Millar, *English Art*; and Waterhouse, *Painting in Britain*.

WARD. Monograph by C. Grundy, London 1909. See also Cat. of Exh., Arts Council, London 1960; and Taylor, *Animal Painting in England*.

WATERCOLOUR. See Constable, *The Painter's Workshop*.

WATTEAU. Monographs by E. Dacier, A. Vuaflart, and J. Hérold, Paris 1922–9 (2 vols.); and H. Adhémar, Paris 1950. For drawings see Sir K. Parker and J. Mathey, Paris 1957 (2 vols.). See also E. and J. de Goncourt, *French 18c. Painters*.

WATTS. Monograph by R. Chapman, London 1945. See also Cat. of Exh., Tate Gall., London 1954–5.

WEENIX. See N. Maclaren, *Cat. of Dutch School*, NG, London 1960.

WEST. Monographs by J. Galt, 2 vols., London 1820; and H. Marceau and F. Kimball, Philadelphia 1938. See also Richardson, *Painting in America*.

WESTMACOTT. See Gunnis, *Dictionary of British Sculptors*; Whinney, *Sculpture in Britain*.

WEYDEN. Monographs by J. Destrée, 2 vols., Brussels 1930 (in French); W. Vogelsang, Amsterdam n.d. (*c.* 1945); and H. Beenken, Munich 1951. See also Friedländer, *Altniederländische Malerei*, ii, xiv, and *Van Eyck to Brueghel*; also Panofsky, *Early Netherlandish Painting*; and Cat. of Exh., Tournai Cathedral, 2 vols., 1964.

WHEATLEY. See Waterhouse, *Painting in Britain*.

WHISTLER. Monographs by E. R. and J. Pennell, London 1908, 2 vols.; and D. Sutton, London 1963. See also Cat. of Exh., London (Arts Council) and New York 1960; and F. Sweet, *Sargent, W., and Mary Cassatt*, Chicago 1954.

WILHELM, MASTER. See Stange, *Deutsche Malerei der Gotik*, ii.

WILIGELMO. Monograph by R. Salvini, Milan 1956. See also Crichton, *Romanesque Sculpture in Italy*.

WILKIE. Monograph by R. Sutherland Gower, London 1902. See also Cat. of Exh., RA, London 1958.

WILSON, BENJAMIN. See Waterhouse, *Painting in Britain*.

WILSON, RICHARD. Monograph by W. G. Constable, London 1953; and B. Ford (on drawings), London 1951.

WILTON. See Gunnis, *Dictionary of British Sculptors*; and Whinney, *Sculpture in Britain*.

WINCKELMANN. Monograph by C. Justi, 3 vols., Leipzig 1866 (4th ed. 1943). There are several editions of his works, e.g. by T. Eiselein, Donauöschingen 1825–9. See also W. Waetzoldt, *Deutsche Kunsthistoriker*, i, Leipzig 1921.

WITTE. Monograph by I. Manke, Amsterdam 1963 (in German).

WITZ. Monographs by J. Ganter, Vienna 1942; and M. Meng-Koehler, Basle 1947 (in German).

WOLGEMUT. See Stange, *Deutsche Malerei der Gotik*, ix.

WOLS. Monograph by G. Dorfles, Milan 1958. See also Haftmann, *Painting in the Twentieth Century*.

WOOTTON. See Waterhouse, *Painting in Britain*.

WORKSHOP PRODUCTION. See Constable, *The Painter's Workshop*; and Thompson, *The Materials of Medieval Painting*.

WOTRUBA. Monograph by E. Canetti, Vienna 1955. See also Giedion-Welcker, *Contemporary Sculpture*.

WOUWERMAN. See Hofstede de Groot, *Dutch Painters*, ii; and Bode, *Great Masters of Dutch and Flemish Painting*.

WRIGHT. See Whinney and Millar, *English Art*; Waterhouse, *Painting in Britain*.

WRIGHT OF DERBY. Monographs by W. Bemrose, Derby 1885; and S. Kaines-Smith and H. C. Bemrose, London 1922. See also Cat. of Exh., Arts Council, London 1958; and Waterhouse, *Painting in Britain*.

WTEWAEL. Monograph by C. M. Lindeman, Utrecht 1929. See also Cat. of Exh., Utrecht 1952.

WYNANTS. See Hofstede de Groot, *Dutch Painters*, viii.

Y

YEATS, J. B. See Cat. of Exh., Arts Council, London 1948.

Z

ZADKINE. Monographs by A. Hammacher, London 1958; and I. Jianou, Paris 1964. See also Cat. of Exh., Tate Gall., London 1961; and Selz, *Modern Sculpture*.

ZAIS. See Levey, *Venice*; and Donzelli, *Pittori Veneziani*.

ZANDOMENEGHI. Monograph by M. Cinotti, Busto Arsizio 1960.

ZICK. Monograph by A. Feulner, Munich 1920. See also Hempel, *Baroque Art . . . in Central Europe*.

ZOFFANY. Monograph by Lady V. Manners and G. C. Williamson, London 1920. See also Waterhouse, *Painting in Britain*; and Cat. of Exh., Arts Council, London 1960–1.

ZOPPO. See Venturi, *Storia*, vii; and Berenson, *The Venetian School*.

ZUCCARELLI. Monograph by G. Rosa, Milan 1952. See also Levey, *Venice*; and Donzelli, *Pittori Veneziani*.

ZUCCARI, F. Zuccari's writings ed. by D. Heikamp, Florence 1961. See also Voss, *Die Malerei der Spätrenaissance*; and Venturi, *Storia*, ix.

ZURBARÁN. Monograph by M. Soria, London 1955 (2nd ed.). See also Kubler and Soria, *Art and Architecture in Spain*.